ESSENTIALS OF
CONTEMPORARY MANAGEMENT

SIXTH EDITION

Gareth R. Jones

Jennifer M. George
Rice University

Jane W. Haddad
Seneca College of Applied Arts and Technology

Essentials of Contemporary Management
Sixth Canadian Edition

The Internet addresses listed in the text were accurate at the time of publication. The inclusion of a Web site does not indicate an endorsement by the authors or McGraw-Hill Ryerson, and McGraw-Hill Ryerson does not guarantee the accuracy of the information presented at these sites.

ISBN-13: 978-1-25-965496-1
ISBN-10: 1-25-965496-6

2 3 4 5 6 7 8 TCP 22 21 20

Printed and bound in Canada.

Care has been taken to trace ownership of copyright material contained in this text; however, the publisher will welcome any information that enables them to rectify any reference or credit for subsequent editions.

Director of Product, Canada: *Rhondda McNabb*
Product Manager: *Amy Clarke-Spencley*
Marketing Manager: *Emily Park*
Product Developer: *Melissa Hudson*
Senior Product Team Associate: *Stephanie Giles*
Supervising Editor: *Janie Deneau*
Photo/Permissions Editor: *Marnie Lamb*
Copy Editor: *Sarah Fulton*
Plant Production Coordinator: *Joelle McIntyre*
Manufacturing Production Coordinator: *Jason Stubner*
Interior and Cover Design: *Michelle Losier*
Cover Image: © *ElenaBs/Alamy Stock Vector*
Page Layout: *MPS Limited*
Printer: *Transcontinental Printing Group*

About the Authors

Jane W. Haddad received her Honours BA from Queen's University, Ontario, in 1984, followed by her MA from the Ontario Institute for Studies in Education at the University of Toronto in 1986. She has taught in the faculties of Sociology and Education at the University of Saskatchewan and the University of Regina, Saskatchewan, and in the Salem International University distance MBA. program. In addition to teaching Liberal Studies, Humanities, and Management Theory for over 30 years at Seneca College of Applied Arts and Technology, Toronto, Ontario, Jane developed the post-graduate certificate program in Non-profit and Social Sector Management in the School of Leadership and Human Resources at Seneca and coordinated the program for five years. She is a co-founder of Skillseed, a not-for-profit aimed at developing community-based skill-sharing activities that sustain household-scale production of personal care products, and was a member for five years of the Board of Directors of Pamoja: Let's Build Together Corporation, a small charity that does development work in the DRC, Africa. Professor Haddad coordinated a SSHRC-funded Community–University Research Alliance (CURA) grant at Seneca from 2000 to 2005 and served on Seneca's Research Ethics Review Board for 10 years. Professor Haddad's research interests include youth training and labour markets, barriers to accessing post-secondary education, social innovation in housing, and social enterprise. She has presented several academic papers at Learned Society and other conferences across Canada and has published her work in journals such as *Canadian Women's Studies Journal* and *The College Quarterly*.

Courtesy of Jane Haddad

Gareth Jones currently offers pro bono advice on solving management problems to nonprofit organizations in Houston, Texas. He received his BA in Economics Psychology and his PhD in Management from the University of Lancaster, U.K. He was formerly Professor of Management in the Graduate School of Business at Texas A&M University and earlier held teaching and research appointments at Michigan State University, the University of Illinois at Urbana–Champaign, and the University of Warwick, U.K.

He continues to pursue his research interests in strategic management and organizational theory and his well-known research that applies transactional cost analysis to explain many forms of strategic and organizational behaviour. He also studies the complex and changing relationships between competitive advantage and information technology in the 2010s.

Courtesy of Gareth Jones

He has published many articles in the leading journals of the field and his research has appeared in the *Academy of Management Review,* the *Journal of International Business Studies,* and *Human Relations*. He published an article about the role of information technology in many aspects of organizational functioning in the *Journal of Management*. One of his articles won the *Academy of Management Journal*'s Best Paper Award, and he is one of the most cited authors in the *Academy of Management Review*, the *Journal of Management*, and *Management Inquiry*.

Gareth Jones has used his academic knowledge to craft leading textbooks in management and three other major areas in the management discipline: organizational behaviour, organizational theory, and strategic management. His books are widely recognized for their innovative, contemporary content and for the clarity with which they communicate complex, real-world issues to students.

Courtesy of Jennifer George

Jennifer George is the Mary Gibbs Jones Professor of Management and Professor of Psychology in the Jesse H. Jones Graduate School of Business at Rice University. She received her BA in Psychology/Sociology from Wesleyan University, her MBA in Finance from New York University, and her PhD in Management and Organizational Behavior from New York University. Prior to joining the faculty at Rice University, she was a professor in the Department of Management at Texas A&M University.

Professor George specializes in organizational behaviour and is well known for her research on mood and emotion in the workplace, their determinants, and their effects on various individual and group-level work outcomes. She is the author of many articles in leading peer-reviewed journals such as the *Academy of Management Journal,* the *Academy of Management Review*, the *Journal of Applied Psychology, Organizational Behavior and Human Decision Processes, Journal of Personality and Social Psychology,* and *Psychological Bulletin.* One of her papers won the Academy of Management's Organizational Behavior Division Outstanding Competitive Paper Award, and another paper won the *Human Relations* Best Paper Award. She is, or has been, on the editorial review boards of the *Journal of Applied Psychology, Academy of Management Journal, Academy of Management Review, Administrative Science Quarterly, Journal of Management, Organizational Behavior and Human Decision Processes, Organization Science, International Journal of Selection and Assessment,* and *Journal of Managerial Issues*; was a consulting editor for the *Journal of Organizational Behavior*; was a member of the SIOP *Organizational Frontiers Series* editorial board; and was an associate editor of the *Journal of Applied Psychology.* She is a fellow in the Academy of Management, the American Psychological Association, the American Psychological Society, the Association for Psychological Science, and the Society for Industrial and Organizational Psychology, and a member of the Society for Organizational Behavior. She has also co-authored a textbook titled *Understanding and Managing Organizational Behavior.*

Brief Contents

Contents

PART III
ORGANIZING

CHAPTER FIVE
Managing Organizational Structure   176

CHAPTER SIX
Managing Communication and Information
Technology (IT)   215

CHAPTER NINE
Managing Leadership 336

CHAPTER TEN
Managing Teams 371

PART V
CONTROLLING

CHAPTER ELEVEN
Managing Control and Operations   416

CHAPTER TWELVE
Managing Change   450

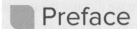# Preface

A manager is a person who makes other people's work meaningful.

When groups of people come together to pursue a common goal, often to satisfy their collective needs, various activities must be structured so that resources can be gathered and used to achieve the goal. The person or people who are assigned the task of keeping the whole group working toward the goal, deciding on timing and strategy, and maintaining the structure of activities and relationships, are those who engage in *management*. The activities of managing are critical to any complex cooperative endeavour. Management is both the art and science of arranging and utilizing the physical and human factors of production toward a socially desirable outcome without interfering in nature's ability to regenerate itself. This book provides you, the student, with an introduction to sustainable management processes. This sixth Canadian edition has a number of new case studies to help you understand the main sets of activities that managers engage in to achieve organizational goals: Planning, Organizing, Leading, and Controlling.

In **Part I: Management, Chapter 1: Managers and Managing,** we discuss who managers are, the types and levels of managers found in organizations, the managerial skills needed to perform their main responsibilities, and the roles they perform in planning, organizing, leading, and controlling. It is important to know how organizational culture and norms and values affect managerial behaviour, and therefore we deal with this topic in the opening chapter.

Chapter 2: Managing the Organizational Environment sets the management process in the environmental context of operating enterprises in Canada and the global economy. The political, economic, socio-cultural, and technological contexts, as well as the immediate agents in the organization's external environment, such as suppliers, customers, distributors, and competitors, are analyzed for the threats and opportunities they present to managers trying to gain a sustainable competitive advantage. The awareness of differences in national cultures is important in being successful in the global economy, and creating shared value among stakeholders is an important breakthrough in making progress to toward a sustainable economy where all stakeholders' interests are highly valued.

Part II: Planning, Chapter 3: Managing Decision Making addresses the fundamental challenge facing managers to make ethical and sustainable decisions. Approaches to socially responsible decision making are addressed here. **Chapter 4, Managing Planning and Strategy,** tackles the process of planning organizational goals, formulating strategies, and finding the best ways to implement and evaluate the success of those goals and strategies. Two common techniques for analyzing the environmental context that is vital to strategy formulation for a competitive advantage, SWOT and Porter's Five Forces model, are examined.

In **Part III: Organizing,** we begin with **Chapter 5: Managing Organizational Structure,** where the elements of organizational design and structure are discussed. Students learn that ways of allocating authority and distributing control over decision making result in different organizational structures. The type of overall organizational structure depends on internal and external environmental factors, such as strategy, technology, human resources, and the degree of environmental change. **Chapter 6: Managing Communication and Information Technology (IT)** begins with examining the communication process, the types and strengths of communication channels, and the importance of changing technological impact on effective communication, including the most important elements of a social media strategy. New to this edition is an expanded discussion of the role of Artificial Intelligence (AI) in disrupting how managers will do their work now and in the near future. **Chapter 7: Managing Human Resources** is focused on how managers can successfully recruit, select, develop, appraise, and compensate valued and diverse employees in the context of the Canadian legal and regulatory environment.

In **Part IV: Leading,** we first look at **Chapter 8: Managing Motivation.** Here we discuss the means by which managers can motivate good work effort and performance from employees. Several *need* and *process* theories are discussed, and the importance of a total rewards strategy utilizing both intrinsic and extrinsic factors is highlighted. In **Chapter 9: Managing Leadership,** the importance of effective leadership in managing organizational performance is analyzed. Trait, behaviour, and contingency theories are explored, and transformational and transactional leadership styles are compared. A section on visionary leadership rounds out this discussion. **Chapter 10: Managing Teams** discusses the types of groups and teams found in contemporary organizations. Students will learn the elements of group dynamics, group decision-making techniques, and what managers can do to create high-performing teams and manage conflict in their organizations.

In **Part V: Controlling,** we start with **Chapter 11: Managing Control and Operations,** where we discuss how managers monitor and measure the use of resources to make sure processes and products are up to standards throughout the entire value chain. Corporate governance practices are examined in light of recent economic crises. The types of controls that managers use impact the success of the organization in achieving high performance and gaining a competitive advantage. And, finally, we conclude our discussion of control by examining theories of organizational change in **Chapter 12: Managing Change.** They say that the only constant is change itself, so understanding how to deal with it is an important skill for managers of organizations.

Continued in this edition is a **Focus on the Social Economy** box, which profiles a social enterprise that has both the function of creating economic value common to traditional for-profit businesses *and* creating social impact common to non-profit and charitable organizations. In each chapter, you will learn how a social enterprise applies business management processes to help people and solve social problems that were once only the responsibility of governments. Social entrepreneurs find innovative ways to deal with some of the fundamental concerns that the "business-as-usual" mentality has created, including a growing gap between rich and poor and environmental degradation. We discuss the awareness that if we continue to operate solely on a "business-as-usual" basis, where profit maximization is the only measurement of success, we will fail all of the stakeholders in any enterprise: employees, customers, partners, suppliers, investors, communities, and nature. We have to embrace innovative and sustainable ways to foster an economy that enables us to clothe, feed, and care for ourselves and others, and enjoy life without interfering with nature's diversity or its ability to regenerate itself.

Also continued in the sixth edition is the running case, **Carrot Tops.** This case gives students the opportunity to apply all the theories and models examined in the text to the management challenges facing the owner/manager of a small business operating in a dynamic organizational environment, where all levels of managers face opportunities and threats.

In addition to the chapter material, appendices are found after each major section. After *Part I: Management,* you will find *Appendix A: History of Management Thought.* After *Part II: Planning,* you will find *Appendix B: Developing a Business Plan. Appendix C: Career Development* is located after *Part III: Organizing.* The online *Appendix D: Operations Management and Competitive Advantage,* available on Connect, rounds out your introduction to the fundamentals of managing an organization successfully.

All of the material in *Essentials of Contemporary Management,* Sixth Canadian Edition, has a direct application to you as a student of organizational management as well as to any business or social enterprise you may own, manage, or work for in the future.

J. W. Haddad
May 2018

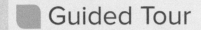

Learning Tools

Learning Outcomes have been highlighted at the beginning of each chapter, identified throughout the text, and discussed in the **Summary and Review.**

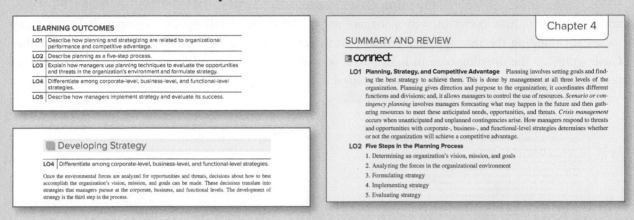

Definitions of Key Terms are highlighted in each chapter of the print text, and a list of these terms is provided at the end of each chapter and in the glossary at the end of the text. Key terms appear as pop-tips in the digital text.

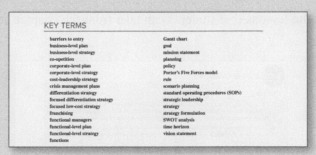

Figures and Tables are interspersed throughout the text to illustrate concepts and provide a visual framework for students.

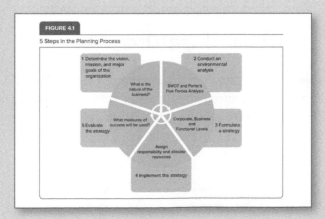

Rich and Relevant Examples

An important feature of our book is the way we use real-world examples and stories about managers and companies to drive home the applied lessons to students. Moreover, unlike boxed material in other books, we integrate more applied and fewer types of boxes seamlessly into the text; they are an integral part of the learning experience, and not tacked on or isolated from the text itself. This is central to our pedagogical approach.

Each chapter begins with an **Opening Case**. These cases pose a real-world, chapter-related challenge and then discuss how companies or managers responded to that challenge, bringing to light the many issues surrounding the management process. At the end of the chapter, the **Wrap-Up to the Opening Case** wraps up the opening case in light of the new information gleaned from the chapter. Students are provided with the answers to the questions raised in the opening case.

Tips for Managers distill the lessons that students can take from the chapter and apply to develop their management skills.

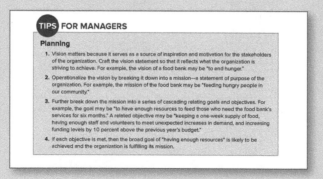

Experiential Learning Features

We have given considerable time and attention to developing state-of-the-art experiential end-of-chapter learning exercises that drive home the meaning of management to students. These exercises are grouped together at the end of each chapter in the section called **Management in Action.**

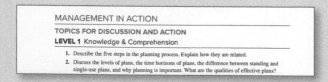

Topics for Discussion and Action are a set of chapter-related questions based on Bloom's three levels of developmental consideration: Level 1 tests students' knowledge and comprehension; Level 2 tests students' ability to apply concepts; and Level 3 tests students' synthesis and evaluation skills.

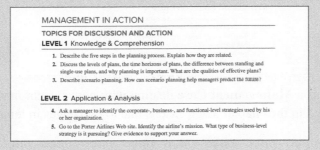

> MANAGEMENT IN ACTION
>
> TOPICS FOR DISCUSSION AND ACTION
>
> **LEVEL 1** Knowledge & Comprehension
>
> 1. Describe the five steps in the planning process. Explain how they are related.
> 2. Discuss the levels of plans, the time horizons of plans, the difference between standing and single-use plans, and why planning is important. What are the qualities of effective plans?
> 3. Describe scenario planning. How can scenario planning help managers predict the future?
>
> **LEVEL 2** Application & Analysis
>
> 4. Ask a manager to identify the corporate-, business-, and functional-level strategies used by his or her organization.
> 5. Go to the Porter Airlines Web site. Identify the airline's mission. What type of business-level strategy is it pursuing? Give evidence to support your answer.

Self-Reflection Exercises are unique exercises that ask students to internalize concepts from the chapter and apply them to their personal lives and situations at this moment, helping them to grasp the relevance of key chapter ideas and concepts.

> SELF-REFLECTION EXERCISE
>
> Think ahead to five years from now to consider what it is that you might like to be doing with your life. Develop your own vision and mission statements. Establish a set of goals that will help you achieve your vision and mission.
>
> Develop a SWOT analysis for considering what you want to be doing in five years. What are your strengths and weaknesses? What are the opportunities and threats in carrying out this plan?
>
> Develop a five-year plan that maps out the steps you need to take in order to get to where you want to be in your life at that time.

Small Group Breakout Exercises are uniquely designed to allow instructors in large classes to utilize interactive experiential exercises in groups of three to four students. The instructor calls on students to form into small groups simply by turning to people around them. All students participate in the exercise in class, and a mechanism is provided for the different groups to share what they have learned with one another.

> SMALL GROUP BREAKOUT EXERCISE
>
> *Form groups of three or four, and appoint one member as the spokesperson who will communicate your findings to the class when called on by the instructor. Then discuss the following scenario:*
>
> You are a team of management consultants hired by a grocery store chain to plan the feasibility of opening a store in your community. You must answer all the questions below and report back to your clients.

Managing Ethically Exercises present students with an ethical scenario or dilemma and ask them, either individually or in a group, to think about an issue from an ethical perspective in order to understand the issues facing practising managers.

> MANAGING ETHICALLY EXERCISE
>
> A major department store has received repeated criticism for selling clothes that are produced at low cost in developing countries. The CEO of the department store knows that suppliers are paying 5 percent

Management Challenge Exercises present a realistic scenario in which a manager or organization faces some kind of challenge or opportunity and the student plays the role of a management consultant offering advice and recommending a course of action based on the chapter content.

> MANAGEMENT CHALLENGE EXERCISE
> Beyond the Green Door
>
> The Green Door is a vegetarian restaurant in Ottawa with a focus on providing local organic food that is wholesome and comforting.[39] The restaurant is situated directly across from Saint Paul University[40] (part of the University of Ottawa and home to about 1000 undergraduate and graduate students in such disciplines as spirituality, philosophy, human sciences, pastoral counselling, and conflict studies). OttawaPlus.ca considers The Green Door the "heaven for vegetarians" and an Ottawa institution.[41]

Management Portfolio Projects present an opportunity for students to follow and analyze an organization of their choice over the course of the semester. Each chapter includes an exercise that asks students to evaluate how the issues discussed in the chapter are dealt with by the organization they are following.

> **MANAGEMENT PORTFOLIO PROJECT**
>
> *Answer the following questions about the organization you have chosen to follow:*
>
> 1. Identify the vision, mission, and major goals of the organization.
> 2. What is the corporate-level strategy of the company?
> 3. What is the business-level strategy of the company?
> 4. Have the strategies supported the vision and mission? How so?
> 5. Has there been a significant shift in strategy over the past decade? If yes, describe it, and try to determine why the organization made the changes.

Each chapter also contains a **Management Case** dealing with how current managers of companies have faced the challenges raised in the chapter. Each case is one to two pages in length, ending with questions for students to consider.

> MANAGEMENT CASE
>
> **STOPPING GLOBAL WATER SHORTAGES**
>
> How much water did it take to manufacture the outfit you are wearing right now? The textile industry has a huge water footprint. First, it takes water to grow cotton, the material that accounts for 90 percent of the textile industry's use of natural fibres.[42] One estimate suggests that 1500 litres of water are needed to produce each cotton T-shirt.[43] The farming of cotton accounts for 2.6 percent of annual global water usage and is the largest water consumption factor in the supply chain of the textile industry.[44] And it's not just quantity. Cotton production has a direct impact on water quality through the use of pesticides, herbicides, and fertilizers.

A **Continuing Case** at the end of each part provides students with an opportunity to integrate and synthesize all the concepts and material learned in the previous sections to the management and organizational challenges of one particular small business. This running case feature helps keep continuity across the entire text and allows students to focus on problems faced by small businesses.

> END OF PART II: CONTINUING CASE
>
> **CARROT TOPS: BUILDING A COMPETITIVE ADVANTAGE**
>
> As the population grew, so too did the competition. Pretty soon it was apparent that Mac's Milk and Shoppers Drug Mart were able to offer customers a wider selection of lower-priced grocery products than Mel's store. Mel had to find a new way to manage his small business if it was going to survive. He began brainstorming new strategies. He researched trends in the food industry. There might be a niche for supplying specialty products, he thought, such as organic and gourmet foods, which were more profitable to sell. He would no longer be competing against giants like Shoppers. He changed the name of his store to Carrot Tops and stocked it with a wide variety of gourmet Canadian food products. He began to offer fine foods, local cheeses, fresh bread, organic fruits and vegetables. Finding a reliable source of products from local farmers and producers could be a stumbling block to his success, but he did have Janet Khan to head up produce procurement and logistics.

Appendices highlight organizational management issues that will be of interest to students wishing to pursue a career in management or wanting to start their own business or social enterprise.

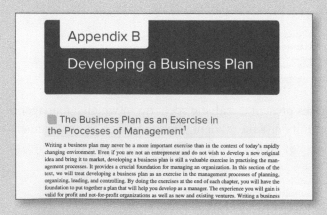

> **Appendix B**
>
> **Developing a Business Plan**
>
> ■ The Business Plan as an Exercise in the Processes of Management[1]
>
> Writing a business plan may never be a more important exercise than in the context of today's rapidly changing environment. Even if you are not an entrepreneur and do not wish to develop a new original idea and bring it to market, developing a business plan is still a valuable exercise in practising the management processes. It provides a crucial foundation for managing an organization. In this section of the text, we will treat developing a business plan as an exercise in the management processes of planning, organizing, leading, and controlling. By doing the exercises at the end of each chapter, you will have the foundation to put together a plan that will help you develop as a manager. The experience you will gain is valid for profit and not-for-profit organizations as well as new and existing ventures. Writing a business

Appendix A: History of Management Thought
Appendix B: Developing a Business Plan
Appendix C: Career Development
Appendix D: Operations Management and Competitive Advantage (on Connect only)

Market-Leading Technology

Learn without Limits

McGraw-Hill Connect® is an award-winning digital teaching and learning platform that gives students the means to better connect with their coursework, with their instructors, and with the important concepts that they will need to know for success now and in the future. With Connect, instructors can take advantage of McGraw-Hill's trusted content to seamlessly deliver assignments, quizzes and tests online. McGraw-Hill Connect is the learning platform that continually adapts to each student, delivering precisely what they need, when they need it, so class time is more engaging and effective. Connect makes teaching and learning personal, easy, and proven.

Connect Key Features:

SmartBook®

As the first and only adaptive reading experience, SmartBook is changing the way students read and learn. SmartBook creates a personalized reading experience by highlighting the most important concepts a student needs to learn at that moment in time. As a student engages with SmartBook, the reading experience continuously adapts by highlighting content based on what each student knows and doesn't know. This ensures that he or she is focused on the content needed to close specific knowledge gaps, while it simultaneously promotes long-term learning.

Connect Insight®

Connect Insight is Connect's new one-of-a-kind visual analytics dashboard—now available for instructors—that provides at-a-glance information regarding student performance, which is immediately actionable. By presenting assignment, assessment, and topical performance results together with a time metric that is easily visible for aggregate or individual results, Connect Insight gives instructors the ability to take a just-in-time approach to teaching and learning, which was never before available. Connect Insight presents data that helps instructors improve class performance in a way that is efficient and effective.

Simple Assignment Management

With Connect, creating assignments is easier than ever, so instructors can spend more time teaching and less time managing.

- Assign SmartBook learning modules.
- Instructors can edit existing questions and create their own questions.
- Draw from a variety of text specific questions, resources, and test bank material to assign online.
- Streamline lesson planning, student progress reporting, and assignment grading to make classroom management more efficient than ever.

Smart Grading

When it comes to studying, time is precious. Connect helps students learn more efficiently by providing feedback and practice material when they need it, where they need it.

- Automatically score assignments, giving students immediate feedback on their work and comparisons with correct answers.
- Access and review each response; manually change grades or leave comments for students to review.

- Track individual student performance—by question, assignment or in relation to the class overall—with detailed grade reports.
- Reinforce classroom concepts with practice tests and instant quizzes.
- Integrate grade reports easily with Learning Management Systems including Blackboard, D2L, and Moodle.

Instructor Resources

- Instructor's Manual updated to reflect changes in this newest edition.
- PowerPoint presentations revised to match the newest edition.
- Test bank and quizzes are unparalleled in the number of test items provided and the depth and currency and make testing student knowledge a simple and efficient process.
  - Video Library with Video Teaching Guide includes:
  - Hotseat videos offer short cases that show real business professionals confronting a variety of workplace challenges.
  - iSeeIt! Animated video explanations clarify some of the most important topics.
  - Video Cases and questions are available on Connect to help students make the connections from chapter concepts to real-world applications.

Assessment Tools

- SmartBook, which holds students accountable for class preparation and engagement.
- Chapter quizzes that are prebuilt to cover all chapter learning objectives.
- Test bank that includes over 100 questions per chapter.
- Application exercises reinforce concepts and facilitate application-level comprehension
- Video assignments help explain difficult concepts and show business concepts in action in companies large and small.
- Application-Based Activities allow students to immerse themselves in critical-thinking and problem-solving opportunities of realistic business scenarios.

Superior Learning Solutions and Support

The McGraw-Hill Education team is ready to help instructors assess and integrate any of our products, technology, and services into your course for optimal teaching and learning performance. Whether it's helping your students improve their grades, or putting your entire course online, the McGraw-Hill Education team is here to help you do it. Contact your Learning Solutions Consultant today to learn how to maximize all of McGraw-Hill Education's resources.

For more information, please visit us online: http://www.mheducation.ca/he/solutions.

Acknowledgements

Producing a textbook is a collective effort and I would like to thank all the people who were involved in reading early drafts of this manuscript and who provided insightful and constructive feedback. I have tried to address your concerns and implement your suggestions. Your input has made this a better book! I would like to acknowledge all the people at McGraw-Hill Ryerson who worked on the production of this edition, especially Melissa Hudson. Without your direction and support, this edition would not have come off the press. And finally, I would like to thank my husband, Klaus Ruland, for supporting and encouraging my work.

This edition is dedicated to all the graduates of the Non-profit and Social Sector Management program at Seneca College. You are changing the world for the better and I'm grateful to have been part of your journeys.

Jane W. Haddad

Part I

Management

Managers and Managing

LEARNING OUTCOMES

LO1	Describe what management is, what managers do, and how managers use resources to achieve organizational goals.
LO2	Distinguish among planning, organizing, leading, and controlling, and explain how managers' abilities to handle each one affect organizational performance.
LO3	Differentiate among the types and levels of management, and understand the responsibilities of managers at different levels in the organizational hierarchy.
LO4	Distinguish among the kinds of managerial skills and roles that managers perform.
LO5	Understand how shared values and norms influence organizational culture and affect managerial behaviour.

OPENING CASE

Management at Brick Brewing Co. Limited

Brick Brewing Co. Limited is Ontario's largest Canadian-owned and Canadian-based publicly held brewery. The company is a regional brewer of award-winning premium quality and value beers. The company, founded by Jim Brickman in 1984, was the first craft brewery to start up in Ontario, and is credited with pioneering the present-day craft brewing renaissance in Canada. Brick has complemented its premium Waterloo craft beer with other popular brands such as Dark, IPA, Pilsner, Amber and Radler.[1] In 2011, the company bought the Canadian rights to the Seagram Coolers brand from Corby Distilleries Limited. In 2014, the company entered into a licensing agreement to sell Seagram Coolers in Quebec under the Blue Spike Beverages brand.[2] By 2016, their LandShark Lager and Margaritaville coolers were on the shelves of The Beer Store and grocery stores, and under its co-packaging agreements, the company produces, sells, markets, and distributes various beer products on behalf of Loblaws Inc. under the licensed President's Choice® trademark. The company also produces the Mott's Caesar brand in bottles under a contract with Canada Dry Mott's, Inc. ("CDMI").

Brick Brewing's chief financial officer, Sean Byrne,[3] is responsible for the timeliness and accuracy of all financial information that is provided to the board and shareholders. Byrne acts as corporate secretary for audit committee and board meetings of the company, and is a key contributor to the company's overall strategy.[4] He was brought on board by Brick Brewing president and CEO, George Croft.

Mr. Byrne graduated from Western University with a Bachelor of Arts, Economics degree and obtained his chartered accountant designation (CMA) while working with Dow Chemical. He also holds an MBA from Heriot-Watt University, Edinburgh Business School. Before joining Brick Brewing in 2013, he held senior finance roles in manufacturing companies operating in Europe and Canada.

Brick Brewing Co. Ltd.

Since 1984, Brick Brewing Co. Limited has supported thousands of cultural, charitable, and community organizations and events. From backing amateur athletes and teams to participating in festival-style events across Ontario, Brick Brewing takes a partnership approach with each sponsorship relationship.

This commitment to the community and to providing innovative products makes Brick Brewing Co. Limited a high-performing organization—one that provides goods and services that customers desire.

After reading and understanding the concepts in this chapter, you should be able to answer the following questions:

1. What kinds of activities or tasks are involved in planning, organizing, leading, and controlling at Brick Brewing?
2. Characterize the type and level of management described in the case.
3. What skills does Sean Byrne bring to the Brick Brewing Co. as a top manager?
4. Which of Mintzberg's managerial roles are illustrated in this case by each manager?

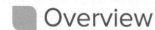 Overview

The actions of the top managers at Brick Brewing Co. Limited illustrate the many challenges managers face. Managing a company is a complex undertaking, and managers must possess the skills and knowledge needed to be effective. Making the right decision is difficult; even effective managers make mistakes. The most effective managers are the ones, like George Croft and Sean Byrne, who continually strive to find ways to improve their companies' performance.

In this chapter we look at what management is, what activities are involved in the management process, the types and levels of managers we find in organizations, how organizational culture affects the style of managing, and the skills and roles that effective managers need to perform well. By the end of this chapter, you will have an appreciation of the role of managers in creating a high-performing organization.

What Is Management?

LO1 | Describe what management is, what managers do, and how managers use resources to achieve organizational goals.

When you think of a manager, what kind of person comes to mind? Do you see someone like Sean Bryne who helps determine the future prosperity of a company? Or do you see the administrator of a not-for-profit organization, such as a school, library, health care organization, or charity? Or do you think of the person in charge of your local McDonald's restaurant or Giant Tiger store? What do all these people have in common and what makes them successful in managing organizations?

First, they all work in **organizations,** which are collections of people who work together and coordinate their actions to achieve a wide variety of goals and desired future outcomes.[5] Organizations provide jobs and employment. Outside of the public sector, most people in Canada are employed in small and medium-sized organizations in the private sector or in the community or social sector. We categorize organizations based on their core purposes (see Figure 1.1). Organizations range from having a strictly social mission, such as a charitable nonprofit organization, funded by grants and donations, to a strictly

FIGURE 1.1

Spectrum of Types of Organizations

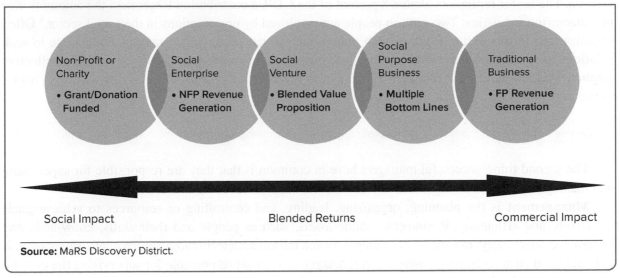

Source: MaRS Discovery District.

commercial for-profit mission, with little regard for achieving socially useful outcomes. *Social enterprises, social ventures,* and *social purpose businesses* combine social and commercial missions to varying degrees and are collectively referred to as organizations in the **social economy.**[6] The concept of the social economy applies to all the organizations that have social objectives central to their mission and their practice, and either have explicit economic objectives or generate some economic value through the services they provide and purchases that they undertake.[7] The social economy is often referred to as the third pillar of the economy; the other two being for-profit (FP) private enterprise and public-sector (government) enterprise. Increasingly, a growing number of enterprising charities, nonprofit or not-for-profit organizations (NPO or NFP), co-operatives, and community organizations are creating businesses with economic as well as social and environmental returns. Public–private partnerships that mobilize private capital rather than relying on tax revenue will become more and more common in the effort to change the way society deals with social problems. The goal of social enterprise is to use market mechanisms to produce or sell goods and services that provide a social or environmental benefit. Social enterprises often employ the clients they serve and thereby provide valuable experience to marginalized groups who can use the skills they acquire in the wider economy. Together, the diverse organizations in the social economy create the infrastructure that helps Canadian communities to grow and prosper. These organizations welcome newcomers, coach kids' sports, deliver meals on wheels, run food banks, daycares, and crisis hotlines, and provide countless other public-benefit services that allow people to be well and participate in civic life. They create social and economic value, known as **blended value.**

organizations Collections of people who work together and coordinate their actions to achieve goals and desired future outcomes.

social economy A bridging concept for organizations that have social objectives central to their mission and their practice, and either have explicit economic objectives or generate some economic value through the services they provide and purchases that they undertake.

blended value Organizations in the social economy that create both social impact and economic value.

Chances are pretty good that you or someone you know works in the social sector of the economy. Canada's nonprofit and voluntary sector is the second largest in the world; the Netherlands' is the largest, while the United States comes in fifth. There are an estimated 162 000 nonprofits and charities in Canada. The sector represents almost 8 percent of the GDP, a contribution larger than the automotive or manufacturing industries. Two million people are employed by organizations in the social sector.[8] Often organizations in this sector, together with public- and private-sector organizations, collaborate to seek solutions to social problems. Working together, instead of in isolation, is the way to achieve **collective impact.** This is why we have included a profile of an organization in the social economy in every chapter of this text.

> **collective impact** Public, private, and nonprofit organizations working together to solve social problems.

The second thing successful managers have in common is that they are responsible for supervising and making the most of an organization's human and other resources to achieve its goals.

Management is the planning, organizing, leading, and controlling of resources to achieve goals effectively and efficiently. **Resources** include assets, such as people and their skills, know-how, and experience; machinery; raw materials; computers and information technology; and patents, financial capital, and loyal customers and employees. A **manager** is a person responsible for supervising the use of a group's or organization's resources to achieve its goals.

> **management** The planning, organizing, leading, and controlling of resources to achieve organizational goals effectively and efficiently.
>
> **resources** Resources include assets such as people and their skills, know-how, and experience; machinery; raw materials; computers and information technology; and patents, financial capital, and loyal customers and employees.
>
> **manager** A person who is responsible for supervising the use of an organization's resources to achieve its goals.

Achieving High Performance: A Manager's Goal

One of the most important goals of organizations and their members is to provide goods or services that customers value. As we saw in the opening case, by purchasing the rights to the Seagram Coolers brand, Brick Brewing Co. is "now able to satisfy a broader range of customers with a wider range of selection in taste and profile for those discerning drinkers."[9] The principal goal of doctors, nurses, and hospital administrators is to increase their hospital's ability to make sick people well; the principal goal of each McDonald's restaurant manager is to produce fast food that people want to eat and are willing to pay for so that they become loyal return customers. Eva's Print Shop is a social enterprise in downtown Toronto with the principal goals of providing training for at-risk youth to gain employment skills and generating revenue to support transitional housing for homeless youth. All of these examples illustrate how serving the needs of customers is key to the goals of managers.

Organizational performance is a measure of how efficiently and effectively managers use resources to satisfy customers and achieve organizational goals. Organizational performance increases in direct proportion to increases in effectiveness and efficiency (see Figure 1.2). What are efficiency and effectiveness?

> **organizational performance** A measure of how efficiently and effectively a manager uses resources to satisfy customers and achieve organizational goals.

FIGURE 1.2

Effectiveness, Efficiency, and Performance in an Organization

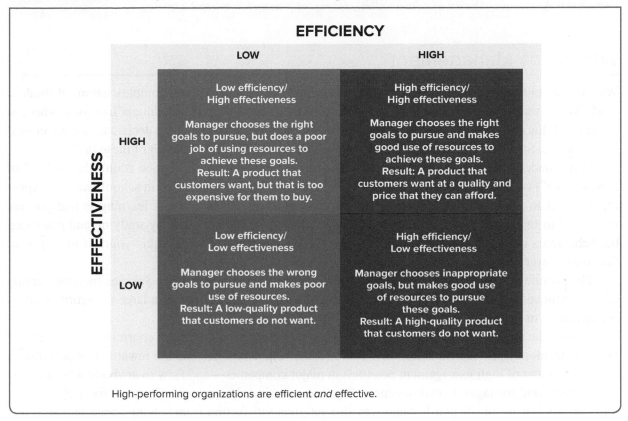

EFFICIENCY

	LOW	HIGH
HIGH	Low efficiency/ High effectiveness	High efficiency/ High effectiveness
	Manager chooses the right goals to pursue, but does a poor job of using resources to achieve these goals. Result: A product that customers want, but that is too expensive for them to buy.	Manager chooses the right goals to pursue and makes good use of resources to achieve these goals. Result: A product that customers want at a quality and price that they can afford.
LOW	Low efficiency/ Low effectiveness	High efficiency/ Low effectiveness
	Manager chooses the wrong goals to pursue and makes poor use of resources. Result: A low-quality product that customers do not want.	Manager chooses inappropriate goals, but makes good use of resources to pursue these goals. Result: A high-quality product that customers do not want.

EFFECTIVENESS

High-performing organizations are efficient *and* effective.

Effectiveness is a measure of the appropriateness of the goals that managers have selected for the organization to pursue and of the degree to which the organization achieves those goals. Management expert Peter Drucker compared the two this way: efficiency is doing things right; effectiveness is doing the right thing.[10] Organizations are effective when managers choose appropriate goals and then achieve them. Some years ago, for example, managers at McDonald's decided on the goal of providing breakfast service to attract more customers. This goal was a smart choice because sales of breakfast food now account for more than 30 percent of McDonald's revenues. Profits continue to grow after beverage and coffee prices were slashed in 2017.

effectiveness A measure of the appropriateness of the goals an organization is pursuing and of the degree to which the organization achieves those goals.

Efficiency is a measure of how well or how productively resources are used to achieve a goal.[11] Organizations are efficient when managers minimize the amount of input resources (such as labour, raw materials, and component parts) or the amount of time needed to produce a given output of goods or services. For example, McDonald's developed a more efficient fat fryer that not only reduces (by 30 percent) the amount of oil used in cooking but also speeds up the cooking of french fries. A manager's responsibility is to ensure that an organization and its members perform, as efficiently as possible, all the activities needed to provide goods and services to customers. High-performing organizations such as

Brick Brewing Co., McDonald's, Walmart, Intel, IKEA, and Habitat for Humanity are simultaneously efficient and effective.

> **efficiency** A measure of how well or productively resources are used to achieve a goal.

Why Study Management?

Why is the study of management currently so popular?[12] The dynamic and complex nature of modern work means that managerial skills are in demand. Organizations need individuals like you, who can understand this complexity, respond to environmental contingencies, and make decisions that are ethical and effective. Studying management helps equip individuals to accomplish each of these tasks.

In a broader sense, individuals generally learn through personal experience (think the "school of hard knocks") or through the experiences of others. By studying management in school, you are exposing yourself to the lessons others have learned. The advantage of such social learning is that you are not bound to repeat the mistakes others have made in the past. Furthermore, by studying and practising the behaviours of good managers and high-performing companies, you will equip yourself to help your future employer succeed.

The economic benefits of becoming a good manager are also impressive. Salaries increase rapidly as people move up the organizational hierarchy, whether it is a school system, a large for-profit business organization, or a not-for-profit charitable or social enterprise.

Indeed, the salaries paid to top managers of private-sector corporations are enormous.[13] These large amounts of money provide some indication of both the responsibilities and the rewards that accompany the achievement of high management positions in major companies—and flow to anybody who successfully creates and manages a small business. Pay, however, is only one type of reward for high achievement, as we will see in Chapter 8. Managers also get great satisfaction from solving social problems and making a lasting contribution to the collective well-being of society. So, what is it that managers actually do to receive such rewards?[14]

▊ Managerial Tasks and Activities

LO2 | Distinguish among planning, organizing, leading, and controlling, and explain how managers' abilities to handle each one affect organizational performance.

The job of management is to help an organization make the best use of its resources to achieve its goals. How do managers accomplish this objective? They do so by performing four essential managerial functions: planning, organizing, leading, and controlling (see Figure 1.3). Henri Fayol first outlined the nature of these managerial tasks in *General and Industrial Management,* published in 1916: a book that remains the classic statement of what managers must do to create a high-performing organization.[15]

Managers at all levels and in all departments—whether in small or large organizations, for-profit or not-for-profit organizations, or organizations that operate in one country or throughout the world—are responsible for performing these four functions, and we will look at each in turn. How well managers perform them determines how efficient and effective their organization is. Individuals who are not managers can also be involved in planning, organizing, leading, and controlling, so understanding these processes is important for everyone.

FIGURE 1.3

Four Tasks of Management

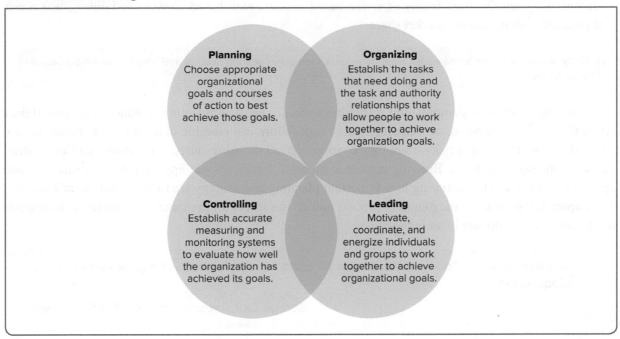

Planning
Choose appropriate organizational goals and courses of action to best achieve those goals.

Organizing
Establish the tasks that need doing and the task and authority relationships that allow people to work together to achieve organization goals.

Controlling
Establish accurate measuring and monitoring systems to evaluate how well the organization has achieved its goals.

Leading
Motivate, coordinate, and energize individuals and groups to work together to achieve organizational goals.

Planning

Planning is a process used to identify and select appropriate goals and courses of action. There are five steps in the planning process:

1. Deciding which goals the organization will pursue
2. Analyzing the organizational environment for threats and opportunities
3. Deciding what courses of action or strategy to adopt
4. Deciding how to allocate organizational resources to implement the plan
5. Evaluating whether the strategy achieved the goals

planning Identifying and selecting appropriate goals and courses of action; one of the four principal functions of management.

How well managers plan determines how effective and efficient their organization is—its **performance level.**[16]

performance level How efficient and effective an organization is in achieving its goals.

The outcome of planning is a **strategy,** a cluster of decisions concerning what organizational goals to pursue, what actions to take, and how to use resources to achieve goals. To illustrate how important planning is, we can look to the strategy Brick Brewing Co. developed. Brick follows a low-cost strategy with its popular Laker brand selling at the lowest legal price, but it also offers specialty coolers and award-winning premium craft beers such as Red Baron Premium Blonde Lager. According to George Croft, president and CEO of Brick Brewing Co. Limited, "It's easy to lose track of a simple foundation for customer satisfaction: Sell a quality product at a reasonable price." Expanding into specialty drinks, including Seagram Coolers' family of vodka-based coolers, malt-based coolers, and ciders, was a risk that paid off with increasing market share.

strategy A cluster of decisions about what goals to pursue, what actions to take, and how to use resources to achieve goals.

Planning strategy is complex and difficult, especially because planning is done under uncertainty when the result is unknown, so that either success or failure is a possible outcome of the planning process. Managers take major risks when they commit organizational resources to pursue a particular strategy. Top managers at Brick Brewing created a successful management approach to the craft beer and specialty drink market, illustrating how important planning and strategy are to an organization's success. In Chapter 4, we focus on the planning process and on the strategies organizations can select to respond to opportunities or threats in an industry.

> "It's easy to lose track of a simple foundation for customer satisfaction: Sell a quality product at a reasonable price."
>
> George Croft, president and CEO of Brick Brewing

Organizing

Organizing is structuring working relationships so organizational members interact and cooperate to achieve organizational goals. Organizing people into departments according to the kinds of job-specific tasks they perform lays out the lines of authority and responsibility between different individuals and groups. Managers must decide how best to organize resources, particularly human resources.

organizing Structuring workplace relationships so organizational members work together to achieve organizational goals; one of the four principal functions of management.

The outcome of organizing is the creation of an **organizational structure,** a formal system of task and reporting relationships that coordinates and motivates organizational members so they work together to achieve organizational goals. Organizational structure determines how an organization's resources can best be used to create goods and services.

organizational structure A formal system of both task and reporting relationships that coordinates and motivates organizational members so that they work together to reach organizational goals.

We examine the organizing process in Chapter 5, where we consider the organizational structures that managers can use to coordinate and motivate people and utilize other resources.

Leading

An organization's *vision* is a short, succinct, and inspiring statement of what the organization intends to become and the goals it is seeking to achieve—its desired future state. In **leading,** managers articulate a clear organizational vision for the organization's members to accomplish, and they energize and enable employees so that everyone understands the part he or she plays in achieving organizational goals. Leadership depends on the use of power, influence, vision, persuasion, and communication skills for two important tasks:

1. To coordinate the behaviours of individuals and groups so that their activities and efforts are in harmony, and

2. To encourage employees to perform at a high level.

> **leading** Articulating a clear vision and energizing and empowering organizational members so that everyone understands his or her individual role in achieving organizational goals; one of the four principal functions of management.

Understanding how to manage and lead effectively is an important skill. You might be interested to know that CEOs have just a few short months to prove to investors that they are able to communicate a vision and carry it out. Studies suggest that investors and analysts give CEOs only 14 to 18 months to show results.[17] The outcome of good leadership is a high level of motivation and commitment among organizational members. As CEO and president of Brick Brewing Co. Limited, George Croft's vision and leadership style have resulted in a hardworking team of employees producing award-winning beverages.[18] "I'm very proud of the hardworking team here who made these achievements possible," says Croft, "and happier still that these awards affirm we are giving our beer drinkers products of extraordinary quality." He adds, "Our success at the Ontario Brewing Awards is a humbling accomplishment."

We discuss the issues involved in managing and leading individuals and groups in Chapters 8 through 10.

Controlling

In **controlling,** the task of managers is to evaluate how well an organization is achieving its goals and take action to maintain or improve performance. For example, managers monitor the performance of individuals, departments, and the organization as a whole to see whether they are all meeting desired performance standards. If standards are not being met, managers take action to improve performance. Individuals working in groups also have the responsibility of controlling because they have to make sure the group achieves its goals and completes its actions. Brick Brewery's goal is to produce beer with a distinctive flavour; they achieve this through their "Craft Quality Assured" brewing method.[19]

> **controlling** Evaluating how well an organization is achieving its goals and taking action to maintain or improve performance; one of the four principal functions of management.

The outcome of the control process is the ability to measure performance accurately and regulate organizational efficiency and effectiveness. In order to exercise control, managers must decide which goals to measure—perhaps goals pertaining to productivity, quality, or responsiveness to customers—and then they must design information and control systems that will provide the data they need to assess performance. These mechanisms provide feedback to managers, and managers provide feedback to employees. The controlling function also allows managers to evaluate how well they themselves are performing the other three functions of management—planning, organizing, and leading—and to take corrective action.

We cover the most important aspects of the control function in Chapter 11, where we outline the basic process of control and examine some control systems that managers can use to monitor and measure organizational performance. Changes in the structure and culture of an organization occur when there is a change in strategy due to a merger, downsizing, expansion, or some other form of restructuring. Leading change successfully requires all of a manager's skills to ensure high levels of organizational performance prevail. In Chapter 12, we look at several models relating to how managers can lead change initiatives.

The four managerial activities —planning, organizing, leading, and controlling—are essential to a manager's job. At all levels in a managerial hierarchy, and across all departments in an organization, effective management means making decisions and managing these four activities successfully.

Types and Levels of Managers

LO3 Differentiate among the types and levels of management, and understand the responsibilities of managers at different levels in the organizational hierarchy.

To perform the four managerial tasks effectively and efficiently, organizations group or differentiate their managers in two main ways—by level in hierarchy and by type of function. First, they differentiate managers according to their level or rank in the organization's hierarchy of authority. The three levels of managers are first-line managers, middle managers, and top managers—arranged in a hierarchy. Typically, first-line managers report to middle managers, and middle managers report to top managers.

Second, organizations group managers into different departments (or functions) according to their specific set of job-related skills, expertise, and experiences, such as a manager's engineering skills, marketing expertise, or sales experience. A **department,** such as the manufacturing, accounting, engineering, or sales department, is a group of managers and employees who work together because they possess similar skills and experience or use the same kind of knowledge, tools, or techniques to perform their jobs. Within each department are all three levels of management. Next, we examine how organizations group managers into the three levels according to their main responsibilities.

department A group composed of subordinates who report to the same supervisor; also called a unit.

Levels of Management

Organizations normally have three levels of management: first-line managers, middle managers, and top managers (see Figure 1.4). Managers at each level have different but related responsibilities for utilizing organizational resources to increase efficiency and effectiveness.

As Figure 1.4 indicates, first-line, middle, and top managers differ from one another by virtue of their job-specific responsibilities, and are found in each of an organization's major departments.

FIRST-LINE MANAGERS

At the base of the managerial hierarchy are **first-line managers** (often called *supervisors*). They are responsible for the daily supervision and coordination of the nonmanagerial employees who perform many of the specific activities necessary to produce goods and services. First-line managers may be found in all departments of an organization. They are responsible for coordinating and supervising the daily work of employees.

first-line managers Managers who are responsible for the daily supervision and coordination of nonmanagerial employees.

FIGURE 1.4

Management Hierarchy

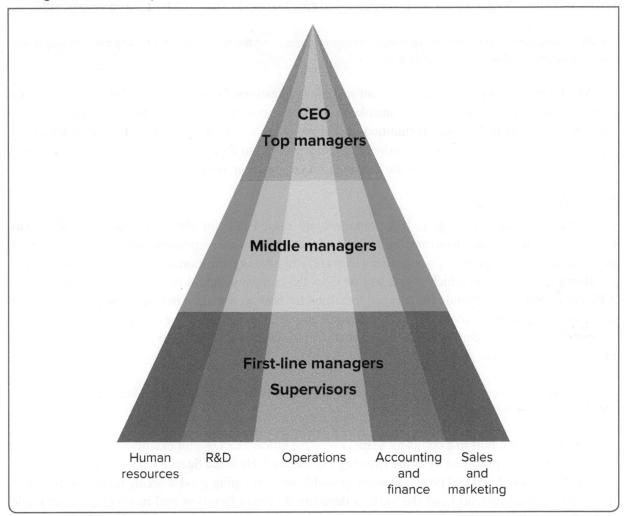

Examples of first-line managers include the supervisor of a work team in the manufacturing department of a car plant, the head nurse in the obstetrics department of a hospital, and the chief mechanic overseeing a crew of mechanics in the service department of a new-car dealership. Functional area titles may include assistant manager of operations, or assistant sales manager.

MIDDLE MANAGERS

Middle managers supervise the first-line managers and have the responsibility of finding the best way to organize human and other resources to achieve organizational goals. To increase efficiency, middle managers try to find ways to help first-line managers and nonmanagerial employees make better use of resources in order to reduce manufacturing costs or improve the way services are provided to customers. To increase effectiveness, middle managers are responsible for evaluating whether the goals that the organization is pursuing are appropriate and for suggesting to top managers ways in which goals should be changed. A major part of the middle manager's job is to develop and fine-tune skills and know-how—manufacturing or marketing expertise, for example—that enable the organization to be efficient and effective. Middle managers also coordinate resources across departments and divisions. Middle managers make the thousands of specific decisions that go into the production of goods and services: Which first-line supervisors should be chosen for this particular project? Where can we find the highest quality resources? How should employees be organized to enable them to make the best use of resources?

> **middle managers** Managers who supervise first-line managers and are responsible for finding the best way to use resources to achieve organizational goals.

Middle managers perform an important role in organizations. For instance, behind a first-class sales team, look for the sales manager responsible for training, motivating, and rewarding assistant sales managers and salespeople. Behind a committed staff of secondary school teachers, look for the principal who energizes them to find ways to obtain the resources they need to do an outstanding and innovative job in the classroom. Functional area titles are human resources manager, operations manager, or sales manager.

TOP MANAGERS

In contrast to middle managers, **top managers** are responsible for the performance of *all* departments.[20] They have *cross-departmental* responsibilities and they are responsible for connecting the parts of the organization together. Top managers help carry out the organizational vision; they establish organizational goals, such as which goods and services the company should produce; they decide how the different departments should interact; and they monitor how well middle managers in each department use resources to achieve goals.[21] Top managers are ultimately responsible for the success or failure of an organization, and their performance is continually scrutinized by people inside and outside the organization, such as employees and investors.[22]

> **top managers** Managers who establish organizational goals, decide how departments should interact, and monitor the performance of middle managers.

Top managers report to a company's *chief executive officer (CEO)*—for example, George Croft is the CEO as well as the president of Brick Brewing Co. Limited. He hired Sean Byrne as the *chief financial officer (CFO)*. The CEO and president are responsible for developing good working relationships among the *senior executives* who head the various departments (manufacturing and marketing, for example) and who usually have the title *vice-president or chief*. A central concern of the CEO is the creation of a smoothly functioning **top-management team,** a group composed of the CEO, the president, and the senior executives most responsible for helping to plan and achieve organizational goals and strategies.[23] The CEO also has the responsibility of setting the vision for the organization.

> **top-management team** (1) Groups composed of the CEO, the president, and the heads of the most important departments; (2) Teams that are responsible for developing the strategies that produce an organization's competitive advantage.

The relative importance of each of the four managerial functions—*planning, organizing, leading, and controlling*—to any particular manager depends on the manager's position in the managerial hierarchy.[24] As managers move up the hierarchy, they spend more time planning and organizing resources to maintain and improve organizational performance (see Figure 1.5). Top managers devote most of their time to *planning* and *organizing,* the functions that are so crucial to determining an organization's long-term performance. The lower a manager's position in the hierarchy, the more time he or she spends *leading* and *controlling* first-line managers or nonmanagerial employees.

FIGURE 1.5

Relative Amounts of Time Managers Spend on the Four Managerial Tasks

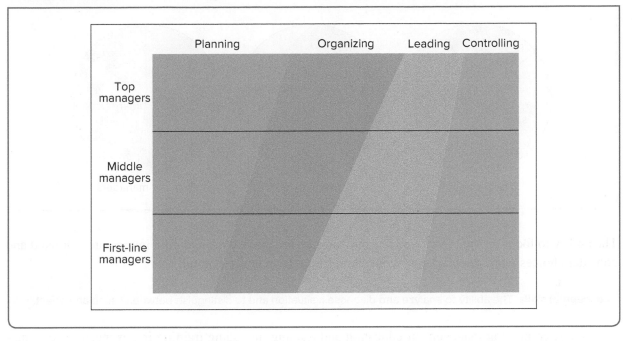

Managerial Skills and Roles

LO4 | Distinguish among the kinds of managerial skills and roles that managers perform.

Managerial Skills

To successfully perform their activities in planning, organizing, leading, and controlling, managers must have certain skills. Research has shown that formal education, training, and experience help managers acquire three principal types of skills: *conceptual, interpersonal,* and *technical.*[25] As you might expect, the level of these skills that a manager needs depends on his or her level in the managerial hierarchy (see Figure 1.6).

CONCEPTUAL SKILLS

Conceptual skills are demonstrated by the ability to analyze and diagnose a situation and to distinguish between cause and effect. Planning and organizing require a high level of conceptual skill. Top managers require the best conceptual skills because their primary responsibilities are planning and organizing.[26] Formal education and training are very important in helping managers develop conceptual skills. Business training at the undergraduate and graduate (MBA) levels provides many of the conceptual tools (theories and techniques in marketing, finance, and other areas) that managers need to perform their roles effectively. Conceptual skills allow managers to understand the big picture confronting an organization.

FIGURE 1.6

Conceptual, Interpersonal, and Technical Skills Used by the Three Levels of Management

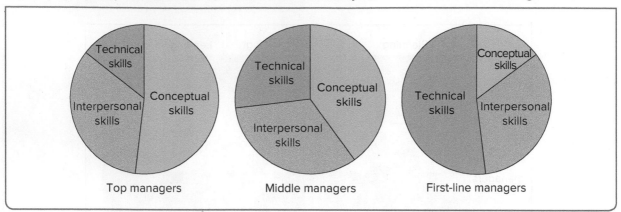

The ability to focus on the big picture lets the manager see beyond the situation immediately at hand and consider choices while keeping the organization's long-term goals in mind.

conceptual skills The ability to analyze and diagnose a situation and to distinguish between cause and effect.

Today, continuing management education and training, including training in advanced IT, are integral in building managerial skills because new theories and techniques are constantly being developed to improve organizational effectiveness, such as *total quality management (TQM), benchmarking, Web-based organization,* and *business-to-business (B2B) networks.* A quick scan through a magazine such as *Canadian Business* reveals a host of seminars on topics such as advanced marketing, finance, leadership, and human resources management that are offered to managers at many levels in the organization, from the most senior corporate executives to middle managers. Suncor, TELUS, BCE, and many other organizations designate a portion of each manager's personal budget to be used at the manager's discretion to attend management development programs.

In addition, organizations may wish to develop a particular manager's abilities in a specific skill area—perhaps to learn an advanced component of departmental skills, such as international bond trading, or to learn the skills necessary to implement total quality management. The organization thus pays for managers to attend specialized programs to develop these skills. Indeed, one signal that a manager is performing well is an organization's willingness to invest in that manager's skill development. Similarly, many nonmanagerial employees who are performing at a high level (because they have studied management) are often sent to intensive management training programs to develop their management skills and to prepare them for promotion to first-level management positions.

INTERPERSONAL SKILLS

Interpersonal skills are people skills. They include the ability to understand, alter, lead, and control the behaviour of other individuals and groups. The ability to communicate and give feedback, to coordinate and motivate people, to give recognition, to mould individuals into a cohesive team, and to play politics effectively distinguishes effective managers from ineffective managers.

interpersonal skills The ability to understand, alter, lead, and control the behaviour of other individuals and groups.

To manage interpersonal interactions effectively, each person in an organization needs to learn how to empathize with other people—to understand their viewpoints and the problems they face. One way to help managers understand their personal strengths and weaknesses is to have their superiors, peers, and subordinates provide feedback about their performance. Thorough and direct feedback allows managers to develop their interpersonal skills. Managers also need to be able to manage politics effectively so that they can deal with resistance from those who disagree with their goals. Effective managers use political strategies to influence others and gain support for their goals, while overcoming resistance or opposition. By all accounts, George Croft and Sean Byrne possess a high level of these interpersonal skills.

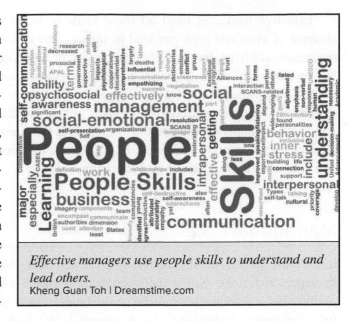

Effective managers use people skills to understand and lead others.
Kheng Guan Toh | Dreamstime.com

Like conceptual skills, interpersonal skills can be learned through education and training, and also can be developed through experience.[27] Organizations increasingly utilize advanced programs in leadership skills and team leadership as they seek to capitalize on the advantages of self-managed teams.[28]

TECHNICAL SKILLS

Technical skills are the job-specific knowledge and techniques that are required to perform an organizational role. Examples include a manager's specific manufacturing, accounting, marketing, and IT skills. Managers need a range of technical skills to be effective. The array of technical skills a person needs depends on his or her position in the organization. The manager of a restaurant, for example, may need cooking skills to fill in for an absent cook, accounting and bookkeeping skills to keep track of receipts and costs and to administer the payroll, and aesthetic skills to keep the restaurant looking attractive for customers.

technical skills Job-specific knowledge and techniques that are required to perform an organizational role.

Today the term **core competency** is often used to refer to the specific set of departmental skills, knowledge, and experience that allows one organization to outperform its competitors. In other words, departmental skills that create a core competency give an organization a competitive advantage. Dell, for example, was the first PC maker to develop a core competency in materials management that allowed it to produce PCs at a much lower cost than its competitors—a major source of competitive advantage. Google is well known for its core competency in research and development (R&D) that allows it to innovate new products at a faster rate than its competitors. From computerized glasses to self-driving cars, Google continues to pioneer the development of technology for the masses.

core competency The specific set of departmental skills, knowledge, and experience that allows one organization to outperform another.

Effective managers need all three kinds of skills—conceptual, interpersonal, and technical. The absence of even one type can lead to failure. One of the biggest problems that people who start small businesses confront, for example, is their lack of appropriate conceptual and people skills. Someone who has the technical skills to start a new business does not necessarily know how to manage the venture successfully. Similarly, one of the biggest problems that scientists or engineers who switch careers from research to management confront is their lack of effective interpersonal skills. Ambitious managers or prospective managers are constantly in search of the latest educational contributions to help them develop the conceptual, interpersonal, and technical skills they need to perform at a high level in today's changing and increasingly competitive global environment.

Managerial Roles

In the early 1970s, McGill University professor Henry Mintzberg detailed 10 specific roles that effective managers undertake in their daily activities. A **role** is a set of specific tasks that a person is expected to perform because of the position he or she holds in an organization. Mintzberg's managerial roles are useful in helping us understand what managers do in a typical hour, day, or week.[29]

role The specific tasks that a person is expected to perform because of the position he or she holds in an organization.

Mintzberg examined all the specific tasks that managers need to perform as they plan, organize, lead, and control organizational resources, and he reduced them to three broad categories and 10 specific roles, outlined in Table 1.1.[30] Managers assume each of these roles in order to influence the behaviour of individuals and groups inside and outside the organization. People inside the organization include other managers and employees. People outside the organization include stakeholders such as shareholders, customers, suppliers, the local community in which an organization is located, and any local or government agency that has an interest in the organization and what it does.[31] Managers often perform several of these roles simultaneously.

TIPS FOR MANAGERS

Personal Development

1. Understand your values, what makes you satisfied from work, and what your level of organizational commitment is.

2. Think about where you see your career heading in two, four, and six years. Make notes.

3. Articulate your hopes and dreams for each time period.

4. As you accomplish your goals and dreams, celebrate your successes and inspire others to action.

TABLE 1.1		

Managerial Roles Identified by Mintzberg

Type of Role	Specific Role	Examples of Role Activities
INTERPERSONAL	Figurehead	Outline future organizational goals to employees at company meetings; open a new corporate headquarters building; state the organization's ethical guidelines and the principles of behaviour employees are to follow in their dealings with customers and suppliers.
	Leader	Provide an example for employees to follow; give direct commands and orders to subordinates; make decisions concerning the use of human and technical resources; mobilize employee support for specific organizational goals.
	Liaison	Coordinate the work of managers in different departments; establish alliances between different organizations to share resources to produce new goods and services.
INFORMATIONAL	Monitor	Evaluate the performance of managers in different functions and take corrective action to improve their performance; watch for changes occurring in the external and internal environment that may affect the organization in the future.
	Disseminator	Inform employees about changes taking place in the external and internal environment that will affect them and the organization; communicate to employees the organization's vision and purpose.
	Spokesperson	Launch a national advertising campaign to promote new goods and services; give a speech to inform the local community about the organization's future intentions.
DECISIONAL	Entrepreneur	Commit organizational resources to develop innovative goods and services; decide to expand internationally to obtain new customers for the organization's products.
	Disturbance handler	Move quickly to take corrective action to deal with unexpected problems facing the organization from the external environment (e.g., a crisis such as an oil spill), or from the internal environment (e.g., producing faulty goods or services).
	Resource allocator	Allocate organizational resources among different functions and departments of the organization; set budgets and salaries of middle and first-level managers.
	Negotiator	Work with suppliers, distributors, and labour unions to reach agreements about the quality and price of input, technical, and human resources; work with other organizations to establish agreements to pool resources to work on joint projects.

The Impact of Values and Attitudes on Organizational Culture and Managerial Behaviour

LO5 | Understand how shared values and norms influence organizational culture and affect managerial behaviour.

What are managers striving to achieve? How do they think they should behave? What do they think about their jobs and organizations? And how do they actually feel at work? We can find some answers to these questions by exploring managers' values, attitudes, and emotions.

Values, attitudes, and moods and emotions capture how managers experience their jobs as individuals. *Values* describe what managers are trying to achieve through work and how they think they should behave. *Attitudes* capture their thoughts and feelings about their specific jobs and organizations. *Moods and emotions* encompass how managers actually feel when they are managing. Although these three aspects of managers' work experience are highly personal, they also have important implications for understanding how managers behave, how they treat and respond to others, and how, through their efforts, they help contribute to organizational effectiveness through planning, leading, organizing, and controlling.

Values: Terminal and Instrumental

The two kinds of personal values are *terminal* and *instrumental*. A **terminal value** is a personal conviction about lifelong goals or objectives; an **instrumental value** is a personal conviction about desired modes of conduct or ways of behaving.[32] Terminal values often lead to the formation of **norms,** which are unwritten, informal codes of conduct, such as behaving honestly or courteously, that prescribe how people should act in particular situations and are considered important by most members of a group or organization. A **value system** shapes what a person wants to achieve in life and how they want to behave.[33]

> **terminal value** A lifelong goal or objective that an individual seeks to achieve.
>
> **instrumental value** A mode of conduct that an individual seeks to follow.
>
> **norms** Unwritten, informal codes of conduct that prescribe how people should act in particular situations and that are considered important by most members of a group or organization.
>
> **value system** The terminal and instrumental values that are guiding principles in an individual's life.

Several terminal values seem to be especially important for managers—such as *a sense of accomplishment (a lasting contribution), equality (brotherhood, equal opportunity for all),* and *self-respect (self-esteem).* A manager who thinks a sense of accomplishment is of paramount importance might focus on making a lasting contribution to an organization by developing a new product that can save or prolong lives, as is true of managers at MaRS (an innovation hub in downtown Toronto that's dedicated to making our work and learning, health, and energy systems more receptive to innovative new ideas, products, and companies), or by mentoring a new startup. A manager who places equality at the top of his or her list of terminal values may be at the forefront of an organization's efforts to support, provide equal opportunities to, and capitalize on the many talents of an increasingly diverse workforce.

Other values are likely to be considered important by many managers, such as *a comfortable life (a prosperous life), an exciting life (a stimulating, active life), freedom (independence, free choice),* and *social recognition (respect, admiration).* The relative importance that managers place on each terminal value helps explain what they are striving to achieve in their organizations and what they will focus their efforts on.

Several of the instrumental values seem to be important modes of conduct for managers, such as being *ambitious (hardworking, aspiring), broad-minded (open-minded), capable (competent, effective), responsible (dependable, reliable),* and *self-controlled (restrained, self-disciplined).* Moreover, the relative importance a manager places on these and other instrumental values may be a significant determinant of actual behaviours on the job. A manager who considers being *imaginative (daring, creative)* to be highly important, for example, is more likely to be innovative and take risks than is a manager who considers this to be less important (all else being equal). A manager who considers being *honest (sincere, truthful)* to be of paramount importance may be a driving force for taking steps to ensure that all members of a unit or organization behave ethically and have purpose in their work.

All in all, managers' value systems signify what managers as individuals are trying to accomplish and become in their personal lives and at work. Thus managers' value systems are fundamental guides to their behaviour and efforts at planning, leading, organizing, and controlling.

Attitudes

An **attitude** is a collection of feelings and beliefs. Like everyone else, managers have attitudes about their jobs and organizations, and these attitudes affect how they approach their jobs. Two of the most important attitudes in this context are job satisfaction and organizational commitment.

attitude A collection of feelings and beliefs.

Job satisfaction is the collection of feelings and beliefs that managers have about their current jobs.[34] Managers who have high levels of job satisfaction generally like their jobs, feel they are fairly treated, and believe their jobs have many desirable features or characteristics (such as interesting work, good pay and job security, autonomy, or nice co-workers). Figure 1.7 shows sample items from two scales

FIGURE 1.7

Sample Items from Two Measures of Job Satisfaction

Sample items from the Minnesota Satisfaction Questionnaire:
People respond to each of the items in the scale by checking whether they are:

[ ] Very dissatisfied
[ ] Dissatisfied
[ ] Can't decide whether satisfied or not
[ ] Satisfied
[ ] Very satisfied

On my present job, this is how I feel about . . .

____ **1.** Being able to do things that don't go against my conscience.
____ **2.** The way my job provides for steady employment.
____ **3.** The chance to do things for other people.
____ **4.** The chance to do something that makes use of my abilities.
____ **5.** The way company policies are put into practice.
____ **6.** My pay and the amount of work I do.
____ **7.** The chances for advancement on this job.
____ **8.** The freedom to use my own judgment.
____ **9.** The working conditions.
____ **10.** The way my co-workers get along with each other.
____ **11.** The praise I get for doing a good job.
____ **12.** The feeling of accomplishment I get from the job.

The Faces Scale
Workers select the face which best expresses how they feel about their job in general.

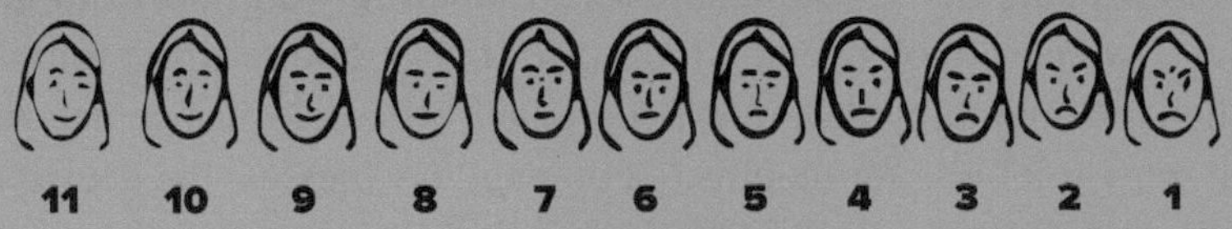
11 10 9 8 7 6 5 4 3 2 1

Source: D.J. Weiss et al., *Manual for the Minnesota Satisfaction Questionnaire*. Copyrighted by the Vocational Psychology Research, University of Minnesota; copyright © 1975 by the American Psychological Association.

that managers can use to measure job satisfaction. Levels of job satisfaction tend to increase as one moves up the hierarchy in an organization. Upper managers, in general, tend to be more satisfied with their jobs than entry-level employees. Managers' levels of job satisfaction can range from very low to very high.

job satisfaction The collection of feelings and beliefs that managers have about their current jobs.

In general, it is desirable for managers to be satisfied with their jobs, for at least two reasons. First, satisfied managers may be more likely to go the extra mile for their organization or perform **organizational citizenship behaviours (OCBs)**—behaviours that are not required of organizational members but that contribute to and are necessary for organizational efficiency, effectiveness, and competitive advantage.[35] Managers who are satisfied with their jobs are more likely to perform these "above and beyond the call of duty" behaviours, which can range from putting in long hours when needed to coming up with truly creative ideas and overcoming obstacles to implement them (even when doing so is not part of the manager's job), or to going out of one's way to help a co-worker, subordinate, or superior (even when doing so entails considerable personal sacrifice).[36]

organizational citizenship behaviours (OCBs) Behaviours that are not required of organizational members but that contribute to and are necessary for organizational efficiency, effectiveness, and competitive advantage.

A second reason why it is desirable for managers to be satisfied with their jobs is that satisfied managers may be less likely to quit.[37] A manager who is highly satisfied may never even think about looking for another position; a dissatisfied manager may always be on the lookout for new opportunities. Turnover can hurt an organization because it results in the loss of the experience and knowledge that managers have gained about the company, industry, and business environment.

A growing source of dissatisfaction for many lower- and middle-level managers, as well as for nonmanagerial employees, is the threat of unemployment and increased workloads from organizational downsizings and layoffs. Organizations that try to improve their efficiency through restructuring and layoffs often eliminate a sizable number of first-line and middle management positions. This decision obviously hurts the managers who are laid off, and it also can reduce the job satisfaction levels of managers who remain. They might fear being the next to be let go. In addition, the workloads of remaining employees often are dramatically increased as a result of restructuring, and this can contribute to dissatisfaction.

How managers and organizations handle layoffs is of paramount importance, not only for the layoff victims but also for employees who survive the layoff and keep their jobs.[38] Showing compassion and empathy for layoff victims, giving them as much advance notice as possible about the layoff, providing clear information about severance benefits, and helping layoff victims in their job search efforts are a few of the ways in which managers can humanely manage a layoff.[39] For example, when Ron Thomas, then vice-president of organizational development for Martha Stewart Living Omnimedia, had to lay off employees as a result of closing the organization's catalogue business, he personally called all the other catalogue businesses he knew to find out about potential positions for laid-off employees.[40] Efforts such as Thomas's to help layoff victims find new jobs can contribute to the job satisfaction of those who survive the layoff. As Thomas puts it, "If you handle a restructuring well, the word gets out that you're a good place to work . . . if we post a job opening today, we'll get 1,500 resumés tomorrow."[41]

Unfortunately, when the unemployment rate is high, laid-off employees sometimes find it difficult to find new jobs and can remain jobless for months.[42] For small businesses, the decision to lay off employees and communicating that decision can be especially painful because managers often have developed close personal relationships with the people they have to let go, know their families, and fear what will happen to them with the loss of a steady income.[43]

Organizational commitment is the collection of feelings and beliefs that managers have about their organization as a whole.[44] Managers who are committed to their organizations believe in what their organizations are doing, are proud of what these organizations stand for, and feel a high degree of loyalty toward their organizations. Committed managers are more likely to go above and beyond the call of duty to help their company and are less likely to quit.[45] Organizational commitment can be especially strong when employees and managers truly believe in organizational values; it also leads to a strong organizational culture.

> **organizational commitment** The collection of feelings and beliefs that managers have about their organization as a whole.

Organizational commitment is likely to help managers perform some of their figurehead and spokesperson roles. It is much easier for a manager to persuade others both inside and outside the organization of the merits of what the organization has done and is seeking to accomplish if the manager truly believes in and is committed to the organization.

Do managers in different countries have similar or different attitudes? Differences in the levels of job satisfaction and organizational commitment among managers in different countries are likely because these managers have different kinds of opportunities and rewards and because they face different political, economic, and sociocultural forces in their organizations' general environments. Levels of organizational commitment from one country to another may depend on the extent to which countries have legislation affecting firings and layoffs and the extent to which citizens of a country are geographically mobile.

Moods and Emotions

Just as you sometimes are in a bad mood and at other times are in a good mood, so too are managers. A **mood** is a feeling or state of mind. When people are in a positive mood, they feel excited, enthusiastic, active, or elated.[46] When people are in a negative mood, they feel distressed, fearful, scornful, hostile, jittery, or nervous.[47] People who are high on extraversion are especially likely to experience positive moods; people who are high on negative affectivity are especially likely to experience negative moods. People's situations or circumstances also determine their moods; however, receiving a raise is likely to put most people in a good mood regardless of their personality traits. People who are high on negative affectivity are not always in a bad mood, and people who are low on extraversion still experience positive moods.[48]

> **mood** A feeling or state of mind.

Emotions are more intense feelings than moods, are often directly linked to whatever caused the emotion, and are more short-lived.[49] However, once whatever has triggered the emotion has been dealt with, the feelings may linger in the form of a less intense mood.[50] For example, a manager who gets very angry when a subordinate has engaged in an unethical behaviour may find his anger decreasing in intensity once he has decided how to address the problem. Yet he continues to be in a bad mood the rest of the day, even though he is not directly thinking about the unfortunate incident.[51]

> **emotions** Intense, relatively short-lived feelings.

Research has found that moods and emotions affect the behaviour of managers and all members of an organization. For example, research suggests that the subordinates of managers who experience positive moods at work may perform at somewhat higher levels and be less likely to resign and leave the organization than the subordinates of managers who do not tend to be in a positive mood at work.[52] Other research suggests that under certain conditions creativity might be enhanced by positive moods, whereas under other conditions negative moods might push people to work harder to come up with truly creative ideas.[53] Recognizing that both mood states have the potential to contribute to creativity in different ways, recent research suggests that employees may be especially likely to be creative to the extent that they experience both mood states (at different times) on the job and to the extent that the work environment is supportive of creativity.[54]

Other research suggests that moods and emotions may play an important role in ethical decision making. For example, researchers at Princeton University found that when people are trying to solve difficult personal moral dilemmas, the parts of their brains that are responsible for emotions and moods are especially active.[55]

More generally, emotions and moods give managers and all employees important information and signals about what is going on in the workplace.[56] Positive emotions and moods signal that things are going well and thus can lead to more expansive, and even playful, thinking. Negative emotions and moods signal that there are problems in need of attention and areas for improvement. So when people are in negative moods, they tend to be more detail-oriented and focused on the facts at hand.[57] Some studies suggest that critical thinking and devil's advocacy may be promoted by a negative mood, and sometimes especially accurate judgments may be made by managers in negative moods.[58]

In understanding the effects of managers' and all employees' moods and emotions, it is important to take into account their levels of emotional intelligence. **Emotional intelligence** is the ability to understand and manage one's own moods and emotions and the moods and emotions of other people.[59] Managers with a high level of emotional intelligence are more likely to understand how they are feeling and why, and they are more able to effectively manage their feelings. When managers are experiencing stressful feelings and emotions such as fear or anxiety, emotional intelligence lets them understand why and manage these feelings so they do not get in the way of effective decision making.[60]

emotional intelligence The ability to understand and manage one's own moods and emotions and the moods and emotions of other people.

Emotional intelligence also can help managers perform their important roles, such as their interpersonal roles (figurehead, leader, and liaison).[61] Understanding how your subordinates feel, why they feel that way, and how to manage these feelings is central to developing strong interpersonal bonds with them.[62] More generally, emotional intelligence has the potential to contribute to effective leadership in multiple ways.[63]

For example, emotional intelligence helps managers understand and relate well to other people.[64] It also helps managers maintain their enthusiasm and confidence and energize subordinates to help the organization attain its goals.[65] Recent theorizing and research suggest that emotional intelligence may be especially important in awakening employee creativity.[66] Managers themselves are increasingly recognizing the importance of emotional intelligence.

Organizational Culture

Personality is a way of understanding why all managers and employees, as individuals, characteristically think and behave in different ways. However, when people belong to the same organization, they tend to share certain beliefs and values that lead them to act in similar ways.[67] **Organizational culture** comprises the shared set of beliefs, expectations, values, norms, and work routines that influence how members of an organization relate to one another and work together to achieve organizational goals. In essence, organizational culture reflects the distinctive ways in which organizational members perform their jobs and relate to others inside and outside the organization. It may, for example, be how customers in a particular hotel chain are treated from the time they are greeted at check-in until they leave; or it may be the shared work routines that research teams use to guide new product development. When organizational members share an intense commitment to cultural values, beliefs, and routines and use them to achieve their goals, a *strong* organizational culture exists.[68] When organizational members are not strongly committed to a shared system of values, beliefs, and routines, organizational culture is *weak*.

> **organizational culture** The shared set of beliefs, expectations, values, norms, and work routines that influence how individuals, groups, and teams interact with one another and cooperate to achieve organizational goals.

The stronger the culture of an organization, the more one can think about it as being the "personality" of an organization because it influences the way its members behave.[69] Organizations that possess strong cultures may differ on a wide variety of dimensions that determine how their members behave toward one another and perform their jobs. For example, organizations differ in how members relate to each other (formally or informally), how important decisions are made (top-down or bottom-up), willingness to change (flexible or unyielding), innovation (creative or predictable), and playfulness (serious or serendipitous). In an innovative design firm like IDEO Product Development in Silicon Valley, employees are encouraged to adopt a playful attitude toward their work, look outside the organization to find inspiration, and adopt a flexible approach toward product design that uses multiple perspectives.[70] IDEO's culture is vastly different from that of companies such as CIBC and SickKids Foundation, in which employees treat each other in a more formal or deferential way, employees are expected to adopt a serious approach to their work, and decision making is constrained by the hierarchy of authority.

MANAGERS AND ORGANIZATIONAL CULTURE

While all members of an organization can contribute to developing and maintaining organizational culture, managers play a particularly important part in influencing organizational culture[71] because of their multiple and important roles. How managers create culture is most vividly evident in startups of new companies. Entrepreneurs who start their own companies are typically also the startups' top managers until the companies grow and become profitable. Often referred to as the firms' founders, these managers literally create their organizations' cultures.

The founders' personal characteristics play an important role in the creation of organizational culture. Benjamin Schneider, a well-known management researcher, developed a model that helps to explain the role that founders' personal characteristics play in determining organizational culture.[72] His model, called the **attraction–selection–attrition (ASA) framework,** posits that when founders hire employees for their new ventures, they tend to be attracted to and choose employees whose personalities are similar to their own.[73] These similar employees are more likely to stay with the organization. Although employees who are dissimilar in personality might be hired, they are more likely to leave the organization over time.[74] As a result of these attraction, selection, and attrition processes, people in the organization tend to have similar personalities, and the typical or dominant personality profile of organizational members determines and shapes organizational culture.[75]

> **attraction–selection–attrition (ASA) framework** A model that explains how personality may influence organizational culture.

For example, when David Kelley became interested in engineering and product design challenges in the late 1970s, he realized that who he was as a person meant he would not be happy working in a typical corporate environment. Kelley is high on openness to experience, driven to go where his interests take him, and not content to follow others' directives. Kelley recognized that he needed to start his own business, and with the help of other Stanford-schooled engineers and design experts, IDEO was born.[76]

From the start, IDEO's culture has embodied Kelley's spirited, freewheeling approach to work and design—from colourful and informal workspaces to an emphasis on networking and communicating with as many people as possible to understand a design problem. No project or problem is too big or too small for IDEO; the company designed the Apple Lisa computer and mouse (the precursor of the Mac) and the Palm as well as the Crest Neat Squeeze toothpaste dispenser and the Racer's Edge water bottle.[77] Kelley hates rules, job titles, big corner offices, and all the other trappings of large traditional organizations that stifle creativity. Employees who are attracted to, selected by, and remain with IDEO value creativity and innovation and embrace this IDEO motto: "Fail often to succeed sooner."[78]

Although ASA processes are most evident in small firms such as IDEO, they also can operate in large companies.[79] According to the ASA model, this is a naturally occurring phenomenon to the extent that managers and new hires are free to make the kinds of choices the model specifies. However, while people tend to get along well with others who are similar to themselves, too much similarity in an organization can impair organizational effectiveness. That is, similar people tend to view conditions and events in similar ways and thus can be resistant to change. Moreover, organizations benefit from a diversity of perspectives rather than similarity in perspectives. At IDEO, Kelley recognized early on how important it is to take advantage of the diverse talents and perspectives that people with different personalities, backgrounds, experiences, and education can bring to a design team. Hence, IDEO's design teams include not only engineers but others who might have a unique insight into a problem, such as anthropologists, communications experts, doctors, and users of a product. When new employees are hired at IDEO, they meet many employees who have different backgrounds and characteristics; the focus is not on hiring someone who will fit in but, rather, on hiring someone who has something to offer and can "wow" different kinds of people with his or her insights.

Managers who are satisfied with their jobs, are committed to their organizations, and experience positive moods and emotions might also encourage these attitudes and feelings in others. The result would be an organizational culture emphasizing positive attitudes and feelings. Research suggests that attitudes like job satisfaction and organizational commitment can be affected by the influence of others. Managers are in a particularly strong position to engage in social influence given their multiple roles. Moreover, research suggests that moods and emotions can be contagious and that spending time with people who are excited and enthusiastic can increase one's own levels of excitement and enthusiasm.

THE ROLE OF VALUES AND NORMS IN ORGANIZATIONAL CULTURE

Shared terminal and instrumental values play a particularly important role in organizational culture. *Terminal values* signify what an organization and its employees are trying to accomplish, and *instrumental values* guide how the organization and its members achieve organizational goals. In addition to values, shared norms also are a key aspect of organizational culture. Recall that norms are unwritten, informal rules or guidelines that prescribe appropriate behaviour in particular situations. For example, norms at IDEO include not being critical of others' ideas, coming up with multiple ideas before settling on one, and developing prototypes of new products.[80]

Managers determine and shape organizational culture through the kinds of values and norms they promote in an organization. Some managers, like David Kelley of IDEO, cultivate values and norms that encourage risk taking, creative responses to problems and opportunities, experimentation, tolerance of failure in order to succeed, and autonomy.[81] Top managers at organizations such as Microsoft and Google encourage employees to adopt such values to support their commitment to innovation as a source of competitive advantage.

Other managers, however, might cultivate values and norms that tell employees they should be conservative and cautious in their dealings with others and should consult their superiors before making important decisions or any changes to the status quo. Accountability for actions and decisions is stressed, and detailed records are kept to ensure that policies and procedures are followed. In settings where caution is needed—nuclear power stations, oil refineries, chemical plants, financial institutions, insurance companies—a conservative, cautious approach to making decisions might be appropriate.[82] In a nuclear power plant, for example, the catastrophic consequences of a mistake make a high level of supervision vital. Similarly, in a bank or mutual fund company, the risk of losing investors' money makes a cautious approach to investing appropriate.

Managers of different kinds of organizations deliberately cultivate and develop the organizational values and norms that are best suited to their task and general environments, strategy, or technology. Organizational culture is maintained and transmitted to organizational members through the values of the founder, the process of socialization, ceremonies and rites, and stories and language (see Figure 1.8).

Values of the Founder From the ASA model just discussed, it is clear that founders of an organization can have profound and long-lasting effects on organizational culture. Founders' values inspire the founders to start their own companies and, in turn, drive the nature of these new companies and their defining characteristics. Thus an organization's founder and his or her terminal and instrumental values have a substantial influence on the values, norms, and standards of behaviour that develop over time within the organization.[83] Founders set the scene for the way cultural values and norms develop because their own values guide the building of the company, and they hire other managers and employees who they believe will share these values and help the organization to attain them. Moreover, new managers quickly learn from the founder what values and norms are appropriate in the organization and thus what is desired of them. Subordinates imitate the style of the founder and, in turn, transmit their values and norms to their subordinates. Gradually, over time, the founder's values and norms permeate the organization.[84]

A founder who requires a great display of respect from subordinates and insists on such things as formal job titles and formal modes of dress encourages subordinates to act this way toward *their* subordinates. Often, a founder's personal values affect an organization's competitive advantage. Frank Stronach, founder of Magna Corporation, based in Aurora, Ontario, believes that his employees should show a "strong sense of ownership and entrepreneurial energy." He practises this belief by diverting 10 percent

FIGURE 1.8

Factors That Maintain and Transmit Organizational Culture

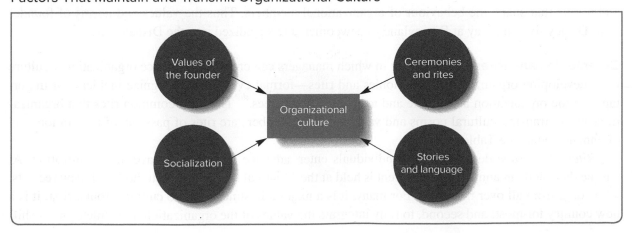

of pre-tax profit to profit-sharing programs for his employees. Similarly, managers' salaries are deliberately set "below industry standards" so that managers will earn more through profit-sharing bonuses. To further emphasize managerial responsibility, Magna's managers are given considerable autonomy over buying, selling, and hiring. Through these policies of profit-sharing and empowerment, Stronach has developed a workforce that has made Magna one of the largest and most profitable companies in the country.

Another success story in "living the dreams" and upholding the values of the founder is the innovative Canadian company Cirque du Soleil. Every travelling Cirque du Soleil show has its own creative director who makes sure the production stays true to the vision and passion of its co-founder Guy Laliberté.[85]

Socialization Over time, organizational members learn from each other which values are important in an organization and the norms that specify appropriate and inappropriate behaviours. Eventually organizational members behave in accordance with the organization's values and norms—often without realizing they are doing so.

Organizational socialization is the process by which newcomers learn an organization's values and norms and acquire the work behaviours necessary to perform jobs effectively.[86] As a result of their socialization experiences, organizational members internalize an organization's values and norms and behave in accordance with them not only because they think they have to but because they think these values and norms describe the right and proper way to behave.[87]

organizational socialization The process by which newcomers learn an organization's values and norms and acquire the work behaviours necessary to perform jobs effectively.

Most organizations have some kind of socialization program to help new employees learn the ropes—the values, norms, and culture of the organization. The military, for example, is well known for the rigorous socialization process it uses to turn raw recruits into trained soldiers. Organizations such as the Walt Disney Company also put new recruits through a rigorous training program to teach them to perform well in their jobs and play their parts in helping Disneyland visitors have fun in a wholesome theme park. New recruits at Disney are called "cast members" and attend Disney University to learn the Disney culture and their parts in it. Disney's culture emphasizes the values of safety, courtesy, entertainment, and efficiency, and these values are brought to life for newcomers at Disney University. Newcomers also learn about the attraction area they will be joining (such as Adventureland or Fantasyland) at Disney University and then receive on-the-job socialization in the area itself from experienced cast members.[88] Through organizational socialization, founders and managers of an organization transmit to employees the cultural values and norms that shape the behaviour of organizational members. Thus the values and norms of founder Walt Disney live on today at Disneyland as newcomers are socialized into the Disney way.

Ceremonies and Rites Another way in which managers can create or influence organizational culture is by developing organizational ceremonies and rites—formal events that recognize incidents of importance to the organization as a whole and to specific employees.[89] The most common rites that organizations use to transmit cultural norms and values to their members are rites of passage, of integration, and of enhancement (see Table 1.2).[90]

Rites of passage determine how individuals enter, advance within, and leave the organization. At Cirque du Soleil, an annual training event is held at the Montreal headquarters studio for all new recruits, who come from all over the world. For many, it is a major adjustment on two cultural fronts: first, it is a new country for most; and second, to fully integrate the values of the organization, the athletes must shift

TABLE 1.2

Organizational Rites

Type of Rite	Example of Rite	Purpose of Rite
Rite of passage	Induction and basic training	Learn and internalize norms and values
Rite of integration	Office holiday party	Build common norms and values
Rite of enhancement	Presentation of annual award	Motivate commitment to norms and values

their focus from a world of competition to a world of expression. The socialization programs developed by all organizations are rites of passage. Likewise, the ways in which an organization prepares people for promotion or retirement are rites of passage.

Sometimes, rites of passage can get out of hand. Fraternities, sororities, sports teams, and even the military have been known to use hazing to initiate members. Activities can include "sleep deprivation, public nudity and childish pranks or, at worst, extreme drunkenness, gross racial slurs, even beatings."[91] The videotaped hazing rituals at CFB Petawawa caused the Airborne Regiment to be disbanded. While the goal of the hazing might have been to desensitize new recruits to the brutality of war, many Canadians felt that the practice had gone too far. In Australia, a court held an organization liable for assault after a teenager, who was wrapped in cling film during a hazing ritual, prosecuted a company and two of its directors for assault under workplace safety laws.

Rites of integration, such as office parties, company cookouts, and shared announcements of organizational successes, build as well as reinforce common bonds among organizational members. WestJet, based out of Calgary, is well known for its efforts to develop ceremonies and rituals to bond employees to the organization by showing them that they are valued members. WestJet holds large profit-sharing parties twice annually, one in the fall and another in the spring, to literally give cheques to workers. "One of the hallmarks of our culture is celebrating success," president and CEO Gregg Saretsky explains. "I can't think of a better way to celebrate success than actually physically handing out checks . . . We have a big party. Live music, an open bar. We have fun. Everybody is standing shoulder to shoulder and it's very much kind of a festival atmosphere."[92]

Rites of enhancement, such as awards dinners, newspaper releases, and employee promotions, let organizations publicly recognize and reward employees' contributions and thus strengthen their commitment to organizational values. By bonding members within the organization, rites of enhancement reinforce an organization's values and norms.

WestJet celebrates success with fun staff meetings.
Mark Blinch/Newscom

Stories and Language Stories and language also communicate organizational culture. At WestJet, you never hear people using the word "passengers," only travelling "guests." Stories (whether fact or fiction) about organizational heroes and villains and their actions provide important clues about values and norms. Such stories can reveal the kinds of behaviours that are valued by the organization and the kinds of practices that are frowned on.[93] Stories about Steve Jobs, the person (hero) who made Apple Computers the company it is today, shed light on many aspects of the company's corporate culture. Stories also about Bill Newnham, founder of Seneca College in Toronto, speak volumes about his spirit and how this spirit lives on in the organizational culture of the college.[94] Language—through slogans, symbols, and jargon—is used to help employees come to know expectations while bonding with one another.

The concept of organizational language encompasses not only spoken language but also how people dress, the offices they occupy, the cars they drive, and the degree of formality they use when they address one another. IBM Canada, long known for its dark-blue suits, introduced less formal clothing in the 1990s so that customers would feel more comfortable when interacting with the company.[95] When employees "speak" and understand the language of their organization's culture, they know how to behave in the organization and what attitudes are expected of them.

MATERIAL SYMBOLS

The organization's layout is a material symbol, and so are the size of offices; whether individuals wear uniforms or have a dress code; and the kinds of cars that top executives are given.[96] Material symbols convey to employees who is important, how much distance there is between top management and employees, and what kinds of behaviour are appropriate. For example, at Toronto-based Willow Manufacturing, an industrial machining firm, everyone from the CEO down wears the same type of uniform. This is typical of industrial environments, especially in Asia, where conformity to group norms is important to the production process. It is not so common in high-tech design firms, where conformity to a dress code is less likely to be part of the culture of the organization.

Midlevel workers at WestJet sit in cubicles that are positioned close to large windows, providing plenty of natural light and a view of aircraft landing and taking off at Calgary International, where the picturesque Rocky Mountains are visible in the background. Senior executives' modern but modest offices are, on the other hand, at the building's interior with no window view. Similarly, at Husky Injection Molding Systems, based in Bolton, Ontario, employees and management share the parking lot, dining room, and even washrooms, conveying the sense of an egalitarian workplace.

CULTURE AND MANAGERIAL ACTION

While founders and managers play a critical role in developing, maintaining, and communicating organizational culture, this same culture shapes and controls the behaviour of all employees, including managers themselves. For example, culture influences how managers perform their four main functions: planning, organizing, leading, and controlling. As we consider these functions, we continue to distinguish between top managers who create organizational values and norms that encourage creative, innovative behaviour and top managers who encourage a conservative, cautious approach by their subordinates. We noted earlier that both kinds of values and norms can be appropriate depending on the situation and type of organization.

Planning Top managers in an organization with an *innovative* culture are likely to encourage lower-level managers to take part in the planning process and develop a flexible approach to planning. They are likely to be willing to listen to new ideas and to take risks involving the development of new products.

In contrast, top managers in an organization with *conservative* values are likely to emphasize formal top-down planning. Suggestions from lower-level managers are likely to be subjected to a formal review, which can significantly slow down decision making. Although this deliberate approach may improve the quality of decision making in a nuclear power plant, it also can have unintended consequences. At conservative IBM, for example, before its more recent turnaround, the planning process became so formalized that managers spent most of their time assembling complex slide shows and overheads to defend their current positions rather than thinking about what they should be doing to keep IBM abreast of the changes taking place in the computer industry.

Organizing What kinds of organizing will managers in innovative and in conservative cultures encourage? Valuing creativity, managers in an *innovative* culture are likely to try to create an organic structure, one that is flat, with few levels in the hierarchy, and in which authority is decentralized so that employees are encouraged to work together to find solutions to ongoing problems. A product team structure may be very suitable for an organization with an innovative culture.

In contrast, managers in a *conservative* culture are likely to create a well-defined hierarchy of authority and establish clear reporting relationships so that employees know exactly whom to report to and how to react to any problems that arise.

Leading In an *innovative* culture, managers are likely to lead by example, encouraging employees to take risks and experiment. They are supportive regardless of employees succeeding or failing.

In contrast, managers in a conservative culture are likely to develop a rigid management by objectives system and to constantly monitor subordinates' progress toward goals, overseeing their every move. We examine leadership in detail in Chapters 8 and 9 when we consider the leadership styles that managers can adopt to influence and shape employee behaviour.

Controlling The ways in which managers evaluate and take actions to improve performance differ depending on whether the organizational culture emphasizes formality and caution or innovation and change. Managers who want to encourage the development of *innovative* values and norms that encourage risk-taking recognize that there are multiple potential paths to success and that failure must be accepted for creativity to thrive. Thus they are less concerned about employees performing their jobs in a specific, predetermined manner and in strict adherence to preset goals and more concerned about employees being flexible and taking the initiative to come up with ideas for improving performance. Managers in innovative cultures are also more concerned about long-term performance than short-term targets because they recognize that real innovation entails much uncertainty that necessitates flexibility.

In contrast, managers in cultures that emphasize caution and maintenance of the status quo often set specific, difficult goals for employees, frequently monitor progress toward these goals, and develop a clear set of rules that employees are expected to adhere to.

Sometimes managers who are hired by a company do not fit into the existing culture. WestJet fired CEO Steve Smith, who was far more controlling than the company's culture warranted. WestJet's founders sent a strong message to the employees by firing Smith in a year when the company had done very well financially.

The values and norms of an organization's culture strongly affect the way managers perform their management functions. The extent to which managers buy into the values and norms of their organization shapes their view of the world and their actions and decisions in particular circumstances.[97] In turn, the actions that managers take can have an impact on the performance of the organization. Thus, organizational culture, managerial action, and organizational performance are linked together.

Although organizational culture can give rise to managerial actions that ultimately benefit the organization, this is not always the case. Sometimes culture can become so much a part of the organization that it becomes difficult to effect change and improve performance.[98] For example, Wayne Sales, the former

CEO of Canadian Tire, tried desperately to revitalize customer service in the company's stores. Canadians had become so used to poor service that employees did not see the need to change. However, with increased competition from Home Depot Canada, RONA, Home Hardware, and Lowe's Canada, lack of customer service is a big issue. Sales set out to "drive away the chain's 'Crappy Tire' image" by changing the culture to encourage employees to be more customer-focused.[99]

> *"Management from the bottom gives employees pride in fulfilling the company's overall objectives without interference from supervisors."*
>
> Clive Beddoe, Chair of the Board of Directors of WestJet

FOCUS ON   *The Social Economy*

Goodwill®

Goodwill inspires hope and self-confidence, helping people from all backgrounds to feel successful, valuable, and dignified.

Goodwill organizations help people earn a living, improve their lives, and strengthen their families and their communities.

The network of 162 independent, community-based Goodwill organizations in the United States and Canada offers employment placement, customized job training, and other services to people facing challenges to finding employment. In 2017, more than 38 million people used computers and mobile devices to access Goodwill education, training, mentoring and online learning services to strengthen their skills. Goodwill helped people train for careers in industries such as information technology, healthcare, retail, hospitality, manufacturing, construction, and automotive services. Goodwill organizations also provide job placement services such as resumé preparation, financial education, and access to transportation and child care.

More than two million people received in-person Goodwill services to build their career and financial assets in 2017. As a result, these individuals increased their collective lifetime earnings and contributed to their communities as productive, tax-paying citizens.

Goodwill meets the diverse needs of people seeking to advance their careers, including people with disabilities, veterans and military families, older workers, youth and young adults, and people reintegrating back into society. In 2017 Goodwill organizations received more than 105 million donations. Local Goodwill organizations sell the donated clothes and household goods at retail stores and online. The revenue generated supports job placement and training programs within the same community.

Goodwills also generate revenue by contracting with businesses and government to provide a wide range of commercial services, including janitorial, manufacturing, warehousing and distribution, packaging and assembly, food preparation, document management, and more.

1. Research Goodwill and find out how they help mitigate or buffer the forces of restructuring and outsourcing.

2. Describe the types and levels of managers found at Goodwill.

Source: http://www.goodwill.org/about-us/. Accessed July 18, 2018.

Chapter 1

SUMMARY AND REVIEW

connect

LO1 What Is Management? A manager is a person responsible for supervising the use of an organization's resources to meet its goals. An organization is a collection of people who work together and coordinate their actions to achieve a wide variety of goals. Management is the process of using organizational resources to achieve organizational goals effectively and efficiently through planning, organizing, leading, and controlling. An efficient organization makes the most productive use of its resources. An effective organization pursues appropriate goals and achieves these goals by using its resources to create the goods or services that customers want.

LO2 Managerial Tasks and Activities The four principal managerial tasks are planning, organizing, leading, and controlling. Managers at all levels and in all departments of the organization perform these functions in varying degrees. Effective management means managing these activities successfully.

LO3 Types and Levels of Managers Managers are characterized by level and function. Functions typically include marketing, operations, human resources, accounting and finance, and research and development. Organizations typically have three levels of management. First-line managers are responsible for the day-to-day supervision of nonmanagerial employees. Middle managers are responsible for developing and utilizing organizational resources efficiently and effectively. Top managers have cross-departmental responsibilities. The job of top managers is to establish appropriate goals for the entire organization and to verify that department managers are using resources effectively and efficiently to achieve those goals.

LO4 Managerial Skills and Roles Three types of skills help managers perform their roles effectively: conceptual, interpersonal, and technical skills. According to Mintzberg, managers enact 10 specific roles in their daily activities: figurehead, leader, liaison, monitor, disseminator, spokesperson, entrepreneur, disturbance handler, resource allocator, and negotiator.

LO5 Values, Attitudes and Organizational Culture

The values, attitudes, and moods and emotions of managers affect the shared set of beliefs, expectations, norms, and work routines—or organizational culture—that shape how managers plan, organize, lead, and control organizational resources to achieve goals. Organizational socialization is the process by which newcomers learn an organization's values and norms and acquire the work behaviours necessary to perform jobs effectively.

KEY TERMS

attitude	department
attraction–selection–attrition (ASA) framework	effectiveness
blended value	efficiency
collective impact	emotional intelligence
conceptual skills	emotions
controlling	first-line managers
core competency	instrumental value
	interpersonal skills

job satisfaction	organizations
leading	organizing
management	performance level
manager	planning
middle managers	resources
mood	role
norms	social economy
organizational citizenship behaviours (OCBs)	strategy
organizational commitment	technical skills
organizational culture	terminal value
organizational performance	top managers
organizational socialization	top-management team
organizational structure	value systems

WRAP-UP TO OPENING CASE

Management at Brick Brewing Co. Limited

In the opening case you were introduced to two top managers at Brick Brewing Co., Sean Byrne, CFO, and George Croft, CEO. After having read and understood the concepts in this chapter you should now be able to answer the following questions:

1. *What kinds of activities or tasks are involved in planning, organizing, leading, and controlling at Brick Brewing?*

   ANSWER: Planning involves setting organizational goals and finding the best ways, or strategy, to achieve them. The top managers at Brick Brewing Company use several strategies concurrently to offer products of quality and value to its customers. Purchasing the rights to Seagram Coolers strengthens their goal to provide specialty beverages. They are credited with founding the craft beer renaissance in Canada and have won awards for their premium craft beers, thereby differentiating themselves from other breweries. Brick Brewing also offers the lowest legally priced beer with its Laker brand, indicating a low-cost strategy can co-exist with a differentiation strategy.

   Organizing involves putting people and allocating resources into jobs and grouping jobs together to coordinate tasks and achieve organizational goals. It involves creating lines of authority and establishing reporting relationships. In this case, Sean Byrne is responsible for the financial management of the company. In his capacity as CFO he allocated the funds necessary to purchase the Seagram Cooler brand from Corby and oversaw the deal to license the brand in Quebec. He reports directly to George Croft, CEO.

   Leading involves creating and communicating a vision for the organization that motivates people to achieve organizational goals. George Croft and Sean Byrne created a high-performing team that won the company recognition for their premium beers, while also providing the cheap brand that is very popular among consumers. The vision: to sell a quality product at a reasonable price.

   Controlling involves determining how well organizational goals have been achieved and taking corrective actions to improve performance. Brick Brewing achieves its goals by using quality assurance techniques to carefully monitor its brewing practices. This ensures a high level of performance.

2. *Characterize the type and level of management described in the case.*

ANSWER: Sean Byrne as chief financial officer (CFO) is a top manager at Brick Brewing Co. His functional or departmental area is finance. He would likely supervise middle and first-line managers in the finance department.

George Croft is the top manager as chief executive officer (CEO). Sean Byrne would be part of his top management team, as would other heads or vice-presidents of other departments. The CEO is responsible for the overall well-being and operation of the whole organization. He or she sets the vision, organizational goals, and strategy.

3. *What skills does Sean Byrne bring to the Brick Brewing Co. as a top manager?*

ANSWER: All three sets of managerial skills are evident in this case on the part of Sean Byrne: conceptual skills are evident in the use of "business judgment and contribution to overall strategy"; interpersonal skills are evident in negotiating the licensing arrangement in Quebec; and technical skills are evident in his role as a professional chartered accountant and secretary to the audit committee of the board.

4. *Which of Mintzberg's managerial roles are illustrated in this case by each manager?*

ANSWER: In performing interpersonal roles, Croft illustrated the specific managerial role of leading when he hired Byrne. Byrne acts as a leader in creating a high-performance auditing team. Brick Brewing's top managers act in the role of a figurehead when they sponsor charitable events and as a liaison when they act in partnership with community organizations. A spokesperson reported the acquisition of the Canadian rights to distribute the Seagram Coolers brands from Corby Distilleries by Brick Brewing Co. In performing decisional roles, the founder of the company acted as an entrepreneur when he started up the first craft brewery in Ontario in 1984. Subsequent managers have acted as entrepreneurs when introducing new brands such as Laker, Red Cap, and Formosa Springs Draft. Top managers acted in the role of entrepreneur when they struck a deal under its co-packaging agreements, to produce, sell, market, and distribute various beer products on behalf of Loblaws Inc. under the licensed President's Choice® ("PC®") trademark and again with bottling the Mott's Caesar brand under a contract with Canada Dry Mott's, Inc. ("CDMI").

MANAGEMENT IN ACTION

TOPICS FOR DISCUSSION AND ACTION
LEVEL 1 Knowledge & Comprehension

1. Describe what management is and what managers do to achieve organizational goals.
2. Describe the difference between efficiency and effectiveness.
3. Describe the primary responsibilities of the three levels of management, and discuss the skills managers use in carrying out their roles and duties.

LEVEL 2 Application & Analysis

4. Ask a middle or top manager, perhaps someone you already know, to give examples of how he or she performs the management functions of planning, organizing, leading, and controlling. How much time does he or she spend in performing each function?

5. Like Mintzberg, try to find a cooperative manager who will allow you to follow him or her around for a day. List the types of roles the manager plays and how much time he or she spends performing them.

6. Study an organizational culture in terms of its socialization processes and write a short report on your findings.

LEVEL 3 Synthesis & Evaluation

7. Evaluate one (real) organization that you believe to be efficient and effective and one organization that you assess to be inefficient and ineffective in its use of resources. Give evidence to support your evaluation.

8. Put yourself in the position of a first-line manager of a men's clothing department in a retail store. What skills and roles would you use in your daily work? What activities would you likely be involved in?

9. Explain how the managerial functions of planning, organizing, leading, and controlling differ in the three levels of management.

SELF-REFLECTION EXERCISE

In each chapter you will find a self-reflection feature, which gives you ideas on how to apply this material to your personal life. We do this to help reinforce the idea that management is not just for managers—all of us manage our lives and can apply many of the concepts in this book.

Think about where you hope to be in your life five years from now (i.e., your major goal). What is your competitive advantage for achieving your goal? What do you need to plan, organize, lead, and control to make sure that you reach your goal? Looking over Mintzberg's managerial roles (see Table 1.1), which roles do you perform in your daily life? Give examples.

SMALL GROUP BREAKOUT EXERCISE

Form groups of three or four people and appoint one member as the spokesperson who will communicate your findings to the whole class when called on by the instructor. Then discuss the following scenario:

Assume you and your teammates belong to a fusion rock band. The leader of the group wrote a proposal that will go before city council to get a licence to hold a concert. The band's leader calls a meeting to tell you that it has been accepted by the council with the strict condition that the band ensures that no laws are violated and the safety of all the concert-goers is maintained. Your group accepts the terms and now must figure out how to manage the event.

1. What set of skills did the leader mostly use in creating the proposal?

2. What must now be done to plan this event effectively and efficiently?

3. What kinds of resources must the band use in organizing the event?

4. Identify the managerial role the leader engaged in:

   a. when he or she called the meeting of the band

b. when he or she met with the council

c. when the group accepted the terms of the agreement

5. How could the leader of the band lead the group to put on a successful concert?

6. What kind of control measures could the group take to fulfill its agreement with the council?

MANAGING ETHICALLY EXERCISE

Recently, six global pharmaceutical companies admitted that they had conspired to artificially raise the prices of vitamins on a global basis. This involved a Swiss firm, a German firm, and four others. The decision to inflate the prices came from senior managers in each company through a joint decision. This unethical action resulted in passing on unfair expenses to the customers. In several meetings around the world, they worked out the details that went undiscovered for many years. Once they were caught, there was jail for some and continuing prosecution for others; all were fired.

The result of this situation was that each company agreed to create a special position of ethics officer to oversee behaviour in the organization. Why are some people unethical, while others would not even consider doing what is described above? Is ethics an internal force in each individual, or can you educate people in ethics, or can people be made to be ethical? How do you define "unethical" in this case? Do you think it is possible for businesses to be ethical? What was the gain for the managers?

MANAGEMENT CHALLENGE EXERCISE
Diagnosing Culture

Think about the culture of the last organization you worked for, your current university, or another organization or club to which you belong. Then answer the following questions:

1. What values are emphasized in this culture?

2. What norms do members of this organization follow?

3. Who seems to have played an important role in creating the culture?

4. In what ways is the organizational culture communicated to organizational members?

MANAGEMENT PORTFOLIO PROJECT

You may be asked to follow and analyze an organization over the semester to help you build your management skills. Each chapter will have an exercise that asks you to evaluate how the issues in the chapter are dealt with by your organization. Choose a large, well-known, publicly traded Canadian company that is easy to research through company websites, newspapers, the Canadian Securities Administrators' website, SEDAR.com, and company annual reports. Cite all your sources of information using an appropriate method.

Answer the following questions about the organization you have chosen to follow:

1. Give a brief profile of the organization. How large is it in terms of number of employees, annual revenues, profits, location of facilities, and so on? What kind of products or services does it provide?

2. Give a brief profile of the industry in which it operates. Under what industrial classification does it fall? How many competitors are active? What is their target market?

3. Identify the top management team. Who is the CEO, and what is his or her background? Give examples of the activities of the CEO that illustrate how he or she engages in the management processes of planning, organizing, leading, and controlling.

4. Describe the organizational culture of the organization. What are some of its rites of passage?

MANAGEMENT CASE

VOLKSWAGEN CEO RESIGNS AS CAR MAKER RACES TO STEM EMISSIONS SCANDAL[100]

BERLIN—Volkswagen AG raced Wednesday to contain the widening scandal threatening Germany's most important company, ousting its chief executive and pledging to prosecute those involved in a scheme to cheat U.S. auto-pollution tests.

CEO Martin Winterkorn's resignation follows a calamitous few days after Friday's disclosure by the U.S. Environmental Protection Agency that Europe's biggest auto maker employed software on some VW and Audi diesel-powered cars to manipulate the results of routine emissions tests.

The crisis threatens to spill beyond the auto maker to the broader German economy. Wolfsburg-based Volkswagen is as much institution as corporation at home, with nearly 300,000 employees, 29 plants across the country and deep ties to the government—Lower Saxony owns 20% of VW.

The company's next CEO faces a daunting task of cleaning up the scandal—the scope of which remains unclear—and keeping its sales expansion on track. Volkswagen hasn't yet said it knows who was responsible or how many employees were involved.

On Tuesday, Volkswagen disclosed that as many as 11 million cars contained software alleged to have duped emissions tests and were possibly subject to a global recall. The company issued a profit warning and disclosed a €6.5 billion ($7.27 billion) charge to earnings to cover the costs of addressing the matter.

In a statement following Wednesday's meeting of the company's top shareholders and labor representatives, Mr. Winterkorn said he would "accept responsibility" for the "irregularities that have been found in diesel engines" and tendered his resignation to the supervisory board.

"I am shocked by the events of the past few days," he said. "Above all, I am stunned that misconduct on such a scale was possible in the Volkswagen Group."

The executive committee of the supervisory board thanked Mr. Winterkorn for his contributions to the company and said the CEO had "no knowledge of manipulation of the emissions data."

The committee said it would seek prosecution of any Volkswagen employees involved in the affair, and it would establish a special investigative committee to uncover what had happened and who was responsible.

The board subcommittee said it would present by Friday's scheduled supervisory board meeting names of candidates to succeed Mr. Winterkorn, but didn't disclose any.

Two prominent Volkswagen executives on many lists are Herbert Diess and Matthias Müller.

Mr. Diess is a former BMW AG executive who joined Volkswagen in July after being passed over at BMW for the CEO's job. He runs its namesake brand, the company's biggest business. Choosing Mr. Diess would send a signal that Volkswagen shareholders are opting for a fresh start, bringing in an outsider with a strong record in cost-cutting.

Some analysts, however, say Volkswagen has never done well with outside executives. The company's culture is famously clubby and success depends on being well-connected in Wolfsburg and striking a balance between boosting profit margins and maintaining strong ties to labor.

Others think that insular culture makes Mr. Müller, CEO of sports car brand Porsche, a more likely candidate. Mr. Müller gets along well with the Porsche and Piech families who control the company, said people familiar with the matter, and he has deep roots in Volkswagen. He is also well respected in financial circles. "We believe shareholders would welcome such a move," said Arndt Ellinghorst, automotive analyst at Evercore ISI.

Whoever becomes the next CEO, the job of boosting profit margins likely will take a back seat to steering the company through what could be years of rebuilding a brand badly wounded over the past few days. The company's market value is off 29% since Friday.

Volkswagen could face more than $18 billion in fines from the EPA, though analysts say it is unlikely that Volkswagen will have to pay that much. The U.S. Department of Justice has launched a criminal investigation that could result in indictments against Volkswagen executives, analysts said.

The crisis is spreading as regulators and justice officials in Europe and Asia launch investigations, and angry investors and customers file lawsuits seeking damages.

The urgency to repair Volkswagen's reputation goes beyond the benefits to shareholders or even the company's 600,000 employees world-wide. Volkswagen is Germany's largest corporation, generating revenue of almost €203 billion ($227 billion) last year in a country where every seventh job is linked to the nation's export-oriented auto industry.

Damage to Volkswagen could prove a major blow to the broader German economy. Some German politicians, though angry at the company for violating U.S. law, say Volkswagen is being singled out by U.S. authorities.

"It's no coincidence that this discussion comes up now," said Oliver Wittke, a conservative German lawmaker. "Economic interests in the U.S. are also playing a role here."

Under Germany's two-tier corporate governance, the supervisory board oversees the executive management board, but doesn't run the company day-to-day. A five-person subcommittee of the supervisory board, including Wolfgang Porsche, whose grandfather was Beetle inventor Ferdinand Porsche, gathered in Wolfsburg for a crisis meeting. The Porsche-Piech families control about 51% of Volkswagen's voting stock. The second-largest shareholder is the state of Lower Saxony, which holds 20% of the voting rights and has special privileges. State Premier Stephan Weil was present at the meeting. Also in attendance were three representatives of the company's workforce and IG Metall trade union, including Bernd Osterloh, the powerful head of its works council.

It is still unclear who at Volkswagen was responsible for the scheme to trick the EPA. The company hasn't offered a rationale, though outside experts speculate it was to ensure strong engine performance and boost fuel economy amid tough U.S. emissions standards.

The members of the executive committee meeting in Wolfsburg said they were convinced that Mr. Winterkorn knew nothing about it. VW is launching an investigation of its own and will tap external experts. It also asked prosecutors in Braunschweig, the county where VW is located, to investigate.

"I'm pleased that Volkswagen is taking such an aggressive stance on admitting the problem and attacking it," Gina McCarthy, EPA administrator, told The Wall Street Journal on Tuesday.

Mr. Winterkorn's resignation is a bitter end to a long career at Europe's biggest car maker. He was hired by its luxury car brand, Audi, in 1981 as assistant to the director of quality control. A stickler for detail, he became known for his obsession with the quality of its vehicles. He became CEO of the company in 2007 and oversaw a period of unparalleled expansion. He aimed to make Volkswagen the biggest, most profitable and best-run car company in the world. It could overtake current market leader Toyota Motor Corp. in annual sales. In the first half of this year, Volkswagen sold more cars than its rival. But profits are falling as higher costs hit margins, and sales in markets such as China and the U.S. decline. Now, he said, it is time to step down. "Volkswagen needs a fresh start," he said. "I have always been driven by my desire to serve this company, especially our customers and employees. Volkswagen has been, is and will always be my life."

1. Was the CEO's resignation the right thing to do? Why or why not?

2. In addition to the economic fallout, what other impact could the emissions scandal have on the company's managers? On its employees?

3. How can the company retain current customers?

Chapter 2

Managing the Organizational Environment

LEARNING OUTCOMES

LO1	Explain the importance of understanding the organizational environment for managerial success.
LO2	Identify the main forces in an organization's external environment and the challenges these forces present to managers.
LO3	Explain the changes in the global economy that lead to opportunities and threats for managing organizations.
LO4	Explain the ways managers can minimize threats and uncertainty from forces in the external environment.
LO5	Evaluate the major challenges managers face in gaining a competitive advantage in the global economy.

OPENING CASE

IKEA Is on Top of the Furniture World[1]

IKEA is the largest furniture chain in the world because it can provide what the average customer wants: well-designed and well-made contemporary furniture at an affordable price. With the acquisition of Task-Rabbit, a website that allows users to hire people to put together IKEA products, and collaborations with internet giants like Amazon and Alibaba to beef up e-commerce sales, the company is poised for massive growth throughout the world in the coming decade. IKEA's ability to provide customers with affordable furniture is very much the result of its approach to globalization, to the way it treats its global employees and operates its global store empire. In a nutshell, IKEA's global approach revolves around simplicity, attention to detail, cost-consciousness, and responsiveness in every aspect of its operations and behaviour.

IKEA's global approach derives from the personal values and beliefs of its founder, Ingvar Kamprad, about how companies should treat their employees and customers. Kamprad, who died in January of 2018, was born in Smaland, a poor Swedish province whose citizens are well known for being entrepreneurial, frugal, and hardworking. Kamprad definitely absorbed these values, for when he entered the furniture business he made them the core of his management approach. He taught store managers and employees his values; his beliefs about the need to operate in a no-frills, cost-conscious way; and his view that they were all in business "together," by which he meant that every person who works in his global empire plays an essential role and has an obligation to everyone else.

What does Kamprad's approach mean in practice? It means that all of IKEA's members fly coach class on business trips, stay in inexpensive hotels, and keep travel expenses to a minimum. It also means that IKEA stores operate on the simplest set of rules and procedures possible and that employees are expected to cooperate to solve problems and get the job done. Many famous stories exist about the frugal Kamprad,

Frank Beecham

such as that he always flew coach class, and that when he took a Coke can from the mini-bar in a hotel room he replaced it with one bought in a store—despite the fact that he was a multibillionaire ranked in the top 20 on the *Forbes* list of the world's richest people!

IKEA's employees see what his global approach means as soon as they are recruited to work in a store in one of the many countries in which the company operates. They start learning about IKEA's global corporate culture by performing jobs at the bottom of the ladder, and they are quickly trained to perform all the various jobs involved in store operations. During this process they internalize IKEA's global values and norms, which centre on the importance the company attaches to their taking the initiative and responsibility for solving problems and for focusing on the customer. Employees are rotated between departments and sometimes stores, and rapid promotion is possible for those who demonstrate the enthusiasm and togetherness that signifies they have bought into IKEA's global culture.

Most of IKEA's top managers rose from its ranks, and the company holds "breaking the bureaucracy weeks" in which they are required to work in stores and warehouses for a week each year to make sure they and all employees stay committed to IKEA's global values. No matter which country they operate in, all employees wear informal clothes to work at IKEA—Kamprad always wore an open-neck shirt—and there are no marks of status such as executive dining rooms or private parking places. Employees believe that if they buy into IKEA's work values, behave in ways that keep its growing global operations streamlined and efficient, and focus on being one step ahead of potential problems, they will share in its success. Promotion, training, above-average pay, a generous store bonus system, and the personal well-being that comes from working in a company where people feel valued are some of the rewards that Kamprad pioneered to build and strengthen IKEA's global approach.

After reading and understanding the concepts in this chapter, you should be able to answer the following questions:

1. Explain how the forces in the external organizational environment affected IKEA's global operations.
2. Discuss how global competition and increasing complexity has impacted management decisions at IKEA.
3. Evaluate how managers at IKEA handle environmental change and uncertainty.
4. Explain how IKEA embraced the challenges of being competitive in the global economy.

Overview

In recent years there has been a marked shift toward a more open global environment in which capital flows more freely as people and companies search for new opportunities to solve social problems and create wealth. This has hastened the process of globalization. **Globalization** is the set of forces that lead to integrated social systems so that nations become increasingly interdependent and similar. The process of globalization has been hastened by declining barriers to international trade. Top managers of a global company like IKEA are always operating in an environment where they are competing with other companies for scarce and valuable resources.

> **globalization** The set of forces that lead to integrated social systems so that nations become increasingly interdependent and similar.

The internal environments of organizations, including the strategy, organizational culture, organizational structure and the way that resources are used to achieve organizational goals are all important aspects of managerial work that are discussed in Parts 3 and 4 of this textbook. Here, we look at how the external environment, that is, the factors and conditions that influence the operations of the organization from beyond the organization's boundaries, must be managed to establish a competitive advantage in the market—both local and, increasingly, global. The nature of the external environmental forces affect a manager's ability to acquire and utilize resources. The two levels of the external environment are often referred to as the specific and general components. These create opportunities and threats that managers must deal with and thus affect the way organizations plan, organize, lead, and control resources to achieve organizational goals. In this chapter we discuss the ways that managers can adjust and respond to forces in the organization's environment to capitalize on opportunities and minimize threats. By the end of the chapter, you will understand the steps managers must take to ensure that organizations adequately address and appropriately respond to the external environment to meet the challenges they face in the global economy.

What Is the Organizational Environment?

LO1	Explain the importance of understanding the organizational environment for managerial success.

The **organizational environment** is a set of forces and conditions that can affect the way the organization operates and the way managers engage in planning and organizing.[2] These forces change over time and thus present managers with opportunities and threats. Changes in the organizational environment, such as the development of efficient new production technology, the availability of lower-cost components, or the opening of new global markets, create opportunities for managers to make and sell more products, obtain more resources and capital, and thereby strengthen their organization. In contrast, the rise of new global competitors, a global economic recession, cyber hacking, or an oil shortage pose threats that can devastate an organization if managers are unable to sell its products and revenues and profits plunge. The quality of managers' understanding of forces in the global environment and their ability to respond appropriately to those forces, such as IKEA's managers' ability to make and sell furniture products that customers around the world want to buy, are critical factors affecting organizational performance.

organizational environment The set of forces and conditions that can affect the way an organization operates.

The organizational environment can be divided into the *internal environment* and the *external environment*. The **internal environment** consists of forces operating within an organization and stemming from the organization's structure and culture, including the strategy, human resources, and technology capabilities. The **external environment** consists of forces operating beyond the boundaries of an organization that affect how an organization functions. The importance or strength of each force varies with the circumstances at any particular time. We generally divide the organization's external environment into two major categories: the *industry-specific or task environment* and the *general environment*. Both of these environments are shown in Figure 2.1. All the persons, groups, and institutions that are directly affected by the internal and external environments are known as the **stakeholders** of the organization. Understanding how each stakeholder group is affected by the actions of the organization helps managers make better decisions about how to balance each group's interests. Managers' ability to perceive what the interests of the stakeholders are and how they are changing will help the organization respond quickly to conditions that affect profitability and opportunities for growth and expansion. Failure to interpret the dynamics of the organizational environment can lead to poor management decisions and business failure. For example, when Eddie Lampert, Chairman of Sears Holding company, made the decision to aggressively push the Shop My Way rewards program using a TripAdvisor and Uber online model to try to stop the company from declining sales, it backfired,

FIGURE 2.1

Forces in the Organizational Environment

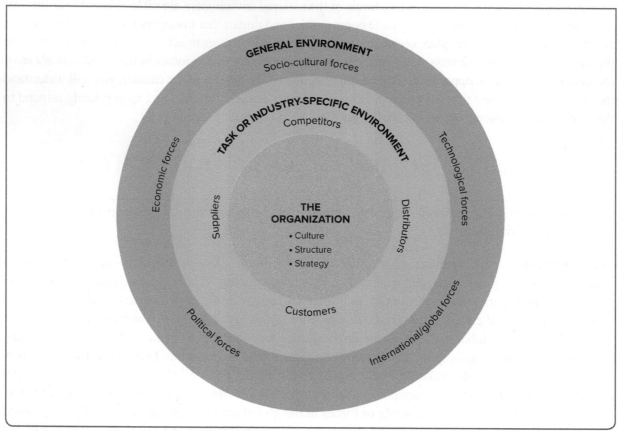

and he ended up selling many of the best store locations in an effort to stave off bankruptcy. The failure to perceive, interpret, and respond to the technological and socio-cultural changes in the retail environment resulted in the 123-year-old company filing for bankruptcy in 2017.[3]

internal environment The forces operating within an organization and stemming from the organization's strategy, structure, and culture.

external environment The forces operating beyond the boundaries of an organization that affect how the organization functions.

stakeholders Persons, groups, and institutions directly affected by the activities and decisions of an organization.

The External Organizational Environment

LO2 Identify the main forces in an organization's external environment and the challenges these forces present to managers.

The **industry-specific or task environment** is a set of external forces and conditions *that affect an organization's ability to obtain inputs and dispose of its outputs*—its finished products or services. The task environment contains the forces that have the most immediate and direct effect on managers because they arise from the specific sector or industry in which the organization conducts its operations. The forces acting on a small publishing company in Saskatchewan are likely to be different from the forces affecting an oil and gas mining company in Alberta and those of a lobster fisher family in Nova Scotia, and so on. The industry-specific forces pressure and influence managers on a daily basis and thus have considerable impact on short-term decision making. When managers turn on the radio or television to their local station, arrive at their offices or stores, open their mail, or look at their computer screens, they are likely to learn about problems facing them because of changing conditions in their organization's task environment.

industry-specific or task environment The set of forces and conditions that affect an organization's ability to obtain inputs and dispose of its outputs because they influence managers on a daily basis.

The **general environment** contains the political, economic, socio-cultural, technological and international (global) forces that affect the industry and hence the organization. The small publishing company in Saskatchewan may not be able to sell a book on religious freedom in Iran because the political regulators prohibit such products. If the price of oil declines below a certain threshold, the mining company in Alberta may put new oil sands production on hold until the economic conditions become more favourable. The Nova Scotian lobster fisher could see an increase in international demand for the crustaceans if the socio-cultural trend toward eating sustainably caught seafood products continues to grow. For the individual manager, opportunities and threats resulting from changes in the general environment are often more difficult to identify and respond to than are events in the task environment. However, changes in these forces can have major impacts on managers and their organizations. The opportunities and threats are not static; they change constantly as technology evolves, economies develop, and societal priorities shift. The implication is clear: Managers must constantly analyze forces in the organizational environment because these forces affect ongoing decision making and planning.

general environment The political, economic, socio-cultural, technological, and international/global forces (PESTI) that affect an organization and its task environment.

The Industry-Specific or Task Environment

The *task or industry-specific environment* includes several stakeholder groups, organizations, and persons that the organization deals with directly in its daily operations and that have an immediate effect on the operations and performance levels of the organization.* These forces can either create a favourable or unfavourable situation for managers. Forces in the task environment result from the actions of suppliers, distributors, customers, and competitors (see Figure 2.1). While firms have little control over what their competitors do, the actions of their competitors affect their operations, as do the actions of suppliers and the actions of consumers. Examples of how each of these four groups affect a manager's ability to obtain resources and distribute outputs on a daily, weekly, or monthly basis are discussed in turn below. Readers will notice the similarity of the forces acting in the industry-specific environment with Porter's Five Forces competitive analysis—a tool used to assess the profitability of an industry—described in Chapter 4. Each force has a significant impact on short-term management decision making and competitive strategy.

SUPPLIERS

Suppliers are the individuals and organizations that provide an organization with the inputs (resources such as raw materials, component parts, financing, or employees) that it needs to produce goods and services. In return, the supplier receives compensation for those goods and services. An important aspect of a manager's job is to ensure a reliable supply of input resources. The ability to obtain inputs necessary for production is as important to a small retail clothing store as it is to a global company. Take, for example, a clothing store located in Vancouver. The store carries lines manufactured in Montreal as well as lines manufactured in Bangladesh and Vietnam. Suppliers will not provide the same brand of clothing to competitors in close proximity. So, while the manager of the clothing store desires to sell a particular brand made in St. John's, he or she may have to make an alternate decision if that line is being sold by a competitor around the corner. And while there may be few logistical problems procuring clothing lines manufactured within Canada, finding high-quality products supplied from overseas nations is more difficult. Suppliers must be able to guarantee delivery of inputs by agreed-upon dates to satisfy the buyer. The manager of the clothing store in Vancouver needs the line of fashion by January for the spring market or risks losing business to a competitor. This illustrates how competition can influence the ability of managers to obtain inputs from suppliers.

suppliers Individuals and organizations that provide an organization with the inputs and resources that it needs to produce and sell goods and services.

The opening case on IKEA illustrates how complex global supply chains have become. IKEA has more than 2000 suppliers that manufacture over 12 000 products in more than 50 countries. The company developed its own software, Electronic Commerce for IKEA Suppliers (ECIS), to coordinate the global supply chain efficiently.

Finding the overseas suppliers that offer the lowest-priced and highest-quality products is an important task facing the managers of local and global organizations. Since these suppliers are located in thousands of cities in many countries around the world, finding them is a difficult business. Often, large companies use the services of overseas intermediaries or brokers, located near these suppliers, to find the one that best meets their input requirements. Li & Fung, now run by brothers Victor and William Fung, is one of the brokers that has helped hundreds of global companies to locate suitable overseas suppliers, especially suppliers in mainland China.[4]

Managing global companies' supply chains is a complicated task. To reduce costs, overseas suppliers are increasingly specializing in just one part of the task of producing a product. For example, in the past, a company such as IKEA might have negotiated with an overseas supplier to manufacture one million units of some particular type of furniture at a certain cost per unit. But with specialization, IKEA might find it can reduce the costs of producing the item even further by splitting apart the operations involved in its production and having different overseas suppliers, often in different countries, perform each operation. For example, to get the lowest cost per unit, rather than negotiating with a single overseas supplier over the price of making a particular sofa, IKEA might first negotiate with a yarn manufacturer in Vietnam to make the yarn, then ship the yarn to a Chinese supplier to weave it into cloth, and then ship the cloth to several different factories in Malaysia and the Philippines to cut the fabric and assemble the sofa. Then, another overseas company might take responsibility for packaging and shipping the items to wherever in the world they are required. Because a company such as IKEA has thousands of different furniture products under production, and they change all the time, the problems of managing such a supply chain to get the full cost savings from global expansion are clearly difficult and costly.

Li & Fung capitalized on this opportunity. Realizing that many global companies do not have the time or expertise to find such specialized low-price suppliers, its founders moved quickly to provide such a service. Li & Fung employs 3600 agents who travel across 37 countries to locate new suppliers and inspect existing suppliers to find new ways to help its global clients get lower prices or higher-quality products. Global companies are happy to outsource their supply chain management to Li & Fung because they realize significant cost savings. Even though they pay a hefty fee to Li & Fung, they avoid the costs of employing their own agents. As the complexity of supply chain management continues to increase, more and more companies like Li & Fung are appearing.

Managing a global supply chain poses a significant challenge to managing effectively and efficiently.
Christos Georghiou | Dreamstime.com

Changes in the nature, number, or types of suppliers lead to opportunities and threats that managers must respond to if their organizations are to prosper. Often, when managers do not respond to a threat, they put their organization at a competitive disadvantage. When a textile factory in Vietnam closes due to poor management, the effects are felt halfway across the globe by a retail clothing store in Vancouver. The rapid growth in the first decade of the 21st century posed a serious challenge for IKEA. "We can't increase by more than 20 stores a year because supply is the bottleneck," said Lennart Dahlgren, former country manager for Russia. Since Russia is a source of timber, IKEA aims to turn it into a major supplier of finished products.[5]

DISTRIBUTORS

Distributors are organizations that help other organizations sell their goods or services to customers. The decisions that managers make about how to distribute products to customers can have important effects on organizational performance. For many years, Apple Computer refused to let others sell its computers, which meant that customers had to buy directly from Apple. Thus, potential customers who shopped at large computer stores with a variety of products were less likely to buy an Apple computer, since it would not be sold there.

distributors Organizations that help other organizations sell their goods or services to customers.

The changing nature of distributors and distribution methods can also bring opportunities and threats for managers. If distributors are so large and powerful that they can control customers' access to a particular organization's goods and services, they can threaten the organization by demanding that it reduce the prices of its goods and services.[6] For example, before Chapters was taken over by Indigo Books & Music, smaller Canadian publishers complained that Chapters had used its market share to force them into dropping their wholesale prices to the book retailer. Because Chapters was the largest distributor of books to customers in Canada, publishers felt compelled to comply with Chapters' demands.

In contrast, the power of a distributor may be weakened if there are too many options for manufacturers and wholesalers. Selling directly to customers on the Internet with B2B and B2C can significantly reduce the demand for distributors' services by eliminating their role as intermediaries. The lobster fisher in Nova Scotia has the opportunity to easily sell directly to markets in Japan via the Internet, thus eliminating the need for paying a distributor.

CUSTOMERS

Customers are the individuals and groups that buy the goods and services an organization produces. Changes in the numbers and types of customers or changes in customers' tastes and needs result in opportunities and threats. Consumer demand for spring fashion is very tricky to predict one year earlier when managers make the decisions about product lines. Zara has minimized the risk of making decisions by cutting their production time to a two-week window made possible by an efficient supply chain. Managers at Zara can make decisions about product lines and in two weeks have it on their shelves. This makes it difficult for smaller boutique clothing stores like the one in Vancouver to be responsive to changes in consumer demands. When IKEA tried to enter the Japanese market, it was a disaster, because consumers wanted high-quality products made of quality materials, not low-cost products made of recycled particle board. IKEA customizes its products for particular national markets. Their research shows that "Americans prefer to store most of their clothes folded, and Italians like to hang." The result is a wardrobe that features deeper drawers for U.S. customers.[7]

customers Individuals and groups that buy the goods and services that an organization produces.

COMPETITORS

One of the most important forces that an organization confronts in its industry-specific environment is competitors. **Competitors** are organizations that produce goods and services that are similar to a particular organization's goods and services. In other words, competitors are organizations that are vying for the same customers. Statistics Canada indicates that 40 percent of successful businesses identified more than 20 competitors each. "Think of the benefit of your product and service and then consider who else can provide that same benefit to your customers. There is only so much money in a consumer or business budget, and a family or company must decide how best to spend it. Your competition is every company that is in some way vying for those same 'benefit' dollars."[8]

competitors Organizations that produce goods and services that are similar to a particular organization's goods and services.

Rivalry between competitors can be the most threatening force that managers must deal with. A high level of rivalry often results in price competition, and falling prices reduce access to resources and cause profits to decrease. In the case of the clothing store in Vancouver, cheap imports from overseas sold by Zara may be seen by consumers as attractive substitutes for the higher quality Canadian-made products, thus drawing them away from the boutique. When there are only a few firms operating in an oligopoly market structure, the high costs of entering the industry and/or the governmental regulations within the industry can prevent new organizations from competing. Such was the case with the telecommunications industry in Canada. Giants like TELUS, Rogers, and Bell dominate the sector, making it difficult for smaller firms like WIND mobile to compete. TELUS and Shaw Media have tremendous rivalry in Western Canada, where they compete for customers in a market worth billions. Shaw appeared to capture customers switching from analogue technology to digital technology with their premium cable packages, which claimed the fastest Internet speeds in Canada. But TELUS came out ahead by offering deep discounts and promotions.[9]

Potential competitors are organizations that are not currently in a task environment but have the resources to enter if they so choose. In 2010, Amazon.com, for example, was not in the furniture or large appliance business, but it could enter these businesses if its managers decided it could profitably sell such products online—and in 2015 it started selling furniture and large appliances. When new competitors enter an industry, competition increases and prices and profits decrease—as furniture and electronic stores such as IKEA and Best Buy have discovered as they battle the global giant, Amazon.com.

potential competitors Organization that are npt currently in a task environment but have the resources to enter if they so choose.

BARRIERS TO ENTRY

In general, the potential for new competitors to enter a task environment (and thus increase competition) is a function of barriers to entry. **Barriers to entry** are factors that make it difficult and costly for a company to enter a particular task environment or industry.[10] In other words, the more difficult and costly it is to enter the task environment, the higher are the barriers to entry. The higher the barriers to entry, the fewer the competitors in an organization's task environment and thus the lower the threat of competition. With fewer competitors, it is easier to obtain customers and keep prices high.

barriers to entry Factors that make it difficult and costly for a company to enter an industry.

Barriers to entry result from three main sources: economies of scale, brand loyalty, and government regulations that impede entry (see Figure 2.2). **Economies of scale** are the cost advantages associated

FIGURE 2.2

Barriers to Entry and Competition

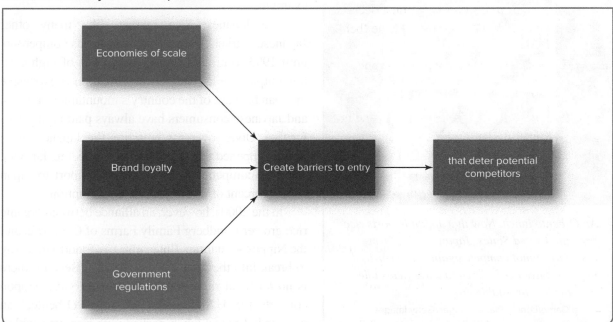

with large operations. Economies of scale result from factors such as manufacturing products in very large quantities, buying inputs in bulk, or making more effective use of organizational resources than do competitors by fully utilizing employees' skills and knowledge. If organizations already in the task environment are large and enjoy significant economies of scale, their costs are lower than the costs that potential entrants will face, and newcomers will find it expensive to enter the industry. Amazon.com, for example, enjoys significant economies of scale relative to most other online companies because of its highly efficient distribution system.[11]

economies of scale Cost advantages associated with large operations.

Brand loyalty is customers' preference for the products of organizations currently in the task environment. If established organizations enjoy significant brand loyalty, a new entrant will find it difficult and costly to obtain a share of the market. Newcomers must bear huge advertising costs to build customer awareness of the goods or services they intend to provide. Today, Google, Amazon.com, and Apple enjoy a high level of brand loyalty and have some of the highest website hit rates, which allows them to increase their marketing revenues.

brand loyalty Customers' preference for the products of organizations.

In some cases, *government regulations* function as a barrier to entry at both the industry and the country levels. Many industries that were deregulated, such as air transport, trucking, utilities, and telecommunications, experienced a high level of new entry after deregulation; this forced existing companies in those industries to operate more efficiently or risk being put out of business. At the national and global levels, administrative barriers are government policies that create barriers to entry and limit imports of goods by overseas companies. Japan is well known for the many ways in which it attempts to restrict the entry of overseas competitors or lessen their impact on Japanese firms. Japan has come under intense pressure to relax and abolish regulations such as those governing the import of rice, for example.

An O-bento lunch. Now that Japan imports rice from the United States, Japanese rice farmers, who cannot compete against lower-priced imports, have been forced to leave fields idle or grow less profitable crops.
Philip Game/Lonely Planet Images/Getty Images

The Japanese rice market, like many other Japanese markets, was closed to overseas competitors until 1993 to protect Japan's thousands of high-cost, low-output rice farmers. Rice cultivation is expensive in Japan because of the country's mountainous terrain, and Japanese consumers have always paid high prices for rice. Under overseas pressure, the Japanese government opened the market, but to protect its farmers, overseas competitors are allowed to export to Japan only 8 percent of its annual rice consumption.

In the 2000s, however, an alliance between organic rice grower Lundberg Family Farms of California and the Nippon Restaurant Enterprise Co. found a new way to break into the Japanese rice market. Because there is no tariff on rice used in processed foods, Nippon converts the U.S. organic rice into "O-bento," an organic hot boxed lunch packed with rice, vegetables, chicken, beef, and salmon, all imported from the United States. The lunches, which cost about four dollars each compared to a Japanese rice bento that costs about nine dollars, are sold at railway stations and other outlets throughout Japan and have become very popular. A storm of protest from Japanese rice farmers arose because the entry of U.S. rice growers forced them to leave their rice fields idle or grow less profitable crops. Other overseas companies are increasingly forming alliances with Japanese companies to find new ways to break into the high-priced Japanese market, and little by little, Japan's restrictive trade practices are being whittled away.

In summary, intense rivalry among competitors creates a task environment that is highly threatening and makes it increasingly difficult for managers to gain access to the resources an organization needs to make goods and services. Conversely, low rivalry results in a task environment where competitive pressures are more moderate and managers have greater opportunities to acquire the resources they need to make their organizations effective.

The General Environment

Managers not only must concern themselves with competitors and finding suppliers and customers, but also must pay attention to the larger environment around them. Political, economic, socio-cultural, technological, and international (acronym: PESTI) forces in an organization's general environment can have profound effects on the organization's specific environment, effects that may be ignored by some managers. For example, technology in the telecommunications industry has made it possible for companies to offer their customers a variety of products. In the past, consumers simply chose the cheapest long-distance package or the best telephone system, but now they are looking at enhanced communication products—such as unlimited wireless data that gives access to the Internet—that are offered as part of the package. Telephone providers who failed to expand their range of offerings quickly have had difficulty keeping customers.

Managers have to constantly analyze the forces arising from the general environment in order to manage effectively. Their decisions and planning will have long-term effects. Below we examine each of the major forces in the general environment in turn, exploring their impact on managing the organization's task environment.

POLITICAL FORCES

Political forces are outcomes of changes in laws and regulations. They result from political and legal developments that take place within a nation, within a world region, or across the world and significantly affect managers and organizations everywhere. Political processes shape a nation's laws and the international laws that govern the relationships among nations. Laws constrain the operations of organizations and managers and thus create both opportunities and threats.[12] For example, in much of the industrialized world, there has been a strong trend toward **deregulation** of industries previously controlled by the state and **privatization** of organizations once owned by the state. Liquor sales have long been controlled and regulated by provincial governments in Canada. Quebec and Ontario have a government monopoly on liquor sales but allow beer and wine to be sold in grocery stores. The government of Alberta privatized all of its liquor trade in 1993–94 but kept a monopoly by contracting only two distribution firms—one for wine, spirits, and imported beer and the other for domestic beer, thus hampering the free market. British Columbia began allowing private liquor retail outlets in 2002, while continuing operate government-run stores. This opened opportunities for small businesses, although it also resulted in higher prices for consumers. For more than a decade, the two systems have operated side by side. When governments deregulate and privatize industries, new opportunities for small business are created and consequences for consumers result.

> **political forces** Outcomes of changes in laws and regulations, such as the deregulation of industries, the privatization of organizations, and increased emphasis on environmental protection.
> **deregulation** Opening industries previously operated and controlled by the state to free market competition.
> **privatization** Selling organizations once owned and operated by the state to individuals or corporations.

Deregulation and privatization are just two examples of political and legal forces that can create challenges for organizations and managers. Others include increased emphasis on safety in the workplace and on environmental protection and the preservation of endangered species. Successful managers carefully monitor changes in laws and regulations in order to take advantage of the opportunities they create and counter the threats they pose in an organization's specific environment.

The *Competition Act* of 1986 provides more legislation that affects how companies may operate. Under this act, the federal Competition Bureau acts to maintain and encourage competition in Canada. For example, when companies merge, they face intense scrutiny from the bureau to make sure there is no unfair competitive advantage t will adversely affect customers, employees, and other stakeholders. Even though Ellis Jacob, CEO of Cineplex Galaxy LP, had the "deal of a lifetime" with a $500-million purchase of rival movie theatre exhibition chain Famous Players from Viacom Inc., he had to sell theatres to meet the demands of regulators. "The federal Competition Bureau sought to maintain competition in pricing and choice by making it a condition of the deal that Cineplex sell 35 theatres in 17 cities across Canada," recalled Jacob, "which would have brought in about 11 percent of the companies' combined revenue of $874 million."[13]

ECONOMIC FORCES

Economic forces affect the general health and well-being of a nation or the regional economy of an organization. They include interest rates, inflation, unemployment, economic growth, and so on. Economic forces produce many opportunities and threats for managers. Low levels of unemployment and falling interest rates mean a change in the customer base: More people have more money to spend, and as a result organizations have an opportunity to sell more goods and services. Good economic times affect supplies: Resources become easier to acquire, and organizations have an opportunity to flourish.

> **economic forces** Interest rates, inflation, unemployment, economic growth, and other factors that affect the general health and well-being of a nation or the regional economy of an organization.

Global financial crises create uncertainty and risk for managers.
©Lawcain | Dreamstime.com

In contrast, worsening macroeconomic conditions pose a threat because they limit managers' ability to gain access to the resources their organization needs. Profit-oriented organizations, such as retail stores and hotels, have fewer customers for their goods and services during economic downturns. Not-for-profit organizations, such as charities and colleges, receive fewer donations during economic downturns. Even a moderate deterioration in national or regional economic conditions can seriously affect the performance of an organization.

Poor economic conditions make the environment more complex and managers' jobs more difficult and demanding. Managers may need to reduce the number of individuals in their departments and increase the motivation of remaining employees, and managers and workers alike may need to identify ways to gain and use resources more efficiently. Debt crises in the eurozone, specifically with Greece, illustrate how important it is for managers to realize the effects that economic forces have on their organizations, and they pay close attention to changes in the national and regional economies in order to respond appropriately.

But when a global economic crisis occurs, dire consequences result for managers, especially in the financial industry. The global financial crisis of 2008 to 2010 demonstrated that too much risk-taking and not enough oversight and governance of economic forces can severely derail economic growth. The credit crunch, precipitated by the largest housing bubble in U.S. history, saw many innovative financial products derived from mortgage-backed securities. When the value of the products collapsed as the bubble broke and houses were foreclosed on, several investment banks in the United States also collapsed. The trading of these debt instruments led to the worst economic meltdown and the largest intervention in the market by governments since the stock market crash of 1929 and the Great Depression.

> In two tumultuous weeks the Federal Reserve and the Treasury between them nationalized the country's two mortgage giants, Fannie Mae and Freddie Mac; took over AIG, the world's largest insurance company; in effect extended government deposit insurance to $3.4 trillion in money-market funds; temporarily banned short-selling in over 900 mostly financial stocks; and, most dramatic of all, pledged to take up to $700 billion of toxic mortgage-backed assets on to its books.[14]

While the unregulated financial instruments called into question banking systems around the world, Canada's banks, which had relatively little exposure to the new and complicated debt products, were ranked the world's most sound with a score of 6.8 out of 7.[15] Canada inched ahead of the banks in five other countries—Sweden, Luxembourg, Australia, Denmark, and the Netherlands—all of which received a score of 6.7 out of 7. The United States was ranked 40th, with a score of 6.1.[16]

SOCIO-CULTURAL FORCES

Socio-cultural forces are pressures emanating from the social structure of a country or society or from the national culture. Pressures from both sources can either constrain or facilitate the way organizations operate and managers behave. **Social structure** is the arrangement of relationships between individuals and groups in a society. Societies differ substantially in social structure. In societies that have a high degree of social stratification, there are many distinctions among individuals and groups. Caste systems in India and Tibet and the recognition of numerous social classes in Great Britain and France produce a multilayered social structure in each of those countries. In contrast, social stratification is lower in relatively egalitarian New Zealand and Canada, where the social structure reveals few distinctions among people. Most top managers in France come from the upper classes of French society, but top managers in Canada come from all strata of society.

socio-cultural forces Pressures emanating from the social structure of a country or society or from the national culture.

social structure The arrangement of relationships between individuals and groups in a society.

Societies also differ in the extent to which they emphasize the individual over the group. For example, the United States emphasizes the primacy of the individual, and Japan emphasizes the primacy of the group. This difference may dictate the methods managers need to use to motivate and lead employees. **National culture** is the set of values that a society considers important and the norms of behaviour that are approved or sanctioned in that society. Societies differ substantially in the values and norms that they emphasize. For example, in the United States individualism is highly valued, and in Korea and Japan individuals are expected to conform to group expectations.[17] National culture also affects the way managers motivate and coordinate employees and the way organizations do business. Ethics, an important aspect of national culture, is discussed in detail in Chapter 3.

national culture The set of values that a society considers important and the norms of behaviour that are approved or sanctioned in that society.

Social structure and national culture not only differ across societies but also change within societies over time. In Canada, attitudes toward the roles of women, love, sex, sexual orientation, and marriage have changed in every past decade. Many people in Asian countries, such as Hong Kong, Singapore, Korea, and Japan think that the younger generation is far more individualistic and "American-like" than previous generations. Currently, throughout much of Eastern Europe, new values that emphasize individualism and entrepreneurship are replacing communist values based on collectivism and obedience to the state. The pace of change is accelerating.

⃰Individual managers and organizations must be responsive to changes in, and differences among, the social structures and national cultures of all the countries in which they operate. In today's increasingly integrated global economy, managers are likely to interact with people from several countries, and many managers live and work abroad. Effective managers are sensitive to differences between societies and adjust their behaviours accordingly.

⃰Managers and organizations also must respond to changing behavourial and consumer trends within a society. In the last few decades, for example, Canadians have become increasingly interested in their personal health and fitness. Managers who recognized this trend early and exploited the opportunities that resulted from it were able to reap significant gains for their organizations. PepsiCo used the opportunity presented by the fitness trend and took market share from archrival Coca-Cola by being the first to introduce diet colas and fruit-based soft drinks. Quaker Oats made Gatorade the most popular sports drink and brought out a whole host of low-fat food products. The health trend, however, did not offer opportunities to all companies; to some it posed a threat. Tobacco companies came under intense pressure due to consumers' greater awareness of negative health impacts from smoking. Laura Secord and other manufacturers of candy have been threatened by customers' desires for low-fat, healthy foods. The rage for "low-carb" foods led to a huge increase in demand for meat and hurt bread and pasta companies. Increased demand for organic and sustainably farmed agricultural products presents opportunities for small scale, local farmers and fisher families.

Cultural variations affect the way managers conduct business.
Gallo Images/AGE Fotostock

A key socio-cultural dimension for managers is changes in the demographic characteristics of a nation. **Demographic forces** are outcomes of changes in the characteristics of a population, such as age, gender, ethnic origin, race, sexual orientation, and social class. Like the other forces in the general environment, demographic forces present managers with opportunities and threats and can have major implications for organizations. The dramatic increase in the number of working women has focused public concern on issues such as equal pay for equal work and sexual harassment at work. One issue in particular that managers will have to address more and more is the lack of women in top positions. This concern is important because managers are responsible for attracting and making full use of the talents of all employees. Women make up almost half of the total workforce and about 4.4 percent of CEOs in the Standard & Poor's 500 Index.[18] Research shows that performance levels are higher in companies where women are well represented in senior positions and where women serve on boards of directors.[19] Needless to say, managers must factor these kinds of circumstances into their decision making.

demographic forces Outcomes of changes in the characteristics of a population, such as age, gender, ethnic origin, race, sexual orientation, and social class.

Changes in the age distribution of a population are another example of a demographic force that affects managers and organizations. Currently, most industrialized nations are experiencing the aging of their populations as a consequence of falling birth and death rates and the aging of the baby boom generation, whereas many emerging nations are experiencing a bulge in their youth populations. The exception to this phenomenon in Canada is with the First Nations, who are experiencing growth in the youth segment of the population. Overall, the number of seniors in the Canadian population is estimated to reach 23.6 percent by 2030, the year the youngest baby boomers turn 65. That compares with 15.3 percent in 2013. By 2063, the number of Canadians aged 80 years and over is expected to reach nearly 5 million, compared with 1.4 million in 2013.[20] The largest proportional youth populations projected by the CIA are in Pakistan, Afghanistan, Saudi Arabia, Yemen, and Iraq.[21] The aging of the population in developed nations is increasing opportunities for organizations that cater to older people. The recreation and home health care industries, for example, are seeing an upswing in demand for their services. As early as 2006, with regard to the aging population, the Auditor General of Canada stated: "The demographic die is cast: there is little we can do to reverse or even slow the aging of Canada's population over the coming decades. But it is certainly within our power to plan better for it. And better planning begins with better information concerning the long-term fiscal implications of the coming demographic shift."[22]

> *"The demographic die is cast: there is little we can do to reverse or even slow the aging of Canada's population over the coming decades. But it is certainly within our power to plan better for it."*
>
> Auditor General of Canada

The aging of the population also has several implications for the workplace. Most significant are a relative decline in the number of young people joining the workforce and an increase in active employees willing to postpone retirement past the old mandatory retirement age of 67. These changes suggest that organizations will need to find ways to motivate older employees and use their skills and knowledge, an issue that many industrialized societies have yet to tackle.

TECHNOLOGICAL FORCES

Technology is the combination of skills and equipment that managers use in the design,

The aging population poses both opportunities and threats to organizations.

Blend Images - JGI/Tom Grill/Getty Images

production, and distribution of goods and services. **Technological forces** are outcomes of changes in the technology that managers use to design, produce, or distribute goods and services. Technological forces have increased greatly since the Second World War because the overall pace of technological change has sped up so much.[23] Computers have become increasingly faster and smaller. Transportation speed has increased. Distribution centres are able to track shipments with technologies such as radio frequency identification (RFID) systems. Unmanned drones are delivering goods to remote regions.

> **technology** The combination of skills and equipment that managers use in the design, production, and distribution of goods and services.
>
> **technological forces** Outcomes of changes in the technology that managers use to design, produce, or distribute goods and services.

Technological forces can have profound implications for managers and organizations. Technological change can make established products obsolete overnight—for example, typewriters, black-and-white televisions, and bound sets of encyclopedias—forcing managers to find new products to make. Although technological change can threaten an organization, it also can create a host of new opportunities for designing, making, or distributing new and better kinds of goods and services. Canadian brand icon BlackBerry capitalized on the boom in demand for secure messaging. Brand powerhouse Lululemon gained a competitive advantage in the global economy based on the use of innovative high-tech fabrics. Managers must move quickly to respond to such changes if their organizations are to survive and prosper.

Changes in information technology also are changing the very nature of work itself within organizations, and the manager's job. Telecommuting, texting, and face-to-face video streaming are now everyday activities that provide opportunities for managers to supervise and coordinate employees working from home or other locations. Even students engage in telecommuting, communicating with classmates and instructors via email, Skype, or Facebook, and completing assignments at home. This has changed the way instructors do their jobs.

INTERNATIONAL/GLOBAL FORCES

Global forces are outcomes of changes in international relationships, changes in nations' economic, political, and legal systems, and changes in technology. Perhaps the most important global force affecting managers and organizations is the increasing economic integration of countries around the world.[24] Developments such as the Transpacific Partnership Agreement (TPP), The Canadian-European Union Comprehensive Economic and Trade Agreement (CETA), and the free-trade agreements enforced by the World Trade Organization (WTO), have led to a lowering of barriers to the free flow of goods and services between nations.[25]

> **global forces** Outcomes of changes in international relationships primarily due to declining trade barriers; changes in nations' economic, political, and legal systems; and changes in technology that allow reliable and instantaneous communication.

Falling trade barriers have created enormous opportunities for organizations in one country to sell goods and services in other countries. But by allowing foreign companies to compete for an organization's domestic customers, falling trade barriers also pose a serious threat because they increase competition in the task environment. After the North American Free Trade Agreement (NAFTA) was signed in 1994, one of the major challenges facing Canadian managers was how to compete successfully against American companies moving into this country. Rona and Home Hardware, for instance, as well as smaller retail

FIGURE 2.3

The Global Environment

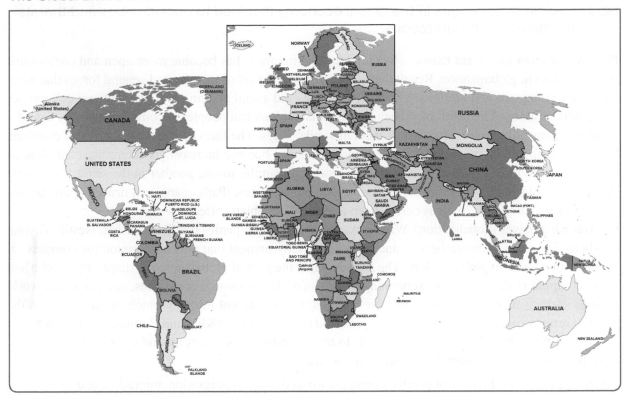

operations in Canada, face strong challenges from American giants Home Depot and Lowes. Similarly, the government of Newfoundland and Labrador is concerned that CETA will cause lost jobs by eliminating minimum processing requirements in the province's fisheries.[26]

In essence, as a result of falling trade barriers, managers view the global environment as open—that is, as an environment in which companies are free to buy goods and services from, and sell goods and services to, whichever companies and countries they choose. (See Figure 2.3.) They also are free to compete against each other to attract customers around the world. They must establish an international network of operations and subsidiaries to build global competitive advantage. Coca-Cola and PepsiCo, for example, have competed aggressively for 30 years to develop the strongest global soft drink empire, just as Toyota and Honda have built hundreds of car plants around the world to provide the vehicles that global customers like. Some products are subject to "regional content" rules that specify a percentage of component parts must be made or assembled in the trade agreement member nations in order for the product to qualify for no tariffs to be levied. IKEA must comply with the regional content rules on furniture production in order to trade its goods tariff-free within the NAFTA member nations of the United States, Mexico, and Canada.[27]

While the current terms of NAFTA state that at least 62.5 percent of a motor vehicle's content must be made in North America to qualify for duty-free access between the U.S., Canada, and Mexico, when renegotiating NAFTA in 2017, the U.S. proposed that vehicles must have "substantial" U.S. content to qualify for duty-free movement within North America. In further moves away from free trade the same year, the Trump administration levied significant tariffs on Canadian softwood lumber and Bombardier's C-Series regional jets, citing unfair competition for U.S. competitors.

◼ The Global Environment

LO3	Explain the changes in the global economy that lead to opportunities and threats for managing organizations.

Perhaps the most important reason why the global environment has become more open and competitive is the increase in globalization. Recall that *globalization* is the set of specific and general forces that work together to integrate and connect economic, political, and social systems *across* countries, cultures, or geographic regions. The result of globalization is that nations and peoples become increasingly *interdependent* because the same forces affect them in similar ways. The fates of peoples in different countries become interlinked as the world's markets and businesses become increasingly interconnected. And as nations become more interdependent, they become more similar to one another in the sense that people develop a similar liking for products as diverse as mobile phones, iPads, jeans, soft drinks, sports teams, Japanese cars, and foods, such as curry, green tea, and Colombian coffee.

But what drives globalization? What makes people and companies like Bombardier, Nestlé, Toyota, or Microsoft want to venture into an uncertain global environment that puts into motion the complex set of forces that result in globalization? The answer is that the path of globalization is shaped by the ebb and flow of capital (valuable wealth-generating assets) as it moves through companies, countries, and world regions seeking its most highly valued use—that is, the investment through which capital can earn the greatest returns (wealth). Managers, employees, and companies like IKEA and Bombardier are motivated to try to profit or benefit by using their skills to make products customers around the world want to buy. Four principal forms of capital flow between countries are:

- *Human capital:* the flow of people around the world through immigration, migration, and emigration.

- *Financial capital:* the flow of money capital across world markets through overseas investment, credit, lending, and aid.

- *Resource capital:* the flow of natural resources and semi-finished products between companies and countries, such as metals, minerals, lumber, energy, food products, microprocessors, and auto parts.

- *Political capital:* the flow of power and influence around the world using diplomacy, persuasion, aggression, and force of arms to protect a country's or world region's or political bloc's access to the other forms of capital.

Globalization refers to the ways that nations are interconnected through trade and culture. Most of the changes associated with globalization are the result of these four capital flows and the interactions among them, as nations compete on the world stage to protect and increase their standards of living and to further the political goals and social causes that are espoused by their societies' cultures. In a positive sense, the faster the flow, the more capital is being utilized where it can create the most value, in the sense of people moving to where their skills earn them more money, or investors switching to the stocks or bonds that give them higher dividends or interest, or companies finding lower-cost sources of inputs. In a negative sense, however, a fast flow of capital also means that individual countries or world regions can find themselves in trouble when companies and investors move their capital to invest it in more productive ways in other countries or world regions, often those with lower labour costs or rapidly expanding markets. When capital leaves a country, the result is higher unemployment, recession, and a lower standard of living for its people.

While declining barriers to trade have increased the pace of globalization, nations still differ widely from each other because they have distinct cultural values and norms that managers must appreciate if they are to compete successfully across countries. How national cultures differ and why it is important for managers to be sensitive to the political and social systems around the world is discussed online. A culturally diverse management team can be a source of strength in the global marketplace. Organizations that employ managers from a variety of cultures better appreciate how national cultures differ than do organizations with culturally similar management teams, and they tailor their management systems and behaviours to the differences. ArcelorMittal (India) and Lenovo (China) are good examples of top global companies with international management teams and they are poised to become role models for all global companies.[28]

Declining Barriers to Trade and Investment

One of the main factors that has speeded globalization by freeing the movement of capital has been the decline in barriers to trade and investment, discussed earlier. During the 1920s and 1930s, many countries erected formidable barriers to international trade and investment in the belief that this was the best way to promote their economic well-being. Many of these barriers were high tariffs on imports of manufactured goods. A **tariff** is a tax that a government imposes on goods imported into one country from another. The aim of import tariffs is to protect domestic industries and jobs, as we saw in the last section with Japanese rice farmers. Import tariffs, such as those in the auto or steel industry, are meant to protect domestic firms from overseas competition by raising the price of these products from abroad. In 2009, for example, the U.S. government increased the tariffs on vehicle tires imported from China to protect U.S. tire makers from unfair competition; in 2012 it imposed a 30 percent tariff on imports of Chinese solar panels after U.S. solar companies complained that the Chinese government was unfairly subsidizing this industry.

tariff A tax that a government imposes on goods imported into one country from another.

The reason for removing tariffs is that, very often, when one country imposes an import tariff, others follow suit, and the result is a series of retaliatory moves as countries progressively raise tariff barriers against each other. This is precisely what happened in 2017 when Canada, Mexico, and the United States began renegotiating NAFTA. In retaliation for the U.S. imposing a 220 percent anti-dumping duty on the C-Series jet made by Bombardier, and a 20 percent tariff on Canadian softwood lumber, Canada imposed provisional duties on gypsum board imported from the U.S. to western Canada in the amount of 105.2 percent to 276.5 percent, depending on the supplier.

Canada also called on the U.S. to respect a World Trade Organization ruling on meat labelling, which found the American system discriminates against foreign livestock, costing Canadian beef and pork industries more than $1 billion a year.

NAFTA: Canada, Mexico, and the United States began renegotiating the North American Free Trade Agreement in 2017.

scibak/iStockphoto/Getty Images

In the 1920s this type of behaviour depressed world demand and helped usher in the Great Depression of the 1930s and massive unemployment. Beginning with the 2008 economic crisis, the governments of most countries have worked hard in the 2010s not to fall into the trap of raising tariffs to protect jobs and industries in the short run because they know the long-term consequences of this would be the loss of even more jobs. Governments of countries that resort to raising tariff barriers ultimately reduce employment and undermine the economic growth of their countries because capital and resources will always move to their most highly valued use—wherever that is in the world.[29]

GATT AND THE RISE OF FREE TRADE

After the Second World War, advanced Western industrial countries, having learned from the Great Depression, committed themselves to the goal of removing barriers to the free flow of resources and capital between countries. This commitment was reinforced by acceptance of the principle that free trade, rather than tariff barriers, was the best way to foster a healthy domestic economy and low unemployment.[30]

The **free-trade doctrine** predicts that if each country agrees to specialize in the production of the goods and services that it can produce most efficiently, this will make the best use of global capital resources and will result in lower prices.[31] For example, if Indian companies are highly efficient in the production of textiles and Canadian companies are highly efficient in the production of computer software, then, under a free-trade agreement, capital would move to India and be invested there to produce textiles, while capital from around the world would flow to Canada and be invested in its innovative computer software companies. Consequently, prices of both textiles and software should fall because each product is being produced where it can be made at the lowest cost, benefiting consumers and making the best use of scarce capital. This doctrine is also responsible for the increase in global outsourcing and the loss of millions of Canadian jobs in textiles and manufacturing as capital has been invested in factories in Asian countries such as China and Malaysia. However, many Canadian jobs have also been created because of new capital investments in the high-tech, IT, and service sectors, which in theory should offset manufacturing job losses in the long run.

free-trade doctrine The idea that if each country specializes in the production of the goods and services that it can produce most efficiently, this will make the best use of global resources.

Historically, countries that accepted this free-trade doctrine set as their goal the removal of barriers to the free flow of goods, services, and capital between countries. They attempted to achieve this through an international treaty known as the General Agreement on Tariffs and Trade (GATT). In the half-century since World War II, there have been eight rounds of GATT negotiations aimed at lowering tariff barriers. The last round, the Uruguay Round, involved 117 countries and succeeded in lowering tariffs by over 30 percent from the previous level. It also led to the dissolving of GATT and its replacement by the World Trade Organization (WTO), which continues the struggle to reduce tariffs and has more power to sanction countries that break global agreements.[32] On average, the tariff barriers among the governments of developed countries declined from over 40 percent in 1948 to about 3 percent today, causing a dramatic increase in world trade.[33]

Declining Barriers of Distance and Culture

Historically, barriers of distance and culture also closed the global environment and kept managers focused on their domestic market. The management problems experienced by Unilever, the huge British-based soap and detergent maker, at the turn of the 20th century illustrate the effect of these barriers.

Founded in London during the 1880s by William Lever, a Quaker, Unilever had a worldwide reach by the early 1900s and operated subsidiaries in most major countries of the British Empire, including India, Canada, and Australia. Lever had a very hands-on, autocratic management style and found his far-flung business empire difficult to control. The reason for Lever's control problems was that communication over great distances was difficult. It took six weeks to reach India by ship from England, and international telephone and telegraph services were unreliable.

Another problem Unilever encountered was the difficulty of doing business in societies that were separated from Britain by barriers of language and culture. Different countries have different sets of national beliefs, values, and norms, and Lever found that a management approach that worked in Britain did not necessarily work in India or Persia (now Iran).*As a result, management practices had to be tailored to suit each unique national culture. After Lever's death in 1925, top management at Unilever decentralized decision-making authority to the managers of the various national subsidiaries so they could develop a management approach that suited the country in which they were operating. One result of this strategy was that the subsidiaries grew distant and remote from one another, which reduced Unilever's performance.[34]

Since the end of the Second World War, a continuing stream of advances in communications and transportation technology has worked to reduce the barriers of distance and culture that affected Unilever and all global organizations. Over the last decades, global communication has been revolutionized by developments in satellites, digital technology, the Internet and global computer networks, and video teleconferencing that allow transmission of vast amounts of information and make reliable, secure, and instantaneous communication possible between people and companies anywhere in the world.[35] This revolution has made it possible for a global organization—a tiny garment factory in Li & Fung's network or a huge company such as Bombardier or Unilever—to do business anywhere, at anytime, and to search for customers and suppliers around the world.

✷ One of the most important innovations in transportation technology that has opened the global environment has been the <u>growth of commercial jet trav</u>el. New York is now closer in travel time to Tokyo than it was to Toronto in the 1880s—a fact that makes control of far-flung international businesses much easier today than in William Lever's era. In addition to speeding travel,✷modern communications and transportation technologies have also helped reduce the cultural distance between countries. The Internet and its millions of websites facilitate the development of global communications networks and media that are helping to create a worldwide culture above and beyond unique national cultures.

Effects of Free Trade on Managers

The lowering of barriers to trade and investment and the decline of distance and culture barriers has created enormous opportunities for companies to expand the market for their goods and services through exports and investments in overseas countries. The shift toward a more open global economy has created not only more opportunities to sell goods and services in markets abroad but also the opportunity to buy more from other countries. For example, the success of clothing companies such as Lands' End has been based on its managers' willingness to import low-cost clothing and bedding from overseas manufacturers. Lands' End works closely with manufacturers in Hong Kong, Malaysia, Taiwan, and China to make the clothing that its managers decide has the quality and styling its customers want at a

Nations in the European Union share a common currency that facilitates trade between member nations.
Brian Jackson/Alamy Stock Photo

price they will pay.[36] A manager's job is more challenging in a dynamic global environment because of the increased intensity of competition that goes hand in hand with the lowering of barriers to trade and investment.

REGIONAL TRADE AGREEMENTS

The growth of regional trade agreements such as the European Free Trade Agreement (EFTA) and the North American Free Trade Agreement (NAFTA) presents opportunities and threats for managers and their organizations. In North America, NAFTA, aimed to abolish the tariffs on 99 percent of the goods traded between Mexico, Canada, and the United States by 2004. Although it did not achieve this lofty goal, NAFTA has removed most barriers on the cross-border flow of resources, giving, for example, financial institutions and retail businesses in Canada and the United States unrestricted access to the Mexican marketplace. After NAFTA was signed, there was a flood of investment into Mexico from the United States and Canada, as well as many other countries such as Japan.

The establishment of free-trade areas creates an opportunity for manufacturing organizations because it lets them reduce their costs. They can do this either by shifting production to the lowest-cost location within the free-trade area (for example, Canadian auto and textile companies shifting production to Mexico) or by serving the whole region from one location rather than establishing separate operations in each country. Some managers, however, view regional free-trade agreements as a threat because they expose a company based in one member country to increased competition from companies based in the other member countries. NAFTA has had this effect; today Mexican managers in some industries face the threat of head-to-head competition against efficient U.S. and Canadian companies. But the opposite is true as well: U.S. and Canadian managers are experiencing threats in labour-intensive industries, such as the flooring tile, roofing, and textile industries, where Mexican businesses have a cost advantage. The more competitive environment NAFTA has brought about has increased both the opportunities that managers can take advantage of and the threats they must respond to in performing their jobs effectively. The Comprehensive and Progressive Agreement for Trans Pacific Partnership (CPTPP) brought this issue to the fore as managers in Canada compete with their counterparts in member nations which include Australia, Brunei, Darussalam, Chile, Japan, Malaysia, Mexico, New Zealand, Peru, Singapore, the United States (until 23 January 2017) and Vietnam. The trade deal was signed in March 2018.

FOCUS ON *The Social Economy*

The Social Purchasing Portal, Winnipeg

The Social Purchasing Portal (SPP) is an online community of suppliers, consumers and job seekers who connect through a network to utilize each other's services and promote sustainable community economic development in Winnipeg. The portal provides a platform for small business suppliers to connect with individual and corporate customers. It also provides employment for job seekers experiencing multiple barriers to employment. The newly employed people find meaning and self-worth through stable employment. Individuals, businesses, nonprofits, and governments register as purchasers and buy goods and services from registered suppliers that are locally owned small businesses, co-ops, and social enterprises. This collaborative model creates blended value for both business and the community. Everybody benefits!

1. Identify the opportunities and threats facing managers deciding to register with the SPP as a purchaser.

Source: Based on http://www.sppwinnipeg.org/. Accessed Jan. 4, 2015.

Managing the External Environment

LO4	Explain the ways managers can minimize threats and uncertainty from forces in the external environment.

As previously discussed, an important task for managers is to understand how forces in the industry-specific and general environments create opportunities for, and threats to, their organizations.* To analyze the importance of opportunities and threats in the external environment, managers must measure (1) the level of complexity in the environment and (2) the rate at which the environment is changing. With this information, they can plan better and choose the best goals and courses of action.

The complexity of the external environment depends on the number and potential impact of the forces that managers must respond to in the task and general environments. A force that seems likely to have a significant negative impact is a potential threat to which managers must devote a high level of organizational resources. A force likely to have a marginal impact poses little threat to an organization and requires only a minor commitment of managerial time and attention. A force likely to make a significant positive impact warrants a considerable commitment of managerial time and effort to take advantage of the opportunity. When Starbucks went to Vienna, the company had to think carefully about its no-smoking policy, since it would be the only coffee shop in the city to ban smoking.

In general, the larger an organization is, the greater is the number of environmental forces that managers must respond to. Consider Tim Hortons. Each year it must consider, to take just one example, the environmental issue of its coffee cups when it announces its "Roll Up the Rim" contest. For some people, it is a chance to win an exciting prize, such as a vehicle or new TV; for environmentalists, however, these cups represent a serious biodegradable hazard, and they also litter the environment.[37] "I don't think it's socially responsible to have a promotion which creates massive waste," said Ronald Colman, executive director of GPI Atlantic, a nonprofit group that researches environmental and quality-of-life issues.[38] A study in Nova Scotia showed that Tim Hortons and McDonald's alone account for one-third of all litter in that province. Thus, managers have to ensure that the organization's practices do not clash with socio-cultural trends, such as environmental sustainability, while responding to customers' preferences and marketing strategies. The movement toward more sustainable decision-making practices is discussed in Chapter 3.

Environmental change is the degree to which forces in the specific and general environments change and evolve over time. Change is problematic for an organization and its managers because the consequences of change can be difficult to predict.[39] Managers can try to forecast or simply guess about future conditions in the environment, such as where and how strong the new competition may be. But, confronted with complex and changing environments, managers cannot be sure that decisions and actions taken today will be suitable in the future. This uncertainty makes their jobs especially challenging. It also makes it vitally important for managers to understand the forces that shape the external environment.

environmental change The degree to which forces in the task and general environments change and evolve over time.

An understanding of the external environment is necessary so that managers can anticipate how it might look in the future and decide on the actions to pursue if the organization is to prosper. McDonald's is a good example of how adaptive an organization must be to remain successful. With the aging population and the emphasis on low-fat foods, McDonald's began changing its menu by including salads and wraps that had fewer fats and carbohydrates. It is also aware of people with food allergies and other food sensitivities and has made adjustments accordingly.[40] Sony Corporation is a good example of how an organization failed to adapt to changes in the organizational environment. Companies in Korea, Taiwan, and China began to innovate new technologies, like digital LCD screens and flash memory, that made Sony's technologies obsolete. Companies such as Apple and Nokia came out with the iPod, smartphones, and tablet computers that better fit customer needs than Sony's "old generation" products, such as the Walkman.

Reducing the Impact of Environmental Forces

Finding ways to reduce the number and potential impact of forces in the external environment is the job of all managers in an organization.

- The principal task of the CEO and the top-management team is to devise strategies that will allow an organization to take advantage of opportunities and counter threats in its organizational environment (see Chapter 4 for a discussion of this vital topic).

- Middle managers in an organization's departments collect relevant information about the environment, such as (1) the future intentions of the organization's competitors, (2) the identity of new customers for the organization's products, and (3) the identity of new suppliers of crucial or low-cost inputs.

- First-line managers find ways to use resources more efficiently to hold costs down or to get close to customers and learn what they want.

Managers at all three levels and in all departments are responsible for reducing the negative impact of environmental forces as they evolve over time (see Figures 2.4 and 2.5).

FIGURE 2.4

Responsibilities for Managing the Forces in the Organization's Environment

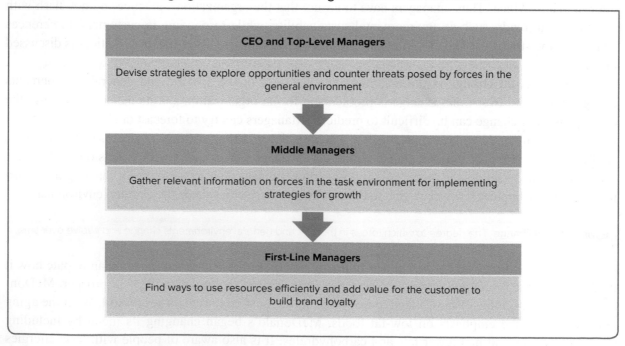

FIGURE 2.5

Managing Forces in the Organizational Environment

Functional Area Managers	Role in Managing the Forces in the Organizational Environment
Sales and Service	Ensure customer satisfaction and brand loyalty
Research and Development	Deal with technological forces
Marketing and Strategy	Deal with pressures from competitors
Accounting and Finance	Handle economic forces
Legal and Public Relations	Deal with political and legal forces
Operations and Materials Management	Deal with pressures from suppliers

Managers as Agents of Change

It is important to note that although much of the change that takes place in the external environment is independent of a particular organization—for example, basic advances in biotechnology or plastics—a significant amount of environmental change is the direct consequence of actions taken by managers within organizations.[41] An organization is an open system: It takes in inputs from the environment and converts them into goods and services that are sent back to the environment. Thus, change in the environment is a two-way process. Often, however, the choices that managers make about which products to produce and even about how to compete with other organizations affect the system as a whole. Our ability to predict and control the course of events is determined by the rate of change in the environment and the complexity of the environment (see Figure 2.6).

Many decisions managers make in response to the forces in the environment are made under conditions of **uncertainty** and risk. As we will see in Chapter 4, it is very difficult to know all the possible outcomes of adopting a particular alternative or strategy. The more complex and dynamic the environment, the greater are the uncertainty and risk. Strategies and organizational structures must be somewhat flexible to be able to accommodate change. However, when managers act under conditions of **certainty,** there is less risk and more complete knowledge of the possible outcomes of their decisions (see Figure 2.7). Managers must minimize threats from changes in the environmental forces while capitalizing on the opportunities they present. They do this by adopting flexible organizational structures and culture. Managers of a global company like IKEA, who have a global supply chain network of over 2000 companies in over 50 nations, necessarily operate under conditions of uncertainty and risk. Managing these risks is made easier with a decentralized organizational structure based on geographical region, which empowers divisional managers so that products can be customized to meet the demand of different cultures and populations. The cultural norm in Japan of companies providing "lifelong" employment was a threat to Sony Corp's ability to manage the forces in the rapidly changing organizational environment. Sony was also the target of technological forces which resulted in a cyberattack on its motion picture division in late 2014, forcing the company to delay the screening of a comedic film perceived to be demeaning to the dictatorship in North Korea. The rate of change in technological developments makes this environmental force particularly important for managers today. Hackers can innovate more quickly than regulators that oversee technological systems. Ensuring that privacy breaches and systems hacking do not occur has become an opportunity for Internet security firms worldwide.

uncertainty The state of environmental forces that is so dynamic that managers cannot predict the probable outcomes of a course of action.

certainty The state of environmental forces that is stable enough to predict possible outcomes of decisions.

FIGURE 2.6

Uncertainty in the Environment and Managerial Action

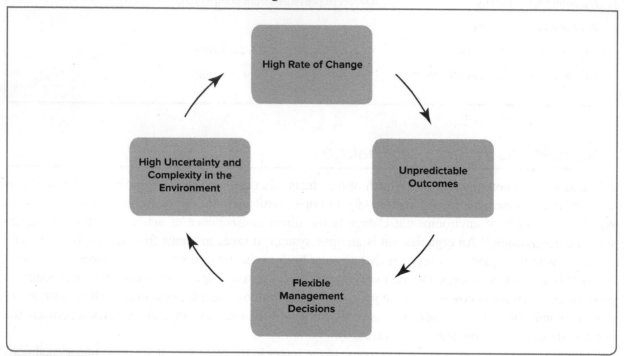

FIGURE 2.7

Uncertainty Matrix

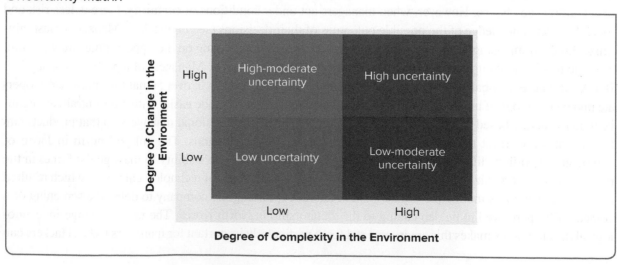

TIPS FOR MANAGERS

Managing the External Environment

Reduce uncertainty and risk associated with a high degree of change in the external environment by:

1. Identifying all the societal needs, benefits, and harms that are or could be embodied in the firm's products.

2. Analyzing underserved markets for their substantial concentrated purchasing power.

3. Exploring societal needs to discover new opportunities for differentiation and repositioning in traditional markets.

4. Adopting technology that can yield net cost savings through enhanced resource utilization, process efficiency, and quality.

Challenges for Management in a Global Environment

LO5 | Evaluate the major challenges managers face in gaining a competitive advantage in the global economy.

Canadian firms are less likely to operate only within their own borders these days. The distinction between the general and industry-specific environments is becoming blurred with globalization. The rise of **global organizations**—organizations that operate and compete in more than one country—has put severe pressure on many organizations to improve their performance and to identify better ways to use their resources. The successes of Indian metals industry giant Arcelor Mittal, German chemical companies Schering and Hoechst, Italian furniture manufacturer Natuzzi, Korean electronics company Samsung, Swedish contemporary furniture retailer IKEA, and Brazilian plane maker Empresa Brasileira de Aeronautica SA (Embraer)—all global companies—are putting pressure on organizations in other countries to raise their level of performance in order to compete successfully.

global organizations Organizations that operate and compete in more than one country.

More than three times as many Canadian companies rank in the world top five in their industry as did 20 years ago.[42] Bombardier, the Canadian aerospace giant, enjoys global success in providing transportation and aerospace products to over 20 nations. Today, managers who make no attempt to learn and adapt to changes in the global environment find themselves reacting rather than innovating, and their organizations often become uncompetitive and fail.[43] Research In Motion (RIM) succumbed to competitive pressure in the global economy when its market share for BlackBerry hand-held devices dropped off in 2012. After rebranding the company name to BlackBerry and focusing on the company's core competency of secure communications, BlackBerry stocks began to climb again in 2015.

*Two major challenges stand out for Canadian managers in today's global economy: building a competitive advantage while maintaining ethical standards, and utilizing new kinds of information systems and technologies. Michael E. Porter and Mark R. Kramer's concept of Creating Shared Value (CSV) is a way for organizations to meet these challenges in a more sustainable and equitable way. **Creating Shared Value** involves rethinking old ways of doing business that rely on simply shifting operations and activities to locations with ever lower wages as a sustainable "solution" to competitive challenges. The concept of shared value can be defined as "policies and operating practices that enhance the competitiveness of a company while simultaneously advancing the economic and social conditions in the communities in which it operates. Shared value creation focuses on identifying and expanding the connections between societal and economic progress"[44] such that all organizations in the supply and distribution chain flourish through enhanced community development. Companies can create economic and social value by reconceiving products and markets to include underserved urban and rural areas, redefining productivity in the supply chain by viewing the prosperity of direct producers as a benefit, not a cost, to business, and by investing in building clusters of development within the communities in which they locate— in other words, supporting community economic development, such as schools, infrastructure, and culture. Business-as-usual practice has been to squeeze suppliers to unsustainable profit margins and exploit resources while degrading the environment to obtain short-term profits. Creating shared value views these old practices as creating costs rather than benefits to business and society. "The concept of shared value resets the boundaries of capitalism. By better connecting companies' success with societal improvement, it opens up many ways to serve new needs, gain efficiency, create differentiation, and expand markets."[45]

> **Creating Shared Value (CSV)** Policies and operating practices that enhance the competitiveness of a company while simultaneously advancing the economic and social conditions in the communities in which it operates.

Building a Competitive Advantage

If managers and organizations are to reach and remain at the top of the competitive environment, they must build a **competitive advantage**, which is the ability of one organization to outperform other organizations because it produces desired goods or services more efficiently and effectively than its competitors. The four building blocks of competitive advantage are superior efficiency, quality, innovation, and responsiveness to customers (see Figure 2.8).

> **competitive advantage** The ability of one organization to outperform other organizations because it produces desired goods or services more efficiently and effectively than competitors do.

INCREASING EFFICIENCY

Organizations increase their efficiency when they reduce the quantity of resources (such as people and raw materials) they use to produce goods or services. In today's competitive environment, organizations are constantly seeking new ways to use their resources to improve efficiency. Many organizations are training their workers in new skills and techniques to increase their ability to perform many new and different tasks. Designers at IKEA work closely with in-house production teams to find the least costly materials and suppliers. They aim to cut the cost of all their products by 2 to 3 percent per year. No product goes on the floor of IKEA without being affordable. Most large items are flat packed in boxes, allowing customers to take the merchandise home with them, and saving IKEA millions of dollars in shipping costs. Walmart, as another example, was able to address costs to the company from excess packaging and greenhouse gas emissions by reducing its packaging and rerouting its trucks to cut 100 million miles from its delivery routes, saving $200 million even as it shipped more products.[46]

FIGURE 2.8

Building Blocks of Competitive Advantage

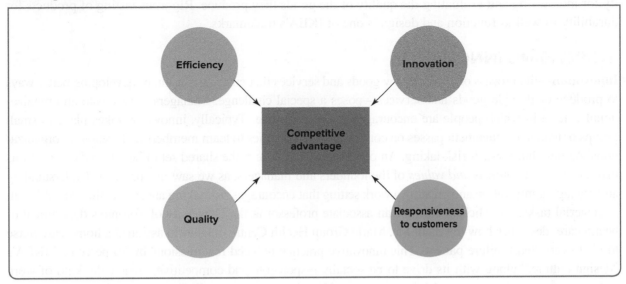

$*$New technological solutions to project management are another way companies can increase efficiency. EllisDon, one of Canada's largest construction companies, developed a software platform technology to help it deal with the "mountains of documents—forms, correspondence, quotes, contracts, schedules, purchase orders, architectural drawings, drawing revisions, photographs, meeting minutes, payroll time sheets, permits, safety inspection reports, and anything else one could think of with respect to building structures in a way that involved clients, consultants, and innumerable subtrades."[47] The result was that the company grew by 50 percent without having to increase staff.

In addition to training staff and introducing new technologies, companies can sometimes work together to increase efficiency. Creating alliances and partnerships, where two companies with their own relative strengths cooperate to produce results that neither could have achieved alone, can result in positive synergies and cost savings. Collaborations help create shared value. (These kinds of network structures and B2B relationships are discussed in more detail in Chapter 6.)

Spin Master, a Canadian toy company, has achieved efficiencies through creating alliances in all aspects of its operations, from designing new products to manufacturing and retailing. The flexibility of outsourcing everything has allowed Spin Master to concentrate on what it does best—bringing products to market faster than any of the big companies, such as Hasbro and Mattel, could ever do. Take, for example, the deal to manufacture and market Catch-a-Bubble. "Six months after the first meeting in Hong Kong, Spin Master shipped 7 million units and invoiced $15 million."[48] Gaining a competitive advantage in the global economy demands that organizations achieve efficiencies in order to provide affordable merchandise to their customers, but not at the expense of the manufacturer or direct producer.

INCREASING QUALITY

The challenge from global organizations such as Korean electronics manufacturers, Mexican agricultural producers, and European marketing and financial firms has also increased pressure on companies to improve the quality of goods and services delivered. One major thrust to improve quality has been to introduce quality-enhancing techniques known as total quality management (TQM). Employees involved in TQM are often organized into quality control teams and are given the responsibility of continually finding new and better ways to perform their jobs—including reducing their environmental footprint by utilizing recycled materials and by-products of production processes. They also are given the responsibility for monitoring and evaluating the quality of the goods they produce. Rigorous testing of products for durability as well as function and design is one of IKEA's trademarks.

INCREASING INNOVATION

Innovation—the process of creating new goods and services that customers want, or developing better ways to produce or provide goods and services—poses a special challenge. Managers must create an organizational culture in which people are encouraged to be innovative. Typically, innovation takes place in small groups or teams; management passes on control of work activities to team members and creates an organizational culture that rewards risk-taking. An organization's culture is the shared set of beliefs and expectations that are shaped by *norms and values* of the founders and managers, as we saw in Chapter 1. Understanding and managing innovation and creating a work setting that encourages risk-taking are among the most difficult managerial tasks. Dr. Michael Rachlis, an associate professor at the University of Toronto's department of health care, describes how the Sault Ste. Marie Group Health Centre in Ontario assigned a home-care nurse to visit every heart-failure patient. This innovative practice reduced readmissions by 70 percent.[49] IKEA's "design culture," along with its drive to be socially responsible and competitive, creates the kind of work setting that fosters innovation. As the president of IKEA Sweden said, "Designing beautiful-but-expensive products is easy... Designing beautiful products that are inexpensive and functional is a huge challenge."[50]

innovation (1) The implementation of creative ideas in an organization. (2) The process of creating new goods and services or developing better ways to produce or provide goods and services.

> "Designing beautiful-but-expensive products is easy...Designing beautiful products that are inexpensive and functional is a huge challenge."
>
> Josephine Rydberg-Dumont, Ikea

Efficiency is a key component of IKEA's competitive strength.
Frank Beecham

Blackberry, (formerly Research In Motion) was particularly good at innovation. Founded in 1984 and headquartered in Waterloo, Ontario, RIM was a leading designer, manufacturer, and marketer of innovative wireless solutions for the worldwide mobile communications market. It first developed in 1999 the BlackBerry device that had the new capability of sending wireless email. One of the strengths of the BlackBerry brand was its secure messaging system, used most notably in organizing the popular protests that toppled many political despots in Arab nations in 2011. Past U.S. President Barack Obama and the U.S. government famously used the BlackBerry exclusively because of its top-notch security. In 2012, however, RIM lost market share to Apple's iPhone and Google's Android when both received U.S. government approval for use. For 13 years, RIM enjoyed a near monopoly in the mobile communications market based on its innovative technology. In 2014, the company rebranded as simply BlackBerry, stopped making hardware, and focused on its niche strength of secure messaging systems to regain competitiveness.

INCREASING RESPONSIVENESS TO CUSTOMERS

Keeping up with trends in consumer demands is tough, but creating products that are actually good for consumers is the way forward. Forget tobacco and fatty, salty foods. Food companies that traditionally concentrated on taste and quantity to drive more and more consumption are refocusing on the fundamental need for better nutrition to the benefit of the whole society.

Organizations must also re-evaluate traditional markets and begin to see the opportunities in serving undersupplied populations with needed goods and services, whether they be low-income workers in an urban desert or female entrepreneurs in a rural area in a developing nation. There is a huge untapped potential for market expansion here. For example, microfinance—which started by providing small, low-interest loans to rural women in India to start their own businesses—is fast becoming a way to meet the financing needs of U.S. citizens, filling an important gap that was unrecognized.[51]

Organizations use their products and services to compete for customers, so training employees to be responsive to customers' needs is vital for all organizations, and particularly for service organizations. Retail stores, banks, and restaurants, for example, depend entirely on their employees to give high-quality service at a reasonable cost.[52] As Canada and other countries become knowledge-based economies (in part because of the loss of manufacturing jobs to China, Malaysia, and other countries with low labour costs), managing customer needs and relationships in service organizations is becoming increasingly important. IKEA offers quality supervised child care for customers while they shop because a substantial proportion of their customer base is families with young children.

In today's global economy, innovations in the fashion industry are quickly replicated at lower costs by knock-off manufacturers in emerging markets. It is not enough to sell uniqueness at premium prices. Harry Rosen CEO, Larry Rosen, explains, "Quality for the customer becomes less a question of what you sell than of how you sell it. When you get to a price point at Rosen, it's the experience you're buying. We don't perceive ourselves as being in the clothing business. We don't just sell suits and sport jackets. It's a relationship-based business. My business is to get to know you, to have you build a relationship with one of my highly trained associates. I want to be your clothier for life. The whole key to our business is loyal clients. I strongly believe we have a corporate culture that has a love of quality and a love of clients. And building customer relationships is a managed process."[53]

Maintaining Ethical Standards

While mobilizing organizational resources, all managers are under considerable pressure to increase the level at which their organizations perform. For example, top managers receive pressure from shareholders to increase the performance of the entire organization in order to boost stock prices, improve profits, or raise dividends. In turn, top managers may then pressure middle managers to find new ways to use organizational resources to increase efficiency or quality in order to attract new customers, earn more revenues, and reduce the ecological footprint of their activities.

Pressure to improve performance can be healthy for an organization because it causes managers to question the organization's operations and encourages them to find new and better ways to plan, organize, lead, and control. However, too much pressure to perform can be harmful.[54] It may induce managers to behave unethically in dealings with individuals and groups both inside and outside the organization.[55] For example, a purchasing manager for a large retail chain might buy inferior clothing as a cost-cutting measure. Or to secure a large foreign contract, a sales manager in a large company might offer bribes to foreign officials. Or overzealous stockbrokers might trade in credit default swaps and other securities derivatives to make a fast buck without due consideration of the risk of total financial collapse, as almost happened in the crisis of 2008. *Codes of ethical conduct* are a useful tool for managers to train and control the behaviour of employees and partners. IKEA has a supplier code of conduct that requires suppliers to meet minimum standards with respect to the environment and social and working conditions for employees, including prohibiting the use of child labour.

When managers act unethically, some individuals or groups may obtain short-term gains, but in the long run the organization and people inside and outside the organization will pay. In Chapter 3, we discuss the nature of ethics and the importance of managers and all members of an organization behaving ethically as they pursue organizational goals.

Utilizing New Information Systems and Technologies

Another important challenge facing managers is the pressure to increase performance through new information systems and technologies.[56] The importance of information systems and new technologies to managers in acquiring and utilizing information is discussed in detail in Chapter 6. Coordinating the production of more than 12 000 products from 50 countries and 2000 suppliers would not be possible in today's global economy without IKEA's own software, Electronic Commerce for IKEA Suppliers (ECIS).

SUMMARY AND REVIEW

Chapter 2

connect

LO1 What Is the Organizational Environment? The organizational environment is the set of forces and conditions that affect a manager's ability to acquire and use resources. The organizational environment has two components: the internal environment and the external environment. The dimensions of the internal environment are the focus of Parts 3 and 4 of this textbook and include the strategy, structure, human resources, organizational culture, and control mechanisms of the organization. The external environment can be divided into the industry-specific or task environment and the general environment. Failure of managers to perceive, interpret, and respond to forces in the organizational environment can lead to failure when competing in the global economy.

LO2 The External Organizational Environment The external organizational environment is understood as having two levels—one general and overarching, and one specific to the sector or industry. The industry-specific or task environment is the set of forces and conditions that originate with suppliers, distributors, customers, and competitors and that influence a manager's ability to obtain inputs and sell outputs on a daily basis. The general environment includes wider-ranging political, economic, socio-cultural, technological, and international/global forces (PESTI) that affect an organization more indirectly.

LO3 The Global Environment In recent years there has been a marked shift toward a more open global environment in which capital flows more freely as people and companies search for new opportunities to create profit and wealth. This has hastened the process of globalization. Globalization is the set of specific and general forces that work together to integrate and connect economic, political, and social systems across countries, cultures, or geographic regions so that nations become increasingly interdependent and similar. The process of globalization has been furthered by declining barriers to international trade and investment and declining barriers of distance and culture.

LO4 Managing the External Environment Two factors affect the nature of the opportunities and threats that organizations face: (1) the level of complexity in the environment and (2) the rate of change in the environment. Managers must learn how to analyze the forces in the environment in order to respond effectively to opportunities and threats. Managers at all three levels and in all functional areas are responsible for reducing the negative impact and embracing the new opportunities posed by environmental forces as they evolve over time.

LO5 Challenges for Management in a Global Environment Today's competitive global environment presents the challenge of creating shared value—that is, economic and social value—by building a competitive advantage through increasing efficiency, quality, innovation, and responsiveness to customers; behaving ethically toward stakeholders inside and outside the organization; and utilizing new information systems and technologies.

KEY TERMS

barriers to entry	globalization
brand loyalty	industry-specific or task environment
certainty	innovation
competitive advantage	internal environment
competitors	national culture
Creating Shared Value	organizational environment
customers	political forces
demographic forces	potential competitors
deregulation	privatization
distributors	social structure
economic forces	socio-cultural forces
economies of scale	stakeholders
environmental change	suppliers
external environment	tariff
free trade doctrine	technological forces
general environment	technology
global forces	uncertainty
global organizations	

WRAP-UP TO OPENING CASE

IKEA Is on Top of the Furniture World

In the opening case you were introduced to the IKEA concept. After having read and understood the concepts in this chapter, you should be able to answer the following questions:

1. *Explain how the forces in the external organizational environment affected IKEA's global operations.*

    ANSWER: The external organizational environment includes forces in the task and general environments. The task environment is made up of forces that present immediate opportunities and threats for managers in acquiring and utilizing resources, while the forces in the organization's general environment pose problems and promises that have a longer-term effect and have a great impact on management planning and decision making. Forces in the task environment result from the actions of suppliers, distributors, customers, and competitors. Forces in the general environment result from political, economic, socio-cultural, technological, and international/global trends. IKEA, as a global company, deals with more than 2000 suppliers of goods manufactured in over 50 nations, producing more than 12 000 products. Suppliers must abide by the IKEA code of conduct if they want to provide the company with goods. This code includes rules for using sustainable materials and providing good working conditions for labour. IKEA is such a large customer for its suppliers that they comply with its rules in order to maintain their contracts. Many companies compete for IKEA's business, thus minimizing the power they exert on the company. IKEA has built brand loyalty among its customers all over the world by providing a unique shopping experience for low cost through modern furniture and household fixtures that customers can usually take home and assemble themselves. Competitors are firms that sell similar products and services. While IKEA provides a unique experience for customers, companies like U.S. giant Target Corp. are offering similar style low-cost furniture, and could pose a threat to IKEA by luring away its customers with a low-cost strategy.

    To minimize the problem of coordinating the great number of suppliers, IKEA developed its own software to manage its supply chain. As the population age rises in developed countries like Canada, IKEA must capitalize on the opportunity for growth by providing goods desired by older people. Catering to the needs of parents by providing quality child care while parents shop has proved to be good for business. During times of recession, customers seek value-based products such as the ones sold by IKEA. The company's low-cost strategy of selling affordable goods that make living better is a strategy that can weather fluctuations in economic conditions. When IKEA locates its stores in different nations, it must abide by those nations' laws governing trade and commerce. While trade barriers are declining, international trade agreements, such as NAFTA, stipulate a minimal amount of member-nation content or assembly that IKEA must meet to sell its goods tariff-free in the member nations. IKEA has taken advantage of the global economy by locating stores in over 40 nations. The challenge for its global operations is to customize products to meet the needs of different national cultures.

2. *Discuss how global competition and increasing complexity has impacted management decisions at IKEA.*

    ANSWER: Global competition and increasing complexity have impacted the decisions IKEA managers make in terms of coordinating the supply of products with the demand for products. Americans like to fold their clothes, while Italians like to hang theirs. This difference in national cultural norms resulted in changes to the design of wardrobes for each nation. The kind of low-cost offerings IKEA provides does not appeal to cultures such as the Japanese culture, which values high-quality, high-cost products. Thus, the demand for IKEA products in Japan was minimal, resulting in failure in that country.

3. *Evaluate how managers at IKEA handle environmental change and uncertainty.*

   ANSWER: Environmental change occurs when the forces in the task and general environments change. An understanding of the external environment is necessary so that managers can anticipate how the task environment might look in the future and decide on the actions to pursue if the organization is to prosper. If the changes in the forces in the external environment can be easily predicted, managers can make decisions with more certainty and less risk. If the changes are complicated and happen quickly, managers are less likely to be able to predict future outcomes of decisions. To minimize uncertainty, companies adopt flexible organizational structures, work processes, and cultures. IKEA has a geographical organizational structure that allows divisional managers to analyze the forces in the environment and create strategy, such as customizing products, to meet the specific needs of the national culture. Work teams that consist of designers and producers try to find environmentally sustainable inputs and more efficient ways to produce affordable, portable products.

4. *Explain how IKEA embraced the challenges of being competitive in the global economy.*

   ANSWER: The challenges for managers in the global economy to be competitive include creating an advantage by developing four building blocks, managing ethically and utilizing information technology systems to make management decisions. The four building blocks of a competitive advantage are 1) increasing efficiencies, 2) focusing on quality, 3) being responsive to customers, and 4) adopting a culture of innovation. IKEA looks for ways to reduce the costs of its products by 2 to 3 percent per year, while using sustainable and recycled materials that do not diminish quality. IKEA creates affordable products that customers can take home and assemble themselves with some basic tools the company provides. Designers continually aim to create appealing household furnishings that can be flat packed and easily transported. The network of more than 2000 global suppliers must adhere to a code of conduct. The entire supply chain is coordinated by IKEA's own software technology. IKEA is a successful company in the competitive global economy.

MANAGEMENT IN ACTION

TOPICS FOR DISCUSSION AND ACTION
LEVEL 1 Knowledge & Comprehension

1. Identify and describe the forces found in an organization's external environment.
2. Describe the implications that globalization has for managers.
3. Describe what each level of manager can do to reduce the impact of the forces in the organizational environment.

LEVEL 2 Application & Analysis

4. Ask the manager of an organization to discuss the types and strengths of forces in the organization's task environment. What are the current opportunities and threats resulting from competitors, customers, and suppliers?

5. Scan the environmental forces affecting local businesses by reading the business section of today's newspaper or listening to a business podcast. Explain the impact of the forces on the ability of local businesses to acquire and use resources.

6. Go to the library and gather information that allows you to compare and contrast the political, economic, demographic, and cultural systems of the United States, Mexico, and Canada. How might the similarities and differences affect the management of an enterprise such as Walmart, which does business in all three countries?

LEVEL 3 Synthesis & Evaluation

7. Illustrate how each force in the organization's task environment can pose an opportunity and a threat for a manager of a Tim Hortons restaurant expanding into the United States.

8. Put yourself in the position of a first-line manager of a retailer such as Giant Tiger. What suggestions would you make to your boss about how to use the four building blocks to gain a competitive advantage?

9. Which organization is likely to face the most complex task environment: a biotechnology company trying to develop a cure for cancer, or a large retailer such as Hudson's Bay? Explain why this is the case with reference to each force in the organization's task environment.

SELF-REFLECTION EXERCISE

You are considering organizing an event to raise funds for a special cause (e.g., children living in poverty, breast cancer research, literacy, or something of your choice). Think about who you might invite to this event (i.e., your "customers"—those who will buy tickets to the event). What type of event might appeal to them? What suppliers might you approach for help in organizing the event? What legal issues might you face in setting up this event? After considering all these issues, how difficult is the environment you face in holding this event?

SMALL GROUP BREAKOUT EXERCISE

Form groups of three or four people and appoint one member as the spokesperson who will communicate your findings to the whole class when called on by the instructor. Then discuss the following scenario: Assume you and your teammates run a management consultancy company. Two of your clients, a multinational pharmaceutical company and a home construction company, are concerned about changing demographic trends in Canada. The population is aging because of declining birth rates, declining death rates, and the aging of the baby boom generation.

1. What might be some of the implications (opportunities and threats) of this demographic trend for your clients?

MANAGING ETHICALLY EXERCISE

You are a manager for a drug company that has developed a pill to cure river blindness, a common disease in Africa. It was a quick and easy solution, but there were no buyers because the people afflicted, or who could be afflicted, are too poor to buy the pills. Should you shelve the pills and wait until the market can pay the price? What other alternatives might you have?

MANAGEMENT CHALLENGE EXERCISE
How to Enter the Copying Business

You have decided to open a small printing and copying business in a college town of 100 000 people. Your business will compete with companies like FedEx Kinko's. You know that over 50 percent of small businesses fail in their first year, so to increase your chances of success, you have decided to do a detailed analysis of the task environment of the copying business to discover what opportunities and threats you will likely encounter.

1. Decide what you must know about (a) your future customers, (b) your future competitors, and (c) other critical forces in the task environment if you are to be successful.

2. Based on this analysis, list some of the steps you would take to help your new copying business succeed.

MANAGEMENT PORTFOLIO PROJECT

Answer the following questions about the organization you have chosen to follow:

1. Describe the main forces in the industry-specific or task environment that are affecting the organization.

2. Describe the main forces in the general environment that are affecting the organization.

3. Try to determine whether the organization's task and general environments are relatively stable or changing rapidly.

4. Explain how these environmental forces affect the job of an individual manager within this organization. How do these forces determine the opportunities and threats that managers must confront?

5. How does the organization utilize the four building blocks of a competitive advantage?

MANAGEMENT CASE

TURNAROUND AT SONY?

Sony, the Japanese electronics maker, used to be renowned for using its innovation and engineering prowess to turn out blockbuster new products such as the Walkman and Trinitron TV. In the 1990s, product engineers at Sony turned out an average of four new product ideas every day. Why? A large part of the answer was Sony's culture, called the "Sony Way," which emphasized communication, cooperation, and harmony between groups of engineers across the company to foster innovation and change. Engineers were given considerable freedom to pursue their own ideas, and the managers of different product groups championed their own innovations, but problems arose with Sony's approach.

Companies in Korea, Taiwan, and China began to innovate new technologies like digital LCD screens and flash memory that made Sony's technologies obsolete. Companies such as Apple and Nokia came out with the iPod, smartphones, and tablet computers that better fit customer needs than Sony's "old-generation" products such as the Walkman. One reason why Sony experienced major problems responding to these changes was that its culture had changed with its success. The top managers of its many divisions had become used to acting as if they had control of a fiefdom, and, protected by the Japanese tradition of lifetime employment, they worked to promote their own division's interests, not their company's. This competition had increased Sony's bureaucracy and slowed its decision making, making it much harder for Sony to take advantage of its pipeline of new product innovations. At the same time, its research was becoming enormously expensive, as divisions demanded more and more funds to create innovative new products.

Sensing this was a crucial turning point in their company's history, Sony's Japanese top managers turned to a *gaijin,* or non-Japanese, executive to lead their company. Their choice was Sir Howard Stringer, a Welshman, who headed Sony's North American operations and had been instrumental in cutting costs and increasing the profits of Sony's U.S. division. Stringer cannot speak Japanese, but luckily for him, many of Sony's top executives speak English.

While he was in command, he faced the problem of reducing costs in Japan, where many Japanese companies have a policy of lifetime employment. He made it clear that layoffs would be forthcoming, as Sony had to reduce its high operating costs. He has also made it clear that the politicking going on between Sony's different product groups must stop and that managers must prioritize new products, investing only in those that have the highest chance of success, in order for Sony to reduce its huge R&D budget. Indeed, he wanted to make engineering, not management, the focus once again at Sony and eliminate the tall, bloated hierarchy that had developed over time—by, for example, downsizing corporate headquarters. In Stringer's own words, the culture or "business of Sony has been management, not making products." However, he had to accomplish this in Japan, which has a national culture known for its collectivist, long-term orientation and for its distrust of *gaijin* or overseas values. And these same values operate inside Sony, so Stringer had to be hard-headed and push Sony to make the best use of its resources. He demonstrated this hard-headed approach in 2009, when, after Sony's losses increased, he replaced his top management team and streamlined the management hierarchy to speed decision making.

In his effort to revamp the company, Stringer confronted difficult, challenging cultural differences while bringing his cost-cutting expertise to bear on Sony's deteriorating situation. Sony was still struggling to regain its former leadership position. When Stringer stepped down in April 2012, replaced by Mr. Kazuo Hirai, the company's television division was losing $80 on each set it sold.[57,58]

While losing market share was bad enough, Sony Pictures Entertainment became the target of a cyberattack in late 2014 that forced the decision to delay the debut of a comedy about the dictatorship in North Korea. After speculating that the regime in North Korea was behind the hack, U.S. president Obama announced sanctions against North Korea.[59] Shortly afterward, the depressed company announced it would close all of its 14 retail stores across Canada.[60]

1. Evaluate how the forces in the organizational environment impacted Sony.

2. How were the actions of management influenced by environmental change in this case?

3. How did the new manager use the building blocks of a competitive advantage to try to turn around the operations at Sony?

END OF PART I: CONTINUING CASE

CARROT TOPS: INTRODUCTION

The main theme of this book is that the management process—planning, organizing, leading, and controlling—is not confined to the top management, but rather is a process in which every manager must engage. Perhaps nowhere is this more apparent than in the typical small service business. Here the owner/operator usually has few staff to rely on. The success of the enterprise often depends on the effectiveness with which the manager structures activities and uses resources to achieve a goal. The activities of managing are critical to any complex cooperative endeavour. Management is both the art and the science of arranging and utilizing the physical and human factors of production toward a desired outcome.

To help illustrate and emphasize the role of the front-line manager we will use a continuing or running case of a business based in southwestern Ontario. Each segment will illustrate how the case's main players—owner/manager Mel Harvey and first-line manager Janet Khan—confront and solve management problems each day by applying the concepts and techniques presented in the book in each particular part: Part I—Management; Part II—Planning; Part III—Organizing; Part IV—Leading; and Part V—Controlling. Here is some background information you'll need to answer the questions that arise in subsequent parts of this book.

CARROT TOPS: A PROFILE

After putting together a typical business plan to meet the requirements of a course on entrepreneurship, Mel Harvey started "Mel's General Store" in 2018. The business plan was about 20 pages long and outlined the usual array of topics: a profile of the organization; a profile of the industry; a profile of the product or service; marketing, organization, operating, and control systems plans; pro forma financial statements; and financial project tables and appendices. The one-page executive summary included a synopsis of the plan and covered "the business," "the market," "strategy," "competition," "management," and "financial details," including how the company intends to generate revenue, as well as a likely exit strategy. In this case, Mel was committed to supplying low-cost, basic groceries to the local community in which he lived in southwestern Ontario. One day, he hoped to sell franchise licences.

Drawing on all segments of this case:

1. What kinds of activities does Mel have to consider in planning, organizing, leading, and controlling his enterprise?

2. What sets of skills will Mel use when planning, organizing, leading, and controlling?

3. Identify an example of an activity that Mel could undertake that illustrates each of Mintzberg's managerial roles.

4. What opportunities and threats might Mel encounter in the organizational environment?

Appendix A

History of Management Thought

The systematic study of management began in the closing decades of the 19th century, after the Industrial Revolution had swept through Europe and America. In the new economic climate, managers of all types of organizations—political, educational, and economic—were increasingly turning their focus toward finding better ways to satisfy customers' needs. Many major economic, technical, and cultural changes were taking place at this time. With the introduction of steam power and the development of sophisticated machinery and equipment, the Industrial Revolution changed the way goods were produced, particularly in the weaving and clothing industries. Small workshops run by skilled workers who produced hand-manufactured products (a system called *crafts production*) were being replaced by large factories in which sophisticated machines controlled by hundreds or even thousands of unskilled or semiskilled workers made products. For example, raw cotton and wool that in the past families or whole villages working together had spun into yarn were now shipped to factories where workers operated machines that spun and wove large quantities of yarn into cloth.

Owners and managers of the new factories found themselves unprepared for the challenges accompanying the change from small-scale crafts production to large-scale mechanized manufacturing. Moreover, many of the managers and supervisors in these workshops and factories were engineers who had only a technical orientation. They were unprepared for the social problems that occur when people work together in large groups (as in a factory or shop system). Managers began to search for new techniques to manage their organizations' resources, and soon they began to focus on ways to increase the efficiency of the worker–task mix. They found help from Frederick W. Taylor.

F.W. Taylor and Scientific Management

Frederick W. Taylor (1856–1915) is best known for defining the techniques of **scientific management,** the systematic study of relationships between people and tasks for the purpose of redesigning the work process to increase efficiency. Taylor was a manufacturing manager who eventually became a consultant and taught other managers how to apply his scientific management techniques. Taylor believed that if the amount of time and effort that each worker expends to produce a unit of output (a finished good or service) can be reduced by increasing specialization and the division of labour, the production process will become more efficient. Taylor believed the way to create the most efficient division of labour could best be determined by using scientific management techniques, rather than intuitive or informal rule-of-thumb knowledge. Based on his experiments and observations as a manufacturing manager in a variety of settings, he developed four principles to increase efficiency in the workplace:[1]

scientific management The systematic study of relationships between people and tasks to increase efficiency.

- Principle 1: *Study the way workers perform their tasks, gather all the informal job knowledge that workers possess, and experiment with ways of improving the way tasks are performed.*

  To discover the most efficient method of performing specific tasks, Taylor studied in great detail and measured the ways different workers went about performing their tasks. One of the main tools he used was a time and motion study, which involves the careful timing and recording of the actions taken to perform a particular task. Once Taylor understood the existing method of performing a task, he then experimented to increase specialization; he tried different methods of dividing up and coordinating the various tasks necessary to produce a finished product. Usually this meant simplifying jobs and having each worker perform fewer, more routine tasks. Taylor also sought to find ways to improve each worker's ability to perform a particular task—for example, by reducing the number of motions workers made to complete the task, by changing the layout of the work area or the type of tool workers used, or by experimenting with tools of different sizes.

- Principle 2: *Codify the new methods of performing tasks into written rules and standard operating procedures.*

  Once the best method of performing a particular task was determined, Taylor specified that it should be recorded so that the procedures could be taught to all workers performing the same task. These rules could be used to further standardize and simplify jobs—essentially, to make jobs even more routine. In this way efficiency could be increased throughout an organization.

- Principle 3: *Carefully select workers so that they possess skills and abilities that match the needs of the task, and train them to perform the task according to the established rules and procedures.*

  To increase specialization, Taylor believed workers had to understand the tasks that were required and be thoroughly trained in order to perform a task at the required level. Workers who could not be trained to this level were to be transferred to a job where they were able to reach the minimum required level of proficiency.[2]

- Principle 4: *Establish a fair or acceptable level of performance for a task, and then develop a pay system that provides a reward for performance above the acceptable level.*

  To encourage workers to perform at a high level of efficiency, and to provide them with an incentive to reveal the most efficient techniques for performing a task, Taylor advocated that workers benefit from any gains in performance. They should be paid a bonus and receive some percentage of the performance gains achieved through the more efficient work process.

By 1910, Taylor's system of scientific management had become nationally known and in many instances faithfully and fully practised.[3] However, managers in many organizations chose to implement the new principles of scientific management selectively. This decision ultimately resulted in problems. For example, some managers using scientific management obtained increases in performance, but rather than sharing performance gains with workers through bonuses as Taylor had advocated, they simply increased the amount of work that each worker was expected to do. Many workers experiencing the reorganized work system found that as their performance increased, managers required them to do more work for the same pay. Workers also learned that increases in performance often meant fewer jobs and a greater threat of layoffs because fewer workers were needed. In addition, the specialized, simplified jobs were often monotonous and repetitive, and many workers became dissatisfied with their jobs.

From a performance perspective, the combination of the two management practices—(1) achieving the right mix of worker–task specialization and (2) linking people and tasks by the speed of the production line—resulted in huge savings in cost and huge increases in output that occur in large, organized work settings. For example, in 1908, managers at the Franklin Motor Company using scientific management principles redesigned the work process, and the output of cars increased from 100 cars a month to 45 cars a day; workers' wages, however, increased by only 90 percent.[4]

Taylor's work has had an enduring effect on the management of production systems. Managers in every organization, whether it produces goods or services, now carefully analyze the basic tasks that workers must perform and try to create a work environment that will allow their organizations to operate most efficiently. We discuss this important issue in Managing Human Resources, Chapter 7.

Weber's Bureaucratic Theory

Side by side with scientific managers studying the person–task mix to increase efficiency, other researchers were focusing on how to increase the efficiency with which organizations were managed. Max Weber, a German professor of sociology, outlined his famous principles of **bureaucracy**—a formal system of organization and administration designed to ensure efficiency and effectiveness—and created bureaucratic theory. A bureaucratic system of administration is based on five principles:

bureaucracy A formal system of organization and administration designed to ensure efficiency and effectiveness.

- Principle 1: *In a bureaucracy, a manager's formal authority derives from the position he or she holds in the organization.*

  Authority is the power to hold people accountable for their actions and to make decisions concerning the use of organizational resources. Authority gives managers the right to direct and control their subordinates' behaviour to achieve organizational goals. In a bureaucratic system of administration, obedience is owed to a manager, not because of any personal qualities—such as personality, wealth, or social status—but because the manager occupies a position that is associated with a certain level of authority and responsibility.[5]

authority The power to hold people accountable for their actions and to allocate organizational resources.

- Principle 2: *In a bureaucracy, people should occupy positions because of their performance, not because of their social standing or personal contacts.*

  This principle was not always followed in Weber's time and is often ignored today. Some organizations and industries are still affected by social networks in which personal contacts and relations, not job-related skills, influence hiring and promotion decisions.

- Principle 3: *The extent of each position's formal authority and their responsibilities, and their relationship to other positions in an organization, should be clearly specified.*

  When the tasks and authority associated with various positions in the organization are clearly specified, managers and workers know what is expected of them and what to expect from each other. Moreover, an organization can hold all its employees strictly accountable for their actions when they know their exact responsibilities.

- Principle 4: *Authority can be exercised effectively in an organization when positions are arranged hierarchically, so employees know whom to report to and who reports to them.*[6]

  Managers must create an organizational hierarchy of authority that makes it clear who reports to whom and to whom managers and workers should go if conflicts or problems arise. This principle is especially important in the armed forces, policing, and other organizations that deal with sensitive issues involving possible major repercussions. It is vital that managers at high levels of the hierarchy be able to hold subordinates accountable for their actions.

- Principle 5: *Managers must create a well-defined system of rules, standard operating procedures, and norms so that they can effectively control behaviour within an organization.*

    Rules are formal written instructions that specify actions to be taken under different circumstances to achieve specific goals (for example, if A happens, do B). **Standard operating procedures (SOPs)** are specific sets of written instructions about how to perform a certain aspect of a task. A rule might state that at the end of the workday employees are to leave their machines in good order, and a set of SOPs specifies exactly how they should do so, itemizing which machine parts must be oiled or replaced. **Norms** are unwritten, informal codes of conduct that prescribe how people should act in particular situations. For example, an organizational norm in a restaurant might be that waiters should help each other if time permits.

rule A formal, written guide to action.

standard operating procedures (SOPs) (1) Written instructions describing the exact series of actions that should be followed in a specific situation; (2) Rules and policies that standardize behaviours.

norms Unwritten, informal codes of conduct that prescribe how people should act in particular situations and that are considered important by most members of a group or organization.

Rules, SOPs, and norms provide behavioural guidelines that increase the performance of a bureaucratic system because they specify the best ways to accomplish organizational tasks. Companies such as McDonald's and Walmart have developed extensive rules and procedures to specify the behaviours required of their employees, such as "Always greet the customer with a smile."

Weber believed that organizations that implement all five principles establish a bureaucratic system that improves organizational performance. The specification of positions and the use of rules and SOPs to regulate how tasks are performed make it easier for managers to organize and control the work of subordinates. Similarly, fair and equitable selection and promotion systems improve managers' feelings of security, reduce stress, and encourage organizational members to act ethically and further promote the interests of the organization.[7]

If bureaucracies are not managed well, many problems can result. Sometimes managers allow rules and SOPs, "bureaucratic red tape," to become so cumbersome that decision making becomes slow and inefficient and organizations are unable to change. When managers rely too much on rules to solve problems and not enough on their own skills and judgment, their behaviour becomes inflexible. A key challenge for managers is to use bureaucratic principles to benefit, rather than harm, an organization.

The Work of Mary Parker Follett

If F. W. Taylor is considered the father of management thought, Mary Parker Follett (1868–1933) serves as its mother.[8] Much of her writing about management and the way managers should behave toward workers was a response to her concern that Taylor was ignoring the human side of the organization. She pointed out that management often overlooks the multitude of ways in which employees can contribute to the organization when managers allow them to participate and exercise initiative in their everyday work lives.[9] Taylor, for example, never proposed that managers involve workers in analyzing their jobs to identify better ways to perform tasks, or even ask workers how they felt about their jobs. Instead, he used time and motion experts to analyze workers' jobs for them. Follett, in contrast, argued that because workers know the most about their jobs, they should be involved in job analysis and managers should allow them to participate in the work development process.

Follett proposed, "Authority should go with knowledge . . . whether it is up the line or down." In other words, if workers have the relevant knowledge, then workers, rather than managers, should be in control of the work process itself, and managers should behave as coaches and facilitators—not as monitors and supervisors. In making this statement, Follett anticipated the current interest in self-managed teams and empowerment. She also recognized the importance of having managers in different departments communicate directly with each other to speed decision making. She advocated what she called "cross-functioning": members of different departments working together in cross-departmental teams to accomplish projects—an approach that is increasingly utilized today.[10] She proposed that knowledge and expertise, not managers' formal authority deriving from their position in the hierarchy, should decide who would lead at any particular moment. She believed, as do many management theorists today, that power is fluid and should flow to the person who can best help the organization achieve its goals. Follett took a horizontal view of power and authority, rather than viewing the vertical chain of command as being most essential to effective management. Thus, Follett's approach was very radical for its time.

The Hawthorne Studies and Human Relations

Probably because of its radical nature, Follett's work went unappreciated by managers and researchers until quite recently. Most continued to follow in the footsteps of Taylor, and to increase efficiency, they studied ways to improve various characteristics of the work setting, such as job specialization or the kinds of tools workers used. One series of studies was conducted from 1924 to 1932 at the Hawthorne Works of the Western Electric Company.[11] This research, now known as the Hawthorne studies, was initiated as an attempt to investigate how characteristics of the work setting—specifically the level of lighting or illumination—affect worker fatigue and performance. The researchers conducted an experiment in which they systematically measured worker productivity at various levels of illumination.

The experiment produced some unexpected results. The researchers found that regardless of whether they raised or lowered the level of illumination, productivity increased. In fact, productivity began to fall only when the level of illumination dropped to the level of moonlight, a level at which presumably workers could no longer see well enough to do their work efficiently.

As you can imagine, the researchers found these results very puzzling. They invited a noted Harvard psychologist, Elton Mayo, to help them. Mayo proposed another series of experiments to solve the mystery. These experiments, known as the relay assembly test experiments, were designed to investigate the effects of other aspects of the work context on job performance, such as the effect of the number and length of rest periods and hours of work on fatigue and monotony.[12] The goal was to raise productivity.

During a two-year study of a small group of female workers, the researchers again observed that productivity increased over time, but the increases could not be solely attributed to the effects of changes in the work setting. Gradually, the researchers discovered that, to some degree, the results they were obtaining were influenced by the fact that the researchers themselves had become part of the experiment. In other words, the presence of the researchers was affecting the results because the workers enjoyed receiving attention and being the subject of study and were willing to cooperate with the researchers to produce the results they believed the researchers desired.

Subsequently, it was found that many other factors also influence worker behaviour, and it was not clear what was actually influencing the Hawthorne workers' behaviour. However, this particular effect—which became known as the **Hawthorne effect**—seemed to suggest that the attitudes of workers toward their managers affect the level of workers' performance. In particular, the significant finding was that a manager's behaviour or leadership approach can affect performance. This finding led many researchers to turn their attention to managerial behaviour and leadership. If supervisors could be trained to behave in ways that would elicit cooperative behaviour from their subordinates, then productivity could be increased. From this view emerged the **human relations movement,** which advocates that supervisors be behaviourally trained to manage subordinates in ways that elicit their cooperation and increase their productivity.

Hawthorne effect Workers' productivity is affected more by observation or attention received than by physical work setting.

human relations movement Advocates behaviour and leadership training of supervisors to elicit worker cooperation and improve productivity.

The importance of behavioural or human relations training became even clearer to its supporters after another series of experiments—the bank wiring room experiments. In a study of workers making telephone-switching equipment, researchers Elton Mayo and F. J. Roethlisberger discovered that the workers, as a group, had deliberately adopted a norm of output restriction to protect their jobs. Other group members subjected workers who violated this informal production norm to sanctions. Those who violated group performance norms and performed above the norm were called "ratebusters"; those who performed below the norm were called "chisellers."[13]

The experimenters concluded that both types of workers threatened the group as a whole. Ratebusters threaten group members because they reveal to managers how fast the work can be done. Chisellers are looked down on because they are not doing their share of the work. Work-group members discipline both ratebusters and chisellers in order to create a pace of work that the workers (not the managers) think is fair. Thus, the work group's influence over output can be as great as the supervisors' influence. Since the work group can influence the behaviour of its members, some management theorists argue that supervisors should be trained to behave in ways that gain the goodwill and cooperation of workers so that supervisors, not workers, control the level of work-group performance.

One of the main implications of the Hawthorne studies was that the behaviour of managers and workers in the work setting is as important in explaining the level of performance as the technical aspects of the task. Managers must understand the workings of the **informal organization,** the system of behavioural rules and norms that emerge in a group, when they try to manage or change behaviour in organizations. Many studies have found that, as time passes, groups often develop elaborate procedures and norms that bond members together, allowing unified action either to cooperate with management in order to raise performance or to restrict output and thwart the attainment of organizational goals.[14] The Hawthorne studies demonstrated the importance of understanding how the feelings, thoughts, and behaviour of work-group members and managers affect performance. It was becoming increasingly clear to researchers that understanding behaviour in organizations is a complex process that is critical to increasing performance.[15] Indeed, the increasing interest in the area of management known as **organizational behaviour,** the study of the factors that have an impact on how individuals and groups respond to and act in organizations, dates from these early studies.

informal organization The system of behavioural rules and norms that emerge in work groups.

organizational behaviour The study of factors that impact how workers respond to and act in an organization.

Theory X and Theory Y

Several studies after the Second World War revealed how assumptions about workers' attitudes and behaviour affect managers' behaviour. Douglas McGregor developed the most influential approach. He proposed that two different sets of assumptions about work attitudes and behaviours dominate the way managers think and affect how they behave in organizations. McGregor named these two contrasting sets of assumptions *Theory X* and *Theory Y.*[16]

According to the assumptions of **Theory X,** the average worker is lazy, dislikes work, and will try to do as little as possible. Moreover, workers have little ambition and wish to avoid responsibility. Thus, the manager's task is to counteract workers' natural tendencies to avoid work. To keep workers' performance at a high level, the manager must supervise them closely and control their behaviour by means of "the carrot and stick"—rewards and punishments.

Theory X The assumption that workers will try to do as little as possible and avoid further responsibility unless rewarded or punished for doing otherwise.

Managers who accept the assumptions of Theory X design and shape the work setting to maximize their control over workers' behaviours and minimize workers' control over the pace of work. These managers believe that workers must be made to do what is necessary for the success of the organization, and they focus on developing rules, SOPs, and a well-defined system of rewards and punishments to control behaviour. They see little point in giving workers autonomy to solve their own problems because they think that the workforce neither expects nor desires cooperation. Theory X managers see their role as to closely monitor workers to ensure that they contribute to the production process and do not threaten product quality. Henry Ford, who closely supervised and managed his workforce, fits McGregor's description of a manager who holds Theory X assumptions.

In contrast, **Theory Y** assumes that workers are not inherently lazy, do not naturally dislike work, and, if given the opportunity, will do what is good for the organization. According to Theory Y, the characteristics of the work setting determine whether workers consider work to be a source of satisfaction or punishment; and managers do not need to closely control workers' behaviour in order to make them perform at a high level, because workers will exercise self-control when they are committed to organizational goals. The implication of Theory Y, according to McGregor, is that "the limits of collaboration in the organizational setting are not limits of human nature but of management's ingenuity in discovering how to realize the potential represented by its human resources."[17] It is the manager's task to create a work setting that encourages commitment to organizational goals and provides opportunities for workers to be imaginative and to exercise initiative and self-direction.

Theory Y The assumption that workers will do what is best for an organization if given the proper work setting, opportunity, and encouragement.

When managers design the organizational setting to reflect the assumptions about attitudes and behaviour suggested by Theory Y, the characteristics of the organization are quite different from those of an organizational setting based on Theory X. Managers who believe that workers are motivated to help the organization reach its goals can decentralize authority and give more control over the job to workers, both as individuals and in groups. In this setting, individuals and groups are still accountable for their activities, but the manager's role is not to control employees but to provide support and advice, to make sure workers have the resources they need to perform their jobs, and to evaluate them on their ability to help the organization meet its goals.

These same kinds of debates are raging today as managers seek to increase both the efficiency and effectiveness of their organizations.

Part II

Planning

Managing Decision Making

LEARNING OUTCOMES

LO1	Differentiate between programmed and nonprogrammed decisions, and explain why nonprogrammed decision making is a complex, uncertain process.
LO2	Compare the assumptions that underlie the classical and administrative models of decision making.
LO3	Describe the seven steps managers should take to make sound decisions.
LO4	Explain how cognitive biases can affect decision making and lead managers to make poor decisions.
LO5	Explain the role played by ethics, corporate social responsibility, and organizational learning in helping managers improve their decisions.

OPENING CASE

Good Decision Making at PUMA

When Jochen Zeitz took over as CEO of PUMA AG at the age of 30, the company was facing major threats.[1] PUMA AG, based in the small German sneaker-producing town of Herzogenaurach,[2] had lost money for the previous eight years and PUMA North America was facing imminent bankruptcy.[3]

Facing tough decisions about how to turn around the company's fortunes, Zeitz decided that rather than trying to compete based on the performance capabilities of its athletic shoes and equipment, PUMA would focus more on style, colours, and sustainably produced lines of shoes. Essentially, Zeitz saw a potential opportunity in trying to start up a new division focused on experimental fashion and sport as lifestyle. Of course, Zeitz also made difficult decisions to respond to the threats the company was facing by, for example, dramatically reducing costs of production and taking back control over distribution of PUMA products in North America.[4] Another example is the decision to update its policies on sustainable production. In collaboration with Greenpeace, PUMA engaged in a detoxification process of all of its operations. PUMA felt that an update of its sustainability policies must be based on sound decisions and has therefore started a dialogue with industry peers, experts, and the chemical industry to investigate which substances could be phased out with existing technology and where more research was needed.[5] PUMA continues to produce high-performance athletic shoes and gear for serious sport.[6]

Nonetheless, Zeitz's bold decision to pursue the world of fashion and style was a major contributor to PUMA becoming the fourth biggest athletic apparel company worldwide. Recognizing the importance of coming up with creative designs and sustainable products, he decided to create a new division called "sport lifestyle" led by Antonio Bertone, then a 21-year-old skateboarder.[7] The division was tasked with creating experimental fashion products. Bertone partnered with German fashion designer Jil Sander to

Eric D ricochet69/Alamy Stock Photo

turn PUMA's traditional 1960s-style cleated soccer shoe into a trendy fashion sneaker using funky colours and suede. At first, this new experimental product line received a lot of skepticism from industry experts and retailers alike; it was hard to believe that a company that had excelled in high-performance sports gear could successfully switch to fashion. As Zeitz indicated, "It took a while—and from my perspective, a lot of energy—to protect this new little child [the lifestyle group] of PUMA from getting killed . . . Eventually, it became the entire company."[8]

Customers loved the more ecologically friendly, retro look and edgy colours of the new line of sneakers, which are now sold in a variety of venues ranging from Foot Locker to high-end stores like Barneys to upscale department stores. PUMA has its own showcase boutique in the meatpacking district of Manhattan, employs more than 13 000 people and distributes its products in 120 countries.[9]

In 2012, Zeitz moved on from Puma. In 2013, Bjørn Gulden (CEO) introduced PUMA's new mission statement: to be the Fastest Sports Brand in the World. The company's mission not only reflects PUMA's new brand positioning of being Forever Faster, it also serves as the guiding principle for the company, expressed through all of its actions and decisions. Their objective is to be fast in reacting to new trends, fast in bringing new innovations to the market, fast in decision making and fast in solving problems for their partners.[10]

2016 was particularly exciting because of big events, such as the Copa América, the UEFA Euro 2016, and the Olympics in Rio—all of which proved to be perfect stages to showcase PUMA as an innovative and design-driven sports brand. The company managed to better capitalize on partnerships with some of the world's best ambassadors. The World's Fastest Man, Usain Bolt; star footballer Antoine Griezmann; golf icons Rickie Fowler and Lexi Thompson, Arsenal Football Club, BVB Borussia Dortmund, the New York City Ballet, pop stars Rihanna and The Weeknd, celebrities Cara Delevingne and Kylie Jenner, and many others made a major impact in creating more brand heat and improving the sales of PUMA products.[11]

The company continues to make decisions in response to opportunities and, in the process, has expanded PUMA's range of products in far-reaching directions.[12] Clearly, the decisions managers make at PUMA are key contributors to the success of PUMA today.[13] And while much uncertainty and ambiguity surrounded these decisions at the time they were made, and they were sometimes met with skepticism, they have propelled PUMA to be a powerhouse of innovation and sustainability.[14]

After reading and understanding the concepts in this chapter, you should be able to answer the following questions:

1. What type of decision was made by Zeitz when PUMA launched into sport lifestyle fashions?
2. Identify the threats and opportunities in the industry-specific environment that impact PUMA's decision making.
3. How does PUMA foster sustainability and promote creativity and innovation? Why is this good decision making?

Overview

The opening scenario in this chapter allows us to see how decision making can have a profound influence on organizational effectiveness. The decisions that managers make at all levels in companies large and small can have a dramatic impact on their growth and prosperity and the well-being of their employees, customers, and other stakeholders. Yet such decisions can be very difficult to make because they are fraught with uncertainty.

In this chapter we examine how managers make decisions and explore how individual styles and organizational factors affect the quality of the decisions they make and thus determine organizational performance. We discuss the nature of managerial decision making and examine two models of the decision-making process that help reveal the complexities of that process. Next we outline the seven steps in the decision-making process that managers can use to make better decisions. We then explore the biases that may cause capable managers to make poor decisions. How ethics influence decision making and how managers can be socially responsible by promoting sustainability, organizational learning, and creativity are examined to help managers improve the quality of their decision making. By the end of this chapter, you will understand the crucial role that decision making plays in creating a high-performing organization.

The Nature of Managerial Decision Making

LO1 | Differentiate between programmed and nonprogrammed decisions, and explain why nonprogrammed decision making is a complex, uncertain process.

Every time a manager acts to plan, organize, direct, or control organizational activities, he or she makes a stream of decisions. In opening a new restaurant, for example, managers have to decide where to locate it, what kinds of food to provide to customers, what kinds of people to employ, and so on. Decision making is a basic part of every task a manager performs.

As we discussed in Chapter 2, one of the main tasks facing a manager is to manage the organizational environment. Forces in the external environment give rise to many opportunities and threats for managers and their organizations. In addition, inside an organization managers must address many opportunities and threats that may arise during the course of utilizing organizational resources. To deal with these opportunities and threats, managers must make decisions—that is, they must select one solution from a set of alternatives. **Decision making** is the process by which managers respond to the opportunities and threats that confront them by analyzing the options and making determinations, or *decisions,* about specific organizational goals and courses of action. Good decisions result in the selection of appropriate goals and courses of action that increase organizational performance; bad decisions result in lower performance.

decision making The process of analyzing options and making determinations about specific organizational goals and courses of action.

Decision making in response to opportunities occurs when managers search for ways to improve organizational performance to benefit customers, employees, and other stakeholder groups. In the opening case, Jochen Zeitz turned around PUMA's fortunes by the decisions he made in response to opportunities the company faced for sustainable growth. *Decision making in response to threats* occurs when events inside or outside the organization are adversely affecting organizational performance and managers are searching for ways to increase performance.[15] When Zeitz became CEO of PUMA, high production costs and an ineffective distribution system were threats that prompted Zeitz to make a number of decisions to improve the performance and viability of the company.[16] Decision making is central to being a manager, and whenever managers engage in planning, organizing, leading, and controlling—their four principal functions—they are constantly making decisions.

Managers are always searching for ways to make better decisions to improve organizational performance. At the same time, they do their best to avoid costly mistakes that will hurt organizational performance. Examples of spectacularly good decisions include Liz Claiborne's decision to focus on producing clothes for the growing number of women entering the workforce—a decision that contributed to making her company one of the largest clothing manufacturers. Also, Bill Gates's decision to buy a computer operating system for $50 000 from a small company in Seattle and sell it to IBM for the new IBM personal computer, turned Gates and Microsoft, respectively, into the richest man and richest software company in the United States. An example of a really bad decision was when Richard Branson invested $20 million designing an MP3 player called the Virgin Pulse that backfired when the product bombed against Apple's iPod and iTunes, and the investment had to be written off.[17]

Programmed and Nonprogrammed Decision Making

Regardless of the specific decision that a manager is responsible for, the decision-making process is either programmed or nonprogrammed.[18]

PROGRAMMED DECISION MAKING

Programmed decision making is a routine, virtually automatic process. Programmed decisions are decisions that have been made so many times in the past that managers have been able to develop rules or guidelines to be applied when certain situations inevitably occur. Programmed decisions are decisions where all the inputs and outcomes are known with a lot of certainty. Examples of when programmed decision making takes place, is when a school principal asks the school board to hire a new teacher whenever student enrollment increases by 40 students; when a manufacturing supervisor hires new workers whenever existing workers' overtime increases by more than 10 percent; and when an office manager orders basic office supplies, such as paper and pens, whenever the inventory of supplies on hand drops below a certain level. Furthermore, in the last example, the office manager probably orders the same amount of supplies each time. The decision-making process involved in such a routine, repetitive task is an example of programmed decision making.

> **programmed decision making** Routine, virtually automatic decision making that follows established rules or guidelines.

This decision making is called *programmed* because an office manager, for example, does not need to repeatedly make new judgments about what should be done. He or she can rely on long-established decision rules such as these:

- *Rule 1*. When the storage shelves are three-quarters empty, order more paper.
- *Rule 2*. When ordering paper, order enough to fill the shelves.

Managers can develop rules and guidelines to regulate all routine organizational activities. For example, rules can specify how a worker should perform a certain task, and rules can specify the quality standards that raw materials must meet to be acceptable. Most decision making that relates to the day-to-day running of an organization is programmed decision making. Examples include decision making about how much inventory to hold, when to pay bills, when to bill customers, and when to order materials and supplies. Programmed decision making occurs when managers have the information they need to create rules that will guide decision making. There is little ambiguity involved in assessing when the stockroom is empty or counting the number of new students in class.

NONPROGRAMMED DECISION MAKING

Suppose, however, managers are not at all certain that a course of action will lead to a desired outcome. Or, in even more ambiguous terms, suppose managers are not even clear about what they are really trying to achieve. Obviously, rules cannot be developed to predict uncertain events.

Nonprogrammed decision making occurs when there are no ready-made decision rules that managers can apply to a situation. Nonprogrammed decision making is required for these *nonroutine* decisions. Nonprogrammed decisions are made in response to unusual or novel opportunities and threats. Rules do not exist because the situation is unexpected or uncertain and managers lack the information they would need to develop rules to cover it. Sometimes managers have to make rapid decisions and don't have the time for careful consideration of the issues involved. They must rely on their *intuition* to quickly respond to a pressing concern. For example, when fire chiefs, captains, and lieutenants manage firefighters battling dangerous, out-of-control fires, they often need to rely on their expert intuition to make on-the-spot decisions that will protect the lives of the firefighters and save the lives of others, contain the fires, and preserve property—decisions made in emergency situations entailing high uncertainty, high risk, and rapidly changing conditions.[19] Other times, managers do have the time available to make reasoned judgments but there are no established rules to guide their decisions, such as when deciding whether or not to proceed with a proposed merger. Unlike the routine decision of reordering materials when supplies drop below a certain level, the decision to merge two companies is a complex and uncertain endeavour that requires research into the likely outcomes of various decision scenarios. The probable results of each decision have to be calculated to the extent possible so that all the outcomes can be determined and the best course of action or decision can be made. Other examples of nonprogrammed decision making include decisions to invest in a new kind of green technology, develop a new kind of product (as Jochen Zeitz did in the opening case), launch a new promotional campaign, enter a new market, expand internationally, or start a new business. None of these types of decisions can be programmed with certainty. Most complex business decisions—those involving a lot of variables—are not programmed (or programmable) decisions where past practice and rules can be relied upon to produce a positive outcome. Nonprogrammed decision making causes the most problems for managers and can result in effective or ineffective decision making.

nonprogrammed decision making Nonroutine decision making that occurs in response to unusual, unpredictable opportunities and threats.

 Two Models of Decision Making

LO2 | Compare the assumptions that underlie the classical and administrative models of decision making.

The *classical* and the *administrative* decision-making models reveal many of the assumptions, complexities, and pitfalls that affect decision making. These models help reveal the factors that managers and other decision makers must be aware of to improve the quality of their decision making. Keep in mind, however, that the classical and administrative models are just guides that can help managers understand the decision-making process. In real life, the process is typically not cut-and-dried, but these models can help a manager understand the decision-making process. We compare and contrast them below.

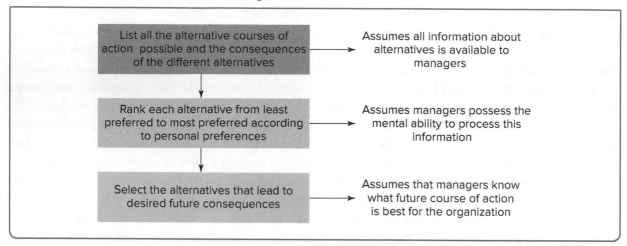

FIGURE 3.1

The Classical Model of Decision Making

The Classical Model

One of the earliest models of decision making, the **classical model** (also referred to as the *rational model*) is prescriptive, which means that it specifies how decisions *should* be made to maximize the benefit to the organization and shareholders. Managers using the rational model make a series of simplifying assumptions about the nature of the decision-making process (see Figure 3.1). The idea behind this model is that once managers recognize the need to make a decision, they should be able to make a complete list of *all* alternatives. For each alternative they should be able to list all consequences, so they can then make the best choice. In other words, the classical model assumes that managers have access to *all* the information they need to make the **optimum decision**, which is the most appropriate decision possible in light of what they believe to be the most desirable future consequences for their organization. Furthermore, the rational model assumes that managers can easily list their own preferences for each alternative and rank them from least to most preferred in order to make the optimum decision.

classical model A prescriptive approach to decision making based on the idea that the decision maker can identify and evaluate all possible alternatives and their consequences and rationally choose the most suitable course of action.

optimum decision The most appropriate decision in light of what managers believe to be the most desirable future consequences for their organization.

The Administrative Model

James March and Herbert Simon disagreed with the underlying assumptions of the classical model of decision making. In contrast, they proposed that managers in the real world do not have access to all the information they need to make a decision. Moreover, they pointed out that even if all information were readily available, many managers would lack the mental or psychological ability to absorb and evaluate it correctly. As a result, March and Simon developed the **administrative model** of decision making to explain why decision making is always an inherently uncertain and risky process—and why managers

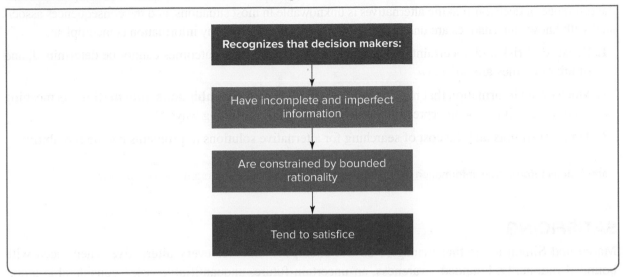

FIGURE 3.2

The Administrative Model of Decision Making

can rarely make decisions in the manner prescribed by the classical model. Simon, who trained as a political scientist, questioned the mainstream economists' view of the economic manager as "a lightning-quick calculator of costs and benefits."[20] Instead, he argued that the manager has to deal with limitations and constraints while making a decision. The administrative model is based on three important concepts: *bounded rationality, incomplete information,* and *satisficing.* See Figure 3.2.

administrative model An approach to decision making that explains why decision making is an inherently uncertain and risky process and why managers usually make satisfactory rather than optimum decisions.

THE NATURE OF RATIONALITY

March and Simon pointed out that human decision-making capabilities are bounded by people's cognitive limitations that constrain their ability to interpret, process, and act on information.[21] When *The Globe and Mail* rejected an offer to partner with Monster.com, they were unaware of the threat of online job advertising. They suffered from **bounded awareness**—the tendency for people to overlook important information that bears on the decision-making process. Our ability to rationally and objectively apply our ethics, demonstrate concern for others rather than ourselves, and plan for the future instead of living for today are all constrained by our inability to interpret, process, and act on information when making decisions. March and Simon argued that the limitations of human intelligence constrain the ability of decision makers to determine the optimum decision; they coined the term **bounded rationality** to describe the situation in which the number of alternatives a manager must identify is so great and the amount of information so vast that it is difficult for the manager to even come close to evaluating it all before making a decision.[22]

bounded awareness The tendency for people to overlook important information that bears on the decision-making process.
bounded rationality Cognitive limitations that constrain one's ability to interpret, process, and act on information.

INCOMPLETE INFORMATION

Even if managers did have an unlimited ability to evaluate information, they still would not be able to arrive at the optimum decision because they would have incomplete information. Information is incomplete because the full range of decision-making alternatives is unknowable in most situations, and the consequences associated with known alternatives are uncertain.[23] There are three reasons why information is incomplete:

1. Because of risk and uncertainty, the probabilities of alternative outcomes cannot be determined, and future outcomes are *unknown*.

2. Much of the information that managers have at their disposal is **ambiguous information**; its meaning is not clear—it can be interpreted in multiple and often conflicting ways.[24]

3. Time constraints and the cost of searching for alternative solutions to problems can be prohibitive.

> **ambiguous information** Information that can be interpreted in multiple and often conflicting ways.

SATISFICING

March and Simon argue that managers do not attempt to discover every alternative when faced with bounded rationality, bounded awareness, an uncertain future, unquantifiable risks, considerable ambiguity, time constraints, and high information costs. Rather, they use a strategy known as **satisficing**, exploring a limited sample of possible alternatives.[25] Consider the situation confronting a purchasing manager at Ford Canada who has one month to choose a supplier (out of thousands) for a small engine part. Given the time available, the purchasing manager cannot contact all potential suppliers and ask each for its terms of trade (price, delivery schedules, and so on). Moreover, even if the time were available, the costs of obtaining the information, including the manager's own time, would be prohibitive. When managers satisfice, they search for and choose acceptable, or satisfactory, ways to respond to problems and opportunities, rather than trying to make the best decision.[26] For instance, the purchasing manager for Ford Canada would likely engage in a limited search to identify suppliers. This might involve asking a limited number of suppliers for their terms, trusting that they are representative of suppliers in general, and making a choice from that set. Although this course of action is reasonable from the point of view of the purchasing manager, it may mean that a potentially superior supplier is overlooked.

> **satisficing** Searching for and choosing acceptable, or satisfactory, ways to respond to problems and opportunities, rather than trying to make the best decision.

> Simon questioned the mainstream economists' view of the economic manager as a "lightning-quick calculator of costs and benefits."

March and Simon pointed out that managerial decision making often is more art than science. In the real world, managers must rely on their intuition and judgment to make what seems to them to be the best decision in the face of uncertainty and ambiguity.[27] **Intuition** is a person's ability to make sound decisions based on past experience and immediate feelings about the information at hand. **Judgment** is a person's ability to develop a sound opinion because of the way he or she evaluates the importance of the information available in a particular context. Managerial decision making is often fast-paced, as managers use their experience and judgment to make crucial decisions under conditions of incomplete information. Although there is nothing wrong with this approach, decision makers should be aware that human judgment is often flawed. As a result, even the best managers sometimes end up making very poor decisions.[28] Cognitive biases that lead to poor decision outcomes are discussed a little later in this chapter.

The administrative model of decision making helps managers understand and be aware of their limitations when it comes to making decisions. Even with the best intentions, optimal decision making is difficult. One technique in helping managers make optimal decisions is to follow a sequence of steps that breaks down the process. We now turn our attention to the steps in the decision-making process.

Calculating risk is a serious challenge for managers.
Image Source/Alamy

intuition Ability to make sound decisions based on past experience and immediate feelings about the information at hand.

judgment Ability to develop a sound opinion based on one's evaluation of the importance of the information at hand.

Steps in the Decision-Making Process

LO3 | Describe the seven steps managers should take to make sound decisions.

The conditions for making an optimum decision rarely exist. To help managers make the best decision possible, researchers have developed a step-by-step model of the decision-making process and the issues and problems that they may confront at each step. There are seven steps that managers should consciously follow to make a good decision (see Figure 3.3).[29] We introduce this model by examining a case where a manager at a small magazine publishing company had to make a nonprogrammed decision.

Step 1: Recognize the Need for a Decision

The first step in the decision-making process is to recognize the need for a decision. Managers face decisions that arise both internally and as a consequence of changes in the external environment.[30] An organization possesses a set of skills, competencies, and resources in its employees and in departments such as marketing, manufacturing, and research and development. Managers who actively pursue opportunities to use these competencies create the need to make decisions. Recognizing the need to make a decision is an important part of the process that generally involves two steps:

1. Stating the problem, and
2. Formulating the decision question.

FIGURE 3.3

Steps in the Decision-Making Process

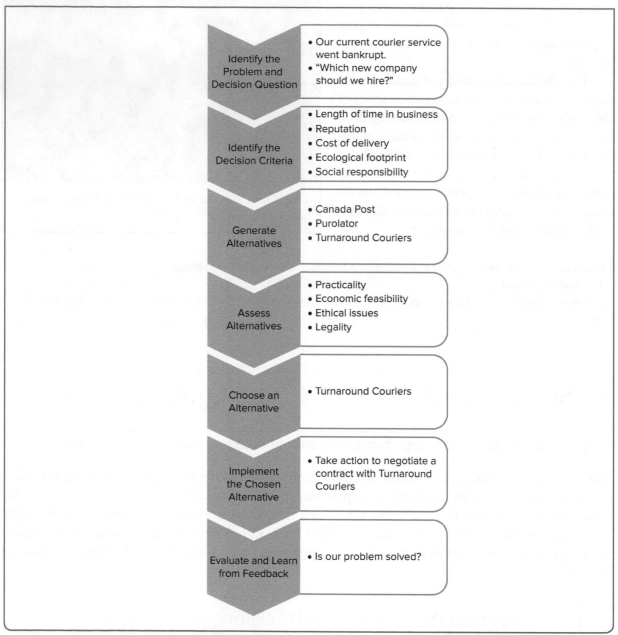

The identification of the problem involves analyzing the current state of affairs and what the future state of affairs should be. It does not suggest a solution. Managers thus can be proactive or reactive in recognizing the need to make a decision, but the important issue is that they must recognize this need and respond in a timely and appropriate way.[31]

Once a decision maker recognizes the need to make a decision, he or she will need to diagnose the issue or problem in order to determine all the factors underlying the problem. In our scenario, the local courier service that was used by the firm folded. This presents a problem for the management. See Figure 3.4.

FIGURE 3.4

Tools to Help Assess the Accuracy of the Problem Statement and Decision Question

- Make sure the current state of the situation is stated clearly and that it does not reflect the symptom of the problem.

- At this point, you are not asking why there is a problem on which a decision has to be made. But you should be asking: Who does the problem affect? What does the problem affect? When does the problem take effect? And how and where is it a problem?

- Ask yourself what the desired future state would look like. What is the goal of the project? Where do you want to be?

- Make sure you focus on only one problem.

- Make sure the problem statement does not suggest a solution or assign any blame.

- The decision question follows from the combined statement of the current situation and the desired future state, or problem statement.

- The decision question avoids asking "Why" but can be formulated as a "What" or "How" question.

In our example, the current situation for our publishing company is that it is without the means to distribute its product around the city because the company it hired to do so went bankrupt. The desired situation is to have a contract with a courier service to distribute their magazines within the city limits. The decision question is, Which company should be hired for the job?

Step 2: Identify Decision Criteria

Having recognized the need to make a decision, managers must consider what variables are important to the decision before they can generate a set of feasible alternative courses of action to take in response to the opportunity or threat. One reason for bad decisions is that managers often fail to specify the criteria that are important in reaching a decision.[32] In our scenario, the manager certainly does not want to run the risk of contracting a company that is on the verge of bankruptcy. To minimize the risk of having the new company go bankrupt, an important variable to the decision is the length of time the company has been in business and their reputation for providing good service. The cost of providing the courier services is also important as is the means by which the transportation is achieved. It is important to the publisher that the ecological footprint of the transportation be minimized. Because the publisher is pro-social, it also wants to ensure that the company pays fair wages to its employees.

Step 3: Generate Alternatives

The failure to properly generate and consider different alternatives is one reason why managers sometimes make bad decisions.[33] In our case, the manager does some research and finds two large companies that operate in the city, Purolator and Canada Post, along with a small local company called Turnaround Couriers, for a total of three alternatives to consider.

Step 4: Assess Alternatives

Once managers have listed a set of alternatives, they must evaluate the advantages and disadvantages of each one, according to the decision criteria developed in Step 2.[34] Moreover, the relative importance assigned to the criteria is something that must be clearly thought through. Not all the criteria will have equal bearing on the decision. The criteria have to be prioritized and assigned relative values; high values are assigned to the most important criteria. In general, successful managers should consider four categories of criteria to evaluate the pros and cons of each alternative (see Figure 3.5).

1. *Practicality Issues.* Managers must decide whether they have the capabilities and resources to implement the alternative, and they must be sure that the alternative will not threaten the ability to reach other organizational goals. At first glance an alternative might seem to be economically superior to other alternatives, but if managers realize that it is likely to threaten other important projects, they might decide that it is not practical after all.

2. *Economic Feasibility Issues.* Managers must decide whether the alternatives make sense economically and fit the organization's performance goals. Typically, managers perform a cost–benefit analysis of the various alternatives to determine which one is likely to have the best financial payoff.

3. *Ethical Issues.* Managers must ensure that a possible course of action is ethical and that it will not unnecessarily harm any stakeholder group. Many of the decisions that managers make may help some organizational stakeholders and harm others.

4. *Legal Issues.* Managers must ensure that a possible course of action is legal and will not violate any domestic and international laws or government regulations.

Very often, a manager must consider these four criteria simultaneously. In our example, the manager categorized the requirements into the categories of criteria and assigned each category a relative weight. The most important criteria in deciding which company to hire were difficult to decide. The manager gave practical concerns a weight of 35 percent, economic feasibility concerns a value of 50 percent, 10 percent to ethical concerns, and 5 percent to legal aspects. See Figure 3.6.

Next, the manager began to research how the alternatives measured up to the criteria in order to arrive at a score out of 10 points. A score of 1 is unfavourable and a score of 10 is most favourable. They

---

FIGURE 3.5

Categories of Criteria for Evaluating Alternatives

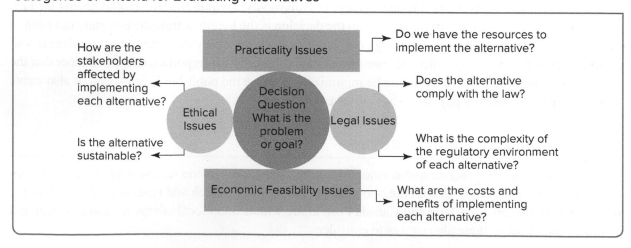

FIGURE 3.6

Weighted Decision Criteria

Criteria	Weight
Practicality Issues	**35%**
Time to deliver	20%
Capacity of each delivery	10%
Service record	5%
Economic Feasibility	**50%**
Cost per delivery	50%
Ethical Issues	**10%**
Greenhouse gas emissions	5%
Fair wages paid	5%
Legal Criteria	**5%**
Lawsuits pending	1%
Company reputation	2%
Length of time in business	2%
Total	**100%**

checked with the Chamber of Commerce to see if the companies had any serious customer complaints. They looked at their Web sites to determine human resource policies. One thing that became clear was that the local company used bicycles instead of trucks as its mode of transportation, and hired couriers who faced barriers to mainstream employment, making it more favourable under the ethical category. But using bicycles instead of trucks meant that the number of magazines that could be delivered in each trip—the capacity of each delivery—was lower than that of the two large companies, increasing the costs to the publisher. Each criterion is researched and assessed. The analysis is displayed in a decision preference matrix (see Figure 3.7).

Step 5: Choose an Alternative

Once the set of alternative solutions has been carefully evaluated, the next task is to rank the various alternatives. When ranking alternatives, managers must be sure that all of the available information is brought to bear on the problem or issue at hand. Identifying all relevant information for a decision does not mean that the manager has complete information. In most instances, information is incomplete. Our manager uses a matrix to determine the highest ranking alternative, and the best choice according to the criteria is Turnaround Couriers (Figure 3.7).

FIGURE 3.7

Decision Preference Matrix

Weighted Criteria	Canada Post Score (1–10)	Weighted Score	Purolator Score (1–10)	Weighted Score	Turnaround Couriers Score (1–10)	Weighted Score
Practicality Issues—35%						
Time to deliver 20%	1	20	1	20	10	200
Capacity of each delivery 10%	10	100	10	100	5	50
Service record 5%	5	25	5	25	5	25
Economic Feasibility—50%						
Cost per delivery 50%	10	500	10	500	8	400
Ethical Issues 10%						
Greenhouse gas emissions 5%	1	5	1	5	10	50
Fair wages paid 5%	10	50	10	50	10	50
Legal Criteria—5%						
Lawsuits pending 1%	5	5	5	5	10	10
Company reputation 2%	8	16	8	16	8	16
Length of time in business 2%	10	20	10	20	5	10
Total 100%		746		746		811

Step 6: Implement the Chosen Alternative

Once a decision has been made and an alternative has been selected, it must be acted upon, and many subsequent and related decisions must be made. As we saw in the opening case with PUMA's launch of sport lifestyle apparel, thousands of subsequent decisions may be necessary for implementation. For PUMA, these decisions involved recruiting designers, obtaining ethically sourced materials, finding high-quality manufacturers, and signing contracts with retail stores to sell the new line. In our magazine publishing company example, the manager would now negotiate a contract with Turnaound Couriers to deliver its magazines.

Managers make good decisions when they further the direction of their organization's mission and goals.
DNY59/Getty Images

Step 7: Evaluate and Learn from Feedback

The final step in the decision-making process is learning from feedback. Managers who do not evaluate the results of their decisions do not learn from experience; instead they stagnate and are likely to make the same mistakes again and again.[35] To avoid this problem, managers must establish a formal procedure for learning from the results of past decisions. The procedure should include these steps:

1. Compare what actually happened to what was expected to happen as a result of the decision.

2. Explore why any expectations for the decision were not met.

3. Develop guidelines that will help in future decision making.

TIPS FOR MANAGERS

Managing the Decision-Making Process

1. When identifying the need to make a decision, avoid assigning blame to any individual or group.

2. Making decisions often means making changes in the organization's strategy, structure, and culture, which creates uncertainty and even anxiety. To reduce anxiety and foster an inclusive culture, involve as many stakeholders in the decision-making process as possible.

3. Give employees and other stakeholders reassurances and confirm their emotional concerns, rather than giving rational explanations, when faced with decisions that create disruptive change.

4. Treat successes and failures as stepping stones in your decision-making practice.

Individuals who always strive to learn from past mistakes and successes are likely to continuously improve their decision making. A significant amount of learning can take place when the outcomes of decisions are evaluated, and this assessment can produce enormous benefits. Did the decision meet the needs of the company and solve the problem? If the problem still exists, the manager may need to go back to the original definition of the problem. Another issue may be failure to execute the decision properly. Or perhaps there was insufficient analysis of the alternatives. Some of the worst managerial decisions can be traced to poor assessment of the alternatives—such as the decision to launch the *Challenger* space shuttle, which ended up killing seven crew members when it crashed. In that case, the desire of NASA and Morton Thiokol managers to demonstrate to the public the success of the U.S. space program in order to ensure future funding (*economic feasibility*) conflicted with the need to ensure the safety of the astronauts (*ethicalness*). Managers deemed the economic criterion more important and decided to launch the space shuttle even though there were unanswered questions about safety. Tragically, some of the same decision-making problems that resulted in the *Challenger* disaster led to the demise of the *Columbia* space shuttle 17 years later, killing all seven astronauts on board.[36] In both the *Challenger* and the *Columbia* tragedies, safety questions were raised before the shuttles were launched; safety concerns took second place to budgets, economic feasibility, and schedules; top decision makers seemed to ignore or downplay the inputs of those with relevant technical expertise; and speaking up was discouraged.[37] Rather than making safety a top priority, decision makers seemed overly concerned with keeping on schedule and within budget.[38] Perhaps the most serious issue is the often-documented tendency of managers to ignore critical information even when it is available. We discuss this tendency in detail below when we examine the operation of cognitive biases in decision making.

Biases in Decision Making

LO4	Explain how cognitive biases can affect decision making and lead managers to make poor decisions.

In the 1970s, two psychologists, Daniel Kahneman and Amos Tversky, suggested that because all decision makers are subject to bounded rationality they tend to use **heuristics,** which are rules of thumb that simplify the process of making decisions.[39] Kahneman and Tversky argued that rules of thumb are often useful because they help decision makers make sense of complex, uncertain, and ambiguous information. Sometimes, however, the use of heuristics can lead to distortions in the way decision makers process information about alternatives and make decisions. **Systematic errors** are errors that people make over and over again and that result in poor decision making.[40] There are many cognitive biases that distort decision making; some common ones are outlined in Figure 3.8.

heuristics Rules of thumb that simplify decision making.

systematic errors Errors that people make over and over again and that result in poor decision making.

When managers work as a *team* to make decisions and solve problems, their choices of alternatives are less likely to fall victim to the biases and errors discussed previously. They are able to draw on the combined skills, competencies, and accumulated knowledge of group members and thereby improve their ability to generate feasible alternatives and make good decisions. Group decision making also allows managers to process more information and to correct one another's errors. And in the implementation phase, all managers affected by the decisions agree to cooperate. When

FIGURE 3.8

Examples of Cognitive Bias and Errors in Decision Making

Bias	Description	Example
Escalating Commitment	The tendency to increase the investment of time and money in a course of action and ignore evidence that it is illegal, unethical, uneconomical, or impractical.	A Stanford University study on the decisions made by financial analysts found that in cases where company earnings forecasts were proving to be wrong, the analysts were reluctant to adjust their estimates to reflect new data. "The more their forecast differed from consensus, the more stubborn they became and the more they escalated their commitment to their erroneous forecast."*
Recency Effect	The error of considering the most recent data to have the most relevance to a problem. This shows the importance of managers to collect long-term data to determine trends, rather than relying on short-term ups and downs that may distort the overall trend.	A sales manager makes a decision to pull a product line off the shelf because of poor sales in the last month. The longer-term data show that the downturn in sales of this product is cyclical.

Continued

Bias	Description	Example
Representativeness Bias	Many decision makers inappropriately generalize from a small sample or even from a single vivid case or episode.	Walmart managers assumed that the model that worked so well in the United States would work in every country. They were wrong. The efficient layout of stores, while suitable for the individualistic culture of the United States, proved to discourage shoppers in Asia, who consider shopping a more social event. This led to Walmart having to rethink its decisions when expanding internationally.
Clustering Illusion	The tendency to see patterns in data where none exist.	A regional manager makes a decision to increase production based on random data that are interpreted to show a pattern of increased sales.
Prior Hypothesis Bias	Decision makers who have strong prior beliefs about the relationship between two variables tend to make decisions based on those beliefs *even when presented with evidence that their beliefs are wrong.*	Sony Corp. associated product innovation with providing lifelong employment. The belief is that stable teams have the opportunity to develop state-of-the-art technology. Sticking with that hypothesis caused Sony to be overtaken by Apple and others who developed innovative new technologies like digital LCD screens and flash memory that made Sony's technologies obsolete. Faced with the crisis of falling profits, Sony only recently changed its lifelong employment strategy to reduce its bureaucracy and cut costs by downsizing.
Confirmation Bias	The tendency to seek information that will prove rather than disprove our ideas. Information that may challenge or completely invalidate our view is overlooked in favour of information that supports our point of view.	A shift manager in a call centre comes out of a performance review with a positive impression even though the manager received feedback that showed low productivity levels and room for improvement in several categories.
Fundamental Attribution Error	The tendency to mistake personality traits or internal factors as the cause of some outcome instead of correctly perceiving the external or situational factors as the cause.	A sales manager views the poor performance of his or her sales agents as resulting from their laziness rather than from the innovative product line of a competitor.
Illusion of Control and Overconfidence Bias	The tendency of decision makers to overestimate their ability to control activities and events.	Richard Branson launched the Virgin Pulse MP3 player to compete with Apple's iPod against the advice of his management team, who argued that very high numbers would have to be sold to make the $20 million investment work. After it bombed, Branson said, "Ignoring my managers' advice and losing millions trying to take down the iPod reminded me: the CEO is not always right."***

*"Really Bad Advice," *Maclean's,* September 19, 2011, p. 43.
***"What Steve Jobs Taught Me by Kicking My Butt," *Canadian Business,* October 10, 2011, p. 17.

a group of managers makes a decision (as opposed to one top manager making a decision and imposing it on subordinate managers), the probability that the decision will be implemented successfully increases. Group decision making techniques are discussed in Chapter 10, Managing Teams.

Individual managers as well as whole companies often have difficulty identifying their own biases and assumptions and seeking help from networks outside of their firms, such as from consulting and marketing firms, to help them uncover their biases.[41] More and more, openness and transparency in revealing and sharing decision-making challenges are becoming popular among progressive companies. For example, PUMA is engaging in frank and candid discussions of its sourcing decisions with its stakeholders and networks in an effort to examine the cri-

Virgin CEO Richard Branson has made both good decisions and poor decisions. Storms Media Group/ Alamy Stock Photo

teria it uses to assess and evaluate the ethicality of alternative courses of action and whether any cognitive biases and heuristics were used to arrive at the chosen options.

Often managers fail to allocate enough time, let alone other resources, to the decision-making process. The development of time-management skills is essential. Experts suggest it can be helpful to managers to recall two recent decisions, one that turned out well and one that turned out poorly, and analyze the decision process, including considering how much time was spent on each of the steps in the decision-making process to determine if it was sufficient.[42] Managers should be sure that enough uninterrupted time is devoted to important activities in the decision-making process, no matter what personal decision-making style prevails.

Decision-Making Styles

Every manager has their own style of making decisions. You may recall working for a manager who was very decisive and would rarely consult with his or her team. Or, on the opposite end of the spectrum, you might have worked for a manager who would go to great lengths to make sure everyone was on board with major decisions that affected them and their jobs. Decision-making styles vary in terms of a person's *way of thinking* and on their *tolerance for ambiguity*. In terms of ways of thinking, managers may act logically and rationally or they might trust their intuition and gut feelings. This dimension reflects the way the manager processes information before making a decision. Some managers require highly structured information that is clear and ordered, while others can tolerate multiple points of view that may conflict with one another, leading to uncertainty and ambiguity. Four decision-making styles result from the degree to which the manager processes information rationally or intuitively and the degree of tolerance for ambiguity and complexity; see Figure 3.9.

Managers with the *directive style* are rational in their way of thinking and have a low tolerance for ambiguity. Often, they make quick decisions based on little information and assessment of alternatives. Directive-style decision makers think in the short term and are effective at handling unexpected crises.

FIGURE 3.9

Decision-Making Styles

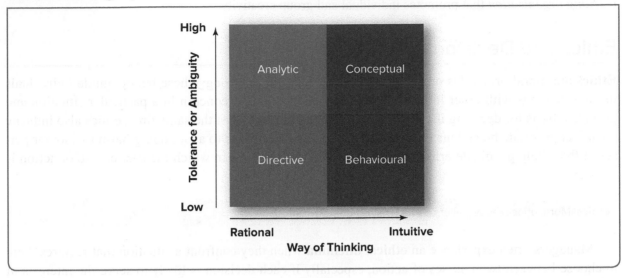

Managers with an *analytic style* are also rational in the way they process information but can handle a greater degree of ambiguity and uncertainty. They tend to consider more alternatives than directive-style decision makers and are good at solving complex problems.

Managers who use a high degree of intuition when making decisions and have a high degree of tolerance for ambiguity are *conceptual* decision makers. They tend to be flexible, adaptive, and give thoughtful consideration and judgment to their decision making over short-term "fix-it" solutions.

Managers who use a high degree of intuition and have a low tolerance for ambiguity have a *behavioural* decision-making style. They tend to be consultative and consensus seeking, ensuring that the people around them feel included and valued.

Most managers have a distinct decision-making style, but some are able to combine styles depending on the situation and context. Despite different personal decision-making styles, managers must be aware of cognitive bias and make the effort needed to make ethical and socially responsible decisions which will lead their organizations to perform at high levels of success.

Ethics, Social Responsibility, and Decision Making

LO5 | Explain the role played by ethics, corporate social responsibility, and organizational learning in helping managers improve their decisions.

No matter which style governs one's decision making, all managers should strive to make good decisions. How can managers avoid the negative effects of cognitive biases and improve their decision-making and problem-solving abilities? They must understand what it means to *behave ethically* and in a *socially responsible* way toward the individuals and groups in their organizational environment. Moreover, they must uncover their biases and use their time wisely, but the quality of decision making ultimately depends on innovative responses to opportunities and threats in the environment. Managers can increase their ability to make good nonprogrammed decisions by adopting a *sustainability strategy* and becoming a *learning organization* that promotes individual and group creativity.

Ethics and Decision Making

Ethics are moral principles or beliefs about what is right or wrong. These beliefs guide individuals in their dealings with other individuals and groups who have a concern in a particular situation and provide a basis for deciding if a behaviour is right and proper.[43] At the same time, ethics also indicate what inappropriate behaviour is and how a person should behave to avoid doing harm to another person. Ethics help people determine moral responses to situations in which the best course of action is unclear.

> **ethics** Moral principles or beliefs about what is right or wrong.

Managers often experience an **ethical dilemma** when they confront a situation that requires them to choose between two courses of action, especially if each decision is likely to serve the interests of one particular stakeholder group to the detriment of another or one's self-interest.[44] People often know they are confronting an ethical dilemma when their moral scruples come into play and cause them to hesitate, debate, and reflect upon the "rightness" or "goodness" of a course of action. *Moral scruples* are thoughts and feelings that tell a person what is right or wrong; they are a part of a person's ethics. The essential problem in dealing with ethical issues, and thus solving moral dilemmas, is that there are no absolute or indisputable set of rules or principles that can be developed to decide if an action is ethical or unethical. Put simply, different people or groups may dispute which actions are ethical or unethical depending on their own personal self-interest and specific attitudes, beliefs, and values. Sometimes, making a decision is easy because some obvious standard, value, or norm of behaviour applies. In other cases, managers have trouble deciding what to do. How, therefore, are we, and companies and their managers and employees, to decide what is ethical and so act appropriately toward other people and groups?

> **ethical dilemma** The quandary people find themselves in when they have to decide if they should act in a way that might help another person or group even though doing so might go against their own self-interest.

Making Ethical Decisions

The first answer to this question is that society as a whole, using the political and legal process, can lobby for and pass laws that specify what people can and cannot do. Many different kinds of laws exist to govern business—for example, laws against fraud and deception and laws governing how companies can treat their employees and customers. Laws also specify what sanctions or punishments will follow if those laws are broken. Different groups in society lobby for which laws should be passed based on their own personal interests and beliefs with regard to what is right or wrong. The group that can summon the most support is able to pass the laws that most closely align with its interests and beliefs. Once a law is passed, a decision about what the appropriate behaviour is with regard to a person or situation is taken from the personally determined ethical realm to the societally determined legal realm. If you do not conform to the law you can be prosecuted, and if you are found guilty of breaking the law you can be punished. You have little say in the matter; your fate is in the hands of the court and its lawyers.

In studying the relationship between ethics and law, it is important to understand that *neither laws nor ethics are fixed principles,* cast in stone, which do not change over time. Ethical beliefs alter and change as time passes, and as they do so, laws change to reflect the changing ethical beliefs of a society. For example, it was seen as ethical, and it was legal, to acquire and possess slaves in ancient Rome and Greece and in the United States until the late 19th century. Ethical views regarding whether slavery was morally right or appropriate changed, however. Slavery was made illegal in the United States when those

Making ethical decisions means deciding what the right thing to do is, regardless of its legality.
Iqoncept | Dreamstime.com

in power decided that slavery degraded the very meaning of being human. In denying freedom to others, we risk losing it ourselves, just as stealing from others opens the door for them to steal from us in return.

There are many types of behaviour—such as murder, theft, slavery, rape, and driving while intoxicated—that most, if not all, people currently believe are unacceptable and unethical and should therefore be illegal. There are also, however, many other kinds of actions and behaviours whose ethical nature is open to dispute. Some people might believe that a particular behaviour—for example, smoking tobacco or gambling—is unethical and so should be made illegal. Others might argue that it is up to the individual or a group to decide if such behaviours are ethical or not and thus whether a particular behaviour should remain legal.

As ethical beliefs change over time, some people may begin to question whether existing laws that make specific behaviours illegal are still appropriate today. They might argue that although a specific behaviour is deemed illegal, this does not make it unethical and thus the law should be changed. In Canada, possession of marijuana (cannabis) was criminalized in 1923. To justify this law, it is commonly argued that smoking marijuana leads people to try more dangerous drugs. Once the habit of taking drugs has been acquired, people can get hooked on them. More powerful drugs, such as heroin, are fearfully addictive, and most people cannot stop using them without help from others. Thus, the argument is that the use of marijuana, because it might lead to further harm, is an unethical practice. However, worldwide research has documented that the criminalization of marijuana has failed to solve the problem for which it was ostensibly created.

Moreover, it has been documented that the use of marijuana has many medical benefits for people with certain illnesses. For example, for cancer sufferers who are undergoing chemotherapy and for those with AIDS who are on potent medications, marijuana offers relief from many of the treatments' side effects, such as nausea and lack of appetite. Medical marijuana is available in Canada with a doctor's prescription and licensed producers approved by Health Canada are actively providing medical marijuana to patients. An estimated 500 000 Canadians use marijuana for medical purposes,[45] and the federal government made it legal for recreational use in 2018 after a widespread popular movement. The provincial governments now regulate how cannabis is sold. Most are controlling how recreational marijuana is sold by establishing government-operated monopolies to regulate and tax the product. Now that it is legal for adults to consume, an ethical debate about whether private sector entrepreneurs should be allowed to produce and sell cannabis products is ensuing. Governments want to treat its sale as a regulated, controlled substance, while entrepreneurs think it should be left to the competitive market.

The important point to note is that while ethical beliefs lead to the development of laws and regulations to prevent certain behaviours or encourage others, laws themselves can and do change or even disappear as ethical beliefs change. In Britain in 1830, there were over 350 different crimes for which a person could be executed, including sheep stealing. Today there are none; capital punishment and the death penalty are no longer legal in Britain. Thus, both ethical and legal rules are relative: No absolute or unvarying standards exist to determine how we should behave, and people are caught up in moral dilemmas all the time. Because of this we have to make ethical choices.

Ethical choices or decisions are important for an organization to survive and prosper. Organizations must effectively satisfy the often competing needs of their *stakeholders.*[46] Shareholders want dividends, managers and employees want salaries and stable employment, and customers want high-quality products at reasonable prices. If stakeholders do not receive these benefits, they may withdraw their support for the organization: shareholders will sell their stock, managers and workers will seek jobs in other organizations, and customers will take their business elsewhere. Since stakeholders can directly benefit or be harmed by its actions, the ethics of a company and its managers are important to them.

Codes of Ethics

Codes of ethics are formal standards and rules, based on beliefs about right or wrong, that managers can use to make appropriate decisions in the best interests of their stakeholders.[47] Ethical standards embody views about abstractions such as justice, freedom, equity, and equality. An organization's code of ethics derives from three main sources in the organizational environment: (1) *societal ethics,* governing how everyone deals with each other on issues such as fairness, justice, poverty, and the rights of the individual; (2) *professional ethics,* governing how members of the profession make decisions when the way they should behave is not clear-cut; and (3) the *individual ethics,* or personal standards for interacting with others, of the organization's top managers (see Figure 3.10).

> **codes of ethics** Formal standards and rules, based on beliefs about right or wrong, that managers can use to make appropriate decisions in the best interests of their stakeholders.

Societal Ethics

Societal ethics are standards that govern how members of a society deal with each other in matters involving issues such as fairness, justice, poverty, and the rights of the individual. Societal ethics emanate from a society's laws, customs, and practices, and from the unwritten attitudes, values, and norms that influence how people interact with each other. People in a particular country may automatically behave ethically because they have internalized values and norms that specify how they should behave in certain situations. Not all values and norms are internalized, however. The typical ways of doing business in a society and laws governing the use of bribery and corruption are the result of decisions made and enforced by people with the power to determine what is appropriate.

> **societal ethics** Standards that govern how members of a society deal with each other on issues such as fairness, justice, poverty, and the rights of the individual.

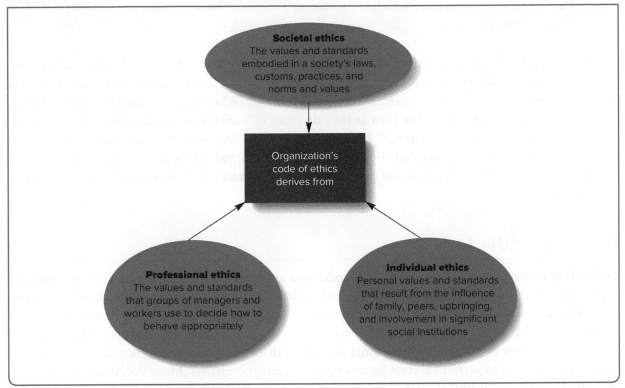

FIGURE 3.10

Sources of an Organization's Code of Ethics

Societal ethics vary among societies. For example, ethical standards accepted in Canada are not accepted in all other countries. In many economically poor countries, bribery is standard practice to get things done, such as getting a telephone installed or a contract awarded. In Canada and many other Western countries, bribery is considered unethical and often illegal.

Societal ethics control self-interested behaviour by individuals and organizations—behaviour threatening to society's collective interests. Laws spelling out what is good or appropriate business practice provide benefits to everybody. Free and fair competition among organizations is possible only when laws and rules level the playing field and define what behaviour is acceptable or unacceptable in certain situations. For example, it is ethical for a manager to compete with managers in other companies by producing a higher-quality or lower-priced product, but it is not ethical (or legal) to do so by spreading false claims about competitors' products, bribing stores to exclude competitors' products, or blowing up competitors' factories.

Professional Ethics

Professional ethics are standards that govern how members of a profession, managers or workers, make decisions when the way in which they should behave is not clear-cut.[48] Medical ethics govern the way doctors and nurses are to treat patients. Doctors are expected to perform only necessary medical procedures and to act in the patient's interest and not in their own. The ethics of scientific research require scientists to conduct their experiments and present their findings in ways that ensure the validity of their conclusions. Like society at large, most professional groups can impose punishments for violations of ethical standards. Doctors and lawyers can be prevented from practising their professions if they disregard professional ethics and put their own interests first.

> **professional ethics** Standards that govern how members of a profession make decisions when the way they should behave is not clear-cut.

Within an organization, professional rules and norms often govern how employees, such as lawyers, researchers, and accountants, make decisions and act in certain situations, and these rules and norms may become part of the organization's code of ethics. When they do, workers internalize the rules and norms of their profession (just as they do those of society) and often follow them automatically when deciding how to behave.[49] Because most people follow established rules of behaviour, people often take ethics for granted. However, when professional ethics are violated, such as when scientists fabricate data to disguise the harmful effects of products, ethical issues rise to the forefront of public attention.

Individual Ethics

Individual ethics are personal values and attitudes that govern how individuals interact with other people.[50] Sources of individual ethics include the influence of one's family, peers, and upbringing in general, and an individual's personality and experience. The experiences gained over a lifetime—through membership in significant social institutions, such as schools and religions, for example—also contribute to the development of the personal standards and values that a person applies to decide what is right or wrong and whether to perform certain actions or make certain decisions. Many decisions or behaviours that one person finds unethical, such as using animals for cosmetics testing, may be acceptable to another person because of differences in their personalities, values, and attitudes.

> **individual ethics** Personal standards that govern how individuals interact with other people.

Managers can emphasize the importance of ethical behaviour and social responsibility by ensuring that ethical values and norms are a central component of organizational culture. An organization's code of ethics guides decision making when ethical questions arise, but managers can go one step further by ensuring that important ethical values and norms are key features of an organization's culture. For example, PUMA's Code of Ethics, first introduced in 2005, prescribes the organization's commitment to ethical and responsible individual and corporate behaviour. All its employees, affiliated brands, and business partners are required to comply with its Code of Ethics. Ethical values and norms that are part of an organization's culture help organizational members resist self-interested action and recognize that they are part of something bigger than themselves.[51]

The role of managers in developing ethical values and standards in other employees is very important. Employees naturally look to those in authority to provide leadership, and managers become ethical role models whose behaviour is scrutinized by their subordinates. If top managers are not ethical, their subordinates are not likely to behave in an ethical manner. Employees may think that if it's all right for a top manager to engage in dubious behaviour, it's all right for them, too. Increasingly, organizations are creating the role of ethics officer, or **ethics ombudsperson,** to monitor their ethical practices and procedures. The ethics ombudsperson is responsible for communicating ethical standards to all employees, for designing systems to monitor employees' conformity to those standards, and for teaching managers and nonmanagerial employees at all levels of the organization how to respond appropriately to ethical dilemmas.[52] Because the ethics ombudsperson has organization-wide authority, organizational members in any department can communicate instances of unethical behaviour by their managers or co-workers without fear of retribution. This arrangement makes it easier for everyone to behave ethically. In addition, the ethics ombudsperson can provide guidance when organizational members are uncertain about whether an action is ethical. Some organizations have an organization-wide ethics committee to provide guidance on ethical issues and help write and update the company code of ethics.

ethics ombudsperson An ethics officer who monitors an organization's practices and procedures to ensure that they are ethical.

Ethical control systems such as codes of ethics and regular training programs help employees and managers learn an organization's values. However, only a third of Canadian businesses provide managers with such training, and generally less than one hour per year is devoted to it.[53] Moreover, strong codes of ethics and good governance practices still do not guarantee ethical behaviour. Enron and Arthur Andersen, the accounting company that certified and audited Enron's fraudulent accounts, both had codes of ethics. Even companies that are recognized and rewarded for good governance can be ethically deceptive, as is illustrated by the case of Satyam, the global software company that provided official IT services for the FIFA World Cup in 2014, when it was the subject of the largest scandal in the global economy since Enron's bankruptcy in 2001.[54] A few months after being awarded the prestigious Golden Peacock Award for Corporate Governance, Ramalinga Raju, the founder and chairman of Satyam, in a statement sent to the stock exchange, admitted to "inflating profits" and the shares of the company immediately plunged by 82 percent. He said "[w]hat started as a marginal gap between actual operating profits and the one reflected in the books of accounts continued to grow over the years . . . It was like riding a tiger, not knowing how to get off without being eaten."

> *"What started as a marginal gap between actual operating profits and the one reflected in the books of accounts continued to grow over the years . . . It was like riding a tiger, not knowing how to get off without being eaten."*
>
> Ramalinga Raju, founder and chairman of Satyam

Social Responsibility and Decision Making

There are many reasons why it is important for managers and organizations to act ethically and do everything possible to avoid harming stakeholders. However, what about the other side of the coin? What responsibility do managers have to provide benefits to their stakeholders and to adopt courses of action that enhance the well-being of society at large? The term **social responsibility** refers to a manager's duty or obligation to make decisions that nurture, protect, enhance, and promote the welfare and well-being of stakeholders and society as a whole. Many kinds of decisions signal an organization's interest in being socially responsible (see Figure 3.11).

social responsibility A manager's duty or obligation to make decisions that promote the well-being of stakeholders and society as a whole.

FIGURE 3.11

Examples of Socially Responsible Behaviour

Managers are being socially responsible and showing their support for their stakeholders when they:

- Provide severance payments to help laid-off workers make ends meet until they can find another job.

- Provide workers with opportunities to enhance their skills and acquire additional education so they can remain productive and do not become obsolete because of changes in technology.

- Allow employees to take time off when they need to and provide extended health care and pension benefits to employees.

- Contribute to charities or support various civic-minded activities in the cities or towns in which they are located.

- Decide to keep a company's operations in Canada to protect the jobs of Canadian workers rather than outsource and move abroad.

- Decide to spend money to improve a new factory so that it will not pollute the environment.

- Procure ethically sourced inputs.

- Decline to invest in countries that have poor human rights records.

- Choose to help poor countries develop an economic base to improve living standards.

APPROACHES TO SOCIAL RESPONSIBILITY BY TRADITIONAL BUSINESSES

The strength of traditional for-profit businesses' commitment to social responsibility ranges from low to high (see Figure 3.12).[55] At the low end of the range is an **obstructionist approach**. Obstructionist managers choose not to behave in a socially responsible way. Instead, they behave unethically and illegally and do all they can to prevent knowledge of their behaviour from reaching other organizational stakeholders and society at large. An example of this approach occurred when media mogul Conrad Black defrauded the shareholders of Hollinger Inc. by using corporate funds for personal use.

FIGURE 3.12

Approaches to Social Responsibility by Traditional Businesses

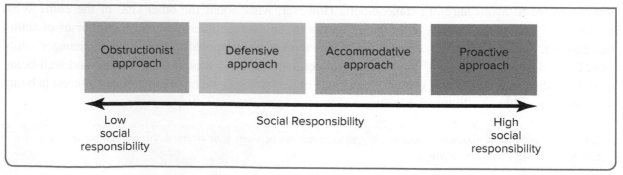

He pleaded not guilty but was found guilty and served 42 months of a 78-month jail sentence. He was released in 2012.

obstructionist approach Disregard for social responsibility; willingness to engage in and cover up unethical and illegal behaviour.

A **defensive approach** indicates at least a minimal commitment to ethical behaviour. Managers adopting this approach do all they can to ensure that their employees behave legally and do not harm others. But when making ethical choices, these managers put the claims and interests of their shareholders first, at the expense of other stakeholders.

defensive approach Minimal commitment to social responsibility; willingness to do what the law requires and no more.

Some economists believe that managers in a capitalist society should always put shareholders' (investors) claims first.[56] From a defensive point of view, it is not managers' responsibility to make socially responsible choices; their job is to abide by the rules that have been legally established. Milton Friedman said: "There is one and only one social responsibility of business—to use its resources and engage in activities designed to increase its profits, so long as it stays within the rules of the game, which is to say, engages in open and free competition without deception or fraud."[57]

But increasingly, going beyond what is legislated may be the only way to do any business at all. Indian mining giant Vedanta Resources was told by the Supreme Court of India that its application to mine bauxite in the pristine Nyuamgiri hills in one of India's poorest states would be turned down by the Supreme Court unless it participated in a joint venture with the state-owned Orissa Mining Corporation to spend 100 million rupees (US$2.4 million) a year, or 5 percent of its operating profits, whichever is greater, on fighting poverty and protecting wildlife and the tribal people.[58]

An **accommodative approach** is an acknowledgment of the need to support social responsibility. Accommodative managers agree that organizational members ought to behave legally and ethically, and they try to weigh the interests of different stakeholders against one another so that the claims of one group of shareholders are seen in relation to the claims of other stakeholders. Managers adopting this approach want to make choices that are reasonable in the eyes of society and want to do the right thing when called on to do so. Walmart Canada was criticized for its policy of doing business with third-party suppliers—such as Hampton Industries, Sutton Creations, Global Gold, Stretch-O-Rama, Cherry Stix, and By Design—that import goods from Myanmar, which engages in forced labour, including that of children. In defence of the company's actions, Walmart Canada spokesman Andrew Pelletier noted, "We have a policy we are looking at, of monitoring vendors sourcing from other countries."[59] The company started with a defensive approach, focusing on not doing anything illegal, but moved to a more accommodative and, more recently, perhaps even a proactive style. Even the ex-president of the famous environmental group the Sierra Club is now "working with the enemy." *Fast Company* magazine reports, "Once the youngest president of the Sierra Club, Adam Werbach used to call [WalMart] toxic. Now the company is his biggest client."[60] Since 2005, Walmart has set goals to become the world's largest and most environmentally sustainable retail company by reducing its ecological footprint and increasing the number of environmentally friendly products it sells, and, after some nasty legal battles, promoting better labour practices and working conditions.[61]

accommodative approach Moderate commitment to social responsibility; willingness to do more than the law requires, if asked.

Managers taking a **proactive approach** actively embrace the need to behave in socially responsible ways, go out of their way to learn about the needs of different stakeholder groups, and are willing to use organizational resources to promote the interests of shareholders as well as other stakeholders. David Suzuki said of Walmart Canada: "[WalMart's] commitment to sustainability acts as an inspiration and incentive to other corporations to follow suit. The company has enormous influence on corporate thinking and I am delighted with the priorities it has selected."[62]

proactive approach Strong commitment to social responsibility; eagerness to do more than the law requires and to use organizational resources to promote the interests of all organizational stakeholders.

WHY BE SOCIALLY RESPONSIBLE?

There are several advantages to social responsibility by managers and organizations. First, employees and society benefit directly because organizations (rather than the government) bear some of the costs of helping employees. Second, it has been said that if all organizations in a society were socially responsible, the quality of life as a whole would be higher.[63] Indeed, several management experts have argued that the way organizations behave toward their employees determines many of a society's values and norms and the ethics of its citizens. Experts point to Japan, Sweden, Germany, the Netherlands, and Switzerland as countries where organizations are socially responsible and where, as a result, crime and unemployment rates are relatively low, the literacy rate is relatively high, and socio-cultural values promote harmony among different groups of people. Other reasons for being socially responsible are that it is the right thing to do and that companies that act responsibly toward their stakeholders benefit from increasing business and see their profits rise.[64] The most pressing reason to practise business in a socially responsible manner is the recognition that Earth cannot support unsustainable practices that focus on short-term profit making. The World Business Council for Sustainable Development put it this way: "Business cannot function if ecosystems and the services they deliver—like water, biodiversity, fibre, food and climate—are degraded or out of balance."[65]

Jason Mogus, principal strategist of Communicopia, finds that being socially responsible is a competitive advantage: "The times that we are in right now are tough times for a lot of high-tech firms, and the ones that are thriving are the ones that really did build community connections and have strong customer and employee loyalty," says Mogus. "If everyone's just there for the stock price and it goes underwater, then what you have is a staff of not very motivated workers."[66]

Given these advantages, why would anyone quarrel over organizations and their managers pursuing social responsibility? One response is that a commitment to social responsibility could benefit some stakeholders and not others. For instance, some shareholders might think they are being harmed financially when organizational resources are used for socially responsible courses of action. Some people, like Friedman, as noted earlier, argue that business has only one kind of responsibility: to use its resources for activities that increase its profits and thus reward its shareholders.[67] See Figure 3.13.

How should managers decide which social issues they will respond to, and to what extent their organizations should trade profits for social gain? With impact investing, managers don't view investing in companies that prioritize social missions as a trade-off to profit making. **Impact investing** involves investing in solving social or environmental challenges, while generating a financial return on investment. There is a growing recognition that societies cannot rely solely on community and government agencies to solve social problems. Shareholders, investors, and businesses have a social responsibility to help solve the immense problems the world faces today, such as environmental degradation and poverty.

impact investing Investments that seek to solve social or environmental problems and generate financial returns to the investor.

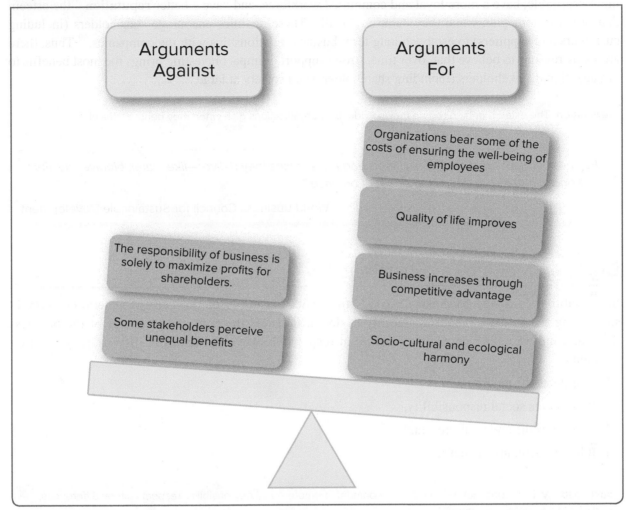

FIGURE 3.13

FIGURE 3.13

Why Be Socially Responsible?

Arguments Against

Arguments For

Organizations bear some of the costs of ensuring the well-being of employees

Quality of life improves

The responsibility of business is solely to maximize profits for shareholders.

Business increases through competitive advantage

Some stakeholders perceive unequal benefits

Socio-cultural and ecological harmony

Impact investors play an important role in unlocking capital for nonprofits and social enterprises that have the ability to generate both financial returns and scale up social impact. The increasingly popular view is that investors need not sacrifice financial return in exchange for social impact. And although it is in its infancy, more and more investors are attracted to this blended value proposition. A **social audit** allows managers to consider both the organizational and the social effects of particular decisions. The audit ranks various courses of action according to both their profitability and their social benefits. The Global Impact Investing Network (GIIN) has compiled a list of 399 metrics that can be used in a social audit to report impacts which range from indicators that describe the organization's environmental footprint to indicators that describe the performance and reach of the organization's products and services.[68] Using these metrics, an organization's social and environmental impacts can be rated, much like Standard & Poor's rates a company's credit risk. This allows investors to make decisions based on standardized, comparable data and will open up access to much-needed capital to social entrepreneurs and social enterprises.

social audit A tool that allows managers to analyze the profitability and social returns of socially responsible actions.

Evidence suggests that, in the long run, managers who behave in a socially responsible way will most benefit all organizational stakeholders (including shareholders). It appears that socially responsible companies, in comparison with less responsible competitors, are less risky investments, tend to be somewhat more profitable, have a more loyal and committed workforce, and have a better **reputation**—the esteem that organizations gain when they behave ethically. These qualities encourage stakeholders (including customers and suppliers) to establish long-term business relationships with the companies.[69] Thus, there are many reasons to believe that, over time, strong support of impact investing brings the most benefits to organizational stakeholders (including shareholders) and society at large.

reputation The esteem or high repute that individuals or organizations gain when they behave ethically.

"Business cannot function if ecosystems and the services they deliver—like water, biodiversity, fibre, food and climate—are degraded or out of balance."

World Business Council for Sustainable Development

Decision Making for Sustainability

Sustainability is a way to make decisions that meet the needs of the current generation without sacrificing the future generation's ability to do so. It serves the core competencies of the business to create, innovate, and enter new markets in responsible ways. A **sustainability** strategy has four elements:

1. It protects the environment,
2. It promotes social responsibility,
3. It respects different cultures, and
4. It has an economic benefit.

sustainability Decisions that protect the environment, promote social responsibility, respect cultural differences, and provide an economic benefit.

Sustainability has to have the support of the top management of the organization but also has to engage the employees. Everyone must internalize the individual responsibility for the good of the whole. Eva's Print Shop, featured in the Focus on the Social Economy feature, does just that.

One way that employees are encouraged to engage in sustainable strategies at Saatchi & Saatchi is to have them embark on their own personal projects inside and outside the office. This might mean making the decision to park as far away from the door of the shopping mall as possible, to get a little walk in on their way to work. Or it might mean deciding to bicycle to work rather than driving. Such forms of engagement create sustainable practices and make for good decision making in every area of life.

Making sustainable decisions becomes particularly important when managers consider the choice of the source(s) of their inputs. Chef Robert Clark of Vancouver promotes sustainable fishing practices in British Columbia through the Ocean Wise program at the Vancouver Aquarium. Part of the program includes purchasing direct from fishers who use organic means of growing, selective harvesting, and exclusive production techniques that support and maintain the diverse marine ecosystem.[70] Compass Group Canada and Sea Choice Canada expanded the Ocean Wise program nationwide to include new purchasing standards, internal compliance mechanisms, and chef and public education and awareness. "As the Canadian leader in food and support services, we are proud to embrace a sustainable seafood policy that will support the health of our oceans. Our purchasing shift can make a significant impact and it is clearly the right thing for us to do,"[71] said Jack MacDonald, CEO of Compass Group Canada.

Many universities and colleges are making the decision to not purchase eggs from caged hens because caging severely limits the ability of the hens to engage in many of their natural behaviours, such as wing stretching, walking, dust bathing, standing on solid ground, or laying eggs in a nest. More than 300 universities and colleges in North America, including the University of Guelph, the University of British Columbia, Langara College, and the British Columbia Institute of Technology, have already stopped purchasing eggs from suppliers that cage their hens.[72] The European Union has banned the practice of caging hens.

Consumers still have trouble identifying the leaders in sustainability.[73] A study by IMC2 on how effectively S&P 100 companies are communicating their sustainability efforts found that financial, media, and entertainment companies had the worst practices and policies related to communicating with the outside world about their sustainability issues, while the automotive and forestry industries had the best.[74]

Decision Making in Learning Organizations

Organizational learning is the process through which managers seek to improve employees' desire and ability to understand and manage the organization and its task environment so that employees can make decisions that constantly raise organizational effectiveness.[75] A **learning organization** is one in which managers do everything possible to maximize the ability of individuals and groups to think and behave creatively and thus maximize the potential for organizational learning to take place. At the heart of organizational learning is **creativity**, the ability of a decision maker to discover original ideas that lead to feasible alternative courses of action. Encouraging creativity among managers is such a pressing organizational concern that many organizations hire outside experts to help them develop programs to train their managers in the art of creative thinking and problem solving.

> **organizational learning** The process through which managers seek to improve employees' desire and ability to understand and manage the organization and its task environment.
>
> **learning organization** An organization in which managers try to maximize the ability of individuals and groups to think and behave creatively and thus maximize the potential for organizational learning to take place.
>
> **creativity** A decision maker's ability to discover original and novel ideas that lead to feasible alternative courses of action.

PROMOTE INDIVIDUAL CREATIVITY

Research suggests that individuals are most likely to be creative when certain conditions are met. First, people must be given the opportunity and freedom to generate new ideas. Creativity declines when managers look over the shoulders of talented employees and try to "hurry up" a creative solution. How would you feel if your boss said you had one week to come up with a new product idea to beat the competition? Creativity results when individuals have an opportunity to experiment, to take risks, and to make mistakes and learn from them. Companies that have a lot of innovation foster intrapreneurship through their formal structure and expectations. An **intrapreneur** is a manager, scientist, employee,

FOCUS ON   *The Social Economy*

Eva's Print Shop

Eva's Print Shop is arguably one of the most successful social purpose enterprises in Toronto, having achieved an enviable balance of its blended value proposition: sustainable business results, remarkable social outcomes, and environmental responsibility.

Eva's Print Shop is a socially and environmentally responsible commercial printer that supports award-winning transitional housing and employment training offered by Eva's Initiatives for Homeless Youth for young people experiencing homelessness. Print services are competitively priced and on-time delivery is guaranteed. Eva's Print Shop is Forestry Stewardship Council (FSC) certified. Some customers include Porter Airline, Crosslinx Transit Solutions, CIBC, Artscape, Creation Crate, Colliers International, and the Toronto Organizing Committee for the 2015 Pan American and Parapan American Games.

Eva's Print Shop recruits young people to participate in a training program to learn the basics of graphic communications and print technologies, including the operation of equipment and machinery. Upon completion of the training program, trainees are supported by Eva's to apply for work. Some trainees find their career passion in the graphics and print industry. The Print Shop also offers its own job opportunities for graduates.

Eva's Print Shop has had significant success over the years. Their innovative profit-for-purpose social enterprise model helps young people build futures free of homelessness. Over 60 percent of the training program students get full-time work, and Eva's provides follow-up support to help them sustain employment. Many return to school, some with the assistance of a bursary from Eva's, and others start their own businesses or jobs. Many young people trained by Eva's Print Shop find stable housing, moving out of a shelter or marginal housing into independent living. Eva's Print Shop provides practical solutions to challenging social issues.

1. Describe how Eva's Print Shop demonstrates ethical and socially responsible decision making.

Source: Adapted from Eva's Initiatives for Homeless Youth, 2018. Print Shop. http://www.evas.ca/what-we-do/print-shop/. Accessed Jul 1, 2018.

or researcher who works inside an organization and notices opportunities to develop new or improved products and better ways to make them. For instance, in one year, 3M launched more than 200 new products, many of which came from employee intrapreneurs.[76] Highly innovative companies such as Google, Apple, and Facebook are well known for the wide degree of freedom they give their managers and employees to experiment and develop innovative goods and services.[77] **Innovation** is the implementation of creative ideas. Top managers must act on the new ideas and cultivate their implementation to achieve innovation. Organizations must reward intrapreneurs equitably if they wish to prevent them from leaving and becoming outside entrepreneurs who might form a competitive new venture. Nevertheless, intrapreneurs frequently do so.

intrapreneurs Employees of existing organizations who notice opportunities for product or service improvement and are responsible for managing the development process.

innovation (1) The implementation of creative ideas in an organization. (2) The process of creating new goods and services or developing better ways to produce or provide goods and services.

Sometimes a manager misses a good opportunity because of decision-making biases, as discussed earlier in this chapter, and sometimes it happens because they do not share their concerns about an idea with others and simply reject it outright. Sharing challenges and getting feedback from a wide variety of channels, including other firms through networking, can help managers make sure they do not miss out on a good idea—as did Hewlett-Packard when it decided not to develop one of its employees' ideas. The result: Steve Wozniak went off with his device to co-found Apple Computer. Other examples of poor decisions are shown in Figure 3.14.

Managers seek to improve employees' desire and ability to understand and manage the organization and its industry-specific environment so that employees can make decisions that continuously raise organizational effectiveness. Employees who believe that they are working on important, vital issues will be motivated to put forth the high levels of effort that creativity demands. Managers must take steps to promote organizational learning and creativity to improve the quality of decision making.

Despite the importance of fostering creativity in organizations, in a survey of 500 CEOs, only six percent felt that they were doing a great job at managing their creative people. John MacDonald, co-founder of MacDonald Dettwiler & Associates Ltd. (MDA), a global communications and information company based in Richmond, B.C., suggests that "managing creative people is a bit like riding herd on a thousand prima donnas. They are all highly individual people who don't follow the herd, so managing them is a challenge."[78]

FIGURE 3.14

Some of the Biggest Mistakes Managers Have Ever Made

- Alexander Graham Bell invented the telephone in 1876, but he had a hard time attracting backers. U.S. President Rutherford B. Hayes used a prototype telephone and thought it was an amazing invention, but couldn't fathom anyone wanting to use one of them! Bell approached Western Union Telegraph Company and offered to sell them the patents. Their decision: They had no use for an electrical toy.

- A young inventor, Chester Carlson, took his idea to 20 corporations, all of which turned him down. He finally got a small New York company named Haloid Co. to purchase the rights to his electrostatic paper-copying process. Haloid became Xerox Corporation, and Carlson's process made both Xerox and Carlson very rich.

- In 1962 four musicians played for executives of Decca Recording Company. One executive later explained that his company just did not like the group's sound, noting that guitar groups were on their way out. Four other record companies turned them down. The Decision Making Hall of Fame will have a special place for Decca, which turned down the Beatles.

- The decision of Ken Olsen, founder of Digital Equipment Corporation, to stay with mainframe computers in the 1980s rather than allowing his engineers to spend the company's resources on creating new kinds of personal computers cost Olsen his job as CEO and almost ruined his company. Why did he do it? Because he thought computers were simply toys!

- Monster.com approached *The Globe and Mail* to collaborate on online job advertising, but was turned down. *The Globe and Mail* lost huge revenues from job advertisement as a result of large numbers of firms moving from print to online.

- BlackBerry CEOs took days to communicate an apology to the public for the power outage in 2011 that caused loyal users around the world to switch to the iPhone or Android.

Chapter 3

SUMMARY AND REVIEW

connect

LO1 **The Nature of Managerial Decision Making** Programmed decisions are routine decisions that are made so often that managers have developed decision rules to be followed automatically. Nonprogrammed decisions are made in response to situations that are unusual or unique; they are nonroutine decisions that require research and analysis.

LO2 **Two Models of Decision Making** The classical model of decision making assumes that decision makers have complete information, are able to process that information in an objective, rational manner, and make optimum decisions. March and Simon in the administrative model argue that managers are subject to bounded rationality, rarely have access to all the information they need to make optimum decisions, and consequently satisfice and rely on their intuition and judgment when making decisions.

LO3 **Steps in the Decision-Making Process** When making decisions, managers should take these seven steps: recognize the need for a decision, develop decision criteria, generate alternatives, assess alternatives, choose among alternatives, implement the chosen alternative, and evaluate and learn from feedback.

LO4 **Biases in Decision Making** Managers are often fairly good decision makers. However, problems result when human judgment is adversely affected by the operation of cognitive biases. Cognitive biases are caused by systematic errors in the way decision makers process information to make decisions.

LO5 **Ethics, Social Responsibility, and Decision Making** Managers can make better decisions when they examine their *ethics* and approaches to *social responsibility*. But to make optimum decisions, managers should make decisions that promote sustainability—ones that are transparent, engaging, and economically beneficial without leaving a large carbon footprint. They must become a learning organization and encourage *creativity* to ensure that new, innovative ideas are not overlooked in the decision-making process.

KEY TERMS

accommodative approach	ethics
administrative model	ethical dilemma
ambiguous information	ethics ombudsperson
bounded awareness	heuristics
bounded rationality	impact investing
classical model	individual ethics
codes of ethics	innovation
creativity	intrapreneur
decision making	intuition
defensive approach	judgment

learning organization

nonprogrammed decision making

obstructionist approach

optimum decision

organizational learning

proactive approach

professional ethics

programmed decision making

reputation

satisficing

social audit

social responsibility

societal ethics

sustainability

systematic errors

WRAP-UP TO OPENING CASE

Good Decision Making at PUMA

PUMA faced considerable threats in its task environment which led to a major decision by past CEO Jochen Zeitz to reduce costs, increase sustainability in operations, and launch a new product. After having read and understood the concepts in this chapter, you should be able to answer the following questions:

1. *What type of decision was made by Zeitz when PUMA launched into sport lifestyle fashions?*

   ANSWER: Decision making is made in response to either routine or unique situations. Programmed decisions are made in response to routine situations where managers can establish rules to guide behaviour. Most decision making that relates to the day-to-day running of an organization is programmed decision making. Examples include decision making about how much inventory to hold, when to pay bills, when to bill customers, and when to order materials and supplies. Nonprogrammed decision making is required for nonroutine situations. Rules do not exist because the situation is unexpected or uncertain and managers lack the information they would need to develop rules to cover it. Zeitz's decision to launch into sport lifestyle gear and apparel is a nonprogrammed decision made under conditions of risk and uncertainty.

2. *Identify the threats and opportunities in the task environment that impact PUMA's decision making.*

   ANSWER: Decision making in response to threats occurs when events inside or outside the organization are adversely affecting organizational performance and managers are searching for ways to increase performance. In this case, PUMA was almost on the brink of bankruptcy in the early 1990s when Zeitz made the nonprogrammed decision to launch a new "sport lifestyle" line of products instead of competing in the high-performance athletic shoe market. In responding to the threats, PUMA decreased costs, took over distribution of PUMA North America, and adopted a sustainable operations strategy. The bold move appealed to consumers and turned around the fortunes of the company. PUMA is the fourth largest athletic apparel company in the world.

   Decision making in response to opportunities occurs when managers search for ways to improve organizational performance to benefit customers, employees, and other stakeholder groups. In this case, Zeitz's decision to focus on lifestyle and fashion products appealed to the younger demographic in the market. PUMA also took advantage of the growing trend among young people to buy products that are made in a sustainable manner, thus reducing the degradation of the environment. PUMA's decisions improved its organizational performance and benefited customers, the environment, and other stakeholders.

3. *How does PUMA foster sustainability and promote creativity and innovation? Why is this good decision making?*

ANSWER: Sustainability involves making decisions that meet the needs of the current generation without sacrificing the future generation's ability to do so. A sustainability strategy protects the environment, promotes social responsibility, respects different cultures, and has an economic benefit to the enterprise. PUMA collaborated with Greenpeace to embark on the "detoxification" of its operations. It collaborated with the chemical industry to determine how to phase out toxic materials in the production of its goods while lowering production costs. Thus PUMA is promoting social responsibility toward the environment while creating an economic benefit to the company.

Creativity is the ability to discover original ideas that lead to feasible alternative courses of action. Zeitz recognized the importance of coming up with creative designs that combined performance with style and hired a young skateboarder, Bertone, to head up the sport lifestyle division. As head of the division, the young manager partnered with experts and designers to create trendy products using sustainable materials. Bertone was able to implement new creative ideas including a limited-edition line called Thrift (products made from vintage clothing) and Mongolian Shoe BBQ (shoes that can be customized online). Zeitz and other managers like Bertone fostered innovation at PUMA.

The decisions Zeitz made at PUMA illustrate good decision making in the face of a highly competitive industry. In responding to those threats, Zeitz sought opportunities to create a high-performing organization by fostering creativity and innovation, and adopting a sustainability strategy in making the decision to change the direction of the company. It was good decision making because all the stakeholders benefit.

MANAGEMENT IN ACTION

TOPICS FOR DISCUSSION AND ACTION

LEVEL 1 Knowledge & Comprehension

1. Define and describe the two types of decisions.
2. Describe the seven steps that managers should take to make the best decisions.
3. Describe the different approaches to corporate social responsibility.

LEVEL 2 Application & Analysis

4. Ask a manager to recall when they experienced an ethical dilemma. Report on how they dealt with the situation.
5. Ask a manager to describe how the company's Code of Ethics influenced a decision they made.
6. Research two organizations and compare and contrast their approaches to social responsibility.

LEVEL 3 Synthesis & Evaluation

7. Compare and contrast the assumptions underlying the classical and administrative models of decision making.

8. You are a first-line manager of a grocery store that has a home delivery service. You tell your boss that you have found a cheaper supplier of insurance for the drivers with the same amount of coverage. Your boss continues to use the more expensive insurer. What decision-making bias is your boss suffering from?

9. When a manager is asked to judge an alternative in terms of a cost–benefit analysis, which decision making criterion are they weighting most highly?

SELF-REFLECTION EXERCISE
How Do You Make Decisions?

Pick a decision that you have made recently that has had important consequences for you. This decision may be your decision concerning which university to attend, which program to select, which part-time job to take, or even whether or not to take a part-time job. Using the material in this chapter, analyze the way in which you made the decision.

1. Identify the criteria you used, either consciously or unconsciously, to guide your decision making.

2. List the alternatives that you considered. Were these all the possible alternatives? Did you unconsciously (or consciously) ignore some important alternatives?

3. How much information did you have about each alternative? Did you base the decision on complete or incomplete information?

4. Try to remember how you reached a decision. Did you sit down and consciously think through the implications of each alternative, or did you make a decision on the basis of intuition? Did you use any rules of thumb to help you make the decision?

5. Do you think that your choice of decision alternative was shaped by any of the cognitive biases discussed in this chapter?

6. Do you think in retrospect that you made a reasonable decision? What, if anything, might you do to improve your ability to make good decisions in the future?

SMALL GROUP BREAKOUT EXERCISE
What Type of Computer Should We Buy?

Form groups of three or four people and appoint one member as the spokesperson who will communicate your findings to the whole class when called on by the instructor. Then discuss the following scenario: Assume your group is charged with solving the problem of replacing the obsolete desktop computer monitors for the human resources department. You must purchase seven new monitors, but are struggling over the decision of what brand to buy. Apply the steps in the decision-making process.

1. State the decision question.

2. Brainstorm the brands of computer monitors available.

3. **a.** List the factors that are important in making the decision, and fit them into the four categories of criteria.

   b. Assign a value or weight to each of the criteria categories and subfactors.

   c. Discuss the advantages and disadvantages of each of the brands in terms of the decision criteria and assign them a score out of 10 (0 is low).

   d. Make a decision preference matrix (see Figure 3.7) to display the weighted scores.

4. Which brand will you choose, and why?

5. How will you go about implementing your decision?

6. How will you know if you made a good decision?

MANAGING ETHICALLY EXERCISE

Managers Struggle with Ethical Decisions[79]

"It's hard to do the right thing as a manager—especially when you are not sure what the "right thing" is. Sometimes you must balance your own sense of ethics with organizational pressures.

"Take the case of employees at a cabinet manufacturing company. A number of them routinely work on their own projects on company time. The manager is aware. But there is a labour crunch in the booming construction sector, and she's concerned about retaining staff. So she turns a blind eye. The organization tacitly supports the manager's decision not to stop the practice because labour is hard to find.

"Nevertheless, the manager is uncomfortable. The decision does not sit right, and she has noticed that allowing the practice has affected other workers. People are taking longer lunches and breaks and talking on the phone during company time. Productivity is starting to slide."

How do you think the manager should deal with this situation?

MANAGEMENT CHALLENGE EXERCISE

George Stroumboulopoulos, former anchor for *Hockey Night in Canada,* initiated a campaign called "One Million Acts of Green,"[80] which was an attempt to get Canadians to engage in something that will prevent greenhouse gas emissions. The act could "be as simple as switching to compact fluorescent lightbulbs, starting a recycling program, or walking to work."

1. As a manager of a small printing/copy shop business, what decisions could you make that will promote sustainability?

MANAGEMENT PORTFOLIO PROJECT

Answer the following questions about the organization you have chosen to follow:

1. Try to find some evidence that managers at the organization made a few poor decisions over the past decade.

2. If poor decisions were made, what role, if any, did decision-making ethics play?

3. Evaluate the approach to sustainability taken by this organization.

MANAGEMENT CASE

WHY DECISION MAKING AT A COMPANY SUFFERS WITH MORE INFORMATION

The following is an excerpt of an interview held in Vancouver in 2016.

MOORE: This is Karl Moore of the Desautels Faculty of Management at McGill University with Talking Management for *The Globe and Mail*. Today I am delighted to be in Vancouver with Julian Birkinshaw from the London Business School.

Julian, the working title of your new book is *Fast Forward*. What are some of the key ideas that are going to be a part of that book?

BIRKINSHAW: So, the book starts with this very simple premise that information in the world is ubiquitous. Search costs have pretty much shrunk to zero, we can pretty much get access to anything whenever we like. That creates a number of pathologies in organizations. We have all heard the concept of analysis paralysis, the idea that essentially we get kind of frozen because there is so much information we can gather we never know when to stop.

As an antidote to that, what we have to do is think in terms of the scarce resource, if you like, of the second half of the information age and that scarce resource is our attention – our capacity to attend to and focus and make decisions on things in an efficient way.

For me the biggest sort of single challenge that large organizations face is how to become more decisive, to basically figure out ways of creating decisive action in order to make things happen more quickly. Learning and experimenting along the way and also to figure out a way of tapping into what you might call the emotional conviction of our people.

The risk of having an information based economy is that our decision making becomes incredibly sterile. If you think about it, everything gets boiled down to numbers and sort of logical rational arguments and we park all this stuff, which goes under the banner of emotion or intuition or gut feeling.

MOORE: How as a manager do I tap into that emotional side that you talk about?

BIRKINSHAW: So, let's be very practical. You are running a meeting and you are trying to tap into views. Let's put the numbers on the table, let's see how far the numbers take us, and then let's say, "Ok, on the basis of that, what additional insights are we now able to bring from our intuition, from our reservoir of experiences, what do we feel about this decision?"

Jeff Bezos at Amazon is very famous for this. He says essentially there are two types of decisions we make at Amazon – there are the purely rational ones, where we have done all the data, where we can prove this website is better than that one. Those are great decisions, he says. But then there are these other decisions – should we launch the Kindle, should we get into movies – where there is no way rational narrowed-down decision making can help us.

He says on those decisions we get the data but then we start brainstorming and we then figure out what our intuition tells us and we defray the risks as much as we can but ultimately we are not afraid to make the big calls because we know you cannot make those decisions in a rational way.

1. Does this case support the classical or administrative model of decision making? Give evidence for your answer.

Source: Karl Moore, "Why Decision Making at a Company Suffers with More Information," *The Globe and Mail,* published Jan. 13, 2016, updated Mar. 25, 2017. https://www.theglobeandmail.com/report-on-business/careers/transcript-why-decision-making-at-a-company-suffers-with-more-information/article28145063/. Accessed Jan. 15, 2018. Reprinted courtesy of Karl Moore.

Chapter 4

Managing Planning and Strategy

LEARNING OUTCOMES

LO1	Describe how planning and strategizing are related to organizational performance and competitive advantage.
LO2	Describe planning as a five-step process.
LO3	Explain how managers use planning techniques to evaluate the opportunities and threats in the organization's environment and formulate strategy.
LO4	Differentiate among corporate-level, business-level, and functional-level strategies.
LO5	Describe how managers implement strategy and evaluate its success.

OPENING CASE

Microsoft CEO Satya Nadella Looks to Future Beyond Windows[1]

The following article appeared on Bloomberg.com in February of 2015.

"Our industry does not respect tradition. It only respects innovation," Satya Nadella said in February 2014, when he was appointed chief executive officer of Microsoft. After 39 years, the company Bill Gates co-founded had come to be perceived as an out-of-touch behemoth that relied too much on its Windows operating system and failed to move into new markets, like mobile. Key products such as Microsoft Office—the suite of applications that includes Word and Excel—had been designed around Windows, with only parts converted to work on Apple's iOS and Google's Android systems. Nadella's accession would be a chance to reorient the company, getting it to introduce products that looked outside Windows and to develop new business models.

Nadella has aggressively pursued this course. Since December, Microsoft has bought two small companies that focus on mobile productivity apps for iOS and Android phones and tablets. To appeal to younger users, the company last September purchased Mojang, maker of the popular Minecraft video game, for $2.5 billion, and it's adding features to Windows such as 3D holograms that users view through a headset and control with hand gestures. The newest version of Microsoft's Power BI (business intelligence) product—a dashboard for data analysis—was released in January, a first for iOS systems. "Microsoft hasn't really shown any sort of vision like this in a long, long time," Michael Silver, an analyst at Gartner and longtime Microsoft watcher, said in January when it unveiled the holograms. "All it took was replacing the senior management."

In Nadella's first year, Microsoft stock rose 14 percent, and sales increased 12 percent. The new CEO, unlike his predecessor Steve Ballmer, is popular with investors, venture capitalists, and startups. Even employees like Nadella, surprising for a chief executive who signed off on the largest layoffs in Microsoft's history—18,000 job cuts were announced last July. Staff say they appreciate Nadella's strategy shifts and attempts to make the company leaner and less bureaucratic.

The big issue Nadella faces is how to generate more revenue with new software and features, such as cloud subscriptions and free apps, replacing pricey Windows and Office licences. Revenue is projected to increase 8.6 percent, to $94.3 billion, this fiscal year, slowing from last year's double-digit growth, according to data compiled by Bloomberg. "He's hit all the low-hanging fruit—that said, these things were not easy to do," says Brad Silverberg, a venture capitalist and former Microsoft executive.

"Where there are execution issues, we will address them," Nadella said on a conference call in January. "Where there are macroeconomic issues, we will weather them." Microsoft declined to make Nadella available for an interview.

Windows, which once dominated computing and ran on more than 90 percent of computing devices, now runs on 11 percent of computers and gadgets, according to a report from Sanford C. Bernstein. Nadella and Windows chief Terry Myerson are looking at ways to update the software.

Nadella uses the Power BI dashboard to track and compile huge amounts of information on product usage and financial performance to see what works and what doesn't, says James Phillips, general manager of the product. Nadella also measures and coordinates executive performance with metrics from the dashboard. "Satya has been leading the charge for everyone in the company to be more data-oriented," says Chief Strategy Officer Mark Penn.

Microsoft's quarterly earnings report in January highlights the hurdles Nadella faces. While cloud software sales to businesses more than doubled in the quarter that ended Dec. 31, sales of traditional Office and Windows software to companies fell short of analysts' estimates. Windows sales to personal computer makers who put the program on their machines dropped 13 percent. In total, profit declined 11 percent from the previous year, to $5.86 billion, while sales rose 8 percent, to $26.5 billion.

Revenue is being hurt by fluctuating currencies, while the Chinese government is investigating Microsoft over alleged anticompetitive practices and seeking to end purchases of its software. The government of Russian President Vladimir Putin says it wants to reduce reliance on Microsoft.

Internally, Nadella and his executives make the point whenever they can that the day could come when new and younger generations of computer and software users might not use its products. At one board meeting last year, Windows chief Myerson showed a slide with pictures of students using Apple Macs and iPads, according to Microsoft spokesman Peter Wootton.

In 2014, Nadella told employees at a town hall that they should skip meetings if they don't really need to be there. And he's advised workers to come to him directly if they feel the bureaucracy is stifling. "The organization knows it's go-time," says Phillips. "There are changes in the market we need to respond to."

Nadella's also changed the way engineering teams are structured, eliminating testers to speed up software releases and adding data scientists and designers to the teams. He's looking at cutting some middle managers to make decisions faster and to eliminate layers of bureaucracy, Wootton says.

Eli Lilly Chief Technology Officer Mike Meadows says Microsoft is more open and listening to what customers need. He was glad to see the company demonstrate its products on iPads at Microsoft's chief information officer conference last fall—Lilly's 20,000 salespeople use Apple tablets, Meadows says. "They're starting to demonstrate more understanding of reality," he says. "They would say, –We were going in this direction already,' but Satya lit a fire."

The bottom line: Nadella is working to push Microsoft out of its Windows slump and into cloud computing and apps for iOS and Android.

After reading and understanding the concepts in this chapter, you should be able to answer the following questions:

1. What kind of planning missteps helped cause Microsoft's decline over the past few years?
2. How is Nadella trying to eliminate some of the bureaucracy that has hurt the company's ability to innovate?
3. What business strategies has Nadella implemented that will help revitalize the technology giant?

Overview

As the opening case suggests, in a fast-changing competitive environment such as mobile computing, managers must continually evaluate how well products are meeting customer needs and engage in thorough, systematic planning to find new strategies to better meet those needs. This chapter explores the manager's role both as planner and as strategist. We first discuss what planning is, who does it, why it's important for high performance, and what qualities make effective plans. We then discuss the five main steps in the planning process: a) determining and communicating an organization's vision, mission, and goals; b) analyzing the forces in the organizational environment; c) formulating strategy at the corporate, business, and functional level; d) implementing strategy; and, finally, e) evaluating the success of the strategy in achieving the mission and goals of the organization. By the end of this chapter, you will understand the vital role managers carry out when they plan, develop, and implement strategies to create a high-performing organization.

Planning and Strategy

LO1 | Describe how planning and strategizing are related to organizational performance and competitive advantage.

Planning, as we noted in Chapter 1, is a process that managers use to identify and select suitable goals and courses of action for an organization.[2] It is one of the four principal managerial functions. The organizational plan that results from the planning process details the goals of the organization and specifies how managers intend to attain those goals. The cluster of decisions and actions that managers take to help an organization attain its goals is its **strategy.** Thus, planning is both a goal-making and a strategy-making process.

> **planning** Identifying and selecting appropriate goals and courses of action; one of the four principal functions of management.
>
> **strategy** A cluster of decisions about what goals to pursue, what actions to take, and how to use resources to achieve goals.

In most organizations, planning is a five-step activity (see Figure 4.1). The first step is to determine the organization's vision, mission, and major goals. The **vision statement** captures the desired end state or change the organization wants to inspire. A **mission statement** is a broad declaration of an organization's overriding purpose and what it is seeking to achieve from its activities; this statement also

FIGURE 4.1

5 Steps in the Planning Process

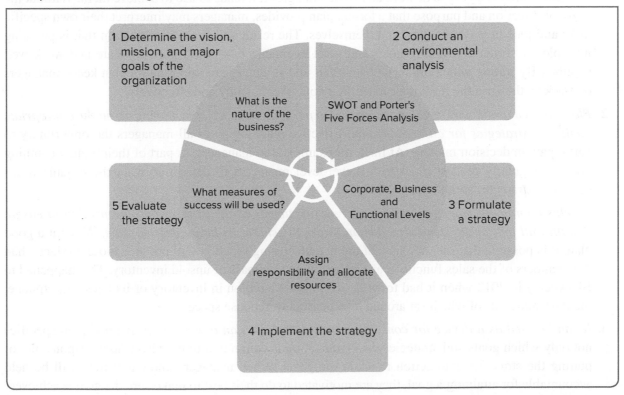

identifies what is *unique or important* about its products to employees and customers and *distinguishes or differentiates* the organization in some ways from its competitors. The second step is to conduct an analysis of the current situation with respect to threats and opportunities in the external environment, and strengths and weaknesses in the internal environment. The third step is to formulate a strategy. Managers analyze the organization's current situation and then conceive and develop the strategies necessary to attain the organization's mission and goals. The fourth step is to implement the strategy. Managers decide how to allocate the resources and responsibilities required to implement the strategies among people and groups within the organization.[3] The final step is to evaluate the strategy. How successful is the organization in achieving its mission and goals? In subsequent sections of this chapter we look in detail at the specifics of these steps. But first we examine why planning is important for a competitive advantage and what types and levels of plans are key to high-performing organizations.

vision statement A broad declaration of the big picture of the organization and/or a statement of its dreams for the future.

mission statement A broad declaration of an organization's purpose that identifies the organization's products and customers and distinguishes the organization from its competitors.

Why Planning Is Important

Almost all managers engage in planning, and all *should* do so because planning helps predict future opportunities and threats. The absence of a plan often results in hesitation, false steps, and mistaken changes of direction that can hurt an organization or even lead to disaster. Planning is important for four main reasons:

1. *It is necessary to give the organization a sense of direction and purpose.*[4] A plan states what goals an organization is trying to achieve and what strategies it intends to use to achieve them. Without the sense of direction and purpose that a formal plan provides, managers may interpret their own specific tasks and jobs in ways that best suit themselves. The result will be an organization that is pursuing multiple and often conflicting goals and a set of managers who do not cooperate and work well together. By stating which organizational goals and strategies are important, a plan keeps managers on track so they use the resources under their control efficiently and effectively.

2. *Planning is a useful way of getting managers to participate in decision making about the appropriate goals and strategies for an organization.* Effective planning gives all managers the opportunity to participate in decision making. At Intel, for example, top managers, as part of their annual planning process, regularly request input from lower-level managers to determine what the organization's goals and strategies should be.

3. *It helps coordinate managers of the different functions and divisions of an organization to ensure that they all pull in the same direction and work to achieve its future desired state.* Without a good plan, it is possible that the members of the manufacturing function will produce more products than the members of the sales function can sell, resulting in a mass of unsold inventory. This happened to Blackberry in 2012 when it had to write off almost $1 billion in inventory of its latest smartphone, the Z10, hundreds of which sat around in expensive warehouse space.

4. *It can be used as a device for controlling managers within an organization.* A good plan specifies not only which goals and strategies the organization is committed to but also *who* is responsible for putting the strategies into action to attain the goals. When managers know that they will be held accountable for attaining a goal, they are motivated to do their best to make sure the goal is achieved.

Henri Fayol, the originator of the model of management we discussed in Appendix A, said that effective plans should have four qualities: unity, continuity, accuracy, and flexibility.[5] *Unity* means that at any time only one central, guiding plan is put into operation to achieve an organizational goal; more than one plan to achieve a goal would cause confusion and disorder. *Continuity* means that planning is an ongoing process in which managers build and refine previous plans and continually modify plans at all levels—corporate, business, and functional—so they fit together into one broad framework. *Accuracy* means that managers need to make every attempt to collect and use all available information in the planning process. Of course managers must recognize that uncertainty exists and that information is almost always incomplete. Despite the need for continuity and accuracy, however, Fayol

A group of managers meets to plot their company's strategy. Their ability to assess opportunities and challenges and to forecast the future doesn't just depend on intelligence. Such tools as SWOT analysis can significantly bolster the accuracy of their predictions.
© Ryan McVay/Getty Images/RF

emphasized that the planning process should be *flexible* enough so plans can be altered and changed if the situation changes; managers must not be bound to a static plan.

Levels of Planning and Types of Plans

In large organizations planning usually takes place at three levels of management: corporate, business or division, and department or functional. Consider how General Electric (GE) operates. One of the world's largest global organizations, GE competes in several businesses or industries.[6] GE has three main levels of management: corporate level, business or divisional level, and functional level (see Figure 4.2). At the corporate level are CEO and Chairman John L. Flannery, his top management team, and their corporate support staff. Together they are responsible for planning and strategy-making for the organization as a whole.

Below the corporate level is the business level. At the business level are the different *divisions* or *business units* of the company that compete in distinct industries. GE has several divisions, including GE Aviation, GE Capital, GE Healthcare, GE Lighting, GE Power, GE Renewable Energy, and GE Transportation. Each division or business unit has its own set of *divisional managers* who control planning and strategy for their particular division or unit. For example, GE Lighting's divisional managers plan how to operate globally to reduce costs while meeting the needs of customers in different countries.

Going down one more level, each division has its own set of *functions* or *departments,* such as manufacturing, marketing, human resource management (HRM), and research and development (R&D). For example, GE Aviation has its own marketing function, as do GE Lighting and GE Transportation. Each division's *functional managers* are responsible for the planning and strategy-making necessary to increase the efficiency and effectiveness of their particular function. So, for example, GE Lighting's marketing managers are responsible for increasing the effectiveness of its advertising and sales campaigns in different countries to improve light bulb sales. Planning at GE, as at all other large organizations, takes place at each level. Figure 4.3 shows the level of manager responsible for the planning and strategy-making process.

FIGURE 4.2

Levels of Planning at General Electric

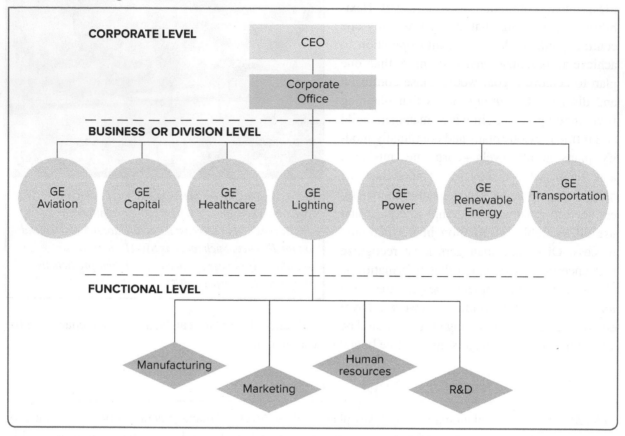

FIGURE 4.3

Level of Manager Responsible for Types of Plans

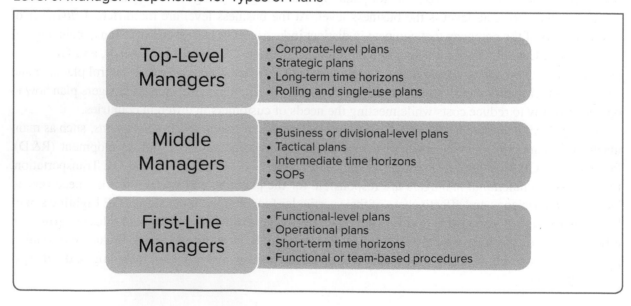

The **corporate-level plan** contains top management's decisions concerning the organization's mission and goals, overall (corporate-level) strategy, and structure. **Corporate-level strategy** specifies in which industries and national markets an organization intends to compete and why. One of the goals stated in GE's corporate-level plan is that GE should be first or second in market share in every industry in which it competes. A division that cannot attain this goal may be sold to another company. GE Medical Systems was sold to Thompson of France for this reason. Another GE goal is to acquire other companies that can help a division build its market share to reach its corporate goal of being first or second in an industry. In 2011, GE sold its NBC division to Comcast Cable at an extremely profitable price.

> **corporate-level plan** Top management's decisions concerning the organization's mission and goals, overall (corporate-level) strategy, and structure.
>
> **corporate-level strategy** Specifies in which industries and national markets an organization intends to compete and why.

In general, corporate-level planning and strategy are the primary responsibility of top or corporate managers, as indicated in Figure 4.3.[7] John L. Flannery and his top management team decide which industries GE should compete in to achieve the corporate-level goal of being the first or second leading company in every industry in which it competes. The corporate-level plan provides the framework within which divisional managers create their business-level plans as illustrated in Figure 4.4. At the business

FIGURE 4.4

Levels and Types of Planning and Strategy-Making

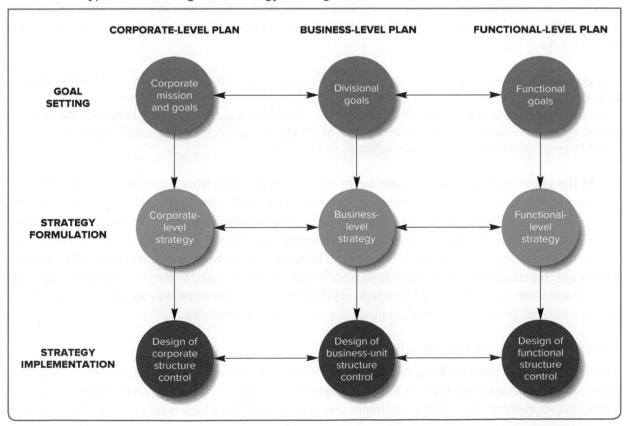

level, the managers of each division create a **business-level plan** that details (1) the long-term divisional goals that will allow the division to meet corporate goals and (2) the division's business-level strategy and structure necessary to achieve divisional goals. **Business-level strategy** outlines the specific methods a division, business unit, or organization will use to compete effectively against its rivals in an industry. Managers at GE's lighting division (currently number two in the global lighting industry, behind the Dutch company Philips NV) develop strategies designed to help their division take over the number one spot and better contribute to GE's corporate goals. The lighting division's specific strategies might focus on ways to reduce costs in all departments to lower prices and so gain market share from Philips. For example, GE has expanded its European lighting operations in Hungary, which is a low-cost location.[8]

> **business-level plan** Includes (1) the long-term divisional goals that will allow the division to meet corporate goals, and (2) the division's business-level strategy and structure necessary to achieve divisional goals.
>
> **business-level strategy** Outlines the specific methods a division, business unit, or organization will use to compete effectively against its rivals in an industry.

At the functional level, the business-level plan provides the framework within which functional managers devise their plans. A **functional-level plan** states the goals that the managers of each function will pursue to help their division attain its business-level goals, which, in turn, will allow the entire company to achieve its corporate goals. **Functional-level strategy** is a plan of action that managers of individual functions (such as manufacturing or marketing) can follow to improve the ability of each function to perform its task-specific activities in ways that add value to an organization's goods and services and thereby increase the value customers receive. Thus, for example, consistent with the lighting division's strategy of driving down costs, its manufacturing function might adopt the goal "To reduce production costs by 20 percent over the next three years," and functional strategies to achieve this goal might include (1) investing in state-of-the-art European production facilities and (2) developing an electronic global business-to-business network to reduce the costs of inputs and inventory holding.

> **functional-level plan** States the goals that the managers of each function will pursue to help their division attain its business-level goals.
>
> **functional-level strategy** A plan of action that managers of individual functions can follow to improve the ability of each function to perform its task-specific activities in ways that add value to an organization's goods and services and thereby increase the value customers receive.

In the planning process, it is important to ensure that planning across the three different levels is *consistent*—functional goals and strategies should be consistent with divisional goals and strategies, which, in turn, should be consistent with corporate goals and strategies, and vice versa. When consistency is achieved, the whole company operates in harmony; activities at one level reinforce and strengthen those at the other levels, increasing efficiency and effectiveness. To help accomplish this, each function's plan is linked to its division's business-level plan, which, in turn, is linked to the corporate plan. Although few organizations are as large and complex as GE, most plan in the same way as GE and have written plans, which are frequently updated, to guide managerial decision making.

TIME HORIZONS OF PLANS

Plans differ in their **time horizon,** or intended duration. Managers usually distinguish among long-term plans with a horizon of five years or more, intermediate-term plans with a horizon between one and five years, and short-term plans with a horizon of one year or less.[9] Typically, corporate- and business-level goals and strategies require long- and intermediate-term plans, and functional-level goals and strategies require intermediate- and short-term plans.

time horizon The intended duration of a plan.

Although most organizations operate with planning horizons of five years or more, it would be inaccurate to infer from this that they undertake major planning exercises only once every five years and then "lock in" a specific set of goals and strategies for that period. Most organizations have an annual planning cycle, which is usually linked to their annual financial budget (even though a major planning effort may be undertaken only every few years).

Although a corporate- or business-level plan may extend over five years (or more), it is typically treated as a *rolling plan,* a plan that is updated and amended every year to take into account changing conditions in the external environment. Thus, the time horizon for an organization's 2025 corporate plan might be 2025, but it might be reviewed and amended in 2021, 2022, 2023, and 2024. The use of rolling plans is essential because of the high rate of change in the environment and the difficulty of predicting competitive conditions five years in the future. Rolling plans allow managers to make any mid-course corrections that environmental changes warrant or to change the thrust of the plan altogether if it no longer seems appropriate. The use of rolling plans allows managers to plan flexibly, without losing sight of the need to plan for the long term.

STANDING PLANS AND SINGLE-USE PLANS

Another distinction often made among plans is whether they are standing or single-use plans. Managers create standing and single-use plans to help achieve an organization's specific goals. *Standing plans* are used in situations where programmed decision making is appropriate. When the same situations occur repeatedly, managers develop policies, rules, and **standard operating procedures (SOPs)** to control the way employees perform their tasks. A **policy** is a general guide to action; a **rule** is a formal, written guide to action; and an SOP is a written instruction describing the exact series of actions that should be followed in a specific situation. For example, an organization may have a standing plan about the ethical behaviour of employees. This plan includes a *policy* that all employees are expected to behave ethically in their dealings with suppliers and customers; a *rule* that requires employees to report any gift worth more than 50 dollars that is received from a supplier or customer; and an *SOP* that obliges the recipient of the gift to make the disclosure in writing within 30 days.

standard operating procedures (SOPs) (1) Written instructions describing the exact series of actions that should be followed in a specific situation; (2) Rules and policies that standardize behaviours.
policy A general guide to action.
rule A formal, written guide to action.

In contrast, *single-use plans* are developed to handle nonprogrammed decision making in unusual or one-of-a-kind situations. Examples of single-use plans include *programs* (integrated sets of plans for achieving certain goals) and *projects* (specific action plans created to complete various aspects of a program). For instance, NASA is working on a major program to launch a rover in 2020 to investigate a specific environment on the surface of Mars. One project in this program is to develop the scientific instruments to bring samples back from Mars.

SCENARIO PLANNING

One of the most difficult aspects of making plans is predicting the future, which can be very uncertain. In the face of uncertainty, one of the most widely used planning techniques is scenario planning.

Scenario planning (also known as *contingency planning*) is the generation of multiple forecasts of future conditions followed by an analysis of how to respond effectively to each of those conditions.

scenario planning The generation of multiple forecasts of future conditions followed by an analysis of how to respond effectively to each of those conditions; also called *contingency planning*.

Scenario planning generates "multiple futures"—or scenarios of the future—based on different assumptions about conditions that *might prevail* in the future, and then develops different plans that detail what a company *should do* in the event that any of these scenarios actually occur. Managers use scenario planning to generate different future scenarios of conditions in the environment. They then develop responses to the opportunities and threats facing the different scenarios and create a set of plans based on these responses. The great strength of scenario planning is its ability not only to anticipate the challenges of an uncertain future but also to educate managers to think about the future—to think strategically.[10]

Traditional forecasting and budgeting systems produce linear projections insufficient for risky, uncertain times. What's needed is scenario planning, where companies stress-test their strategies and processes against a wide range of future scenarios to identify their vulnerabilities. Thus informed, the companies can adjust them to be more responsive and resilient. But scenario planning often takes a backseat to more immediate concerns, such as developing new products, fighting an aggressive competitor, and meeting earnings targets. So when large-scale external events hit, their impact is seismic.[11]

Apple apologized in 2017 for intentionally slowing down the operating systems of older iPhones.
Mark Dierker/McGraw-Hill Education

CRISIS MANAGEMENT

In many cases, managers cannot predict the conditions that might give rise to a contingency plan. In cases where unpredictable and unforeseeable conditions prevail, usually a disaster that can seriously damage the organization is in the making. The degree to which the organization can recover from such a crisis largely hinges on how transparent and open the top managers are with the stakeholders. **Crisis management plans** are formulated to deal with possible future crises.[12] Management crisis software can help formulate a response that minimizes the potential damage to reputation and consumer confidence that comes along with a disaster. Several companies have faced crises that had to be managed for damage control (see Figure 4.5).

crisis management plans Plans formulated to deal with possible future crises.

As we discussed earlier, determining the organization's mission and goals is the first step of the planning process. Once the mission and goals are agreed upon and formally stated in the corporate plan, they guide the next steps in determining which strategies are appropriate for the current competitive environment.[13]

We now turn to an in-depth examination of the each of the steps in the planning process.

FIGURE 4.5

Notable Corporate Responses to Crisis Management

1. Johnson & Johnson's response to the case of tampered Tylenol is widely cited as the gold standard response to a crisis. In 1982, in Chicago, seven people died after taking extra-strength Tylenol that had been laced with cyanide. The company yanked the product off the shelves across the United States. It would ultimately introduce three-way, tamper-proof pill bottles. Within a year, Tylenol had regained its market share.

2. In March 2007, the president of Canadian pet food company Menu Foods apologized to pet owners amid a recall of products found to contain Chinese-supplied wheat gluten laced with poisonous melamine. Company shares dropped following deaths of cats and dogs. Executives were asked to take pay cuts, and the company downsized its workforce after millions of packages of pet food were recalled and dozens of lawsuits were launched. The recall cost Menu Foods an estimated $55 million.*

3. After a massive data breach that impacted up to 70 million people, the CEO of Target resigned, leaving the Chief Marketing Officer to write to all employees via LinkedIn that "The Truth Hurts," and "The culture of Target is an enormous strength and might be our current Achilles heel."

4. After being sued by thousands of its independent-contractor drivers, Uber retaliated for the negative press coverage by digging up dirt on reporters who covered Uber unfavourably, which led to a 14-part Twitter apology by Uber management.**

5. In December 2017, Apple apologized and admitted to intentionally slowing down older iPhones, which resulted in a global class action suit against the company.***

Sources:
*Parts one and two: CBC Licensing. "How Maple Leaf Foods Is Handling the Listeria Outbreak." Website:www.cbc.ca/money/story/2008/08/27/f-crisisresponse.html. Accessed Nov. 13, 2008.
**Parts three and four: "The Top 10 Organizational Culture Crises of 2014." http://switchandshift.com/the-top-10-organizational-culture-crises-of-2014.
***Part five: "Apple's Apology for iPhone Software Glitch May Soothe Ill Feelings." https://www.ctvnews.ca/business/apple-s-apology-for-iphone-software-glitch-may-soothe-ill-feelings-1.2024317. Accessed Jan 17, 2018.

TIPS FOR MANAGERS

Planning

1. Vision matters because it serves as a source of inspiration and motivation for the stakeholders of the organization. Craft the vision statement so that it reflects what the organization is striving to achieve. For example, the vision of a food bank may be "to end hunger."

2. Operationalize the vision by breaking it down into a mission—a statement of purpose of the organization. For example, the mission of the food bank may be "feeding hungry people in our community."

3. Further break down the mission into a series of cascading relating goals and objectives. For example, the goal may be "to have enough resources to feed those who need the food bank's services for six months." A related objective may be "keeping a one-week supply of food, having enough staff and volunteers to meet unexpected increases in demand, and increasing funding levels by 10 percent above the previous year's budget."

4. If each objective is met, then the broad goal of "having enough resources" is likely to be achieved and the organization is fulfilling its mission.

Steps in the Planning Process

LO2 | Describe planning as a five-step process.

In most organizations, planning is a five-step process (refer to Figure 4.1). The first step is *determining the organization's vision, mission, and goals.* The second step involves analyzing the forces in the organizational environment to determine where the opportunities lie and how to counter any threats. Managers use several techniques to *analyze the current situation,* two of which, SWOT and Porter's Five Forces analysis, we examine in this chapter. The third step is *formulating strategy.* Managers analyze the organization's current situation and then conceive and develop the strategies necessary to attain the organization's mission and goals. The fourth step is *implementing strategy.* Managers decide how to allocate the resources and responsibilities required to implement the chosen strategies among individuals and groups within the organization.[14] The last step is *evaluation.* How does a manager know if the strategy was successful? In subsequent sections of this chapter, we look in detail at the specifics of each of these steps.

Defining the Vision, Mission, and Goals

DETERMINING THE VISION

A vision statement reveals the big picture of the organization, its dream for the future. What is the long-term outcome or change the organization wants to achieve? Vision differs from other forms of organizational direction setting in several ways:

> A vision has clear and compelling imagery that offers an innovative way to improve, which recognizes and draws on traditions, and connects to actions that people can take to realize change. Vision taps people's emotions and energy. Properly articulated, a vision creates the enthusiasm that people have for sporting events and other leisure time activities, bringing that energy and commitment to the workplace.[15]

The organization's vision is generally set by the founder and CEO. When Sandhra Khan started Sandy's Bike Shop, his vision was "a sustainable, healthy, fun mode of transportation for all."

See Appendix B for more examples of vision statements.

SETTING THE MISSION

The organization's mission is supposed to flow from the vision for the organization. As noted previously, a mission statement is a broad declaration of an organization's overriding purpose; this statement is intended to identify an organization's products and customers, as well as to distinguish the organization in some way from its competitors.

To determine an organization's mission, managers must first *define its business* so that they can identify what kind of value they will provide to customers. To define the business, managers must ask three questions[16]: (1) Who are our customers? (2) What customer needs are being satisfied? and (3) How are we satisfying customer needs? Answering these questions helps managers identify not only what customer needs they are satisfying now but also what needs they should try to satisfy in the future and who their true competitors are. All of this information helps managers determine the mission and then establish appropriate goals. Amazon's purpose hasn't changed since founder Jeffrey P. Bezos published the first letter to shareholders in 1997 where he promised to create the earth's most customer-focused company for three primary market segments: consumers, sellers, and enterprises.[17]

ESTABLISHING MAJOR GOALS

Once the business is defined, managers must establish a set of primary goals to which the organization is committed. A **goal** is a desired future outcome that an organization strives to achieve within a specified time frame. Generally, the goals are set based on the vision and mission of the organization. Once the mission and goals are agreed upon and formally stated in the corporate plan, they guide the next steps by defining which strategies are appropriate and which are inappropriate.[18] A goal of Campbell's Soup is to expand into high-growth markets. At the corporate level this translates into expanding internationally to China and Indonesia. At the business level, they aim to compete in new market segments such as fresh food and simple organic meals for children, thereby differentiating their brand from other processed food companies.[19]

> **goal** A desired future outcome that an organization strives to achieve within a specified timeframe.

Developing organizational goals gives the organization a sense of direction or purpose. Thus, as we showed in this chapter's opening case, Microsoft is committed to serving its customers in a very challenging environment. The best statements of organizational goals are ambitious—that is, they stretch the organization and require that all its members work to improve its performance.[20] The role of **strategic leadership,** the ability of the CEO and top managers to convey a compelling vision of what they want to achieve to their subordinates, is important here. If subordinates buy into the vision, and model their behaviours on the leader, they develop a willingness to undertake the hard, stressful work that is necessary for creative, risk-taking strategy making.[21] Many popular books, such as *Built to Last,* provide lucid accounts of strategic leaders establishing "big, hairy, audacious goals (BHAGs)" that serve as rallying points for their subordinates.[22]

> **strategic leadership** The ability of the CEO and top managers to convey a compelling vision of what they want the organization to achieve to their subordinates.

Other elements of effective goals are represented by the acronym "SMART + C."[23] See Figure 4.6. To be effective, goals should be *specific*, not vague; be *measurable*—that is, quantifiable whenever possible; be *attainable*; be *realistic*; fall within an appropriate *time frame*; and be *communicated* to all stakeholders. Although goals should be challenging, they should also be realistic. Challenging goals give

FIGURE 4.6

Qualities of Good Goal Formulation: Make Them SMART + C

	Qualities of Good Goal Formulation
S	Specific
M	Measurable
A	Assignable (Achievable, Attainable, Action-oriented, Acceptable, Agreed-upon, Accountable)
R	Realistic (Relevant, Result-oriented)
T	Time-related (Timely, Time-bound, Tangible, Traceable)
C	Communicated

managers at all levels an incentive to look for ways to improve organizational performance, but a goal that is clearly unrealistic and impossible to attain may prompt managers to give up.[24]

The period in which a goal is expected to be achieved should be stated. Time constraints are important because they emphasize that a goal must be reached within a reasonable period; they inject a sense of urgency into goal attainment and act as a motivator.

After determining the vision, mission and goals, the next step is to analyze the current environment to determine the strengths and weaknesses of the company and the opportunities and threats that top managers must navigate to achieve their vision and mission. We now turn to step 2.

Analyzing the Environment

LO3 | Explain how managers use planning techniques to evaluate the opportunities and threats in the organization's environment and formulate strategy.

Strategy formulation includes analyzing an organization's current situation and then developing strategies to accomplish the organization's mission and achieve its goals.[25] Strategy formulation begins with managers analyzing the factors within an organization and outside—in the industry-specific and general environments—that affect or may affect the organization's ability to meet its current and future goals. Several techniques can be used to analyze the organization's environment, including *SWOT analysis* and the *Five Forces model.* Once the environmental forces are analyzed for opportunities and threats, decisions about how to best accomplish the organization's vision, mission, and goals can be made. These decisions translate into strategies that managers pursue at the corporate, business, and functional levels.

strategy formulation Analysis of an organization's current situation followed by the development of strategies to accomplish the organization's mission and achieve its goals.

SWOT Analysis

SWOT analysis is a planning exercise in which managers identify organizational strengths (S) and weaknesses (W), and environmental opportunities (O) and threats (T). Based on a SWOT analysis, managers at the different levels of the organization select corporate-, business-, and functional-level strategies to best position the organization to achieve its mission and goals (see Figure 4.7).

SWOT analysis A planning exercise in which managers identify organizational strengths (S) and weaknesses (W), and environmental opportunities (O) and threats (T) relative to the competition.

The first step in SWOT analysis is to identify an organization's strengths and weaknesses that characterize the present state of the organization *relative to its competition,* and then consider how the strengths will be maintained and the weaknesses overcome to gain a competitive advantage.

Identifying the strengths of an organization involves an analysis of the things it does well (such as high-quality skills in marketing and in research and development). When conducting a SWOT on a competitor, the manager looks at the internal organizational forces, such as the strategy, resources (assets and people), management competencies, organizational structure, capacity and capabilities, location, trademarks and patents, length of time in business, and source of competitive advantage. When identifying weaknesses, managers look at the internal organizational forces that are done poorly, such as gaps in capabilities, lack of competitive strength, financials (debt to equity, ROI), reputation, level of

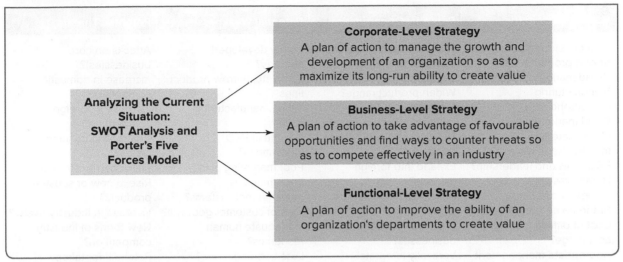

FIGURE 4.7

Environmental Assessment and Strategy Formulation

Analyzing the Current Situation: SWOT Analysis and Porter's Five Forces Model

Corporate-Level Strategy
A plan of action to manage the growth and development of an organization so as to maximize its long-run ability to create value

Business-Level Strategy
A plan of action to take advantage of favourable opportunities and find ways to counter threats so as to compete effectively in an industry

Functional-Level Strategy
A plan of action to improve the ability of an organization's departments to create value

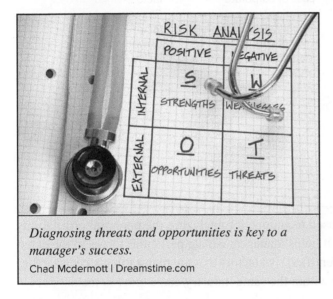

Diagnosing threats and opportunities is key to a manager's success.
Chad Mcdermott I Dreamstime.com

employee morale, outdated technology, and lack of management competencies. As the opening case in this chapter illustrates, a major weakness of Microsoft was to fail to see changes in the computer mobile market and myopically stick to PC operating systems.

The second step in SWOT analysis begins when managers identify potential opportunities and threats in the environment that affect the organization now or may affect it in the future. Examples of possible opportunities and threats that must be anticipated are listed in Table 4.1. Scenario planning is often used to strengthen this analysis.

Opportunities are found in the external organizational environment. Opportunities are chances for increasing market share and growth. Managers look for things in the organizational environment that present such opportunities. Threats are things in the external environment that hinder profitability and growth, such as shifts in market demand and legal and political changes.

When managers are able to identify potential opportunities and threats in their environments that affect the organization at the present and may affect it in the future, they can then consider how best to take advantage of the opportunities for growth and overcome any threats. Nadella, Microsoft's CEO is doing just that.

With the SWOT analysis completed, and strengths, weaknesses, opportunities, and threats identified, managers can continue the planning process and determine industry-specific strategies for achieving the organization's mission and goals. The resulting strategies should enable the organization to attain its goals by taking advantage of opportunities, countering threats, building strengths, and correcting organizational weaknesses.

TABLE 4.1

Questions Managers Ask in a SWOT Analysis

Potential Strengths	Potential Opportunities	Potential Weaknesses	Potential Threats
Well-developed strategy?	Expand core business(es)?	Poorly developed strategy?	Attacks on core business(es)?
Strong product lines?	Exploit new market segments?	Obsolete, narrow product lines?	Increase in domestic competition?
Broad market coverage?	Widen product range?	Rising manufacturing costs?	Increase in foreign competition?
Manufacturing competence?	Extend cost or differentiation advantage?	Decline in R&D innovations?	Change in consumer tastes?
Good marketing skills?	Diversify into new growth businesses?	Poor marketing plan?	Fall in barriers to entry?
Good materials management systems?	Expand into foreign markets?	Poor materials management systems?	Rise in new or substitute products?
R&D skills and leadership?	Apply R&D skills in new areas?	Loss of customer goodwill?	Increase in industry rivalry?
Human resource competencies?	Enter new related businesses?	Inadequate human resources?	New forms of industry competition?
Brand-name reputation?	Vertically integrate forward?	Loss of brand name?	Potential for takeover?
Cost of differentiation advantage?	Vertically integrate backward?	Growth without direction?	Changes in demographic factors?
Appropriate management style?	Overcome barriers to entry?	Loss of corporate direction?	Changes in economic factors?
Appropriate organizational structure?	Reduce rivalry among competitors?	Infighting among divisions?	Downturn in economy?
Appropriate control systems?	Apply brand-name capital in new areas?	Loss of corporate control?	Rising labour costs?
Ability to manage strategic change?	Seek fast market growth?	Inappropriate organizational structure and control systems?	Slower market growth?
Others?	Others?	High conflict and politics?	Others?
		Others?	

The Five Forces Model

Michael **Porter's Five Forces model** is a widely used technique for analyzing the potential profitability of entering and competing in a particular industry. It helps managers isolate particular forces in the external environment that are potential threats. Porter identified five factors that are major threats because they affect how much profit organizations that compete within the same industry can expect to make:

Porter's Five Forces model A technique managers use to analyze the potential profitability of entering and competing in a particular industry.

- *The level of rivalry among organizations in an industry.* The degree of rivalry is the extent of the competition—the amount that companies compete against one another for customers. For example, by lowering the prices of products or by increasing advertising, the lower will be the level of industry profits. Low prices mean less profit. The degree to which firms vigorously compete with one another used to be conceptualized in terms of the entire operation of one firm against another. Recently, as Peter Drucker predicted,[26] firms have begun to swallow their pride and cooperate in specific areas while maintaining fierce competition in others. Automobile manufacturers and airlines have long since adopted these networked strategic alliances to achieve economies of scale by collaborating on vehicle platforms and sharing check-in facilities, but recently industries such as media and courier companies have increased their cooperation, coined **co-opetition** by professors at Yale University.[27] In a 10-year deal, the German-owned parcel-delivery company DHL paid rival American UPS to carry its packages in the United States, Canada, and Mexico in order to reduce its losses in North America while taking advantage of UPS's excess capacity. Even though the two companies cooperated, a UPS executive said "nothing will change the fact that we are a rabid competitor of DHL."[28]

co-opetition Arrangements in which firms compete vigorously with one another, while also cooperating in specific areas to achieve economies of scale.

"Our industry does not respect tradition. It only respects innovation."

Satya Nadella, CEO, Microsoft

- *The potential for entry into an industry.* This refers to how easy it is for another firm to enter the industry. The easier it is for companies to enter an industry—because, for example, **barriers to entry** are low—the more likely it is for industry prices and therefore industry profits to be low. For example, there are huge barriers to entry in the oil and aerospace industries because of the large investment of capital needed to start up and operate. Moreover, brand loyalty protects profits. Industries that rely on the "difficulty of change," such as Microsoft's Windows operating system and drug companies that enjoy long-term patents on proprietary drugs, make it harder for new firms to compete, create large barriers to entry, and thus enjoy a stronger potential for profits.

barriers to entry Factors that make it difficult and costly for a company to enter an industry.

- *The power of suppliers.* If there are only a few suppliers of an important input, then (as discussed in Chapter 2) suppliers can drive up the price of that input, and expensive inputs result in lower profits for the producer. Samsung is Apple's most important supplier in the smartphone and tablet-computer markets. Samsung components, which include all the product's application processors, account for 16 percent of the value of an iPhone. This much reliance on one supplier has Apple searching for ways to diversify its supply chain.[29] The airline industry suffers from threats posed by the suppliers of expensive fuel. As jet fuel prices increase, airlines have little choice but to pay the higher prices.

- *The power of customers.* The bargaining power of your customers is affected by their size and how much revenue they generate for your company. If only a few large customers are available to buy an industry's output, they can bargain to drive down the price of that output. As a result, producers make lower profits. For example, Walmart, as the largest retailer in the global economy, has a huge impact on firms that supply it with goods to sell. If Walmart refuses to carry a company's products, it would be unlikely for the company to become successful in the global economy. Walmart is such a large customer, it purchases so much inventory and accounts for such a large proportion of a supplier's revenue, that most companies will do anything to protect their business with it.

- *The threat of substitute products.* Often, the output of one industry is a substitute for the output of another industry (e.g., plastic may be a substitute for steel in some applications). Companies that produce a product with a known substitute cannot demand high prices for their products, and this constraint keeps their profits low. On the other hand, industries that have few, if any, substitutes can command very high profits as long as there remains a demand for the product. For example, there is no widespread substitute for oil. If gasoline prices go too high, people may switch to hybrid or electric vehicles, or pay the high price because they cannot easily find a substitute for gasoline-powered cars. With clothing, on the other hand, if the price of designer clothing goes up, people

FIGURE 4.8

FIGURE 4.8

Porter's Five Forces Competitive Analysis Summary

Threat	Outcome
Level of rivalry	Increased competition results in lower profits
Potential for entry	Easy entry leads to lower prices and profits
Power of suppliers	If there are only a few suppliers of important items, supply costs rise
Power of customers	If there are only a few large buyers, they can bargain down prices
Substitutes	More available substitutes tend to drive prices and profits lower

Source: Based on Michael E. Porter, "The Five Competitive Forces That Shape Strategy," *Harvard Business Review* (57, 2), 1979, pp. 137–45.

have the option of buying many cheaper no-name brands. When a substitute for their product exists, companies cannot demand very high prices for it or customers will switch to the substitute, and this constraint keeps their profits low.

Porter argued that when managers analyze opportunities and threats, they should pay particular attention to these five forces because they are likely to affect the levels of profitability. See Figure 4.8. It is the job of managers at the corporate, business, and functional levels to formulate strategies to counter

FOCUS ON *The Social Economy*

Prince George Native Friendship Centre

The Prince George Native Friendship Centre (PGNFC) is a social service agency whose goal is to foster community growth by promoting friendship. PGNFC has four meeting rooms which can be rented out and used for community events. Their social enterprise is their Smokehouse Restaurant and Catering Services, which operates an employment training program and bridging program to continuing education.

The Smokehouse Kitchen Training Program provides indigenous participants with practical knowledge, skills, and experience based on Level 1 curriculum leading to employment in the food industry or to access to post-secondary education in a related field. Participants are trained in a full commercial kitchen with a restaurant and catering department that cater events ranging from box-lunch drop-off to full-service in-house catering. In addition, participants receive information workshops to develop employability skills that include career planning, cover letters, interview skills, job search, and networking skills. Students also benefit from a work placement to gain employment experience. The Smokehouse Kitchen Program graduates have the prerequisites to pursue employment or further education in the food service and hospitality industry.

1. Research the PGNFC on the Internet. Identify the organization's vision and mission.

2. Perform a SWOT analysis on PGNFC. What strategies would you recommend the organization pursue to achieve their vision and mission?

Source: Based on http://www.pgnfc.com/programs_services.html. Accessed July 11, 2018.

these threats so that an organization can respond to both its industry-specific and general environments, perform at a high level, and generate high returns and social impact. The Focus on the Social Economy feature illustrates how the Prince George Native Friendship Centre generates high social impact.

Developing Strategy

LO4 | Differentiate among corporate-level, business-level, and functional-level strategies.

Once the environmental forces are analyzed for opportunities and threats, decisions about how to best accomplish the organization's vision, mission, and goals can be made. These decisions translate into strategies that managers pursue at the corporate, business, and functional levels. The development of strategy is the third step in the process.

Corporate-Level Strategy

Corporate-level strategy is a plan of action concerning which industries and countries an organization should invest its resources in to achieve its mission and goals. In developing a corporate-level strategy, managers ask: How should the growth and development of the company be managed in order to increase its ability to create value for its customers (and thus increase performance) over the long run? Managers of most organizations have the goal to grow their enterprises and actively seek out new opportunities to use the organization's resources to create more goods and services for customers. Seeking out new opportunities occurs when companies and their strategies are able to adapt to changing circumstances due to changing forces in the task or general environment. For example, customers may no longer be buying the kinds of goods and services a company is producing (high-salt soup, bulky analogue televisions, or gas-guzzling SUVs), or other organizations may have entered the market and attracted customers away (this happened to Sony after Apple and Samsung began to produce better MP3 players, laptops, and flat-screen LCD televisions). Top managers aim to find corporate strategies that can help the organization strengthen its business-level strategies and thus respond to these changes and improve performance.

The principal corporate-level strategies either help a company grow, maintain it when its on top of its industry, or helps it retrench and reorganize in order to stop its decline. Common corporate-level strategies are *concentration on a single business; diversification; vertical integration;* and *international expansion.* Corporate-level plans contain decisions relating to the organization's mission, strategy, and structure that increase the value to customers and other stakeholders by either (1) lowering the costs of developing and making products, or (2) increasing product differentiation so that more customers want to buy the products even at higher or premium prices. Both of these outcomes strengthen a company's competitive advantage and increase its performance. In **franchising,** a company (the franchiser) sells to another organization (the franchisee) the rights to use its brand name and operating know-how in return for a lump-sum payment and share of the franchisee's profits. The advantage of franchising is that the franchiser does not have to bear the development costs of expansion and avoids the many problems associated with setting up operations. The downside is that the organization that grants the franchise may lose control over how the franchisee operates, and product quality may fall. In this way franchisers, such as Tim Hortons, Avis, and McDonald's, risk losing their good names. Canadian customers who buy Tim Hortons coffee and Timbits in the Philippines may reasonably expect the products to be as good as the ones they get at home. If they are not, Tim Hortons' reputation will suffer over time. The advantage of using the franchising strategy domestically, as do Giant Tiger and Home Hardware Stores, is that the franchisees know their communities and can tailor the products they sell to meet their customers' needs in a way that corporate-owned store expansion cannot.

> **franchising** A corporate-level strategy that licenses the rights to use the brand name and trademarks of the franchiser to an independent owner (the franchisee) in exchange for a lump-sum payment and a percentage of sales.

Business-Level Strategy

Michael Porter, the researcher who developed the Five Forces model, also developed a theory of how managers can select a business-level strategy—a plan to gain a competitive advantage in a particular market or industry. Porter argued that business-level strategy creates a competitive advantage because it allows an organization (or a division of a company) to *counter and reduce* the threat of the five industry forces. That is, successful business-level strategy reduces rivalry, prevents new competitors from entering the industry, reduces the power of suppliers or buyers, and lowers the threat of substitutes—and this raises prices and profits.[30] According to Porter, managers must choose between the two basic ways of increasing the value of an organization's products: higher quality or lower costs. Porter also argues that managers must choose between serving the whole market or serving just one segment or part of a market. Given those choices, managers choose to pursue one of four business-level strategies: *cost-leadership, differentiation,* and *focused low-cost* or *focused differentiation* (see Table 4.2).

COST-LEADERSHIP STRATEGY

With a **cost-leadership strategy,** managers try to gain a competitive advantage by focusing the energy of all the organization's departments or functions on driving the organization's costs down below the costs of its rivals. This strategy means manufacturing managers must search for new ways to reduce production costs, R&D managers must focus on developing new products that can be manufactured more cheaply, and marketing managers must find ways to lower the costs of attracting customers. According to Porter, organizations following a low-cost strategy can sell a product for less than their rivals and still make a profit because more customers will be attracted to their lower costs. Thus, organizations that pursue a low-cost strategy hope to enjoy a competitive advantage based on their low prices. Giant Tiger pursues a cost-leadership strategy as it offers extremely low prices every day on a broad assortment of products, including clothing and accessories for women, men and children, housewares and groceries.

> **cost-leadership strategy** Driving the organization's costs down below the costs of its rivals.

TABLE 4.2

Porter's Business-Level Strategies

Strategy	Number of Market Segments Served	
	Many	**Few**
Cost-leadership	√	
Differentiation	√	
Focused low-cost		√
Focused differentiation		√

DIFFERENTIATION STRATEGY

With a **differentiation strategy,** managers try to gain a competitive advantage by focusing all the energies of the organization's departments or functions on distinguishing the organization's products from those of competitors in one or more important dimensions, such as product design, quality, or after-sales service and support. For instance, Canada's oldest confectionary, Ganong Bros. Ltd., based in St. Stephen, New Brunswick, is a small player in the Canadian chocolate market. It differentiates itself from bigger chocolate makers by focusing on innovative products. In the 1890s the company was one of the first, if not the first, Canadian confectioner to produce a lollipop. In 1910, the family owner-managers began experimenting by sprinkling nuts into their own brand of milk chocolate, and shaping the product into long narrow pieces. They created the first chocolate nut bar in the world, which they began mass producing and selling.[31] Best Buy Co. Inc. aims to woo shoppers with more personalized service. Best Buy's customer-centric strategy allowed the company to differentiate its offerings from those of gargantuan Walmart, as well as rivals Giant Tiger and Amazon.

> **differentiation strategy** Distinguishing an organization's products from the products of competitors in dimensions such as product design, quality, or after-sales service.

Often, the process of making products unique and different is expensive. This strategy, for example, often requires managers to increase spending on product design or R&D to make the product stand out, and costs rise as a result. However, organizations that successfully pursue a differentiation strategy may be able to charge a *premium price* for their products, a price usually much higher than the price charged by a low-cost organization. The premium price allows organizations pursuing a differentiation strategy to recoup their higher costs. Coca-Cola, PepsiCo, and Procter & Gamble are some of the many well-known companies that pursue a strategy of differentiation. They spend enormous amounts of money on advertising to differentiate, and create a unique image for, their products. Also, differentiation makes industry entry difficult because new companies have no brand name to help them compete and customers don't perceive other products to be close substitutes, so this also allows for premium pricing and results in high profits.

"STUCK IN THE MIDDLE"

According to Porter's theory, managers cannot simultaneously pursue both a cost-leadership strategy and a differentiation strategy. Porter identified a simple correlation: Differentiation raises costs and thus necessitates premium pricing to recoup those high costs. According to Porter, managers must choose between a cost-leadership strategy and a differentiation strategy. He says that managers and organizations that have not made this choice are "stuck in the middle." According to Porter, organizations stuck in the middle tend to have lower levels of performance than do those that pursue a low-cost or a differentiation strategy. To avoid being stuck in the middle, top managers

Brick Brewing offers both Laker, a low-cost brand, and expensive premium lagers, showing that low-cost and differentiation strategies can be used successfully by the same firm.

Courtesy of Brick Brewery Co. Ltd., www.brickbeer.com

must instruct departmental managers to take actions that will result in either low cost or differentiation in formulating functional-level strategies.

However, exceptions to this rule can be found. In many organizations, managers have been able to drive costs down below those of rivals and simultaneously differentiate their products from those offered by rivals.[32] For example, Toyota's production system is reportedly the most efficient in the world. This efficiency gives Toyota a low-cost strategy vis-à-vis its rivals in the global car industry. At the same time, Toyota has differentiated its cars from those of rivals on the basis of superior design and quality. This superiority allows the company to charge a premium price for many of its popular models.[33] Thus, Toyota seems to be simultaneously pursuing both a low-cost and a differentiated business-level strategy. Brick Brewing Company Limited follows a cost-leadership strategy with its lowest priced brand, Laker, while simultaneously brewing award-winning premium-priced brands. These examples suggest that although Porter's ideas may be valid in most cases, very well-managed companies, such as Toyota and Brick Brewery, have both low-cost and differentiated products.

FOCUSED LOW-COST AND FOCUSED DIFFERENTIATION STRATEGIES

Both the differentiation strategy and the cost-leadership strategy are aimed at serving most or all segments of the market. Porter identified two other business-level strategies that aim to serve the needs of customers in only one or a few market segments.[34] A company pursuing a **focused low-cost strategy** serves one or a few segments of the overall market and aims to be the lowest-cost company serving that segment. In the last decade, the global soft-drink environment has undergone a major change because of Gerald Pencer, a Canadian entrepreneur who came up with a new strategy for competing against powerful differentiators in the soft drink industry—Coke and Pepsi. Pencer's strategy was to produce a high-quality, low-priced cola, manufactured and bottled by the Cott Corporation, of which he was CEO at the time, but to sell it as the private-label house brand of major retail stores such as Walmart (Sam's Cola brand) and supermarket chains such as Kroger's (Big K brand), thus bypassing the bottlers. Pencer could implement his *focused low-cost* strategy and charge a low price for his soft drinks because he did not need to spend any money on advertising (the retail stores did that) and because Cott's soft drinks are distributed by the store chains and retailers using their efficient national distribution systems, such as the nationwide trucking system developed by giant retailer Walmart. Retailers are willing to do this because Cott's low-cost soft drinks allow them to make much more profit than they receive from selling Coke or Pepsi. At the same time, the products build their store-brand image. By 2004, Cott was the world's largest supplier of retailer-branded carbonated soft drinks.[35] It has manufacturing facilities in Canada, the United States, and the United Kingdom, and a syrup-concentrate production plant in Columbus, Georgia, which supply most of the private-label grocery store, drugstore, mass-merchandising, and convenience store chains in these countries. However, note that while Cott is the leading supplier of retailer-branded sodas, it is still focusing on its low-cost strategy. It makes no attempt to compete with Coke and Pepsi, which pursue differentiation strategies and whose brand-name soft drinks dominate the global market.

> **focused low-cost strategy** Serving only one segment of the overall market and being the lowest-cost organization serving that segment.

By contrast, a company pursuing a **focused differentiation strategy** serves just one or a few segments of the market and aims to be the most differentiated company serving that segment. BMW, for example, pursues a focused differentiation strategy, producing cars exclusively for higher-income customers. By contrast, Toyota pursues a differentiation strategy and produces cars that appeal to consumers in almost *all* segments of the car market, from basic transportation (Toyota Corolla) through the middle of the market (Toyota Camry) to the high-income end of the market (Lexus).

> **focused differentiation strategy** Serving only one segment of the overall market and trying to be the most differentiated organization serving that segment.

As these examples suggest, companies pursuing either of these focused strategies have chosen to specialize in some way—by directing their efforts at a particular kind of customer (such as serving the needs of babies or affluent customers) or even the needs of customers in a specific geographical region (customers on the east coast or the west coast).

Functional-Level Strategy

A functional-level strategy is a plan of action to improve the ability of an organization's departments to create value that is consistent with the business-level and corporate-level strategies. It is concerned with the actions that **functional managers** of individual departments (such as manufacturing or marketing **functions**) can take to add value to an organization's goods and services and thereby increase the value customers receive.

> **functional managers** Managers who supervise the various functions—such as manufacturing, accounting, and sales—within a division.
>
> **functions** Units or departments in which people have the same skills or use the same resources to perform their jobs.

There are two ways in which departments can add value to an organization's products:

1. Departmental managers can lower the costs of creating value so that an organization can attract customers by keeping its prices lower than its competitors' prices.

2. Departmental managers can add value to a product by finding ways to differentiate it from the products of other companies.

For instance, the marketing and sales departments at Molson-Coors create value by building brand loyalty and finding more effective ways to attract customers. And as discussed previously, General Electric's Lighting division's strategy to drive costs down might translate into a functional-level plan for the manufacturing department to "reduce production costs by 20 percent over three years." The functional-level strategy to accomplish this might include investing in state-of-the-art production facilities and developing an electronic global business-to-business network to reduce the cost of inputs and inventory-holding costs. Each organizational function has an important role to play in lowering costs or adding value to a product or service (see Table 4.3).

Cott Corporation offers a focused low-cost strategy.
©Joshua Blake/Getty Images

> **TABLE 4.3**

Examples of Functional-Level Strategies

Department or Functional Area	Ways to Lower the Cost of Creating Value (Low-Cost Advantage)	Ways to Add Value (Differentiation Advantage)
Sales and marketing	• Find new customers • Find low-cost advertising methods	• Promote brand-name awareness and loyalty • Tailor products to suit customers' needs
Materials management	• Use just-in-time inventory system/computerized warehousing • Develop long-term relationships with suppliers and customers	• Develop long-term relationships with suppliers to provide high-quality inputs • Reduce shipping time to customers
Research and development	• Improve efficiency of machinery and equipment • Design products that can be made more cheaply	• Create new products • Improve existing products
Manufacturing	• Develop skills in low-cost manufacturing	• Increase product equity and reliability
Human resource management	• Reduce turnover and absenteeism • Raise employee skills	• Hire highly skilled employees • Develop innovative training programs

Implementing and Evaluating Strategy

LO5 | Describe how managers implement strategy and evaluate its success.

Strategy Implementation

After conducting a SWOT analysis and analyzing the forces in the organization's industry using Porter's Five Forces model, managers formulate appropriate strategies at the corporate, business, and functional level that support the organization's vision, mission, and goals. The next step in the planning process, *implementation*, now confronts managers with the challenge of how to put those strategies into action. Strategy implementation is a five-step process in itself:

1. Allocating responsibility for implementation to the appropriate individuals or groups.
2. Drafting detailed action plans that specify how a strategy is to be implemented.
3. Establishing a timetable for implementation that includes precise, measurable goals linked to the attainment of the action plan. A **Gantt chart** can be used to manage the project.[36] A Gantt chart is a graphic bar chart managers use to schedule tasks in a project showing what tasks need to be done, who will do them, and by what time frame they will be completed.
4. Allocating appropriate resources to the responsible individuals or groups.
5. Holding specific individuals or groups responsible for reaching corporate, divisional, and functional goals.

Gantt chart A graphic bar chart managers use to schedule tasks in a project showing what tasks need to be done, who will do them, and by what timeframe.

The planning process goes beyond the mere identification of strategies; it also includes actions taken to ensure that the organization actually implements its strategies. Normally the plan for implementing a new strategy requires the development of new functional strategies, the redesign of an organization's structure, and the development of new control systems; it might also require a new program to change an organization's culture.

Evaluating Strategy

The last step in the process of planning is evaluating whether or not the strategy has been successful in achieving the major goals set out in Step One. How do managers know when they are successful?

In evaluating the success of a strategy, managers must monitor progress, evaluate performance levels, and make corrective adjustments if there is a substantial gap between the goal and the actual performance. This is essentially the *control process* more fully discussed in Chapter 11. Managers monitor and measure actual performance levels and compare the results with the initial goal for a particular strategy. If the business-level strategy is to position the company as the low-cost leader in the industry, managers must assess the market to determine if it has achieved that position and determine what role it has been playing within the industry and how well it is performing on key financial metrics, such as return on investment and other financial indicators. How can managers determine if the organization is achieving its goals and performance targets? A gap analysis can be performed to determine if there is a significant enough deviation between major goals and actual performance levels from following a particular strategy. If there is a significant gap, corrective action must be taken and strategy revisited. See Figure 4.9.

FIGURE 4.9

Strategy Evaluation Framework

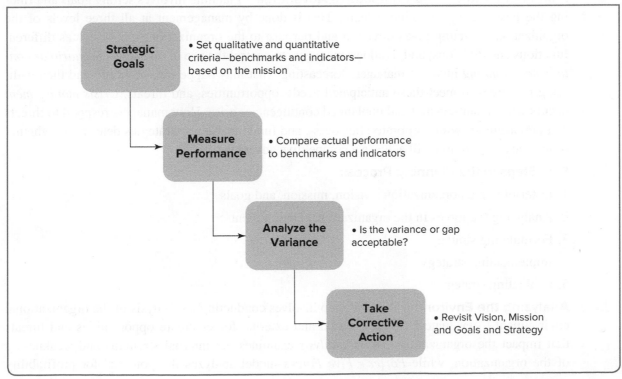

For example, following a corporate-level strategy of international expansion, CIBC decided to enter the U.S. retail banking market by putting branches in grocery stores. But after about a decade of losses, amounting to hundreds of millions of dollars, the strategy was abandoned. CIBC largely pulled out of the United States after this strategy failed. Instead, CIBC bought a stake in a troubled Irish bank. Looking overseas to expand internationally may be motivated, in part, by its disastrous venture into the United States.[37] Campbell's Soup Company did an about-face after it lost its competitive advantage to General Mills when the latter began offering a more health-conscious line of soup in the early 2000s. Campbell's responded to this threat by realigning its products to meet the changing nutrition needs of consumers. Among the changes, it reduced the amount of sodium in soups. But, sales were sluggish and CEO Denise Morrison reversed the low-sodium strategy to try to regain market share. Premium Select Harvest soups had sodium levels raised to 650 milligrams from 480 milligrams a serving.[38]

When goals are unmet, strategy must be rethought in such a way as to stay true to the vision and mission of the organization. This is exactly what Microsoft must do to remain competitive in the computing industry.

Chapter 4

SUMMARY AND REVIEW

connect

LO1 Planning, Strategy, and Competitive Advantage Planning involves setting goals and finding the best strategy to achieve them. This is done by management at all three levels of the organization. Planning gives direction and purpose to the organization; it coordinates different functions and divisions; and, it allows managers to control the use of resources. *Scenario or contingency planning* involves managers forecasting what may happen in the future and then gathering resources to meet these anticipated needs, opportunities, and threats. *Crisis management* occurs when unanticipated and unplanned contingencies arise. How managers respond to threats and opportunities with corporate-, business-, and functional-level strategies determines whether or not the organization will achieve a competitive advantage.

LO2 Five Steps in the Planning Process

1. Determining an organization's vision, mission, and goals
2. Analyzing the forces in the organizational environment
3. Formulating strategy
4. Implementing strategy
5. Evaluating strategy

LO3 Analyzing the Environment This step involves conducting an analysis of the organizational environment to evaluate how the internal and external forces create opportunities and threats that impact the organization. *SWOT analysis* examines the internal strengths and weaknesses of the organization, while *Porter's Five Forces* model analyzes the potential for profitability within a particular industry by looking at the degree of competitive rivalry, the ease of entry, the power of buyers, the power of suppliers, and the threat of substitute products. Managers use these techniques to evaluate what strategy would gain them a competitive advantage in the current environment.

LO4 Developing Strategy   At the *corporate level,* organizations use strategies such as franchising to help increase the value of the goods and services provided to customers. At the *business or divisional level,* managers are responsible for developing a low-cost or differentiation strategy, either for the whole market or for a particular segment of it (focus strategy). At the *functional level,* departmental managers try to add value to the product or service by differentiation or increasing efficiencies by reducing costs. All levels of strategy support the mission of the organization.

LO5 Implementing and Evaluating Strategy   These steps require managers to allocate responsibilities to individuals or groups, draft detailed action plans that specify how a strategy is to be implemented, establish a timetable for implementation that includes specific measurable goals, allocate necessary resources, and hold the individuals or groups accountable for reaching goals. Managers monitor the progress of goal achievement and make corrective adjustments when strategies fail to accomplish the organization's mission and goals.

KEY TERMS

barriers to entry
business-level plan
business-level strategy
co-opetition
corporate-level plan
corporate-level strategy
cost-leadership strategy
crisis management plans
differentiation strategy
focused differentiation strategy
focused low-cost strategy
franchising
functional managers
functional-level plan
functional-level strategy
functions

Gantt chart
goal
mission statement
planning
policy
Porter's Five Forces model
rule
scenario planning
standard operating procedures (SOPs)
strategic leadership
strategy
strategy formulation
SWOT analysis
time horizon
vision statement

WRAP-UP TO OPENING CASE

Microsoft CEO Satya Nadella Looks to Future Beyond Windows

Nadella's accession to CEO of Microsoft would be a chance to reorient the company, getting it to introduce products that looked outside Windows and to develop new business models.

After having read and understood the concepts in this chapter, you should now be able to answer the following questions:

1. *What kind of planning missteps helped cause Microsoft's decline over the past few years?*

   ANSWER: Microsoft relied too much on its Windows operating system and failed to move into new markets, like mobile. Key products such as Microsoft Office—the suite of applications that includes Word and Excel—had been designed around Windows, with only parts converted to work on Apple's iOS and Google's Android systems.

2. *How is Nadella trying to eliminate some of the bureaucracy that has hurt the company's ability to innovate?*

   ANSWER: Nadella told employees at a town hall that they should skip meetings if they don't really need to be there. And he's advised workers to come to him directly if they feel the bureaucracy is stifling. Nadella also changed the way engineering teams are structured, eliminating testers to speed up software releases and adding data scientists and designers to the teams. He's looking at cutting some middle managers to make decisions faster and to eliminate layers of bureaucracy.

3. *What business strategies has Nadella implemented that will help revitalize the technology giant?*

   ANSWER: Microsoft bought two small companies that focus on mobile productivity apps and released a new dashboard for data analysis. Nadella uses the Power BI dashboard to track and compile huge amounts of information on product usage and financial performance to see what works and what doesn't. Nadella also measures and coordinates executive performance with metrics from the dashboard.

MANAGEMENT IN ACTION

TOPICS FOR DISCUSSION AND ACTION

LEVEL 1 Knowledge & Comprehension

1. Describe the five steps in the planning process. Explain how they are related.
2. Discuss the levels of plans, the time horizons of plans, the difference between standing and single-use plans, and why planning is important. What are the qualities of effective plans?
3. Describe scenario planning. How can scenario planning help managers predict the future?

LEVEL 2 Application & Analysis

4. Ask a manager to identify the corporate-, business-, and functional-level strategies used by his or her organization.

5. Go to the Porter Airlines Web site. Identify the airline's mission. What type of business-level strategy is it pursuing? Give evidence to support your answer.

6. Go to the Bombardier Web site. Identify the vision, mission, and major goals for the company. What is the business-level strategy of its largest division?

LEVEL 3 Synthesis & Evaluation

7. Research a well-known company that you can easily find information about. What is the main industry that the company competes in? Apply Porter's Five Forces model to this industry to determine its potential for profitability.

8. Present an argument for having lower-level managers participate in the company's strategic planning process. What might happen if they were to have no input?

9. Research two firms in the same industry, and perform a competitive SWOT analysis. What type of business-level and functional-level strategies would you recommend for the firms, and why?

SELF-REFLECTION EXERCISE

Think ahead to five years from now to consider what it is that you might like to be doing with your life. Develop your own vision and mission statements. Establish a set of goals that will help you achieve your vision and mission.

Develop a SWOT analysis for considering what you want to be doing in five years. What are your strengths and weaknesses? What are the opportunities and threats in carrying out this plan?

Develop a five-year plan that maps out the steps you need to take in order to get to where you want to be in your life at that time.

SMALL GROUP BREAKOUT EXERCISE

Form groups of three or four, and appoint one member as the spokesperson who will communicate your findings to the class when called on by the instructor. Then discuss the following scenario:

You are a team of management consultants hired by a grocery store chain to plan the feasibility of opening a store in your community. You must answer all the questions below and report back to your clients.

1. List the major supermarket chains in your city, and identify their strengths and weaknesses relative to one another. What opportunities and threats exist for each chain?

2. What business-level strategies are these supermarkets currently pursuing?

3. What kind of supermarket strategy would do best against the competition?

4. What would you recommend to your clients, and why?

MANAGING ETHICALLY EXERCISE

A major department store has received repeated criticism for selling clothes that are produced at low cost in developing countries. The CEO of the department store knows that suppliers are paying 5 percent better than the going rate of wages in these countries and feels that this is fair enough. Working conditions at suppliers' factories are no worse than at other factories in those countries. The CEO has come to you to check her assumptions that as long as the suppliers are buying from manufacturing plants that have better-than-average working conditions for the country where the company is located, nothing further needs to be done. What would you advise her? How would you justify your advice?

MANAGEMENT CHALLENGE EXERCISE
Beyond the Green Door

The Green Door is a vegetarian restaurant in Ottawa with a focus on providing local organic food that is wholesome and comforting.[39] The restaurant is situated directly across from Saint Paul University[40] (part of the University of Ottawa and home to about 1000 undergraduate and graduate students in such disciplines as spirituality, philosophy, human sciences, pastoral counselling, and conflict studies). OttawaPlus.ca considers The Green Door the "heaven for vegetarians" and an Ottawa institution.[41]

1. Name some vegetarian restaurants in the city where you live. Do a SWOT analysis as to their strengths and weaknesses.
2. Look up reviews of The Green Door on the Internet. If The Green Door wanted to expand, what kind of business-level strategy should it pursue?

MANAGEMENT PORTFOLIO PROJECT

Answer the following questions about the organization you have chosen to follow:

1. Identify the vision, mission, and major goals of the organization.
2. What is the corporate-level strategy of the company?
3. What is the business-level strategy of the company?
4. Have the strategies supported the vision and mission? How so?
5. Has there been a significant shift in strategy over the past decade? If yes, describe it, and try to determine why the organization made the changes.
6. How successful is the organization's planning process?

MANAGEMENT CASE

STOPPING GLOBAL WATER SHORTAGES

How much water did it take to manufacture the outfit you are wearing right now? The textile industry has a huge water footprint. First, it takes water to grow cotton, the material that accounts for 90 percent of the textile industry's use of natural fibres.[42] One estimate suggests that 1500 litres of water are needed to produce each cotton T-shirt.[43] The farming of cotton accounts for 2.6 percent of annual global water usage and is the largest water consumption factor in the supply chain of the textile industry.[44] And it's not just quantity. Cotton production has a direct impact on water quality through the use of pesticides, herbicides, and fertilizers.

Second, problems continue beyond the growing of raw materials. The textile industry uses and pollutes water while dyeing fabrics. It can take more than 22 litres of water to dye one T-shirt. The polyester apparel industry alone uses 8.8 trillion litres of water a year.[45] The process of treating, rinsing, and dyeing fabric accounts for about 20 percent of the world's industrial water pollution.[46] Dye houses in China and India have been accused of overusing local water supplies as well as dumping toxic wastewater into local waterways.[47] In response to concerns about the use and pollution of water to make fabric and garments, several manufacturers have sought no-water and reduced-water ways of working in their supply chains.

In 2014 Levi Strauss & Co. made more than 100 000 pairs of jeans using 100 percent recycled water in China. This batch alone saved about 11 million litres of water in addition to the 750 million litres the company's Water<Less jeans brand had already saved.[48] The company also plans to retrofit facilities in Nicaragua and South Asia to recycle water in the production process.

Nike and Adidas also are cutting back on water use in their supply chains by using an innovative process that dyes polyester without using water or chemicals. The process, developed by DyeCoo Textile Systems in the Netherlands, dyes fabric by turning carbon dioxide into a liquid by putting it under extreme pressure. As the carbon dioxide cools, it turns back into a gas that can be recycled and used again.[49] The first garment produced by Nike using the process was the running singlet worn by Kenyan marathoner Abel Kirui in the 2012 Olympics. The company began selling products manufactured using the process in 2014 under the name Nike ColorDry.[50] Adidas also started waterless dyeing in 2012, producing a limited collection of 50 000 T-shirts with the Yeh Group, which owns a textile mill in Thailand. A full line of "DryDye" apparel is now available around the world.[51]

Nike COO Eric Sprunk said, "NIKE, Inc., innovates not only in the design of our products but also in how they are made. We see sustainability and business growth as complementary, and our strategy is to prioritize relationships with factory groups that demonstrate a desire to invest in sustainable practices and technologies. Our collaboration with Far Eastern and DyeCoo, to develop and scale the ColorDry process, is an important milestone on our path toward manufacturing innovation."[52]

1. Describe the strategy in this case.

END OF PART II: CONTINUING CASE

CARROT TOPS: BUILDING A COMPETITIVE ADVANTAGE

As the population grew, so too did the competition. Pretty soon it was apparent that Mac's Milk and Shoppers Drug Mart were able to offer customers a wider selection of lower-priced grocery products than Mel's store. Mel had to find a new way to manage his small business if it was going to survive. He began brainstorming new strategies. He researched trends in the food industry. There might be a niche for supplying specialty products, he thought, such as organic and gourmet foods, which were more profitable to sell. He would no longer be competing against giants like Shoppers. He changed the name of his store to Carrot Tops and stocked it with a wide variety of gourmet Canadian food products. He began to offer fine foods, local cheeses, fresh bread, organic fruits and vegetables. Finding a reliable source of products from local farmers and producers could be a stumbling block to his success, but he did have Janet Khan to head up produce procurement and logistics.

His plan worked. Customers loved his new upscale supermarket concept. The premium products he had chosen to stock sold quickly. Realizing that he needed to capitalize on his success to protect his growing business, Mel continually expanded the variety of premium organic foods and drinks he sold. Taking advantage of the popularity of the name Carrot Tops, he began to offer his own store-label products. Today, more than 80 percent of the products Carrot Tops sells sport its own label. Every product adheres to sustainable environmental production practices.

To compete in the premium-quality segment of the supermarket business and keep customers buying high-priced organic products, Carrot Tops needed to provide excellent customer service. Mel provided training and support. The store employees feel valued by Mel and provide excellent customer service and develop personal relationships with customers, who are often on first-name terms. Mel feels really good about the approach Carrot Tops is taking toward its stakeholders. He is considering formalizing a Code of Ethics to guide new employees and introduce them to the culture of the organization.

Drawing on all segments of this case:

1. Identify the mission of Carrot Tops.

2. Identify the stakeholders and their issues in this case.

3. What threats and opportunities exist in the task and general environments for Carrot Tops? Recommend how Mel should deal with them.

4. How would you characterize the Carrot Tops approach to ethics and social responsibility?

Appendix B

Developing a Business Plan

The Business Plan as an Exercise in the Processes of Management[1]

Writing a business plan may never be a more important exercise than in the context of today's rapidly changing environment. Even if you are not an entrepreneur and do not wish to develop a new original idea and bring it to market, developing a business plan is still a valuable exercise in practising the management processes. It provides a crucial foundation for managing an organization. In this section of the text, we will treat developing a business plan as an exercise in the management processes of planning, organizing, leading, and controlling. By doing the exercises at the end of each chapter, you will have the foundation to put together a plan that will help you develop as a manager. The experience you will gain is valid for profit and not-for-profit organizations as well as new and existing ventures. Writing a business plan gives you practice in thinking about managing activities such as:

- Developing an idea to solve a problem
- Tapping into opportunities and countering threats in competitive conditions
- Organizing resources to achieve goals
- Targeting potential customers with promotional opportunities
- Designing an effective organizational structure
- Securing sources of finance
- Controlling for risk

What Is a Business Plan?

A business plan is a recognized management tool used to document the organization's objectives and to set out how these objectives will be achieved within a specific time frame. It is a written document that describes who you are, what you intend to accomplish, how you will organize resources to attain your goals, and how you will overcome the risks involved to provide the anticipated returns. In general, a business plan comprises several elements, each giving the reader a piece of the overall picture of the project you are undertaking, and provides convincing reasons why you will be successful in this undertaking. Managers and entrepreneurs use a business plan to seek support and financing to expand an existing business or to finance a new venture.

TABLE B.1

Major Business Plan Components

	Check off and date when completed and add any notes of interest
1. Nondisclosure Statement	☐
2. Executive Summary	☐
3. Profile of the Organization	☐
4. Profile of the Industry or Sector	☐
5. Profile of the Product or Service	☐
6. Marketing Plan	☐
7. Organizational Plan	☐
8. Operating and Control Systems Plan	☐
9. Financial Plan	☐
10. Appendices	☐

Putting It All Together

Throughout this course, you may have been asked to complete the end-of-chapter exercises on developing a business plan. Now is the time to start to put all the pieces together to create your comprehensive plan. Draw on the work that you have already done to write the major components of the business plan. See Table B.1.

At this point, you should familiarize yourself with a business planning software package. There are several on the market. Your professor will instruct you as to which is appropriate for your course.[2] The software will help you compile the main elements in your plan and calculate the financial statements.

1. Nondisclosure Statement

A nondisclosure statement is optional in a business plan. When used, it usually states that the information in the plan is proprietary and not to be shared, copied, or disclosed. The agreement should have a unique "copy number" that is the same as a number on the title page of the plan and a place for the recipient's signature. The agreement should be either a loose-leaf page or a page that can be torn out of the plan and retained by you.

2. Executive Summary

The executive summary is the first thing, besides the Table of Contents and title page, that the reader will view, but it is generally the last thing the writer creates. The executive summary is a maximum one-page précis of your business plan. It is probably the most important part of your plan because readers will use it to make a judgment as to whether or not they want to continue to examine your plan. The executive summary tells the reader the following information:

• Who you are and what your company/organization does

• The products and/or services that you provide or intend to provide

- Your target markets; that is, who are or will be your customers
- How you will promote your product/service to your customers
- What your financial projections are for a given period
- How you will achieve your goals, that is, your strategy for gaining a competitive advantage
- The strengths of your management team and why the reader should believe you can do what you are proposing
- The major risks you expect and your solutions to minimize these threats

The executive summary should be no longer than one page.

3. Profile of the Organization

This section of the business plan tells the reader your vision, mission, and goals for the organization. Consider the following questions when preparing this section.

- What is the name of your company/organization?
- What is the legal structure and form of ownership?
- What are your reasons for going into business?
- What problem does your product or service solve, or what needs gap does it fill?
- What experience do you have that would enable you to pursue this venture successfully?
- Who makes up your management team, and what roles and responsibilities will they have?

VISION STATEMENT

The vision for your company or organization is set out in a written statement telling the reader what direction or change you wish your company to pursue for the next three to five years. Write this statement in the future tense. See Chapter 4 for examples of what should be included in your venture's vision statement. The vision statement should convey an idea of the future state or end-goal that drives your organization's work. For example, a food bank may have the vision of "A world without hunger." It is a broad statement that contains no specific course of action on how to achieve the desired state.

   Refer to the business planning exercise you did for Chapter 4: Managing Planning and Strategy on Connect. Write the vision statement for your venture. Keep it short and sweet.

MISSION STATEMENT

The mission statement tells the reader what the purpose of your company or organization is. Refer to Chapter 4 for examples of mission statements. Ask yourself what the essence of your business is. What will the business really be doing? Why does it exist? What values is it premised on? Every noun, adjective, and verb in the statement is important and should explain the problem that will be solved or the need that will be fulfilled if your plan is implemented. Your mission statement should reflect your basic beliefs, values, and principles. You must include what product or service you offer, how you will provide it to your customers or clients, and who your target market is (in a general sense). For example, the mission statement for a restaurant venture whose vision is to bring gourmet vegan cuisine into everyday life might look like this: "Karma Foods caters to people who want to make a conscious decision to eat well and minimize their impact on the planet by serving fresh, organic, vegan cuisine." The food bank whose vision is "a world without hunger" may have as it's mission statement, "ABC Food Bank provides healthy food to families in need within its community."

- Refer to the value statement and code of ethics you created for the Business Planning exercise you did in Connect Online for Chapter 3: Managing Decision Making. Incorporate these values and principles into your mission statement.
- Refer to the mission statement you wrote for the Business Planning exercise you did in Connect Online for Chapter 4: Managing Planning and Strategy.

Write the mission statement for your venture. Keep it to 50 words or fewer.

ORGANIZATIONAL GOALS

Organizational goals must be made for the business as a whole and for each functional area. Organization-wide goals are longer term and are strategic in nature, while functional-level goals are shorter term and are more operational in nature. For example, corporate- and divisional-level goals are generally made in the areas of market share, profitability, and return on investment. Functional-level goals include how departments will add value for the customer and reduce costs in the production of a good or service. Goals and objectives are statements of the level of performance desired within a certain time frame. Goals must be formulated so that they are S.M.A.R.T plus C:

- **S**pecific
- **M**easurable
- **A**ttainable
- **R**ealistic, within a
- **T**ime frame
- Plus **C**ommunicated to the relevant stakeholders.

An example of a SMART goal relating to market share might look like the following:

> *"By the end of the first year of operation, ABC company will have a 20-percent market share for its product, XYZ."*

MEC might formulate the goal of . . .

> *"...giving 5 percent of gross profits to the major charitable organizations in the environmental movement by the year 2022."*

This goal must be consistent with the company's mission and strategic vision, as stated above. ABC Food Bank may also set a goal of having enough food to service its community for a two-week period. Once goals are developed, plans must be formulated to achieve the objectives. These plans are generally referred to as strategies. The formulation of strategies depends upon the opportunities and threats facing your company from the forces in the organizational environment. You will formulate your strategy after doing an analysis of the current situation. The competitive analysis and strategy is analyzed in the context of the industry as a whole and detailed in the Marketing Plan component of the business plan.

Formulate the major goal for the venture as a whole, using a one-year time frame.

FORM OF OWNERSHIP

If you are writing a business plan for an existing organization, the legal entity has no doubt been established already; however, it may make sense to consider a separate legal entity for the new product or service. If you are an entrepreneur or a group of entrepreneurs, you must decide what form of legal entity (form of ownership) will best suit the nature of the business, the competitive strategy, and the organizational structure of the business. Will you need a partner? Should you incorporate or simply operate as a sole proprietor? What advantages, if any, would there be in forming a cooperative structure? Refresh your memory about the advantages and disadvantages of each legal structure by reviewing an introductory business textbook. Now that you have developed your ideas and business plan up to this point, describe the legal form of your organization.

Which legal structure do you think is most appropriate, and why?

THE MANAGEMENT TEAM

At the beginning of a new venture, the principal person who writes the business plan generally has overriding authority over the other members of the management team, if a team exists at all. In the case that several people are involved in the management team, the positions they will hold and roles they will play should be described and justified on the basis of their experience and expertise.

Provide a brief biography[3] of each member of the management team, and describe their roles and responsibilities in the venture.

4. Profile of the Industry or Sector

Industries are classified and coded according to specific criteria that are common across North America. The North American Industrial Classification System (NAICS)[4] (pronounced "Nakes") is used to codify industries and sectors. It is useful to know which NAICS code, and hence which industrial group, applies to your venture to research the changing trends from the forces acting in its organizational environment (Chapter 2). For example, if your business plan is to start a family restaurant, you would find that this type of venture is part of the Accommodation and Food Services Industry, NAICS 72211. From there, you can research the active forces within the industry that are providing opportunities for growth or proving to be a threat to your venture. Use Porter's Five Forces model to analyze the threats to profitability within the industry (Chapter 4). Information on changing industrial trends can be found from Statistics Canada and industry associations. For our family restaurant example, we could go to the Restaurants Canada Web site to learn about industry trends.[5] From this site, we learn that people's favourite way to spend time with friends and family is by going to a restaurant together. Statistics on the profit margins in the food services industry show they are relatively unchanged at around 4.3 percent.[6] Statistics showing trends in the industry either support your business plan or tell the reader the type and severity of the risks involved in investing in this industry. If the trend in the industry is toward contraction, rather than expansion, you have to tell the reader how you intend to deal with the risks.

Describe the trends in the industry and whether or not they pose an opportunity for growth or a threat to the profitability of your venture. State how you will minimize the potential risks.

5. Profile of the Product/Service

This part of the business plan provides the reader with a complete overview of all the products and services you will offer.

PRODUCT OR SERVICE DESCRIPTION

It is important to stress to the reader the uniqueness of your offering. What will you provide or do that is different from your competitors? Why would consumers purchase your product or service over someone else's?

Describe in as much detail as possible the uniqueness of the product or service you will be offering.

REGULATIONS, LICENCES, AND PERMITS

All businesses in Canada are subject to regulations at various levels of government. Consult BizPal,[7] a Web site designed to help businesses figure out all the regulations they must comply with and the permits and licences that are necessary to operate their venture. If you have developed a prototype of an original product or a modification of an existing product, you should apply for a patent and/or protection of your intellectual property. This can be done online at http://strategis.ic.gc.ca/sc_mrksv/cipo/welcome/welcom-e.html.

Describe the permits and licences that are required for your venture. Factor the costs into your financial plan projections.

FUTURE PRODUCT DEVELOPMENT/INNOVATION

In this section, tell the reader how you expect your product or service offering to change in the future. Do you have plans for expansion? Will you bring new products and services on board, and when? How will you sustain your growth once the business reaches maturity? Give the reader a sense of how you will end the venture. Do you intend to sell the venture, franchise, or dissolve the company?

Describe your future product development and exit strategies.

6. Marketing Plan

This part of the business plan includes an analysis of your venture's strengths and weaknesses relative to your competition (SWOT) as well as an analysis of the four Ps in the marketing mix: product, place (distribution channels), price, and promotion. Detailed research must be gathered on who will buy the product or service; what the potential size of the market is and whether there is potential for growth; the prices that should be charged; the distribution channel and the most effective promotion strategy to reach the target market.

SWOT ANALYSIS

Referring to the SWOT analysis you did in Chapter 4, identify your strengths and weaknesses relative to one major competitor. Direct competitors can be found by searching the Yellow Pages and the Web sites of associations, trade magazines, chambers of commerce, and Statistics Canada. Things to compare might include:

Strengths	Weaknesses
• Resources (assets/people)	• Gaps in capabilities
• Experience	• Reputation
• Diversity	• Poor customer responsiveness
• Location and hours of operation	• Resources (assets/people)
• Sustainability strategy	• Inexperience
• Quality of product/service	• Lack of quality

Opportunities	Threats
• Market demand/changing trends	• Legal /political
• Competitors' vulnerabilities	• Demographic trends
• Partnerships	• Competitive advantages
• Innovation	• Barriers to entry
• Competitive advantages	• Suppliers

STRATEGIES FOR A COMPETITIVE ADVANTAGE

After completing the SWOT analysis relative to your competition and remembering the analysis of the industry you did in section 4, you are now ready to articulate the kind of strategy that will gain you a competitive advantage. Refer to Chapter 4. Will you adopt a cost-leadership or a differentiation strategy? How will you focus that strategy?

Describe the business-level strategy you intend to use to gain a competitive advantage.

TARGET MARKET PROFILE(S)

Which segment of the market will buy your product or service? Demographic characteristics such as age, income, geographic location, and buyer behaviour need to be researched and documented. This is usually done through conducting focus groups, giving surveys, interviewing potential market segments, and through observing and recording pre- and post-purchase behavioural habits of customers. Association Web sites and Statistics Canada[8] are good sources of data, including the 2016 census.

For each market segment, create a customer profile by researching the following:

- Demographic questions
- Customer attitudes on price and quality
- Where customers currently buy the product/service
- Where customers wish to buy the product/service
- The influence of advertising
- How much of the product/service the customer buys and how often
- Why the customer buys this product/service

Characteristics of the Customer	Customer Profile for Your Venture's Product/Service/Offering	Potential for Growth/Trends	Source/Reference
Demographic information			
Frequency of purchase			
No. of units purchased yearly			
Price sensitivity			
Lifestyle/personality			
Advertising influences			
Motivation			
Buying decisions based on:			
Other			

Describe your target market(s).

PRICING

Before setting the price of your product or service, you must evaluate your costs per unit, what the markup should be, and what the competition charges for a similar product or service. Cost of goods should include material and labour overhead (utilities, rent, insurance, salaries), and costs from suppliers. You must add up the costs based on an estimate of the volume of sales. Markups or margins in your industry can be found by reading a trade journal or by asking the suppliers. The markup usually includes a degree of profit that represents the industry standard. Industry standards can be found from Statistic Canada, association Web sites, and organizations such as Dun & Bradstreet.[9]

If you plan to increase market penetration by using pricing specials or volume discounts, you should describe them. Before deciding to discount in order to undercut the competition and gain market share, you should consider that the competition could also lower its prices and therefore reduce the profit margins for everyone.

If you adopt a differentiation business-level strategy for your product or service, you may be able to justify charging more than the competition. To do this, you will offer customers a product or service that is unique and/or of better quality such that people will pay the higher price relative to the competition.

Describe your pricing strategy and how that compares with the competition.

DISTRIBUTION (PLACE)

How will you make it convenient for your customers to access your product or service? The market conditions, attributes of the product or service, cost benefits, and characteristics of the venture should all be considered when deciding on a channel of distribution. It may be appropriate to sell directly to the customer or to a retailer if the target market is concentrated in a particular geographic area. If not, it may be appropriate to use a distributor or wholesaler. If the product is large, bulky, perishable, hazardous, or expensive, the rule of thumb is to channel the product through direct sales. If the cost of indirect sales (using a middle person such as a retailer or wholesaler) is minimal and the benefit is great in terms of reaching a dispersed market, it may be more appropriate to channel indirectly. And finally, if the venture has great financial strength, multiple channels may be considered.

If you intend to use dealers or distributors, discounts or commissions will be required and should be described.

Describe your distribution strategy.

When deciding on a *location* for your facilities, you must consider how much space you will need for the operation and whether or not the facility will be accessible to the consumer (direct sales). If you are considering purchasing or renting a building, further criteria may become relevant: Is it zoned for commercial use? Is it in need of renovation? Is there potential for expansion? Is there ample parking? What is the cost per square foot? How many competitors are in the area? Other criteria may be relevant to your location decision. Compare two or three sites against your criteria to come up with the best location for your venture.

Criteria	Site X	Site Y	Site Z
Cost per square foot			
Parking			
Accessibility			
History of the building			
Number of competitors in the area			
Zoning laws			
Potential for expansion			
Features of the area (specify)			
Other (specify)			

Describe the location of your venture.

PROMOTION

The success of your venture will largely depend on your promotional plan. Advertising, public relations, and Internet marketing are common ways of promoting your organization to your target market. Consider that each market segment may require different promotional activities. Also consider the degree to which your target market is influenced by advertising. Would a slogan be appropriate to capture the vision of your organization or capitalize on the uniqueness of your product or service?

Develop a slogan and/or logo that promotes the image you want to project about your organization/product/service.

Decide whether you will "pull" or "push" your promotions. Things to consider include:

- The pull strategy requires direct contact with the customer. This requires a major commitment to advertising. The objective is to attract the customers to every channel outlet for your product or service. If enough customers demand your product, the channels will want to carry it. The price and quality of your product is important here.

- The push strategy requires less investment in advertising. The push strategy maximizes the use of all available channels of distribution to "push" the offering into the marketplace, usually by giving large discounts or commissions as incentives to the channels to promote the offering. Research must be done into the channel discount requirements and the relationship that the competition has with the channel.

Create a list of public relations, social media activities, and types of advertising that you can undertake to generate awareness of your venture in your target market(s). Expected returns include the audience reached and how this exposure will benefit you. Include the costs of the promotion plan in the financial plan section of the business plan.

Promotional Activity	Date and Contact Person	Cost and Length of Run	Expected Returns
Send a press kit with your company's profile, pictures, and press releases to newspapers and trade journals			
Host an open house			
Go to a trade show			
Write letters to the editors of various papers			
Develop a company Web site			
Social media blog			
Register with search engines			
Banner ads			
Billboard ads			
Radio/TV ads			
Other			

Write your promotional strategy for each market segment.

7. Organizational Plan

This section provides a description of the organizational structure, culture, and human resources plan for your venture.

ORGANIZATIONAL STRUCTURE

When designing the *organizational structure,* some things to consider are:

- How should similar jobs be grouped together into units or departments?
- Who should be accountable to whom to ensure the coordination of activities?
- How many levels of authority are needed?

The relationships that jobs have with one another are depicted in an organizational chart. The organizational chart shows the positions of all members. Refer to the Business Planning exercise in Connect Online for Chapter 5, Managing Organizational Structure.

Draw an organizational chart for year one of your venture.

ORGANIZATIONAL CULTURE

The organizational structure creates the foundation for the coordination of work that needs to be done. But finding the right mix of people to assume the responsibilities outlined in the structure is just as critical to the success of the organization as having a marketable product.

When building *organizational culture,* the founder and management team will foster the values and principles embodied in your vision and mission statements. The desired culture must be consistently role-modelled for employees. It must be deliberately embodied in the symbols and practices of the organization if it is to be successful.

Describe the values, principles, and norms that underlie your organizational culture.

HUMAN RESOURCES MANAGEMENT PLAN

The objective of human resources planning is to match the right people to the right job at the right time. This section of the business plan provides the reader with a job analysis of the key positions and how the management will recruit, select, train, appraise, and compensate employees. Things to consider are:

- What kinds of labour (specifications) are needed to fulfill the duties of the positions (descriptions)?
- How will they be recruited?
- What selection techniques will be used to determine the best candidates?
- What kind of training and development will be offered?
- How will you know if they have learned the jobs?
- What levels of pay and pay structures will you offer that are consistent with the strategy of the venture?

JOB ANALYSIS

In conducting a job analysis for the venture, consult Chapter 7 as well as industry and association Web sites to determine what you need to include for each position. Consider the degree of enrichment you build into each job as a motivating factor.

For each position in the organizational chart, research and write a job description and a set of job specifications.

RECRUITMENT

Where will you find the employees you need for your venture? Is there a need for highly specialized/qualified human resources? If so, determine if there will be a shortage in supply for those positions in the first year of operation.

Make a list of the external sources of potential applicants for each position.

SELECTION

What methods will you use to pick the most qualified and best-suited applicant for a position? The techniques you use, such as interviews, ability testing, background checks and so on must be valid and reliable.

Describe the selection techniques you will use to hire new employees and why they are valid and reliable.

TRAINING AND DEVELOPMENT

Once you have offered a candidate a job, you must orient and train them in the roles and responsibilities of the position. Referring to Chapter 7, determine what types of training and development programs are suitable for each position.

Describe the types of training you will provide for each position.

PERFORMANCE APPRAISALS

In order to determine if the employee has learned how to do the job, their performance levels must be appraised by management. The Human Resources Plan section of the business plan should describe how performance appraisals will be conducted and in what time frame.

How will employee performance appraisals be conducted and feedback given?

PAY AND COMPENSATION

Research the pay levels and structures for the types of occupations you need for your venture. Industry standards can be found from Statistics Canada.[10] The amount of pay you offer should be consistent with the *strategy* you have adopted. For example, if our family restaurant intends to differentiate itself from the competition by focusing on high-income households as a target market, it makes sense that it can pay its waitstaff higher wages than if it adopted a cost-leadership strategy focusing on low-income households. Generally, if the competitive advantage is derived from superior quality, customer service, and innovation, higher than industry wages can be paid. If, on the other hand, the competitive advantage is derived from efficiency, lower than standard industry wages generally will be paid.

Will you offer wages at, above, or below the industry standards? Justify your answer in terms of the strategy of the venture.

8. Operating and Control Systems Plan

This section of the business plan describes the flow of goods and services from the input stage, through the conversion stage, and in the post-production stage. Standards must be set for the use of resources at every stage and control measures implemented to ensure that the standards are being met. This involves an analysis of the whole supply chain. In particular, a supplier analysis, an inventory control analysis, and an assessment of how the goods will flow to the customer must be considered, whether the venture is a retail operation, a service provider, or a manufacturer.

RETAIL OPERATION OR SERVICE PROVIDER

If your venture is a retail operation or a service provider, you should consider the following questions:

1. From whom will merchandise be purchased?

   • Consider the supplier's reputation, past record, prices versus other suppliers, delivery methods, whether or not it supplies your competitors, and how important your business is to it.

2. How will the inventory and quality control system operate?
   - Consider how you will inspect the goods received and what you will do if materials are defective.
   - What are your storage and processing space needs?
   - What is your ordering materials process?
3. How will the goods flow to the customer?
   - What steps are involved in a business transaction?
   - What technology (debit machines, scanners) will you need to serve customers effectively?

Referring to Chapter 11, create standards for each phase of the operation, and describe what methods of control you will use to ensure they are met.

	Standard/Goal	Control Measures
Supplier analysis		
Inventory and quality control		
Flow of goods to customers		
Customer satisfaction		

MANUFACTURING OPERATION

If you are proposing a manufacturing operation, you should describe the complete operations management process. Some of the issues will be the same as above, but some will be different. In the *supplier analysis* area, you would include how much, if any, of the manufacturing process is subcontracted out to another firm. Who will perform such work, and how will you decide what to outsource and what operations to keep in-house? What specialized machinery and equipment is needed, and who will supply this? What are the capital equipment needs and expenditures? Include the costs in your financial plan and a full list of equipment in the appendices. In analyzing the *flow of goods,* illustrate the layout and all the steps in the production process.

Both service providers and manufacturers should have standards set for being responsive to customers. For example, a goal for customer service might be, "100-percent satisfaction or your money back guaranteed!" Enterprises must build in feedback control measures that allow customers to complain and praise the service and/or products, such as questionnaires and surveys.

Describe the risks that could arise in managing the operations of the venture and how you can minimize them.

9. Financial Plan

The financial plan tells the reader what level of potential investment commitment is needed and whether or not the business plan is feasible. It details the needed capital requirements for starting the venture, or new strategy, the forecast sales, and the expenses incurred in selling the product/service over a number of months and years.

Anyone reading your financial projections will want to know what assumptions went into the creation of the projections. This includes assumptions about, for example, the size of the market and your ability to penetrate it, staffing plans, management salaries, inventory turnover, receivables and payables periods, and expectations for investment or loans.

Refer to the business planning exercise for Chapter 11: Managing Control and an accounting textbook to help you calculate the financial statements for your venture for a period of two years. Or simply follow the instructions in a business planning software program. This will create the spreadsheets for your plan.

PRO FORMA INCOME STATEMENT

The income statement subtracts all the costs incurred to operate your enterprise from the amounts received from selling goods and services. The result is a net income or a net loss for the year. You will be asked to enter revenue and expenses for each month of the first year, and for each quarter of the second year.

CASH FLOW PROJECTIONS

The cash flow statement will show the amount of cash you have available at any given time during your business plan. If a negative cash balance occurs, you will have to examine your revenue and expense projections. To address the negative cash balance, you will have to increase revenues, decrease expenses, or arrange to get cash through a loan or capital investment. Cash flow is projected for each month of the first year and for each quarter of the second year.

PRO FORMA BALANCE SHEET

The balance sheet is divided into two sections: assets and liabilities plus shareholders' equity. The two sections must always be in balance. A dollar amount or a "balance" represents each asset, liability, and component of shareholders' equity reported in the balance sheet. The balance sheet is projected for each month of the first year and for each quarter of the second year.

BREAK-EVEN ANALYSIS

The projection of when the revenue will surpass the expenses of the venture is called the break-even point and is generally depicted graphically.

ALTERNATIVE SCENARIOS

When presenting your business plan to an investor or to your management, it is of value to show projections for revenues and expenses that represent the best possible case and the worst possible case. It is recommended you provide some explanation for the circumstances that might precipitate either the best or worst case in the financial assumptions section.

Create a pro forma income statement, a cash flow statement, a balance sheet, and a break-even analysis for your business plan.

10. Appendices

The appendix of the business plan generally contains all the documents that are referenced in the plan itself and any backup material that is not necessary in the text of the document. You might consider including the following:

- Product/service samples
- Market research data
- Legal forms and documents
- Leases or contracts
- Price lists from suppliers, if applicable
- Promotional material examples
- Resumés of the management team
- Other backup material

Part III

Organizing

Managing Organizational Structure

LEARNING OUTCOMES

LO1	Identify the elements involved in designing organizational structures.
LO2	Explain how managers arrange tasks to create jobs that are motivating and satisfying for employees.
LO3	Describe how managers cluster jobs into departments and units.
LO4	Explain the ways that managers allocate authority and decision-making responsibilities.
LO5	Evaluate the factors that managers consider when deciding on a formal or flexible overall structure.

MACEWAN BOOKSTORE - CC
10700 - 104 AVE
EDMONTON   AB

CARD   * * * * * * * * * * * *3771
CARD TYPE   INTERAC
ACCOUNT TYPE
                 FLASH DEFAULT
DATE   2023/01/05
TIME   0012 12:20:41
RECEIPT NUMBER
 H84067120-001-088-087-0

REFUND
TOTAL

         $78.50

Interac
A0000002771010010000000003
CD7FF85627EE0D3A
8080008000-

APPROVED

AUTH# 142041   00-001
THANK YOU

        CARDHOLDER COPY

OPENING CASE

Samsung Reorganizes for the 21st Century

From a humble beginning as a noodle maker in 1938 in Korea, Samsung has grown to become Asia's largest conglomerate, comprising 83 individual networked companies held under an umbrella company called Everland, with products ranging from transistor radios to insurance and credit card services. Similar to General Electric in the United States, the Samsung Group conglomerate is in dozens of unrelated industries. The largest company within the network, Samsung Electronics Co. Ltd., is a leader in electronics technology, making more televisions, memory chips, and LCD flat screens than any other company in the world. Within Samsung Electronics, there were traditionally two main product groups—Digital Media and Communications, and Device Solutions—with 10 operating divisions.

In 2010, Samsung reorganized the company structure to give more autonomy to each business division by eliminating the Global Business Manager (GBS) layer responsible for overseeing the major product divisions.[1] The reorganization replaced the "two business group structure with seven independent companies under a single corporate entity."[2] Prior to the change, business units did not control their own budgets—they didn't even have their own balance sheets and income statements.[3] The change gave the business divisions independence to act as standalone companies with their own president and CFO. Each product division head now reports directly to the newly created executive position—the COO for all divisions. The new COO, who happened to be the heir apparent to the empire, would help expedite decision making, improve efficiency, and mediate between business units. This model is used by many multinational corporations. The management hierarchy went from three to two levels, increasing the speed of decision making and shortening the time to market for new products.

Steve Marcus/Newscom

In terms of sales, Samsung Electronics galloped to the front of the pack, yet the company is diversifying away from consumer electronics before the low profit margins, falling prices, and fast product cycles take the company's profits down.[4] Believing that green technologies will drive future growth, Chairperson Lee Kun-hee told his executives in 2011, "The majority of our products today will be gone in ten years."[5] Accordingly, the company plans to invest $20 billion over the next decade in five new industries: solar panels, LED lighting, electric vehicle batteries, healthcare and medical devices, and biotech drugs. To be successful in these new endeavours, Samsung realizes it has to partner with startups in each industry. For example, in healthcare, Samsung has partnered with Canadian company AdvancedCare.com to collaborate on telehealth and remote patient monitoring systems.

These new businesses move Samsung away from electronic products toward green technology and health care products that it believes will be in high demand in the 21st century, even though in 2017 mobile phones and semiconductors were its most important source of income, moving it up to sixth place in global brand value.[6] Samsung's new organizational structure consists of three main business divisions: Device Solutions Division (DS), Consumer Electronics Division (CE), and IT and Mobile Communications Division (IM), signifying a new structure for a new strategy.[7]

After reading and understanding the concepts in this chapter, you should be able to answer the following questions:

1. How would you characterize Samsung Electronics' organizational structure?
2. How did the changes to Samsung's organizational structure affect the hierarchy of authority and span of control?
3. How is Samsung's strategy related to its structure?

 Overview.

In Part 3, we examine how managers can organize human and other resources to create high-performing organizations. To organize, managers must design a structure that makes the best use of resources to produce the goods and services customers want. They must consider how rapidly the organization's environment is changing to align the strategy and culture with the organizational structure. Managers design organizational structures to fit the factors or circumstances that are affecting the company the most, and causing them the most uncertainty.[8] With rapid changes in the global economy and production techniques, organizational structures are changing to become more responsive to changing conditions. Leaders need to make decisions on how best to adapt and change to remain competitive. The family-owned and controlled Samsung Group has done just that. Our opening case illustrates how a powerhouse company like Samsung Group changed its organizational structure to better fit with its strategy for the 21st century.

By the end of this chapter, you will be familiar with various organizational structures and with the typical factors that determine the organizational design choices that managers make.

> "The majority of our products today will be gone in ten years."
>
> Lee Kun-Hee, Chairperson, Samsung Group

Designing Organizational Structure

LO1 | Identify the elements involved in designing organizational structures.

Recall from Chapter 1 that organizing is the process of establishing the structure of the organization. This includes:

- Arranging tasks to create jobs and a division of labour
- Grouping jobs into departments
- Creating working relationships among employees, teams, and departments
- Distributing authority, accountability, and control over decision making
- Coordinating the efforts of each department and division to achieve organizational goals
- Allocating sufficient resources to enable employees to achieve organizational goals effectively and efficiently

The outcome of organizing is the creation of an **organizational structure,** the formal system of task and reporting relationships that determines how employees use resources to reach organizational goals.[9] Typically, organizational structures are either comprised of brick and mortar departments or divisions, teams (temporary, permanent, face-to-face, or virtual), or networks comprised of business-to-business (B2B) strategic alliances. Examples are illustrated in Figure 5.1. But before we look at the characteristics

organizational structure A formal system of both task and reporting relationships that coordinates and motivates organizational members so that they work together to reach organizational goals.

FIGURE 5.1

Types of Organizational Structures

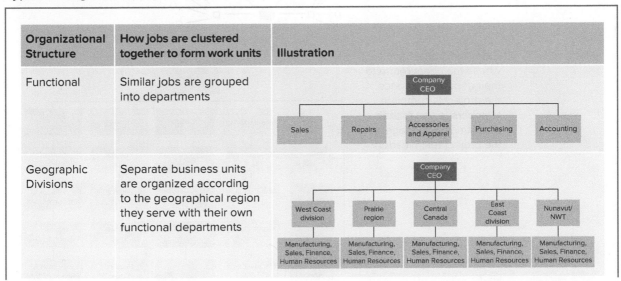

Organizational Structure	How jobs are clustered together to form work units	Illustration
Functional	Similar jobs are grouped into departments	Company CEO → Sales, Repairs, Accessories and Apparel, Purchasing, Accounting
Geographic Divisions	Separate business units are organized according to the geographical region they serve with their own functional departments	Company CEO → West Coast division, Prairie region, Central Canada, East Coast division, Nunavut/NWT — each with Manufacturing, Sales, Finance, Human Resources

(Continued)

FIGURE 5.1

Types of Organizational Structures (*Continued*)

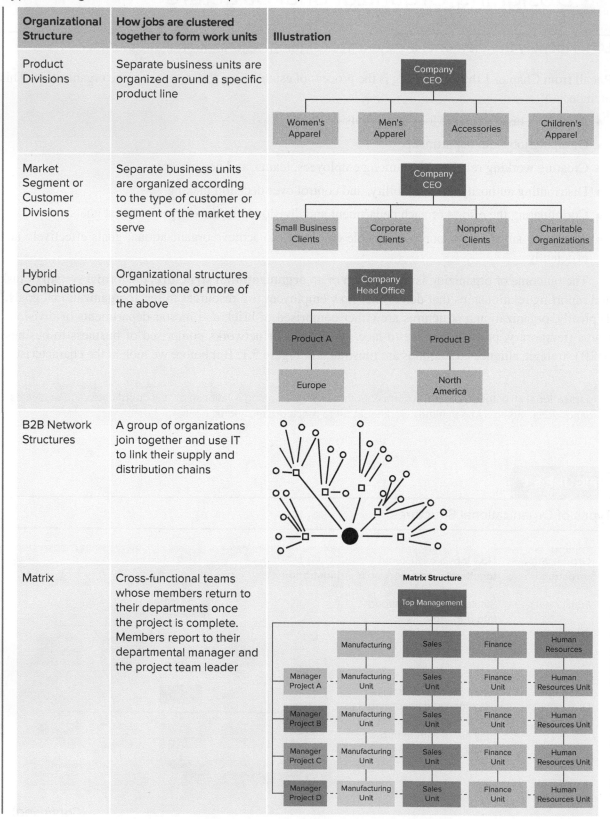

Organizational Structure	How jobs are clustered together to form work units	Illustration
Product Divisions	Separate business units are organized around a specific product line	Company CEO → Women's Apparel, Men's Apparel, Accessories, Children's Apparel
Market Segment or Customer Divisions	Separate business units are organized according to the type of customer or segment of the market they serve	Company CEO → Small Business Clients, Corporate Clients, Nonprofit Clients, Charitable Organizations
Hybrid Combinations	Organizational structures combines one or more of the above	Company Head Office → Product A (Europe), Product B (North America)
B2B Network Structures	A group of organizations join together and use IT to link their supply and distribution chains	
Matrix	Cross-functional teams whose members return to their departments once the project is complete. Members report to their departmental manager and the project team leader	Matrix Structure: Top Management → Manufacturing, Sales, Finance, Human Resources; Manager Project A–D with Manufacturing Unit, Sales Unit, Finance Unit, Human Resources Unit

(Continued)

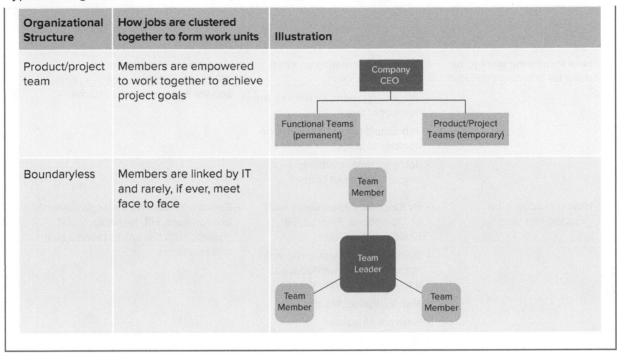

FIGURE 5.1

Types of Organizational Structures (*Continued*)

Organizational Structure	How jobs are clustered together to form work units	Illustration
Product/project team	Members are empowered to work together to achieve project goals	Company CEO → Functional Teams (permanent); Product/Project Teams (temporary)
Boundaryless	Members are linked by IT and rarely, if ever, meet face to face	Team Leader with Team Members

of these organizational structures in detail, we have to understand the kinds of questions managers need to ask when deciding on an appropriate organizational structure.

When managers make decisions about what the organizational structure will be, they are engaged in *organizational design*. **Organizational design** is the process by which managers make specific organizing choices that result in the construction of a particular organizational structure.[10] The questions managers ask and the criteria that provide the answers are outlined in Figure 5.2. Managers design organizational structures with four important elements in mind:

1. How to group tasks into individual jobs that are interesting and motivating for employees.

2. How to group jobs into departments and divisions as organizations grow.

3. How to allocate authority among functional areas and divisions to ensure coordination and integration.

4. Whether to pursue a more formal or flexible structure.

organizational design The process by which managers make specific organizing choices that result in a particular kind of organizational structure.

As the opening case illustrates, a company's organizational design and structure is closely aligned with its strategy and culture. The ability to make the right kinds of organizing choices is often what differentiates effective from ineffective managers and creates a high-performing organization.

FIGURE 5.2

Organizational Design Questions and Answers

Questions to Consider	Design Options	Criteria
How should the work to be done be grouped into jobs?	• Job design: creating an initial division of labour • Job enlargement: increasing the number of tasks • Job simplification: reducing the number of tasks • Job enrichment: adding responsibility and control	• Based on the most effective and efficient way to produce the product/service and serve the customer
How should jobs be grouped into units?	• By function: departments such as Operations, Finance, HR, Sales, and Marketing • By division: product, geographic, market or customer-focused, and hybrid (combinations) • Matrix, product team • Network structures • Outsourcing	• Based on matching the organization's environment, HR, technology and strategy with the organization's size and resources
How should authority be distributed so that the organization can coordinate and control its activities?	• Hierarchy of authority: tall or flat • Span of control • Chain of command • Centralized or decentralized control over decision making • Integrating mechanisms	• Based on the minimum chain of command principle, which states that the managerial hierarchy should have the fewest levels necessary to use organizational resources efficiently and effectively while balancing centralized and decentralized decision making and coordination across work units
Should the overall organizational structure be formal or flexible?	• Mechanistic structures: formal, stable, and rigid • Organic structures: fluid, dynamic, and flexible	• Depends on the degree of change in the organizational environment, the use of industrial or new technology, the use of skilled or unskilled labour, and the type of strategy (low cost or differentiation)

Grouping Tasks into Jobs: Job Design

LO2 | Explain how managers arrange tasks to create jobs that are motivating and satisfying for employees.

The most fundamental step in organizational design is **job design,** the process by which managers decide how to divide the work to be done into specific jobs. These are the tasks that have to

job design The process by which managers decide how to divide the work to be done into specific jobs.

be performed to provide customers with goods and services. Managers at McDonald's, for example, have decided how best to divide the tasks required to provide customers with fast, cheap food in each McDonald's restaurant. After experimenting with different job arrangements, McDonald's managers decided on a basic division of labour among chefs and food servers. Managers allocated all the tasks involved in actually cooking the food (putting oil in the fat fryers, opening packages of frozen french fries, putting beef patties on the grill, making salads, and so on) to the job of chef. They allocated all the tasks involved in giving the food to customers (such as greeting customers, taking orders, putting fries and burgers into bags, adding salt, pepper, and napkins, and taking money) to food servers. In addition, they created other jobs—the job of dealing with drive-thru customers, the job of keeping the restaurant clean, and the job of overseeing employees and responding to unexpected events. The result of the job design process is a **division of labour** among employees, one that McDonald's managers have discovered through experience is most effective and efficient. The degree to which the job is focused on particular tasks or multiple tasks is called **work specialization.**

division of labour Splitting the work to be performed into particular tasks and assigning tasks to individual workers.

work specialization The degree to which the job is focused on particular tasks or multiple tasks.

Establishing an appropriate division of labour among employees is a critical part of the organizing process, one that is vital to increasing efficiency and effectiveness. At McDonald's, the tasks associated with chef and food server were split into different jobs because managers found that, for the kind of food McDonald's serves, this approach was most efficient. It is efficient because when each employee is given fewer tasks to perform (so that each job becomes more specialized), employees become more productive at performing the particular tasks that constitute each job.

Work Specialization

At Subway sandwich shops, however, managers chose a different kind of job design. At Subway, there is no division of labour among the people who make the sandwiches, wrap the sandwiches, give them to customers, and take the money. The multiple tasks of chef and food server are combined into one job. This different division of tasks and jobs is effective and efficient for Subway and not for McDonald's because Subway serves a limited menu of mostly submarine-style sandwiches that are prepared to order. Subway's production system is far simpler than McDonald's. McDonald's menu is much more varied and its chefs must cook many different kinds of foods. At Subway, the roles of chef and server are combined into one, making the job "larger" than the jobs of the more specialized food servers at McDonald's.

Managers of every organization must analyze the range of tasks to be performed and then create jobs that best allow the organization to give customers the goods and services they want. In deciding how to assign tasks to individual jobs, however, managers must be careful not to go too far with **job simplification**—the process of reducing the number of tasks that each employee performs.[11] Too much job simplification may reduce effectiveness and efficiency rather than increase it if workers find their simplified jobs boring and monotonous, become demotivated and unhappy, and, as a result, perform at a low level.

job simplification Reducing the number of tasks that each worker performs.

At Subway, the roles of chef and server are combined into one, making the job "larger" than the jobs of the more specialized food servers at McDonald's. The idea behind job enlargement is that increasing the range of tasks performed by employees will reduce boredom.
Education & Exploration 3/Alamy Stock Photo

Researchers have looked at ways to create a division of labour and design individual jobs to encourage employees to perform at a higher level and be more satisfied with their work. Based on this research, they have proposed job enlargement and job enrichment as better ways than job simplification to group tasks into jobs.

Job enlargement increases the number of different tasks in a given job by changing the division of labour.[12] For example, because Subway food servers make the food as well as serve it, their jobs are "larger" than the jobs of McDonald's food servers. The idea behind job enlargement is that increasing the range of tasks performed by an employee will reduce boredom and fatigue and may increase motivation to perform at a high level—increasing both the quantity and the quality of goods and services provided.

job enlargement Increasing the number of different tasks in a given job by changing the division of labour.

Job enrichment increases the degree of responsibility a worker has over his or her job by, for example, (1) empowering employees to experiment to find new or better ways of doing the job, (2) encouraging employees to develop new skills, (3) allowing employees to decide how to do the work and giving them responsibility for deciding how to respond to unexpected situations, and (4) allowing employees to monitor and measure their own performance.[13] The idea behind job enrichment is that increasing employees' responsibility increases their involvement in their jobs and thus increases their interest in the quality of the goods they make or the services they provide.

job enrichment Increasing the degree of responsibility a worker has over his or her job.

Increasing job enrichment relies on empowering employees with more control over decision making. Employees who perform a variety of tasks and who are allowed and encouraged to discover new and better ways to perform their jobs are likely to act flexibly and creatively. Thus, managers who enlarge and enrich jobs create a flexible organizational structure, and those who simplify jobs create a more formal structure. If, in addition to job enrichment, employees are also grouped into self-managed work teams, the organization is likely to be flexible because team members provide support to each other and can learn from one another.

The Job Characteristics Model

J. R. Hackman and G. R. Oldham's job characteristics model is an influential model of job design that explains in detail how managers can make jobs more interesting and motivating.[14] Hackman and Oldham's model also describes the likely personal and organizational outcomes that will result from enriched and enlarged jobs.

According to Hackman and Oldham, every job has five characteristics that determine how motivating the job is. These characteristics determine how employees react to their work and lead to outcomes such as high performance and satisfaction and low absenteeism and turnover. Hackman and Oldham's five characteristics are:

- *Skill variety:* The extent to which a job requires that an employee use a wide range of different skills, abilities, or knowledge. Example: The skill variety required by the job of a research scientist is higher than that called for by the job of a McDonald's food server.

- *Task identity:* The extent to which a job requires that a worker perform all the tasks necessary to complete the job from the beginning to the end of the production process. Example: A craftsperson who takes a piece of wood and transforms it into a custom-made desk has higher task identity than does a worker who performs only one of the numerous operations required to assemble a flat-screen TV.

- *Task significance:* The degree to which a worker feels his or her job is meaningful because of its effect on people inside the organization, such as co-workers, or on people outside the organization, such as customers. Example: A teacher who sees the effect of his or her efforts in a well-educated and well-adjusted student enjoys high task significance compared to a restaurant dishwasher who monotonously washes dishes as they come into the kitchen.

- *Autonomy:* The degree to which a job gives an employee the freedom and discretion needed to schedule different tasks and decide how to carry them out. Example: Salespeople who have to plan their schedules and decide how to allocate their time among different customers have relatively high autonomy compared to assembly-line workers whose actions are determined by the speed of the production line.

- *Feedback:* The extent to which actually doing a job provides a worker with clear and direct information about how well he or she has performed the job. Example: An air traffic controller whose mistakes may result in a midair collision receives immediate feedback on job performance; a person who compiles statistics for a business magazine often has little idea of when he or she makes a mistake or does a particularly good job.

Hackman and Oldham argue that these five job characteristics affect an employee's motivation because they, in conjunction with the employee's need for growth, or *growth need strength*, affect three critical psychological states. Employees with high growth need strength excel when they feel that their work is *meaningful* and that they are *responsible for work outcomes* and *responsible for knowing how those outcomes affect others*. The more motivating the work becomes, the more likely these employees are to be satisfied and to perform at a high level. Moreover, employees who have jobs that are highly motivating are called on to use their skills more and to perform more tasks, and they are given more responsibility for doing the job. All of the foregoing are characteristic of jobs and employees in flexible structures where authority is decentralized and where employees commonly work with others and must learn new skills to complete the range of tasks for which their group is responsible.

◼ Departmentalization

LO3 Describe how managers cluster jobs into departments and units

Once managers have decided which tasks to allocate to which jobs, they face the next organizing decision: how to group jobs together into units to best match the needs of the organization's environment, strategy, technology, and human resources. This is known as **departmentalization.** When managers move away from a

departmentalization Grouping jobs together into units to best match the needs of the organization's environment, strategy, technology, and human resources.

simple structure where the owner-operator carries out all the functions in the management process and makes all the decisions, they first decide to group jobs into departments. As an organization grows and becomes more difficult to control, managers must choose a more complex organizational design, such as *product, geographical,* or *market (customer)* divisions. Each more complex structure has both benefits and drawbacks for the organization. The more complex structures may anticipate the needs of customers and formulate strategy that gives the organization a competitive advantage. At the same time, communication issues and other problems associated with rigid bureaucracies arise that may make the organizational structure more inefficient and ineffective. To overcome these difficulties, organizations today are adopting more flexible organizational structures that rely more on *cross-functional teamwork* and less on formal departments. *Matrix, product or project teams,* and *network* structures overcome some of the rigidity of the older common ways to departmentalize.

Simple Structure

Small businesses and entrepreneurial startups often adopt a very **simple structure** where the owner is the general manager responsible for the activities in all the functions. Take, for example, the enterprise of a restaurant. It is not uncommon for the owner-manager to make all the initial decisions including hiring and surpervision. Then as the business grows, the owner-manager may need to delegate responsibility to the head chef to manage the "back of the house," or the food purchasing and hiring/supervision of the kitchen staff, while another manager operates the "front of the house," including supervising the wait staff and bartender/sommelier. The manager may decide to contract out the noncore functions that are necessary to the operation of the restaurant but not central to its mission, like payroll and accounting. As the organization grows, the owner-manager cannot continue to make all the decisions and must hire employees and managers and delegate responsibility and authority. Take, for another example, Sandy's Bike Shop. Sandy sells and services bicycles. Over the years, Sandy has built an excellent reputation and attracted a lot of customers. Recently, however, a Sport Chek has opened in the neighbourhood, selling a wider range of sporting goods and clothing. Sandy's Bike Shop was organized as a simple structure: Sandy did all the purchasing, sales, and repairs and contracted out all the HR, accounting, and payroll functions. With the increase in competition, Sandy has decided the best way to compete is to invest in a new product line—sports apparel—to gain a competitive advantage. To accommodate this growth, he has had to rethink the organizational structure. He definitely will have to hire employees. With the expansion, it makes sense to perform the functions of purchasing and accounting in-house and hire managers to supervise all the functional departments—bicycle sales, repairs, and accessories and apparel—as illustrated in Figure 5.3.

> **simple structure** An organizational structure where the owner is the general manager responsible for the activities in all the functions.

FIGURE 5.3

Functional Structure for Sandy's Bike Shop

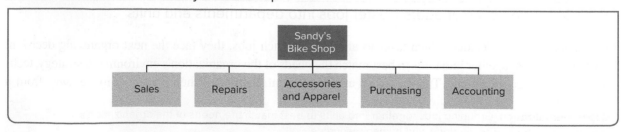

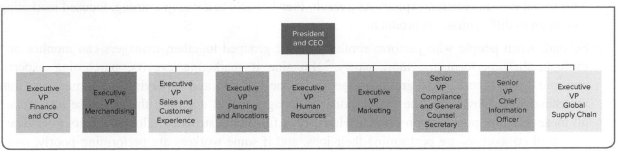

FIGURE 5.4

The Functional Structure of Pier 1 Imports

President and CEO

- Executive VP Finance and CFO
- Executive VP Merchandising
- Executive VP Sales and Customer Experience
- Executive VP Planning and Allocations
- Executive VP Human Resources
- Executive VP Marketing
- Senior VP Compliance and General Counsel Secretary
- Senior VP Chief Information Officer
- Executive VP Global Supply Chain

Functional Structure

People working together in a single department possess similar skills and use the same kind of knowledge, tools, or techniques to perform their jobs. Similar jobs are grouped in this way to create functional departments that are efficient and effective. The vertical, up-and-down communication channels within the work unit allow each department to specialize. As noted in Chapter 1, human resources, sales and marketing, research and development, operations, and accounting and finance are typical departments found in *functional departmental structures.* A **functional structure** is an organizational structure composed of all the departments that an organization requires to produce its goods or services. Pier 1 Imports, a home furnishings company, uses a functional structure to supply its customers with a range of goods from around the world to satisfy their desires for new and innovative products. Figure 5.4 shows the functional structure that Pier 1 Imports uses.

functional structure An organizational structure composed of all the departments that an organization requires to produce its goods or services.

Pier 1's main functions are finance and administration, merchandising (purchasing the goods), stores (managing the retail outlets), logistics (managing product distribution), marketing, human resources, and real estate. Each job inside a department exists because it helps the employees perform the activities necessary for high organizational performance. Thus, within the logistics department are all the jobs necessary to distribute and transport products efficiently to stores. Inside the marketing department are all the jobs (such as promotion, photography, and visual communication) that are necessary to increase the appeal of Pier 1's products to customers.

There are several advantages to grouping jobs according to function. See Figure 5.5.

- First, when people who perform similar jobs are grouped together, they can learn from watching one another. Thus they become more specialized and can perform at a higher level. The tasks associated with

Pier 1 Imports uses a functional structure.
Clark Brennan/Alamy Stock Photo

one job often are related to the tasks associated with another job, which encourages cooperation within a function. In Pier 1's planning department, for example, the person designing the photography program for an ad campaign works closely with the person responsible for designing store layouts and with visual communication experts. As a result, Pier 1 is able to develop a strong, focused marketing campaign to differentiate its products.

- Second, when people who perform similar jobs are grouped together, managers can monitor and evaluate their performance more easily.[15] Imagine if marketing experts, purchasing experts, and real-estate experts were grouped together in one function and supervised by a manager from merchandising. Obviously, the merchandising manager would not have the expertise to evaluate all these different people appropriately. However, a functional structure allows workers to evaluate how well co-workers are performing their jobs, and if some workers are performing poorly, more experienced workers can help them develop new skills.

- Finally, managers like functional structure because it allows them to create the set of functions they need for scanning and monitoring the competitive environment and to obtain information about the way it is changing.[16] With the right set of functions in place, managers are then in a good position to develop a strategy that allows the organization to respond to its changing situation. Employees in the marketing group can specialize in monitoring new marketing developments that will allow Pier 1 to better target its customers. Employees in merchandising can monitor all potential suppliers of home furnishings both at home and abroad to find the goods most likely to appeal to Pier 1's customers and manage Pier 1's global outsourcing supply chain.

As an organization grows and its strategy changes to produce a wider range of goods and services for different kinds of customers, several problems can make a functional structure less efficient and effective.[17] See Figure 5.5.

- First, managers in different functions may find it more difficult to communicate and coordinate with one another when they are responsible for several different kinds of products, especially as the organization grows both domestically and internationally.

- Second, functional managers may become so preoccupied with supervising their own specific departments and achieving their departmental goals that they lose sight of organizational goals. If that happens, organizational effectiveness will suffer because managers will be viewing issues and problems facing the organization only from their own, relatively narrow, departmental perspectives.[18] Both of these problems can reduce efficiency and effectiveness.

FIGURE 5.5

The Advantages and Disadvantages of Functional Departmentalization

	Advantages for Managers	Disadvantages for Managers
Grouping similar jobs together into departments	• People learn from each other and cooperation is encouraged • Control is easier as is employee performance evaluation • Targeted environmental scanning allows managers to develop better strategy and minimize risk	• Difficulty in communicating across functions as organizations grow • Organizational goals take second place to departmental goals • Organizational effectiveness and efficiency can be compromised

TIPS FOR MANAGERS

Choosing a Divisional Structure

1. As the manager of a small business, you often end up performing all the functions in-house, but this may not be the most efficient and effective way of organizing.

2. The decision to "make-or-buy" depends on relative costs. Sometimes an outside firm can perform the function both better and cheaper because of greater specialization, superior technology, or some other advantage.

3. Decisions to contract out noncore functions must be made in relation to the capabilities and competencies of your staff.

4. Form and function or structure and strategy have to fit well together, but be flexible to accommodate unpredictable changes in the organization's environment.

Divisional Structures: Product, Geographic, and Market

As the problems associated with growth and diversification increase over time, managers must search for new ways to organize their activities to overcome the problems linked with a functional structure. Most managers of large organizations choose a **divisional structure** and create a series of business units to produce a specific kind of product for a specific kind of customer. Each division is a collection of functions or departments that work together to produce the product. The goal behind the change to a divisional structure is to create smaller, more manageable units within the organization. There are three forms of divisional structure (refer to Figure 5.1).[19]

divisional structure An organizational structure composed of separate business units within which are the functions that work together to produce a specific product for a specific customer.

When managers organize divisions according to the *type of good or service* they provide, they adopt a product structure. When managers organize divisions according to the *area of the country or world they operate in*, they adopt a geographic structure. When managers organize divisions according to the *types of customers* they focus on, they adopt a market structure.

PRODUCT DIVISIONS

Imagine the problems that managers at Pier 1 would encounter if they decided to diversify into producing and selling cars, fast food, and health insurance—in addition to home furnishings—and tried to use their existing set of functional managers to oversee the production of all four kinds of products. No manager would have the necessary skills or abilities to oversee those four products. No individual marketing manager, for example, could effectively market cars, fast food, health insurance, and home furnishings at the same time. To perform a functional activity successfully, managers must have experience in specific markets or industries. Consequently, if companies decide to diversify into new industries or to expand their range of products, they commonly design a product division structure to organize their operations. Using a **product division** structure (refer to Figure 5.1), managers place each distinct product line or business

product division An organizational structure in which each product line or business is handled by a self-contained division.

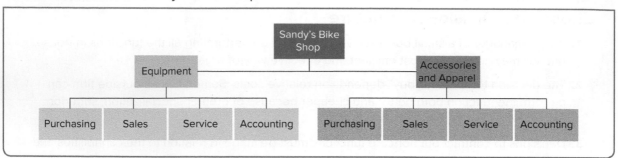

FIGURE 5.6

Product Structure for Sandy's Bike Shop

in its own self-contained division and give divisional managers the responsibility for devising an appropriate business-level strategy to allow the division to compete effectively in its industry or market.[20] Each division is self-contained because it has a complete set of all the functions—marketing, R&D, finance, and so on—that it needs to produce or provide goods or services efficiently and effectively. Functional managers report to divisional managers, and divisional managers report to top or corporate managers.

Small businesses can also organize along product lines within, for example, the same store. A shoe store may sell children's as well as men's and women's shoes in the same location. As the company grows, it may be appropriate for individual managers to oversee each product category, thus gaining from the same advantages as a product divisional structure. Sandy's Bike Shop decides that a *product divisional* structure is the best way to move forward and reorganize to effectively compete with the big box sports stores. See Figure 5.6.

Grouping functions into divisions focused on particular products or services has several advantages for managers at all levels in the organization.

- First, a product structure allows functional managers to specialize in only one product area, so they are able to build expertise and fine-tune their skills in this particular area.

- Second, each division's managers can become experts in their industry; this expertise helps them choose and develop a business-level strategy to differentiate their products or lower their costs while meeting the needs of customers.

- Third, a product structure frees corporate managers from the need to supervise each division's day-to-day operations directly; this latitude allows corporate managers to create the best corporate-level strategy to maximize the organization's future growth and ability to create value.

Corporate managers are likely to make fewer mistakes about which businesses to diversify into or how best to expand internationally, for example, because they are able to take an organization-wide view.[21] Corporate managers also are likely to better evaluate how well divisional managers are doing, and they can intervene and take corrective action as needed.

The extra layer of management, the divisional management layer, can improve the use of organizational resources. Moreover, a product structure puts divisional managers close to their customers and lets them respond quickly and appropriately to the changing task environment.

GEOGRAPHIC DIVISION

When organizations expand rapidly both at home and abroad, functional structures can create special problems because managers in one central location may find it increasingly difficult to deal with the different problems and issues that may arise in each region of a country or area of the world. In these cases, a **geographic division** structure, in which divisions are broken down by geographical location, is often chosen (refer to Figure 5.1). To achieve the corporate mission of providing next-day mail service, Fred Smith, chair, president, and CEO of Federal Express, and a man "with transportation in his blood,"[22] chose a geographic structure and divided up operations by creating a division in each region. Large retailers often use a geographic structure. Since the needs of retail customers differ by region—for example, umbrellas in Vancouver and down-filled parkas in the Prairies—a geographic structure gives regional retail managers the flexibility they need to choose products that best meet the needs of regional customers.

> **geographic division** An organizational structure in which each region of a country or area of the world is served by a self-contained division.

MARKET SEGMENT DIVISION

Sometimes, the pressing issue managers face is how to group functions according to the type of customer buying the product, in order to tailor the organization's products to each customer's unique demands. TELUS, based in Burnaby, B.C., is structured around six customer-focused business units: Consumer Solutions, focused on households and individuals; Business Solutions, focused on small- to medium-sized businesses and entrepreneurs; Client Solutions, focused on large organizations in Canada; Partner Solutions, focused on Canadian and global carriers into and within Canada; Wireless Solutions, focused on people and businesses on the go; and TELUS Québec, a TELUS company for the Quebec marketplace.

To satisfy the needs of diverse customers, TELUS adopts a **market segment division** structure (also called a customer divisional structure), which groups divisions according to the particular kinds of customers they serve (refer to Figure 5.1). A market structure allows managers to be both responsive to the needs of their customers and able to act flexibly to make decisions in response to customers' changing needs.

> **market segment division** An organizational structure in which each kind of customer is served by a self-contained division; also called customer divisional structure.

In the case of co-operative organizations, the customers are the owners and members. Organizations structured as co-operatives that are involved in providing similar services often have an apex or umbrella co-op that coordinates and supports member organizations. They do this by either acting as a broker to market member-produced goods or by acting as a purchasing agent, allowing the member organizations to achieve economies of scale in procuring the inputs they need for their businesses. The Canadian co-operative Arctic Co-operatives Ltd. (ACL) is organized with this co-operative structure. ACL is owned by 32 community-based co-operative businesses located in Nunavut and the Northwest Territories. These organizations are its customers as well as its member-owners. The ACL provides financing, purchasing of goods and services needed by the member co-ops, and the marketing of Indigenous art produced by the Inuit, Métis, and Dene owners of the member businesses. As with co-operatives in general, each owner-member has one voting share that allows them to participate in the governance of ACL. Surplus revenues are distributed among the 32 owner-members based on their use of ACL's services.[23] In 2013, the redistributed funds paid to the members totalled $11.2 million.[24]

Home Hardware Stores Ltd.

Home Hardware Stores Ltd. is a retailers' co-operative operating throughout Canada with 1100 independently owned member stores under the brands Home Hardware, Home Hardware Building Centre, Home Building Centre, and Home Furniture. It is the largest independent home improvement retailer in Canada, serving communities in some of the remotest corners of the country. Each owner-operator is a cornerstone of their community and a survivor of the big box retailer explosion. It is estimated that over 1000 small business hardware stores closed when the big box retailers, like Home Depot and RONA, entered the landscape because they couldn't compete with the economies of scale the new competitors could take advantage of.

In 1964, Walter Hachborn championed the Home Hardware co-operative model that enabled independent small business owners to share buying power, advertising costs, and distribution and delivery services, enabling them to focus on inventory that served community needs and to compete with multinational retail corporations while remaining independent and sharing in the benefits of a nationally recognized brand.

Member stores, known as Home Owners, participate in the decision making of the company on an equal footing. This fosters democratic control and shared decision making: one vote per member.

1. How does management in co-operative organizational structures such as Home Hardware Stores Ltd. compare to management in other organizational structures used by traditional businesses?

Source: Based on https://www.homehardware.ca/history-of-home-hardware. Accessed July 11, 2018.

Team-Based Organizational Structures

Moving to a product, market, or geographic divisional structure means managers can respond more quickly and flexibly to the particular set of circumstances they confront. However, when information technology or customer needs are changing rapidly and the environment is very uncertain, even a divisional structure may not provide managers with enough flexibility to respond to the environment quickly. To operate effectively under these conditions, managers must design a more flexible team-based organizational structure: a matrix or a product/project team structure (refer to Figure 5.1).

MATRIX

In a **matrix team** structure, managers group people and resources in two ways simultaneously: by function and by product.[25] Employees are grouped into functions to allow them to learn from one another and become more skilled and productive. Employees are also grouped into product teams, in which members of different functions work together to develop a specific product. The result is a complex network of reporting relationships among product teams and functions that make the matrix structure very flexible (refer to Figure 5.1). Each person in a product team reports to two managers: (1) a functional manager, who assigns individuals to a team and evaluates their performance from a functional point of view, and (2) the manager of the product team, who evaluates their performance on the team. Thus, team members are known as two-boss employees.

matrix team An organizational structure that simultaneously groups people and resources by function and by product.

The functional employees assigned to product teams change over time as the specific skills that the team needs change. At the beginning of the product development process, for example, engineers and R&D specialists are assigned to a product team because their skills are needed to develop new products. When a provisional design has been established, marketing experts are assigned to the team to gauge how customers will respond to the new product. Manufacturing personnel join when it is time to find the most efficient way to produce the product. As their specific jobs are completed, team members leave and are reassigned to new teams. In this way, the matrix structure makes the most use of human resources.

To keep the matrix team structure flexible:

- Product teams are empowered and team members are responsible for making most of the important decisions involved in product development.[26]
- The product team manager acts as a facilitator, controlling the financial resources and trying to keep the project on time and within budget.
- The functional managers try to ensure that the product is the best that it can be in order to make the most of its differentiated appeal.

High-tech companies have been using matrix teams successfully for many years. These companies operate in environments where new product developments happen monthly or yearly and the need to innovate quickly is vital to the organization's survival. The matrix team structure provides enough flexibility for managers to keep pace with a changing and increasingly complex environment. For this reason, matrixes also have been designed by managers who want to control international operations as they move abroad and face problems of coordinating their domestic and foreign divisions.[27] Virtual teams, discussed in Chapter 10, are becoming increasingly common as a way of organizing product and service matrixes in global companies.

PRODUCT/PROJECT TEAM

The dual reporting relationships that are at the heart of a matrix team structure have always been difficult for managers and employees to deal with. Often, the functional manager and the product manager make conflicting demands on team members, who do not know which manager to satisfy first. Also, functional and product team managers may come into conflict over precisely who is in charge of which team members and for how long. To avoid these problems, managers have devised a way of organizing people and resources that still allows an organization to be flexible but makes its structure easier to operate: a *product or project* team structure.

The **product/project team** structure differs from a matrix structure in two ways: (1) it does away with dual reporting relationships for employees, and (2) functional employees are permanently assigned to a *cross-functional team* that is empowered to work on a new project, such as bringing a new or redesigned product to market. A **cross-functional team** is a group of individuals brought together from different departments to perform organizational tasks. When individuals are grouped into cross-departmental teams, the artificial boundaries between departments disappear, and a narrow focus on departmental goals is replaced with a general interest in working together to achieve organizational goals. The results of such changes have been dramatic. For example, Chrysler Canada's use of cross-functional teams has reduced the time it takes to retool for a new product from months to just weeks.

product/project team An organizational structure in which employees are permanently assigned to a cross-functional team and report only to the project team manager or to one of his or her direct subordinates.

cross-functional team A group of individuals from different departments brought together to perform organizational tasks.

Members of a cross-functional team report only to the project team manager or to one of his or her direct subordinates. The functional managers have only an informal, advisory relationship with members of the project teams. These managers counsel and help cross-functional team members, share knowledge among teams, and provide new technological developments that can help improve each team's performance (refer to Figure 5.1).[28] Teams can be permanent or temporary.

B2B Network Structures

Recently, increasing globalization and the use of new IT have brought about changes in organizational architecture that are sweeping through North American and European companies. They are *business-to-business (B2B) network structures* and *strategic alliances*. A **strategic alliance** is a formal agreement that commits two or more companies to exchange or share their resources in order to produce and market a product.

> **strategic alliance** A formal agreement that commits two or more companies to exchange or share their resources in order to produce and market a product.

Most commonly, strategic alliances are formed because the companies share similar interests and believe they can benefit from cooperating. For example, Japanese car companies such as Toyota and Honda have formed many strategic alliances with particular suppliers of inputs such as car axles, gearboxes, and air-conditioning systems. Over time, these car companies work closely with their suppliers to improve the efficiency and effectiveness of the inputs so that the final product—the car produced—is of higher quality and very often can be produced at lower cost. Toyota and Honda have also established alliances with suppliers throughout Canada, the United States, and Mexico because both companies now build several models of cars in these countries.

The growing sophistication of IT, with global intranets and teleconferencing, has made it much easier to manage strategic alliances and allow managers to share information and cooperate. One outcome of this has been the growth of strategic alliances into a network structure. A **network structure** is a series of global strategic alliances that an organization creates with suppliers, manufacturers, and/or distributors to produce and market a product. Network structures allow an organization to manage its global value chain in order to find new ways to reduce costs and increase the quality of products—without incurring the high costs of operating a complex organizational structure (such as the costs of employing many managers). Many of the 83 companies in the Samsung Group supply inputs to other product divisions. For example, micro-processing chips (Device Solutions Division) are used in household appliances and microwaves (Consumer Electronics Division).

> **network structure** A series of global strategic alliances that an organization creates with suppliers, manufacturers, and/or distributors to produce and market a product.

More and more Canadian, American, and European organizations are relying on global network structures to gain access to low-cost foreign sources of inputs. This approach allows managers to keep costs low. As discussed in Chapter 3, PUMA is a company that has used this approach extensively. Nike, the most profitable shoe manufacturer in the world, also uses a network structure to produce and market shoes. As noted in Chapter 4, many successful companies today are trying to pursue a low-cost and a differentiation strategy simultaneously. Nike Chairman Emeritus, Phil Knight, (then CEO) decided early that to do this at Nike he needed an organizational architecture that would allow his company to focus on some functions, such as design, and to leave others, such as manufacturing, to other organizations.

By far the largest function at Nike's Oregon headquarters is the design function, composed of talented designers who pioneered innovations in sports shoe design, such as the air pump and Air Jordans that Nike introduced so successfully. Designers use computer-aided design (CAD) to design Nike shoes, and they electronically store all new product information, including manufacturing instructions. When the designers have finished their work, they electronically transmit all the blueprints for the new products to a network of Southeast Asian suppliers and manufacturers with which Nike has formed strategic alliances.[29] Instructions for the design of a new sole may be sent to a supplier in Taiwan, and instructions for the leather uppers to a supplier in Malaysia. The suppliers produce the shoe parts and send them for final assembly to a manufacturer in China with which Nike has established another strategic alliance. From China, the shoes are shipped to distributors throughout the world. Ninety-nine percent of the 120 million pairs of shoes that Nike makes each year are made in Southeast Asia. This network structure gives Nike two important advantages:

- First, Nike is able to respond to changes in sports shoe fashion very quickly. Using its global IT system, Nike can change the instructions it gives each of its suppliers literally overnight, so that within a few weeks its foreign manufacturers are producing new kinds of shoes.[30] Any alliance partners that fail to perform up to Nike's standards are replaced with new partners.

- Second, Nike's costs are very low because wages in Southeast Asia are a fraction of what they are in the United States, and this difference gives Nike a low-cost advantage. Also, Nike's ability to **outsource**—that is, use foreign manufacturers to produce all its shoes abroad—allows Nike to keep the organization's U.S. structure flat and flexible. Nike is able to use a relatively inexpensive functional structure to organize its activities. However, sports shoe manufacturers' attempts to keep their costs low have led to many charges that Nike and others are supporting sweatshops that harm foreign workers.

outsource To use outside suppliers and manufacturers to produce goods and services.

The ability of managers to develop networks to produce or provide the goods and services customers want, rather than creating a complex organizational structure to do so, has led many researchers and consultants to popularize the idea of a **boundaryless organization** composed of people who are linked by computers, computer-aided design systems, and video teleconferencing, and who rarely, if ever, see one another face to face. People are used when their services are needed, much as in a matrix structure, but they are not formal members of an organization. They are functional experts who form an alliance with an organization, fulfill their contractual obligations, and then move on to the next project.

boundaryless organization An organization whose members are linked by computers, faxes, computer-aided design systems, and video teleconferencing, and who rarely, if ever, see one another face to face.

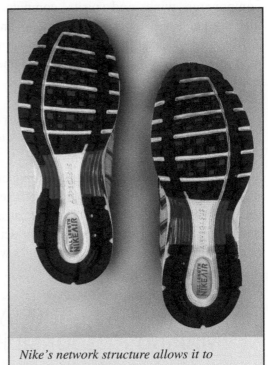

Nike's network structure allows it to remain competitive by keeping up with fashion trends and keeping costs low.
Mark Steinmetz

Large consulting companies such as Accenture utilize their global consultants in this way. Consultants are connected by laptops to an organization's **knowledge management system,** its company-specific information system that systematizes the knowledge of its employees and provides them with access to other employees who have the expertise to solve the problems that they encounter as they perform their jobs. iGEN Knowledge Solutions Inc., based in New Westminster, B.C., operates as a boundaryless organization to bring technical solutions to its business clients. Associates work from home offices connected by wireless technologies and the Internet and collaborate to solve client problems. The virtual model allows fast cycle times for idea implementation, service delivery, and product development. The model makes it easy to set up operations in different regions of the world without large overhead costs.

knowledge management system A company-specific virtual information system that allows workers to share their knowledge and expertise and find others to help solve ongoing problems.

The use of outsourcing and the development of network structures is increasing rapidly as organizations recognize the many opportunities they offer to reduce costs and increase organizational flexibility. The push to lower costs has led to the development of electronic **business-to-business (B2B) networks,** in which most or all of the companies in an industry (e.g., automakers) use the same software platform to link to each other and establish industry specifications and standards. Then, these companies jointly list the quantity and specifications of the inputs they require and invite bids from the thousands of potential suppliers around the world. Suppliers also use the same software platform so that electronic bidding, auctions, and transactions are possible between buyers and sellers around the world. Canada's Mediagrif has B2B networks in nine areas: electronics components, wines and spirits, computer equipment, telecommunications equipment, automotive aftermarket parts, truck parts, government e-tendering (which includes the MERX electronic tendering system used by the federal government of Canada), medical equipment, and IT parts and equipment.[31] The idea is that high-volume, standardized transactions can help drive down costs at the industry level.

business-to-business (B2B) networks A group of organizations that join together and use software to link themselves to global suppliers and distributors to increase efficiency and effectiveness.

Today, with advances in IT, designing organizational structure is becoming an increasingly complex management function. To maximize efficiency and effectiveness, managers must carefully assess the relative benefits of having their own organization perform a functional activity versus forming an alliance with another organization to perform the activity. It is still not clear how B2B networks and other forms of electronic alliances between companies will develop in the future.

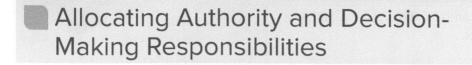

Allocating Authority and Decision-Making Responsibilities

LO4 Explain the ways that managers allocate authority and decision-making responsibilities.

Allocating Authority

Having discussed how managers divide organizational activities into jobs, departments, and divisions to increase efficiency and effectiveness, we now look at how they get people in the organization to carry out the tasks and jobs. How do managers decide who will be responsible and accountable for achieving organizational goals? They do this by designing the hierarchy of authority.[32] **Authority** is the power to hold people accountable for their actions and to make decisions concerning the use of organizational resources. The **hierarchy of authority** is an organization's chain of command—the relative authority that each manager has—extending from the CEO at the top, down through the middle managers and first-line managers, to the nonmanagerial employees who actually make goods or provide services. Every manager, at every level of the hierarchy, supervises one or more subordinates. The term **span of control** refers to the number of subordinates who report directly to a manager. The span of control determines the number of managers needed in the hierarchy. The wider the span of control, the fewer levels of managers. Figure 5.7 illustrates a company with a narrow span of control and one with a wider span of control. Can you tell which one has the wider span of control?

> **authority** The power to hold people accountable for their actions and to allocate organizational resources.
>
> **hierarchy of authority** An organization's chain of command, specifying the relative authority of each manager.
>
> **span of control** The number of subordinates who report directly to a manager.

Figure 5.8 shows a simplified picture of the hierarchy of authority and the span of control of managers in McDonald's as of January 2017. The fast-food giant's new president and CEO, Steve Easterbrook, has taken bold steps to revise the company's organizational structure in a successful effort to turn around the business. Easterbrook, who took over as CEO in March 2015, is the manager who has the ultimate responsibility for the company's overall performance, and he has the authority to decide how to use organizational resources to benefit the stakeholders of McDonald's.

The company's four divisions—USA, High Growth Markets, International Lead Markets, and Foundational Markets—focus on grouping markets with similar needs, challenges, and opportunities for

FIGURE 5.7

Span of Control

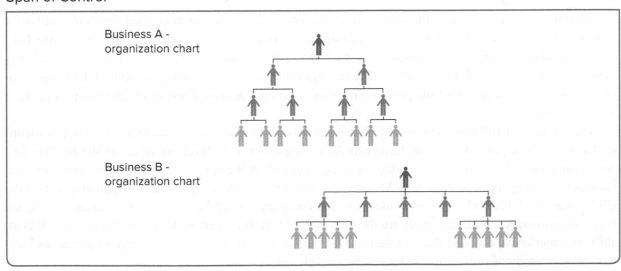

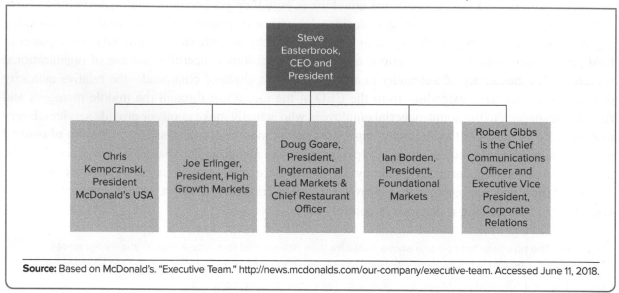

FIGURE 5.8

Simplified Hierarchy of Authority and Span of Control at McDonald's Corporation

Source: Based on McDonald's. "Executive Team." http://news.mcdonalds.com/our-company/executive-team. Accessed June 11, 2018.

growth rather than taking a geographic approach to company operations. Also in the top management hierarchy is Robert Gibbs, Chief Communications Officer and Executive Vice President, Corporate Relations. Unlike other managers, Gibbs is not a **line manager,** that is, someone in the direct line or chain of command who has formal authority over people and resources. Rather, Gibbs is a **staff manager,** responsible for one of the specialist functions at McDonald's—communications. He reports directly to Easterbrook.[33]

line manager Someone in the direct line or chain of command who has formal authority over people and resources at lower levels.

staff manager Someone responsible for managing a support function, such as finance or human resources.

Managers at each level of the hierarchy confer on managers at the next level down the authority to make decisions about how to use organizational resources. Accepting this authority, those lower-level managers then become responsible for their decisions and are accountable for how well they make those decisions. Managers who make the right decisions are typically promoted, and organizations motivate managers with the prospect of promotion and increased responsibility within the chain of command.

Have a look at the left-most box in Figure 5.8, where the president of McDonald's USA is identified as Chris Kempczinski. Below Kempczinski are the other main levels or layers in the McDonald's American chain of command—executive vice presidents of its West, Central, and East regions, regional managers, and supervisors. Note how McDonald's uses a geographical approach to organizing within the USA division. A hierarchy is also evident in each company-owned McDonald's restaurant. At the top is the store manager; at lower levels are the first assistant, shift managers, and crew personnel. McDonald's managers have decided that this hierarchy of authority best allows the company to pursue its business-level strategy of providing fast food at reasonable prices.

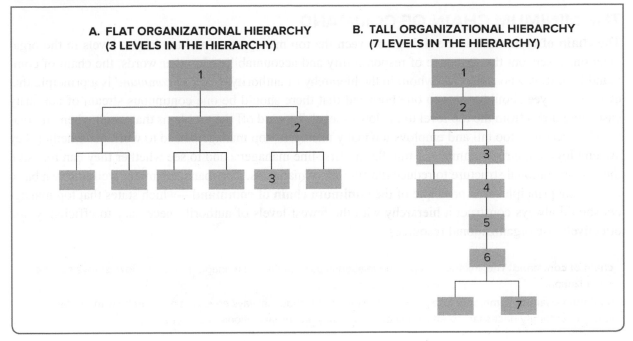

FIGURE 5.9

Flat and Tall Organizations

A. FLAT ORGANIZATIONAL HIERARCHY (3 LEVELS IN THE HIERARCHY)

B. TALL ORGANIZATIONAL HIERARCHY (7 LEVELS IN THE HIERARCHY)

TALL AND FLAT ORGANIZATIONS

As an organization grows in size (normally measured by the number of its managers and employees), its hierarchy of authority normally lengthens, making the organizational structure taller and the span of control more narrow. A tall organization has many levels of authority relative to company size; a flat organization has fewer levels relative to company size (see Figure 5.9).[34] As a hierarchy becomes taller, problems may result that make the organization's structure less flexible and slow managers' responses to changes in the organizational environment.

For instance, communication problems may arise. When an organization has many levels in the hierarchy, it can take a long time for the decisions and orders of upper-level managers to reach managers further down in the hierarchy, and it can take a long time for top managers to learn how well their decisions worked out. Feeling out of touch, top managers may want to verify that lower-level managers are following orders and may require written confirmation from them. Middle managers, who know they will be held strictly accountable for their actions, start devoting more time to the process of making decisions in order to improve their chances of being right. They might even try to avoid responsibility by making top managers decide what actions to take.

Another communication problem that can result is the distortion of commands and messages being transmitted up and down the hierarchy, which causes managers at different levels to interpret differently what is happening. Distortion of orders and messages can be accidental, occurring because different managers interpret messages from their own narrow functional perspectives. Or it can be intentional, when managers low in the hierarchy decide to interpret information to increase their own personal advantage.

Another problem with tall hierarchies is that usually they indicate an organization is employing too many managers, and managers are expensive. Managerial salaries, benefits, offices, and secretaries are a huge expense for organizations. Large companies such as Bombardier, Magna International, and General

Motors pay their managers billions of dollars a year. During the 2008–2010 recession, hundreds of thousands of managers were laid off as companies restructured and downsized their workforces to reduce costs. Since the economic recovery, layoffs are less frequent.

THE MINIMUM CHAIN OF COMMAND

The **chain of command** is the linkage between the top management and the lowest levels in the organization. It sets out the sequence of responsibility and accountability. In other words, the chain of command identifies who reports to whom in the hierarchy of authority. *Unity of command* is a principle that every employee should report to one boss and that there should be one continuous stream of authority cascading down from the top level to the lowest level. To ward off the problems that result when an organization becomes too tall and employs too many managers, top managers need to work out whether they are employing the right number of middle and first-line managers, and to see whether they can redesign their organizational structure to reduce the number of managers. Top managers might well follow a basic organizing principle—the principle of the **minimum chain of command**—which states that top managers should always construct a hierarchy with the fewest levels of authority necessary to efficiently and effectively use organizational resources.

> **chain of command** The linkage of reporting relationships from the top management to the lowest levels in the organization.
>
> **minimum chain of command** The idea that top managers should always construct a hierarchy with the fewest levels of authority necessary to efficiently and effectively use organizational resources.

Effective managers constantly scrutinize their hierarchies to see whether the number of levels can be reduced—for example, by eliminating one level and giving the responsibilities of managers at that level to managers above and empowering employees below. One organization that is trying to empower staff is Ducks Unlimited Canada of Stonewall, Manitoba, a nonprofit charitable organization founded by sportsmen that is devoted to preserving wetlands and associated waterfowl habitats.[35] The company went through a reorganization to flatten its management hierarchy. Gary Goodwin, past director of human resources, explains that "the reorganization was essentially to help empower employees, making it easier for people working in the field to make decisions quickly without having to go up and down the proverbial power ladder."[36] This practice has become more common in Canada and the United States as companies that are battling low-cost foreign competitors search for new ways to reduce costs.

> *"[T]he reorganization was essentially to help empower employees, making it easier for people working in the field to make decisions quickly without having to go up and down the proverbial power ladder."*
>
> Gary Goodwin, Ducks Unlimited

Centralization and Decentralization of Decision Making

Another way in which managers can keep the organizational hierarchy flat is by **decentralizing decision-making authority**—that is, by giving lower-level managers and nonmanagerial employees

> **decentralizing decision-making authority** Giving lower-level managers and nonmanagerial employees the right to make important decisions about how to use organizational resources.

the right to make important decisions about how to use organizational resources.[37] If managers at higher levels give lower-level employees the responsibility to make important decisions and only manage by exception, then the problems of slow and distorted communication noted previously are kept to a minimum. Moreover, fewer managers are needed because their role is not to make decisions but to act as coach and facilitator and to help other employees make the best decisions. In addition, when decision making is done at the low level in the organization and near the customer, employees are better able to recognize and respond to customer needs.

Managers must ask how much central control is needed.
©Abhirama Arjun Kharidehal | Dreamstime.com

Samsung Group decentralized authority to divisional managers when it eliminated the Global Business Manager function.

Decentralizing decision-making authority allows an organization and its employees to behave flexibly even as the organization grows and becomes taller. This is why managers are so interested in empowering employees, creating self-managed work teams, establishing cross-functional teams, and establishing liaisons among groups, teams, and departments to increase communication and coordination among functions and divisions.

While more organizations are taking steps to decentralize authority, too much decentralization has certain disadvantages:

1. If divisions, functions, or teams are given too much decision-making authority, they may begin to pursue their own goals at the expense of organizational goals. Managers in engineering design or R&D, for example, may become so focused on making the best possible product that they fail to realize that the best product may be so expensive that few people will be willing or able to buy it.

2. Also, with too much decentralization, lack of communication among functions or among divisions may prevent possible synergies or cost savings among them from ever materializing, and organizational performance suffers.

Top managers have to look for the balance between centralization and decentralization of decision-making authority that best meets the organization's needs. If managers are in a stable environment, using well-understood technology, and producing staple kinds of products (such as cereal, canned soup, books, or televisions), there is no pressing need to decentralize authority, and managers at the top can maintain control of much of the organizational decision making.[38] However, in uncertain, changing environments where high-tech companies are producing state-of-the-art products, top managers must empower employees and allow teams to make important strategic decisions so that the organization can keep up with the changes taking place.

Loblaws chose to centralize its management structure after years of decentralized regional offices created their own dysfunctional fiefdoms. T&T, the Asian-focused supermarket chain that Loblaws acquired in 2009, was being run separately out of two offices—one in British Columbia and one in Ontario. Non-food merchandising was consolidated in 2010, strengthening the centralized operation and giving Loblaws more clout as the largest retailer in Canada.[39]

Linking and Coordinating Activities

The more complex the organizational structure a company uses to group its activities is, the greater the problems of linking and coordinating its different functions and divisions. Coordination becomes a problem because each function or division develops a different orientation toward the other groups that affects the way it interacts with them. Each function or division comes to view the problems facing the company from its own particular perspective; for example, they may develop different views about the major goals, problems, or issues facing a company.

At the functional level, the manufacturing function typically has a very short-term view; its major goal is to keep costs under control and get the product out the factory door on time. By contrast, the product development function has a long-term viewpoint because developing a new product is a relatively slow process and high product quality is seen as more important than low costs. Such differences in viewpoint may make manufacturing and product development managers reluctant to cooperate and coordinate their activities to meet company goals. At the divisional level, in a company with a product structure, employees may become concerned more with making their division's products a success than with the profitability of the entire company. They may refuse, or simply not see the need, to cooperate and share information or knowledge with other divisions.

Much coordination takes place through the hierarchy of authority. However, several problems are associated with establishing contact among managers in different functions or divisions. As discussed earlier, managers from different functions and divisions may have different views about what must be done to achieve organizational goals. But if the managers have equal authority (as functional managers typically do), the only manager who can tell them what to do is the CEO, who has the ultimate authority to resolve conflicts. The need to solve everyday conflicts, however, wastes top management time and slows strategic decision making; indeed, one sign of a poorly performing structure is the number of problems sent up the hierarchy for top managers to solve.

To increase communication and coordination among functions or between divisions and to prevent these problems from emerging, top managers incorporate various **integrating mechanisms** into their organizational architecture. The greater the complexity of an organization's structure, the greater is the need for coordination among people, functions, and divisions to make the organizational structure work efficiently and effectively.[40] Thus when managers adopt a divisional, matrix, or product/project team structure, they must use complex integrating mechanisms to achieve organizational goals. Several integrating mechanisms are available to managers to increase communication and coordination.[41] Two are discussed below and illustrated in Figure 5.10.

integrating mechanisms Ways to increase effective and efficient communication and coordination among departments and divisions.

LIAISON ROLES

Managers can increase coordination among functions and divisions by establishing **liaison roles.** When the volume of contacts between two functions increases, one way to improve coordination is to give one manager in each function or division the responsibility for coordinating with the other. These managers may meet daily, weekly, monthly, or as needed. A liaison role is the person within a function who has

liaison roles The responsibility for coordinating with the other functional departments or divisions.

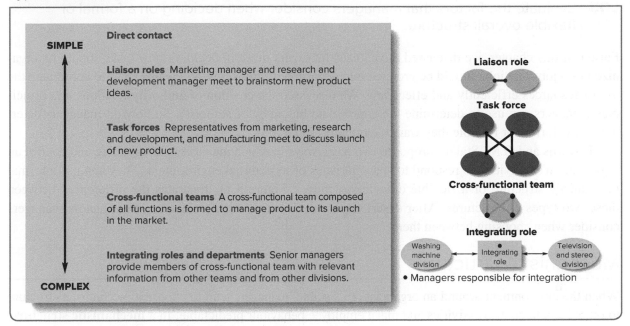

FIGURE 5.10

Types and Examples of Integrating Mechanisms

responsibility for coordinating with the other functions. Coordinating is part of the liaison's full-time job, and usually an informal relationship develops among the people involved, greatly easing strains between functions. Furthermore, liaison roles provide a way of transmitting information across an organization, which is important in large organizations whose employees may know no one outside their immediate function or division.

INTEGRATING ROLES

An **integrating role** is a role whose only purpose is to increase coordination and integration among functions or divisions to achieve performance gains from synergies. Usually managers who perform integrating roles are experienced senior managers who can envisage how to use the resources of the functions or divisions to obtain new synergies. One study found that DuPont, the giant chemical company, had created 160 integrating roles to coordinate the different divisions of the company and improve corporate performance.[42] The more complex an organization and the greater the number of its divisions, the more important are the integrating roles.

integrating role The responsibility to increase coordination and integration across departments or divisions to achieve performance gains.

In summary, to keep an organization responsive to changes in its task-specific and general environments as it grows and becomes more complex, managers must increase coordination among departments and divisions by using complex integrating mechanisms. We now turn to a discussion of how managers decide on the best way to organize their overall structures—that is, choose the structure that allows them to make the best use of organizational resources.

Choosing a Formal or Flexible Overall Structure

LO5 | Evaluate the factors that managers consider when deciding on a formal or flexible overall structure.

Earlier in this chapter, we discussed the choices managers make in deciding how tasks should be organized into jobs and jobs should be grouped into departments, divisions, and teams so as to coordinate the use of resources efficiently and effectively. We discussed the creation of authority relations and principles managers can use to determine the appropriate hierarchy of authority. So how do managers determine how formal or flexible they want the organization to be?

T. Burns and G.M. Stalker proposed two basic ways in which managers can organize and control an organization's activities to respond to characteristics of its external environment: They can use a formal mechanistic structure or a flexible organic structure.[43] Figure 5.11 illustrates the differences between these two types of structures. After describing these two structures, we discuss what factors managers consider when choosing between them.

Mechanistic Structures

When the environment around an organization is stable, managers tend to choose a mechanistic structure to organize and control activities and make employee behaviour predictable. In a **mechanistic structure,** authority is centralized at the top of the managerial hierarchy, and the vertical hierarchy of authority is the main means used to control subordinates' behaviour. Tasks and roles are clearly specified, subordinates are closely supervised, and the emphasis is on strict discipline and order. Everyone knows his or her place, and there is a place for everyone. A mechanistic structure provides the most efficient way to operate in a stable environment because it allows managers to obtain inputs at the lowest cost, giving an organization the most control over its conversion processes and enabling the most efficient production of goods and services with the smallest expenditure of resources. This explains the mechanistic structure at McDonald's.

mechanistic structure An organizational structure in which authority is centralized at the top of the hierarchy, tasks and roles are clearly specified, and employees are closely supervised.

FIGURE 5.11

Mechanistic versus Organic Organizations

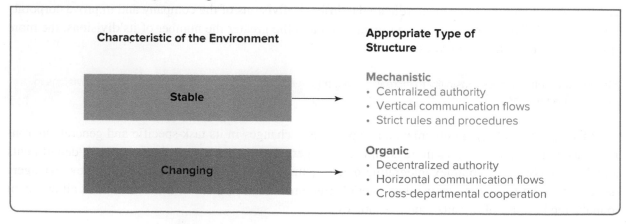

Organic Structures

In contrast, when the environment is changing rapidly it is difficult to obtain access to resources. Managers need to organize their activities in a way that allows them to cooperate, to act quickly to obtain resources (such as new types of wood to produce new kinds of furniture), and to respond effectively to the unexpected. In an **organic structure,** authority is decentralized to middle and first-line managers to encourage them to take responsibility and act quickly to pursue scarce resources. Departments are encouraged to take a cross-departmental or functional perspective, and authority rests with the individuals and departments best positioned to control the current problems the organization is facing. Control in an organic structure is much looser than it is in a mechanistic structure, and reliance on shared norms to guide organizational activities is greater.

> **organic structure** An organizational structure in which authority is decentralized to middle and first-line managers and tasks and roles are left ambiguous to encourage employees to cooperate and respond quickly to the unexpected.

Managers in an organic structure can react more quickly to a changing environment than can managers in a mechanistic structure. However, an organic structure is generally more expensive to operate, so it is used only when needed—when the organizational environment is unstable and rapidly changing. Organic structures may also work more effectively if managers establish semi-structures that govern "the pace, timing, and rhythm of organizational activities and processes." In other words, introducing a bit of structure while preserving most of the flexibility of the organic structure may reduce operating costs.[44]

Factors Affecting Choice of Overall Organizational Structure

Organizational structures need to fit the factors or circumstances that affect the company the most and cause them the most uncertainty.[45] Thus, there is no "best" way to design an organization: Design reflects each organization's specific situation. Four factors are important determinants of organizational structure: the nature of the organizational environment, the type of strategy the organization pursues, the technology the organization uses, and the characteristics of the organization's human resources (see Figure 5.12).[46]

THE ORGANIZATIONAL ENVIRONMENT

In general, the more quickly the external environment is changing and the greater the uncertainty within it, the greater are the problems a manager faces in trying to gain access to scarce resources. In this situation, to speed decision making and communication and make it easier to obtain resources, managers typically make organizing choices that bring flexibility to the organizational structure.[47] They are likely to decentralize authority and empower lower-level employees to make important operating decisions.

In contrast, if the external environment is stable, if resources are readily available, and if uncertainty is low, then less coordination and communication among people and functions is needed to obtain resources, and managers can make organizing choices that bring more formality to the organizational structure. Managers in this situation prefer to make decisions within a clearly defined hierarchy of authority and use extensive rules, standard operating procedures, and restrictive norms to guide and govern employees' activities—a more mechanistic form of organizing.

Factors Affecting Overall Organizational Structure

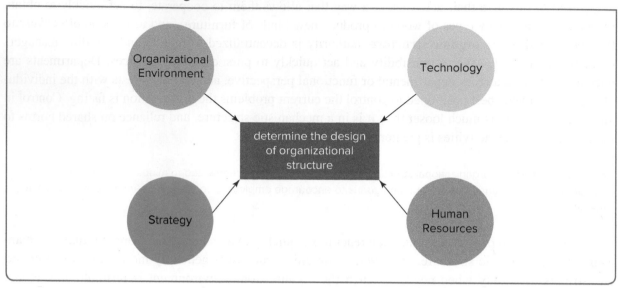

As we discussed in Chapter 2, change is rapid in today's marketplace, and increasing competition both at home and abroad is putting greater pressure on managers to attract customers and increase efficiency and effectiveness. Thus, there has been growing interest in finding ways to structure organizations—such as through empowerment and self-managed teams—to allow people and departments to behave flexibly. A case in point is media executive Kathleen Dore, past president of television and radio at Canwest Mediaworks Inc., and her unique empowerment management style. In a world dominated by men, she has become a role model for other women. She uses a term, "force multiplier," which focuses on "using your skills, abilities, and experience as a magnet which pulls others toward you and makes them want to engage in the undertaking you're about."[48]

Flexibility helps managers cope with rapidly changing environments.
© Adonis1969 | Dreamstime.com

STRATEGY

As discussed in Chapter 4, once managers decide on a strategy, they must choose the right means to implement it. Different strategies often call for the use of different organizational structures. For example, a differentiation strategy aimed at increasing the value customers perceive in an organization's goods and services usually succeeds best in a flexible structure. Flexibility assists a differentiation strategy because managers can develop new or innovative products quickly—an activity that requires extensive cooperation among functions or departments. In contrast, a low-cost strategy that is aimed at driving down costs in all functions usually fares best in a more formal structure, which gives managers greater control over the expenditures and actions of the organization's various departments.[49]

In addition, at the corporate level, when managers decide to expand the scope of organizational activities by, for example, vertical integration or diversification, they need to design a flexible structure to provide sufficient coordination among the different business divisions.[50] By moving to a more flexible structure, such as a product division structure, divisional managers gain more control over their different businesses.

Finally, expanding internationally and operating in many different countries challenges managers to create organizational structures that allow organizations to be flexible on a global level.[51]

TECHNOLOGY

Recall that technology is the combination of skills, knowledge, tools, machines, computers, and equipment that are used in the design, production, and distribution of goods and services. As a rule, the more complicated the technology an organization uses, the more difficult it is for managers and employees to impose strict control on technology or to regulate it efficiently.[52] Thus, the more complicated the technology, the greater is the need for a flexible structure to enhance managers' and employees' ability to respond to unexpected situations and give them the freedom to work out new solutions to the problems they encounter. In contrast, the more routine the technology, the more appropriate a formal structure is because tasks are simple and the steps needed to produce goods and services have been worked out in advance.

The nature of an organization's technology is an important determinant of its structure. Today, there is a growing use of computer-controlled production, and a movement toward using self-managed teams (groups of employees who are given the responsibility for supervising their own activities and for monitoring the quality of the goods and service they provide) to promote innovation, increase quality, and reduce costs. As a result, many companies are trying to make their structures more flexible to take advantage of the value-creating benefits of complex technology. What makes a technology routine or complicated? One researcher who investigated this issue, Charles Perrow, argued that two factors determine how complicated or nonroutine technology is: task variety and task analyzability.[53] Task variety is the number of new or unexpected problems or situations that a person or function encounters in performing tasks or jobs. Task analyzability is the degree to which programmed solutions are available to people or functions to solve the problems they encounter. Nonroutine or complicated technologies are characterized by high task variety and low task analyzability; this means that many varied problems occur and that solving these problems requires significant nonprogrammed decision making. In contrast, routine technologies are characterized by low task variety and high task analyzability; this means that the problems encountered do not vary much and are easily resolved through programmed decision making.

Examples of nonroutine technology are found in the work of scientists in an R&D laboratory who develop new products or discover new drugs, and they are seen in the planning exercises an organization's top-management team uses to chart the organization's future strategy. Examples of routine technology include typical mass-production or

Assembling fine-dining dinner plates requires motivated and skilled staff, while serving fast food is very routine.
Shutterstock/Semen Kuzmin

assembly operations, where workers perform the same task repeatedly and where managers have already identified the programmed solutions necessary to perform a task efficiently. Similarly, in service organizations such as fast-food restaurants, the tasks that crew members perform in making and serving fast food are very routine.

HUMAN RESOURCES

A final important factor affecting an organization's choice of structure and culture is the characteristics of the human resources it employs. In general, the more highly skilled an organization's workforce and the more people required to work together in groups or teams to perform their tasks, the more likely the organization is to use a flexible, decentralized structure. Highly skilled employees or those who have internalized strong professional values and norms of behaviour as part of their training usually desire freedom and autonomy and dislike close supervision. Accountants, for example, have learned the need to report company accounts honestly and impartially, and doctors and nurses have absorbed the obligation to give patients the best care possible without being watched over by a supervisor.

Flexible structures, characterized by decentralized authority and empowered employees, are well suited to the needs of highly skilled people. Similarly, when people work in teams, they must be allowed to interact freely, which also is possible in a flexible organizational structure. Thus, when designing an organizational structure and culture, managers must pay close attention to the needs of the workforce and to the complexity and kind of work employees perform.

In summary, an organization's external environment, strategy, technology, and human resources are the factors to be considered by managers seeking to design the best structure and culture for an organization. The greater the level of uncertainty in an organization's environment, the more complex its strategy and technology, and the more highly qualified and skilled its workforce, the more likely managers will design a structure and culture that are flexible, can change quickly, and allow employees to be innovative in their responses to problems, customer needs, and so on. The more stable an organization's environment, the less complex and better understood its strategy or technology, and the less skilled its workforce, the more likely managers will design an organizational structure that is formal and controlling and a culture whose values and norms prescribe how employees should act in particular situations.

Chapter 5

SUMMARY AND REVIEW

Mc Graw Hill Education **connect**

LO1 Designing Organizational Structure Organizational structure is the formal system of both task and reporting relationships that determines how employees use resources to achieve organizational goals. The way organizational structures work depends on how tasks are grouped into individual jobs; how jobs are grouped into functional departments and divisions; how authority is allocated and decisions are made; and whether the structure is formal or flexible.

LO2 Grouping Tasks into Jobs: Job Design Job design is the initial process by which managers group tasks into jobs. To create more interesting jobs, and to get workers to act flexibly, managers can enlarge and enrich jobs. Hackman and Oldman's job characteristics model provides a tool managers can use to measure how motivating or satisfying a particular job is.

LO3 Departmentalization Managers can choose from many kinds of organizational structures to make the best use of organizational resources. Depending on the specific organizing problems they face, managers can choose from functional, divisional (based on product, geography, or market segment (customer)), matrix, product/project team, and network structures or a combination of several forms of organizing.

LO4 Allocating Authority and Decision-Making Responsibilities No matter which structure managers choose, they must decide how to distribute authority in the organization, how many levels in the hierarchy of authority to have, and what balance to strike between centralization and decentralization to keep the number of levels in the hierarchy to a minimum. As organizations grow, managers must increase integration mechanisms to ensure coordination among functions and divisions.

LO5 Choosing a Formal or Flexible Overall Structure Overall organizational structure is determined by four main factors: the external environment, strategy, technology, and human resources. In general, the higher the level of uncertainty associated with these factors, the more appropriate a flexible, adaptable structure is as opposed to a formal, rigid one.

KEY TERMS

authority	liaison roles
boundaryless organization	line manager
business-to-business (B2B) networks	market segment division
chain of command	matrix team
cross-functional team	mechanistic structure
decentralizing decision-making authority	minimum chain of command
departmentalization	network structure
division of labour	organic structure
divisional structure	organizational design
functional structure	organizational structure
geographic division	outsource
hierarchy of authority	product division
integrating mechanisms	product/project team
integrating role	simple structure
job design	span of control
job enlargement	staff manager
job enrichment	strategic alliance
job simplification	work specialization
knowledge management system	

WRAP-UP TO OPENING CASE

Samsung Reorganizes for the 21st Century

As noted in Chapter 4, an organization's design and structure must be closely aligned with its strategy. The strategy depends on the nature of the business and the competitive and environmental landscape. Strategy is successful when the leaders and management teams recognize the opportunities and threats in the environment and effectively organize the resources to compete in such a market. Leaders need to make decisions on how best to adapt and change to remain competitive. The family-owned and controlled Samsung Group of companies has done just that. After having read and understood the concepts in this chapter, you should be able to answer the following questions:

1. *How would you characterize Samsung Group's organizational structure?*

    ANSWER: After its reorganization, Samsung Group is using a global product structure common to many multinational organizations. This is a form of divisional structure, where autonomous business units are set up to produce a specific product for a specific customer. Each division is self-contained with its own president and CFO. Product division managers manage their own budgets and global value chains and decide where to establish foreign subsidiaries to distribute and sell their products to customers in foreign countries.

2. *How did the changes to Samsung's organizational structure affect the hierarchy of authority and span of control?*

    ANSWER: The hierarchy of authority is the organization's chain of command. Samsung Group's change in organizational structure has reduced the levels in the hierarchy of authority by eliminating one level of management. The span of control refers to the number of subordinates who report directly to a manager. In this case, the president and chief financial officer of each global product division—Device Solutions (DS) Division, Consumer Electronics (CE) Division, and IT and Mobile Communications (IM) Division—now reports directly to the president and CEO of Samsung Group.

3. *How is Samsung's strategy related to its structure?*

    ANSWER: Samsung has pursued a corporate-level strategy of unrelated diversification, resulting in 83 different companies in several industrial sectors including financial services and electronics. Its global operations were overseen by individual Global Business Management (GBM) divisions, creating a top-heavy hierarchy of authority, which slowed down decision making, speed to market, and customer responsiveness. Samsung Group reorganized to a global product structure, including where each product division manager takes responsibility for deciding where to manufacture its products and how to market them in countries worldwide. Removing one level of management, by eliminating the GBM, allowed each product to be managed in its own self-contained division and gave divisional managers the responsibility for devising an appropriate business-level strategy to allow the product to compete effectively in its industry or market. Decision time was reduced, divisional managers could focus on developing strategies that focus on their particular customers, and the time it takes to get new products to market became faster. The global product structure is a more efficient way of organizing resources.

By adopting a global product divisional structure, Samsung will be better positioned to compete in new industries over the next 10 years. To compete in the new industries, Samsung is using strategic alliances and networks of strategic alliances which take advantage of expertise and knowledge sharing through cooperation between two or more companies. For example, it has partnered with AdvancedCare.com to provide telehealth and remote patient monitoring systems. Of the 83 companies under the Samsung Group umbrella, several provide inputs to each other's business products. Thus, we can say that Samsung's new strategy lends itself to a series of strategic alliances, resulting in a global network structure.

MANAGEMENT IN ACTION

TOPICS FOR DISCUSSION AND ACTION

LEVEL 1 Knowledge & Comprehension

1. Describe the things managers must consider when engaging in organizational design.

2. How do matrix structures and product/project team structures differ? Why is the product team structure more widely used?

3. Using the job characteristics model as a guide, discuss how a manager might enlarge or enrich a salesperson's or secretary's job to make it more motivating.

LEVEL 2 Application & Analysis

4. Google's organizational structure has been described as being similar to the "Brownian motion," the way that molecules of food colouring move through water in a bottle. Research and report on Google's organizational structure.

5. Find and interview a manager and identify the kind of organizational structure that his or her organization uses to coordinate people and resources. Discuss the distribution of authority. Does the manager think that decentralizing authority and empowering employees is appropriate? Why or why not?

6. Research the organizational structure of Branson's Virgin Group Investments Ltd. Would you characterize the Branson empire as mechanistic or organic in overall structure?

LEVEL 3 Synthesis & Evaluation

7. Compare the pros and cons of using a network structure to perform organizational activities and performing all activities in-house (within one organizational hierarchy).

8. Would a flexible or a more formal structure be appropriate for these organizations: (a) a large department store, (b) a big accounting firm, (c) a biotechnology company? Explain your reasoning.

9. When and under what conditions might a manager change from a functional structure to (a) a product, (b) a geographic, or (c) a market structure?

SELF-REFLECTION EXERCISE

Choose an organization for which you have worked. How did the structure of your job and the organization affect your job satisfaction? Did the tasks within your job make sense? In what ways could they be better organized? What structural changes would you make to this organization? Would you consider making this a taller or flatter organization? How would the changes you have proposed improve responsiveness to customers and your job satisfaction?

SMALL GROUP BREAKOUT EXERCISE

Bob's Appliances

Form groups of three or four, and appoint one member as the spokesperson who will communicate your findings to the whole class when called on by the instructor. Then discuss the following scenario:

Bob's Appliances sells and services household appliances such as washing machines, dishwashers, stoves, and refrigerators. Over the years, the company has developed a good reputation for the quality of its customer service, and many local builders are customers at the store. Recently, some new appliance retailers, including Best Buy, have opened stores that also sell numerous appliances. In addition to appliances, however, to attract more customers, these stores carry a complete range of consumer electronics products, including television sets, stereos, and computers. Bob Lange, the owner of Bob's Appliances, has decided that to stay in business he must widen his product range and compete directly with the chains.

In 2019, he decided to build a new 1800-square-foot store and service centre, and he is now hiring new employees to sell and service the new line of consumer electronics. Because of his company's increased size, Lange is not sure of the best way to organize the employees. Currently, he uses a functional structure; employees are divided into sales, purchasing and accounting, and repair. Bob is wondering whether selling and servicing consumer electronics is so different from selling and servicing appliances that he should move to a product structure (see the figure below) and create separate sets of functions for each of his two lines of business.[54]

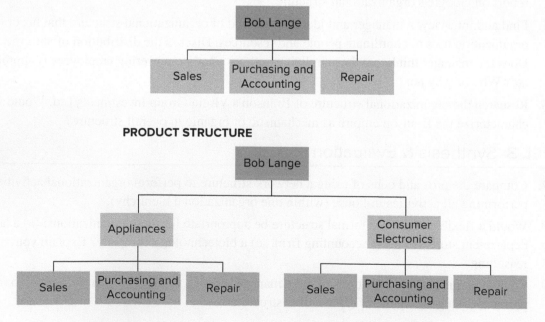

FUNCTIONAL STRUCTURE

Bob Lange
- Sales
- Purchasing and Accounting
- Repair

PRODUCT STRUCTURE

Bob Lange
- Appliances
  - Sales
  - Purchasing and Accounting
  - Repair
- Consumer Electronics
  - Sales
  - Purchasing and Accounting
  - Repair

You are a member of a team of local consultants that Bob has called in to advise him as he makes this crucial choice. Which structure would you recommend? Why?

MANAGING ETHICALLY EXERCISE

In many businesses—such as chicken-processing plants, small engineering companies, furniture makers, warehouses, and offices—unskilled workers perform the same repetitive tasks for many hours a day, day in and day out, and often for years if they stay at the same job. Boredom is common, as is the development of physical ailments such as skin problems, muscle fatigue, and carpal tunnel syndrome. Is it ethical for managers to allow workers to perform repetitive tasks for long periods of time? What kinds of standards would you use to settle this issue? To what degree should job redesign be used to change such a situation and enrich jobs if it also would raise costs and make a company less competitive? How could organizational structure be redesigned to make this problem less prevalent?

MANAGEMENT CHALLENGE EXERCISE

Speeding Up Website Design

You have been hired by a website design, production, and hosting company whose new animated website designs are attracting a lot of attention and a lot of customers. Currently, employees are organized into different functions such as hardware, software design, graphic art, and website hosting, as well as functions such as marketing and human resources. Each function takes its turn to work on a new project from initial customer request to final online website hosting.

The problem the company is experiencing is that it typically takes one year from the initial idea stage to the time that the website is up and running; the company wants to shorten this time by half to protect and expand its market niche. In talking to other managers, you discover that they believe the company's current functional structure is the source of the problem—it is not allowing employees to develop websites fast enough to satisfy customers' demands. They want you to design a better one.

1. Discuss ways in which you can improve how the current functional structure operates so that it speeds website development.

2. Discuss the pros and cons of moving to a (a) multidivisional, (b) matrix, or (c) product team structure to reduce website development time.

3. Which of these structures do you think is most appropriate, and why?

MANAGEMENT PORTFOLIO PROJECT

Answer the following questions about the organization you have chosen to follow:

1. Describe the organizational structure of the firm.

2. Does the enterprise have centralized or decentralized control over decision making?

3. How many levels are present in the hierarchy of authority? Is the structure tall or flat?

4. Is the structure suitable for the strategy, technology, human resources, and organizational environment in which the firm operates? If not, suggest ways in which it could better align its structure to support its mission.

MANAGEMENT CASE

LOBLAW ACQUIRES SHOPPERS DRUG MART

When the deal to purchase Shoppers Drug Mart concluded in 2015, Loblaw had to reorganize its corporate structure. To satisfy the Competition Bureau of Canada, Loblaw had to sell 18 Shoppers Drug Mart stores and 19 of its own in-store pharmacies.[55] Below is the new organizational chart for Loblaw since the acquisition.

1. Describe the type of organizational structure at Loblaw.

2. Can you recommend a more efficient and effective way for the company to organize?

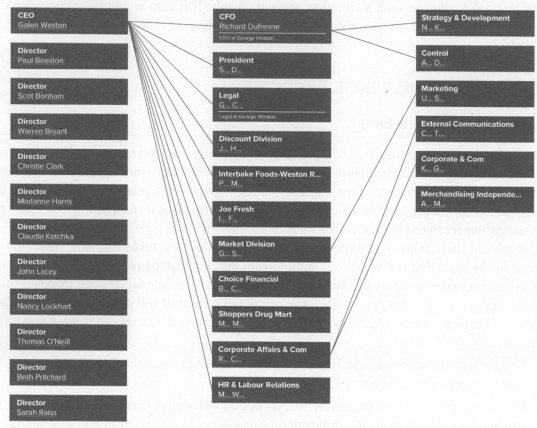

Source: Reprinted by permission of The Official Board

Managing Communication and Information Technology (IT)

LEARNING OUTCOMES

LO1	Explain why effective communication helps an organization gain a competitive advantage.
LO2	Describe the communication process and communication styles.
LO3	Describe the organizational communication networks and channels available to managers.

LO4	Explain how the use of information technology (IT) can be vital to organizational communication.
LO5	Describe how managers are using social media to communicate.

OPENING CASE

Amazon's Newest IT Revolution

Amazon opened a grocery store in Seattle, Washington, in early 2018 that will revolutionize the way we shop.[1]

As you enter the store and go through the turnstile, you swipe your smartphone. This registers your identity and tracks your progress through the store. You then pick up the items you want to purchase and walk out. The Amazon account on your smartphone is automatically charged with the items you chose. The process relies heavily on new technology involving hundreds of overhead cameras with computer vision and weight sensors in the shelves that enable Amazon to know what products you pick up. If you change your mind and put an item back on the shelf, Amazon automatically takes it off the bill in your virtual cart. This revolutionary new store signifies more than just the disruption of conventional bricks-and-mortar shopping for consumers; it is also representative of Amazon's long-term strategy to expand its presence in the physical retail arena. It now owns 470 grocery stores, including the Whole Foods chain, as well as several bookstores. It also has floor space in some Kohl's department stores where, among other things, Amazon.com returns can be processed.[2]

Walmart introduced its scan-and-go technology in about 20 Canadian stores at the same time as Amazon Go rolled out in Seattle. Walmart shoppers in these stores scan the barcodes of items they want to purchase using either using a portable scanner or a smartphone app, then place the items in their shopping cart. When they have finished their shopping, customers pay the automatically tallied bill either at a cashier or a self-checkout, showing their receipt to the "exit greeter" as proof of purchase when they leave the store.[3]

Driven by consumers' increasing impatience with waiting in line, it seems a foregone conclusion that retailers will continue to use automation to revolutionize physical shopping. Once regarded as cutting-edge, according to London-based research and consulting group RBR, there were over a quarter million self-checkout machines around the world by the end of 2016—a number that RBR predicted would rise to 400 000 by 2022.[4]

Amazon Go disrupts the grocery shopping experience.
Paul Christian Gordon/Alamy Stock Photo

After reading and understanding the concepts in this chapter, you should be able to answer the following question:

1. How will Amazon Go disrupt the grocery industry?

◼ Overview

As Amazon's success suggests, developing new IT to improve operations and decision making is a vital managerial task. Communication is an essential component in the fabric of a healthy workplace. In addition to warding off toxic work environments, effective communication can be <u>the lifeblood</u> of work each day. Ineffective communication is detrimental for managers, employees, and organizations; it can lead to conflict, poor performance, strained interpersonal relations, poor service, and dissatisfied customers. Managers at all levels need to be good communicators in order for an organization to be effective and gain a competitive advantage. Increasingly, new information technology (IT) is fundamentally changing the way we communicate and, as the opening case illustrates, even the way we complete day-to-day tasks such as shopping for groceries.

In this chapter, we describe the nature of communication and the communication process and explain why it is so important for all managers and their subordinates to be effective communicators. We describe the communication skills that help individuals be effective senders and receivers of messages and how barriers that create ineffective communication can be overcome. We describe the communication networks available to managers, and the factors that managers need to consider in selecting a communication method for each message they send. Next, we discuss the utilization of information technology (IT) and how management information systems (MIS) are changing the way managers collect, interpret, and communicate information. Finally, we discuss the ways that managers and organizations are using social media to communicate with employees and with external stakeholders. By the end of this chapter, you will have an appreciation of the nature of communication and the steps that all organizational members can take to ensure that they are effective communicators. You will also become aware of the skills necessary to manage organizational conflict.

◼ The Importance of Communication in Organizations

LO1 | Explain why effective communication helps an organization gain a competitive advantage.

Communication is the sharing of information between two or more individuals or groups to reach a common understanding.[5] Some organizations are more effective at doing this than are others. First and foremost, communication, no matter how electronically based, is a human endeavour and involves individuals and groups. Second, communication does not take place unless a common understanding is reached. Thus, if you try to call a business to speak to a person in customer service or billing and you are bounced back and forth between endless automated messages and menu options and eventually hang up in frustration, communication has not taken place.

> **communication** The sharing of information between two or more individuals or groups to reach a common understanding.

In Chapter 2, we explained that in order for an organization to gain a competitive advantage managers must strive to increase efficiency, quality, responsiveness to customers, and innovation. Good communication is essential for attaining each of these four goals and thus is a necessity for gaining a competitive advantage.

✸ Managers can *increase efficiency* by updating the production process to take advantage of new and more efficient technologies and by training workers to operate the new technologies and expand their skills. Good communication is necessary for managers to learn about new technologies, implement them in their organizations, and train workers in how to use them. Similarly, *improving quality* hinges on effective communication. Managers need to communicate to all members of an organization the meaning and importance of high quality and the routes to attaining it. Subordinates need to communicate quality problems and suggestions for increasing quality to their superiors, and members of self-managed work teams need to share their ideas for improving quality with each other.

Good communication can also help to increase *responsiveness to customers*. When the organizational members who are closest to customers, such as salespeople in department stores and tellers in banks, are empowered to communicate customers' needs and desires to managers, managers are better able to respond to these needs. Managers, in turn, must communicate with other organizational members to determine how best to respond to changing customer preferences. As discussed in Chapter 4, effective communication is particularly important when managing crises. Maple Leaf Foods is widely considered a textbook example of successfully communicating with customers for the way it handled Canada's largest food recall ever due to a deadly outbreak of listeria at one of its meat plants in August 2008. CEO Michael McCain quickly responded to the recall by holding a press conference, as well as recording a YouTube video detailing the steps Maple Leaf was taking to resolve the problems. The company also bought advertisements in newspapers and on television to inform customers further. The CEOs of Research In Motion (now BlackBerry), on the other hand, waited until the problem of the worldwide BlackBerry outage in 2011 was essentially resolved before co-CEO Mike Lazaridis went on YouTube to give an update. Ten years later, Apple had to apologize to customers after they learned the company was deliberately slowing down older iPhone models.

Effective communication skills are important for managers.
©Arne9001 | Dreamstime.com

✸*Innovation,* which often takes place in cross-functional teams, also requires effective communication. Members of a cross-functional team developing a new mobile app, for example, must communicate effectively with each other to develop an app that customers will want, that will be of high quality, and that can work across platforms efficiently. Members of the team also must communicate with managers to secure the resources they need to develop the app and keep the managers informed of progress on the project.

✸ Effective communication is necessary for managers and all members of an organization to increase efficiency, quality, responsiveness to customers, and innovation and thus gain a competitive advantage for their organization. Managers therefore must have a good understanding of the communication process if they are to perform effectively. Work that is truly team-based entails a number of highly interdependent yet distinct components, and involves team members with distinct areas of expertise who need to closely coordinate their efforts.

The Communication Process and Communication Styles

LO2 | Describe the communication process and communication styles.

The Communication Process

The communication process consists of two phases. In the *transmission phase,* information is shared between two or more individuals or groups. In the *feedback phase,* a common understanding is reached. In both phases, a number of distinct stages must occur for communication to take place (see Figure 6.1).[6]

The **sender** (the person or group wishing to share information with some other person or group) starts the transmission phase by deciding on the **message** (the information to communicate). Then the sender translates the message into symbols or language, a process called **encoding.** Often, messages are encoded into words but they could also be symbols, such as :-) or a stop sign. **Noise** is a general term that refers to anything that hampers any stage of the communication process.

sender The person or group wishing to share information.

message The information that a sender wants to share.

encoding Translating a message into understandable symbols or language.

noise Anything that hampers any stage of the communication process.

Once encoded, a message is transmitted through a medium to the **receiver,** the person or group for which the message is intended. A **medium** is simply the pathway—such as social media, a phone call, a letter, a memo, or face-to-face communication in a meeting—through which an encoded message is

FIGURE 6.1

The Communication Process

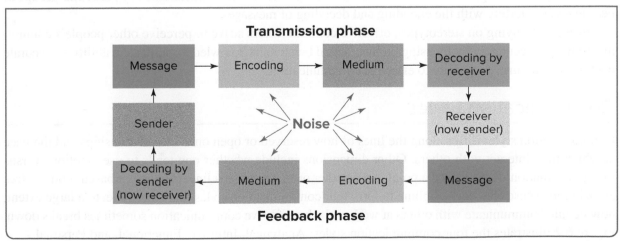

transmitted to a receiver. At the next stage, the receiver interprets and tries to make sense of the message, a process called **decoding.** This is a critical point in communication.

> **receiver** The person or group for which a message is intended.
> **medium** The pathway through which an encoded message is transmitted to a receiver.
> **decoding** Interpreting and trying to make sense of a message.

The feedback phase is begun by the receiver (who becomes a sender). The receiver decides what message to send to the original sender (who becomes a receiver), encodes it, and transmits it through a chosen medium (see Figure 6.1). The message might contain a confirmation that the original message was received and understood, a restatement of the original message to make sure that it was correctly interpreted, or a request for more information. The original sender decodes the message and makes sure that a common understanding has been reached. If the original sender determines that a common understanding has not been reached, the sender and receiver go through the whole process as many times as needed to reach a common understanding. Failure to listen to employees prevents many managers from receiving feedback and reaching a common understanding with their employees. Feedback eliminates misunderstandings, ensures that messages are correctly interpreted, and enables senders and receivers to reach a common understanding. The communication loop is successful only when the sender can confirm that the receiver understands the intent of the message.

Perception plays a central role in communication and affects both transmission and feedback. **Perception** is the process through which people select, organize, and interpret sensory input to give meaning and order to the world around them. But it is inherently subjective and influenced by people's personalities, values, attitudes, and moods, as well as by their culture, experience, and knowledge. Thus, when senders and receivers communicate with each other, they are doing so based on their own subjective perceptions. The encoding and decoding of messages and even the choice of a medium hinge on the perceptions of senders and receivers.

> **perception** The process through which people select, organize, and interpret sensory input to give meaning and order to the world around them.

In addition, perceptual biases can hamper effective communication. Recall from Chapter 3 that *biases* are systematic tendencies to use information about others in ways that result in inaccurate perceptions and poor decisions. These same biases also can lead to ineffective communication. For example, stereotypes—simplified and often inaccurate beliefs about the characteristics of particular groups of people—can interfere with the encoding and decoding of messages.

Instead of relying on stereotypes, effective communicators strive to perceive other people's communication style accurately by focusing on their actual behaviours, knowledge, skills, and abilities. Accurate perceptions, in turn, contribute to effective communication.

Communication Styles

Communication styles differ along the lines of how reserved or open one is to relationships and the pace at which they interact with others. Other dimensions include whether one tends to use emotions versus using information/data to make a point and whether one's thinking is linear/logical or based more on free association. These elements combine to form four communication styles that determine, to a large extent, how people communicate with others at work and why effective communication sometimes breaks down. Figure 6.2 illustrates the four communication styles: Analytical, Intuitive, Functional, and Personal.

FIGURE 6.2

Communication Styles

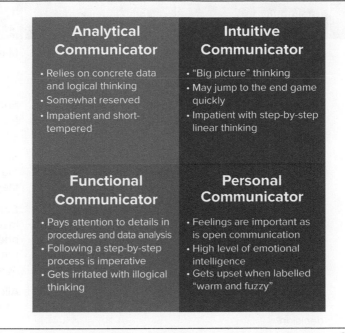

Analytical Communicator
- Relies on concrete data and logical thinking
- Somewhat reserved
- Impatient and short-tempered

Intuitive Communicator
- "Big picture" thinking
- May jump to the end game quickly
- Impatient with step-by-step linear thinking

Functional Communicator
- Pays attention to details in procedures and data analysis
- Following a step-by-step process is imperative
- Gets irritated with illogical thinking

Personal Communicator
- Feelings are important as is open communication
- High level of emotional intelligence
- Gets upset when labelled "warm and fuzzy"

Source: Based on Murphy, M. (2015, August 6). Which of these four communication styles are you? *Forbes*. https://www.forbes.com/sites/markmurphy/2015/08/06/which-of-these-4-communication-styles-are-you/#6c5a40953adb. Accessed Sept. 4, 2018.

We find it much easier to communicate with people who share our style, but, of course, effective communicators must understand how to communicate with all styles if miscommunication is to be avoided. Table 6.1 offers some tips on communicating effectively with each style. For example, if you are communicating with an analytical communicator, try to get to the point quickly in a clear and succinct manner, speak at a fast pace, and so on.

Verbal and Nonverbal Communication

The encoding of messages into words, written or spoken, is **verbal communication.** We also encode messages without using written or spoken language; **nonverbal communication** shares information by means of facial expressions (smiling, raising an eyebrow, frowning, dropping one's jaw), body language (posture, gestures, nods, shrugs), and even style of dressing (casual, formal, conservative, trendy). "People make judgments about you based on how you look. If you're sloppily dressed or look like you're going to the beach, you'll leave a negative impression on clients and other employees," warned Natasha VandenHoven when she was senior vice president of human resources at Aon Consulting in Toronto.[7]

verbal communication The encoding of messages into words, either written or spoken.

nonverbal communication The encoding of messages by means of facial expressions, body language, and styles of dressing.

TABLE 6.1

Tips for Communicating with Different Styles

The Analytic Communicator	The Intuitive Communicator	The Functional Communicator	The Personal Communicator
Get to the point quickly in a clear and succinct manner	Use less intense eye contact	Be more formal in your speech and manner	Make direct eye contact
Speak at a fast pace	Speak at a moderate pace with a softer voice and moderate tone	Don't speak in a loud or fast-paced voice	Speak in an energetic and fast-paced manner
Be specific and don't overexplain or repeat yourself	Seek their opinions and ideas, then listen	Present the pros and cons of an idea along with options	Support your ideas with the opinions of people they respect
Make direct eye contact	Try not to counter their ideas with logical arguments	Follow up in writing	Confirm any agreements made; follow up with a brief "to do" list so they remember what they agreed to do
Minimize small talk	To reduce pressure, allow time for them to make a decision	Be punctual	Allow some socializing time in meetings
Be organized and well prepared	Encourage them to express their concerns without getting upset with them	Present information in an organized, planned, and comprehensive manner	Talk about experiences, people, opinions, and facts
Focus on results to be achieved	Aim for mutual agreement on work goals and completion dates	Accept that options requiring risk-taking are generally not welcomed	Ask about their "gut" feeling
Be punctual and stick to guidelines			Maintain balance between fun and achieving results

Source: Adapted from "Understanding Communication Styles in the Workplace" by Anne Toner Fung. Reprinted by permission of Anne Toner Fung.

> *"People make judgments about you based on how you look. If you're sloppily dressed or look like you're going to the beach, you'll leave a negative impression on clients and other employees."*
>
> Natasha Vandenhoven, partner, Davies Ward Phillips & Vineberg LLP

Nonverbal communication can reinforce verbal communication. Just as a warm and genuine smile can support words of appreciation for a job well done, a concerned facial expression can support words of sympathy for a personal problem. In such cases, similarity between verbal and nonverbal communication helps ensure that a common understanding is reached. This is not always as straightforward as it appears. Nonverbal gestures are culturally constructed; that is, different cultures perceive and interpret nonverbal symbols differently. For example, the thumbs-up sign in Western cultures indicates "all is good," but in the Middle East it is a gesture of insult. Similarly, maintaining eye contact is viewed as a sign of engagement and attentiveness in Canada, but in Japan it is viewed as rude behaviour and an invasion of privacy.[8]

Nonverbal cues, such as an intense look exchanged by two people, can provide managers and employees with vital information that helps them make better decisions. Sometimes when members of an organization decide not to express a message verbally, they inadvertently do so nonverbally. People tend to have less control over nonverbal communication, and often a verbal message that is withheld gets expressed through body language or facial expressions. For instance, a manager who agrees to a proposal that she or he actually is not in favour of may unintentionally communicate disfavour by grimacing.

Sometimes nonverbal communication is used to send messages that cannot be sent through verbal channels. Many lawyers are well aware of this communication tactic. Law-

Body language conveys culturally specific messages.
E. Audras/PhotoAlto

yers are often schooled in techniques of nonverbal communication, such as choosing where to stand in the courtroom for maximum effect and using eye contact during different stages of a trial. Lawyers sometimes get into trouble for using inappropriate nonverbal communication in an attempt to influence juries.

It is important to be aware of nonverbal aspects of communication, as well as the literal meanings of words. You should particularly be aware of contradictions between the messages. A manager may say it is a good time to discuss a raise but then keep looking at the clock. This nonverbal signal may indicate that this is really *not* a good time to talk. Thus, actions can speak louder (and more accurately) than words. A variety of popular books help one interpret body language. However, do use some care. For instance, while it is often thought that crossing your arms in front of your chest conveys resistance to a message, one might do this simply because they feel cold.

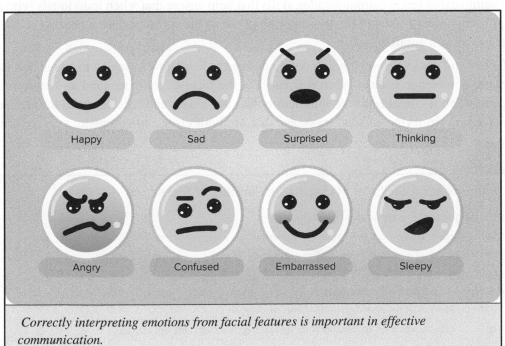

Correctly interpreting emotions from facial features is important in effective communication.

Good communication is essential for organizations to function effectively. Managers spend about 85 percent of their time engaged in some form of communication, whether in meetings, in telephone conversations, through email, or in face-to-face interactions. Employees also need to be effective communicators.[9] When all members of an organization are able to communicate effectively with each other and with people outside the organization, the organization is much more likely to perform highly and gain a competitive advantage.

Developing Communication Skills

There are various kinds of barriers to effective communication in organizations. Some barriers have their origins in senders. When messages are unclear, incomplete, or difficult to understand, when they are sent over an inappropriate medium, or when no provision for feedback is made, communication suffers. Other communication barriers have their origins in receivers. When receivers pay no attention to, do not listen to, or make no effort to understand the meaning of a message, communication is likely to be ineffective.

To overcome these barriers and effectively communicate with others, managers (as well as other organizational members) must possess or develop certain communication skills. Some of these skills are particularly important when individuals send messages, and others are critical when individuals receive messages. These skills help ensure not only that individuals will be able to share information but also that they will have the information they need to make good decisions and take action and be able to reach a common understanding with others.

Communication Skills for Senders

Individuals can make sure that they consider all of the steps of the communication process when they are engaging in communication.

IMPROVING THE COMMUNICATION PROCESS

Table 6.2 summarizes seven communication skills that help ensure that when individuals send messages, they are properly understood and the transmission phase of the communication process is effective. Let us see what each skill entails.

1. *Send clear and complete messages.* Individuals need to learn how to send a message that is clear and complete. A message is clear when it is easy for the receiver to understand and interpret, and it is complete when it contains all the information that the sender and receiver need to reach a common understanding. In trying to send messages that are both clear and complete, managers must learn

---

TABLE 6.2

Seven Communication Skills for Managers as Senders of Messages

1. Send messages that are clear and complete.
2. Encode messages in symbols the receiver understands.
3. Select a medium that is appropriate for the message.
4. Select a medium that the receiver monitors.
5. Avoid filtering and information distortion.
6. Ensure that a feedback mechanism is built into messages.
7. Provide accurate information to ensure that misleading rumours are not spread.

to anticipate how receivers will interpret messages and adjust messages to eliminate sources of misunderstanding or confusion.

2. *Encode messages in symbols the receiver understands.* Individuals need to appreciate that when they encode messages, they should use symbols or language that the receiver understands. When sending messages in English to receivers whose native language is not English, for example, it is important to use commonplace vocabulary and to avoid clichés that, when translated, may make little sense and in some cases are unintentionally comical or insulting.

   Jargon, specialized language that members of an occupation, group, or organization develop to facilitate communication among themselves, should never be used to communicate with people outside the occupation, group, or organization. For example, truck drivers refer to compact cars as "roller skates," highway dividing lines as "paints," and orange barrels around road construction areas as "Schneider eggs." Using this jargon among themselves results in effective communication because they know precisely what is being referred to, but if a truck driver used this language to send a message (such as "That roller skate can't stay off the paint") to a receiver who did not drive trucks, the receiver would not know what the message meant.[10]

3. *Select a medium appropriate for the message.* When choosing among communication media, individuals need to take into account the level of information richness required, time constraints, and the need for a paper or electronic trail. A primary concern in choosing an appropriate medium is the nature of the message. Is it personal, important, nonroutine, and likely to be misunderstood and in need of further clarification? If it is, face-to-face communication is likely to be in order.

4. *Select a medium that the receiver monitors.* Another factor that individuals need to take into account when selecting a communication medium is whether it is one that the receiver uses. Not everyone checks voice mail and email routinely. Many people simply select the medium that they themselves use the most and are most comfortable with, but doing this can often lead to ineffective communication. No matter how much an individual likes email, sending an email message to someone else who never checks his or her email is useless. Learning which individuals like things in writing and which prefer face-to-face interactions and then using the appropriate medium enhances the chance that receivers will actually receive and pay attention to messages.

   A related consideration is whether receivers have disabilities that limit their ability to decode certain kinds of messages. A visually impaired receiver, for example, cannot read a written message. Managers should ensure that their employees with disabilities have resources available to communicate effectively with others.

5. *Avoid filtering and information distortion.* **Filtering** occurs when senders withhold part of a message because they (mistakenly) think that the receiver does not need the information or will not want to receive it. Filtering can occur at all levels in an organization and in both vertical and horizontal communication. Rank-and-file employees may filter messages they send to first-line managers, first-line managers may filter messages to middle managers, and middle managers may filter messages to top managers. Such filtering is most likely to take place when messages contain bad news or problems that subordinates are afraid they will be blamed for.

   Information distortion occurs when the meaning of a message changes as the message passes through a series of senders and receivers. Some information distortion is accidental—due to faulty encoding and decoding or to a lack of feedback. Other information distortion is deliberate. Senders may alter a message to make themselves or their groups look good and to receive special treatment.

Managers themselves should avoid filtering and distorting information. But how can they eliminate these barriers to effective communication throughout their organization? They need to establish trust throughout the organization. Subordinates who trust their managers believe that they will not be blamed for things beyond their control and will be treated fairly. Managers who trust their subordinates provide them with clear and complete information and do not hold things back.

6. *Include a feedback mechanism in messages.* Because feedback is essential for effective communication, individuals should build a feedback mechanism into the messages they send. They either should include a request for feedback or indicate when and how they will follow up on the message to make sure that it was received and understood. When writing letters and memos or sending faxes, one can request that the receiver respond with comments and suggestions in a letter, memo, or fax; schedule a meeting to discuss the issue; or follow up with a phone call. Building feedback mechanisms such as these into messages ensures that messages are received and understood.

7. *Provide accurate information.* **Rumours** are unofficial pieces of information of interest to organizational members but with no identifiable source. Rumours spread quickly once they are started, and usually they concern topics that organizational members think are important, interesting, or amusing. Rumours, however, can be misleading and can cause harm to individual employees and to an organization when they are false, malicious, or unfounded. Managers can halt the spread of misleading rumours by providing organizational members with accurate information on matters that concern them.

jargon Specialized language that members of an occupation, group, or organization develop to facilitate communication among themselves.

filtering Withholding part of a message out of the mistaken belief that the receiver does not need or will not want the information.

information distortion Changes in the meaning of a message as the message passes through a series of senders and receivers.

rumours Unofficial pieces of information of interest to organizational members but with no identifiable source.

Communication Skills for Receivers

Senders also receive messages, and thus they must possess or develop communication skills that allow them to be effective receivers of messages. Table 6.3 summarizes three of these important skills, which we examine in greater detail.

1. PAY ATTENTION

When individuals are overloaded and forced to think about several things at once, they sometimes do not pay sufficient attention to the messages they receive. To be effective, however, individuals should always

TABLE 6.3

Three Communication Skills for Managers as Receivers of Messages

1. Pay attention.
2. Be a good listener.
3. Be empathetic.

pay attention to messages they receive, no matter how busy they are. For example, when discussing a project with a subordinate, an effective manager focuses on the project and not on an upcoming meeting with his or her own boss. Similarly, when individuals are reading written forms of communication, they should focus their attention on understanding what they are reading and not be sidetracked into thinking about other issues.

2. BE A GOOD LISTENER

Part of being a good communicator is being a good listener. This is an essential communication skill for all organizational members. Being a good listener is surprisingly more difficult than you might realize, however. The average person speaks at a rate of 125 to 200 words per minute, but the average listener can effectively process up to 400 words per minute. Therefore listeners are often thinking about other things when someone is speaking to them.

It is important to engage in active listening, which requires paying attention, interpreting, and remembering what was said. Active listening requires making a conscious effort to hear what a person is saying and interpreting it to see that it makes sense. Being a good listener is an essential communication skill in many different kinds of organizations, from small businesses to large corporations.

Organizational members can practise the following behaviours to become active listeners[11]:

1. *Make eye contact if it is culturally appropriate.* Eye contact lets the speaker know that you are paying attention, and it also lets you pick up nonverbal cues. In Japan, making eye contact is considered rude behaviour, however. Being a good listener requires being culturally sensitive.

2. *Exhibit affirmative nods and appropriate facial expressions.* By nodding your head and exhibiting appropriate facial expressions, you further show the speaker that you are listening.

3. *Avoid distracting actions or gestures.* Do not look at your watch, shuffle papers, play with your pencil, or engage in similar distractions when you are listening to someone. These actions suggest to the speaker that you are bored or uninterested. They also mean that you probably are not paying full attention to what is being said.

4. *Ask questions.* The critical listener analyzes what he or she hears and asks questions. Asking questions provides clarification and reduces ambiguity, leading to greater understanding. It also assures the speaker that you are listening.

5. *Paraphrase.* Paraphrasing means restating in your own words what the speaker has said. The effective listener uses such phrases as "What I hear you saying is . . ." or "Do you mean . . .?" Paraphrasing is a check on whether you are listening carefully and accurately.

6. *Avoid interrupting the speaker.* Interruptions can cause the speaker to lose his or her train of thought and cause the listener to jump to wrong conclusions based on incomplete information.

7. *Do not overtalk.* Most of us prefer talking to listening. However, a good listener knows the importance of taking turns in a conversation.

8. *Make smooth transitions between the roles of speaker and listener.* The effective listener knows how to make the transition from the listener role to the speaker role, and then back to being a listener. It is important to listen rather than plan what you are going to say next.

3. BE EMPATHETIC

Receivers are empathetic when they try to understand how the sender feels and try to interpret a message from the sender's perspective, rather than viewing a message from only their own point of view.

Organizational Communication Networks and Channels

LO3 | Describe the organizational communication networks and channels available to managers.

Communication within organizations can be formal or informal, top down or bottom up, horizontal among employees in teams or diagonal cutting across work units, departments, and levels in the hierarchy of authority, such as with email. Communication networks are established channels by which communication flows throughout the organization. Typically, we find five communication networks available to managers, illustrated in Figure 6.3.

- *The Wheel* network has a manager at the centre who plays the role of liaison and is responsible for integrating other work groups by controlling the information communicated from the central source.
- *The Circle* network is generally used among work groups and teams who may collaborate using file sharing and reply-all email.
- *The All-Channel* network allows information to flow freely among and between members of a department or work unit.
- *The Chain* symbolizes either formal horizontal or lateral communication among people at the same level of the organization or formal top-down or bottom-up vertical networks.
- *The "Y"* network branches out from a chain network to reach others.

The **grapevine** is the informal way of communicating information throughout an organization that is based on a gossip network or cluster network. Surprisingly, the information that is sent and received through the grapevine is seldom distorted. Not only is the information accurate, it also travels remarkably quickly. See Figure 6.4.

grapevine An informal communication network among people in organizations.

FIGURE 6.3

Formal Communication Networks

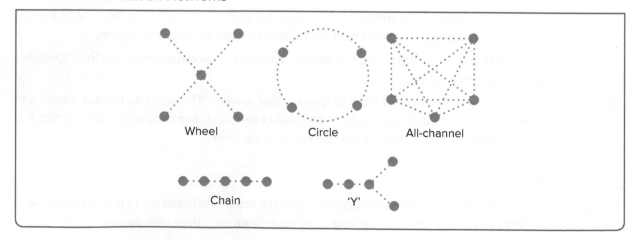

FIGURE 6.4

The Grapevine Communication Network

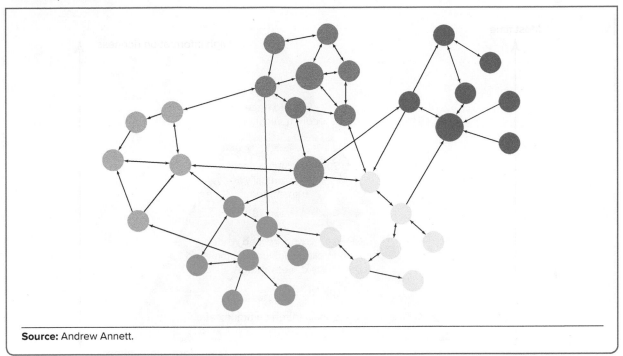

Source: Andrew Annett.

Choosing a Communication Network and Channel

To be effective communicators, individuals need to select an appropriate communication network for *each* message they send. Should a change in procedures be communicated to subordinates using an all-channel network? Should the information be in a memo or sent as email? Should a congratulatory message about a major accomplishment be communicated in a letter, in a phone call, or informally over lunch? Should a layoff announcement be made in a memo or at a plant meeting? Should the members of a purchasing team travel to Europe to finalize a major agreement with a new supplier, or should they do this through electronic files and faxes? Managers deal with these questions day in and day out.

There is no one best communication network or medium. The most appropriate choice depends on variables such as the level of information richness needed (which relates to the sensitivity of the information involved), time constraints, and the need for a permanent record to be kept.

- *The level of information richness that is needed.* **Information richness** is the amount of information a communication medium can carry and the extent to which the medium enables sender and receiver to reach a common understanding.[12] The communication media that managers use vary in their information richness (see Figure 6.5).[13] Media high in information richness are able to carry a lot of information and generally enable receivers and senders to come to a common understanding.

- *The time needed for communication.* Managers' and other organizational members' time is valuable, and this affects the way messages should be sent.

- *The need for a paper or electronic trail.* An individual may want written documentation that a message was sent and received.

FIGURE 6.5

The Information Richness of Communication Media

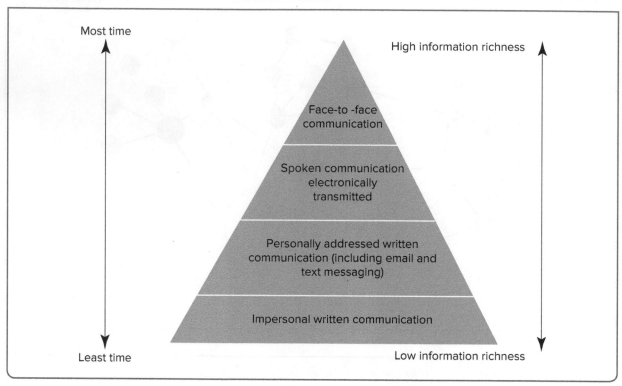

Most time

High information richness

Face-to -face communication

Spoken communication electronically transmitted

Personally addressed written communication (including email and text messaging)

Impersonal written communication

Least time

Low information richness

information richness The amount of information that a communication medium can carry and the extent to which the medium enables sender and receiver to reach a common understanding.

In the remainder of this section, we examine four types of communication media that vary along these three dimensions: information richness, time, and need for a paper or electronic trail.[14]

Face-to-Face Communication

Face-to-face communication has the highest information richness. When individuals communicate face to face, they not only can take advantage of verbal communication but also can interpret each other's nonverbal signals, such as facial expressions and body language. A look of concern or puzzlement can sometimes tell more than a thousand words, and individuals can respond to these nonverbal signals on the spot. Face-to-face communication also enables instant feedback. Points of confusion, ambiguity, or misunderstanding can be resolved, and individuals can cycle through the communication process as many times as they need to in order to reach a common understanding.

Management by wandering around (MBWA) is a face-to-face communication technique that is effective for many managers at all levels in an organization.[15] Rather than scheduling formal meetings with subordinates, managers walk around work areas and talk informally with employees about issues and concerns that both employees and managers may have. These informal conversations provide managers and subordinates with important information and at the same time foster the development of positive relationships. William Hewlett and David Packard, founders and former top managers of Hewlett-Packard, found management by wandering around to be a highly effective way to communicate with their employees.

management by wandering around (MBWA) A face-to-face communication technique in which a manager walks around a work area and talks informally with employees about issues and concerns.

Because face-to-face communication is highest in information richness, you might think that it should always be the medium of choice. This is not the case, however, because of the amount of time it takes and the lack of a paper or electronic trail resulting from it. For messages that are important, personal, or likely to be misunderstood, it is often well worth the time to use face-to-face communication and, if need be, supplement it with some form of written communication documenting the message.

Advances in information technology are providing managers with new and close alternative communication media for face-to-face communication. Many organizations are using videoconferences to capture some of the advantages of face-to-face communication (such as access to facial expressions), while saving time and money because individuals in different locations do not have to travel to meet with one another. In addition to saving travel costs, videoconferences can speed up decisions, shorten new product development time, and lead to more efficient meetings. Some managers have found that meetings are 20 to 30 percent shorter when they use videoconferences instead of face-to-face formats.[16]

Spoken Communication Electronically Transmitted

After face-to-face communication, spoken communication electronically transmitted over the phone is second-highest in information richness (see Figure 6.5). Although individuals communicating over the phone do not have access to body language and facial expressions, they do have access to the tone of voice in which a message is delivered, the parts of the message the sender emphasizes, and the general manner in which the message is spoken, in addition to the actual words themselves. Thus, phone conversations have the capacity to convey extensive amounts of information. Individuals also can ensure that mutual understanding is reached because they can get quick feedback over the phone and can answer questions.

Voice mail systems and answering machines also allow people to send and receive verbal electronic messages. Voice mail systems are companywide systems that enable senders to record messages for members of an organization who are away from their desks and allow receivers to access their messages when hundreds of kilometres away from the office. Such systems are obviously a necessity when managers or employees are frequently out of the office, and those on the road are well advised to check their voice mail periodically.

Teleconferencing can effectively facilitate meetings by retaining a personal feeling.
©Ariel Skelley/Blend Images LLC

Personally Addressed Written Communication

Lower than electronically transmitted verbal communication in information richness is personally addressed written communication, including text messaging (see Figure 6.5). One of the advantages of face-to-face communication and verbal communication electronically transmitted is that they both tend to demand attention, which helps ensure that receivers pay attention. Personally addressed written communication such as a memo or letter also has this advantage. Because it is addressed to a particular person, the chances are good that the person will actually pay attention to (and read) it. Moreover, the sender can write the message in a way that the receiver is most likely to understand it. Like voice mail, written communication does not enable a receiver to have his or her questions answered immediately, as is the case with face-to-face communication, but when messages are clearly written and feedback is provided, common understanding can still be reached.

Even if managers use face-to-face communication, a follow-up in writing is often needed for messages that are important or complicated and need to be referred to later on. This is precisely what Karen Binder, a disability claims administrator at Manulife Financial, did when she needed to tell one of her subordinates about an important change in the way the company would be handling denials of insurance benefits. Binder met with the subordinate and described the changes face-to-face. Once she was sure that the subordinate understood them, she handed her a sheet of instructions to follow, which essentially summarized the information they had discussed.

EMAIL, TWITTER, FACEBOOK, AND BLOGS

Email, Twitter, Facebook, and blogs also fit into this category of communication media because senders and receivers are communicating through personally addressed written words. However, the words are appearing on their personal mobile devices rather than on pieces of paper. Short forms of written words and symbols are often used when space is limited, as it is on Twitter. All too often people forget the importance of using business etiquette when communicating up and down the hierarchy of the organization. For instance, email and text messages in capital letters are often perceived as being shouted or screamed.

While the growing use of email and texting has enabled better communication within organizations, not all the effects have been positive. Many individuals complain of "email overload," and being unable to keep up with all the emails and texts that arrive. In addition, employees often find their electronic mailboxes clogged with junk mail. In a recent survey, more than half of the organizations surveyed acknowledged some problems with their email systems.[17]

To avoid these and other costly forms of email abuse, managers need to develop a clear policy specifying what company email can and should be used for and what is out of bounds. Managers also should clearly communicate this policy to all members of an organization as well as describe both the procedures that will be used when email abuse is suspected and the consequences that will result when email abuse is confirmed.

The increasing use of voice mail and email in companies large and small has led to some ethical concerns. These forms of communication are not necessarily private. The federal *Privacy Act* and the *Access to Information Act* apply to all federal government departments, most federal agencies, and some federal Crown corporations, but many private-sector employees are not covered by privacy legislation. Only Quebec's *Act Respecting the Protection of Personal Information in the Private Sector* applies to the entire private sector in that province.

The ethics of listening to other people's voice mail or reading their email is likely to be a growing concern for many managers. A survey of more than 2000 large American firms found that 38 percent reported that they "store and review" employee email messages.[18] The Ontario, Manitoba, and British Columbia governments have told their employees that email will be monitored if abuse is suspected. The governments' positions are that the Internet and email should be used only for business purposes.

Impersonal Written Communication

Impersonal written communication is lowest in information richness and is well suited for messages that need to reach a large number of receivers. Because such messages are not addressed to particular receivers, feedback is unlikely, so managers must make sure that messages sent by this medium are written clearly in language that all receivers will understand.

Managers can use impersonal written communication, including company newsletters, for various types of messages, including rules, regulations, policies, newsworthy information, and announcements of changes in procedures or the arrival of new organizational members. Impersonal written communication also can be used to communicate instructions about how to use machinery or how to process work orders or customer requests. For these kinds of messages, the paper trail left by this communication medium can be invaluable for employees. Much of this information is also being posted to company intranets. The danger with impersonal communication, however, is that some individuals will not read it, so it is important that employees are made aware of important messages.

Like personal written communication, impersonal written communication can be delivered and retrieved electronically, and this is increasingly being done in companies large and small. Unfortunately, the ease with which electronic messages can be spread has led to their proliferation. The electronic inboxes of many managers and workers are backlogged, and they rarely have time to read all the electronic work-related information available to them. The problem with such **information overload**—a superabundance of information—is the potential for important information to be ignored or overlooked while tangential information receives attention. Moreover, information overload can result in thousands of hours and millions in dollars in lost productivity.

information overload A superabundance of information that increases the likelihood that important information is ignored or overlooked and tangential information receives attention.

Advances in Information Technology

LO4 | Explain how the use of information technology (IT) can be vital to organizational communication.

Computer-based information technology can greatly facilitate and improve the communication process. It has allowed managers to develop computer-based management information systems that provide timely, complete, relevant, and high-quality information. IT allows companies to improve their responsiveness to customers, minimize costs, and thus improve their competitive position. The link between information systems, communication, and competitive position is an important one that may determine the success or failure of organizations in an increasingly competitive global environment.

A trend of considerable significance for information systems has been the rapid growth of wireless communication technologies, particularly digital communications. Wireless communication is significant

TIPS FOR MANAGERS

Information Richness and Communication Media

1. When you have something to communicate that is important, emotion-based, and personal, use face-to-face communication.

2. Use videoconferencing when distance, weather, or cost hinders face-to-face communication.

3. Consider introducing "Email-Free Friday," recommended by Sport England.

4. Whether or not privacy is protected by law or contract, foster a workplace culture where privacy is valued and respected.

for the information technology revolution because it facilitates linking together people and computers, which greatly increases their decision-making ability. An engineer or salesperson working in the field can send information to, and receive information from, the home office by using the wireless capability built into smartphones, laptops, and tablets.

The tumbling price of computing power and information and the use of wireless communication channels have facilitated **networking,** the exchange of information through a group or network of inter-linked computers. The most common arrangement now emerging is a three-tier network consisting of clients, servers, and a mainframe situated externally in the cloud. At the outer nodes of a typical three-tier network are the personal computers (PCs) that sit on the desks of individual users. These personal computers, referred to as *clients,* are linked to a local *server,* a high-powered midrange computer that "serves" the client personal computers. Servers often store power-hungry software programs that can be run more effectively on a server than on individuals' personal computers. Servers may also manage several printers that can be used by hundreds of clients, and they store data files and handle email communications between clients. The client computers linked directly to a server constitute a *local area network (LAN).* Within any organization there may be several LANs—for example, one in every division and function.

networking The exchange of information through a group or network of interlinked computers.

At the hub of a three-tier system are *mainframe computers,* large and powerful computers that can be used to store and process vast amounts of information. The mainframe can also be used to handle electronic communications between personal computers situated in different LANs. In addition, the mainframe may be connected to mainframes in other organizations and, through them, to LANs in other organizations. Increasingly, the Internet, a worldwide network of interlinked computers, is used as the conduit for connecting the computer systems of different organizations.

A manager with a personal computer hooked into a three-tier system can access data and software stored in the local server, in the mainframe, or through the Internet in computers based in another organization. When the storage of organizational data happens on an external mainframe, it is called "cloud computing." A manager can therefore communicate electronically with other individuals hooked into the system, whether they are in the manager's LAN, in another LAN within the manager's organization, or in another organization altogether. Moreover, because of the growth of wireless communications, an individual with the proper equipment can hook into the system from any location—at home, on a boat, on the beach, in the air—anywhere a wireless communications link can be established.

Software Developments

If computer hardware has been developing rapidly, so has computer software. **Operating system software** tells the computer hardware how to run. **Applications software,** such as programs for word processing, spreadsheets, graphics, and database management, is software developed for a specific task or use. The increase in the power of computer hardware has allowed software developers to write increasingly powerful programs that are, at the same time, increasingly user-friendly. By harnessing the rapidly growing power of microprocessors, applications software has vastly increased the ability of managers to acquire, organize, manipulate, and transmit information. In doing so, it also has increased the ability of managers to coordinate and control the activities of their organization and to make decisions, as discussed in Chapter 3.

operating system software Software that tells computer hardware how to run.

applications software Software designed for a specific task or use.

FOCUS ON *The Social Economy*

Framework Foundation

Framework Foundation is a charitable organization that has a core program called Timeraiser. Timeraiser is a silent art auction with a difference. People bid time, not money, on works of art by local emerging artists. Timeraiser artists are paid fair market value for their work. During the event, people match their skills to the needs of the agencies and groups seeking volunteers. After finding a match, the volunteers bid their time on the artwork.*

Framework uses online applications (website and blog) to showcase interesting nonprofit initiatives across Canada and paves the way for volunteers to get involved. Since 2017, they have hosted nearly 30 Timeraiser auctions, thereby generating as much as 95 000 volunteer hours throughout the participants' various communities; provided financial support for emerging artists to the tune of almost half a million dollars; helped almost 400 charitable organizations to find volunteers; and inspired 6043 Canadians to contribute their service to a cause that interests them.**

On the communication front, Framework has several challenges to overcome. They operate in several time zones, making accessible, collaborative documents available to staff and volunteers, regardless of their location. They require up-to-date records of their contacts in order to plan and execute events. To communicate with the public they use Facebook, Twitter, and a blog and also produce YouTube videos.

1. What are the communication challenges for Framework's Timeraiser program?

*https://www.canadahelps.org/en/charities/frameworktimeraiser/. Accessed July 22, 2018.
**http://imaginationforpeople.org/en/project/timeraiser/. Accessed January 23, 2018.

As illustrated by the nonprofit organization Framework Foundation in our Focus on the Social Economy feature, the need for real-time information can be crucial to the success of a venture.

Another software development that is starting to have an impact on the manager's job is speech recognition software. Currently, speech recognition software must be "trained" to recognize and understand each individual's voice, and it requires the speaker to pause after each word. The increasing power of microprocessors, however, has enabled the development of faster speech recognition programs that can handle more variables and much greater complexity. Now, a manager driving down the road may be able to communicate with a computer through a wireless link and give that computer complex voice instructions.[19]

Management Information Systems (MIS)

Computer-based information gathering and processing systems are central to the operation of most organizations today. **Management information systems (MIS)** are electronic systems of interconnected components designed to collect, process, store, and disseminate information to facilitate management decision making, planning, and control. They are designed specifically to help managers make decisions when planning, leading, organizing, and controlling and to communicate those decisions efficiently and effectively.

> **management information systems (MIS)** Electronic systems of interconnected components designed to collect, process, store, and disseminate information to facilitate management decision making, planning, and control.

There are six types of management information systems (MIS) that have been particularly helpful to managers as they perform their management tasks: transaction-processing systems, operations information systems, decision support systems, expert systems, enterprise resource planning systems, and e-commerce systems. In Figure 6.6, these MIS systems are arranged along a continuum according to the sophistication of the IT they are based on—IT that determines their ability to give managers the information they need to make nonprogrammed decisions.

Recall from Chapter 3 that nonprogrammed decision making occurs in response to unusual, unpredictable opportunities and threats.) We examine each of these systems next.

Transaction-Processing Systems A **transaction-processing system** is a system designed to handle large volumes of routine, recurring transactions. Transaction-processing systems began to appear in the

---

FIGURE 6.6

Six Computer-Based Management Information Systems

Transaction-processing systems	Operations information systems	Decision support systems	Expert systems

Programmed decision making	←——————→	Nonprogrammed decision making

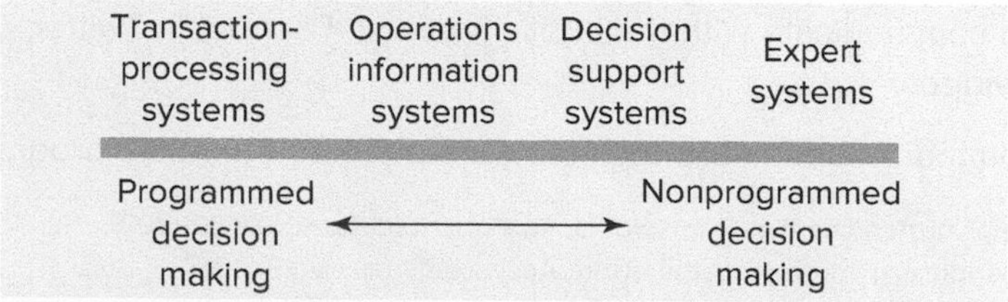

early 1960s with the advent of commercially available mainframe computers. They were the first type of computer-based IT adopted by many organizations, and today they are commonplace. Bank managers use a transaction-processing system to record deposits into, and payments out of, bank accounts. Supermarket managers use a transaction-processing system to record the sale of items and to track inventory levels. More generally, most managers in large organizations use a transaction-processing system to handle tasks such as payroll preparation and payment, customer billing, and payment of suppliers.

transaction-processing system A management information system designed to handle large volumes of routine, recurring transactions.

Operations Information Systems Many types of management information systems followed hard on the heels of transaction-processing systems in the 1960s. An **operations information system** is a system that gathers comprehensive data, organizes it, and summarizes it in a form that is of value to managers. Whereas a transaction-processing system processes routine transactions, an operations information system provides managers with information that they can use in their nonroutine coordinating, controlling, and decision-making tasks. Most operations information systems are coupled with a transaction-processing system. An operations information system typically accesses data gathered by a transaction-processing system, processes those data into useful information, and organizes that information into a form accessible to managers. As described in the opening case, the data collected by wireless cameras and scanners in the Amazon cashierless supermarket are part of an operations information system.

operations information system A management information system that gathers, organizes, and summarizes comprehensive data in a form that managers can use in their nonroutine coordinating, controlling, and decision-making tasks.

Decision Support Systems A **decision support system** is an interactive computer-based system that provides models that help managers make better nonprogrammed decisions.[20] Recall from Chapter 3 that nonprogrammed decisions are decisions that are relatively unusual or novel, such as decisions to invest in new productive capacity, develop a new product, launch a new promotional campaign, enter a new market, or expand internationally. Although an operations information system organizes important information for managers, a decision support system gives managers a model-building capability and so provides them with the ability to manipulate information in a variety of ways. Managers might use a decision support system to help them decide whether to cut prices for a product. The decision support system might contain models of how customers and competitors would respond to a price cut. Managers could run these models and use the results as an *aid* to decision making.

decision support system An interactive, computer-based management information system that managers can use to make nonroutine decisions.

The emphasis on the word *aid* is important, for in the final analysis, a decision support system is not meant to make decisions for managers. Rather, its function is to provide valuable information that managers can use to improve the quality of their decision making.

Artificial Intelligence and Expert Systems **Artificial intelligence (AI)** has been defined as behaviour by a machine that, if performed by a human being, would be called "intelligent." This behaviour has already made it possible to write programs that can solve problems and perform many tasks. For example, software programs variously known as *bots*, *softbots*, or *knowbots* can be used to perform simple managerial tasks such as sorting through reams of data or incoming email messages to look for important ones. The interesting feature of these programs is that from "watching" a manager sort through such data, they can "learn" what the manager's preferences are when reviewing information. With this type of capability, these "smart" programs can take over some of the work for managers, freeing them up to work on other tasks. Many of these programs are still in the development stage but could be commonplace within the next several years.[21] There are 100 000 bots (AI assisted software programs) on Facebook Messenger.[22]

artificial intelligence (AI) Behaviour performed by a machine that, if performed by a human being, would be called "intelligent."

Expert systems, the most advanced management information systems available, incorporate AI in their design. An **expert system** is a system that utilizes human knowledge embedded in computer software to solve problems that ordinarily require human expertise. Mimicking human expertise (and intelligence) requires technology that can, at a minimum, (1) recognize, formulate, and solve a problem; (2) explain the solution; and (3) learn from the experience. Self-driving cars are an example of how AI will disrupt the future of work. The Google Car has driven 1.3 million miles autonomously. It is estimated that 15 million vehicle operators could be replaced by driverless vehicles in the U.S. alone and 10 million service and warehouse jobs are at risk of displacement in the next 5 to 10 years due to AI. One hundred million new jobs will be needed to replace those lost to AI in the next two decades.[23]

expert system A management information system that utilizes human knowledge embedded in computer software to solve problems that ordinarily require human expertise.

Recent advances in artificial intelligence that go by names such as "fuzzy logic" or "neural networks" have resulted in computer programs that try to mimic human thought processes. Although artificial intelligence is still in the development stage, an increasing number of business applications are beginning to emerge in the form of expert systems.

Enterprise Resource Planning Systems To achieve high performance, it is not sufficient just to develop a management information system within each of a company's functions or divisions to provide better information and knowledge. It is also vital that managers in the different functions and divisions have access to information about the activities of managers in other functions and divisions. The greater the flow of information and knowledge among functions and divisions, the more learning can take place, and this builds a company's stock of knowledge and expertise. This knowledge and expertise are the source of its competitive advantage and profitability. The global AI market is estimated to grow to 16 billion U.S. dollars by 2022.[24]

Over the past 25 years, another revolution has taken place in IT as software companies have worked to develop enterprise resource planning systems, which essentially incorporate most MIS aspects just discussed, as well as much more. **Enterprise resource planning (ERP) systems** are multimodule application software packages that allow a company to link and coordinate the entire set of functional activities and operations necessary to move products from the initial design stage to the final customer stage. Some of the business applications in these software packages may include accounting, customer relationship management (CRM), human resources, manufacturing, and inventory and supply chain management.[25] Essentially ERP systems (1) help each individual function improve its functional-level skills and (2) improve integration among all functions so they work together to build a competitive advantage for the company. Today, choosing and designing an ERP system to improve how a company operates is the biggest challenge facing the IT function inside a company. By 2021, 800 000 new jobs driven by AI in CRM software will be created worldwide.[26]

> **enterprise resource planning (ERP) systems** Multimodule application software packages that coordinate the functional activities necessary to move products from the design stage to the final customer stage.

E-Commerce Systems **E-commerce** is trade that takes place between companies and between companies and individual customers using technology and the Internet. **Business-to-business (B2B) commerce** is trade that takes place between companies using technology and the Internet to link and coordinate the value chains of different companies. The goal of B2B commerce is to increase the profitability of making and selling goods and services. Through the use of technology, B2B commerce increases profitability because it allows companies to reduce operating costs and may improve overall quality. A principal B2B software application is **B2B marketplaces,** which are Internet-based online trading platforms set up in many industries to connect buyers and sellers. To participate in a B2B marketplace, companies adopt a common software standard that allows them to search for and share information with each other. The companies can work together over time to reduce costs or improve quality. **Business-to-customer (B2C) commerce** is trade that takes place between a company and individual customers using technology and the Internet. Using technology to connect directly to customers allows companies to avoid using intermediaries, such as wholesalers and retailers, who capture a significant part of the profit in the value chain. The use of websites and online stores also lets companies give their customers and other consumers much more information about the value of their products. This use of technology often allows companies to attract more customers and thus generate higher sales revenues.

> **e-commerce** Trade that takes place between companies, and between companies and individual customers, using technology and the Internet.
>
> **business-to-business (B2B) commerce** Trade that takes place between companies using technology and the Internet to link and coordinate the value chains of different companies.
>
> **B2B marketplaces** Internet-based trading platforms set up to connect buyers and sellers in an industry.
>
> **business-to-customer (B2C) commerce** Trade that takes place between a company and individual customers using technology and the Internet.

These days, software companies such as Salesforce, Microsoft, Oracle, SAP, and IBM are using AI and cloud computing to make their products work seamlessly while responding to global companies' growing demand for e-commerce software. Previously, their software was configured to work only on a particular company's internal website. Today, software must be able to network a company's IT systems to other companies, such as suppliers and distributors. The challenge facing managers now is to select e-commerce software that allows a seamless exchange of information between companies anywhere in the world. The Canadian company Descartes Systems is a global leader in this area. The stakes are high because global competitive advantage goes to the company that is first with a new major technological advance. By acquiring Whole Foods grocery chain, Amazon has the perfect opportunity to configure its IT systems to create a seamless and cashless shopping transaction with Amazon Go.

In summary, by using advanced types of MIS, managers have more control over a company's activities and operations and can work to improve its competitive advantage and profitability. The IT function has become increasingly important because IT managers decide which kind of hardware and software a company will use and then train other functional managers and employees on how to use it effectively as part of daily business operations. AI is revolutionizing MIS systems.

Limitations of Information Systems

Despite their usefulness, information systems have some limitations. A serious potential problem is the one noted at the beginning of this chapter. In all of the enthusiasm for management information systems, electronic communication by means of a computer network, and the like, a vital human element of communication may be lost. The human brain is 360 000 times more powerful than the fastest supercomputer.[27] Some kinds of information cannot be aggregated and summarized on an MIS report because of issues surrounding information richness. Very rich information, far beyond that which can be quantified and aggregated, is often required to coordinate and control an enterprise and to make informed decisions.

The importance of information richness is a strong argument in favour of using electronic communication to *support* face-to-face communication, not to replace it. For example, it would be wrong to make a judgment about an individual's performance merely by "reading the numbers" provided by a management information system. Instead, the numbers should be used to alert managers to individuals who may have a performance problem. The nature of this performance problem should then be explored in a face-to-face meeting, during which rich information can be gathered. As a top Boeing manager noted, "In our company, the use of email and videoconferencing has not reduced the need to visit people at other sites; it has increased it. Email has facilitated the establishment of communications channels between people who previously would not communicate, which is good, but direct visits are still required to cement any working relationships that evolve out of these electronic meetings."[28]

Social Media

LO5 | Describe how managers are using social media to communicate.

One would be hard-pressed to find an organization operating today that does not have a social media strategy to communicate with internal and external stakeholders. As social media continues to change the way people communicate, it is an increasingly important tool for managers. A social media strategy has three interrelated functions. See Figure 6.7.

FIGURE 6.7

Functions of a Social Media Strategy

1. It communicates the brand or identity of the organization—telling the potentially massive audience who they are and what they stand for, with very little investment.

2. It allows rapid and real-time engagement with peers, suppliers, employees, customers, communities, and anyone else in an easy, accessible, and direct way.

3. It provides the opportunity to learn from instant feedback and gather instant statistics and data on the users.

Functions of a social media strategy:

1. *It communicates the brand or identity of the organization—telling the potentially massive audience who they are and what they stand for, with very little investment.* Most companies have a Facebook page where customers and potential customers can interact after identifying the company through its name, trademarks, and logos.

2. *It allows rapid and real-time engagement with peers, suppliers, employees, customers, communities, and anyone else in an easy, accessible, and direct way.* Likes, comments, surveys and other types of posts are instantaneously shared among the users of the site.

3. *It provides the opportunity to learn from instant feedback and gather statistics and data on the users.* Collecting data on users is essential to the successful functioning of a social media strategy. Managers collect data on all demographic characteristics of the users of the site in order to better serve their needs. Being able to track data from users, known as *analytics,* does not guarantee the social media strategy will be successful, however. Being liked on Facebook, or having fans on Twitter and connections on LinkedIn, doesn't necessarily mean you will get more customers or generate more revenue. Unless you track new subscribers, start new conversations, and interact and engage your target market, the strategy is likely to fail. Managers often make several social media mistakes. Having all the elements in Figure 6.8 (and discussed below) can result in a successful social media strategy.

FIGURE 6.8

Important Elements of a Social Media Strategy

> 1. Spend time identifying the target audience.
>
> 2. Craft a well-thought-out message.
>
> 3. Choose the correct Internet sites.
>
> 4. Provide engaging material, not just promotions.
>
> 5. Monitor and measure the effectiveness of social media sites.

---

1. *Spend time identifying the target audience.* First, every goal established in the social media strategy should follow from the vision and mission of the organization. The values of the business and the target market are reflected in which platforms are chosen. Your social media strategy has to match the values of your organization and your customers.

2. *Craft a well-thought-out message.* Second, to be successful, a social media campaign needs to have consistency in the usefulness of the information it includes and the frequency of communication. Companies like Hootsuite provide the service of scheduling and hosting reoccurring, regular communications with users that are developed well in advance. Companies can post regular status updates which can be kept track of in an electronic file, like a spreadsheet, that contains a deadline, target keywords, the format of the content, call to action, and status. These features are important to crafting and communicating a well-thought-out message.

3. *Choose the correct platforms.* Third, many managers may lump all social media outlets into the same category, often not recognizing their differences. While Pinterest is appropriate for a restaurant

to use as a channel to reach foodies who love to look at images of meals, it may not be a very effective platform for an insurance company to reach its customers. Facebook has the most users of any network, and for that reason alone the chances of reaching your target market are good there. Each network has specific demographics that it appeals to. Choose the ones your customers use.

4. *Provide engaging material, not just promotions.* Fourth, effectiveness comes from engaging the customer, not from constantly pushing products or promotions. Managers must ask themselves why users would want to like, share, or comment on their content and not the content of others. Developing unique content tailored to the organization's customers is a challenge for social media managers. A mistake managers make is putting out sales pitches and promotions all the time, rather than listening to customers to find out what they really want to read and share.

5. *Monitor and measure the effectiveness of social media sites.* Finally, monitoring and measuring the effectiveness of social media sites will help managers determine if their social media strategy is working. If you don't know which sites your customers are using, you can't reach them.

Chapter 6

SUMMARY AND REVIEW

connect

LO1 The Importance of Communication in Organizations Effective communication is the sharing of information between two or more individuals or groups to reach a common understanding. Good communication is essential for attaining increased efficiency, quality, responsiveness to customers, and innovation—the four goals for gaining a competitive advantage.

LO2 The Communication Process and Communication Styles Communication takes place in a cyclical process that has two phases: *transmission* and *feedback*. The communication loop is successful only when the sender can confirm that the receiver understands the intent of the message. Communication styles differ along the lines of how reserved or open one is to relationships and the pace at which one interacts with others, yielding four distinct approaches to communication. Communication occurs verbally and nonverbally. Managers can learn skills that make them better senders and receivers of messages.

LO3 Organizational Communication Networks and Channels Communication networks are established mechanisms by which communication flows throughout the organization. They can be formal or informal. Typically, we find five communication networks available to managers: the wheel, the circle, the all-channel, the chain, and the "Y." Four important categories of communication channels are *face-to-face communication* (includes videoconferences), *spoken communication electronically transmitted* (includes voice mail), *personally addressed written communication* (includes email and texting), and *impersonal written communication*. Each channel varies in the extent to which it enables the sender and receiver to reach a common understanding.

LO4 Advances in Information Technology Information technology (IT) can be vital to organizational communication. Computer-based information gathering and processing systems are central to the operation of most organizations. Management information systems (MIS) are electronic systems of interconnected components designed to collect, process, store, and disseminate information to facilitate management decision making, planning, and control. Artificial Intelligence (AI) and expert systems are paving the way for innovative business transactions that are fundamentally changing the nature of management.

LO5 Social Media As social media continues to change the way people communicate, it is an increasingly important tool for managers. A social media strategy includes five important elements and has three interrelated functions.

KEY TERMS

applications software	jargon
artificial intelligence	management by wandering around (MBWA)
B2B marketplaces	management information systems (MIS)
business-to-business (B2B) commerce	medium
business-to-customer (B2C) commerce	message
communication	networking
decision support system	noise
decoding	nonverbal communication
e-commerce	operating system software
encoding	operations information system
enterprise resource planning (ERP) systems	perception
expert system	receiver
filtering	rumours
grapevine	sender
information distortion	transaction-processing system
information overload	verbal communication
information richness	

WRAP-UP TO OPENING CASE

Amazon's Newest IT Revolution

Amazon opened a grocery store in Seattle, Washington in early 2018 that will revolutionize the way we shop. After reading and understanding the concepts in this chapter, you should be able to answer the following question:

1. *How will Amazon Go disrupt the grocery industry?*

   ANSWER: Digital disruption can be described as using IT to change a long-standing, often industry-specific, business model to gain a competitive advantage. Amazon Go has fundamentally changed the way we shop by using IT and MIS to track, record, and compute all the data involved in buying groceries, including the payment transaction. As you enter the store and go through the turnstile, you swipe your smartphone. This registers your identity and tracks your progress through the store. You then pick up the items you want to purchase and walk out. The Amazon account on your smartphone is automatically charged with the items you chose. The new process relies heavily on new technology involving hundreds of overhead cameras with computer vision and shelves with weight sensors that enable the machines to know what products you pick up. If you put an item back on the shelf, Amazon removes it from your virtual cart. This is different from the self-checkout scan-and-go technology used in many grocery stores, because the only task the customer is responsible for is swiping their smartphone upon entering the store: A true disruption to the industry.

MANAGEMENT IN ACTION

TOPICS FOR DISCUSSION AND ACTION

LEVEL 1 Knowledge & Comprehension

1. Describe the communication process. Why is perception important?
2. Describe the communication skills for senders and receivers of messages.
3. Explain the communication styles outlined in the chapter.

LEVEL 2 Application & Analysis

4. Explain why ineffective communication occurs.
5. Which type of communication network is suitable for a large bureaucratic organization and why?
6. Which medium (or media) do you think would be appropriate for a manager to use when sending the following messages to a subordinate? Explain your choices.
   a. Getting a raise.
   b. Not receiving a promotion.
   c. Disciplining an employee for being consistently late.
   d. Adding job responsibilities.
   e. Creating the schedule for company holidays for the upcoming year.

LEVEL 3 Synthesis & Evaluation

7. Explain how best to deal with each communication style and why the method would be effective.
8. Evaluate the advances in information technology and discuss their limitations for the manager who wants to communicate effectively.
9. How can managers overcome some common errors that lead to social media strategy failure?

SELF-REFLECTION EXERCISE

Consider a person with whom you have had difficulty communicating. Using the communication skills for senders as a start, analyze what has gone wrong with the communication process with that person. What can be done to improve communication? To what extent did sender and receiver problems contribute to communication breakdown?

SMALL GROUP BREAKOUT EXERCISE

Form groups of three or four and appoint one member as the spokesperson who will communicate your findings to the whole class when called on by the instructor. Then discuss the following scenario:

Assume you are a team assigned the task of creating a social media strategy for an organic food store in Halifax. The store specializes in sustainable fishery products and sells to the growing local population of discerning consumers with high enough incomes to afford good-quality fish, meat, and vegetables.

MANAGING ETHICALLY EXERCISE

About 75 percent of medium and large companies that were surveyed engaged in some kind of monitoring of employees' email and Internet activities. Critics say this is an invasion of privacy. Proponents say that Web surfing costs millions of dollars in lost productivity. What is your opinion of Web surfing? To what extent should it be allowed? When does Internet use at work become unethical? To what extent should it be monitored? When does monitoring become unethical?

MANAGEMENT CHALLENGE EXERCISE

Assume you are a middle-level manager at a data processing company. After monitoring the online user statistics, it is evident that several employees are using company time to send personal emails. You have been asked by your boss to create a company policy on personal emails at work and send a memo to the employees describing it. Share your thoughts with two other students, and consolidate everyone's thoughts on the policy into one memo.

MANAGEMENT PORTFOLIO PROJECT

Answer the following questions about the organization you have chosen to follow:

1. What kinds of communication media are commonly used in this organization for the various types of messages? Are the media appropriate for the messages?
2. What kinds of MIS does the organization use?
3. Describe the organization's social media strategy.

MANAGEMENT CASE

HOOTSUITE CONNECTS BUSINESS TO SOCIAL MEDIA

How Can Managers Use Technology to Help Improve Communications?

Hootsuite provides businesses with a social media platform which enables them to connect with over 35 popular social media networks to promote online marketing, e-commerce, and customer engagement from one place through a single dashboard.[29] They provide over 90 apps to enhance customer service, collaboration among teams, social campaigns/contests, tracking performance with analytics reports, and just about anything else to do with effective communication for small to medium businesses, agencies, governments, and enterprises.[30]

Founded in 2008 by Ryan Holmes of Vancouver, B.C., the company grew from a user base of zero to five million in the first three years without a budget for marketing. Using a low-cost strategy called *freemium economics* and word-of-mouth community *crowdsourcing*, they soon attracted millions more. With freemium economics, the majority of users pay nothing for basic services and as they grow, businesses can upgrade to premium services that allow them to schedule, manage, and measure results from their social media communications. Hootsuite also got volunteers through crowdsourcing to translate their programs into several languages, which allowed them to expand internationally and develop a worldwide community of collaborators. After surveying 600 business professionals, G2Crowd found Hootsuite to be one of three top social media platforms.[31]

1. Describe Hootsuites' social media strategy.
2. How did the company achieve such success?

Managing Human Resources

LEARNING OUTCOMES

LO1	Describe the legal framework of human resource management in Canada and why effectively managing diversity is good for business.
LO2	Explain why strategic human resource management and human resource planning can help an organization gain a competitive advantage.
LO3	Describe the five components of human resource management and explain how they fit together with the strategy and structure of the organization.
LO4	Explain the role of the human resource manager in dealing with workplace harassment.

OPENING CASE

Effectively Managing Human Resources at the Four Seasons Hotels & Resorts

Four Seasons Hotels & Resorts is one of only about 14 companies to be ranked among the "100 Best Companies to Work For" every year since *Fortune* magazine started its annual ranking of companies almost 20 years ago.[1] In addition, Four Seasons often receives other awards and recognition based on customer ratings.[2] In an industry in which annual turnover rates are over 35 percent, turnover for Four Seasons is among the lowest at 12.7 percent.[3] Evidently, employees and customers alike are very satisfied with the way they are treated at Four Seasons. Understanding that these two facts are causally linked is perhaps the key to Four Seasons' success. As Four Seasons' founder, chairman of the board, and CEO Isadore Sharp suggests, "How you treat your employees is how you expect them to treat the customer."[4]

Four Seasons was founded by Canadian-born Sharp in 1960. After opening and running both small and large hotels, Sharp decided that he could provide customers with a very different kind of hotel experience by trying to combine the best features of both kinds of hotel experiences—that is, the sense of closeness and personal attention that a small hotel brings with the amenities of a big hotel to suit the needs of business travellers.[5]

Sharp sought to provide the kind of personal service that would really help business travellers on the road—providing them with the amenities they have at home and in the office and miss when travelling on business. Thus, Four Seasons was the first hotel chain to provide many conveniences such as bathrobes and shampoo.[6] While these are relatively concrete ways of personalizing the hotel experience, Sharp realized that the ways in which employees treat customers are just as, or perhaps even more, important. When employees view each customer as an individual with his or her own needs and desires and try to meet these needs and desires and help customers both overcome any problems or challenges they face and truly enjoy their hotel experience, customers are likely to be both loyal and highly satisfied.[7]

Sharp has always realized that in order for employees to treat customers well, Four Seasons needs to treat its employees well. Salaries are relatively high at Four Seasons, by industry standards (i.e., between the 75th and 90th percentiles), employees participate in a profit-sharing plan, and the company contributes to their pension plans. All employees are provided with free meals in the hotel cafeteria, have access to staff showers and a locker room, and are provided with an additional, highly attractive benefit: once a new employee has worked for Four Seasons for six months, he or she can stay for three nights free at any Four Seasons hotel or resort in the world. After a year of employment, this benefit increases to six free nights and it continues to increase as tenure with the company increases.[8]

All aspects of human resource management at Four Seasons are oriented around ensuring that the guiding principle behind all Four Seasons operations is upheld. This, according to Sharp, is that all employees and managers should "deal with others—partners, customers, co-workers, everyone—as we would want them to deal with us."[9]

Roussel Photography/Alamy Stock Photo

All job applicants to Four Seasons, regardless of level or area, have a minimum of four interviews, one of which is with the general manager of the property.[10] Four Seasons devotes so much attention to hiring the right people because of the importance of each and every employee providing a consistently high level of empathetic and responsive customer service.[11]

New hires participate in a three-month training program that includes improvisation activities to help them learn how to anticipate guests' needs, requirements, and actions, and appropriately respond to them.[12] The aim of training is to help ensure that all employees, regardless of area or function, provide consistently high-quality and highly responsive customer service. Since customer service is everyone's responsibility, Four Seasons has no separate customer service department, per se. Training is an ongoing activity at Four Seasons and never really stops.[13]

Four Seasons also tends to promote from within. Thirty-seven percent of all jobs were filled internally in 2017.[14] For example, while recent college graduates may start out as assistant managers, those who do well and have high aspirations could potentially become general managers in less than 15 years. This helps to ensure that managers have empathy and respect for those in lower-level positions as well as the ingrained ethos of treating others (employees, subordinates, co-workers, and customers) the way they would like to be treated themselves. All in all, the way in which Four Seasons manages its human resources helps to ensure that customers are treated very well indeed.[15]

After reading and understanding the concepts in this chapter, you should be able to answer the following questions:

1. How does Isadore Sharp employ a human resource system that creates an outstanding experience for customers at Four Seasons?
2. How does Four Seasons manage the components of its HR system?

◼ Overview

Managers are responsible for acquiring, developing, protecting, and using the resources that an organization needs to be efficient and effective. One of the most important resources in all organizations is human resources (HR)—the people involved in the production and distribution of goods and services. Human resources include all members of an organization, ranging from top managers to entry-level employees. Effective human resource managers—like Isadore Sharp in the opening case—realize how valuable human resources are and take active steps to make sure that their organizations build and fully utilize their human resources to gain a competitive advantage.

This chapter examines how managers can tailor their human resource management system to their organization's strategy, structure, and culture. We discuss in particular the major components of human resource management in the context of the Canadian legal framework and labour force diversity. By the end of this chapter, you will understand the central role that human resource management plays in creating a high-performing organization.

As shown in Figure 7.1, an organization's **human resource management (HRM)** system has five major components: (1) recruitment and selection, (2) training and development, (3) performance appraisal and feedback, (4) pay and benefits, and (5) employee engagement. Managers use *recruitment and selection,* the first component of an HRM system, to attract and hire new employees who have the abilities, skills, and experiences that will help the organization achieve its goals. For example, Cirque du Soleil recruits its

---

FIGURE 7.1

Components of a Human Resource Management System

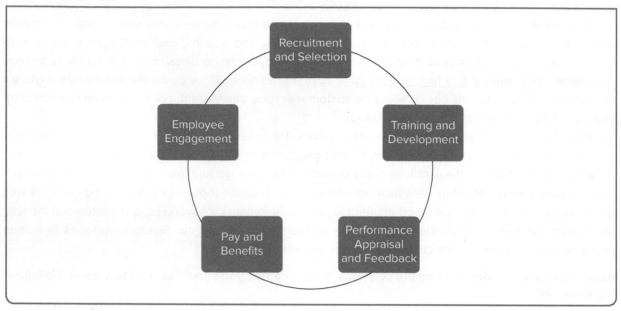

---

members from all over the world; about 70 percent of recruits come from a sports background, which is well suited for training in acrobatics, a core part of Cirque de Soleil's entertainment experience.

human resource management (HRM) Activities that managers engage in to attract and retain employees and to ensure that they perform at a high level and contribute to the accomplishment of organizational goals.

After recruiting and selecting employees, managers use the second component, *training and development,* to ensure that organizational members develop skills and abilities that will enable them to perform their jobs effectively in the present and the future. Training and development is an ongoing process because changes in technology and the environment, as well as in an organization's goals and strategies, often require organizational members to learn new techniques and ways of working. Extensive training at Four Seasons Hotels & Resorts removes this gap and positions the company to gain a competitive advantage.

The third component, *performance appraisal and feedback,* serves two purposes in HRM. First, performance appraisal can provide managers with the information they need to make good human resources decisions—decisions about how to orient, train, motivate, and reward organizational members.[16] Thus, the performance appraisal and feedback component is a kind of control system that can be used with management by objectives (discussed in Chapter 11). Second, performance feedback from performance appraisals serves a developmental purpose for the members of an organization. When managers regularly evaluate their subordinates' performance, they can provide subordinates with valuable information about their strengths and weaknesses and the areas in which they need to concentrate. On the basis of performance appraisals, managers distribute pay to employees.

In the fourth component of HRM, *pay and benefits,* managers distribute pay to employees, first by determining their starting salaries, and later by determining whether raises or bonuses should be given. By rewarding high-performing organizational members with pay raises, bonuses, and the like, managers increase the likelihood that an organization's most valued human resources are motivated to continue their high levels of contribution to the organization. Moreover, when pay is linked to performance, high-performing employees are more likely to stay with the organization, and managers are more likely to be able to fill open positions with highly talented individuals. Benefits such as health insurance are important outcomes that employees receive by virtue of their membership in an organization. At Four Seasons Hotels & Resorts, even part-time employees get health insurance benefits.

Last but not least, *employee engagement* includes the steps that managers take to develop and engage all of the people working in the organization. When an organization is unionized, the HR manager represents the interests of the employer, while the labour unions represent the interests of the employees when negotiating working conditions such as wages, vacation, and hours worked. An organization's HR managers develop labour relations policies that provide safe working conditions and fair labour practices in their offices and plants.

Managers must ensure that all five of these components fit together and complement their companies' structure, strategy, and control systems.[17] For example, if managers decide to decentralize authority and empower employees, they need to invest in training and development to ensure that lower-level employees have the knowledge and expertise they need to make the decisions that top managers would make in a more centralized structure.

Each of the five components of HRM influences the others.[18] The kind of people that the organization attracts and hires through recruitment and selection, for example, determines (1) the training and development that are necessary, (2) the way performance is appraised, and (3) the appropriate levels of pay and benefits. Managers at Microsoft ensure that their organization has highly qualified program designers by (1) recruiting and selecting the best candidates, (2) guiding new hires with experienced team members, (3) appraising program designers' performance in terms of their individual contributions and their teams' performance, and (4) basing programmers' pay on individual and team performance. Before we look at each component of an HR system in detail, we first examine the legal context in which human resource management takes place.

HRM Legislation and Managing Diversity

LO1	Describe the legal framework of human resource management in Canada and why effectively managing diversity is good for business.

The Legal Framework of HRM in Canada

Several key pieces of legislation govern the management of human resources in Canada. The laws have been developed to protect the rights of employers and employees. HR managers must be aware of the legal and political environment in which they do their work. Failure to adhere to the legislation governing employment standards, labour relations, health and safety, employment equity, and other employment-related regulations, such as the *Charter of Rights and Freedoms,* knowingly or unknowingly, can result in severe penalties to managers and employers. The HR manager has the responsibility to avoid **intentional discrimination** (deliberately using prohibited grounds, such as race, religion, and sex, when making employment decisions) and **unintentional discrimination** (unfair practices and policies that have an adverse impact on specific groups for reasons that are unrelated to the job). In this chapter, we look at two pieces of legislation that make up the legal environment of HR management in Canada: the *Employment Standards Act* and the *Canadian Human Rights Act.*

intentional discrimination The illegal practice of deliberately using prohibited grounds, such as race, religion, and sex, when making employment decisions.

unintentional discrimination Unfair practices and policies that have an adverse impact on specific groups for reasons unrelated to the job.

"How you treat your employees is how you expect them to treat the customer."

Isadore Sharp, CEO, Four Seasons

The *Employment Standards Act* sets out minimum standards for the private sector in federal, provincial, and territorial legislation. It deals with the minimum age for employment, hours of work and overtime pay, minimum wages, equal pay, the weekly rest day, general holidays with pay, annual vacations with pay, parental leave, and individual and group terminations of employment. It also deals with mandatory retirement and whistleblower protection rights. Minimum employee entitlements are established for each element covered by the Act.

The *Canadian Human Rights Act* covers all businesses under federal jurisdiction. This typically includes businesses that operate in more than one province, such as telecommunications and transportation. Each province and territory has its own human rights legislation that prohibits discrimination based on specific grounds. There are differences across the nation. For example, in certain jurisdictions, such as Newfoundland and Labrador and the Northwest Territories, it is considered discriminatory to reject an applicant for employment based on a record of criminal conviction. In other jurisdictions, such as Nova Scotia and Saskatchewan, there are no such protections. All jurisdictions prohibit discrimination on the grounds of race, colour, religion or creed, physical and mental disability, sex (including pregnancy and childbirth), and marital status. All areas have policies related to discrimination on the basis of age; however, the protected age groups differ. Human resource managers must act according to the legislation that governs their jurisdiction in hiring and firing employees. Failure to do so may result in charges of discrimination and may lead to increasingly large fines and settlements.

It is important to note that the *Employment Standards Act* and the *Human Rights Act* do not restrict employers' right and ability to reward high-performing employees and discipline employees for not meeting productivity standards or following company rules, as long as such rewards and punishments are based on *job-related criteria* and not on prohibited grounds.

Every human resource manager must pay attention to maintaining a healthy and safe working environment. It is estimated that indirect costs of an accident can be as much as two to ten times more than the direct costs. The Canadian government has recognized the importance of health and safety as well. However, in Canada, unlike in the United States, there is no federal body to which organizations report. Rather, Canada has health and safety regulations and enforcement agencies by province and territory. What can be called Canadian health and safety net legislation would include the following: the *Canada Labour Code*,[19] WHMIS (Workplace Hazardous Materials Information System),[20] Workers' Compensation,[21] Canadian Centre for Occupational Health and Safety,[22] and the *Occupational Health and Safety Act*.[23]

Managing Diversity

One of the most important issues in management to emerge over the past 30 years has been the increasing diversity of the workforce. **Diversity** is dissimilarity, or differences, among people due to age, gender, race, ethnicity, religion, sexual orientation, socioeconomic background, capabilities or disabilities, position, status, seniority, parental status, and so on. Managing diversity raises important ethical and social responsibility issues. Managers must treat their employees fairly and consistently, regardless of the dissimilarities in their characteristics. Failure to do so can lead to charges of discrimination, conflict among groups and individuals, and disgruntled stakeholders. High-performing organizations manage diversity well. At Four Seasons Hotels & Resorts, 65 percent of the labour force is comprised of people from minority populations. [24]

diversity Differences among people in age, gender, race, ethnicity, ability, and sexual orientation.

L. Gardenswartz and A. Rowe explain the complexity of diversity in a model that involves four layers. See Figure 7.2. The model illustrates the organizational dimensions of sources of diversity in the

---

FIGURE 7.2

Sources of Diversity in the Workforce

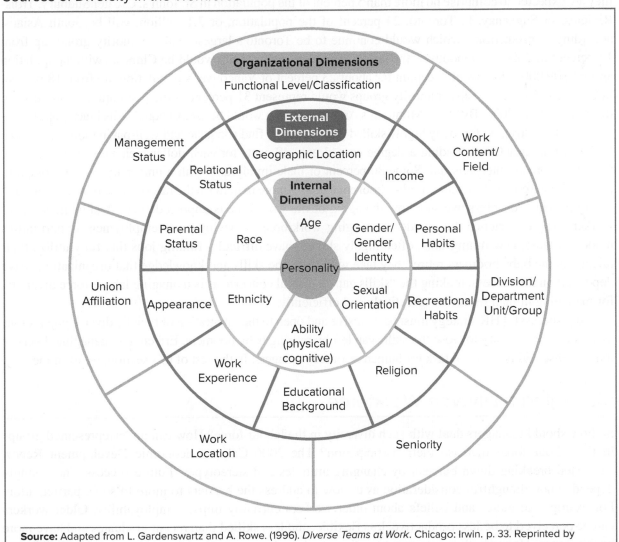

Source: Adapted from L. Gardenswartz and A. Rowe. (1996). *Diverse Teams at Work*. Chicago: Irwin. p. 33. Reprinted by permission of L. Gardenswartz and A. Rowe.

workplace that affect individuals, such as seniority and status, as well as the external and internal environmental dimensions that influence diversity. The most immediate layer of factors that create diversity relate to one's age, gender, ability, ethnicity, race, and sexual orientation.

Diversity in Canada

Canada has become a truly diverse country, especially with respect to the dimensions of age, race, and ethnicity. With respect to race and ethnicity, Statistics Canada[25] projects that by 2031, between 25 and 28 percent of the population could be foreign-born. About 55 percent of this population would be born in Asia. Between 29 and 32 percent of the population could belong to a visible minority group, as defined in the *Employment Equity Act.* This would be nearly double the proportion reported by the 2006 Census. More than 200 different ethnic origins were reported in the 2006 Census. The Indigenous birth rate is 1.5 times that of non-Indigenous peoples. The distribution of the visible minority population will vary widely across the country. For example, by 2031, visible minority groups are projected to comprise 63 percent of the population of Toronto, 59 percent in Vancouver and 31 percent in Montreal. In contrast, they are expected to comprise no more than 5 percent of the population in St. John's, Greater Sudbury, Trois-Rivières, or Saguenay. In Toronto, 24 percent of the population, or 2.1 million, will be South Asians, according to predictions, which would continue to be Toronto's largest visible minority group, up from 13 percent in 2006. In Vancouver, the largest visible minority group would be Chinese, with a population around 809 000. They would account for about 23 percent of Vancouver's population, up from 18 percent in 2006. In Montreal, visible minority groups would represent 31 percent of the population, nearly double the 16 percent in 2006. By 2031, Montreal's Arab population would be almost equal to its black population.

It is still a struggle for many highly skilled immigrants to find adequate and well-paying jobs in Canada. In 2008, immigrant men holding a degree earned only 48 cents for each dollar their university-educated, Canadian-born counterparts did. Some 30 percent of male immigrants with a university degree worked in jobs that required no more than a high-school education—more than twice the rate of those born in Canada.[26]

In previous chapters, we saw how the aging of the workforce is unprecedented. And while younger workers may experience the upside of an aging workforce by having more employment opportunities made available, new immigrants, often highly skilled, have difficulty finding jobs that fully utilize their talent. As the baby boomers retire, they take with them the skills and knowledge that organizations have depended on for success, making the "skills gap" a central concern, as is managing labour force diversity, for managing human resources effectively and efficiently.

Any successful HR strategy must be inclusive and open to the integration of racially diverse populations as well as age diversity to close the skills gap left by retiring baby boomers. Effectively managing diversity makes sense and is a critical task for human resource managers. In the rest of this section, we examine why.

Managing a Diverse Workforce

So how should managers deal with such diversity in the labour force? How can underrepresented groups in the labour force increase their participation? The 2006 Calgary Economic Development Report suggested breaking down barriers by changing attitudes and stereotypes. Future success "increasingly depends upon thoughtful consideration as to how to address the barriers to more fulsome participation. For example, attitudes and beliefs about older workers currently impact employability. Older workers can be perceived to be less productive, less flexible, and less skilled than recent graduates and have more health issues. Hence both employer perceptions and worker perceptions would need to be modified in order to attract and retain older workers."[27]

Age diversity presents managers with unique challenges. Older workers are staying longer in the labour force since mandatory retirement was abolished. At the same time, **Generation Y** or millennials are entering the labour force. A challenge for managers is to gain respect and commitment from this group of stakeholders. Managers must be aware of some of the myths about Generation Y and adopt positive strategies to help integrate them into the labour force.

Generation Y Also known as *millennials*; people born between 1981 and 1992.

For example, to combat the perception that Gen Ys are disrespectful and vocal when dissatisfied, managers must earn their respect by engaging them and listening to their concerns and ideas, and explain why things are done the way they are. As the generation that has grown up with technology, they have immediate access to information that they can collect and share with others, including information about industry standards for salaries. Managers should be prepared for questions and provide clear realistic job previews to cultivate trust.

Several reasons explain why diversity is such a pressing issue for managers and organizations:

1. Effectively managing diversity can improve organizational effectiveness. When managers manage diversity well, they not only encourage other managers to treat diverse members of an organization fairly and justly but they also demonstrate that diversity is an important resource that can help an organization gain a competitive advantage.

2. Embracing diversity encourages employee engagement and thus encourages differences in opinions or ideas that can be beneficial to the organization.

3. There is a strong ethical imperative in many societies to see that all people receive equal opportunities and are treated fairly and justly. Unfair treatment is also illegal.

We now turn to the activities that managers engage in to attract, develop, and retain high-performing employees.

Strategic Human Resource Management

LO2 | Explain why strategic human resource management and human resource planning can help an organization gain a competitive advantage.

As we discussed at the beginning of this chapter, human resource management (HRM) includes all the activities that managers engage in to attract and retain employees and to ensure that they perform at a high level and contribute to the accomplishment of organizational goals. These activities make up an organization's human resource management system, which has five major components: recruitment and selection, training and development, performance appraisal and feedback, pay and benefits, and employee engagement. (See Figure 7.1.) **Strategic human resource management** is the process by which managers design the components of an HRM system to be consistent with each other, with other elements of organizational architecture, and with the organization's strategy and goals.[28] The objective of strategic HRM is the development of an HRM system that enhances an organization's efficiency, quality, innovation, and responsiveness to customers—the four building blocks of competitive advantage, which we discussed in Chapter 2. More and more organizations are turning to technology to help plan and manage the components of their HR system. Human resource information systems (HRIS) collect and sort data relevant to help HR managers make strategic decisions about how to best manage current and future staffing needs. At Four Seasons, featured in the opening case, the HRM system ensures that all employees provide excellent customer service.

strategic human resource management The process by which managers design the components of a human resource management system to be consistent with each other, with other elements of organizational architecture, and with the organization's strategy and goals.

Human Resource Planning

Human resource planning includes all the activities that managers use to forecast their current and future needs for human resources. Current human resources are the employees an organization needs today to provide high-quality goods and services to customers. Future human resources are the employees the organization will need at some later date to achieve its longer-term goals. Workforce planning involves analyzing the gap in current and future needs, developing strategies to meet those needs, and implementing and evaluating the strategy. See Figure 7.3.

human resource planning Activities that managers use to forecast their current and future needs for human resources.

FIGURE 7.3

Human Resource Workforce Planning Cycle

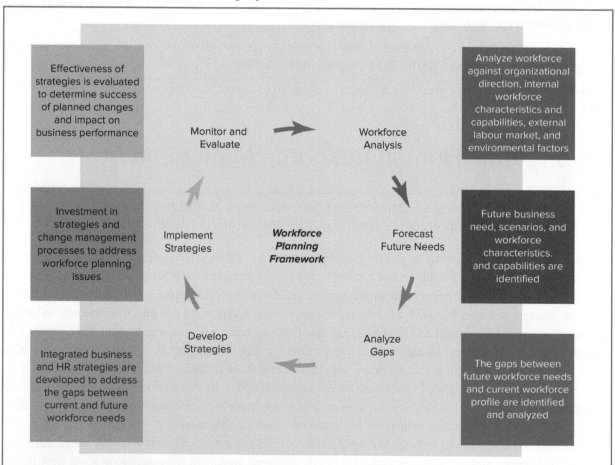

Source: http://vpsc.vic.gov.au/html-resources/workforce-planning-toolkit-a-guide-for-workforce-planning-in-small-to-medium-sized-victorian-public-sector-organisations/2-how-to-implement-workforce-planning/.

As part of the human resource workforce planning cycle, managers must make both demand forecasts and supply forecasts as part of forecasting future needs. *Demand forecasts* estimate the qualifications and numbers of employees an organization will need given its goals and strategies. *Supply forecasts* estimate the availability and qualifications of current employees now and in the future and the supply of qualified workers in the external labour market. Strategies must be developed, implemented, and evaluated to ensure an adequate pool of qualified candidates exists to fill the demand. One of the factors facing some amusement parks is that not enough teenagers are available or willing to work at them. With low supply, they have had to look to senior citizens as an alternative supply of labour.

As a result of human resource planning, managers sometimes decide to **outsource** to fill some of their HR needs. Instead of recruiting and hiring employees to produce goods and services within the organization, managers contract people who are not members of their organization to produce goods and services for them. This contracting out of work, rather than doing it "in-house" is outsourcing. Managers in publishing companies, for example, frequently contract freelance editors to copy-edit books that they intend to publish. The People Bank is an organization that provides temporary typing, clerical, and secretarial workers to managers who want to use outsourcing to fill some of their human resource requirements in these areas. EMBERS Staffing Solutions, featured in the Focus on the Social Economy feature later in this chapter, provides contract construction and warehouse staff.

outsource To use outside suppliers and manufacturers to produce goods and services.

Two reasons why human resource planning sometimes leads managers to outsource are flexibility and cost. First, outsourcing can give managers increased *flexibility,* especially when accurately forecasting human resource needs is difficult, human resource needs fluctuate over time, or finding skilled workers in a particular area is a challenge. Second, outsourcing can sometimes allow managers to make use of human resources at a lower *cost.* When work is outsourced, costs can be lower for a number of reasons: the organization does not have to provide benefits to workers; managers are able to contract for work only when the work is needed; and managers do not have to invest in training. Outsourcing can be used for functional activities such as after-sales service on appliances and equipment, legal work, and the management of information systems.

Outsourcing does have its disadvantages, however.[29] When work is outsourced, managers may lose some control over the quality of goods and services. Also, individuals performing outsourced work may have less knowledge of organizational practices, procedures, and goals, and less commitment to an organization than regular employees. In addition, unions resist outsourcing because it has the potential to eliminate some of their members. To gain some of the flexibility and cost savings of outsourcing and avoid some of its disadvantages, a number of organizations, such as Microsoft and IBM, rely on a pool of temporary employees to, for example, debug programs.

A major trend reflecting the increasing globalization of business is the outsourcing of office work, computer programming, and technical jobs from Canada, the United States and countries in Western Europe with high labour costs to countries like India and China, where there are lower labour costs.[30] For example, computer programmers in India and China earn a fraction of what their U.S. counterparts earn. According to estimates by Gartner Inc., outsourcing (or *offshoring,* as it is also called when work is outsourced to other countries) of information technology and business process work is valued at over $34 billion per year.

As companies gain experience in outsourcing software and technological services, managers are learning what kinds of work can be effectively outsourced and what work should probably not be outsourced. In India, for example, the workforce is highly trained and motivated, and cities like Bangalore are bustling with high-tech jobs and companies like Infosys Technologies, providing software services to companies abroad. Managers who have outsourcing experience have found that outsourcing works best for tasks that can be rule-based, do not require closeness/familiarity with customers and/or the customs and culture of the country in which the company is based, and do not require creativity.[31] When the work requires the recognition and solution of problems rather than the application of pre-existing algorithms, creativity in developing solutions, and independent thinking and judgment without the guidance of standard operating procedures, performance might suffer from outsourcing. Essentially, the more complex and uncertain the work and the more it depends on being close to customers and the company itself, the less advantageous outsourcing tends to be.[32]

Nonetheless, there are many kinds of tasks that can be effectively outsourced, and the cost savings for these tasks can be considerable.[33] And some managers believe that many tasks can be effectively outsourced, even those requiring creativity. Some of the advantages and disadvantages of outsourcing HR are shown in Table 7.1.

Job Analysis

The assessment of both current and future human resource needs helps managers determine whom they should be trying to recruit and select to achieve organizational goals *now* and in the *future*. As workers age and retire, they take with them valuable knowledge about the ins and outs of getting a job done. This is why succession planning is becoming a critical need. In recent years, Montreal-based BCE has created a new position, "chief talent officer," who is responsible for executive recruitment, compensation, and succession planning in order to make sure that BCE's companies have the right leadership and talent as BCE looks toward the future.[34]

Succession planning helps ensure that valuable knowledge is not lost to the organization when workers leave or retire. It must be well thought out. HR managers often use **personnel replacement charts** as tools in this process. A personnel replacement chart is an examination of all current positions, along with who holds them, what their skills and qualifications are, and whether or not their performance levels make them suitable for promotion as positions become available. In order to create a replacement chart, a thorough analysis of each position—a *job analysis*—is required. See Figure 7.4 for an example of a typical personnel replacement chart.

TABLE 7.1

Advantages and Disadvantages of Outsourcing Human Resources

Examples	Advantages	Disadvantages
Computer software companies outsourcing programming work to India Contracting out activities to companies that specialize in HRM	Takes advantage of lower labour costs Provides flexibility by allowing the company to focus on core competencies Reduces costs: when a company outsources, it does not have to provide benefits to full-time workers or invest in training	Lose control over the quality of goods and services. Companies hired to do the work have less knowledge of organizational practices, procedures, and goals. Outsourced employees have less commitment to an organization than do regular, full-time employees. The potential to eliminate members' jobs creates resistance to outsourcing by labour unions.

FIGURE 7.4

A Typical Personnel Replacement Chart

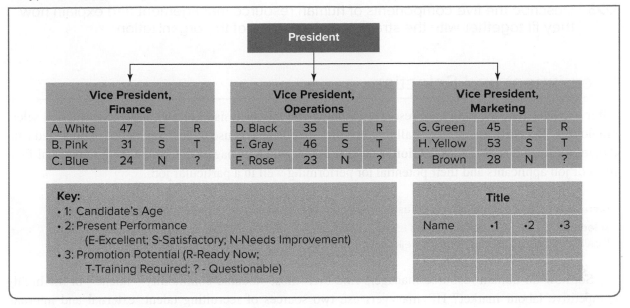

Vice President, Finance			
A. White	47	E	R
B. Pink	31	S	T
C. Blue	24	N	?

Vice President, Operations			
D. Black	35	E	R
E. Gray	46	S	T
F. Rose	23	N	?

Vice President, Marketing			
G. Green	45	E	R
H. Yellow	53	S	T
I. Brown	28	N	?

Key:
- 1: Candidate's Age
- 2: Present Performance
    (E-Excellent; S-Satisfactory; N-Needs Improvement)
- 3: Promotion Potential (R-Ready Now;
    T-Training Required; ? - Questionable)

Title			
Name	•1	•2	•3

personnel replacement charts Graphic illustrations of current positions, who holds them, and whether they have the skills and qualifications necessary for succession planning.

Job analysis is the process of identifying (1) the tasks, duties, and responsibilities that make up a job (the *job description*), and (2) the knowledge, skills, and abilities needed to perform the job (the *job specifications*).[35] For each job in an organization, a job analysis needs to be done. Recall from Chapter 5 the five core job characteristics involved in job design according to Hackman and Oldham's job characteristics model. An analysis of the skill variety, task identity, task significance, degree of autonomy, and the degree to which doing the job itself provides the worker with feedback is useful in conducting a job analysis.

job analysis Identifying the tasks, duties, and responsibilities that make up a job and the knowledge, skills, and abilities needed to perform the job.

A job analysis can be done in a number of ways, including by observing current employees as they perform the job or by interviewing them. Often, managers rely on questionnaires completed by job holders and their managers. The questionnaires ask about the skills and abilities needed to perform the job, job tasks and the amount of time spent on them, responsibilities, supervisory activities, equipment used, reports prepared, and decisions made.[36]

A trend in some organizations is toward more flexible jobs in which tasks and responsibilities change and cannot be clearly specified in advance. For these kinds of jobs, job analysis focuses more on determining the skills and knowledge workers need to be effective and less on specific duties.

When managers complete human resource planning and job analyses for all jobs in an organization, they know their human resource needs and the jobs they need to fill. They also know what knowledge, skills, and abilities potential employees will need to perform those jobs. At this point, the first component of HRM, recruitment and selection, can begin.

The Components of HRM

LO3 | Describe the five components of human resource management and explain how they fit together with the strategy and structure of the organization.

Recruitment and Selection

After managers engage in human resource planning and job analysis, they can start to recruit and select employees. **Recruitment** includes all the activities that managers use to develop a pool of qualified candidates for open positions.[37] **Selection** is the process by which managers determine the relative qualifications of job applicants and their potential for performing well in a particular job.

> **recruitment** Activities that managers use to develop a pool of qualified candidates for open positions.
>
> **selection** The process that managers use to determine the relative qualifications of job applicants and the individuals' potential for performing well in a particular job.

So, how do human resource managers find their most valuable commodity—talent—in the highly competitive labour market? HR managers use two sources of recruiting talent: external and internal, which are now supplemented by recruiting over the Internet.

EXTERNAL RECRUITING

When managers do external recruiting to fill open positions, they look outside the organization for people who have not worked for the organization before. There are many ways in which managers can recruit externally—advertisements in newspapers and magazines, open houses for students, career counsellors at high schools and colleges, career fairs at colleges and universities, recruitment meetings with groups in the local community, and job sites on the Internet.

Many large organizations send teams of interviewers to college campuses to recruit new employees. External recruitment can also take place through informal networks, such as when current employees inform friends about open positions in their companies or recommend people they know to fill vacant spots. Some organizations use employment agencies for external recruitment, and some external recruitment takes place simply through walk-ins, where job hunters come to an organization and inquire about employment possibilities. An example of an employment agency that provides a source of labour in the construction and maintenance sectors is featured in our Focus on the Social Economy box.

With all the downsizing and corporate layoffs that have taken place in recent years, you might think that external recruiting would be a relatively easy task for managers. However, often it is not, because even though many people may be looking

Managers seek to develop a pool of qualified candidates when recruiting.
opolja/Dreamstime.com/Getstock.com

FOCUS ON *The Social Economy*

EMBERS (Eastside Movement for Business & Economic Renewal Society)

EMBERS (Eastside Movement for Business & Economic Renewal Society) is a nonprofit agency that works to combat poverty and assists in the revitalization of Vancouver's inner city by facilitating community-based business development. They do this by helping individuals and groups start small businesses and social enterprises. They offer self-employment training and one-on-one business coaching, and they work with residents, community groups, and other stakeholders to develop plans, strategies, and specific ventures to improve the lives of residents and build a healthy community.

In 2008, EMBERS launched EMBERS Staffing Solutions as a way to connect people with barriers to employment to businesses seeking employees and to have a strong social impact in the community. The only socially responsible, nonprofit staffing agency in Vancouver, they provide companies with high-quality blue-collar workers on a monthly, weekly, or daily basis. Their candidates are talented, reliable, and proven workers in construction, warehousing, and other sectors. All profits from EMBERS Staffing Solutions are reinvested back into EMBERS Staffing Solutions employment programs to help to improve the lives and skills of workers.

1. Describe how EMBERS Staffing Solutions helps organizations with a vital component of HRM.

Source: Based on http://www.embersvancouver.com/staffing-solutions/. Accessed February 15, 2018.

for jobs, many of the jobs that are opening up require skills and abilities that these job hunters do not have. Managers needing to fill vacant positions and job hunters seeking employment opportunities are increasingly relying on the Internet to make connections with each other through employment websites such as Indeed, Monster. com[38] and Jobline International. Jobline is Europe's largest electronic recruiting site, with operations in 12 countries.[39] Major corporations such as Coca-Cola, Cisco, Ernst & Young, Canon, and Telia have relied on Jobline. net to fill global positions.[40] Job postings for international recruitment are often placed online in trade journals and news magazines like *The Times* and *The Economist*.

Dr. Marilyn Mackes, the executive director for the U.S. National Association of Colleges and Employers, suggests that whereas in the past employers used social networking sites "to check profiles of potential hires," today "more than half will use the sites to network with potential candidates."[41] Job seekers are wise to not upload anything on the Internet that may be viewed unfavourably, as hiring managers are likely to see it.

External recruiting has both advantages and disadvantages for managers. These are summarized in Table 7.2.

Advantages of recruiting externally include having access to a potentially large applicant pool; being able to hire people who have the skills, knowledge, and abilities the organization needs to achieve its goals; and being able to bring in newcomers who may have a fresh approach to problems and be up to date on the latest technology. These advantages have to be weighed against the disadvantages, however, including lower morale if current employees feel that there

Selecting the right people for the job leads to high-performing organizations.
©Stockbyte/Getty Images

TABLE 7.2

Advantages and Disadvantages of External and Internal Recruitment

External Recruitment		Internal Recruitment	
Advantages	Disadvantages	Advantages	Disadvantages
Access to a large labour pool	Current employees may feel bypassed	Promotions or lateral moves boost levels of employee motivation and morale	A limited pool of candidates
Newcomers have a fresh approach to problems	High costs of training	Candidates are already familiar with the organization, thus reducing the costs of orientation and training	Set in the organization's existing ways, thus resistant to change
Tend to have up-to-date knowledge of new technology	Uncertainty of fit and performance	Managers know internal candidates' skills and abilities and actual behaviour on the job	Use existing/old technology

are individuals within the company who should be promoted, but are bypassed. External recruitment also has high costs. Employees recruited externally lack knowledge about the inner workings of the organization and may need to receive more training than those recruited internally. Finally, with external recruitment, there is always uncertainty about whether the new employees actually will be good performers. Nonetheless, there are steps managers can take to reduce some of the uncertainty surrounding external recruitment. For example, Vancouver-based Angiotech Pharmaceuticals Inc. solves this problem by working with potential employees years before they are ready to be hired. The company provides research money to graduate students at the University of British Columbia who are working on projects closely related to Angiotech's needs.

INTERNAL RECRUITING

When recruiting is internal, managers turn to existing employees to fill open positions. Employees recruited internally want either **lateral moves** (job changes that entail no major changes in responsibility or authority levels) or promotions. Internal recruiting has several advantages. First, internal applicants are already familiar with the organization (including its goals, structure, culture, rules, and norms). Second, managers already know internal candidates; they have considerable information about their skills and abilities and actual behaviour on the job. Third, internal recruiting can help boost levels of employee motivation and morale, both for the employee who gets the job and for other workers. Those who are not seeking a promotion or who may not be ready for a promotion can see that it is a possibility for the future, or a lateral move can alleviate boredom once a job has been fully mastered and also provide a useful way to learn new skills. Finally, internal recruiting is normally less time-consuming and expensive than external recruiting. As is discussed in the opening case, the Four Seasons hotel chain often promotes from within. A new college graduate can start as an assistant manager and, if they have the right stuff, advance within 15 years to become a hotel general manager.

lateral moves Job changes that entail no major changes in responsibility or authority levels.

Given the advantages of internal recruiting, why do managers rely on external recruiting as much as they do? The answer lies in the disadvantages to internal recruiting—among them, a limited pool of candidates and a tendency among those candidates to be set in the organization's ways. Often, the organization simply does not have suitable internal candidates. Sometimes, even when suitable internal applicants are available, managers may rely on external recruiting to find the very best candidate or to help bring new ideas and approaches into the organization. When organizations are in trouble and performing poorly, external recruiting is often relied on to bring in managerial talent with a fresh approach.

THE SELECTION PROCESS

Once managers develop a pool of applicants for open positions through the recruitment process, they need to find out whether each applicant is

Selection techniques must be valid and reliable.
Daving photography/Getty Images

qualified for the position and whether he or she is likely to be a good performer. If more than one applicant meets these two conditions, managers must further determine which applicants are likely to be better performers than others. They have several selection tools to help them sort out the relative qualifications of job applicants and to appraise applicants' potential for being good performers in a particular job.

All selection techniques must be valid *and* reliable. To be a **valid selection technique,** it must determine the candidates' likely performance (success or failure) on the job. Validity is the degree to which a test predicts performance on the tasks or job in question. Does a physical ability test used to select firefighters, for example, actually predict on-the-job performance? Do assessment centre ratings actually predict managerial performance? Do keyboarding tests predict secretarial performance? These are all questions of validity. Honesty tests, for example, are controversial because it is not clear that they validly predict honesty in such jobs as retailing and banking.

valid selection technique A test or tool that measures the candidates' likely success or failure in performing the job.

If a candidate is given a test that is unrelated to performing the job, it is invalid, and managers can be subject to charges of discrimination if the candidate is not chosen. For example, it would be invalid for a manager to use a test of strength to select a candidate for a word-processing job. The test of strength has no relation to how the candidate will perform the tasks of a word processor. Women have long been unable to access many of the jobs traditionally held by men because of invalid selection techniques. To be a **reliable selection technique,** it must yield consistent results when repeated over time. Reliability is the degree to which the test or tool measures the same thing each time it is administered. In the previous example, if the word-processing candidate is given a typing test that is reliable, it should yield similar performance results, without a significant deviation, when repeated some time later. Selection techniques include background information and reference checks, interviews, and tests.[42] See Figure 7.5.

reliable selection technique A test or tool that yields consistent results when repeated.

Background Information and Reference Checks To aid in the selection process, managers obtain background information from job applications and from resumés. Such information might include highest levels of education obtained, university or college majors and minors, type of college or university

FIGURE 7.5

Selection Techniques

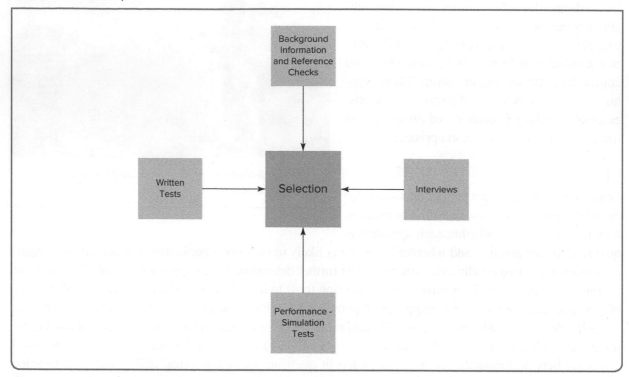

attended, years and type of work experience, and mastery of foreign languages. Background information can be helpful both to screen out applicants who are lacking key qualifications (such as a post-secondary degree) and to determine which qualified applicants are more promising than others (e.g., applicants with a BSc may be acceptable, but those who also have an MBA are preferable).

Increasing numbers of organizations are performing background checks to verify that the background information prospective employees provide is accurate (and also to uncover any negative information such as crime convictions).[43] Companies performing background checks on prospective employees can uncover inaccuracies, inconsistencies, and negative information such as prior convictions or driving violations.[44] It is important to remember that not all negative information about someone's past can legally be used to screen them out of the competition. At all times, the HR manager must be in compliance with the laws governing human resource management referred to earlier in the chapter.

Applicants for many jobs are required to provide references from former employers or other knowledgeable sources (such as a college instructor or adviser) who know the applicant's skills, abilities, and other personal characteristics. These individuals are asked to provide candid information about the applicants. References are often used at the end of the selection process to confirm a decision to hire. Yet, the fact that many former employers are reluctant to provide negative information in references sometimes makes it difficult to interpret what a reference is really saying about an applicant.

In fact, several recent lawsuits filed by applicants who felt that they were unfairly denigrated or had their privacy invaded by unfavourable references from former employers have caused managers to be increasingly wary of providing any kind of negative information in a reference, even if it is accurate. For jobs in which the job holder is responsible for the safety and lives of other people, however, failing to provide accurate negative information in a reference does not just mean that the wrong person might get hired but may also mean that other people's lives will be at stake.

Interviews Virtually all organizations use interviews during the selection process. The interview process is intended to create a perception of the candidate to try to determine if they are a good match for the job and fit well with the culture of the organization.

Two general types of interviews are *structured* and *unstructured*. In a structured interview, managers ask each applicant the same standard questions (such as "What are your unique qualifications for this position?" and "What characteristics of a job are most important for you?"). Particularly informative questions may be those where the actual answering

Interviews provide the employer and candidate with valuable information.
Wernerheiber/Dreamstime.com/Getstock.com

allows an interviewee to demonstrate skills and abilities needed for the job. Sometimes called *situational interview questions,* these questions present interviewees with a scenario that they would likely encounter on the job and ask them to indicate how they would handle it.[45] For example, applicants for a sales job may be asked to indicate how they would respond to a customer who complains about waiting too long for service, a customer who is indecisive, and a customer whose order is lost.

An **unstructured interview** or *nondirective interview* proceeds more like an ordinary conversation. The interviewer feels free to ask probing questions to discover what the applicant is like and does not ask a fixed set of questions prepared in advance. In general, a **structured interview,** where a standard set of questions based on the job analysis are asked in set sequence and evaluated based on predetermined answers, is superior to the unstructured interview because it is more likely to yield information that will help identify qualified candidates and is less subjective.

unstructured interview Unplanned questions asked as points of interest arise in the conversation.

structured interview Formal, standardized questions are asked in a set sequence.

Many types of questions are used in structured interviews. We deal with three common types below. **Situational interview questions** ask candidates how they would deal with a specific situation *in the future.* For example, "What would you do if a customer walked out of the store without paying for an item?" **Behavioural interview questions** ask candidates to describe how they reacted to a specific situation *in the past.* Behavioural interview questions focus on relevant past job-related or *job knowledge* behaviours. They involve describing a situation and asking the candidate how they handled it. For example, "How did you inform a subordinate that you had to let them go?" **Worker-requirements questions** assess candidates' willingness to perform under prevailing job conditions, such as nonstandard job shifts. See Figure 7.6 for additional examples.

situational interview questions Questions that ask candidates how they would respond to a particular work situation in the future.

behavioural interview questions Questions that ask candidates how they dealt with a situation they encountered on the job in the past.

worker-requirements questions Questions that ask candidates about their willingness to work under specific job conditions.

FIGURE 7.6

Examples of Interview Question Types

Situational interview questions

- How would you deal with an irate customer?
- What would you do if you had to persuade someone to change their opinion?

Behavioural interview questions

- Describe a situation in which you successfully used conflict resolution skills
- Tell me about a situation in which you had to use persuasion to influence someone's opinion

Worker-requirements interview questions

- Sometimes we have customers complaining about slow service. How do you feel about working in a hostile environment?
- You will be asked to mediate customer complaints. Are you willing to handle the stress?

Even when structured interviews are used, however, there is always the potential for the biases of the interviewer to influence his or her judgment. The *similar-to-me effect* can cause people to perceive others who are similar to themselves more positively than they perceive those who are different. This illustrates how stereotypes can result in inaccurate perceptions. It is important for interviewers to be trained to avoid these biases and sources of inaccurate perceptions as much as possible. Many of the approaches to increasing diversity awareness and diversity skills can be used to train interviewers to avoid the effects of biases and stereotypes, as discussed later in this chapter. In addition, using multiple interviewers can be advantageous, for their individual biases and idiosyncrasies may cancel one another out.[46] *Panel interviews,* where several managers interview each candidate, may be used in combination with structured interviews to minimize the possibility of bias.

When conducting interviews, managers have to be careful not to ask questions that are irrelevant to the job in question, or their organizations run the risk of costly lawsuits. It is inappropriate and illegal, for example, to inquire about an interviewee's spouse or to ask questions about whether an interviewee plans to have children. Questions such as these, which are irrelevant to job performance, are *invalid* and may be viewed as discriminatory and violate human rights legislation. Thus, interviewers also need to be instructed in what is required under the legislation and informed about questions that may be seen as violating those laws.

Written Tests   Potential employees may be asked to take written tests. The two main kinds of written tests used for selection purposes are *ability tests* and *personality tests*. **Ability tests** assess the extent to which applicants possess the skills necessary for job performance, such as verbal comprehension or numerical skills. Autoworkers hired by General Motors, Chrysler, and Ford, for example, are typically tested for their ability to read and to do mathematics.[47]

ability tests Assess the skills necessary to perform the job well.

Personality tests measure personality traits and characteristics relevant to job performance. Employers keen to find and retain the right workers are turning to personality testing to help everything from recruiting to promoting to team building. Proponents call them essential, but critics worry that they sometimes can be invasive, ineffective, even borderline illegal.[48] Some retail organizations, for example, give job applicants honesty tests to determine how trustworthy they are. The use of personality tests (including honesty tests) for hiring purposes is controversial. Some critics maintain that honesty tests do not really measure honesty (i.e., they are not valid) and can be subject to faking by job applicants. Before using any written tests for selection purposes, managers must have sound evidence that the tests are actually good predictors of performance on the job in question. Managers who use tests without such evidence may be subject to costly discrimination lawsuits.

personality tests Measure personality traits and characteristics relevant to job performance.

For jobs that require physical abilities—such as firefighting, garbage collecting, and package delivery—managers' selection tools include **physical ability tests** that measure physical strength and stamina. Autoworkers are typically tested for mechanical dexterity because this physical ability is an important skill for high job performance in many auto plants.[49]

physical ability tests Measure physical strength and stamina.

Performance-Simulation Tests **Performance-simulation tests** measure job applicants' performance on actual job tasks. Applicants for secretarial positions, for example, are typically required to complete a typing test that measures how quickly and accurately they are able to type. Applicants for middle- and top-management positions are sometimes given short-term simulated projects to complete—projects that mirror the kinds of situations that arise in the job being filled—to assess their knowledge and problem-solving capabilities.[50]

performance-simulation tests Measure the candidate's ability to perform actual job tasks.

In summary, managers have an ethical and legal obligation to use reliable and valid selection tools. Yet reliability and validity are matters of degree rather than all-or-nothing characteristics. Thus, managers should strive to use selection tools in such a way that they can achieve the greatest degree of reliability and validity. For ability tests of a particular skill, managers should keep up to date on the latest advances in the development of valid written tests and use the test with the highest reliability and validity ratings for their purposes. Regarding interviews, managers can improve reliability by having more than one person interview job candidates. While background checks can reveal inaccuracies, the usefulness of reference checking is limited due to the reluctance of managers to provide negative information. See Figure 7.7 for a summary of the typical steps in the hiring process.

Once a candidate is offered a position but before accepting, they should be given a *realistic job preview*. Usually occurring in the final interview, a **realistic job preview (RJP)** involves communicating the good and bad aspects of a job to a candidate to prevent mismatched expectations and high turnover. Increasingly, big data analytics are being used to help hire the right people and predict when they are at risk of leaving.[51] Four Seasons has a substantially lower turnover rate than the rest of the industry because potential employees understand from the beginning the difficulties and rewards of creating a first-class hotel experience for customers.

realistic job preview (RJP) Communicating the good and bad aspects of a job to a candidate to prevent mismatched expectations and high turnover.

FIGURE 7.7

Typical Steps in the Hiring Process

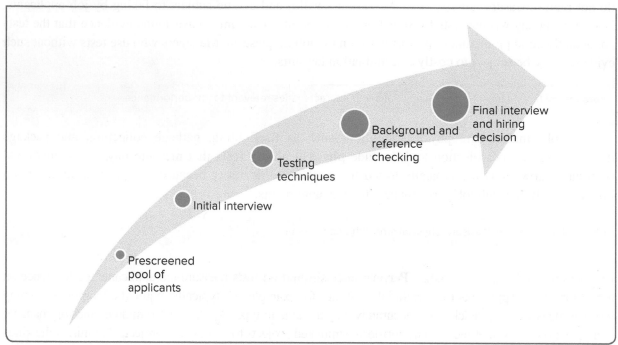

Prescreened pool of applicants

Initial interview

Testing techniques

Background and reference checking

Final interview and hiring decision

TIPS FOR MANAGERS

Recruitment and Selection

1. Be transparent with potential new recruits as to the advantages and disadvantages of a job.

2. Be aware that older workers may be your solution to a skills gap in your company.

3. Think through the leadership talent you will need to build future organizational success.

4. Make sure your selection tools are reliable and valid.

Training and Development

If the candidate accepts the position, they must be introduced to the culture and norms of the organization and their work unit. This is the **orientation.** During this introduction, the new hire learns the ropes of the job and relevant HR policies about benefits and working conditions, procedures, history and values, and the vision and mission of the organization. Training and development help ensure that organizational members have the knowledge and skills they need to perform their jobs effectively, take on new responsibilities, and adapt to changing conditions. **Training** focuses mainly on teaching organizational members how to perform their current jobs and on helping them acquire the knowledge and skills they need to be effective performers. New hires at Four Seasons participate in a three-month training program that includes improvisation activities to help them learn how to anticipate guests' needs, requirements, and actions and appropriately respond to them.

> **orientation** The introduction to the culture, norms, policies, values, and vision and mission of the organization.
>
> **training** Teaching organizational members how to perform their current jobs and helping them acquire the knowledge and skills they need to be effective performers.

Development focuses on building the knowledge and skills of organizational members so that they will be prepared to take on new responsibilities and challenges. Training tends to be used more often at lower levels of an organization; development tends to be used more often with professionals and managers.

> **development** Building the knowledge and skills of organizational members so that they will be prepared to take on new responsibilities and challenges.

Before creating training and development programs, managers should perform a **needs assessment** in which they determine which employees need training or development and what type of skills or knowledge they need to acquire.[52]

> **needs assessment** An assessment to determine which employees need training or development and what type of skills or knowledge they need to acquire.

TYPES OF TRAINING AND DEVELOPMENT

There are many methods of training and development. See Figure 7.8. Each has advantages and disadvantages in terms of cost, time consumption, levels of interaction, and so on. Employees may be trained in both *hard* and *soft* skills. Hard skills refer to the specialized technical skills and knowledge needed to do the job, while soft skills refer to interpersonal skills like communication, effective team building, conflict resolution, and motivation skills.

FIGURE 7.8

Training and Development Methods

Online Delivery	Using videoconferencing • Saves time and reduces costs
e-Learning	Using interactive simulations or games • Key aspects of the work situation and job tasks are duplicated as closely as possible in an artificial setting
On-the-Job Training	Using actual work situations • Keeps up to date with changes in goals, technology, products, or customer needs and desires
Mentoring	Using an experienced member of an organization who provides advice and guidance to a less experienced member • Formal and informal channels give trainees varied work experiences
Diversity Training	Using films, focus groups, forums, role play, experiential exercises, and group exercises • Uncovers biases, stereotypes, and systemic racism

Training can be delivered in many ways. *Online* delivery using videoconferencing technologies is popular as it saves travel and time costs and modules can be customized to fit the needs in a particular organization. Also popular is *e-learning,* where employees participate in interactive simulations or games that mirror the types of decisions they would make on the job. In a simulation, key aspects of the work situation and job tasks are duplicated as closely as possible in an artificial setting. For example, air traffic controllers are trained by simulations because of the complicated nature of the work, the extensive amount of learning involved, and the very high costs of air traffic control errors. Managers often use *on-the-job training* on a continuing basis to ensure that their subordinates keep up to date with changes in goals, technology, products, or customer needs and desires. For example, sales representatives at Mary Kay Cosmetics Inc. receive ongoing training so that they not only are knowledgeable about new cosmetic products and currently popular colours but also are reminded of Mary Kay's guiding principles.

Another development approach is mentoring. A *mentor* is an experienced member of an organization who provides advice and guidance to a less experienced member, called a *protegé.* Having a mentor can help managers seek out work experiences and assignments that will contribute to their development and can enable them to gain the most possible from varied work experiences.[53] While some mentors and protegés hook up informally, organizations have found that formal mentorship programs can be valuable ways to contribute to the development of managers and all employees.

Formal mentoring programs which assign protegés to mentors give structure to the process and ensure that diverse organizational members have equal access to mentors. Mentors receive formal training and efforts are focused on matching up mentors and protegés so that meaningful developmental relationships ensue and organizations can track reactions and assess the potential benefits of the program. A study conducted by David A. Thomas, a professor at the Harvard Business School, found that members of racial minority groups at three large corporations who were very successful in their careers had had the benefit of mentors. Formal mentorship programs help organizations make this valuable development tool available to all employees.[54]

When diverse members of an organization lack mentors, their progress in the organization and advancement to high-level positions can be hampered. Ida Abbott, a lawyer and consultant on work-related issues, concluded, "The lack of adequate mentoring has held women and minority lawyers back from achieving professional success and has led to high rates of career dissatisfaction and attrition."[55]

Mentoring can benefit all kinds of employees in all kinds of work.[56] John Washko, a former manager at the Four Seasons hotel chain, benefited from the mentoring he received from Stan Bromley regarding interpersonal relations and how to deal with employees; Bromley, in turn, found that participating in the Four Seasons' mentoring program helped him develop his own management style.[57] More generally, development is an ongoing process for all managers, and mentors often find that mentoring contributes to their own personal development.

> "The lack of adequate mentoring has held women and minority lawyers back from achieving professional success and has led to high rates of career dissatisfaction and attrition."
>
> Ida Abbott, lawyer and consultant

Many *diversity awareness training* programs in organizations strive to increase managers' and employees' awareness of (1) their own attitudes, biases, and stereotypes and (2) the differing perspectives of diverse managers, subordinates, co-workers, and customers. Diversity awareness programs often have these goals:[58]

1. Providing organizational members with accurate information about diversity.

2. Uncovering personal biases and stereotypes.

3. Assessing personal beliefs, attitudes, and values and learning about other points of view.

4. Overturning inaccurate stereotypes and beliefs about different groups.

5. Developing an atmosphere in which people feel free to share their differing perspectives.

6. Improving understanding of others who are different from oneself.

Many managers use a varied approach to increase diversity awareness and skills in their organizations: Films and printed materials are supplemented by experiential exercises to uncover any hidden **bias** (the systematic tendency to use information about others in ways that result in inaccurate perceptions) or **stereotype** (simplistic and often inaccurate belief about the typical characteristics of particular groups of people). Sometimes simply providing a forum for people to learn about and discuss their differing attitudes, values, and experiences can be a powerful means for increasing awareness. Also useful are role-playing exercises in which people act out problems that result from lack of awareness and then indicate the increased understanding that comes from appreciating others' viewpoints. Accurate information and training experiences can debunk stereotypes. Group exercises, role plays, and diversity-related experiences can help organizational members develop the skills they need to work effectively with a variety of people.

bias The systematic tendency to use information about others in ways that result in inaccurate perceptions.
stereotype Simplistic and often inaccurate belief about the typical characteristics of particular groups of people.

Managers sometimes hire outside consultants to provide diversity training. For instance, Trevor Wilson, past CEO of Toronto-based Omnibus Consulting, has presented employment equity programs to such clients as IBM Canada Ltd., Molson Inc., and National Grocers Co. Ltd.[59] Some organizations have their own in-house diversity experts, such as at Union Gas, based in Chatham, Ontario.

When top management is truly committed to diversity, human resource managers embrace diversity through their actions and work to break down barriers and systemic racism. Diversity can be a source of competitive advantage when managers deal effectively with diverse employees and are willing to commit organizational resources to managing diversity. That last step alone is not enough. If top managers commit resources to diversity (such as providing money for training programs) but as individuals do not value diversity, any steps they take are likely to fail. Although some steps prove unsuccessful, it is clear that managers must make a long-term commitment to diversity. Training sessions oriented toward the short term are doomed to failure: Participants quickly slip back into their old ways of doing things and systemic barriers are not challenged. The effective management of diversity, like the management of the organization as a whole, is an ongoing process: It never stops and never ends.

Whenever training and development take place off the job or in a classroom setting, it is vital for managers to promote the transfer of the knowledge and skills acquired *to the actual work situation*. Trainees should be encouraged and expected to use their newfound expertise on the job.

Performance Appraisal and Feedback

The recruitment/selection and the training/development components of a human resource management system ensure that employees have the knowledge and skills they need to be effective now and in the future. Performance appraisal and feedback complement recruitment, selection, training, and development. **Performance appraisal** is the evaluation of employees' job performance and contributions to their organization. **Performance feedback** is the process through which managers share performance appraisal information with their subordinates, give subordinates an opportunity to reflect on their own performance, and develop, with subordinates, plans for the future. In order for performance feedback to occur, performance appraisal must take place. Performance appraisal could take place without providing performance feedback, but wise managers are careful to provide feedback because it can contribute to employee motivation and performance.

> **performance appraisal** The evaluation of employees' job performance and contributions to their organization.
>
> **performance feedback** The process through which managers share performance appraisal information with subordinates, give subordinates an opportunity to reflect on their own performance, and develop, with subordinates, plans for the future.

Performance appraisal and feedback contribute to the effective management of human resources in two ways. Performance appraisal gives managers important information on which to base human resource decisions.[60] Decisions about pay raises, bonuses, promotions, and job moves all hinge on the accurate appraisal of performance. Performance appraisal also can help managers determine which workers are candidates for training and development and in what areas. Performance feedback encourages high levels of employee motivation and performance. It alerts good performers that their efforts are valued and appreciated and alerts poor performers that their lacklustre performance needs improvement. Performance feedback can provide both good and poor performers with insight into their strengths and weaknesses and ways in which they can improve their performance in the future.

TYPES OF PERFORMANCE APPRAISAL

Performance appraisal focuses on the evaluation of traits, behaviours, and results.[61]

Trait Appraisals   When trait appraisals are used, managers assess subordinates on personal characteristics that are relevant to job performance, such as skills, abilities, or personality. A factory worker, for example, may be evaluated based on her ability to use computerized equipment and perform numerical calculations. A social worker may be appraised based on his empathy and communication skills.

Three disadvantages of trait appraisals often lead managers to rely on other appraisal methods. First, possessing a certain personal characteristic does not ensure that the personal characteristic will actually be used on the job and result in high performance. For example, a factory worker may possess superior computer and numerical skills but be a poor performer due to low motivation. The second disadvantage of trait appraisals is linked to the first. Because traits do not always show a direct association with performance, workers and courts of law may view trait appraisals as unfair and potentially discriminatory. The third disadvantage of trait appraisals is that they often do not enable managers to provide employees with feedback that they can use to improve performance. Because trait appraisals focus on relatively enduring human characteristics that change only over the long term, employees can do little to change their behaviour in response to performance feedback from a trait appraisal. Telling a social worker that he lacks empathy provides him with little guidance about how to improve his interactions with clients, for example. These disadvantages suggest that managers should use trait appraisals only when they can demonstrate that the assessed traits are accurate and important indicators of job performance.

Behaviour Appraisals   Through behaviour appraisals, managers assess how workers perform their jobs—the actual actions and behaviours that workers exhibit on the job. Whereas trait appraisals assess what workers are *like,* behaviour appraisals assess what workers *do.* For example, with a behaviour appraisal, a manager might evaluate a social worker on the extent to which he looks clients in the eye when talking with them, expresses sympathy when they are upset, and refers them to community counselling and support groups geared toward the specific problem they are encountering. Behaviour appraisals are especially useful when *how* workers perform their jobs is important. In educational organizations such as high schools, for example, the number of classes and students taught is important, but also important are how they are taught and the methods teachers use to ensure that learning takes place.

Behaviour appraisals have the advantage of providing employees with clear information about what they are doing right and wrong and how they can improve their performance. And because behaviours are much easier for employees to change than traits, performance feedback from behaviour appraisals is more likely to lead to performance improvements.

Graphic Rating Scale Method   The most popular method of employee performance appraisal is called the graphic rating scale method. In this method, the appraiser scores the employee on a number of characteristics that reflect performance levels in such areas as quality, productivity, job knowledge, reliability, availability, and ability to work independently or in a team. Specific behavioural descriptions are used for each area that relate to the current job requirements. Points are assigned for each rating and are totalled and averaged for an overall performance score. See Figure 7.9.

Result Appraisals   For some jobs, *how* people perform the job is not as important as *what* they accomplish or the results they obtain. With result appraisals, managers appraise performance by the results or the actual outcomes of work behaviours. Take the case of two new-car salespersons. One salesperson strives to develop personal relationships with her customers. She spends hours talking to them and frequently calls them up to see how their decision-making process is going. The other salesperson has a much more hands-off approach. He is very knowledgeable, answers customers' questions, and then waits for them to come to him. Both salespersons sell, on average, the same number of cars, and the customers

FIGURE 7.9

Elements Included in a Graphic Rating Scale Performance Appraisal

Factors	Rating	Scale	Points and comments
Quality—The degree of excellence and thoroughness of the work performed	Outstanding—Performance is exceptional and superior to others	100–90	☐
Productivity—The amount of work done in a specific period	Very good—High levels of performance that consistently exceed requirements	90–80	☐
Job knowledge—The specialized skills and information used on the job	Good—Competent and reliable level of performance	80–70	☐
Reliability—The degree of trustworthiness to complete the task and follow up	Improvement needed—Performance falls below requirements in some areas	70–60	☐
Availability—The rate of absenteeism and punctuality of the employee	Unsatisfactory—Performance levels are unacceptable	Below 60	☐
Independence—The degree to which the employee must be supervised		·	☐
Team work—The ability to work well as a member of a group			☐

FIGURE 7.10

Who Appraises Performance?

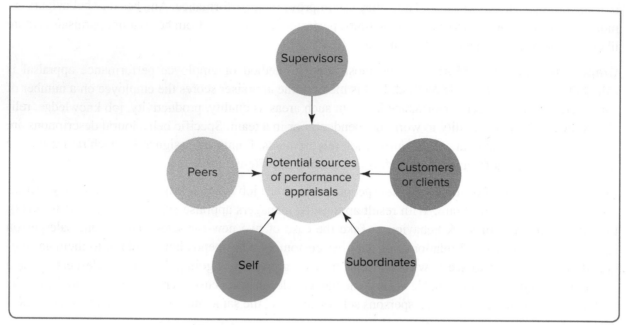

of both are satisfied with the service they receive, according to postcards that the dealership mails to customers asking for an assessment of their satisfaction. The manager of the dealership appropriately uses result appraisals (sales and customer satisfaction) to evaluate the salespeople's performance because it does not matter which behaviour salespeople use to sell cars as long as they sell the desired number and satisfy customers. If one salesperson sells too few cars, however, the manager can give that person performance feedback about his or her low sales.

Who Appraises Performance? We have been assuming that managers or the supervisors of employees evaluate performance. This is a pretty fair assumption, as supervisors are the most common appraisers of performance. Performance appraisal is an important part of most managers' job duties. It is managers' responsibility to motivate their subordinates to perform at a high level, and managers make many of the decisions that hinge on performance appraisals, such as decisions about pay raises or promotions. Appraisals by managers can, however, be usefully supplemented by appraisals from other sources (see Figure 7.10).

360-Degree Performance Appraisals To improve motivation and performance, some organizations include **360-degree appraisals** and feedback in their performance appraisal systems, especially for managers. In a 360-degree appraisal, an individual's performance is appraised by a variety of people, including the individual him or herself, peers or co-workers, subordinates, superiors, and sometimes even customers or clients. The individual receives feedback based on evaluations from these multiple sources.

360-degree appraisals Performance appraisals by peers, subordinates, superiors, and sometimes clients who are in a position to evaluate a manager's performance.

Although appraisals from each of these sources can be useful, managers need to be aware of potential issues that may arise when they are used. Subordinates sometimes may be inclined to inflate self-appraisals, especially if organizations are downsizing and they are worried about their job security. Managers who are appraised by their subordinates may fail to take needed but unpopular actions for fear that their subordinates will appraise them negatively. Some of these potential issues can be mitigated to the extent that there are high levels of trust in an organization. Online surveys that ensure anonymity are increasingly being used by large companies to solicit performance appraisals.

Peers often are very knowledgeable about performance but may be reluctant to provide an accurate and negative appraisal of someone they like or a positive appraisal of someone they dislike. In addition, whenever peers, subordinates, or anyone else evaluates an employee's performance, managers must be sure that the evaluators are actually knowledgeable about the performance dimensions being assessed. For example, subordinates should not evaluate their supervisor's decision making if they have little opportunity to observe this dimension of his or her performance.

These potential problems with 360-degree appraisals and feedback do not mean that they are not useful. Rather, they suggest that in order for 360-degree appraisals and feedback to be effective, trust is needed throughout the organization. More generally, trust is a critical ingredient in any performance appraisal and feedback procedure. Managers using 360-degree appraisals and feedback also have to consider carefully the pros and cons of using anonymous evaluations and of using the results of the appraisals for decision-making about important issues such as pay raises.[62]

Even when 360-degree appraisals are used, it is sometimes difficult to design an effective process by which subordinates' feedback can be communicated to their managers. Advances in information technology provide organizations with a potential solution to this problem. For example, ImproveNow.com has online questionnaires that subordinates fill out to evaluate the performance of their managers and provide the managers with feedback. Each subordinate of a particular manager completes the questionnaire independently, all responses are tabulated, and the manager is given specific feedback on behaviours in a variety of areas, such as rewarding good performance, looking out for subordinates' best interest and being supportive, and having a vision for the future.[63]

EFFECTIVE PERFORMANCE FEEDBACK

In order for the performance appraisal and feedback component of a human resource management system to encourage and motivate high performance, managers must provide their subordinates with performance feedback. To generate useful information to pass on to subordinates, managers can use both formal and informal appraisals. **Formal appraisals** are conducted at set times during the year and are based on performance dimensions and measures that have been specified in advance. A salesperson, for example, may be evaluated by his or her manager twice a year on the performance dimensions of sales and customer service, sales being measured from sales reports and customer service being measured by the number of complaints received. **Informal appraisals**—unscheduled appraisals of ongoing progress and areas for improvement—may occur at the request of the employee. Moreover, when job duties, assignments, or goals change, informal appraisals can provide workers with timely feedback concerning how they are handling their new responsibilities.

formal appraisals Appraisals conducted at a set time during the year and based on performance dimensions and measures that were specified in advance.

informal appraisals Unscheduled appraisals of ongoing progress and areas for improvement.

An integral part of a formal appraisal is a meeting between the manager and the subordinate in which the subordinate is given feedback on his or her performance.

Managers often dislike providing performance feedback, especially when the feedback is negative, but doing so is an important managerial activity. Some guidelines for effectively giving performance feedback that will contribute to employee motivation and performance are outlined in Figure 7.11.

FIGURE 7.11

Effective Performance Feedback

Performance Feedback Guidelines	Example of Poor Feedback	Example of Good Feedback
Be specific and focus on behaviours or outcomes that are correctable and within a worker's ability to improve	Telling a salesperson that he or she is too shy when interacting with customers —likely to do nothing more than lower the person's self-confidence and prompt him or her to become defensive	Giving the salesperson feedback about specific behaviours to engage in—greeting customers as soon as they enter the department, asking customers whether they need help, and volunteering to help customers find items if they seem to be having trouble
Approach performance appraisal as an exercise in problem-solving and solution-finding, not criticizing	Criticizing a financial analyst for turning reports in late	Helping the analyst determine why the reports are late and identify ways to better manage time
Express confidence in a subordinate's ability to improve	Being skeptical and questioning the employee's ability to handle a task	Telling a subordinate how they can increase quality levels
Provide performance feedback both formally and informally	Waiting until the formal feedback meeting to comment on performance levels	Providing frequent informal feedback such as complimenting staff members on creative ideas for special projects, noticing when they do a particularly good job, and pointing out when they provide inadequate supervision of subordinates
Praise instances of high performance and areas of a job in which an employee excels	Focusing on just the negative, such as lack of punctuality	Discussing the areas the subordinate excels in as well as areas in need of improvement.
Avoid personal criticisms, and treat subordinates with respect	Pointing out performance problems to subordinates and criticizing them personally	Acknowledging subordinates' expertise and treating them as professionals
Agree to a timetable for performance improvements	Setting no time frame to meet again to evaluate the subordinate's performance improvements	Deciding to meet again in one month to determine whether quality has improved

In following these guidelines, managers need to keep in mind *why* they are giving performance feedback: to encourage high levels of motivation and performance. Moreover, the information that managers gather through performance appraisal and feedback helps them determine how to distribute pay raises and bonuses.

Pay and Benefits

Pay includes employees' base salaries, pay raises, and bonuses and is determined by a number of factors such as characteristics of the organization and the job and levels of performance. Employee *benefits* are based on membership in an organization (and not necessarily on the particular job held) and include sick days, vacation days, and medical and life insurance. In Chapter 8, we discuss the ways in which pay can be used to motivate organizational members to perform at a high level, as well as the different kinds of pay plans managers can use to help an organization achieve its goals and gain a competitive advantage. It is important for pay to be linked to behaviours or results that contribute to organizational effectiveness. Here we focus on how organizations determine their pay levels and pay structures.

PAY LEVEL

Pay level is a broad comparative concept that refers to how an organization's pay incentives compare, in general, to those of other organizations in the same industry employing similar kinds of workers. Managers must decide whether they want to offer relatively high wages, average wages, or relatively low wages. At Four Seasons, as we saw in the opening case, pay levels are set at the high end of the industry, between the 75th and 90th percentile. High wages help ensure that an organization is going to be able to recruit, select, and retain high performers, but high wages also raise costs. Low wages give an organization a cost advantage but may undermine the organization's ability to select and recruit high performers and motivate current employees to perform at a high level. Either of these situations may lead to inferior quality or inferior customer service.

pay level The relative position of an organization's pay incentives in comparison with those of other organizations in the same industry employing similar kinds of workers.

In determining pay levels, managers should take their organization's strategy into account. A high pay level may prohibit managers from effectively pursuing a low-cost strategy. But a high pay level may be well worth the added costs in an organization whose competitive advantage lies in superior quality and excellent customer service, as is the case with Four Seasons. As one might expect, hotel and motel chains with a low-cost strategy, such as Days Inn and Holiday Inn, have lower pay levels than do chains striving to provide high-quality rooms and services, such as Four Seasons and Hyatt Regency.

PAY STRUCTURE

After deciding on a pay level, managers have to establish a pay structure for the different jobs in the organization. A **pay structure** clusters jobs into categories that reflect their relative importance to the organization and its goals, levels of skills required, and other characteristics that managers consider important. Pay ranges are established for each job category. Individual job holders' pay within job categories is then determined by such factors as performance, seniority, and skill levels.

pay structure The arrangement of jobs into categories that reflect their relative importance to the organization and its goals, levels of skill required, and other characteristics.

There are some interesting global differences in pay structures. Large corporations based in the United States tend to pay their CEOs and top managers higher salaries than do their Canadian, European, or Japanese counterparts. Also, the pay differential between employees at the bottom of the corporate hierarchy and those higher up is much greater in U.S. companies than in other companies.[64]

Concerns have been raised over whether it is equitable or fair for CEOs of large companies to be making millions of dollars in years when their companies are restructuring and laying off a large portion of their workforces.[65] Additionally, the average CEO in the United States typically earns over 430 times what the average hourly worker earns.[66] In Canada, the top CEOs earn about 209 times the pay of the average worker.[67] The Canadian Centre for Policy Alternatives' (CCPA) annual report on executive pay in Canada shows CEO salaries are on the rise, widening the gap between the rich and poor.[68] Is a pay structure with such a huge differential ethical? Shareholders and the public are increasingly asking this very question and asking large corporations to rethink their pay structures.[69] Also troubling are the millions of dollars in severance packages that some CEOs receive when they leave their organizations. In an era when many workers are struggling to find and keep jobs and make ends meet, more and more people are questioning whether it is ethical for some top managers to be making so much money.[70] Income inequality was at the root of the Occupy Wall Street and subsequent "Occupy" protests in cities in Canada and around the world in 2011.

BENEFITS

Employee benefits are based on membership in an organization (and not necessarily on the particular job held) and include sick days, vacation days, and medical and life insurances. Mandatory employee benefits vary across provinces; however, organizations are legally required to pay into workers' compensation, social insurance, and employment insurance for their employees. Workers' compensation provides employees with financial assistance if they become unable to work because of a work-related injury or illness. Social insurance provides financial assistance to retirees and disabled former employees. Employment insurance provides financial assistance to employees who lose their jobs through no fault of their own.

Other benefits—such as extended health insurance, dental insurance, vacation time, pension plans, life insurance, flexible working hours, company-provided daycare, and employee assistance and wellness programs—are provided at the option of employers. Recall from the opening case how a very attractive benefit at Four Seasons is being able to stay for free in any of the company's hotels and resorts. Benefits enabling workers to simultaneously balance the demands of their jobs and of their lives away from the office or factory are of growing importance for many workers who have competing demands on their all-too-scarce time and energy. Benefits mandated by public policy and benefits provided at the option of employers cost organizations a substantial amount of money.

CEOs in Canada made an average of 209 times the average Canadian income in 2017.
Reprinted with permission of Khalil Bendib

In some organizations, top managers decide which benefits might best suit the organization and employees and offer the same benefit package to all employees. Other organizations, realizing that employees' needs and desires for benefits might differ, offer **cafeteria-style benefit plans** that let employees themselves choose the benefits they want from among such options as day care, flex-time, tuition credits, on-site fitness centres, and extended medical and dental plans. Cafeteria-style benefit plans sometimes assist managers in dealing with employees who feel unfairly treated because they are unable to take advantage of certain benefits available to other employees who, for example, have children. Some organizations have success with cafeteria-style benefit plans; others find them difficult to manage.

cafeteria-style benefit plans Plans from which employees can choose the benefits that they want.

Employee Engagement

Employee engagement involves the activities that managers engage in to ensure that fair and consistent treatment of all employees is maintained. Organizations that have good employee engagement are likely to have a human resource strategy that places a high value on employees as stakeholders in the organization. When treated as stakeholders with legitimate interests and rights within the organization, employees can be expected to be treated with dignity and respect. Organizations with good employee engagement allow their employees to balance multiple work–life commitments with empathy and the perception of fairness. Managers should listen to and understand the competing needs of their employees and keep them informed about how management decisions will affect their jobs. Employees should be able to discuss how they feel about management decisions. While there may be good reasons for not changing a management decision, they should listen to the grievance at the very least.

employee engagement Activities that managers engage in to ensure that fair and consistent treatment of all employees is maintained.

Effective employee engagement requires cooperation among managers and HR employee relations representatives, who ensure that company policies are followed and problems are dealt with effectively and efficiently. Employee relations policies are designed to provide channels to resolve any problems before they become serious. *Employee attitude surveys* are developed to measure workers' likes and dislikes of various aspects of their jobs and working conditions. Levels of satisfaction can be monitored and used to shape human resource policies. For example, an *appeals procedure* should be developed as a mechanism for employees to voice their reactions to management decisions and to enhance their perception that the organization is fair and has just employment policies.

Employee assistance programs (EAPS) help employees cope with personal issues and problems that interfere with their job performance, such as alcohol or drug abuse, elder care, compulsive gambling, and domestic violence. All employee problems are handled with confidentiality. Helping employees deal with stress in their personal lives and at work is part of an effective EAP. The cost savings of supporting and retaining good employees who might otherwise be let go due to poor performance outweighs the combined costs of high employee turnover, absenteeism, workers' compensation, and disability insurance that might mount up if no action is taken.

Where organizations have unionized employees an HR specialist engages in **labour relations,** ensuring they have effective working relationships with the labour unions that represent their employees' interests. As a way to deal with the unethical and unfair treatment of workers, the federal and provincial governments created the *Canada Labour Code*, the *Canadian Human Rights Act,* and provincial employment standards laws. However, some employees believe that unions will be more effective than codes and laws in protecting their rights.

labour relations The activities that managers engage in to ensure that they have effective working relationships with the labour unions that represent their employees' interests.

Unions exist to represent workers' interests in organizations. Given that managers have more power than rank-and-file workers and that organizations have multiple stakeholders, there is always the potential that managers might take steps that benefit one set of stakeholders, such as shareholders, while hurting another, such as employees. For example, managers may decide to speed up a production line to lower costs and increase production in the hopes of increasing returns to shareholders. Speeding up the line, however, could hurt employees forced to work at a rapid pace that may increase the risk of injuries. Also, employees would receive no additional pay for the extra work they are performing. Unions would represent workers' interests in a scenario such as this one.

The first step in the labour relations process is for workers to seek collective representation to further their interests in the organization. The reasons they might desire to unionize are many:

- Shareholder interests overshadow those of the workers
- Dissatisfaction with wages, benefits, and working conditions
- Lack of a safe work environment
- Lack of job security
- Lack of proper training
- Perceived inequities in pay
- Unfair policies and practices
- Dissatisfaction with management
- Inability to communicate concerns and effect change

Canada Post backtracked on its threat to lock out its workers in February 2018, and the Canadian Union of Postal Workers did not issue a strike notice.
JSMimages/Alamy Stock Photo

- Lack of opportunities for advancement, growth, and a role in decision making
- The belief that unionization may improve working conditions
- The belief that a united group wields more power than an individual

Although these would seem to be potent forces for unionization, some workers are reluctant to join unions. Individual workers may reject unionization for a number of reasons, including the perception that the leaders are corrupt, or because they simply do not want to pay union dues. Employees also might not want to be forced into doing something they do not want to, such as striking because the union thinks it is in their best interest. Moreover, although unions can be a positive force in organizations, sometimes they also can be a negative force, impairing organizational effectiveness. For example, when union leaders resist needed changes in an organization or are corrupt, organizational performance can suffer.

In order for a union to become the bargaining unit for a group of employees, it must attain acceptance by the majority of eligible employees and be certified by the Labour Relations Board (LRB). See Figure 7.12. During an organizing campaign, employers must make sure they do not question employees about their union activities or use "undue influence" by promising to increase wages

FIGURE 7.12

The Process of Labour Relations

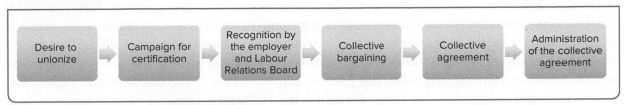

and benefits in a way that could be perceived as a bribe for remaining non-unionized or, for that matter, by threatening employees' jobs if they support unionization.

Once a union is recognized by the employer and the LRB as the bargaining unit for a group of employees, **collective bargaining**—negotiations between the labour union and the employer—take place to arrive at a mutually acceptable **collective agreement** pertaining to the terms and conditions of employment for a specified period of time. Once a collective agreement is signed, both the union members and the management are required to abide by the provisions. When disagreements over the administration of the agreement or violations of the terms arise, they are handled and settled by the *grievance procedure*. When the time frame of the agreement has ended and a new collective agreement has not been reached, neither party is bound by its terms and conditions. In such a case, the union is in a legal strike position, and the employer has the potential to lock out the workers. Both *strikes* and *lockouts* involve work stoppages that affect the productivity of the economy. In 2018, Canada Post threatened to lock out the Canadian Union of Postal Workers. In the end, the employer did not lock out the workers, nor did the union strike, averting a work stoppage. In 2017 in Canada, there were 186 work stoppages from strikes and lockouts that amounted to 10 or more person-days not worked.[71]

> **collective bargaining** Negotiations between labour unions and managers to resolve conflicts and disputes about issues such as working hours, wages, working conditions, and job security.
>
> **collective agreement** A mutually agreed upon set of provisions that govern working conditions between a union and an employer for a set period of time.

TRENDS IN LABOUR RELATIONS

Every year, the Workplace Information and Research Division of the Labour Program of the federal government undertakes a survey of all labour organizations in Canada that represent bargaining units of 50 or more workers. The results from the 2015 survey show the total number of workers paying dues to a union in Canada was 4.83 million at the end of 2015, up from 4.75 million at the end of 2014.

Dues-paying unionized workers comprised 31.8 percent of all employees in Canada in 2015, an increase of 0.3 percentage points from 2014. [72]

Canada and the United States have differential rates of unionization. In the United States, only approximately 15 percent of workers are unionized. Declines in the industrial sectors of the economy, such as manufacturing, where unions have traditionally been strong, are often viewed as the reason for declining unionization in the United States. The growth in service sector employment, which is often viewed as more difficult to organize, is also seen as a reason. In Canada, however, almost 40 percent of public service workers are unionized, while approximately 7 percent belong to unions in the United States. On the macro level, the main argument for differences between the countries is labour law and the structure of the political system in each country.[73]

The impact of labour relations on human resource management is considerable. Once a collective agreement is signed, the HR department typically expands to include a labour relations specialist and this affects the organizational structure of the company. Managers may have their power to make decisions diminished as union leaders typically increase their participation in issues that affect their members. Reward power is lessened, as pay levels and pay structures are set out in the terms of the collective agreement. Some managers resent the loss of authority that having to abide by the collective agreement sometimes entails. HR managers tend to keep more paper records of employee assignments and behaviours, as this is crucial at grievance and arbitration hearings. Overall, long before they get to the bargaining table to negotiate a collective agreement, union leaders and managers must recognize the need to build effective cooperative working relationships in order to remain competitive . It is in their mutual interests to ensure that labour strife is avoided.

Harassment in the Workplace

LO4 Explain the role of the human resource manager in dealing with workplace harassment.

Harassment in the workplace can take many forms. It refers to any behaviour directed toward an employee that is known to be or ought to be known to be offensive and unwelcome. According to Service Canada, "[i]t comprises objectionable conduct, comment or display made on either a one time or continuous basis that demeans, belittles, or causes personal humiliation or embarrassment to an employee of the department. It includes harassment within the meaning of the *Canadian Human Rights Act*, which is based on any of the prohibited grounds of discrimination listed in that Act."[74] Abuse of authority and sexual harassment are two common forms of **workplace harassment**, which we will discuss here. Abuse of authority occurs when the legitimate power vested in a position is used improperly to influence the behaviour of an employee. Threats that intimidate and coerce employee behaviour are examples of abuse of authority, as is blackmail. When "an individual improperly uses the power and authority inherent in his or her position to endanger an employee's job, undermine the performance of that job, threaten the economic livelihood of the employee, or in any way interfere with or influence the career of the employee," they are committing an abuse of authority.[75] The abuse of authority in Hollywood made headlines worldwide when, in 2017, Miramax producer Harvey Weinstein was accused of decades of sexual misconduct and coercive behaviour toward several actresses, starting a cascading ripple effect that has challenged the culture of the industry. Bullying is another form of abuse of authority when committed by a boss. Bullies are overbearing, intimidating, and regularly try to coerce others, often by humiliation. The Canada Safety Council cites a study by the Workplace Bullying Institute that reports 37 percent of workers have been bullied; 57 percent of targets are women; 72 percent of bullies are persons in authority (peer bullies sit at 18 percent); and the most common victims are women in their forties.[76]

workplace harassment Any behaviour directed toward an employee that is known to be or ought to be known to be offensive and unwelcome.

Sexual harassment is defined by the Supreme Court of Canada as unwelcome behaviour of a sexual nature in the workplace that negatively affects the work environment or leads to adverse job-related consequences for the employee. Sexual harassment is prevalent in many organizations today. Many former and current female employees of the RCMP have come forward to disclose that they were the victims of sexual harassment and gender abuse for many years. They charge that the culture of the traditionally male-dominated organization supported and tacitly encouraged abuse of its female officers. The women launched a class action suit against the RCMP for failing to protect them. And although in 1987 the Supreme Court ruled that employers will be held responsible for harassment by their employees and that employers should promote a workplace free of harassment, one is left to wonder if the Supreme Court of Canada's regulations have any teeth after one RCMP officer who confessed to years of sexual misconduct was transferred from Ontario to British Columbia to serve at another branch of the RCMP instead of being fired or compelled to attend mandatory counselling.[77] Many were outraged at what was perceived to be a reward rather than a punishment.

In the wake of the Harvey Weistein revelations, women are speaking out about sexual harassment in the #MeToo movement.
Michele Paccione/Shutterstock

sexual harassment Unwelcome behaviour of a sexual nature in the workplace that negatively affects the work environment or leads to adverse job-related consequences for the employee.

Although women are the most frequent victims of sexual harassment—particularly those in male-dominated occupations, or those who occupy positions stereotypically associated with certain gender relationships (such as a female secretary reporting to a male boss)—men can be victims, too. Several male employees at Jenny Craig in the United States reported that they were subject to lewd and inappropriate comments from female co-workers and managers.[78]

Sexual harassment seriously damages the victims as well as the reputation of the organization. It is not only unethical but also illegal. Beyond the negative publicity, sexual harassment can cost organizations large amounts of money. Managers have an ethical obligation to ensure that they, their co-workers, and their subordinates never engage in sexual harassment, even unintentionally.

Forms of Sexual Harassment

There are two basic forms of sexual harassment: *quid pro quo sexual harassment* and *hostile work environment sexual harassment*. **Quid pro quo sexual harassment** occurs when a harasser asks or forces an employee to perform sexual favours to keep a job, receive a promotion or raise, obtain some other work-related opportunity, or avoid receiving negative consequences such as demotion or dismissal.[79] This "Sleep with me, honey, or you're fired" form of harassment is the more extreme form and leaves no doubt in anyone's mind that sexual harassment has taken place.[80] In October 2017, in the aftermath of the Harvey Weinstein scandal, women took to social media to share their experiences of sexual harassment. The #MeToo movement went viral, spurring a national and global discussion on the issue. An online study published in 2018, found that 81 percent of women and 43 percent of men in the U.S. reported experiencing some form of sexual harassment and/or assault in their lifetime.[81]

quid pro quo sexual harassment Asking or forcing an employee to perform sexual favours in exchange for some reward or to avoid negative consequences.

Unwanted touching is unacceptable behaviour.
Shutterstock/Kaspars Grinvalds

Hostile work environment sexual harassment is more subtle. It occurs when organizational members are faced with an intimidating, hostile, or offensive work environment because of their gender.[82] Lewd jokes, sexually oriented comments, displays of pornography, displays or distribution of sexually oriented objects, and sexually oriented remarks about someone's physical appearance are examples of hostile work environment sexual harassment. About 45 percent of working Canadian women reported this form of harassment in a recent study at York University. Barbara Orser, a researcher with the Conference Board of Canada, noted that "sexual harassment is more likely to occur in workplace environments that tolerate bullying, intimidation, yelling, innuendo, and other forms of discourteous behaviour."[83]

hostile work environment sexual harassment Telling lewd jokes, displaying pornography, making sexually oriented remarks about someone's personal appearance, and other sex-related actions that make the work environment unpleasant.

A hostile work environment interferes with organizational members' ability to perform their jobs effectively and has been deemed illegal by the courts. Managers who engage in hostile work environment harassment or allow others to do so risk costly lawsuits for their organizations. This was the case with auto parts giant Magna International Inc. based in Aurora, Ontario, which was successfully sued for discrimination and harassment after sales managers routinely entertained clients at strip clubs, engaged in heavy drinking and then harassed female employees upon returning to work.[84]

Steps Managers Can Take to Eradicate Workplace Harassment

Human resource managers have an ethical obligation to eradicate workplace harassment in their organizations. There are many ways to accomplish this objective. Four initial steps that managers can take to deal with the problem include the following[85]:

1. *Develop and clearly communicate a workplace harassment policy endorsed by top management.* This policy should include prohibitions against both general workplace and sexual harassment. It should contain (1) examples of types of behaviour that are unacceptable, (2) a procedure for employees to use to report instances of harassment, (3) a discussion of the disciplinary actions that will be taken when harassment has taken place, and (4) a commitment to educate and train organizational members about sexual harassment.

2. *Use a fair complaint procedure to investigate charges of workplace harassment.* Such a procedure should (1) be managed by a neutral third party, (2) ensure that complaints are dealt with promptly and thoroughly, (3) protect and fairly treat victims, and (4) ensure that alleged harassers are fairly treated.

3. *When it has been determined that workplace harassment has taken place, take corrective actions as soon as possible.* These actions can vary depending on the severity of the harassment. When

harassment is extensive, prolonged over a period of time, of a quid pro quo nature, or severely objectionable in some other manner, corrective action may include firing the harasser.

4. *Provide workplace harassment education and training to organizational members, including managers.* Managers at Du Pont, for example, developed Du Pont's "A Matter of Respect" program to help educate employees about workplace harassment and prevent it from happening.

Barbara Orser of Ottawa University notes that most large Canadian organizations have harassment policies on paper; however, many lack a clear resolution process.

Chapter 7

SUMMARY AND REVIEW

connect

LO1 HRM Legislation and Managing Diversity Several key pieces of legislation govern the management of human resources in Canada. The Canadian *Human Rights Act* and the *Employment Standards Act* ensure minimum employee entitlements are standardized across the country and that *intentional and unintentional discrimination* is prohibited based on specific grounds. Managing diversity effectively can improve organizational effectiveness that leads to gaining a competitive advantage, engages all employees, and is ethically and legally sound.

LO2 Strategic Human Resource Management Human resource management (HRM) includes all the activities managers use to ensure their organizations are able to attract, retain, and utilize human resources effectively. *Strategic HRM* is the process by which managers design the components of an HRM system to be consistent with each other, and with the organization's strategies, structure, and goals. *Human resource planning* includes all the activities managers engage in to forecast their current and future needs for human resources. *Job analysis* is the process of identifying (1) the tasks, duties, and responsibilities that make up a job and (2) the knowledge, skills, and abilities needed to perform the job.

LO3 The Components of HRM The five major components of human resource management are (i) recruitment and selection, (ii) training and development, (iii) performance appraisal and feedback, (iv) pay and benefits, and (v) employee engagement.

LO4 Harassment in the Workplace Human resource managers can deal with unwanted behaviour that is offensive and abusive by communicating anti-harassment policies and procedures, investigating complaints, and taking corrective action such as discipline and training to eradicate harassment in the workplace.

KEY TERMS

ability tests
behavioural interview questions
bias

cafeteria-style benefit plans
collective agreement
collective bargaining

development
diversity
employee engagement
formal appraisals
Generation Y
hostile work environment sexual harassment
human resource management (HRM)
human resource planning
informal appraisals
intentional discrimination
job analysis
labour relations
lateral moves
needs assessment
orientation
outsource
pay level
pay structure
performance appraisal
performance feedback
performance-simulation tests

personality tests
personnel replacement charts
physical ability tests
quid pro quo sexual harassment
realistic job preview (RJP)
recruitment
reliable selection technique
selection
sexual harassment
situational interview questions
stereotype
strategic human resource
   management
structured interview
360-degree appraisals
training
unintentional discrimination
unstructured interview
valid selection technique
worker-requirements questions
workplace harassment

WRAP-UP TO OPENING CASE

Effectively Managing Human Resources at Four Seasons Hotels & Resorts

Four Seasons Hotels & Resorts is one of only about 14 companies to be ranked among the "100 Best Companies to Work For" every year since *Fortune* magazine started its annual ranking of companies over 20 years ago.[86]

After having read and understood the concepts in this chapter, you should be able to answer the following questions:

1. *How does Isadore Sharp employ a human resource system that creates an outstanding experience for customers at Four Seasons?*

   ANSWER: Isadore Sharp creates a competitive advantage in an industry with extremely high turnover rates by building outstanding customer responsiveness. Sharp has always realized that in order for employees to treat customers well, Four Seasons needs to treat its employees well. When employees view each customer as an individual with his or her own needs and desires, and try to meet these needs and desires and help customers overcome any problems or challenges they face and truly enjoy their hotel experience, customers are likely to be both loyal and highly satisfied.

2. *How does Four Seasons manage the components of its HR system?*

ANSWER: The five components of a human resource system are: (1) recruitment and selection, (2) training and development, (3) performance appraisal and feedback, (4) pay and benefits, and (5) employee engagement. In this case, we find that Four Seasons focuses a lot of attention on the selection of employees. Applicants are interviewed a minimum of four times to make sure they can provide a high level of empathy to the customer. Internal recruiting through promotion is evident. Recent graduates may start out as assistant managers but those who do well and have high aspirations could potentially become general managers in less than 15 years. This helps to ensure that managers have empathy and respect for those in lower-level positions as well as the ingrained ethos of treating others (employees, subordinates, co-workers, and customers) the way they would like to be treated themselves. Training of employees and development of potential managers is ongoing at Four Seasons. New hires participate in a three-month training program that includes improvisation activities to help them learn how to anticipate guests' needs, requirements, and actions and appropriately respond to them. Varied work experiences such as mentoring of managers is used at Four Seasons. A mentor is an experienced member of an organization who provides advice and guidance to a less experienced member. No mention of how employee performance is appraised is made in this case, nor how employees and management negotiated working conditions. Pay and benefits, however, are discussed. Salaries are relatively high at the Four Seasons by industry standards (i.e., between the 75th and 90th percentiles), employees participate in a profit-sharing plan, and the company contributes to their pension plans. All employees are provided with free meals in the hotel cafeteria, have access to staff showers and a locker room, and are provided with an additional, highly attractive benefit: once a new employee has worked for Four Seasons for six months, he or she can stay for three nights free at any Four Seasons hotel or resort in the world. After a year of employment, this benefit increases to six free nights and it continues to increase as tenure with the company increases. The Four Seasons' human resource management philosophy and practice translate into happy employees—which means happy customers.

MANAGEMENT IN ACTION

TOPICS FOR DISCUSSION AND ACTION

LEVEL 1 Knowledge & Comprehension

1. Describe the five components of an HRM system.

2. Discuss the reasons why an organization might outsource its human resources. What problems can arise?

3. Describe the best way for managers to give performance feedback to subordinates.

LEVEL 2 Application & Analysis

4. Discuss why it is important for the components of the HRM system to be in sync with an organization's strategy and structure and with each other.

5. Interview a manager in a local organization to determine how that organization recruits and selects employees.

6. How can managers avoid charges of discrimination in their hiring practices? Describe the legal framework of HRM in Canada and why managing diversity is good for business.

LEVEL 3 Synthesis & Evaluation

7. Evaluate the pros and cons of 360-degree performance appraisals and feedback. Would you like your performance to be appraised in this manner? Why, or why not?

8. Discuss why two restaurants in the same community might have different pay levels.

9. What is the role of the HR manager in eradicating workplace harassment?

SELF-REFLECTION EXERCISE
Analyzing Human Resource Management Systems

Think about your current job or a job that you had in the past. If you have never had a job, then interview a friend or family member who is currently working. Answer the following questions about the job you have chosen:

1. How are people recruited and selected for this job? Are the recruitment and selection procedures that the organization uses effective or ineffective? Why?

2. What training and development do people who hold this job receive? Is it appropriate? Why, or why not?

3. How is performance of this job appraised? Does performance feedback contribute to motivation and high performance on this job?

4. What levels of pay and benefits are provided for this job? Are these levels of pay and benefits appropriate? Why, or why not?

SMALL GROUP BREAKOUT EXERCISE
Building a Human Resource Management System

Form groups of three or four, and appoint one group member as the spokesperson who will communicate your findings to the whole class when called upon by the instructor. Then discuss the following scenario:

You and your two or three partners are engineers with a business minor who have decided to start a consulting business. Your goal is to provide manufacturing-process engineering and other engineering services to large and small organizations. You forecast that there will be an increased use of outsourcing for these activities. You have discussed with managers in several large organizations the services you plan to offer, and they have expressed considerable interest. You have secured funding to start the business and are now building the HRM system. Your human resources planning suggests that you need to hire between five and eight experienced engineers with good communication skills, two clerical/secretarial workers, and two MBAs who between them will have financial, accounting, and human resources skills. You are striving to develop an in-house approach to building your human resources that will enable your new business to prosper.

1. Describe the steps you will take to recruit and select (a) the engineers, (b) the clerical/secretarial workers, and (c) the MBAs.

2. Describe the training and development the engineers, the clerical/secretarial workers, and the MBAs will receive.

3. Describe how you will appraise the performance of each group of employees and how you will provide feedback.

4. Describe the pay level and pay structure of your consulting firm.

MANAGING ETHICALLY EXERCISE

Nadia Burowsky has recently been promoted to a managerial position in a large downtown bank. Before her promotion, she was one of a group of bank tellers who got together weekly and complained about their jobs. Burowsky enjoyed these get-togethers because she is recently divorced, and they provided a bit of a social life for her. In Burowsky's new role, she will be conducting performance appraisals and making decisions about pay raises and promotions for these same tellers. Burowsky reports to you, and you are aware of her former weekly get-togethers with the tellers. Is it ethical for her to continue attending these social functions? How might she effectively manage having relationships with co-workers and also evaluating them?

MANAGEMENT CHALLENGE EXERCISE

As Canada's economy grew stronger heading into the 2020s, a new power emerged in the executive suite. Many companies began shifting from cutback-survival mode to embracing such enlightened concepts as growth, expansion, and a healthy corporate culture. Canada's human resource specialists finally began getting away from planning layoffs and calculating severance packages to building productive teams, enhancing employee motivation, and creating a winning corporate culture. In some companies, HR's new role is not just evolutionary but revolutionary. A prominent medical products company, for instance, recently appointed its HR vice-president as VP of marketing. One large retailer promoted its former head of HR to country manager. In a recovering economy, it figured its biggest challenge is not merchandising, but improving the quality of customer service and building staff morale. Similarly, a high-tech firm created a senior HR position to forge a new corporate culture. The company knew it had more than enough software engineers on staff (most of them recruited right out of school) but realized it now needed more people who could challenge the culture—develop new markets, build relationships, and foster risk-taking in a company that had always talked things to death. The HR executive's mandate: Find tech-savvy business leaders and hire them now, even if their job does not exist yet. Because of your expertise, your advice is now being sought by these executives.

1. What course of action would you recommend to the executives to fulfill their mandates?

MANAGEMENT PORTFOLIO PROJECT

Answer the following questions about the organization you have chosen to follow:

1. Find out and report on how your organization plans for its human resources. What are the forces operating on this firm that make it easy or difficult to forecast its future supply of and demand for employees?

2. Describe the training and development programs for employees and managers in this organization.

3. What methods of employee performance appraisals are used in this company? How are they different for different categories of employees?

4. Describe the company's compensation and benefits system. Would this system motivate you to work for this company? Why, or why not?

5. Discuss whether or not the company's HRM system is compatible with its strategy and organizational structure. If not, make recommendations as to how to reach a better fit.

6. Describe the employee relations policies of the organization.

MANAGEMENT CASE

THE UNPAID INTERNSHIP DEBATE

It is estimated that around 300 000 unpaid internships existed in Canada in 2014, more than a third more than in Great Britain, which has a population of almost double that of Canada and passed legislation to ban the practice.[87] Moreover, most unpaid internships are found in large federally regulated, profitable telecommunication businesses like Rogers and Bell. Should unpaid internships be allowed in Canada? Do they help young people gain real-world experience or are they unfair labour practices that exploit young people?

The Canadian Intern Association has raised concern about the practice of allowing young people, often fresh out of post-secondary education, to work without pay or benefits across Canada. In a survey of unpaid interns, the authors were shocked to learn that neither federal nor provincial governments track the data on the number and location of unpaid internships and there is little if any legislation governing the practice. They found that many would not speak up about poor working conditions at their unpaid placements in fear of being blacklisted by the potential future employer. "When you ask a lot of these companies, like Bell—which has a massive internship program—they make it sound like they're doing people a favour, that they're generously providing work and experience," says the author, "But it's really nothing more than a way to save money; they're obviously not doing it out of generosity."[88] If companies need workers, they should be paid according to the legislation governing labour relations. Anything else, so the argument goes, is slave labour.

In the face of growing controversy, many companies are abandoning the practice. But some defend the idea of unpaid internships, calling the practice relief from the "scarring" of long-term unemployment. The Bank of Canada governor suggested that young people should accept no wages for working if it means getting out of their parents' basements after graduating—that they should grab the chance to beef up their resumés.[89] The practice certainly helps companies with their hiring needs, because it is a cost-effective way of getting talented workers. At General Electric Canada in Toronto, for example, about 40 percent of entry-level employees hired start out as interns. By the end of the internship, the company knows who they want to offer paid employment to and who they don't. In that way, it is like an extended job interview.[90]

1. Summarize the debate on the "for" and "against" sides of paid versus unpaid internships.

2. Where do you stand and why?

END OF PART III: CONTINUING CASE

CARROT TOPS: STRUCTURE

As the CEO, Mel oversees the outsourcing of the production of his brand-name labels and manages the store employees while Janet sources organic produce and runs the delivery drivers. Both need their people to perform at a high level, but they approach employee motivation very differently. Mel's approach was to decentralize authority, empowering salespeople to take responsibility for meeting customer needs. Mel created a store environment in which employees were treated as individuals and felt valued as people. Rather than forcing employees to follow strict operating rules, Mel gave them autonomy to make decisions and provide personalized customer service. The result is that employees feel they "own" their supermarket. Janet, on the other hand, has been accused of micro-managing the drivers. Even though she doesn't know the city as well as the drivers, she insists on controlling the scheduling of deliveries. This practice results in few deliveries being made on time: drivers find nobody home because they arrive early or arrive late. Drivers feel frustrated with the complicated rules and the endless paperwork they have to fill out for Janet. One was so dissatisfied, he quit and went to work for the competition; now Janet will have to go through the hassle of recruiting, hiring, and keeping a new driver.

Drawing on all segments of this case:

1. Draw an organizational chart for Carrot Tops and describe the hierarchy of authority.
2. Would you describe Carrot Tops as an organic or a mechanistic structure?
3. Using all the components of human resource management, describe the process Janet should use to hire a new driver for Carrot Tops.
4. How might Janet use management information systems to increase efficiencies?
5. Suggest a social media strategy for Carrot Tops.

Appendix C

Career Development

Types of Careers

Managers face several challenges both in the course of their own careers and in facilitating effective career management for their subordinates. A career is the sum total of work-related experiences throughout a person's life.[1] Careers encompass all of the different jobs people hold and the different organizations they work for. Careers are important to most people for at least two reasons. First, a career is a means to support oneself and one's loved ones, providing basic necessities and opportunities to pursue outside interests. Second, a career can be a source of personal fulfillment and meaning. Many managers find that making a difference in an organization and helping improve organizational efficiency and effectiveness are personally as well as financially rewarding.

Career development is a concern for managers both in terms of how their own careers unfold over time and how careers are managed in their organizations. In the development of their own careers, managers seek out challenging and interesting jobs that will develop their skills, lead to future opportunities, and allow them the opportunity to do the kind of work that will be personally meaningful. Similarly, in motivating and leading subordinates, managers need to be attuned to subordinates' career development. When careers (of both managers and rank-and-file employees) are effectively managed in an organization, the organization makes the best use of its human resources and employees tend to be motivated by, and satisfied with, their jobs.

Both employees and managers play an important role in effectively managing careers. For example, employees need to understand themselves, the kind of work they find motivating and fulfilling, and their own future aspirations for their careers. Employees then need to proactively seek the education, training, and kinds of work experiences that will help them to have the careers they want. Managers can motivate employees to make meaningful contributions to organizations by providing them with work assignments, experiences, training, and opportunities that contribute to employees' career development.[2]

While every person's career is unique, the different types of careers that people have fall into four general categories: steady-state careers, linear careers, spiral careers, and transitory careers.[3]

Steady-State Careers

A person with a **steady-state career** makes a one-time commitment to a certain kind of job that he or she maintains throughout his or her working life.[4] People with steady-state careers can become very skilled and expert at their work. A playwright who starts writing plays upon graduation from university and continues to write plays until retiring at age 70 has a steady-state career. So too does a dentist who maintains a steady dental practice upon graduation from dental school until retirement.

steady-state career A career consisting of the same kind of job during a large part of an individual's work life.

Some managers choose to have a steady-state career, holding the same kind of job during a large part of their work life, often becoming highly skilled and expert in what they do. A talented and creative graphic artist at a magazine publishing company, for example, may turn down promotions and other "opportunities" so that he can continue to work on designing attractive magazine spreads and covers, what he really likes to do. Similarly, some department store managers have steady-state careers as area sales managers because they enjoy the direct supervision of salespeople and the opportunity to "stay close to" customers.

Linear Careers

A person who has a **linear career** moves through a sequence of jobs in which each new job entails additional responsibility, a greater impact on an organization, new skills, and upward movement in an organization's hierarchy.[5] The careers of many managers are linear, whether they stay with the same company or frequently switch organizations. A linear career traces a line of upward progress in the positions held.

linear career A career consisting of a sequence of jobs in which each new job entails additional responsibility, a greater impact on an organization, new skills, and upward movement in an organization's hierarchy.

Top managers in large corporations have moved through a series of lower-level positions in a variety of organizations before they became CEOs. An assistant manager in a Red Lobster may have started out in an entry-level position as a cashier. A linear career at a department store may include the following sequencing of positions: executive trainee, area sales manager, assistant buyer, buyer, assistant store manager of merchandising, store manager, and divisional merchandise manager.[6] Managers' subordinates also may have linear careers, although some subordinates may have other types of careers.

Spiral Careers

A person who has a **spiral career** tends to hold jobs that, while building off each other, tend to be fundamentally different.[7] An associate professor of chemical engineering who leaves university teaching and research to head up the R&D department of a chemical company for 10 years and then leaves that position to found her own consulting firm has a spiral career. Similarly, a marketing manager in a large corporation who transfers to a job in public relations and then, after several years in that position, takes a job in an advertising firm has a spiral career. Those three jobs tend to be quite different from each other and do not necessarily entail increases in levels of responsibility.

spiral career A career consisting of a series of jobs that build on each other but tend to be fundamentally different.

Transitory Careers

Some people change jobs frequently and each job is different from the one that precedes it; this kind of career is a **transitory career**.[8] A high school teacher who leaves teaching after two years to work as an administrative assistant in a consumer products company for a year and then moves on to do carpentry work has a transitory career.

transitory career A career in which a person changes jobs frequently and in which each job is different from the one that precedes it.

◼ Career Stages

Every person's career is unique, but there are certain career stages that people generally appear to progress through. Even if a person does not progress through all the stages, typically some of the stages are experienced. Each stage is associated with certain kinds of activities, hurdles, and potential opportunities. Regardless of the extent to which a person experiences each stage, and regardless of the exact number of the stages—about which there is some disagreement among researchers—here we discuss five stages that are useful to understand and manage careers.[9]

These career stages apply to managers and nonmanagers alike. Thus, understanding the stages is important for managers both in terms of their own career development and in terms of the career development of their subordinates. Importantly, and increasingly, these career stages are experienced by most people in a variety of organizations. That is, while in the past, at least some people might have spent most of their careers in a single organization (or in just a few organizations); this is becoming increasingly rare. Rapid changes in technology, increased global competition, environmental uncertainty, outsourcing, and the layoffs many organizations resort to at one point or another to reduce costs are just some of the factors responsible for people's careers unfolding in a series of positions in a number of different organizations. Thus, a **boundaryless career**, or a career that is not attached or bound to a single organization, is becoming increasingly common, and most people have a variety of work experiences in multiple organizations throughout their careers.[10]

boundaryless career A career that is not attached to or bound to a single organization and consists of a variety of work experiences in multiple organizations.

Preparation for Work

During this stage, people decide what kind of career they desire and learn what qualifications and experiences they will need in order to pursue their chosen career.[11] Deciding on a career is no easy task and requires a certain degree of self-awareness and reflection. Sometimes people turn to professional career counsellors to help them discover the kinds of careers in which they are most likely to be happy. A person's personality, values, attitudes, and moods impact the initial choice of a career.[12]

After choosing a career area, a person must gain the knowledge, skills, and education necessary to get a good starting position. A person may need an undergraduate or graduate degree or may be able to acquire on-the-job training through an apprenticeship program (common in Germany and some other countries).

Organizational Entry

At this stage, people are trying to find a good first job. The search entails identifying potential opportunities in a variety of ways (such as reading advertisements, attending career/job fairs, and mining personal contacts), finding out as much as possible about alternative positions, and making oneself an attractive candidate for prospective employers. Organizational entry is a more challenging stage for some kinds of careers than for others. An accounting major who knows she wants to work for an accounting firm already has a good idea of her opportunities and of how to make herself attractive to such firms. An English major who wants a career as an editor for a book publisher may find entry-level positions that seem a "good" start to such a career few and far between and may decide her best bet is to take a position as a sales representative for a well-respected publisher. More often than not, managers do not start out in management positions but rather begin their careers in an entry-level position in a department such as finance, marketing, or engineering.

Early Career

The early-career stage begins after a person obtains a first job in his or her chosen career. At this stage there are two important steps: establishment and achievement. *Establishment* means learning the ropes of one's new job and organization—learning, for example, specific job responsibilities and duties, expected and desired behaviours, and important values of other organizational members such as the boss.[13] A person who has acquired the basic know-how to perform a job and function in the wider organization is ready to take the second step. *Achievement* means making one's mark, accomplishing something noteworthy, or making an important contribution to the job or organization.[14]

The achievement step can be crucial for future career progression. It is a means of demonstrating one's potential and standing out from others who are aspiring to become managers and are competing for desired positions. Downsizing and restructuring have reduced the number of management positions at many large companies, making it very important for individuals to manage the early-career stage effectively and thus increase their chances of advancement. By identifying where and how you can make a truly significant contribution to an organization, you can enhance your career prospects both inside and outside the organization.

Some people find that seeking out and gaining the assistance of a mentor can be a valuable asset for the early-career and subsequent stages. A mentor is an experienced member of an organization who provides advice and guidance to a less experienced worker (the protegé, or mentee). The help that a mentor provides can range from advice about handling a tricky job assignment, dealing with a disagreement with a supervisor, and what kind of subsequent positions to strive for, to information about appropriate behaviour and what to wear in various situations. Mentors often seek out protegés, but individuals also can be proactive and try to enlist the help of a potential mentor. Generally, especially good potential mentors are successful managers who have had a variety of experiences, genuinely desire to help junior colleagues, and are interpersonally compatible with the would-be protegé. Research has found that receiving help from a mentor is associated with an increase in pay, pay satisfaction, promotion, and feeling good about one's accomplishments.[15]

Midcareer

The midcareer stage generally occurs when people have been in the workforce between 20 and 35 years. Different managers experience this stage in quite different ways. For some managers, the midcareer stage is a high point—a time of major accomplishment and success. For other managers, the midcareer stage is a letdown because their careers plateau.

Managers reach a **career plateau** when their chances of being promoted into a higher position in their current organizations or of obtaining a more responsible position in another organization dwindle.[16] Some managers inevitably will experience a career plateau because fewer and fewer managerial positions are available as one moves up an organization's hierarchy. In some organizations upper-level positions are especially scarce because of downsizing and restructuring.

career plateau A position from which the chances of being promoted or obtaining a more responsible job are slight.

Plateaued managers who are able to come to terms with their situation can continue to enjoy their work and make important contributions to their organization. Some plateaued managers, for example, welcome lateral moves, which give them the chance to learn new things and contribute in different ways to the organization. Some find being a mentor especially appealing and a chance to share their wisdom and make a difference for someone starting out in their field.

Late Career

This stage lasts as long as a person continues to work and has an active career. Many managers remain productive at this stage and show no signs of slowing down.

 # Effective Career Management

Managers face the challenge of ensuring not only that they have the kind of career they personally desire but also that **effective career management** exists for all employees in their organization. Effective career management means that at all levels in the organization there are well-qualified workers who can assume more responsible positions as needed and that as many members of the organization as possible are highly motivated and satisfied with their jobs and careers. As you might imagine, effectively managing careers in a whole organization is no easy task. At this point, however, it is useful to discuss two import-ant foundations of effective career management in any organization: a commitment to ethical career prac-tices and accommodations for workers' multidimensional lives

> **effective career management** Ensuring that at all levels in the organization there are well-qualified workers who can assume more responsible positions as needed.

Commitment to Ethical Career Practices

Ethical career practices are among the most important ingredients in effective career management and, at a basic level, rest on honesty, trust, and open communication among organizational members. Ethi-cal career practices include basing promotions on performance, not on irrelevant considerations such as personal friendships and ties, and ensuring that diverse members of an organization receive the career opportunities they deserve. Supervisors must never abuse their power to make career decisions affecting others and must never behave unethically to advance their own careers. Managers at all levels must abide by and be committed to ethical career practices and actively demonstrate this commitment; they must communicate that violation of these practices will not be tolerated; and they must make sure that organi-zational members who feel that they were not ethically treated can communicate their concerns without fear of retaliation.

Accommodations for Workers' Multidimensional Lives

Effectively managing careers also means being sensitive to and providing accommodations for the mul-tiple demands that many organizational members face in their lives. The dual-career couple is now the norm rather than the exception, the number of single parents is at an all-time high, and more and more midcareer workers need to care for their elderly and infirm parents. By limiting unnecessary moves and travel, adopting flexible work arrangements and schedules, providing on-site day care, and allowing workers to take time off to care for children or elderly parents, managers make it possible for workers to have satisfying and productive careers while fulfilling their other commitments.

Careers are as important for managers' subordinates as they are for managers themselves. Under-standing the many issues involved in effectively managing careers helps ensure that both managers and their subordinates will have the kinds of careers they want while helping an organization achieve its goals.

Part IV

Leading

Chapter 8

Managing Motivation

LEARNING OUTCOMES

LO1	Describe the nature of motivation and how it leads to the attainment of intrinsic and extrinsic outcomes.
LO2	Explain how need theories of motivation help managers determine the needs of employees and provide outcomes that satisfy them.
LO3	Describe how process theories of motivation help managers explain high and low performance levels.
LO4	Identify the motivation lessons that managers can learn from Learning theories of motivation.
LO5	Explain how managers use reward systems to increase employee motivation.

OPENING CASE

"People Matter" Is at the Heart of Irving Oil's Culture

What's at the root of Irving Oil's success? "It all starts with our people—our employees and our customers," says Executive Vice-President Sarah Irving. "They're the reason why we're here today."

This sentiment stems from the company's beginnings, she notes. "My grandfather, K.C. Irving, who founded the company in 1924, always gave credit to Irving Oil's employees and customers for helping him to build the business. My dad, Arthur Irving, and his late brother, Jack, similarly commended our employees' hard work and our customers' loyalty in helping our company grow."

"That spirit remains at the heart of Irving Oil today," says Irving. "It is the energy that our employees bring to the business every day that drives this company forward."

Kevin Brine - Editorial/Alamy Stock Photo

Julianne deSoto has spent 25 years with the Saint John, N.B.-based downstream oil and gas company. She says that the company's "People Matter" ethos, "is hugely important to me. I would not enjoy my job as much as I do if I didn't feel connected to the people whom I work for and with."

DeSoto started at Irving Oil's Saint John refinery—Canada's largest, processing 330 000 barrels of oil a day—as a plant technical services engineer involved in day-to-day operations. She was promoted in 2015 to a technical manager role and, in May 2017, to Director, Technical & Planning. In her current position, she is responsible for some 80 employees and has a more strategic focus.

"Irving Oil certainly invested in me and gave me the chance to grow," says deSoto.

The company supported deSoto's education by providing her with the opportunity to attend technical courses and conferences, such as the American Fuel and Petrochemical Manufacturers' annual meeting, which is considered the world's premier refining event.

Already an accredited chemical engineer when she first joined the company, deSoto benefited from its support in earning her MBA degree from the University of New Brunswick in 2012.

Helping employees to set, and meet, professional development goals is important to Irving Oil—so important that the company includes a development objective in every employee's annual performance plan.

The company has been in hiring mode this past year [2017]. There were 115 new positions created at Irving Oil in Canada in the last 12 months. The majority of these jobs involved IT, supply management, finance/accounting, professional drivers and engineers.

"In our recruiting efforts," says Irving, "we look for a strong cultural fit—for individuals who want to be a part of a team, to learn and to grow with our company."

As part of its efforts to promote diversity and inclusion, Irving Oil has two employee resource groups that organize networking and learning and development events for their members. The Women's Forum has been in place for more than 10 years and has more than 700 members focused on engaging and empowering females in the workforce. The "eMERGe" group, led by millennials, started in early 2017 and now has close to 400 members.

As part of its broader commitment to the community, the company provides employees with meaningful opportunities to volunteer with local organizations.

Says Irving, "Across our business, whether we're delivering fuel to a neighbour or volunteering at a local event, we're committed to our customers and to our communities—to provide the best possible experience. That all starts right here with our team."

This article appeared in the magazine announcing this year's Canada's Top 100 Employers winners, published November 7, 2017 in The Globe and Mail. This article was prepared with the financial support of the employer, which reviewed but did not write its contents.

Source: "'People Matter' Is at the Heart of Irving Oil's Culture." *Mediacorp Canada.* https://content.edu.eluta.ca/top-employer-irving-oil. Accessed March 2, 2018. Reprinted with permission of Mediacorp Canada.

After reading and understanding the concepts in this chapter, you should be able to answer the following questions:

1. Apply Herzberg's motivator-hygiene theory to this case.
2. Apply Vroom's expectancy theory to this case.
3. How does Irving Oil use a total reward strategy to motivate employee performance?

Overview

Even with the best strategy in place and an appropriate organizational architecture, an organization will be effective only if its members are motivated to perform at a high level. Sarah Irving clearly realizes this. One reason why leading is such an important managerial activity is that it entails ensuring that each member of an organization is motivated to perform highly and help the organization achieve its goals. When managers are effective, the outcome of the leading process is a highly motivated workforce. A key challenge for managers of organizations both large and small is to encourage employees to perform at a high level.

In this chapter, we describe what motivation is, where it comes from, and why managers need to promote high levels of it for an organization to be effective and achieve its goals. In Figure 8.1 we list some of the important theories of motivation that we discuss in this chapter.

Each of the theories found in Figure 8.1 provides managers with important insights about how to motivate organizational members. The theories are complementary in that each focuses on a somewhat different aspect of motivation. *Need theories* of motivation help managers understand how human needs motivate us to act to satisfy them either extrinsically or intrinsically. *Process theories* help managers explain why people act the way they do and thus help managers understand the roots of high and low performance levels among employees. *Learning theories* help managers see the link between giving rewards for high performance behaviour and the repetition of that behaviour among employees. Considering all of the theories together helps managers gain a rich understanding of the many issues and problems involved in encouraging high levels of motivation throughout an organization. We end this chapter with a discussion of a *total reward strategy* as a motivation tool. By the end of this chapter, you will understand what it takes to have a highly motivated workforce.

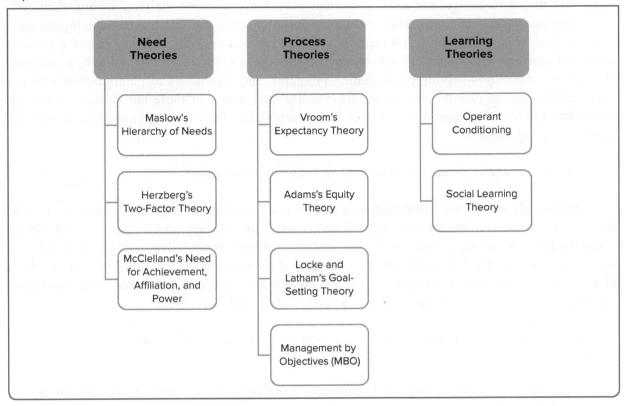

FIGURE 8.1

Important Theories of Motivation

Need Theories
- Maslow's Hierarchy of Needs
- Herzberg's Two-Factor Theory
- McClelland's Need for Achievement, Affiliation, and Power

Process Theories
- Vroom's Expectancy Theory
- Adams's Equity Theory
- Locke and Latham's Goal-Setting Theory
- Management by Objectives (MBO)

Learning Theories
- Operant Conditioning
- Social Learning Theory

The Nature of Motivation

LO1 | Describe the nature of motivation and how it leads to the attainment of intrinsic and extrinsic outcomes.

The term **motivation** refers to the psychological forces that determine the *direction* of a person's behaviour in an organization, a person's *commitment* or *effort,* and a person's *persistence* in the face of obstacles.[1] The *direction of a person's behaviour* refers to the many possible behaviours that a person could engage in. *Effort* refers to how hard people work and their commitment to the work. Employees such as Julianne deSoto at Irving Oil, featured in the opening case, exert high levels of effort to provide superior customer service. *Persistence* refers to whether, when faced with roadblocks and obstacles, people keep trying or give up.

motivation Psychological forces that determine the direction of a person's behaviour in an organization, a person's commitment or effort, and a person's persistence.

Motivation is central to management because it explains *why* people behave the way they do in organizations. Motivation also explains why a waiter is polite or rude and why a kindergarten teacher really tries to get children to enjoy learning or just goes through the motions. It explains why some managers truly put their organizations' best interests first, whereas others are more concerned with maximizing their salaries and why—more generally—some workers put forth twice as much effort as others.

Motivation can come from *intrinsic* or *extrinsic* sources. **Intrinsically motivated behaviour** is behaviour that is performed for its own sake; the source of motivation is actually performing the behaviour, and motivation comes from doing the work itself. Many managers are intrinsically motivated; they derive a sense of accomplishment and achievement from helping the organization to achieve its goals and gain competitive advantages. Jobs that are interesting and challenging are more likely to lead to intrinsic motivation than are jobs that are boring or do not make use of a person's skills and abilities. An elementary school teacher who really enjoys teaching children, a computer programmer who loves solving programming problems, and a commercial photographer who relishes taking creative photographs are all intrinsically motivated. For these individuals, motivation comes from performing their jobs, whether it be teaching children, finding bugs in computer programs, or taking pictures.

intrinsically motivated behaviour Behaviour that is performed for its own sake.

Extrinsically motivated behaviour is behaviour that is performed to acquire material or social rewards or to avoid punishment; the source of motivation is the consequences of the behaviour, not the behaviour itself. A car salesperson who is motivated by receiving a commission on all cars sold, a lawyer who is motivated by the high salary and status that go along with the job, and a factory worker who is motivated by the opportunity to earn a secure income are all extrinsically motivated. Their motivation comes from the consequences they receive as a result of their work behaviours.

extrinsically motivated behaviour Behaviour that is performed to acquire material or social rewards or to avoid punishment.

People can be intrinsically motivated, extrinsically motivated, or both intrinsically and extrinsically motivated.[2] A top manager who derives a sense of accomplishment and achievement from managing a large corporation and strives to reach year-end targets to obtain a hefty bonus is both intrinsically and extrinsically motivated. Similarly, a nurse who enjoys helping and taking care of patients and is motivated by having a secure job with good benefits is both intrinsically and extrinsically motivated. At Enterprise Rent-A-Car, employees are both extrinsically motivated, because of opportunities for promotions and having their pay linked to the performance of their branches or units, and intrinsically motivated, because they get a sense of satisfaction out of serving customers and learning new things.

Whether workers are intrinsically motivated, extrinsically motivated, or both depends on a wide variety of factors: (1) workers' own personal characteristics (such as their personalities, abilities, values, attitudes, and needs), (2) the nature of their jobs (such as whether they are interesting and challenging), and (3) the nature of the organization (such as its structure, its culture, its control systems, its human resource management system, and the ways in which rewards such as pay are distributed to employees).

An elementary school teacher gets satisfaction from helping students learn to read.
Pressmaster/Shutterstock

In addition to being intrinsically or extrinsically motivated, some people are prosocially motivated by their work.[3] **Prosocially motivated behaviour** is behaviour that is performed to benefit or help others.[4] As Bugg-Levine and Emerson suggest, "Talented young people increasingly hunger for employment opportunities that allow them to address social and environmental benefit, a hunger no longer satiated by participating in the annual corporate charity run or pro bono assignment or the classic nonprofit approach that ignores the positive potential of business."[5] Behaviour can be prosocially motivated in addition to being extrinsically and/or intrinsically motivated. An elementary school teacher who not only enjoys the process of teaching young children (has high intrinsic motivation) but also has a strong desire to give children the best learning experience possible, help those with learning disabilities overcome their challenges, and keep up with the latest research on child development and teaching methods in an effort to continually improve the effectiveness of his teaching has high prosocial motivation in addition to high intrinsic motivation. A surgeon who specializes in organ transplants and enjoys the challenge of performing complex operations, has a strong desire to help her patients regain their health and extend their lives through successful organ transplants, and also is motivated by the relatively high income she earns has high intrinsic, prosocial, and extrinsic motivation. A social entrepreneur who creates a business that employs people marginalized from mainstream society, as illustrated in the Focus on the Social Economy feature in this chapter, is motivated by all three principles. Recent preliminary research suggests that when workers have high prosocial motivation, also having high intrinsic motivation can be especially beneficial for job performance.[6]

prosocially motivated behaviour Behaviour that is performed to benefit or help others.

Regardless of whether people are intrinsically, extrinsically, or prosocially motivated, they join and are motivated to work in organizations to obtain certain outcomes. An **outcome** is anything a person gets from a job or organization. Some outcomes, such as autonomy, responsibility, a feeling of accomplishment, and the pleasure of doing interesting or enjoyable work, result in intrinsically motivated behaviour. Outcomes such as improving the lives or well-being of other people and doing good by helping others result in prosocially motivated behaviour. Other outcomes, such as pay, job security, benefits, and vacation time, result in extrinsically motivated behaviour.

outcome Anything a person gets from a job or organization.

Organizations hire people to obtain important *inputs*. An **input** is anything a person contributes to his or her job or organization, such as time, effort, education, experience, skills, knowledge, and actual work behaviours. Inputs such as these are necessary for an organization to achieve its goals. Managers strive to motivate members of an organization to contribute inputs—through their behaviour, effort, and persistence—that help the organization achieve its goals. They do this by making sure that members of an organization obtain the outcomes they desire when they make valuable contributions to the organization. Managers use outcomes to motivate people to contribute their inputs to the organization. Giving people outcomes when they contribute inputs and perform well aligns the interests of employees with the goals of the organization as a whole because when employees do what is good for the organization, they personally benefit.

input Anything a person contributes to his or her job or organization.

FIGURE 8.2

The Motivation Equation

INPUTS FROM ORGANIZATIONAL MEMBERS	PERFORMANCE	OUTCOMES RECEIVED BY ORGANIZATIONAL MEMBERS
Time Effort Education Experience Skills Knowledge Work behaviours	Contributes to organizational efficiency, organizational effectiveness, and the attainment of organizational goals	Pay Job security Benefits Vacation time Job satisfaction Autonomy Responsibility A feeling of accomplishment The pleasure of doing interesting work

"Talented young people increasingly hunger for employment opportunities that allow them to address social and environmental benefit. . ."

Bugg-Levine and Emerson, *Impact Investing*

This alignment between employees and organizational goals as a whole can be described by the motivation equation shown in Figure 8.2. Managers aim to ensure that people are motivated to contribute important inputs to the organization, that these inputs are put to good use or focused in the direction of high performance, and that high performance results in employees obtaining the outcomes they desire.

Each of the theories of motivation we discuss in this chapter focuses on one or more aspects of the motivation equation in Figure 8.2. Together, the theories provide a comprehensive set of guidelines for managers to follow to promote high levels of employee motivation. Effective managers tend to follow many of these guidelines, whereas ineffective managers often fail to follow them and seem to have trouble motivating organizational members.

Need Theories of Motivation

LO2 | Explain how need theories of motivation help managers determine the needs of employees and provide outcomes that satisfy them.

A **need** is a requirement or necessity for survival and well-being. The basic premise of need theories is that people are motivated to obtain outcomes at work that will satisfy their needs. **Need theories** suggest that in order to motivate a person to contribute valuable inputs to a job and perform at a high level, a manager must determine what needs the person is trying to satisfy at work and ensure that the person receives outcomes that help satisfy those needs when the person performs at a high level and helps the organization achieve its goals.

Furniture Bank

Furniture Bank is a registered charitable organization dedicated to helping people and families in need by providing them with refurbished home furnishings that have been donated by corporations and individuals. Its social enterprise—the Leg Up program—trains people from vulnerable populations to refurbish, repair, and reupholster the donated furniture. This serves the dual functions of providing skills training and employment opportunities to people in marginalized communities while diverting recyclable material from landfills.

Furniture Bank's Leg Up program aims to train up to 20 participants per year and to partner with corporate players to source full-time employment opportunities for participants.

Says Tom Bendo, a participant in the Leg Up program, "It has been very rewarding being able to experience and contribute to the front line of client interaction, delivering to people in need and picking up donations from people who want to help. Being able to do that while being a part of an organization that is learning and growing has been nothing short of inspiring!"

1. Would you describe the motivation of the Leg Up program participants like Tom Bendo intrinsic or extrinsic and why?

2. How would you describe the motivation of the people who run the Furniture Bank?

Source: http://furniturebank.org/emplyment-program/. Accessed July 19, 2018 and August 1, 2018.

need A requirement or necessity for survival and well-being.

need theories Theories of motivation that focus on what needs people are trying to satisfy at work and what outcomes will satisfy those needs.

There are several need theories. We discuss three need theories below: Abraham Maslow's *hierarchy of needs*, Frederick Herzberg's *two-factor or motivator-hygiene theory,* and David McClelland's *need for achievement, affiliation, and power.* These theories describe needs that people try to satisfy at work. In doing so, the theories provide managers with insights about what outcomes will motivate members of an organization to perform at a high level and contribute inputs to help the organization achieve its goals.

Maslow's Hierarchy of Needs

Psychologist Abraham Maslow proposed that everyone aims to satisfy five basic kinds of needs: physiological needs, safety needs, belongingness needs, esteem needs, and self-actualization needs (see Figure 8.3).[7] He suggested that these needs constitute a **hierarchy of needs**, with the most basic or compelling needs—physiological and safety needs—at the bottom. Maslow argued that these lowest-level needs must be met or almost completely met before a person will be motivated to satisfy needs higher up in the hierarchy, such as self-esteem needs. Once a need is satisfied, he proposed, it no longer is a source of motivation, and needs in the next level become motivators, driving people to take action to fulfill them.

hierarchy of needs An arrangement of five basic needs that, according to Maslow, motivate behaviour. Maslow proposed that the lowest level of unmet needs is the prime motivator and that only one level of needs is motivational at a time.

FIGURE 8.3

Maslow's Hierarchy of Needs

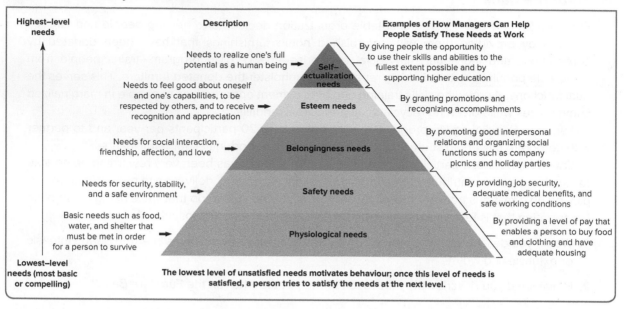

Although Maslow's theory identifies needs that are likely to be important sources of motivation for many people, research does not support his contention that there is a needs hierarchy or his notion that only one level of needs is motivational at a time.[8] Nevertheless, a key conclusion can be drawn from Maslow's theory: People differ in what needs they are trying to satisfy at work. To have a motivated workforce that achieves goals, managers must determine which needs employees are trying to satisfy in organizations and then make sure that individuals receive outcomes that will satisfy their needs when they perform at a high level and contribute to organizational effectiveness. By doing this, managers align the interests of individual members with the interests of the organization as a whole. By doing what is good for the organization (that is, performing at a high level), employees receive outcomes that satisfy their needs.

In an increasingly global economy, it is also important for managers to realize that citizens of different countries might differ in the needs they try to satisfy through work.[9] Some research suggests, for example, that people in Greece and Japan are especially motivated by safety needs and that people in Sweden, Norway, and Denmark are motivated by belongingness needs.[10] In poor countries with lower standards of living, physiological and safety needs are likely to be the prime motivators of behaviour. As countries become wealthier and have higher standards of living, it is likely that needs related to personal growth and accomplishment (such as esteem and self-actualization) become important as motivators of behaviour.

Herzberg's Motivator-Hygiene Theory

Adopting an approach different from Maslow's, Frederick Herzberg focuses on two factors: (1) outcomes that can lead to high levels of motivation and job satisfaction, and (2) outcomes that can prevent people from being dissatisfied. According to **Herzberg's motivator-hygiene theory**, also known as the *two-factor theory,* people have two sets of needs or requirements: motivator needs and hygiene needs.[11] *Motivator needs* are related to the nature of the work itself and how challenging it is. Outcomes such as interesting work, autonomy, responsibility, being able to grow and develop on the job, and a sense of accomplishment and achievement help satisfy motivator needs. In order to have a highly motivated and satisfied workforce, Herzberg suggested, managers should take steps to ensure that employees' motivator needs are being met. Over the 25 years she has been with the company, Irving Oil has provided the opportunity for Julianne deSoto to advance her career to become a managing director, satisfying her motivator needs for growth and development on the job.

> **Herzberg's motivator-hygiene theory** A need theory that distinguishes between motivator needs (related to the nature of the work itself) and hygiene needs (related to the physical and psychological context in which the work is performed). Herzberg proposed that motivator needs must be met in order for motivation and job satisfaction to be high. This theory is also known as the *two-factor theory*.

Hygiene needs are related to the physical and psychological context in which the work is performed. Hygiene needs are satisfied by outcomes such as pleasant and comfortable working conditions, fair pay, job security, good relationships with co-workers, and effective supervision. According to Herzberg, when hygiene needs are not met, workers will be dissatisfied, and when hygiene needs are met, workers are not dissatisfied. Satisfying hygiene needs, however, does not result in high levels of motivation or even high levels of job satisfaction. For motivation and job satisfaction to be high, motivator needs must be met.

Herzberg measures dissatisfaction and satisfaction on two different continua because the factors causing each are different. According to Herzberg, the opposite of satisfaction is not dissatisfaction but, rather, *no* satisfaction. Similarly, the opposite of dissatisfaction is *no* dissatisfaction. Hygiene factors must be adequate for employees to feel no dissatisfaction, while jobs must be sufficiently empowered in order for employees to feel satisfaction. This is illustrated in Figure 8.4.

FIGURE 8.4

Herzberg's Motivator-Hygiene Theory

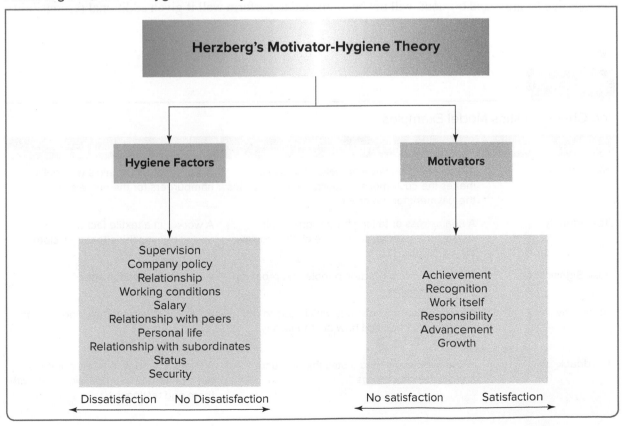

Many research studies have tested Herzberg's propositions, and, by and large, the theory fails to receive support.[12] Nevertheless, Herzberg's formulations have contributed to our understanding of motivation in at least two ways. First, Herzberg helped researchers and managers focus attention on the important distinction between intrinsic motivation (related to motivator needs) and extrinsic motivation (related to hygiene needs), covered earlier in the chapter. Second, his theory prompted researchers and managers to study how jobs can be designed or redesigned so that they are intrinsically motivating. Recall from Chapter 5 how the job characteristics model can help managers design jobs that are more interesting and motivating.

Hackman and Oldham's job characteristics model outlines five core job dimensions that when incorporated into the design of a job can lead to positive personal and organizational outcomes. Jobs that require the employee to do a broad range of tasks instead of a narrow range of tasks have a high level of *skill variety*. *Task identity* is the degree to which one associates oneself with the work or profession. The extent that one controls the entire process of production or simply a small part of it determines the task identity. Jobs that involve conceptualizing the product and executing the tasks involved in its production have high levels of task identity. *Task significance* is the degree to which the job is socially relevant and important. The above three core job dimensions have the potential to create a sense of meaningfulness for employees and generally result in positive personal and organizational outcomes. When *autonomy* is built into a job, employees direct their own work. The results of the work activity are known to the employee from the degree of *feedback* they get from doing the work itself. The degree of feedback can be high or low. See Table 8.1 for examples.

The degree to which the core job characteristics should be built into the design of the job depends on the state of the employee's need for growth—that is, the desire and ability to take on responsibility and challenging goals. Employees with a strong growth need will be motivated to perform well when the job design has high levels of the core job characteristics, while an employee who has a low need for growth, perhaps due to stress and burnout, will not be motivated to perform well if given additional responsibility.

TABLE 8.1

Job Characteristics Model Examples

Job Characteristics	Example of High Levels	Example of Low Levels
Skill Variety	A worker at Subway who bakes the buns, makes the customer's sandwich, and processes the payment for the order	A worker at McDonald's who grills hamburgers for the entire shift
Task Identity	A seamstress or tailor who designs a suit, creates the pattern, selects the cloth, and sews the garment	A worker in a textile factory who operates a machine that cuts cloth
Task Significance	A firefighter who rescues people and property from devastation	A cashier at a coffee shop
Autonomy	An electrician who decides which jobs to do, when to do them, and how best to fix any problems that arise	An automotive assembly-line worker
Feedback	A chef who cooks and tastes the dish and adjusts the seasonings	A kitchen hand who peels potatoes but has no role in preparing a dish with them and tasting it

McClelland's Need for Achievement, Affiliation, and Power

Psychologist David McClelland has extensively researched the needs for achievement, affiliation, and power.[13] The **need for achievement** is the extent to which an individual has a strong desire to perform challenging tasks well and to meet personal standards for excellence. People with a high need for achievement often set clear goals for themselves and like to receive performance feedback. The **need for affiliation** is the extent to which an individual is concerned about establishing and maintaining good interpersonal relations, being liked, and having the people around him or her get along with each other. The **need for power** is the extent to which an individual desires to control or influence others.[14]

> **need for achievement** The extent to which an individual has a strong desire to perform challenging tasks well and to meet personal standards for excellence.
>
> **need for affiliation** The extent to which an individual is concerned about establishing and maintaining good interpersonal relations, being liked, and having the people around him or her get along with each other.
>
> **need for power** The extent to which an individual desires to control or influence others.

While each of these needs is present in each of us to some degree, their importance in the workplace depends upon the position one occupies. For example, research suggests that high needs for achievement and for power are assets for first-line and middle managers and that a high need for power is especially important for upper managers.[15] One study found that U.S. presidents with a relatively high need for power tended to be especially effective during their terms of office.[16] A high need for affiliation may not always be desirable in managers and other leaders because it might lead them to try too hard to be liked by others (including subordinates) rather than doing all they can to ensure that performance is as high as it can and should be. Although most research on these needs has been done in the United States, some studies suggest that the findings may be applicable to people in other countries as well, such as India and New Zealand.[17]

Other Needs

Clearly, more needs motivate employees than those described by these theories. For example, more and more employees are feeling the need for work–life balance and time to take care of their loved ones while also being highly motivated at work. Interestingly enough, recent research suggests that being exposed to nature (even just by being able to see some trees from your office window) has many beneficial effects and that a lack of such exposure can actually impair well-being and performance.[18] Thus, having some time during the day when one can at least see nature may be another important need.

Managers of successful companies often strive to ensure that as many of their valued employees' needs as possible are satisfied in the workplace.

Process Theories of Motivation

LO3 | Describe how process theories of motivation help managers explain high and low performance levels.

Process theories explain the processes by which employee behaviour can be aroused and then directed. Within the process theories, we cover *expectancy theory, equity theory,* and *goal-setting theory.*

> **process theories** Theories that explain the processes by which employee behaviour can be aroused and then directed.

Expectancy Theory

Victor H. Vroom believed that employees consciously decide whether or not to perform at high levels at work. This decision solely depends on the employee's motivation level, which in turn depends on three interrelated factors of expectancy, instrumentality, and valence. **Expectancy theory**, formulated by Vroom in the 1960s, states that motivation will be high when:

- *Effort is linked to performance*—employees believe that high levels of effort will lead to high performance

- *Performance is linked to rewards*—high performance will lead to receiving rewards such as a salary increase or a bonus

- *Rewards satisfy personal goals*—rewards will be desirable to the employee.

> **expectancy theory** The theory that motivation will be high when employees believe that high levels of effort will lead to high performance, that high performance will lead to the attainment of rewards, and rewards will be desired by the employee.

Expectancy theory is one of the most popular theories of work motivation because it focuses on all three parts of the motivation equation: inputs, performance, and outcomes. Expectancy theory identifies three major factors that determine a person's motivation: *expectancy, instrumentality,* and *valence* (see Figure 8.5).[19]

EXPECTANCY

Expectancy is a person's perception about the extent to which effort (an input) will result in a certain level of performance. A person's level of expectancy determines whether he or she believes that a high level of effort will result in a high level of performance. People are motivated to put forth a lot of effort on their jobs only if they think that their effort will pay off in high performance—that is, if they have a high expectancy. Think about how motivated you would be to study for a test if you thought that no matter how hard you tried, you would get only a D. Think about how motivated a marketing manager would be who thought that no matter how hard he or she worked, there was no way to increase sales of an unpopular product. In these cases, expectancy is low, so overall motivation is also low.

> **expectancy** In expectancy theory, a perception about the extent to which effort will result in a certain level of performance.

FIGURE 8.5

Expectancy, Instrumentality, and Valence

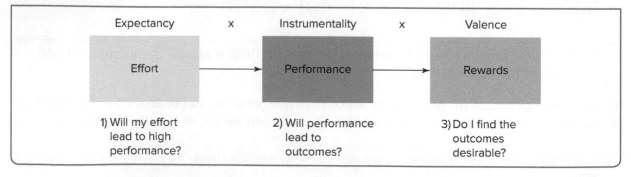

Members of an organization are motivated to put forth a high level of effort only if they think that doing so leads to high performance.[20] In other words, in order for people's motivation to be high, expectancy must be high. In trying to influence levels of expectancy, managers need to make sure that their skilled subordinates believe that if they do try hard, they actually can succeed. In addition to expressing confidence in subordinates, another way for managers to boost subordinates' expectancy levels and motivation is by providing training so that people have all the expertise they need for high performance. As illustrated in the opening case, managers at Irving Oil—a family-owned and privately held regional energy processing, transporting, and marketing company headquartered in Saint

Irving Oil provides leadership training to increase expectancy levels. This is one reason it is consistently ranked one of the top 100 Canadian Employers.
Mikecphoto/Dreamstime.com/Getstock.com

John, New Brunswick— eagerly look forward to leadership training through a variety of programs that instill lifelong learning and development of the individual, including undergraduate and graduate business programs in partnership with New Brunswick universities and leadership discussion forums focused on world issues and current events.[21]

The training increases the organizational member's expectancy by improving his or her ability to perform well.

INSTRUMENTALITY

Expectancy captures a person's perceptions about the relationship between effort and performance. **Instrumentality**, the second major concept in expectancy theory, is a person's perception about the extent to which performance at a certain level will result in receiving outcomes or rewards. According to expectancy theory, employees will be motivated to perform at a high level only if they think that high performance will lead to (or is *instrumental* for attaining) rewards such as pay, job security, interesting job assignments, bonuses, or a feeling of accomplishment. In other words, instrumentality must be high for motivation to be high—people must perceive that because of their high performance they will receive rewards.[22]

instrumentality In expectancy theory, a perception about the extent to which performance will result in the attainment of rewards.

Managers promote high levels of instrumentality when they clearly link performance to desired rewards and communicate this. By making sure that rewards are given to organizational members based on their performance, managers promote high instrumentality and motivation. When rewards are linked to performance in this way, high performers receive more than low performers. In the case of Cognos Inc., the Ottawa-based software company (now a subsidiary of IBM), when employees realized there would be more feedback, more recognition, and more help in meeting their personal goals, they were more motivated to stay with the company. They saw the link between performance and reward. MEC (Mountain Equipment Co-op) pays its employees more if they complete specific training modules. This improves the skill levels of employees (performance) and links the accomplishment to tangible rewards (desired outcomes). Sarah Irving, executive vice-president and chief brand officer of Irving Oil, raises levels of instrumentality and motivation for employees by linking opportunities for promotion and pay to high levels of performance.

VALENCE

Although all members of an organization must have high expectancies and instrumentalities, expectancy theory acknowledges that people differ in their preferences for outcomes or rewards. For many people, pay is the most important outcome of working. For others, a feeling of accomplishment or enjoying one's work is more important. The term **valence** refers to how desirable each of the outcomes/rewards available from a job or organization is to a person. To motivate organizational members, managers need to determine which rewards have high valence—are highly desired—and make sure that those rewards are provided when members perform at a high level. If the reward holds no value for the employee, they will not be motivated to expend the effort to perform at high levels. If the employee perceives the value of the outcome/reward negatively, motivation is low. Rewards must be linked to individual personal goals. From the opening case, it appears that not only pay but also autonomy, responsibility, and opportunities for promotion are highly desirable outcomes for employees like Julianne deSoto at Irving Oil.

> **valence** In expectancy theory, how desirable each of the rewards available from a job or organization is to a person.

BRINGING IT ALL TOGETHER

According to expectancy theory, high motivation results from high levels of expectancy, instrumentality, and valence (see Figure 8.6). If any one of these factors is low, motivation is likely to be low. No matter how tightly desired outcomes are linked to performance, if a person thinks that it is practically impossible for him or her to perform at a high level, then motivation to perform at a high level will be exceedingly low. Similarly, if a person does not think that rewards are linked to high performance, or if a person does not desire the outcomes that are linked to high performance, then motivation to perform at a high level will be low.

For example, think about your motivation to succeed in your classes. If you believe that spending four hours per week studying (effort) the principles of management outside of class time will end up getting you an A+ in the course (performance), then you have a high level of *expectancy,* which contributes to a high level of motivation. At the same time, the teacher has a reputation of never giving out an A+, so you are skeptical that achieving high marks will result in being awarded the A+. If you believe that the teacher will not award you the A+ (outcome) even if your marks exceed 90 percent (performance), you have a low level of *instrumentality* and your motivation to study will decrease. Moreover, even if you believe that you can achieve high marks by putting extra effort into studying, and that achieving the high marks will result in being awarded a high grade in the course, if you do not desire a high grade (*valence*)—if you just want to pass the course with a D—then you will not be motivated to put forth the effort required to achieve the level of performance to get the A+ anyway.

Managers can use expectancy theory to better understand why some employees work hard to achieve organizational goals and others do not. Take a business example. A marketing manager sets up a sales contest for a particular product. The sales associate who sells the most product by the end of the month will win the contest and get the reward of an all-expenses-paid trip for two to Las Vegas for four nights plus $1000 spending money. The manager communicates the details to the sales force and begins the contest. Shortly thereafter, the manager notices that Hoo is working every lead by email and telephone to

FIGURE 8.6

Expectancy Theory in Action

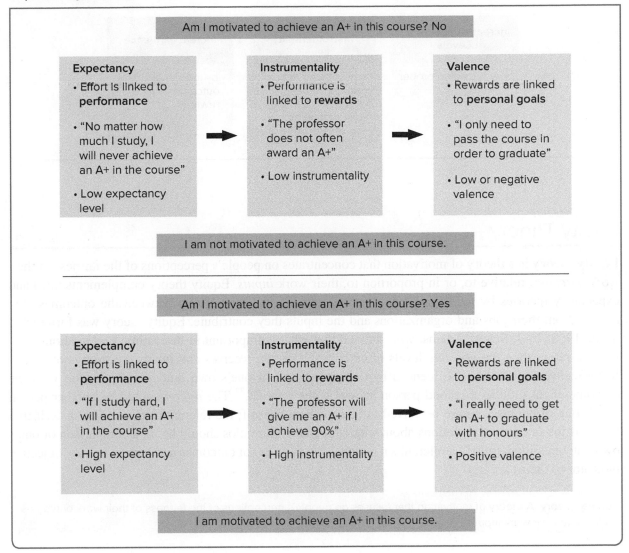

Am I motivated to achieve an A+ in this course? No

Expectancy
- Effort is linked to **performance**
- "No matter how much I study, I will never achieve an A+ in the course"
- Low expectancy level

Instrumentality
- Performance is linked to **rewards**
- "The professor does not often award an A+"
- Low instrumentality

Valence
- Rewards are linked to **personal goals**
- "I only need to pass the course in order to graduate"
- Low or negative valence

I am not motivated to achieve an A+ in this course.

Am I motivated to achieve an A+ in this course? Yes

Expectancy
- Effort is linked to **performance**
- "If I study hard, I will achieve an A+ in the course"
- High expectancy level

Instrumentality
- Performance is linked to **rewards**
- "The professor will give me an A+ if I achieve 90%"
- High instrumentality

Valence
- Rewards are linked to **personal goals**
- "I really need to get an A+ to graduate with honours"
- Positive valence

I am motivated to achieve an A+ in this course.

try to get the most sales and win the trip, while Selma is getting coffee and chatting with her office mates. Later the manager learns that the reward was very attractive to Hoo because he loves to gamble, and that Selma's has a low level of motivation to win the sales contest because she doesn't value the trip as an outcome for high performance. Selma is unmotivated not because she doesn't believe that if she puts in the effort she could make the most sales and win the contest (high levels of expectancy and instrumentality); rather, it is her negative valence toward the prize that demotivates her from putting the effort into performing at a high level in the first place. Selma is a mother of three children with no interest in going to Las Vegas for four nights. Had the manager been more aware of the rewards that employees desire, and provided choices for rewards, he or she would have been more likely to create an inclusive and motivating environment. Managers of successful companies try to ensure that employees' levels of expectancy, instrumentality, and valence are all high so that they will be highly motivated (see Figure 8.7).

FIGURE 8.7

How Managers Can Apply Expectancy Theory

Increase Expectancy Levels	Increase Instrumentality Levels	Increase Valence
• by providing proper training	• by keeping their word and being transparent in the distribution of outcomes (rewards)	• by individualizing outcomes and rewards

Equity Theory

Equity theory is a theory of motivation that concentrates on people's perceptions of the fairness of their work *outcomes* relative to, or in proportion to, their work *inputs*. Equity theory complements need and expectancy theories by focusing on how people perceive the relationship between the outcomes they receive from their jobs and organizations and the inputs they contribute. Equity theory was formulated in the 1960s by J. Stacey Adams, who stressed that what is important in determining motivation is the *relative* rather than the *absolute* levels of outcomes a person receives and inputs a person contributes. Specifically, motivation is influenced by the comparison of one's own outcome–input ratio with the outcome–input ratio of a second person known as the referent.[23] The *referent* could be another person or a group of people who are perceived to be similar to oneself; the referent also could be oneself in a previous job or one's expectations about what outcome–input ratios should be. In a comparison of one's own outcome–input ratio to a referent's ratio, one's *perceptions* of outcomes and inputs (not any objective indicator of them) are key.

> **equity theory** A theory of motivation that focuses on people's perceptions of the fairness of their work outcomes relative to their work inputs.

EQUITY

Equity exists when a person perceives his or her own outcome–input ratio to be equal to a referent's outcome–input ratio. Under conditions of equity (see Table 8.2), if a referent receives more outcomes than you receive, the referent contributes proportionally more inputs to the organization, so his or her outcome–input ratio still equals your outcome–input ratio. Maria Lau and Claudia King, for example, both work in a shoe store in a large mall. Lau is paid more per hour than King but also contributes more inputs, including being responsible for some of the store's bookkeeping, closing the store, and periodically depositing cash in the bank. When King compares her outcome–input ratio to Lau's (her referent), she perceives the ratios to be equitable because Lau's higher level of pay (an outcome) is proportional to her higher level of inputs (bookkeeping, closing the store, and going to the bank).

> **equity** The justice, impartiality, and fairness to which all organizational members are entitled.

TABLE 8.2		

Equity Theory

Perceived Condition	Person 1 compared to Person 2 (Referent)	Example
Equity	Outcomes:Inputs *equals* Outcomes:Inputs	An engineer (person 1) perceives that he contributes the same inputs (time and effort), and receives the same outcomes as person 2 (his referent) does.
Underpayment inequity	Outcomes:Inputs *is less than* Outcomes:Inputs	An engineer (person 1) perceives that he contributes the same inputs (time and effort) but receives less outcomes than person 2 (his referent) does.
Overpayment inequity	Outcomes:Inputs *is greater than* Outcomes:Inputs	An engineer (person 1) perceives that he contributes the same inputs (time and effort) but receives more outcomes than person 2 (his referent) does.

Similarly, under conditions of equity, if you receive more outcomes than a referent, then your inputs are perceived to be proportionally higher. Continuing with our example, when Lau compares her outcome–input ratio to King's (her referent's) ratio, she perceives them to be equitable because her higher level of pay is proportional to her higher level of inputs.

When people perceive that equity exists, they are motivated to continue contributing their current levels of inputs to their organizations to receive their current levels of outcomes. There is no motivation to change anything. If people wish to increase their outcomes under conditions of equity, they are motivated to increase their inputs.

INEQUITY

Inequity, or lack of fairness, exists when a person's outcome–input ratio is not perceived to be equal to a referent's. Inequity creates pressure or tension inside people and motivates them to restore equity by bringing the two ratios back into balance.

There are two types of inequity: underpayment inequity and overpayment inequity (see Table 8.2). **Underpayment inequity** exists when a person's own outcome–input ratio is perceived to be *less* than that of a referent: In comparing yourself to a referent, you think that you are *not* receiving the outcomes you should be receiving, given your inputs. **Overpayment inequity** exists when a person perceives that his or her own outcome–input ratio is *greater* than that of a referent: in comparing yourself to a referent, you think that you are receiving *more* outcomes than you should be, given your inputs.

Managers must promote a perception of fairness and equity.
Wesley VanDinter/Getty Images

inequity Lack of fairness.

underpayment inequity Inequity that exists when a person perceives that his or her own outcome– input ratio is less than the ratio of a referent.

overpayment inequity Inequity that exists when a person perceives that his or her own outcome – input ratio is greater than the ratio of a referent.

FIGURE 8.8

Possible Actions Taken to Restore Equity

Actions Taken to Restore Equity

Underpayment Inequity	Overpayment Inequity	Equity
• Change the perception of one's own or the referent's inputs and outcomes • Reduce inputs • Increase outcomes • Change the referent • Quit the job	• Change the perception of one's own or the referent's inputs and outcomes • Change the referent	• Continue contributing current levels of inputs to receive current levels of outcomes • No changes are made to inputs or outcomes

WAYS TO RESTORE EQUITY

According to equity theory, both underpayment inequity and overpayment inequity create tension that motivates most people to restore equity by bringing the ratios back into balance.[24] See Figure 8.8. When people experience *underpayment* inequity, they may be motivated to lower their inputs by reducing their working hours, putting forth less effort on the job, or being absent, or they may be motivated to increase their outcomes by asking for a raise or a promotion. Take an employee like Mary Campbell, a financial analyst at a large corporation. She noticed that she was working longer hours and getting more work accomplished than a co-worker who had the same position, yet they both received the exact same pay and other outcomes. To restore equity, Campbell decided to stop coming in early and staying late. Alternatively, she could have tried to restore equity by trying to increase her outcomes by, for example, asking her boss for a raise.

When people experience underpayment inequity and other means of equity restoration fail, they can change their perceptions of their own or the referent's inputs or outcomes. For example, they may realize that their referent is really working on more difficult projects than they are or that they really take more time off from work than their referent does. Alternatively, if people who feel that they are underpaid have other employment options, they may leave the organization. As an example, John Steinberg, an assistant principal in a high school, experienced underpayment inequity when he realized that all of the other assistant principals of high schools in his school district had received promotions to the position of principal even though he had been an assistant principal longer than they had. Steinberg's performance had always been appraised as being high, so after his repeated requests for a promotion went unheeded, he found a job as a principal in a different school district.

When people experience *overpayment* inequity, they may try to restore equity by changing their perceptions of their own or their referents' inputs or outcomes. Equity can be restored when people "realize" that they are contributing more inputs than they originally thought. Equity also can be restored by perceiving the referent's inputs to be lower or the referent's outcomes to be higher than one originally thought. When equity is restored in this way, actual inputs and outcomes are unchanged and the person being overpaid takes no real action. What has changed is how people think about or view their own or the referent's inputs and outcomes. For example, employee Susan Martineau experienced overpayment inequity when she realized that she was being paid $2 an hour more than a co-worker who had the same job as hers in a record store and who contributed the same amount of inputs. Martineau restored equity by changing her perceptions of her inputs. She "realized" that she worked harder than her co-worker and solved more problems that came up in the store. Thus, she rationalized the inequity by changing her perception of herself and her inputs.

Experiencing either overpayment or underpayment inequity, you might decide that your referent is not appropriate because, for example, the referent is too different from yourself. Choosing a more appropriate referent may bring the ratios back into balance. Angela Martinez, a middle manager in the engineering department of a chemical company, experienced overpayment inequity when she realized that she was being paid quite a bit more than her friend, who was a middle manager in the marketing department of the same company. After thinking about the discrepancy for a while, Martinez decided that engineering and marketing were so different that she should not be comparing her job to her friend's job even though they were both middle managers. Martinez restored equity by changing her referent; she picked a middle manager who had a similar pay scale in the engineering department as a new referent.

Tough economic times and increased global competition often result in some workers putting in longer and longer working hours (i.e., increasing their inputs) without any kind of increase in their outcomes. For those whose referents are not experiencing a similar change, perceptions of inequity are likely.

Motivation is highest when as many people as possible in an organization perceive that they are being equitably treated; that is, their outcomes and inputs are in balance. Top contributors and performers are motivated to continue contributing a high level of inputs because they are receiving the outcomes they deserve. Mediocre contributors and performers realize that if they want to increase their outcomes, they have to increase their inputs. Managers of effective organizations, like Sarah Irving of Irving Oil, realize the importance of equity for motivation and performance and continually strive to ensure that employees believe they are being equitably treated.

Goal-Setting Theory

Goal-setting theory focuses on motivating workers to contribute their inputs to their jobs and organizations; in this way it is similar to expectancy theory and equity theory. But goal-setting theory takes this focus a step further by considering as well how managers can ensure that organizational members focus their inputs in the direction of high performance and the achievement of organizational goals.

goal-setting theory A theory that focuses on identifying the types of goals that are most effective in producing high levels of motivation and performance and explaining why goals have these effects.

Ed Locke and Gary Latham, the leading researchers on goal-setting theory, suggest that the nature of the goals that organizational members strive to achieve determines their motivation and subsequent performance. A *goal* is what a person is trying to accomplish through his or her efforts and behaviours.[25] Just as you may have a goal to get a good grade in this course, members of an organization have goals that they strive to meet. For example, salespeople at men's clothing retailer Harry Rosen strive to meet sales goals, while top managers pursue market share and profitability goals.

Goal-setting theory suggests that in order to result in high motivation and performance, goals must be *specific and difficult*.[26] Specific goals are often quantitative—a salesperson's goal to sell $200 worth of merchandise each day, a scientist's goal to finish a project in one year, a CEO's goal to reduce debt by

40 percent and increase revenues by 20 percent, a restaurant manager's goal to serve 150 customers each evening. In contrast to specific goals, vague goals such as "doing your best" or "selling as much as you can," do not have much motivational force. Difficult goals are ones that are hard but not impossible to attain. In contrast to difficult goals, easy goals are those that practically everyone can attain, and moderate goals are goals that about one-half of the people can attain. Both easy and moderate goals have less motivational power than difficult goals.

Regardless of whether specific difficult goals are set by managers, workers, or managers and workers together, they lead to high levels of motivation and performance. When managers set goals for their subordinates, it is important that their subordinates accept the goals or agree to work toward them and also that they are committed to them or really want to attain them. Some managers find that having subordinates participate in the actual setting of goals boosts their acceptance of and commitment to the goals. It is also important for organizational members to receive *feedback* about how they are doing; feedback can often be provided by the performance appraisal and feedback component of an organization's human resource management system (see Chapter 7).

MANAGEMENT BY OBJECTIVES (MBO)

A systematic approach to goal setting is found in management by objectives (MBO). **Management by objectives (MBO)** is a formal system of evaluating subordinates on their ability to achieve specific organizational goals or performance standards.[27] Most organizations use some form of an MBO system because it is pointless to establish goals and then fail to evaluate whether they are being achieved. Management by objectives involves three specific steps:

- Step 1: *Specific goals and objectives are established at each level of the organization.*

  MBO starts when top managers establish overall organizational objectives, such as specific financial performance goals or targets. Then, objective-setting cascades down throughout the organization as managers at the divisional and functional levels set their goals to achieve corporate objectives.[28] Finally, first-level managers and employees jointly set goals that will contribute to achieving departmental objectives.

- Step 2: *Managers and their subordinates together determine the subordinates' goals.*

  An important characteristic of management by objectives is its participatory nature. Managers at every level sit down with each of the subordinate managers who report directly to them, and together they determine appropriate and feasible goals for the subordinate and bargain over the budget that the subordinate will need to achieve his or her goals. The participation of subordinates in the objective-setting process is a way of strengthening their commitment to achieving their goals and meeting their budgets.[29] Another reason why it is so important for subordinates (both individuals and teams) to participate in goal setting is that doing so enables them to tell managers what they think they can realistically achieve.[30]

- Step 3: *Managers and their subordinates periodically review the subordinates' progress toward meeting goals.*

management by objectives (MBO) A formal system of evaluating subordinates on their ability to achieve specific organizational goals or performance standards.

Once specific objectives have been agreed on for managers at each level, managers are accountable for meeting those objectives. Periodically they sit down with their subordinates to evaluate their progress.

Normally salary raises and promotions are linked to the goal-setting process, and managers who achieve their goals receive greater rewards than those who fall short.

In the companies that have decentralized responsibility for the production of goods and services to empowered teams and cross-functional teams, management by objectives works somewhat differently. Managers ask each team to develop a set of goals and performance targets that the team hopes to achieve—goals that are consistent with organizational objectives. Managers then negotiate with each team to establish its final goals and the budget the team will need to achieve them. The reward system is linked to team performance, not to the performance of any one team member.

MBO does not always work out as planned, however. Managers and their subordinates at all levels must believe that performance evaluations are accurate and fair. Any

Goals must be challenging to be motivating.
© Dan Bar I Dreamstime.com

suggestion that personal biases and political objectives play a part in the evaluation process can lower or even destroy MBO's effectiveness as a control system. This is why many organizations work so hard to protect the integrity of their systems.

Similarly, when people work in teams, each member's contribution to the team, and each team's contribution to the goals of the organization, must be fairly evaluated. This is no easy thing to do. It depends on managers' ability to create an organizational control system that measures performance accurately and fairly and links performance evaluations to rewards so employees stay motivated and coordinate their activities to achieve the organization's mission and goals.

Learning Theories

LO4	Identify the motivation lessons that managers can learn from learning theories of motivation.

The basic premise of **learning theories** as applied to organizations is that managers can increase employee motivation and performance by the ways they link the outcomes that employees receive to the performance of desired behaviours and the attainment of goals. Thus, learning theory focuses on the linkage between performance and outcomes in the motivation equation (refer back to Figure 8.2).

learning theories Theories that focus on increasing employee motivation and performance by linking the outcomes that employees receive to the performance of desired behaviours and the attainment of goals.

Learning can be defined as a relatively permanent change in a person's knowledge or behaviour that results from practice or experience.[31] Learning takes place in organizations when people learn to perform certain behaviours to receive certain outcomes. For example, a person learns to perform at a higher level than in the past or to come to work earlier because he or she is motivated to obtain the outcomes that result from these behaviours, such as a pay raise or praise from a supervisor.

learning A relatively permanent change in knowledge or behaviour that results from practice or experience.

Of the different learning theories, operant conditioning or *reinforcement theory* and *social learning theory* provide the most guidance to managers in their efforts to have a highly motivated workforce. According to **operant conditioning theory**, developed by psychologist B.F. Skinner, people learn to perform behaviours that lead to desired consequences and learn not to perform behaviours that lead to undesired consequences.[32] Hence, it is a motivation theory that looks at the relationship between behaviour and its consequences. Skinner's theory suggests that people will be motivated to perform at a high level and attain their work goals to the extent that high performance and goal attainment allow them to obtain outcomes they desire. Similarly, people avoid performing behaviours that lead to outcomes they do not desire. By linking the performance of *specific behaviours* to the attainment of *specific outcomes,* managers can motivate organizational members to perform in ways that help an organization achieve its goals.

> **operant conditioning theory** The theory that people learn to perform behaviours that lead to desired consequences and learn not to perform behaviours that lead to undesired consequences.

Operant conditioning theory provides four tools that managers can use to motivate high performance and prevent workers from engaging in absenteeism and other behaviours that detract from organizational effectiveness. These tools are positive reinforcement, negative reinforcement, extinction, and punishment.[33]

Positive reinforcement and punishment involve presenting a *stimulus* or *reinforcer*, while negative reinforcement and extinction involve removing the stimulus or reinforcer. A **reinforcer** is any stimulus that causes a behaviour to be repeated. See Table 8.3. Managers use these four techniques to modify the dysfunctional workplace behaviours of employees, such as absenteeism and lack of punctuality.

> **reinforcer** Any stimulus that causes a given behaviour to be repeated.

TABLE 8.3

Four Operant Conditioning Techniques

	Type of Stimulus	
Action	Positive	Negative
Present the reinforcer or stimulus	**Positive reinforcement**—increases the desired behaviour. Give a reward when desired actions are exhibited.	**Punishment**—decreases the undesired behaviour. Take something of value away when the undesired action is exhibited.
	For example: Jon arrives at work early (desired action) and is given praise (positive stimulus) by his manager.	**For example:** Sarah consistently arrives at work late (undesired action) and is made to stay late (negative stimulus) by her manager to make up the time.
Remove the reinforcer or stimulus	**Extinction**—decreases the undesired behaviour. Ignore the undesired behaviour when it occurs to stop it from being repeated.	**Negative reinforcement**—increases the desired behaviour. Remove the unpleasant consequence or punishment when the desired behaviour is exhibited.
	For example: Ash constantly asks inappropriate questions at staff meetings. Rather than acknowledging Ash (positive stimulus is removed) and giving her a platform to be heard, her manager ignores her raised hand.	For example: When Sarah arrives at work on time (desired action), her manager does not demand that she work late (negative stimulus is removed).

Positive Reinforcement

Positive reinforcement gives people outcomes they desire when they perform well. These outcomes, called *positive reinforcers,* include any outcome that a person desires, such as good pay, praise, or a promotion. Performing well might include producing high-quality goods and services, providing high-quality customer service, and meeting deadlines. By linking positive reinforcers to positive performance, managers motivate people to perform the desired behaviours. For instance, managers at Brandon's hog slaughterhouse offer a variety of incentives to encourage workers to show up for their shifts. To be eligible for a truck raffle, held every three months, employees have to show up for every one of their shifts during that period. Employees get bonuses on top of their regular wage for perfect attendance during shorter periods. The incentive program has paid off. Before the rewards, 12 percent of the employees skipped work each day. Since the rewards, absenteeism has dropped to about 7 to 8 percent.

People respond poorly to punishment and coercion, and favourably to praise and positive reinforcement.
Tupungato | Dreamstime.com

positive reinforcement Giving people outcomes they desire when they perform organizationally functional behaviours.

Negative Reinforcement

Negative reinforcement also can be used to encourage members of an organization to perform desired or organizationally functional behaviours. Managers using negative reinforcement actually eliminate or remove undesired outcomes once the desired behaviour is performed. These undesired outcomes, called *negative reinforcers,* can include unpleasant assignments, a manager's constant nagging or criticism, or the ever-present threat of termination. When negative reinforcement is used, people are motivated to perform behaviours because they want to avoid or stop receiving undesired outcomes. For example, when a salesperson exceeds the sales quota, his or her manager cancels the pep-talk meetings. In this case, the reinforcer or negative stimulus is removed (the pep-talk lecture) because the salesperson has performed the desired behaviour (booked more than expected sales).

negative reinforcement Eliminating or removing undesired outcomes once people have performed organizationally functional behaviours.

Whenever possible, managers should try to use positive reinforcement. Negative reinforcement can make for a very unpleasant work environment and even a negative culture in an organization. No one likes to be nagged, threatened, or exposed to other kinds of negative outcomes. The use of negative reinforcement sometimes causes subordinates to resent managers and try to get back at them.

Even managers who use positive reinforcement (and refrain from using negative reinforcement) can get into trouble if they are not careful to identify the right behaviours to reinforce—behaviours that are truly functional for the organization. Doing this is not always as straightforward as it might seem. First, it is crucial for managers to choose behaviours over which subordinates have control; in other words, subordinates must have the freedom and opportunity to perform the behaviours that are being reinforced. Second, it is crucial that these behaviours contribute to organizational effectiveness.

Extinction

Sometimes members of an organization are motivated to perform behaviours that actually detract from organizational effectiveness. According to the theory, all behaviour is controlled or determined by its consequences. One way for managers to curtail the performance of dysfunctional behaviours is to eliminate whatever is reinforcing them. This process is called **extinction**.

extinction Stopping the performance of dysfunctional behaviours by eliminating whatever is reinforcing them.

Suppose a manager has a subordinate who frequently stops by the office to chat—sometimes about work-related matters but at other times about various topics ranging from politics to last night's football game. The manager and the subordinate share certain interests and views, so these conversations can get quite involved, and both seem to enjoy them. The manager, however, realizes that these frequent and sometimes lengthy conversations are actually causing him to stay at work later in the evenings to make up for the time he loses during the day. The manager also realizes that he is actually reinforcing his subordinate's behaviour by acting interested in the topics the subordinate brings up and responding at length to them. To extinguish this behaviour, the manager stops acting interested in these non–work-related conversations and keeps responses polite and friendly but brief. No longer being reinforced with a pleasant conversation, the subordinate eventually ceases to be motivated to interrupt the manager during working hours to discuss non-work issues.

Punishment

Sometimes managers cannot rely on extinction to eliminate dysfunctional behaviours because they do not have control over whatever is reinforcing the behaviour or because they cannot afford the time needed for extinction to work. When employees are performing dangerous behaviours or those that are illegal or unethical, the behaviours need to be stopped immediately. Sexual harassment, for example, is an organizationally dysfunctional behaviour that cannot be tolerated. In such cases managers often rely on **punishment**, administering undesired or negative consequences to subordinates when they perform the dysfunctional behaviours. Punishments used by organizations range from verbal reprimands to pay cuts, temporary suspensions, demotions, and terminations. Punishment, however, can have unintended side effects—resentment, loss of self-respect, a desire for retaliation, and so on—and should be used only when absolutely necessary.

punishment Administering an undesired or negative consequence when dysfunctional behaviour occurs.

To avoid the unintended side effects of punishment, managers should keep in mind these guidelines:
- Downplay the emotional element involved in punishment. Make it clear that you are punishing a person's performance of a dysfunctional behaviour, not the person himself or herself.
- Try to punish dysfunctional behaviours as soon after they occur as possible, and make sure the negative consequence is a source of punishment for the individuals involved. Be certain that organizational members know exactly why they are being punished.

- Try to avoid punishing someone in front of others, for this can hurt a person's self-respect and lower esteem in the eyes of co-workers as well as make co-workers feel uncomfortable.[34] Even so, making organizational members aware that an individual who has committed a serious infraction has been punished can sometimes be effective in preventing future infractions and teaching all members of the organization that certain behaviours are unacceptable. For example, when organizational members are informed that a manager who has sexually harassed subordinates has been punished, they learn or are reminded of the fact that sexual harassment is not tolerated in the organization.

Managers and students alike often confuse negative reinforcement and punishment. To avoid such confusion, keep in mind the two major differences between them. First, negative reinforcement is used to promote the performance of functional behaviours in organizations; punishment is used to stop the performance of dysfunctional behaviours. Second, negative reinforcement entails the *removal* of a negative consequence when functional behaviours are performed while punishment entails the *administration* of negative consequences when dysfunctional behaviours are performed.

Non-productive workplace behaviours go the way of the dinosaur when extinction is used as a reinforcement technique.
Shutterstock/kikujungboy

Social Learning Theory

Social learning theory proposes that motivation results not only from direct experience of rewards and punishments but also from a person's thoughts and beliefs. Social learning theory extends operant conditioning's contribution to managers' understanding of motivation by explaining (1) how people can be motivated by observing other people perform a behaviour and be reinforced for doing so (*vicarious learning*), (2) how people can be motivated to control their behaviour themselves (*self-reinforcement*), and (3) how people's beliefs about their ability to successfully perform a behaviour affect motivation (*self-efficacy*).[35] We look briefly at each of these motivators.

social learning theory A theory that takes into account how learning and motivation are influenced by people's thoughts and beliefs and their observations of other people's behaviour.

VICARIOUS LEARNING

Vicarious learning, often called *observational learning,* occurs when a person (the learner) becomes motivated to perform a behaviour by watching another person (the model) perform the behaviour and be positively reinforced for doing so. Vicarious learning is a powerful source of motivation on many jobs in which people learn to perform functional behaviours by watching others. Salespeople learn how to be helpful to customers, medical school students learn how to treat patients, law clerks learn how to practise law, and nonmanagers learn how to be managers, in part, by observing experienced members of an organization perform these behaviours properly and be reinforced for them. In general, people are more likely to be motivated to imitate the behaviour of models that are highly competent, are (to some extent) experts in the behaviour, have high status, receive attractive reinforcers, and are friendly or approachable.[36]

vicarious learning Learning that occurs when the learner becomes motivated to perform a behaviour by watching another person perform it and be reinforced for doing so; also called *observational learning.*

To promote vicarious learning, managers should strive to have the learner meet the following conditions:

- The learner observes the model performing the behaviour.
- The learner accurately perceives the model's behaviour.
- The learner remembers the behaviour.
- The learner has the skills and abilities needed to perform the behaviour.
- The learner sees or knows that the model is positively reinforced for the behaviour.[37]

SELF-REINFORCEMENT

Although managers are often the providers of reinforcement in organizations, sometimes people motivate themselves through self-reinforcement. People can control their own behaviour by setting goals for themselves and then reinforcing themselves when they achieve the goals.[38] **Self-reinforcers** are any desired or attractive outcomes or rewards that people can give to themselves for good performance, such as a feeling of accomplishment, going to a movie, having dinner out, downloading a new song, or taking time out for a golf game. When members of an organization control their own behaviour through self-reinforcement, managers do not need to spend as much time as they ordinarily would trying to motivate and control behaviour through the administration of consequences because subordinates are controlling and motivating themselves. In fact, this self-control is often referred to as the *self-management of behaviour.*

self-reinforcers Any desired or attractive outcome or reward that a person gives to himself or herself for good performance.

When employees are highly skilled and are responsible for creating new goods and services, managers typically rely on self-control and self-management of behaviour, as is the case at Google. Employees at Google are given the flexibility and autonomy to experiment, take risks, and sometimes fail as they work on new projects. They are encouraged to learn from their failures and apply what they learn to subsequent projects.[39] Google's engineers are given one day a week to work on their own projects that they are highly involved with, and new products such as Google News often emerge from these projects.[40]

SELF-EFFICACY

Self-efficacy is a person's belief about his or her ability to perform a behaviour successfully.[41] Even with all the most attractive consequences or reinforcers hinging on high performance, people are not going to be motivated if they do not think that they can actually perform at a high level. Similarly, when people control their own behaviour, they are likely to set for themselves difficult goals that will lead to outstanding accomplishments only if they think that they have the capability to reach those goals. Thus, self-efficacy influences motivation both when managers provide reinforcement and when workers themselves provide it.[42] The greater the self-efficacy, the greater is the motivation and performance. In the opening case, managers at Irving Oil boost self-efficacy by providing employees like Julianne deSoto with training, increasing their levels of autonomy and responsibility as they gain experience with the company, and expressing confidence in their ability to manage their own units. Such verbal persuasion, a person's own past performance and accomplishments, and the accomplishments of other people all play a role in determining a person's self-efficacy.

self-efficacy A person's belief about his or her ability to perform a behaviour successfully.

Total Reward Strategy

LO5 | Explain how managers use reward systems to increase employee motivation.

Everyone has experienced not wanting to go in to work at one time or another. Maybe it is because you're not feeling well or didn't get a good night's sleep. But about one quarter of us experience other reasons for not wanting to put forth the effort needed for high performance at work. A 2013 Gallup survey of 143 countries (about 180 million employees) found that only 13 percent of employees feel they are engaged at work, while 63 percent say they lack motivation. Respondents in Canada and the U.S. reported the most motivation at work with 29 percent saying they feel they are engaged in their workplaces. However, 54 percent said they are not engaged while 18 percent said they are actively disengaged.[43] This presents a serious challenge for managers and begs the question of how managers can use rewards to motivate employees.

A **total reward strategy** encompasses both intrinsically and extrinsically motivating factors such as giving positive reinforcement, recognition, opportunities for advancement and personal growth, responsibility, adequate training to raise expectancy levels, and individualized benefits such as flexible hours for work–life balance. We have already discussed training and benefits in Chapter 7. Here we focus on the basic principle that managers must recognize that reward systems must be tailored to individual needs if they are to be motivating.

total reward strategy A total reward strategy encompasses both intrinsically and extrinsically motivating factors.

When it comes to employees' perceptions of fair rewards, the top concern is neither total pay nor increases in salary. It is access to career development opportunities. A 2011 survey reveals the top five concerns in reward fairness are:

1. Career development opportunities

2. Merit increases

3. Base pay amounts

4. Non-financial recognition

5. Employee development and training[44]

One thing that motivation theories help managers understand is that people are motivated by the outcomes they receive for their efforts. These outcomes can be either intrinsically motivating or extrinsically motivating. A total reward strategy encompasses both of these elements. Receiving non-financial recognition for a job well done is one of the top five concerns in fairness and one of the simplest forms of engaging an employee. It makes people feel good to have their efforts appreciated by managers. **Employee recognition programs** are based on the principle of giving personal attention to employee performance, and expressing interest, approval, and appreciation for a job well done. When employees are recognized by managers for the important contributions they make to the organization, they are more likely to be motivated toward high levels of performance.

employee recognition programs Management expressions of interest, approval, and appreciation for a job well done by individuals or groups of employees.

Pay and Motivation

Managers can also use pay to motivate employees to perform at a high level and attain their work goals. Pay is used to motivate entry-level workers, first-line and middle managers, and even top managers such as CEOs. Pay is an extrinsic motivator, and is only one part of a total rewards strategy. How compensation and benefit structures and levels are determined is discussed in Chapter 7. Here we focus on how pay can be used to motivate people to perform behaviours that help an organization achieve its goals, and how it can be used to motivate people to join and remain with an organization.

As illustrated in Figure 8.9, pay is an important extrinsic motivating factor addressed by both *need* and *process theories.*

- *Need theories*: Physiological needs are satisfied through earning wages needed to purchase food, clothing, and shelter. Pay levels must be adequate to avoid feeling dissatisfaction but do not contribute to one's level of satisfaction, according to Herzberg.

- *Expectancy theory*: Instrumentality, the linkage between performance and rewards such as pay, must be high for motivation to be high. Pay is an outcome that has a positive valence.

- *Goal-setting theory*: Outcomes such as pay should be linked to the attainment of goals.

- *Equity theory*: Outcomes such as pay should be distributed in proportion to the level of inputs.

- *Learning theories*: The distribution of pay and other rewards should depend on the performance of desirable workplace behaviours.

As these theories suggest, to promote high motivation, managers should base the distribution of pay on performance levels so that high performers receive more pay than do low performers (other

---

FIGURE 8.9

How Pay Motivates

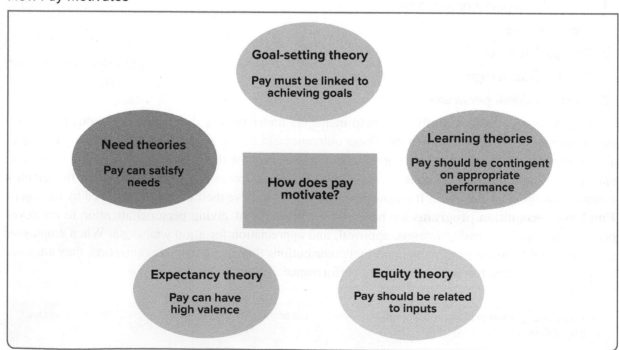

things being equal).[45] It should be remembered that pay is, however, only *one* part of a total reward strategy.

In deciding whether to pay for performance, managers also have to determine whether to use salary increases or bonuses. Thus some pay-for-performance programs (particularly those that use bonuses) are *variable-pay programs* or **merit pay plans**, where earnings go up and down annually based on performance.[46] Thus, there is no guarantee that an individual will earn as much this year as the last.

merit pay plan A compensation plan that bases pay on performance.

The number of employees affected by variable-pay plans has been rising in Canada. Keri Humber, a past senior compensation consultant with Hewitt Associates, remarked, "In this economy, especially, employers must continue to ensure their corporate pay strategies are properly executed. . . . In order to remain competitive and continue to attract quality talent, organizations will need to look beyond base salary for ways to reward and motivate their employees. . . . Variable pay plans are one alternative."[47] These programs are more common among nonunionized workers.[48] Prem Benimadhu, a former vice-president of the Conference Board of Canada notes, "Canadian unions have been very allergic to variable compensation."[49] In addition to wage uncertainty, employees may object to pay for performance if they feel that factors out of their control might affect the extent to which bonuses are possible.

"Appreciate everything your associates do for the business. Nothing else can quite substitute for a few well-chosen, well-timed, sincere words of praise. They're absolutely free and worth a fortune."[50]

Sam Walton

BASING VARIABLE PAY PLANS ON INDIVIDUAL, GROUP, OR ORGANIZATIONAL PERFORMANCE

Managers can base merit pay on individual, group, or organizational performance. Perhaps this is why a recent survey on reward fairness found that variable pay, such as bonuses and incentives, was not among the top five concerns (listed above). When individual performance (such as the dollar value of merchandise a salesperson sells, the number of loudspeakers a factory worker assembles, and a lawyer's billable hours) can be accurately determined, individual motivation is likely to be highest when pay is based on individual performance.[51] When members of an organization work closely together and individual performance cannot be accurately determined (as in a team of computer programmers developing a single software package), pay cannot be based on individual performance, and a group- or organization-based plan must be used. When the attainment of organizational goals hinges on members working closely together and cooperating with each other (as in a small construction company that builds custom homes), group- or organization-based plans may be more appropriate than individual-based plans.[52]

It is possible to combine elements of an individual-based plan with a group or organization-based plan to motivate each individual to perform highly and, at the same time, motivate all individuals to work well together, cooperate with one another, and help one another as needed. Employees also are motivated to contribute their inputs to the organization because their contributions determine their share of the bonus fund.

SALARY INCREASE OR BONUS?

Managers can distribute merit pay to people in the form of a salary increase or a bonus on top of regular salaries. Although the dollar amount of a salary increase or bonus might be identical, bonuses tend to have more motivational impact for at least three reasons. First, salary levels are typically based on performance levels, cost-of-living increases, and so forth from the day people start working in an organization, which means that the absolute level of the salary is based largely on factors unrelated to *current* performance. A 5 percent merit increase in salary, for example, may seem relatively small in comparison to one's total salary. Second, a current salary increase may be affected by other factors in addition to performance, such as cost-of-living increases or across-the-board market adjustments. Third, because organizations rarely reduce salaries, salary levels tend to vary less than performance levels do. Related to this point is the fact that bonuses give managers more flexibility in distributing outcomes. If an organization is doing well, bonuses can be relatively high to reward employees for their contributions. However,

Pay is only one aspect of a total rewards strategy.
Tektite/Dreamstime.com/Getstock.com

unlike salary increases, bonus levels can be reduced when an organization's performance lags. All in all, bonus plans have more motivational impact than salary increases because the amount of the bonus can be directly and exclusively based on performance.[53]

Consistent with the lessons from motivation theories, bonuses can be linked directly to performance and vary from year to year and employee to employee. In addition to receiving pay raises and bonuses, high-level managers and executives are sometimes granted employee stock options. **Employee stock options** are financial instruments that entitle the bearer to buy shares of an organization's stock at a certain price during a certain period of time or under certain conditions.[54] For example, in addition to salaries, stock options are sometimes used to attract high-level managers. The exercise price is the stock price at which the bearer can buy the stock, and the vesting conditions specify when the bearer can actually buy the stock at the exercise price. The option's exercise price is generally set equal to the market price of the stock on the date it is granted, and the vesting conditions might specify that the manager has to have worked at the organization for 12 months or perhaps met some performance target (increase in profits) before being able to exercise the option. In high-technology firms and startups, options are sometimes used in a similar fashion for employees at various levels in the organization.[55]

employee stock options Financial instruments that entitle the bearer to buy shares of an organization's stock at a certain price during a certain period of time or under certain conditions.

From a motivation standpoint, stock options are used not so much to reward past individual performance but, rather, to motivate employees to work in the future for the good of the company as a whole. This is true because stock options issued at current stock prices have value in the future only if an organization does well and its stock price appreciates; thus, giving employees stock options should encourage them to help the organization improve its performance over time.[56] At high-technology startups and dot-coms, stock options have often motivated potential employees to leave promising jobs in larger companies and work for the startups. In the late 1990s and early 2000s, many dot-commers were devastated to learn not only that their stock options were worthless, because their companies went out of business or were doing poorly, but also that they were unemployed. Unfortunately, stock options have also led to unethical behaviour; for example, sometimes individuals seek to artificially inflate the value of a company's stock to increase the value of stock options.

EXAMPLES OF MERIT PAY PLANS

Managers can choose among several merit pay plans, depending on the work that employees perform and other considerations. Using *piece-rate pay,* an individual-based merit plan, managers base employees' pay on the number of units each employee produces, whether televisions, computer components, or welded auto parts. Advances in information technology are currently simplifying the administration of piece-rate pay in a variety of industries. For example, farmers typically allocated piece-rate pay to farm workers through a laborious, time-consuming process. Now, they can rely on metal buttons the size of a dime that farm workers clip to their shirts or put in their pockets. Made by Dallas Semiconductor Corporation, these buttons are customized for use in farming by Agricultural Data Systems, based in Laguna Niguel, California.[57] Each button contains a semiconductor linked to payroll computers by a wand-like probe in the field.[58] The wand relays the number of boxes of fruit or vegetables that each worker picks as well as the type and quality of the produce picked, the location it was picked in, and the time and the date. The buttons are activated by touching them with the probe; hence, they are called Touch Memory Buttons. Managers generally find that the buttons save time, improve accuracy, and provide valuable information about their crops and yields.[59]

Using *commission pay,* another individual-based merit pay plan, managers base pay on a percentage of sales. Managers at the successful real-estate company Re/Max International Inc. use commission pay for their agents, who are paid a percentage of their sales. Some department stores use commission pay for their salespeople.

Examples of organizational-based merit pay plans include the Scanlon plan and profit sharing. The *Scanlon plan* (developed by Joseph Scanlon, a union leader in a U.S. steel and tin plant in the 1920s) focuses on reducing expenses or cutting costs; members of an organization are motivated to come up with and implement cost-cutting strategies because a percentage of the cost savings achieved during a specified time is distributed to the employees.[60] Under *profit sharing,* employees receive a share of an organization's profits. Approximately 16 percent of the employees in medium or large firms receive profit sharing, and about 25 percent of small firms give their employees a share of the profits.[61] Regardless of the specific kind of plan that is used, managers should always strive to link pay to the performance of behaviours that help an organization achieve its goals.

Japanese managers in large corporations have long shunned merit pay plans in favour of plans that reward seniority. However, more and more Japanese companies are adopting merit-based pay due to its motivational benefits; among such companies are SiteDesign,[62] Tokio Marine and Fire Insurance, and Nissho Iwai, a trading organization.[63]

SUMMARY AND REVIEW

connect

LO1 The Nature of Motivation Motivation encompasses the psychological forces within a person that determine the direction of his or her behaviour in an organization, level of effort, and level of persistence in the face of obstacles. Managers strive to motivate employees to contribute their inputs to an organization, to focus these inputs in the direction of high performance, and to ensure that people receive the outcomes they desire when they perform at a high level. People are motivated to work hard *extrinsically* to acquire material rewards or avoid punishment, *intrinsically* for its own sake, and *prosocially* to help others.

LO2 Need Theories of Motivation *Need theories* suggest that to motivate their workforces, managers should determine what needs people are trying to satisfy in organizations and then ensure that people receive outcomes that satisfy these needs when they perform at a high level and contribute to organizational effectiveness. Managers can design jobs with five core dimensions in mind to make them more interesting and motivating.

LO3 Process Theories of Motivation *Process theories* help managers explain why people act the way they do and thus help managers understand the roots of high and low performance levels among employees.

LO4 Learning Theories *Learning theories* help managers see the link between giving rewards for high performance behaviour and the repetition of that behaviour among employees.

LO5 Total Reward Strategy Each of the motivation theories discussed in this chapter alludes to the importance of pay and suggests that pay should be based on performance. Pay is only one part of a *total reward strategy,* which includes both extrinsic elements such as pay and intrinsic elements such as providing opportunities for growth and development and non-financial recognition.

KEY TERMS

employee recognition programs	inequity
employee stock options	input
equity	instrumentality
equity theory	intrinsically motivated behaviour
expectancy	learning
expectancy theory	learning theories
extinction	management by objectives (MBO)
extrinsically motivated behaviour	merit pay plan
goal-setting theory	motivation
Herzberg's motivator-hygiene theory	need
hierarchy of needs	need for achievement

need for affiliation

need for power

need theories

negative reinforcement

operant conditioning theory

outcome

overpayment inequity

positive reinforcement

process theories

prosocially motivated behaviour

punishment

reinforcer

self-efficacy

self-reinforcers

social learning theory

total reward strategy

underpayment inequity

valence

vicarious learning

WRAP-UP TO OPENING CASE

"People Matter" Is at the Heart of Irving Oil's Culture

What's at the root of Irving Oil's success? "It all starts with our people—our employees and our customers," says Executive Vice-President Sarah Irving. "They're the reason why we're here today." After having read and understood the concepts in this chapter, you should be able to answer the following questions:

1. *Apply Herzberg's motivator-hygiene theory to this case.*

   ANSWER: Frederick Herzberg focuses on two factors: outcomes that can lead to high levels of motivation and job satisfaction, and outcomes that can prevent people from being dissatisfied. According to Herzberg's motivator-hygiene theory, people have two sets of needs or requirements: motivator needs and hygiene needs. *Motivator needs* are related to the nature of the work itself and how challenging it is. Outcomes such as interesting work and responsibility help to satisfy motivator needs. To have a highly motivated and satisfied workforce, managers should take steps to ensure that employees' motivator needs are being met. At Irving Oil, managers ensure that employees experience a great deal of autonomy, responsibility, and empowerment in making day-to-day operating decisions and creating superior customer service. Moreover, they provide ample opportunities for growth and development—all factors that lead to high motivation and employee satisfaction.

   Hygiene needs are related to the physical and psychological context in which the work is performed. Hygiene needs are satisfied by outcomes such as pleasant working conditions, adequate pay, and job security. When hygiene needs are not met, workers are dissatisfied. Many employees, like Julianne deSoto have been with the company for many years, enjoying job security and avoiding feelings of dissatisfaction. However, satisfying hygiene needs alone does not result in high levels of motivation or job satisfaction. For motivation and job satisfaction to be high, motivator needs must also be met.

2. *Apply Vroom's expectancy theory to this case.*

   ANSWER: Expectancy theory posits that motivation will be high when workers believe that high levels of effort will lead to high performance and high performance will lead to the attainment of desired outcomes. A person's level of expectancy determines whether he or she believes that a high level of effort will result in a high level of performance. Managers can strengthen employees' levels of expectancy by providing training and mentoring opportunities so that they have the expertise they need for high performance. Managers at Irving Oil provide extensive training in technical courses and conference attendance to employees which strengthens confidence and expectancy levels. Employees will be motivated to perform at a high level only if they think that high performance will lead to desirable outcomes. This is referred to as one's perception of instrumentality and it must be high if employees are to be motivated to perform well. At Irving, employees observe that if they perform well after some time, they will be promoted to the positions of management, as was deSoto. With the commitment to promote from within, employees have strong levels of instrumentality. They believe they will be promoted (receive the outcome) if they put in the effort (input). Promotion is valued highly by employees at Irving and thus the valence or desirability placed on the outcome is high. High motivation results from high levels of expectancy, instrumentality, and valence. Irving Oil provides strong links among all three elements, resulting in a highly motivated workforce.

3. *How does Irving Oil use a total reward strategy to motivate employee performance?*

   ANSWER: A total reward strategy motivates employees by encompassing both intrinsically and extrinsically motivating factors as outcomes for high performance. Intrinsically motivating factors—such as receiving recognition for a job well done and giving employees the opportunity to volunteer for charitable causes that they are passionate about—and extrinsically motivating factors—such as setting professional development goals as part of annual pay and performance reviews—are two examples of how Irving uses a total reward strategy to motivate high performance among employees.

MANAGEMENT IN ACTION

TOPICS FOR DISCUSSION AND ACTION

LEVEL 1 Knowledge & Comprehension

1. Define motivation, and describe how it is related to behaviours that concern managers in organizations.

2. What are the qualities of organizational goals that make them motivating?

3. Discuss how each theory of motivation treats pay as a part of a total reward strategy.

LEVEL 2 Application & Analysis

4. From the point of view of expectancy theory, evaluate what managers should do to have a highly motivated workforce.

5. From the point of view of equity theory, assess what managers should do to have a highly motivated workforce.

6. Describe Maslow's hierarchy of needs *or* Herzberg's two-factor theory *or* McClelland's need theory and suggest what managers could do to apply them in the workplace.

LEVEL 3 Synthesis & Evaluation

7. How can managers use social learning theory to develop a highly motivated work team?

8. Discuss why two people with similar abilities may have very different expectancies for performing at a high level. What steps could a manager take to influence people's levels of expectancy, instrumentality, and valence?

9. Under what circumstances should a manager use each of the techniques in operant conditioning theory? Which technique is the best for long-term changes in behaviour?

SELF-REFLECTION EXERCISE

The following is a typical situation that students often face: you are in a team with six other management students, and you have a major case analysis due in four weeks. This assignment will count for 25 percent of your course mark. *You are the team's leader.*

The problem: Several of your team members are having difficulty getting motivated to start work on the project.

The task: Identify ways you could motivate your team members by using the following theories of motivation as studied in this chapter:

1. Need theories
2. Expectancy theory
3. Goal setting
4. Operant conditioning or reinforcement theory
5. Equity theory

SMALL GROUP BREAKOUT EXERCISE

Form groups of three or four, and appoint one member as the spokesperson who will communicate your findings to the whole class when called on by the instructor. Then discuss the following scenario:

Assume you are the manager of a small company that hired five employees, two of them at minimum wage. One of these employees, Khan, tends to slack off when you are not around to directly supervise his work. When you are around, he puts out more work effort to avoid being disciplined, but he just does not seem motivated. Jack is the company clown. He spends most of the day telling jokes and making the other employees laugh. Jack is almost always late for work. The last time he was late you reprimanded him in front of all the other staff, and Jack felt very uncomfortable but made a joke out of it anyway. Lately, Khan has been taking a lot of sick time. Something is not right.

1. What can you do to motivate high performance from Khan and Jack?
2. Identify the behaviours you would like to see Khan increase and Jack decrease.
3. Design a program using operant conditioning theory to:
   a. Increase the frequency of the functional behaviours you want the employees to exhibit, and
   b. Decrease the frequency of the undesirable behaviours.

MANAGING ETHICALLY EXERCISE

You are the new CEO of a pharmaceutical company that has a reputation for compensating managers well but not employees. Top and middle managers get a 15 percent across-the-board increase, while the employees receive a 4 percent increase annually. The justification is that managers take the risks, make the decisions, and figure out the strategies. But, in fact, for years the company has been using teams to make many of the most crucial decisions for the company. And everyone has input into strategic planning. Employees also have to work extra-long hours during the busiest seasons with no overtime pay. You find that employee morale is very low. While they seem motivated because they have a passion for the work, developing drugs to help cure major diseases, many are threatening to leave if they are not rewarded more fairly. What would you do?

MANAGEMENT CHALLENGE EXERCISE

Handing Over the Reins

Recently a former colleague at a company of 100 employees called you in. You know this company very well because you worked there for seven years before becoming a motivational consultant. It is a family-owned business. Your former colleague is the daughter of the founder, who is very reluctant to hand over the reins of management completely to his daughter. He knows he must, but he keeps saying that he needs that "little extra push"! Your former colleague believes that you have the "motivational key" for this transfer of power.

1. Using the motivational theories from this chapter, what theory or theories would you utilize to try to work this current challenge?

2. What motivational plan are you reasonably comfortable with that you can present to your former colleague?

MANAGEMENT PORTFOLIO PROJECT

Answer the following questions about the organization you have chosen to follow:

1. What evidence can you find on the types of motivation theories that are at work in this organization? For example, if it has an "employee of the month" award, what needs does this fulfill?

2. What kinds of things does the management do to increase the expectancy levels of employees? What about levels of instrumentality?

3. What practices does the management engage in to ensure there is a perception of equity within the organization? Do the outcomes appear to be distributed fairly?

MANAGEMENT CASE

TRAINER TO THE STARS HARLEY PASTERNAK ON KEEPING PEOPLE MOTIVATED[64]

"Real motivation comes from within. You either want to succeed or you don't."

Harley Pasternak, the personal trainer to some of Hollywood's biggest stars and a bestselling author on diet and fitness several times over shares his secrets to keeping people motivated, how to choose a partner for new business lines, and taking branding advice from Oprah.

You've trained some of the most famous people in the world—Halle Berry, Katy Perry, Robert Downey Jr., Kanye West. These are not people who are accustomed to taking orders.

Well, it helps that they come to me, so it's not a case of bossing anybody around. I'm not the kind of trainer who's showing up at someone's house and dragging them out of bed. Most of the people who come to my office are already highly motivated.

I would imagine working as a trainer is a bit like being a turnaround CEO, in that people come to you when they need to make a change. Do you have a standard "time to get real" spiel?

It's not really a spiel, so much as I want to find out about a person's behaviour. That's the way to make a change. I'm meeting with a very successful business person later today, one of the top chocolatiers. We'll go over movement habits, eating habits, sleeping habits. And then we'll talk about very simple, basic changes. People tend to get excited about the simplicity of what I ask them to do.

How do you motivate people?

I don't believe you can motivate another person in any sustainable way. Real, lasting motivation comes from within. There's extrinsic motivation: Maybe someone's paying you to do something or you have a job coming up. Part of the reason I enjoy working with the clients I work with is that they are more motivated than the average person. Most of us want to look and feel better, but if you're about to do a sex scene the whole world is going to see, you're probably more motivated than a school teacher.

So if we all signed on to film sex scenes, everyone would get fit?

Exactly! Really, if somebody doesn't show up for their workout, if they don't eat the right things, there's nothing I can say to make them do it—you either want to succeed or you don't.

You also work with corporate honcho types. What are the specific challenges there?

It mostly comes down to sitting. Business people tend to sit more. And then there are the business lunches, business dinners, business drinks. None of that is good.

What about the fact that the suit and tie crowd can't squeeze in midday yoga classes or what have you?

So move before work, move throughout the day. Walk to the water cooler or to a coffee shop that's a block or two away. Walk to get lunch. Just keep moving—there's always a way.

You are a huge supporter of the 10 000 steps revolution.

It just makes everything so simple. People have so many questions—which machine? what intensity? how often?—and that becomes off-putting. You just need to move as much as you can from the moment you wake up to the moment you go to bed.

How did you break into the world of celebrity training?

I was doing some local training for film people in Toronto when I got a call from someone who was producing the movie *Gothika* in Montreal. He said Halle Berry wanted to work with me, but they were only budgeted for a local trainer. I didn't even ask about the fee. I just packed up my car and went. Two weeks in, Halle asked if I would train her for *Catwoman* in California. It really blew up from there.

You later got a lesson in branding from Oprah?

Right. I developed my program while I was working as a scientist for the Canadian military. I called it multiple variation training. One day, I got a call from Halle. She said, I'm here with Oprah. She wants to talk to you. Oprah got on the phone and asked me what my program was called. I told her and she said, "No, it's not." It was after that conversation that I came up with the 5-Factor Diet.

Now you have snack bars, Xbox games, fitness equipment, running shoes. How do you decide which brand opportunities to pursue?

I have certain rules. I won't endorse weight-loss pills or quick fixes—anything that doesn't jell with my brand or my philosophy. Lately I have been trying to make all of my partnerships synergistic. So when I'm considering a new partner, I think about the other brands I am already working with: What would they think of this company? Would they feel comfortable having their product at the same event?

1. What are the challenges facing Harley Pasternak in motivating celebrities?

2. How would you characterize Pasternak's approach to motivation?

Source: Courtney Shea

Chapter 9

Managing Leadership

LEARNING OUTCOMES

LO1	Explain what leadership is and on what bases of power leaders influence others.
LO2	Describe the early trait and behavioural theories of leadership and their limitations.
LO3	Explain how contingency models of leadership enhance our understanding of effective leadership and management in organizations.
LO4	Compare and contrast visionary models of leadership.
LO5	Explain how gender, culture, and emotional intelligence affect leadership effectiveness.

OPENING CASE

How Can a Manager Foster Creativity in a Rapidly Changing Environment?

Red Hat Inc., the world's largest open-source software company, founded by Bob Young, the Canadian entrepreneur who owns the Hamilton Tiger-Cats, sealed a remarkable deal in 2018, when IBM bought it for the price of $34 billion U.S. dollars.[1]

Jim Whitehurst, president and CEO of Red Hat, Inc. recognizes the vital role that creativity plays in organizations in rapidly changing arenas like open-source software and acknowledges it as a big part of what made Red Hat such a covetable acquisition. As he puts it, "In today's workforce, creativity is a critical skill. I strive every day at Red Hat to be a catalyst with our associates to fuel and spark their creativity and not stifle it by simply telling people what to do."[2]

Red Hat, headquartered in Raleigh, North Carolina, fully embraces the open-source development model, which relies on global communities of contributors to develop, service, and improve software. Red Hat earns revenues through a variety of sources from its business and organizational customers. For example, software is provided via subscriptions (annual or multiyear) that include software support, new editions and updates of software, security upgrades, improvements and solutions to problems, advances in technology, functionality upgrades, and other services.[3]

Red Hat also offers paid technical support to help clients most effectively utilize software as well as keep up to date with latest developments and integrate software offerings with other applications. Consulting services are also offered by Red Hat. Thus, Red Hat provides its customers with the benefits of having a global community to develop and improve open-source software while at the same time providing expert software support and assistance to fully utilize the software to meet business needs while keeping current with the latest developments and improvements.[4]

Jim Whitehurst has been CEO and president of Red Hat for over 10 years. Prior to joining Red Hat, he was the chief operating officer for Delta Airlines.[5] Before joining Delta, he was a managing director at the Boston Consulting Group. He has a bachelor's degree from Rice University in economics and computer science and an MBA from the Harvard Business School.[6] Thus, his prior education and work experience have given him a broad base of expertise to draw upon in his leadership role at Red Hat.

At Red Hat, Whitehurst emphasizes that respect is earned by everyone (including top managers like himself) by what they do and how they contribute. In fact, Whitehurst believes that in order for leaders to be effective, they need to be respected by organizational members for their words and deeds and not just their titles. According to Whitehurst, three important means by which leaders like himself can gain the respect of organizational members is by being passionate about their mission and vision, being confident, and engaging other organizational members.[7] At Red Hat, Whitehurst is passionate about creatively developing better technology and software in an open-source manner involving communities of contributors, partners, and customers. Whitehurst is very competent and confident both in his own abilities and in the capabilities of teams at Red Hat. Whitehurst engages Red Hat employees by encouraging and supporting their creative ideas and perspectives and being inspirational, open, and honest. Mutual trust and respect are important to Whitehurst (and at Red Hat) as are honesty, integrity, and open communication.[8]

A strong believer in empowerment and trusting employees to do what they think is right, Whitehurst also thinks that leaders and all employees must feel accountable to each other. Whitehurst holds himself accountable to employees by his performance, by the ways in which he provides explanations for his decisions and for Red Hat's performance, and for his sincere apologies when things don't go as planned.[9] In fact, Whitehurst often asks employees for feedback before he makes decisions so as to make the best decisions possible. Whitehurst strives to create an environment in which employees will be creative, motivated, energetic, inspired, enthusiastic, and excited and use these sentiments to help Red Hat achieve its mission. Importantly, Whitehurst empowers employees and gives them the freedom to be creative in the ways in which they contribute to Red Hat's mission.[10]

Red Hat has performed well under Whitehurst's leadership. Thus, it's not surprising that he has received recognition for his accomplishments. For example, in April 2014, Whitehurst gave the keynote address at The Cloud Factory conference in Banff, Alberta.[11] The Cloud Factory is a major enterprise technology conference.[12] All in all, Whitehurst's approach to leadership has made Red Hat the centre of the largest tech deal ever.[13]

After reading and understanding the concepts in this chapter, you should be able to answer the following questions:

1. What makes Jim Whitehurst an effective leader?
2. Is Jim Whitehurst a transformational leader? Why, or why not?

 Overview

In the opening scenario, we see a vision of leadership that goes beyond simply the traditional model of leader–follower and looks at the value an inspiring leader can bring to an organization. In Chapter 1, we explained that one of the four principal tasks of managers is leading. Thus, it should come as no surprise that leadership is a key ingredient in effective management. When leaders are effective, their subordinates or followers are highly motivated, committed, and high-performing. When leaders are ineffective, chances are good that their subordinates do not perform up to their capabilities, are demotivated, and may be dissatisfied as well. Leadership is an important ingredient for managerial success at all levels of an organization: top management, middle management, and first-line management. Moreover, leadership is a key ingredient for managerial success for organizations large and small.

In this chapter, we describe what leadership is, how it is different from management, and the foundations of power that leaders use to influence others. We then examine the major leadership models that shed light on the factors that help make a manager an effective leader. See Figure 9.1. *Trait and behavioural models* focus on what leaders are like and what they do. *Contingency models*—Fiedler's contingency model, Hersey-Blanchard's situational leadership theory, path-goal theory, and the leader substitutes model—take into account the context in which leadership takes place and the role of the situation in leader effectiveness. The quest to do great things by inspiring employees to put forth extraordinary effort is what constitutes *visionary leadership* approaches. We describe how managers can have dramatic effects in their organizations by means of *transformational, charismatic,* and *turnaround* leadership. We also examine the relationship between gender and leadership, culture and leadership, and emotional intelligence and leadership. By the end of this chapter, you will have a good appreciation of the many factors and issues that managers face in their quest to be effective leaders.

FIGURE 9.1

Leadership Models

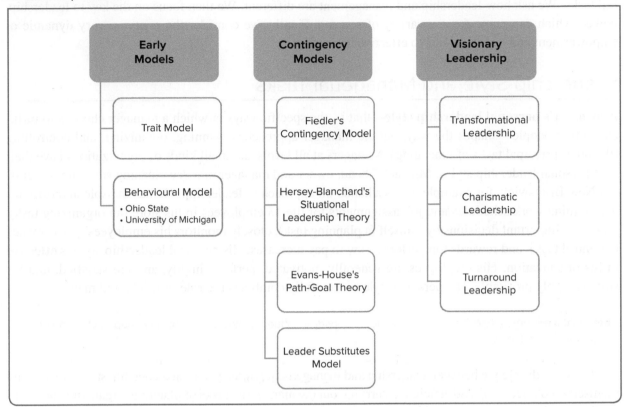

The Nature of Leadership

LO1 | Explain what leadership is and on what bases of power leaders influence others.

Leadership is the process by which a person exerts influence over other people and inspires, motivates, and directs their activities to help achieve group or organizational goals.[14] The person who exerts such influence is a **leader.** When leaders are effective, the influence they exert over others helps a group or organization achieve its performance goals. When leaders are ineffective, their influence does not contribute to, and often detracts from, goal attainment. As the opening case suggests, Jim Whitehurst is taking multiple steps to inspire and motivate his employees to help achieve the organization's mission.

leadership The process by which an individual exerts influence over other people and inspires, motivates, and directs their activities to help achieve group or organizational goals.

leader An individual who is able to exert influence over other people to help achieve group or organizational goals.

Beyond facilitating the attainment of performance goals, effective leadership increases an organization's ability to meet all the contemporary challenges discussed throughout this book, including the need to obtain a competitive advantage, the need to foster ethical behaviour, and the need to manage a diverse workforce fairly and equitably. Leaders who exert influence to help meet these goals increase their organization's chances of success.

In considering the nature of leadership, we first look at leadership styles and how they affect managerial tasks. We ask how leadership and management are different. We then focus on the key to leadership, power, which can come from a variety of sources. Finally, we consider the contemporary dynamic of empowerment and how it relates to effective leadership.

Leadership Style and Managerial Tasks

A manager's **personal leadership style**—that is, the specific ways in which a manager chooses to influence other people—shapes the way that the manager approaches planning, organizing, and controlling (the other principal tasks of managing). Managers at all levels and in all kinds of organizations have their own personal leadership styles. Michael Tibeau, owner and manager of a dry-cleaning store in northeastern New Brunswick, for example, takes a hands-on approach to leadership. He has the sole authority for determining work schedules and job assignments for the 15 employees in his store (an organizing task), makes all important decisions by himself (a planning task), closely monitors his employees' performance (a control task), and rewards top performers with pay increases. His personal leadership style is effective in his organization. His employees are generally motivated, perform highly, and are satisfied, and his store is highly profitable. His personal style successfully combines the role of leader and manager.

> **personal leadership style** The ways a manager chooses to influence others and how they approach planning, organizing, and controlling.

Is there a difference between leadership and management? Some personal leadership styles do not lend themselves to effectively and efficiently carrying out the managerial tasks of planning, organizing, and controlling. And so, we need to ask if there is a distinction between leaders and managers. Harvard Business School Professor John Kotter suggests that "managers promote stability, while leaders press for change and only organizations that embrace both sides of the contradiction can survive in turbulent times."[15] Professor Rabindra Kanungo of McGill University reports growing agreement "among management scholars that the concept of 'leadership' must be distinguished from the concept of 'supervision/management.'"[16] Leaders look to the big picture, providing vision and strategy. Managers are charged with implementing vision and strategy. They coordinate and staff the organization and handle day-to-day-transactions. Managers are appointed to their jobs and rely on the authority vested in the position to get employees to comply and conform to their directives. Leaders are not necessarily appointed and may emerge organically within a work group. Leaders influence others to follow their vision and ideas not because they are the boss, but rather for reasons that go beyond formal authority. While ideally all managers should be leaders, not all leaders can be successful at carrying out the four managerial functions effectively and efficiently.

Consider Jim Whitehurst's personal leadership style as described in the opening case. He empowers employees to be creative. He respects employees as much as other partners and collaborators and makes sure he models the values he wants them to follow. His style creates a highly motivated and successful staff. Although Whitehurst's approach is very different from that of Michael Tibeau, owner-manager of the New Brunswick dry cleaner, the two have been equally successful at combining leadership and management. As the Focus on the Social Economy feature illustrates, the ME to WE leadership training program helps youth learn the leadership skills that will make a difference in managing the lives of thousands worldwide.

Henry Mintzberg and other contemporary leadership theorists agree that no matter what one's leadership style, a key component of effective leadership is found in the *power* the leader uses to affect other people's behaviour and to get them to act in certain ways.[17]

Power: The Key to Leadership

R.P. French Jr. and B. Raven depict five types of managerial power: *legitimate, reward, coercive, expert,* and *referent* (see Figure 9.2)[18]

LEGITIMATE POWER

Legitimate power is the authority a manager has by virtue of his or her position in an organization's hierarchy. Personal leadership style often influences how a manager exercises legitimate power. Take the case of Carol Loray, who is a first-line manager in a greeting card company and leads a group of 15 artists and designers. Loray has the legitimate power to hire new employees, assign projects to the artists and designers, monitor their work, and appraise their performance. She uses this power effectively. She always makes sure that her project assignments match the interests of her subordinates as much as possible so that they will enjoy their work. She monitors their work to make sure they are on track but does not engage in close supervision, which can hamper creativity. She makes sure her performance appraisals are developmental, providing concrete advice for areas where improvements could be made. Recently, Loray negotiated with her manager to increase her legitimate power so that now she can initiate and develop proposals for new card lines.

> **legitimate power** The authority that a manager has by virtue of his or her position in an organization's hierarchy.

REWARD POWER

Reward power is the ability of a manager to give or withhold tangible rewards (pay raises, bonuses, choice job assignments) and intangible rewards (verbal praise, a pat on the back, respect). As you learned in Chapter 8, members of an organization are motivated to perform at a high level by a variety of rewards. Being able to give or withhold rewards based on performance is a major source of power

---

FIGURE 9.2

Sources of Managerial Power

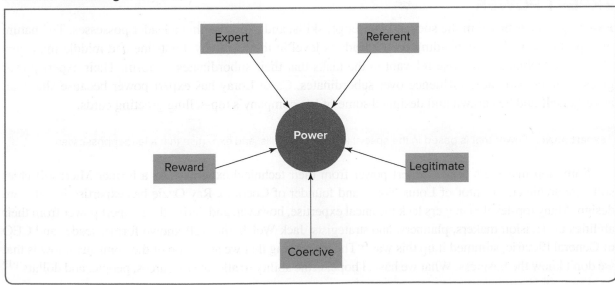

that allows managers to have a highly motivated workforce. Managers of salespeople in retail organizations like Harry Rosen and Best Buy, in car dealerships like General Motors and Ford, and in software development organizations like Red Hat (profiled in the opening case), often use their reward power to motivate their subordinates. Subordinates in organizations such as these often receive commissions on whatever they sell and rewards for the quality of their customer service, which motivates them to do the best they can. Effective managers use their reward power in such a way that subordinates feel that they are doing a good job and their efforts are appreciated.

> **reward power** The ability of a manager to give or withhold tangible and intangible rewards.

COERCIVE POWER

Coercive power is similar to reward power in that it can be used to manipulate the giving of rewards that are valued by others. It rests on the expectation of being punished if one doesn't conform to the influence of the leader. The power comes from the ability of a manager to persuade someone to do something that he or she otherwise would not. It includes the use of psychological and physical threats and actually perpetrating physical and mental harm. Sexual harassment is a form of coercive power. Other forms of power can be used in a coercive way. For example, reward power can be used to punish employees by withholding valuable outcomes like pay when the employee demonstrates undesirable behaviour such as frequent absenteeism. Referent power can become coercive if it is used to deceive people as happens in some religious cults. Managers who rely heavily on coercive power tend to be ineffective as leaders and sometimes even get fired themselves because at some threshold the threat of punishment ceases to encourage conformity.

> **coercive power** The ability to persuade someone to do something that he or she otherwise would not.

Excessive use of coercive power seldom produces high performance and is ethically questionable. Sometimes it amounts to a form of mental abuse, robbing workers of their dignity and causing excessive levels of stress. Overuse of coercive power can even result in dangerous working conditions. Better results and, importantly, an ethical workplace that respects employee dignity can be obtained by using reward power.

EXPERT POWER

Expert power is based in the special knowledge, skills, and expertise that a leader possesses. The nature of expert power varies depending on the leader's level in the hierarchy. First-line and middle managers often have technical expertise relevant to the tasks that their subordinates perform. Their expert power gives them considerable influence over subordinates. Carol Loray has expert power because she is an artist herself and has drawn and designed some of her company's top-selling greeting cards.

> **expert power** Power that is based in the special knowledge, skills, and expertise that a leader possesses.

Some top managers derive expert power from their technical expertise. As a former Microsoft chief software architect, inventor of Lotus Notes, and founder of Cocomo, Ray Ozzie has expertise in software design. Many top-level managers lack technical expertise, however, and derive their expert power from their abilities as decision makers, planners, and strategists. Jack Welch, the well-known former leader and CEO of General Electric, summed it up this way: "The basic thing that we at the top of the company know is that we don't know the business. What we have, I hope, is the ability to allocate resources, people, and dollars."[19]

Effective leaders take steps to ensure that they have an adequate amount of expert power to perform their leadership roles. They may obtain additional training or education in their fields, make sure they keep up to date with the latest developments and changes in technology, stay abreast of changes in their fields through involvement in professional associations, and read widely to be aware of momentous changes in the organization's task and general environments. Expert power tends to be best used in a guiding or coaching manner rather than in an arrogant, high-handed manner.

REFERENT POWER

Referent power is <u>more informal</u> than the other kinds of power. **Referent power** is a function of the personal characteristics of a leader. It is the power that comes from subordinates' and co-workers' respect, admiration, and loyalty. Leaders who are likeable and whom subordinates wish to use as a role model are especially likely to possess referent power. Jim Whitehurst shows us he has referent power in his decisions to empower employees.

> **referent power** Power that comes from subordinates' and co-workers' respect, admiration, and loyalty.

In addition to being a valuable asset for top managers, referent power can help first-line and middle managers be effective leaders. Sally Carruthers, for example, is the first-level manager of a group of office workers in the finance department of a large university. Carruthers's secretaries are known to be among the best in the university. Much of their willingness to go above and beyond the call of duty has been attributed to Carruthers's warm and caring nature, which makes each of them feel important and valued. Managers can take steps to increase their referent power, such as taking time to get to know their subordinates and showing interest in and concern for them. Referent power is the power that managers derive from the trust and commitment given to them by their colleagues because of who they are and how they are perceived by their followers. This is a precarious power source because if the respect and trust afforded to you falters, you <u>can easily lose</u> it, as is often the case with charismatic leaders in politics and religion.[20]

Early Models of Leadership

LO2	Describe the early trait and behavioural theories of leadership and their limitations.

Leading is such an important process in all organizations—nonprofit organizations, government agencies, and schools, as well as for-profit corporations—that it has been researched for decades. Early approaches to leadership, called the *trait model* and the *behavioural model*, sought to determine what effective leaders are like as people and what they do that makes them so effective.

Leadership theories developed before 1980 <u>focused on the supervisory nature of leadership</u>. Thus they were concerned with managing the day-to-day functions of employees. These theories took two different approaches to how supervision could be viewed: (1) Do leaders have traits different from non-leaders? If yes, then people with specific traits should be carefully selected for leadership positions; (2) Should leaders engage in particular behaviours? If yes, this implies that leadership behaviours and skills can be learned and that leaders are not born but are made. We briefly examine these approaches below.

The Trait Model

The trait model of leadership focused on identifying the personal characteristics that are responsible for effective leadership. Researchers thought effective leaders <u>must have certain personal qualities</u> that set them apart from ineffective leaders and from people who never become leaders. Decades of research (beginning in the 1930s) and hundreds of studies indicate that certain personal characteristics do appear to be associated with effective leadership (see Table 9.1 for a list of these).[21] Notice that although this model is called the "trait" model, some of the personal characteristics that it identifies are not personality traits per se; rather, they are concerned with a leader's skills, abilities, knowledge, and expertise. Leaders who do not possess these traits may be ineffective, but a person who does possess many of the traits on the list may not be an effective leader.

Some effective leaders do not possess all of these traits, and some leaders who do possess them are not effective in their leadership roles. This lack of a consistent relationship between leader traits and leader effectiveness led researchers to search for new explanations for effective leadership. <u>Traits alone are not the key to understanding leader effectiveness</u>. Rather than focusing on what leaders are like (the traits they possess), researchers began to turn their attention to what effective leaders actually do—in other words, to the behaviours that allow effective leaders to influence their subordinates to achieve group and organizational goals.

The Behavioural Model

A variety of behavioural models of leadership exist, including the Ohio State University Studies[22] and the University of Michigan Studies.[23] These models attempted to identify the dimensions of leader behaviour. The Ohio State studies identified two basic kinds of leader behaviours used to influence subordinates, *consideration behaviours* and *initiating structure*.

TABLE 9.1

Traits and Personal Characteristics Related to Effective Leadership

Trait	Description
Intelligence	Helps managers understand complex issues and solve problems
Knowledge and expertise	Help managers make good decisions and discover ways to increase efficiency and effectiveness
Dominance	Helps managers influence their subordinates to achieve organizational goals
Self-confidence	Contributes to managers' effectively influencing subordinates and persisting when faced with obstacles or difficulties
High energy	Helps managers deal with the many demands they face
Tolerance for stress	Helps managers deal with uncertainty and make difficult decisions
Integrity and honesty	Help managers behave ethically and earn their subordinates' trust and confidence
Maturity	Helps managers avoid acting selfishly, control their feelings, and admit when they have made a mistake

Leaders engage in **consideration** when they show subordinates that they trust, respect, and care about them. This behavioural leadership modelling is borne out with enthusiastic employees.[24] According to the company Sirota, survey intelligence specialists in attitude research, employees start out with a company feeling enthusiastic. What eventually gets in the way is management!

consideration Behaviour indicating that a manager trusts, respects, and cares about subordinates.

"In today's workforce, creativity is a critical skill. I strive every day at Red Hat to be a catalyst with our associates to fuel and spark their creativity and not stifle it by simply telling people what to do."

Jim Whitehurst, President and CEO, Red Hat Inc.

Managers who truly look out for the well-being of their subordinates and who do what they can to help subordinates feel good and enjoy their work are performing consideration behaviours. With the increasing focus on the importance of high-quality customer service, many managers are realizing that when they are considerate to subordinates, subordinates are more likely to be considerate to customers and vice versa. In the opening case, Jim Whitehurst engages in consideration when he fosters a culture based on trust and respect.

Leaders engage in **initiating structure** when they attempt to define and structure their role and the roles of their subordinates in order to achieve organizational goals. They focus on the goal or outcome rather than the process by taking steps to make sure that work gets done, subordinates perform their jobs acceptably, and the organization is efficient and effective. Assigning tasks to individuals or work groups, letting subordinates know what is expected of them, deciding how work should be done, making schedules, encouraging adherence to rules and regulations, and motivating subordinates to do a good job are all examples of initiating structure.[25] Michael Teckel, the manager of an upscale store selling imported men's and women's shoes in Winnipeg, engages in initiating structure when he establishes weekly work, lunch, and break schedules to ensure that the store has enough salespeople on the floor. Teckel also initiates structure when he discusses the latest shoe designs with his subordinates so that they are knowledgeable with customers, when he encourages adherence to the store's refund and exchange policies, and when he encourages his staff to provide high-quality customer service and to avoid a hard-sell approach.

initiating structure Behaviours that managers engage in to define and structure their role and the roles of their subordinates in order to achieve organizational goals.

The University of Michigan studies also found two main behavioural dimensions in effective leaders: *employee-centred leaders* and *production-oriented* leaders. Similar to *consideration,* **employee-centred leaders** placed a strong emphasis on the well-being of employees and interpersonal relations. They took a personal interest and demonstrated that they cared about subordinates. **Production-oriented leaders** placed a strong emphasis on task-related and goal-achievement behaviours, including technical aspects of the job. In this way, it is similar to the Ohio State notion of initiating structure. The two dimensions appear to be polar opposites, one being relationship-oriented and the other being task-oriented. Each set of studies strived to determine which leader behaviour was demonstrated by effective leaders.

employee-centred leaders Leaders who place a strong emphasis on the well-being of employees and interpersonal relations.

production-oriented leaders Leaders who place a strong emphasis on task-related and goal-achievement behaviours.

You might expect that effective leaders and managers would perform both kinds of behaviours, but research has found that this is not necessarily the case. The relationship between consideration/employee-centred leaders and initiating-structure/production-oriented behaviours and leader effectiveness is not clear-cut. Some leaders are effective even when they do not perform people and task behaviours, and some leaders are ineffective even when they do perform both kinds of behaviours. Leaders with more focus on interpersonal skills and concern for the well-being of employees tend to have followers that are more satisfied, motivated, and have more respect for their leaders. Leaders with more focus on task behaviours have higher performance evaluations and gain higher levels of productivity from groups and teams. Like the trait model of leadership, the behaviour model alone cannot explain leader effectiveness.

Just as the behavioural theories emerged as a critique of trait theory—by saying it is not the characteristics of the leader that matter but what they do—so too were the behavioural models criticized for assuming one style of leadership behaviours were appropriate in all situations. Realizing this, researchers began building more complicated models of leadership that focused not only on the leader's traits and behaviours but also on the situation or context in which leadership occurs. In the evolution of leadership theory, this led to the development of *contingency models of leadership*.

Contingency Models of Leadership

LO3 Explain how contingency models of leadership enhance our understanding of effective leadership and management in organizations.

Simply possessing certain traits or performing certain behaviours does not ensure that a manager will be an effective leader in all situations calling for leadership. Some managers who seem to possess the "right" traits and perform the "right" behaviours turn out to be ineffective leaders. Managers lead in a wide variety of situations and organizations and have various kinds of subordinates performing diverse tasks in many environmental contexts. Given the wide variety of situations in which leadership occurs, what makes a manager an effective leader in one situation (such as certain traits or certain behaviours) is not necessarily what that manager needs in order to be equally effective in a different situation. An effective army general might not be an effective university president, an effective manager of a restaurant might not be an effective manager of a clothing store, an effective coach of a hockey team might not be an effective manager of a fitness centre, and an effective first-line manager in a manufacturing company might not be an effective middle manager. The traits or behaviours that may contribute to a manager being an effective leader in one situation might actually result in the same manager being an ineffective leader in another situation.

Contingency models of leadership take into account the situation or context within which leadership occurs. So, for instance, while behavioural theories asked whether managers should be more employee-centred or more task-centred, contingency theories answer like this: It depends (or is contingent) on the situation. According to contingency models, whether or not a manager is an effective leader is the result of the interplay between what the manager is like, what he or she does, and the situation in which leadership takes place. In this section, we discuss

Leaders need to adapt to situational factors.
©Mawerix | Dreamstime.com

four prominent contingency models that shed light on what makes managers effective leaders: Fiedler's contingency model, Hersey-Blanchard's situational leadership theory, Evans-House's path-goal theory, and the leader substitutes model. As you will see, these leadership models are complementary. Each focuses on a somewhat different aspect of effective leadership in organizations.

contingency models of leadership Models of leadership that take into account the variables in the situation or context in which leadership occurs.

Fiedler's Contingency Model

Fred E. Fiedler was among the first leadership researchers to acknowledge that effective leadership depends on the characteristics of the leader *and* of the situation. Fiedler's contingency model helps explain why a manager may be an effective leader in one situation and ineffective in another; it also suggests which kinds of managers are likely to be most effective in which situations.[26]

As with the trait approach, Fiedler hypothesized that personal characteristics can influence leader effectiveness. He used the term *leader style* to refer to a manager's characteristic approach to leadership and identified two basic leader styles similar to the behavioural models: relationship-oriented and task-oriented. According to Fiedler, all managers can be described as having one style or the other.

Relationship-oriented leaders are mainly concerned with developing good relationships with their subordinates and being liked by them. Relationship-oriented managers focus on having high-quality interpersonal relationships with subordinates. This does not mean, however, that the job does not get done when such leaders are at the helm. It does mean that the quality of interpersonal relationships with subordinates is a prime concern for relationship-oriented leaders. *Task-oriented leaders* are mainly concerned with ensuring that subordinates perform at a high level. Task-oriented managers focus on task accomplishment and making sure the job gets done.

According to Fiedler, leadership style is an enduring characteristic; managers cannot change their style, nor can they adopt different styles in different kinds of situations. With this in mind, Fiedler identified three *situational characteristics* that are important determinants of how favourable a situation is for leading given the leader's style. See Figure 9.3.

- **Leader–member relations:** The extent to which followers like, trust, and are loyal to their leader. Situations are more favourable for leading when leader–member relations are good.

leader–member relations The extent to which followers like, trust, and are loyal to their leader; can be good or poor.

FIGURE 9.3

Three Situational Characteristics and Favourability for Leading

Threat	Outcome
Leader–member relations	Favourable when good
Task structure	Favourable when high
Position power	Favourable when strong

- **Task structure:** The extent to which the work to be performed is clear-cut so that a leader's subordinates know what needs to be accomplished and how to go about doing it. When task structure is high, situations are favourable for leading. When task structure is low, goals may be vague, subordinates may be unsure of what they should be doing or how they should do it, and the situation is unfavourable for leading.

> **task structure** The extent to which the work to be performed is clear-cut so that a leader's subordinates know what needs to be accomplished and how to go about doing it; can be high or low.

- **Position power:** The amount of legitimate, reward, and coercive powers a leader has by virtue of his or her position in an organization. Leadership situations are more favourable for leading when position power is strong.

> **position power** The amount of legitimate, reward, and coercive power that a leader has by virtue of his or her position in an organization; can be strong or weak.

He further determined in which situations a relationship-oriented leader and a task-oriented leader were most effective. When a situation is favourable for leading, it is relatively easy for a manager to influence subordinates so that they perform at a high level and contribute to organizational efficiency and effectiveness. Therefore, it makes the most sense to be task-oriented because the relationship is already going well. In a situation unfavourable for leading, it is much more difficult for a manager to exert influence. This makes being task-oriented the most desirable behaviour for the leader because of their command and control style. In situations that are only moderately favourable because of the combination of the three situational characteristics, a relationship-oriented leader is more successful because they can support the subordinates through uncertainty. By taking all possible combinations of good and poor leader–member relations, high and low task structure, and strong and weak position power, Fiedler identified eight leadership situations, which vary in their favourability for leading for both styles of leaders. See Figure 9.4. After extensive research, Fiedler determined that relationship-oriented leaders are most effective in moderately favourable situations (IV, V, VI, and VII in Figure 9.4), and task-oriented leaders are most effective in very favourable situations (I, II, and III) or very unfavourable situations (VIII).

FIGURE 9.4

Fiedler's Contingency Theory of Leadership

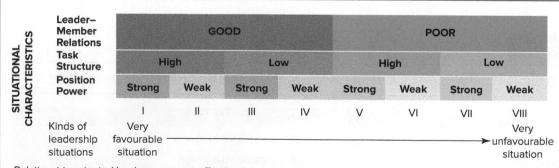

Relationship-oriented leaders are most effective in moderately favourable situations for leading (IV, V, VI, VII).
Task-oriented leaders are most effective in very favourable situations (I, II, III) or very unfavourable situations (VIII) for leading.

According to Fiedler, individuals cannot change their leadership style. Therefore, managers need to be placed in leadership situations that fit their style, or situations need to be changed to suit the manager. Situations can be changed—for example, by giving a manager more position power or by taking steps to increase task structure such as by clarifying goals. Take the case of Mark Compton, a relationship-oriented leader employed by a small construction company, who was in a very unfavourable situation and having a rough time leading his construction crew. His subordinates did not trust him to look out for their well-being (poor leader–member relations); the construction jobs he supervised tended to be novel and complex (low task structure); and he had no control over the rewards and disciplinary actions his subordinates received (weak position power). Recognizing the need to improve matters, Compton's supervisor gave him the power to reward crew members with bonuses and overtime work as he saw fit and to discipline crew members for poor-quality work and unsafe on-the-job behaviour. As his leadership situation improved to moderately favourable, so too did Compton's effectiveness as a leader and the performance of his crew.

Research studies tend to support some aspects of Fiedler's model but also suggest that, like most theories, it needs some modifications.[27] Some researchers also find fault with the model's premise that leaders cannot alter their styles. That is, it is likely that at least some leaders can diagnose the situation they are in and, when their style is inappropriate for the situation, modify their style so that it is more in line with what the leadership situation calls for.

Hersey-Blanchard's Situational Leadership Theory

Paul Hersey and Ken Blanchard's **situational leadership theory (SL)**[28] has been incorporated into leadership training programs at numerous Fortune 500 companies. More than a million managers a year are taught its basic elements.[29]

situational leadership theory (SL) A contingency model of leadership that focuses on the followers' readiness.

SL compares the leader–follower relationship to that between a parent and a child. Just as parents need to give more control to a child as the child becomes more mature and responsible, so too should leaders do this with employees. Hersey and Blanchard identify four specific leadership behaviours that managers can use to lead their employees: telling, selling, participating, and delegating. The styles vary in their degree of task-oriented behaviour and relationship-oriented behaviour. The appropriate style depends on the follower's ability and motivation:

- *Telling.* If a follower is *unable* and *unwilling* to do a task, the leader needs to give clear and specific directions (in other words, the leader needs to be highly directive).

- *Selling.* If a follower is *unable* but *willing*, the leader needs to display both high task orientation and high relationship orientation. The high task orientation will compensate for the follower's lack of ability. The high relationship orientation will encourage the follower to "buy into" the leader's desires (in other words, the leader needs to "sell" the task).

- *Participating.* If the follower is *able* but *unwilling*, the leader needs to use a supportive and participative style.

- *Delegating.* If the employee is both *able* and *willing*, the leader does not need to do much (in other words, a laissez-faire approach will work).

Figure 9.5 illustrates the relationship of leader behaviours to follower readiness.

FIGURE 9.5

Hersey-Blanchard's Situational Leadership Styles

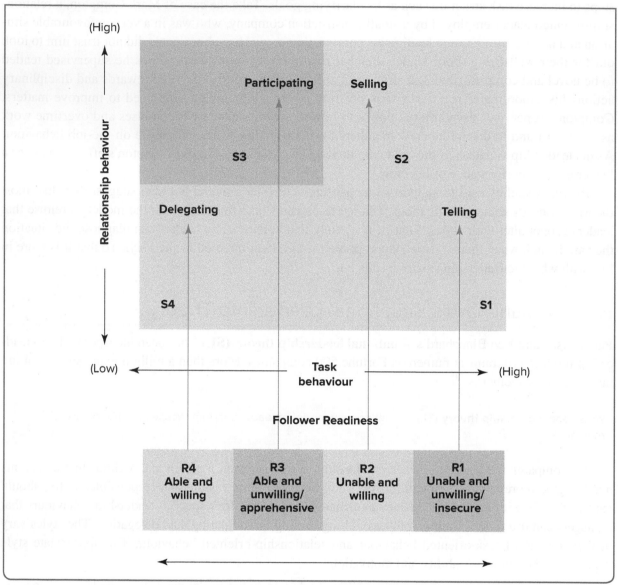

Path-Goal Theory

Developed by Rotman School of Management professor Martin Evans in the late 1960s, and then expanded on by Robert House, **path-goal theory** focuses on what leaders can do to motivate their subordinates to reach group and organizational goals.[30] The premise of path-goal theory is that effective leaders motivate subordinates to achieve goals by (1) clearly identifying the outcomes that subordinates are trying to obtain from the workplace, (2) rewarding subordinates with these outcomes for high performance and the attainment of work goals, and (3) clarifying for subordinates the *paths* leading to the attainment of work *goals*. Path-goal theory is a contingency model because it proposes that the steps that managers should take to motivate subordinates depend on both the nature of the subordinates and the type of work they do.

path-goal theory A contingency model of leadership proposing that leaders can motivate subordinates by helping them find the right path to achieve personal and organizational goals.

Based on the expectancy theory of motivation (see Chapter 8), path-goal theory provides managers with three guidelines to follow to be effective leaders:

1. *Find out what outcomes your subordinates are trying to obtain from their jobs and the organization.* These outcomes can range from satisfactory pay and job security to reasonable working hours and interesting and challenging job assignments. After identifying what these outcomes are, the manager should make sure that he or she has the reward power needed to distribute or withhold them.

2. *Reward subordinates for high performance and goal attainment with the outcomes they desire.*

3. *Clarify the paths to goal attainment for subordinates, remove any obstacles to high performance, and express confidence in subordinates' capabilities.* This does not mean that a manager needs to tell his or her subordinates what to do. Rather, it means that a manager needs to make sure that subordinates are clear about what they should be trying to accomplish and have the capabilities, resources, and confidence levels they need to be successful.

Path-goal theory identifies <u>four kinds</u> of <u>behaviours</u> that leaders can use to motivate subordinates:

- *Directive behaviours* include setting goals, assigning tasks, showing subordinates how to complete tasks, and taking concrete steps to improve performance.

- *Supportive behaviours* include expressing concern for subordinates and looking out for their best interests.

- *Participative behaviours* give subordinates a say in matters and decisions that affect them.

- *Achievement-oriented behaviours* motivate subordinates to perform at the highest level possible by, for example, setting very challenging goals, expecting that they be met, and believing in subordinates' capabilities.

Which of these behaviours should managers use to lead effectively? The answer to this question depends, or is contingent, on the nature of the subordinates and the kind of work they do.

Directive behaviours may be beneficial when subordinates are having difficulty completing assigned tasks, but they might

Direct supervision is helpful when subordinates are first learning a task.
Echo/Getty Images

be detrimental when subordinates are independent thinkers who work best when left alone. *Supportive* behaviours are often advisable when subordinates are experiencing high levels of stress. *Participative* behaviours can be particularly effective when subordinates' support of a decision is required. *Achievement-oriented* behaviours may increase motivation levels of highly capable subordinates who are bored from having too few challenges, but they might backfire if used with subordinates who are already pushed to their limits. Effective managers seem to have a knack for determining the kinds of leader behaviours that are likely to work in different situations and result in increased efficiency and effectiveness.

To illustrate the importance of understanding that situations are different, and can require different styles, consider the fate of some of the Americans who have been recruited to run Canadian companies. Retailer Millard Barron was brought north to turn Zellers around, and American Bill Fields was supposed to save Hudson's Bay Co. Neither could replicate their U.S. successes in Canada. Texas oilman J. P. Bryan was given the chance to restore profitability at two Canadian companies—Gulf Canada Resources Limited (now ConocoPhillips Co.) and Canadian 88 Energy Corp. (now Esprit Exploration Ltd.)—and failed at both attempts.[31] Chief operating officer Gary Daichendt and chief technology officer Gary Kunis walked away from Nortel Corp. over management differences or "divergent management styles and different views of the future of the business" with then-CEO Bill Owens. These examples show the importance of understanding that one's leadership style may need to be adjusted for different companies, for different employees, and perhaps even for different countries.

The Leader Substitutes Model

The leader substitutes model suggests that leadership is sometimes unnecessary because substitutes for leadership are present. A **leader substitute** is something that acts in place of the influence of a leader and makes leadership unnecessary. This model suggests that under certain conditions managers do not have to play a leadership role—that members of an organization sometimes can perform highly without a manager exerting influence over them.[32] The leader substitutes model is a contingency model because it suggests that in some situations leadership is unnecessary. Take the case of David Cotsonas, a young graduate who teaches English at a foreign-language school in Cyprus, an island in the Mediterranean Sea. Cotsonas is fluent in Greek, English, and French, is an excellent teacher, and is highly motivated. Many of his students are businesspeople who have some rudimentary English skills and wish to increase their fluency to be able to conduct more of their business in English. He enjoys not only teaching them English but also learning about the work they do, and he often keeps in touch with his students after they finish his classes. Cotsonas meets with the director of the school twice a year to discuss semiannual class schedules and enrollments.

leader substitute Characteristics of subordinates or characteristics of a situation or context that act in place of the influence of a leader and make leadership unnecessary.

With practically no influence from a leader, Cotsonas is a highly motivated top performer at the school. In his situation, leadership is unnecessary because substitutes for leadership are present. Cotsonas's teaching expertise, his motivation, and his enjoyment of his work all are substitutes for the influence of a leader—in this case, the school's director. If the school's director were to try to exert influence over the way Cotsonas goes about performing his job, Cotsonas would probably resent this infringement on his autonomy, and it is unlikely that his performance would improve because he is already one of the school's best teachers.

As in Cotsonas's case, both the *characteristics of subordinates*—such as their skills, abilities, experience, knowledge, and motivation—and the *characteristics of the situation or context*—such as the extent to which the work is interesting and enjoyable—can be substitutes for leadership.[33] When work is interesting and enjoyable, as it is for Cotsonas, job holders do not need to be coaxed into performing because performing is rewarding in its own right. Similarly, when managers empower their subordinates or use *self-managed work teams* (discussed in detail in Chapter 10), the need for leadership influence from a manager is decreased because team members manage themselves.

TIPS FOR MANAGERS

Applying Contingency Models of Leadership

1. When two individuals are engaged in conflict and take a competing stance, they tend to be highly assertive and unmotivated to find a solution to the problem. In this case, apply the Hersey-Blanchard SL's *participating* style of leadership to encourage the parties to find a solution they can live with.

2. Increases in absenteeism and being late for work may be indications that the employee is burning out. Use positive reinforcement (Chapter 8) and *supportive* leader behaviours to reduce the lower level of performance.

3. Cultivate an inclusive culture with a highly skilled and highly motivated workforce so that employees can work in self-managed teams effectively. This will free up your time to develop and communicate a vision that inspires others to achieve the organization's goals.

Substitutes for leadership can increase organizational efficiency and effectiveness because they free up some of managers' valuable time and allow managers to focus their efforts on discovering new ways to improve organizational effectiveness. The director of the language school, for example, was able to spend much of his time making arrangements to open a second school in Rhodes, an island in the Aegean Sea, because of the presence of leadership substitutes, not only in the case of Cotsonas but in that of most of the other teachers at the school as well.

Summary of Contingency Theories of Leadership

Effective leadership in organizations occurs when managers take steps to lead in a way that is appropriate for the situation or context in which leadership occurs and the subordinates who are being led. The four contingency models of leadership just discussed help managers identify the necessary ingredients for effective leadership. They are complementary in that each one looks at the leadership question from a different angle. Fiedler's contingency model explores how, for maximum effectiveness, a manager's leadership style needs to be matched to the leadership situation that the manager is in. Hersey-Blanchard's situational leadership theory examines the need for leaders to adjust their style to match their followers' ability and motivation. Evans-House's path-goal theory focuses on how managers should motivate subordinates and describes the specific kinds of behaviours that managers can engage in to have a highly motivated workforce. The leadership substitutes model alerts managers to the fact that sometimes they do not need to exert influence over subordinates and thus can free up their time for other important activities. Table 9.2 recaps these four contingency models of leadership.

TABLE 9.2

Contingency Models of Leadership

Model	Focus	Key Contingencies
Fiedler's contingency model	Describes two leader styles, relationship-oriented and task-oriented, and the kinds of situations in which each kind of leader will be most effective	The favourableness for leading depends on three contingency factors: leader–member relations, task-structure, and position power.
Hersey-Blanchard's situational leadership theory	Describes how leaders adjust their styles to match their followers' ability and motivation	The styles that managers should use are contingent on the ability and motivation of subordinates
House's path-goal theory	Describes how effective leaders motivate their followers	The behaviours that managers should engage in to be effective leaders are contingent on the nature of the subordinates and the work they do
Leader substitutes model	Describes when leadership is unnecessary	Whether or not leadership is necessary for subordinates to perform highly is contingent on characteristics of the subordinates and the situation

Visionary Models of Leadership

LO4 | Compare and contrast visionary models of leadership.

The leadership theories that focus on traits, behaviours, and context do a poor job at discussing the importance of motivation to effective leadership. What kind of leader can motivate employees to put forth good work effort and develop their potential? Recall from Chapter 8 that employee motivation comes from satisfying unmet needs, seeing a clear link between effort and performance, transparency and equity in the distribution of rewards, and challenging goals to pursue. Nothing captures the motivating potential of employees better than leaders who espouse a strong, compelling vision for the organization. Think of Steve Jobs of Apple and Jack Welch of General Electric; these men were visionary leaders. Hierarchical organizations still dominate Canada's "Most Admired Corporations,"[34] but many organizations are becoming more innovative, faster moving, and more responsive to customer and employee needs. These organizations have turned to a different style of leadership where leaders and managers not only are expected to perform supervisory tasks but also need to focus on vision-setting activities.

In this section, we look at *transformational* leadership, *charismatic* leadership, and leaders who manage to change the fortunes of struggling companies, known as *turnaround* leadership. These theories try to explain how certain leaders can achieve extraordinary performance from their followers, and they emphasize symbolic and emotionally appealing leadership behaviours.[35]

Transformational Leadership

Transformational leadership is often contrasted with transactional leadership. **Transactional leadership** occurs when managers guide or motivate their subordinates in the direction of established goals. Transactional leaders use rewards to recognize appropriate behaviour. Under this kind of leadership, employees will generally meet performance expectations, though rarely will they exceed expectations.[36] When managers reward high performers, reprimand or otherwise punish low performers, and motivate subordinates by reinforcing desired behaviours and extinguishing or punishing undesired ones, they are engaging in transactional leadership. Simply getting subordinates to perform their jobs adequately is the essence of transactional leadership. Most of the theories discussed in this chapter are transactional approaches to leadership. This style has been criticized for discouraging innovation and initiative in the workplace.[37]

transactional leadership Leaders who guide their subordinates toward expected goals by rewarding them for high performance and reprimanding them for low performance, with no expectation of exceeding expected behaviour.

When managers have dramatic effects on their subordinates and on an organization as a whole, they are engaging in transformational leadership. **Transformational leadership:**

- provides a compelling vision and sense of mission in subordinates that instills pride and trust.
- inspires subordinates to exceed standards by setting high expectations.
- stimulates the intelligence of subordinates through empowerment and problem solving.
- shows developmental consideration for the personal growth needs of subordinates.

transformational leadership Leadership that makes subordinates aware of the importance of their jobs and performance to the organization and aware of their own needs for personal growth, and that motivates subordinates to work for the good of the organization.

When leaders engage in these four activities, they change (or transform) their subordinates in three important ways[38]:

1. Subordinates have increased awareness of the importance of their jobs and high performance to the organization as a whole.
2. Subordinates are made aware of their own needs for growth, development, and accomplishment.
3. Subordinates work for the good of the organization as a whole, not just for their own personal gain or benefit.

Transformational managers openly share information with their subordinates so that subordinates are aware of problems and the need for change. The transformational manager enables subordinates to view problems in their groups and throughout the organization from different perspectives, and ultimately from the perspective that is consistent with their inspiring vision. In many organizations, subordinates may not be aware of many of upper management's organizational problems or may view them as a solely a "management issue" beyond their concern. Some may view such problems as insurmountable. The transformational manager's **intellectual stimulation** leads subordinates to view organizational problems as challenges that they can meet and conquer. The manager engages and empowers subordinates to take personal responsibility for helping to solve organizational problems.[39] For example, unlike other companies that often ask a team for an idea or to solve a problem and then tell them how much money they have to do it, Cirque du Soleil's founder, Guy Laliberté, instead would decide how much could be spent on a new show and then "expect the creative team to come up with their vision within its financial boundaries."[40]

intellectual stimulation Behaviour a leader engages in to make followers aware of problems and view these problems in new ways, consistent with the leader's vision.

When a manager engages in **developmental consideration**, he or she not only performs the consideration behaviours described earlier, such as demonstrating true concern for the well-being of subordinates, but also goes one step further. The transformational manager goes out of his or her way to support and encourage subordinates, giving them opportunities to enhance their skills and capabilities and to grow and excel in their jobs.[41]

developmental consideration Behaviour a leader engages in to support and encourage followers and help them develop and grow in the job.

The evidence supporting the superiority of transformational leadership is overwhelmingly impressive. For example, studies of Canadian, American, and German military officers found, at every level, that transformational leaders were considered more effective than their transactional counterparts.[42] When at the University of Western Ontario, professor Jane Howell and her colleagues studied 250 executives and managers at a major financial services company and found that "transformational leaders had 34 percent higher business unit performance results than other types of leaders."[43] Studies also find that when leaders engage in transformational leadership, their subordinates tend to have higher levels of job satisfaction and performance.[44] Additionally, subordinates of transformational leaders may be more likely to trust their leaders and their organizations and feel that they are being fairly treated, which in turn may positively influence their work motivation (see Chapter 8).[45]

Transformational leaders enhance transactional leadership. They reward subordinates for a job well done and notice and respond to substandard performance. But they also have their eyes on the bigger picture of how much better things could be in their organizations, how much more their subordinates are capable of achieving, and how important it is to treat their subordinates with respect and to help them reach their full potential. See Table 9.3 for a comparison of transactional and transformational leaders.

TABLE 9.3

Transactional versus Transformational Leadership

Transactional Leadership	Transformational Leadership
Managers guide and motivate subordinates to achieve organizational goals through conventional methods such as direct supervision.	Managers produce dramatic effects for the organization's performance by inspiring subordinates to go above and beyond stated goals by modelling desired behaviours.
The status quo daily activities of planning, leading, organizing, and controlling are carried out effectively and efficiently.	Manager's vision goes beyond the status quo, entailing changes in the organization's structure, culture, strategy, decision making, and other critical variables for gaining a competitive advantage.
Subordinates meet performance expectations but rarely exceed them.	Subordinates perform at levels exceeding expectations.
Formal rules, regulations, and the fear of punishment discourage risk taking and innovation.	Managers show excitement and enthusiasm, trust and respect, and concern for subordinates' growth and development, and encourage risk taking and initiative.
Managers rely on legitimate and reward power to exercise authority and recognize high and low levels of performance.	Managers are charismatic, possess referent power, intellectually stimulate subordinates and engage in developmental consideration to foster high performance.
The model is effective and efficient in a stable organizational environment.	The model is effective in an unstable, dynamic environment where a change in the organization's course is desired or necessary to gain a competitive advantage.

From ME to WE Leadership

Craig Kielburger was moved to do something about child slave labour in 1995 when he was just 12 years old. After reading an article about a child his same age who was sold into slavery and spent six years chained to a carpet weaving loom, Kielburger and a few school friends started a charity in Canada called Free the Children. Free the Children's mission is to end child poverty and exploitation through education and training for social change. Free the Children, now WE Charity, is the largest network of children helping children in the world, with over one million youth in 45 countries participating in the movement.

One of the social enterprises used to fund the charitable work of WE Charity is called ME to WE. ME to WE leadership courses and camps provide youth with hands-on training in leading for social change. Youth facilitators teach young people about making environmentally sustainable decisions at home and abroad. Volunteer travel excursions to communities in which WE Charity is building schools and so on give youth the chance to use leadership skills to help change the world. The leadership programs at ME to WE create life-altering experiences for youth who want to make a difference.

1. Go to the ME to WE website. Does the leadership training offered at ME to WE support or refute the behavioural models of leadership? Why?

2. In what ways does the leadership training at ME to WE provide youth with transformational versus transactional skills?

Source: http://www.metowe.com/charity. Accessed June 9, 2012.

Charismatic Leadership

Transformational managers tend to be *charismatic leaders*. **Charismatic leaders** have a vision of how their work groups and organizations should operate in contrast with the status quo. Their vision usually entails dramatic improvements in group and organizational performance as a result of changes in the organization's structure, culture, strategy, decision making, and other critical processes and factors. This vision paves the way for gaining a competitive advantage.

charismatic leaders Enthusiastic, self-confident leaders who are able to communicate clearly their vision of how good things could be.

Charismatic leaders are excited and enthusiastic about their vision and clearly communicate it to their subordinates. The excitement, enthusiasm, and self-confidence of a charismatic leader contribute to the leader's being able to inspire followers to enthusiastically support his or her vision.[46] People often think of charismatic leaders or managers as being "larger than life." Past Prime Minister of Canada Pierre Elliott Trudeau was a charismatic political leader, and his son Justin Trudeau also exhibits the charismatic tendency to go against the status quo. The vision such leaders espouse makes them seem like gurus to their followers. They have a vision and enthusiastically communicate it to others.

The most comprehensive analysis of charismatic leadership was conducted by professor Rabindra Kanungo at McGill University, together with Jay Conger.[47] Based on studies of managers from Canada, the United States, and India, they identified five dimensions that characterize charismatic leadership. These are shown in Table 9.4.

TABLE 9.4

Key Characteristics of a Charismatic Leader

1. *Vision and articulation.* Has a vision—expressed as an idealized goal—that proposes a future better than the status quo; is able to clarify the importance of the vision in terms that are understandable to others.
2. *Personal risk.* Willing to take on high personal risk, incur high costs, and engage in self-sacrifice to achieve the vision.
3. *Environmental sensitivity.* Able to make realistic assessments of the environmental constraints and resources needed to bring about change.
4. *Sensitivity to follower needs.* Perceptive of others' abilities and responsive to their needs and feelings.
5. *Unconventional behaviour.* Engages in behaviours that are perceived as novel and counter to norms.

Source: Adapted from J.A. Conger and R.N. Kanungo, *Charismatic Leadership in Organizations* (Thousand Oaks, CA: Sage, 1998), Table 3.11, p. 94. Adapted by permission of Sage.

Does charismatic leadership really make a difference? An unpublished study by Robert House and his colleagues studying 63 American and 49 Canadian companies (including Nortel Networks, Molson [now Molson-Coors], Gulf Canada [now ConocoPhillips], and Manulife Financial) found that "between 15 and 25 percent of the variation in profitability among the companies was accounted for by the leadership qualities of their CEO."[48] Charismatic leaders led the more profitable companies.

An increasing body of research shows that people who work for charismatic leaders are motivated to exert extra work effort and, because they like their leaders, they express greater satisfaction.[49] One of the most cited studies of the effects of charismatic leadership was done at the University of British Columbia in the early 1980s by Jane Howell (now at the Richard Ivey School of Business, University of Western Ontario) and Peter Frost.[50] The two found that those who worked under a charismatic leader generated more ideas, produced better results, reported higher job satisfaction, and showed stronger bonds of loyalty. Howell, in summarizing these results, says, "Charismatic leaders know how to inspire people to think in new directions."[51]

The accounting scandals and high-profile bankruptcies of North American companies including Enron and WorldCom suggest some of the dangers of charismatic leadership. WorldCom Inc.'s Bernard Ebbers and Enron Corp.'s Kenneth Lay "seemed almost a breed apart, blessed with unique visionary powers" when their companies saw increasing stock prices at phenomenal rates in the 1990s.[52] After the scandals and resultant bankruptcies, however, there was some desire for CEOs with less vision and more ethical and corporate responsibility to be at the helm. After a scandal or a drastic drop in market share, organizations sometimes turn to leaders who they believe will be able to turn the fortunes of the company around. These leaders are known as turnaround leaders.

Turnaround Leadership

When organizations are in need of an extreme overhaul, they often look for leadership to turn the company's fortunes around. In 2013, BlackBerry brought in John Chen after stock prices plummeted, market share was lost, employees were laid off and new product launches were delayed. When asked why he took the top job at BlackBerry, Chen said "BlackBerry is an iconic company, and one that's definitely worth saving. So I just took the job."[53] Chen had a reputation for being a turnaround artist. Before replacing Thorsten Heins as CEO of BlackBerry, he headed up a struggling electronic database company called Sybase that was once a leader in the sector. Chen cut costs and jobs and changed the strategy of the company to focus on database solutions for the mobile market. His approach worked, and Chen brought the company back to profitability. Shortly thereafter it was sold to SAP for almost $6 billion. What is it about turnaround leadership that creates such success stories? In leading a company that requires turning around, Chen gives us the following lessons:

1. *Dialogue with customers and employees*—always start with talking to the customers and the employees to find out what's going on. He said the most difficult thing is to collect all the information.

2. *Refocus strategy*—figure out core strengths and refocus the organization in that direction. BlackBerry was trying to be all things to all customers instead of focusing on enterprise customers.

3. *Add value for customers*—the new server BES12 handles all existing platforms. BBM Protected offers BlackBerry's trademark secure communication, and the BlackBerry Technology Solutions division focuses on technology that connects automobiles to the Internet.

4. *Be honest and realistic*—"People don't necessarily love what I say, but they know it's the truth."[54]

Frances Hesselbein did the same thing with the Girl Scouts of America. When she took the helm in the late 1970s, the organization was struggling and membership was declining. During her 24 years as CEO, the membership quadrupled, diversity increased, and management guru Peter Drucker called it "the best managed organization around." [55] Hesselbein's strategy included three important elements[56]:

1. *Create an inspiring identity*—her vision was to see the Girl Scout organization as a professional, well-managed organization that helps girls become women.

2. *Promote human value*—she appreciated the worthiness and dignity of all people and became a role model for local leaders to emulate.

3. *Increase information flows*—Hesselbein developed a circular management process that created an inclusive communication network.

CEO and President of Red Hat Inc., Jim Whitehurst, profiled in the opening case illustrates that a role-model leader can instill the confidence in individuals to go beyond performance expectations and achieve high levels of success. From the examples in this section, we see that transformational leadership, charismatic leadership, and turnaround leadership have the common element of being able to envision how an organization could be in the future and are able to articulate it to followers in a way that inspires them to be part of the change that is needed. Managing change is best suited to visionary leadership, as we will see in Chapter 12.

Gender, Culture, Emotional Intelligence, and Leadership

LO5	Explain how gender, culture, and emotional intelligence affect leadership effectiveness.

There are many questions about whether men and women have different leadership styles and whether observed differences have more to do with personality differences across people than with explicit gender differences. Others questions consider whether leadership styles are the same cross-culturally and whether our North American leadership theories apply in other countries. More recently, the effects of *moods and emotions* of leaders on their effectiveness have gained notable attention. We consider these issues in the following sections.

Gender and Leadership

The increasing number of women entering the ranks of management as well as the problems some women face in their efforts to be hired as managers or promoted into management positions have prompted researchers to explore the relationship between gender and leadership. Although relatively more women are in management positions today than 10 years ago, relatively few women are in top management in larger organizations, and, in some organizations, even in middle management.

According to Rosenzweig & Company, a global talent-management firm that has studied gender diversity in the largest publicly traded Canadian companies for over a decade, 8.5 percent of the highest paid executive positions were held by women in Canada in 2015.[57] In 2017, 5.6 percent of the CEOs of the top S&P 500 companies were women.[58] When women do advance to top-management positions, special attention is often focused on the fact that they are women. For example, women CEOs of large companies are still rare; those who make it to the very top spot—such as Monique Leroux, Chair of the Board of Investissement, Quebec,—are part of a unique club. While women have certainly made inroads into leadership positions in organizations, they continue to be very underrepresented in top leadership posts. However, a spotlight on the subject is making female representation at the executive level more visible. In 2015, rules put in place by the Ontario Securities Commission asked companies listed on the Toronto Stock Exchange to report on how many women they have serving on their boards of directors and in executive positions. "Never have I felt more hopeful that real change is in the air and gender will have nothing to do with people reaching or not reaching leadership positions in Canadian business," says Jay Rosenzweig.[59] Nine best practices that help companies achieve greater gender equality are outlined in Table 9.5.[60]

A widespread stereotype of women is that they are nurturing, supportive, and concerned with interpersonal relations. Men are stereotypically viewed as being directive and focused on task accomplishment. Such stereotypes suggest that women tend to be more relationship-oriented as managers and engage in more consideration behaviours, whereas men are more task-oriented and engage in more initiating structure behaviours. Does the behaviour of actual male and female managers bear out these stereotypes? Do female managers lead in different ways than males? Are male or female managers more effective as leaders?

Research suggests that male managers and female managers who have leadership positions in organizations behave in similar ways.[61] Women do not engage in more consideration than do men, and men do not engage in more initiating structure than do women. Research does suggest, however, that leadership

TABLE 9.5

Best Practices for Achieving Gender Diversity

- Using accountable search techniques
- Identifying talent and providing succession planning initiatives
- Setting up mentoring and coaching programs
- Offering job rotation opportunities
- Ensuring ongoing measurement
- Creating an inclusive work environment through awareness training
- Avoiding the glass cliff and token females
- Highlighting role models and communicating success
- Ensuring senior management support

style may vary between women and men. Women tend to be somewhat more participative as leaders than men, involving subordinates in decision making and seeking their input.[62] Male managers tend to be less participative than female managers, making more decisions on their own and wanting to do things their own way. Moreover, research suggests that men tend to be more harsh when they punish their subordinates than are women.[63]

There are at least two reasons why female managers may be more participative as leaders than are male managers.[64] First, subordinates may try to resist the influence of female managers more than they do the influence of male managers. Some subordinates may never have reported to a woman before, some may incorrectly see management roles as being more appropriate for men than for women, and some may just resist being led by a woman. To overcome this resistance and encourage subordinates' trust and respect, female managers may adopt a participative approach.

A second reason why female managers may be more participative is that they sometimes have better interpersonal skills than do male managers.[65] A participative

Monique Leroux, Chair of the Board of Investissement, Quebec.
Mathieu Belanger/Newscom

approach to leadership requires high levels of interaction and involvement between a manager and his or her subordinates, sensitivity to subordinates' feelings, and the ability to make decisions that may be unpopular with subordinates but necessary for reaching goals. Good interpersonal skills may help female managers have the effective interactions with their subordinates that are crucial to a participative approach.[66] To the extent that male managers have more difficulty managing interpersonal relationships, they may shy away from the high levels of interaction with subordinates that are necessary for true participation.

The key finding from research on leader behaviours, however, is that male and female managers do *not* differ significantly in their propensities to perform different leader behaviours. Even though they may be more participative, female managers do not engage in more consideration or less initiating structure than male managers.

Perhaps a question even more important than whether male and female managers differ in the leadership behaviours they perform is whether they differ in effectiveness. Consistent with the findings about leadership behaviours, research suggests that across different kinds of organizational settings, male and female managers tend to be equally *effective* as leaders.[67] Thus, there is no logical basis for stereotypes favouring male managers and leaders or for the existence of the **glass ceiling** (an invisible barrier that seems to prevent women from advancing as far as they should in some organizations). Because women and men are equally effective as leaders, the increasing number of women in the workforce should result in a larger pool of highly qualified candidates for management positions in organizations, ultimately enhancing organizational effectiveness.[68]

glass ceiling An invisible barrier that prevents women from advancing as far as they should in some organizations.

Nevertheless, the challenges remain. All executives encounter difficulty with balancing work and life. With the demands of the job, which can easily add up to 60 to 80 hours of work per week, it is hard for executives to find time for life outside of work. Organizations must recognize that female and male executives in general face different work–life issues, and that the organization's culture regarding flexibility, control, capacity, and practical solutions must be tailored to the individual executive's needs if they want to support and encourage greater gender diversity in leadership roles.

> *"Never have I felt more hopeful that real change is in the air and gender will have nothing to do with people reaching or not reaching leadership positions in Canadian business."*
>
> Jay Rosenzweig, managing partner of Rosenzweig & Company

Leadership Styles across Cultures

Some evidence suggests that leadership styles vary not only among individuals but also among countries or cultures. Some research suggests that European managers tend to be more humanistic or people-oriented than Japanese and American managers. The collectivistic culture in Japan places prime emphasis on the group rather than the individual, so the importance of individuals' own personalities, needs, and desires is minimized. Organizations in North America tend to be very profit-oriented and thus tend to downplay the importance of individual employees' needs and desires. Many countries in Europe have a more individualistic outlook than does Japan and a more humanistic outlook than does the United States, which may result in some European managers being more people-oriented than their Japanese or American counterparts. European managers, for example, tend to be reluctant to lay off employees, and when a layoff is absolutely necessary, they take careful steps to make it as painless as possible.[69]

Another cross-cultural difference that has been noted is in the perception of time horizons. Managers in any two countries often differ in their time horizons, but there also may be cultural differences. Canadian and American organizations tend to have a short-run profit orientation, which results in a leadership style emphasizing short-run performance. By contrast, Japanese organizations tend to have a long-run growth orientation, which results in Japanese managers' personal leadership styles emphasizing long-run performance. The big international firms in Europe have a philosophy between the Japanese long term and the United States short term.[70] Research on these and other global aspects of leadership is in its infancy, but as it continues, more cultural differences in managers' personal leadership styles may be discovered.

Emotional Intelligence and Leadership

Do the moods and emotions leaders experience on the job influence their behaviour and effectiveness as leaders? Research suggests that this is likely to be the case. For example, one study found that when store managers experienced positive moods at work, salespeople in the stores they led provided high-quality customer-service and were less likely to quit.[71] Another study found that groups whose leaders experienced positive moods had better coordination, while groups whose leaders experienced negative moods exerted more effort; members of groups with leaders in positive moods also tended to experience more positive moods themselves; and members of groups with leaders in negative moods tended to experience more negative moods.[72]

Emotional intelligence is the ability to understand and manage one's own emotions and the emotions of other people. A leader's level of emotional intelligence may play a particularly important role in leadership effectiveness.[73] For example, emotional intelligence may help leaders develop a vision for their organizations, motivate their subordinates to commit to this vision, and energize them to enthusiastically work to achieve this vision. Moreover, emotional intelligence may enable leaders to develop a significant identity for their organization and instill high levels of trust and cooperation throughout the organization while maintaining the flexibility needed to respond to changing conditions.[74]

> **emotional intelligence** The ability to understand and manage one's own moods and emotions and the moods and emotions of other people.

Emotional intelligence also plays a crucial role in how leaders relate to and deal with their followers, particularly when it comes to encouraging followers to be creative.[75] Creativity in organizations is an emotion-laden process, as it often entails challenging the status quo, being willing to take risks and accept and learn from failures, and doing much hard work to bring creative ideas to fruition in terms of new products, services, or procedures and processes when uncertainty is bound to be high.[76] Leaders who are high on emotional intelligence are more likely to understand all the emotions surrounding creative endeavours, to be able to awaken and support the creative pursuits of their followers, and to provide the kind of support that enables creativity to flourish in organizations.[77] Overall, the research suggests that the better able leaders are in recognizing the emotions of others, the better able they are to influence others effectively.[78] This is the essence of leadership.

Chapter 9

SUMMARY AND REVIEW

connect

LO1 The Nature of Leadership Leadership is different from management. Leadership is the process by which a person exerts influence over other people and inspires, motivates, and directs their activities to help achieve group or organizational goals. Leaders have their own personal leadership style that influences how they go about planning, organizing, and controlling. Leaders are able to influence others because they possess power. The five types of power available to managers are *legitimate power, reward power, coercive power, expert power,* and *referent power.*

LO2 Early Models of Leadership The *trait model* of leadership describes personal characteristics or traits that contribute to effective leadership. However, some managers who possess these traits are not effective leaders, and some managers who do not possess all the traits are nevertheless effective leaders. The *behavioural model* of leadership describes two kinds of behaviour that most leaders engage in: consideration or employee-oriented leaders and initiating structure or production-oriented leaders.

LO3 Contingency Models of Leadership Contingency models take into account the complexity surrounding leadership and the role of the situation in determining whether a manager is an effective or ineffective leader. *Fiedler's contingency model* explains why managers may be effective leaders in one situation and ineffective in another. *Hersey-Blanchard's situational leadership theory* examines the need for leaders to adjust their style to match their followers' level of ability and motivation. *Path-goal theory* describes how effective managers motivate their subordinates by clarifying the paths to goal attainment. The *leader substitutes model* suggests that sometimes managers do not have to play a leadership role because their subordinates perform highly without the manager having to exert influence over them.

LO4 Visionary Models of Leadership Whereas transactional leaders generally motivate their subordinates to meet expectations by rewarding high performance and extinguishing undesirable behaviours, *transformational leadership* occurs when managers have dramatic effects on their subordinates and on the organization as a whole and inspire and energize subordinates to solve problems and improve performance. Managers can engage in transformational leadership by stimulating subordinates intellectually, and by engaging in developmental consideration. *Charismatic leadership* inspires extraordinary performance by followers by articulating a vision that challenges the status quo and relies heavily on referent power. *Turnaround leadership* relies on seeing a better future for struggling organizations and making the necessary changes to achieve renewed success.

LO5 Gender, Culture, Emotional Intelligence, and Leadership Women continue to be underrepresented in top executive positions. Female and male managers do not differ in the leadership behaviours that they perform, contrary to stereotypes suggesting that women are more relationship-oriented and men more task-oriented. Research has found that women and men are equally effective as managers and leaders. Studies have found differences in leadership styles across cultures in terms of people-orientation and time orientations. The emotions leaders experience on the job, and their ability to effectively perceive these feelings in others, can influence their effectiveness as leaders. Moreover, *emotional intelligence* has the potential to contribute to leadership effectiveness in multiple ways, including encouraging and supporting creativity among followers.

KEY TERMS

charismatic leaders

coercive power

consideration

contingency models of leadership

developmental consideration

emotional intelligence

employee-centred leaders

expert power

glass ceiling

initiating structure

intellectual stimulation

leader

leader–member relations

leader substitute

leadership

legitimate power

path-goal theory

personal leadership style

position power

production-oriented leaders

referent power

reward power

situational leadership theory (SL)

task structure

transactional leadership

transformational leadership

WRAP-UP TO OPENING CASE

How Can a Manager Foster Creativity In a Rapidly Changing Environment?

Jim Whitehurst, president and CEO of Red Hat, Inc. recognizes the vital role that creativity plays in organizations in rapidly changing arenas like open-source software that made Red Hat a covetable $34 billion U.S. acquisition by IBM.

After having read and understood the concepts in this chapter, you should be able to answer the following questions:

1. *What makes Jim Whitehurst an effective leader?*

    ANSWER: Hundreds of studies since the 1930s have indicated that certain personal characteristics as well as skills and abilities are found in effective leaders like Jim Whitehurst. Traits such as intelligence, knowledge and expertise, dominance, self-confidence, high energy, tolerance for stress, integrity, honesty, and maturity are on the list. It is important to remember that some effective leaders may possess some or all of these traits, while some leaders who do possess them are not effective in their leadership roles. Jim Whitehurst, however, is an effective leader who demonstrates several leader traits as president and CEO of Red Hat Inc., including self-confidence, integrity, and honesty. Whitehurst exhibits consideration and respect for employees by creating a culture based on fostering empowerment and creativity. He could certainly be characterized as a relationship-oriented leader who holds the same standards for behaviour for himself as he does for his employees. Whitehurst had the self-confidence, energy, integrity, and maturity to grow the open-software company's fortunes, such that when IBM bought it in 2018 for $34 billion U.S., it was the largest tech company buyout in history.

2. *Is Whitehurst a transformational leader? Why, or why not?*

    ANSWER: Transformational leadership occurs when managers change (or transform) their subordinates in three important ways:

    1. Transformational managers make subordinates aware of how important their jobs are for the organization and how necessary it is for them to perform those jobs as best they can so that the organization can attain its goals. Whitehurst is competent and confident both in his own abilities and in the capabilities of teams at Red Hat. Mutual trust and respect are important to Whitehurst (and at Red Hat) as are honesty, integrity, and open communication.

    2. Transformational managers make their subordinates aware of their own needs for personal growth, development, and accomplishment. Whitehurst encourages and supports employees' creative ideas and perspectives. He encourages open and honest communication. In this way, Whitehurst stimulates employees' intellect and engages in developmental consideration. He acts as a catalyst "to fuel and spark their creativity and not stifle it by simply telling people what to do."

    3. Transformational managers motivate their subordinates to work for the good of the organization as a whole, not just for their own personal gain or benefit. Whitehurst is passionate about creatively developing better technology and software in an open-source manner involving communities of contributors, partners, and customers. And so are his employees. Whitehurst empowers employees and gives them the freedom to be creative in the ways in which they contribute to Red Hat's mission. His effective leadership has led the company to prosperity.

MANAGEMENT IN ACTION

TOPICS FOR DISCUSSION AND ACTION

LEVEL 1 Knowledge & Comprehension

1. What is meant by "leadership," and on what bases of power do leaders influence others to take action that achieves organizational goals?

2. How does one's personal leadership style affect how they carry out the managerial tasks of planning, organizing, and controlling?

3. Describe trait and behavioural theories of leadership and their limitations.

LEVEL 2 Application & Analysis

4. Think of specific situations in which it might be especially important for a manager to engage in consideration and in initiating structure.

5. Interview a manager to find out how the three situational characteristics that Fiedler identified are affecting the manager's ability to provide leadership.

6. Discuss why substitutes for leadership can contribute to organizational effectiveness.

LEVEL 3 Synthesis & Evaluation

7. Which leader behaviour from path-goal theory might be appropriate in each of these situations, and why:

   a. a highly motivated and skilled teacher is resisting changes to the curriculum

   b. a new hire on an assembly line consistently makes errors

   c. the leader of a task force finishes writing the final report for a project

8. Compare and contrast transactional and transformational leadership styles.

9. Discuss why some people still think that men make better managers than do women, even though research indicates that men and women are equally effective as managers and leaders.

SELF-REFLECTION EXERCISE

Your school is developing a one-day orientation program for new students majoring in business. You have been asked to consider leading the group of students who will design and implement the orientation program. Develop a two- or three-page "handout" that shows whether the position is a natural fit for you. To do this, (1) identify your strengths and weaknesses in the sources of power you can bring to the project, and (2) discuss whether you would be a transactional leader or a transformational leader and why. Provide a strong concluding statement about whether or not you would be the best leader for this task.

SMALL GROUP BREAKOUT EXERCISE

Improving Leadership Effectiveness

Form groups of three to five, and appoint one member as the spokesperson who will communicate your findings and conclusions to the whole class when called on by the instructor. Then discuss the following scenario:

You are a team of human resource consultants who have been hired by Carla Caruso, an entrepreneur who started her own interior decorating business. At first, she worked on her own as an independent contractor. Then, because of a dramatic increase in the number of new homes being built, she decided to form her own company.

She hired a secretary/bookkeeper and four interior decorators. Caruso still does decorating jobs herself and has adopted a hands-off approach to leading the four decorators because she feels that interior design is a very personal, creative endeavour. Rather than paying the decorators on some kind of commission basis, she pays them a higher-than-average salary so that they are motivated to do what is best for their customers, not what will result in higher billings and commissions.

Caruso thought everything was going smoothly until customer complaints started coming in. These complaints were about the decorators being hard to reach, promising unrealistic delivery times, being late for or failing to keep appointments, and being impatient and rude when customers had trouble making up their minds. Caruso knows that her decorators are competent people and is concerned that she is not effectively leading and managing them. She has asked for your advice.

1. What advice can you give Caruso to either increase her power or use her existing power more effectively?

2. Does Caruso seem to be performing appropriate leadership behaviours in this situation? What advice can you give her about the kinds of behaviours she should perform?

3. How can Caruso increase the decorators' motivation to deliver high-quality customer service?

4. Would you advise Caruso to try engaging in transformational leadership in this situation? If not, why not? If so, what steps would you advise her to take?

MANAGING ETHICALLY EXERCISE

One of your subordinates has noticed that your expense account reports have repeatedly overstated your expenses because you always bill for an extra day, at the "daily rate," when you go out of town on company business. Your assistant knows that you have always been in town and working from home on that extra day. He has questioned your reports, as you have now submitted 15 of these for the year. How would you use your knowledge of power to resolve this dilemma? Which use of power would be most ethical, and why?

MANAGEMENT CHALLENGE EXERCISE
Napoleon on Leadership[79]

Jim Warthin is a friend of yours; he is also CEO of a small plastics firm and has invited you in to discuss a new book he has recently read on leadership and Napoleon Bonaparte.[80] He tells you in an email that Jerry Manas, author of Napoleon on Project Management, identifies the emperor's six managerial principles. Jim wants to discuss these principles in the context of the leadership course that you both took when in business school together. He wants your trusted feedback.

1. *Exactitude:* Napoleon sought pinpoint precision through extensive research, continuous planning, and constant awareness of the situation he faced, which included meditating on what might occur—in other words, awareness, research, and continuous planning.

2. *Speed:* He recognized that momentum—mass times velocity—applied to achieving goals with people as well. "He knew that resistance causes momentum to fade. Increasing speed is about reducing resistance, increasing urgency, and providing focus by employing concentration of force and economy of force," the author says—in other words, reducing resistance, increasing urgency, and providing focus.

3. *Flexibility:* Napoleon ensured that his armies could react quickly to situations, yet operate according to a strategic plan. He organized his troops into mobile units and empowered them by providing knowledge of the mission and structuring them to operate independently; yet he also made sure they were operating under a unified doctrine and serving one ultimate leader—in other words, building teams that are adaptable, empowered, and unified.

4. *Simplicity:* He ensured his objectives were simple, his messages were simple, and his processes were simple, reducing confusion. "The art of war does not require complicated manoeuvre. The simplest are the best," Napoleon declared—in other words, clear simple objectives, messages, and processes.

5. *Character:* While driven by his ambition, Napoleon always maintained honour and integrity, calmness and responsibility, and encouraged respect of other cultures.

6. *Moral force:* "In war, everything depends upon morale," Napoleon said. People do their best work when they have self-confidence, feel what they are doing is worthwhile, and are recognized for their effort—in other words, providing order, purpose recognition, and rewards.

Question: Are Napoleon's six principles more suited to a transformational leader or a transactional leader? Why?

MANAGEMENT PORTFOLIO PROJECT

Answer the following questions about the organization you have chosen to follow:

1. How would you characterize the leadership style of the CEO?

2. Do you consider the CEO to be a transactional or transformative leader, and why? Is the style appropriate for the environmental context in which the organization is situated?

3. What sources of power does he or she rely on most heavily?

MANAGEMENT CASE

MANAGERS NEED TO MAKE TIME FOR FACE TIME

Alan Buckelew, chief operations officer of Carnival Corp., moved to Shanghai last September so he could help the world's biggest cruise-ship company expand in China. He still supervises five executives at its Miami headquarters.

A heavy workload forced Mr. Buckelew to conduct year-end performance reviews for three of those deputies via videoconference but he wasn't happy about it.

"A review is probably the one time when you want to be physically present," Mr. Buckelew says. He says he apologized to them about his Miami absence, and vows to evaluate every lieutenant face to face this year.

As businesses expect more senior leaders to both manage more far-flung teams and spend more time with distant clients, face time has become a precious commodity—and a source of professional agita. Technologies like videoconferencing and enterprise social networks claim to enable true connection over great distances, but the reality is often is far from perfect.

When it comes down to it, there is still no good substitute for being in the same room with a direct report or a high-level boss, many executives say. Yet there is little consensus about how much face time it takes to manage effectively.

"Few executives can deliver business results quickly and engage their people at the same time," says Matt Paese, vice president of succession management and C-suite services for leadership consultants Development Dimensions International. "But increasingly, our corporate clients try to hire or grow ones who can," because they recognize "they can't sustain business growth without a healthy culture."

Hands-off leadership carries career risks. Take, for example, Louis Chenevert, who abruptly relinquished command of conglomerate United Technologies Corp. in November 2014 amid criticism that he was too detached from his top team.

Travelling frequently for work can leave employees without adequate feedback or a boss wondering whether you manage well, suggests Bruce Tulgan, author and chief executive of Rainmaker Thinking Inc., a management research and training firm. "You have to be there to problem-solve."

Ramesh Tainwala, CEO of luggage maker Samsonite International S.A., says that after advancing into the top job in October, he quickly replaced its head of Latin America because the man ran the region from Denver and spent only 40 days a year in Latin America. (Samsonite previously had been based in Denver.)

"Unless you are in the field with your people, it's difficult for you to manage it," he adds.

The new head of Latin America is based in Chile but is almost constantly on the road. Mr. Tainwala told him, "You need to be traveling 20 to 25 days a month" in the new role.

Mr. Tainwala himself travels 25 days a month for Samsonite from his base in Hong Kong. Since becoming CEO last fall, he has held four face-to-face sessions with his senior management team, stationed in four regions world-wide. An April 13 session in Mansfield, Mass., will be his third far from Hong Kong.

"A conference call cannot substitute for face-to-face interactions," Mr. Tainwala continues. "When we meet in person, we almost hear each other's thoughts."

Yet a distant boss with a sudden yen for face time may encounter resistance from subordinates. That happened to a senior manager at an environmental consulting firm in 2012.

The manager realized she had been too hands-off with her team, missing meetings due to conflicting client demands, she told Mr. Tulgan of Rainmaker Thinking after attending his seminar about being a highly engaged boss. She soon scheduled half-hour sessions with each team member.

Several staffers bristled at the sudden outreach, complaining that she was micromanaging them, according to Mr. Tulgan. She convened a meeting to explain how her increased engagement could be helpful. "I want you to help me help you," she said. Her team adjusted over time, and that helped her land a higher-level role at a larger rival early last year, Mr. Tulgan says.

Even when the team is nearby, isolated bosses must find ways to appear present. When Rick Russell managed 1100 people as chief commercial officer of Sunovian Pharmaceuticals Inc., a small drug maker in Marlborough, Mass., his dozen deputies occupied the second floor at headquarters. He toiled behind closed doors in the executive suite two floors above.

After a 2012 employee survey concluded that people felt walled off from their leaders, he decided to make himself more visible. He created a second-floor satellite office surrounded by glass on three sides. Dubbed his "fish-bowl," he worked from the office nearly every Friday, with a deliberately light schedule and no executive assistant.

Wary colleagues gradually grew comfortable about dropping by, Mr. Russell recalls. The chief medical officer adopted the satellite-office idea, too.

The next year's poll showed Sunovian employees' trust for the top brass improved a lot.

"You have to rally the troops. You can't do it from a memo," says Mr. Russell, now CEO of Greer Laboratories Inc., a midsize biologies concern.

Mel Berning, chief revenue officer at A+E Networks in New York, takes a different approach. He travels two weeks a month for the cable network. While at headquarters, he says he tries to, avoid "antiseptic" formal meetings and calls with his six direct reports.

Instead, he breezes into somebody's office at 8:30 a.m. "You have a conversation that is less hurried and less guarded," Mr. Berning notes. "Face-to-face encounters are so much more revealing than a text or an email."

1. Why might making sure to incorporate time for face-to-face interactions be an important component for many managers' personal leadership styles?

2. How might face-to-face interactions contribute to managers effectively engaging in consideration and initiating structure?

3. How might face-to-face interactions help managers effectively engage in transformational leadership?

4. How might emotional intelligence help managers to ensure that they have effective face-to-face interactions?

Source: "Managers Need to Make Time for Face Time" by J. S. Lublin. *The Wall Street Journal*, March 18, 2015, p. B6.

Chapter 10

Managing Teams

LEARNING OUTCOMES

LO1	Explain why groups and teams are key contributors to organizational effectiveness.
LO2	Identify the different types of groups and teams that help managers and organizations achieve their goals.
LO3	Explain how different elements of group dynamics influence the functioning and effectiveness of groups and teams.
LO4	Explain how group decision making can be improved.
LO5	Describe how managers can create high-performing teams.

OPENING CASE

Teams Benefit from Deviance and Conformity at IDEO

IDEO has designed many products we now take for granted: the first Apple mouse, the Palm handheld organizer, stand-up toothpaste containers, flexible shelving for offices, self-sealing drink bottles for sports, blood analyzers, and even equipment used in space travel.[1] Managers and designers at IDEO take pride in being experts at the process of innovation in general, rather than any particular domain. Of course, the company has technical design experts, such as mechanical and electrical engineers, who work on products requiring specialized knowledge; but on the same team with the engineers might be an anthropologist, a biologist, and a social scientist.[2]

A guiding principle at IDEO is that innovation comes in many shapes and sizes and it is only through diversity in thought that people can recognize opportunities for innovation. To promote such diversity in thought, new product development at IDEO is a team effort.[3] Moreover, both conformity and deviance are encouraged on IDEO teams.

Deviance—thinking differently and not conforming to expected mindsets and ways of doing things—is encouraged at IDEO. In fact, innovative ideas often flow when designers try to see things as they really are and are not blinded by thoughts of what is appropriate, what is possible, or how things should be. Often constraints on new product design are created by designers themselves conforming to a certain mindset about the nature of a product or what a product can or should do and look like. IDEO designers are encouraged to actively break down these constraints in their design teams.[4]

Managers at IDEO realize the need for a certain amount of conformity so members of design teams can work effectively together and achieve their goals. Thus, conformity to a few central norms is emphasized in IDEO teams. These norms include understanding what the team is working on (the product, market, or client need), observing real people in their natural environments, visualizing how new products might work and be used, evaluating and refining product prototypes, encouraging wild ideas, and never rejecting an idea simply because it sounds too crazy.[5] As long as these norms are followed, diversity of thought and even deviance promote innovation at IDEO. In fact, another norm at IDEO is to study "rule breakers"—people who don't follow instructions for products, for example, or who try to put products to different uses—because these individuals might help designers identify problems with existing products and unmet consumer needs.[6] All in all, IDEO's focus on encouraging both deviance and conformity in design teams has benefited all of us—we use IDEO-inspired products that seem so familiar we take them for granted. We forget these products did not exist until a design team at IDEO was called on by a client to develop a new product or improve an existing one.[7]

After reading and understanding the concepts in this chapter, you should be able to answer the following questions:

1. How do teams at IDEO help the organization achieve a competitive advantage?
2. What types of teams are encouraged in this case?
3. How do IDEO managers encourage deviance and conformity to group norms and why is this important for high performance?

Overview

IDEO is not alone in using groups and teams to gain a competitive advantage. Managers in companies large and small are using groups and teams to enhance performance, increase responsiveness to customers, spur innovation, and motivate employees. In this chapter, we look in detail at how groups and teams can contribute to organizational effectiveness and at the types of groups and teams used in organizations. We discuss how different elements of group dynamics influence the functioning and effectiveness of groups, how group decision making can increase innovation and creativity, and how managers can motivate group members to achieve organizational goals and reduce social loafing. By the end of this chapter, you will appreciate why the effective management of groups and teams is a key ingredient for organizational performance and effectiveness. See Figure 10.1.

Groups, Teams, and Organizational Effectiveness

LO1	Explain why groups and teams are key contributors to organizational effectiveness.

It is difficult to escape reading about teams if you pick up almost any business magazine. Teams are widely used these days. A Conference Board of Canada report found that more than 80 percent of its 109 respondents used teams in the workplace.[8] In the United States, at least half of the employees at 80 percent of Fortune 500 companies work in teams, while 68 percent of small manufacturers use teams in their production areas.[9]

A **group** may be defined as two or more people who interact with each other to reach certain goals or meet certain needs.[10] A **team** is a group whose members work *intensely* with each other and have regular interaction to achieve a specific common goal or vision. As these definitions imply, all teams

---

FIGURE 10.1

Groups' and Teams' Contributions to Organizational Effectiveness

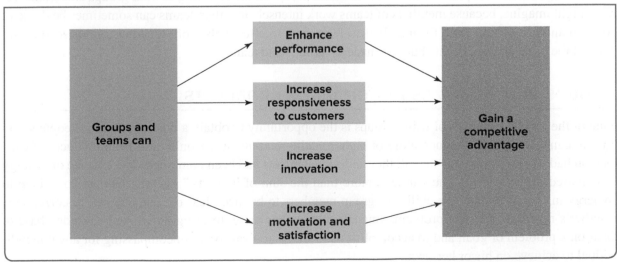

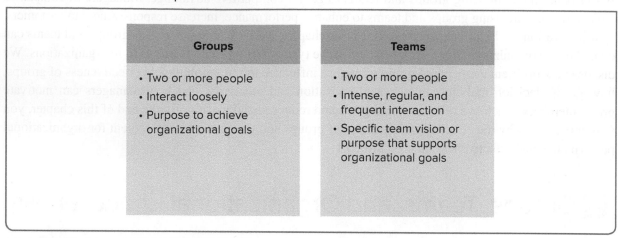

FIGURE 10.2

Differences between Groups and Teams

Groups	Teams
• Two or more people • Interact loosely • Purpose to achieve organizational goals	• Two or more people • Intense, regular, and frequent interaction • Specific team vision or purpose that supports organizational goals

are groups, but not all groups are teams. The two characteristics that distinguish teams from groups are the *intensity* with which team members work together, the *frequency* of interaction, and the presence of a *specific, overriding team goal or objective*. See Figure 10.2. At IDEO, managers form teams that work intensively to achieve the goal of developing a new product or improving an existing one. In contrast, the accountants who work in a small chartered accounting firm are a group: they may interact infrequently with one another to achieve goals, such as keeping up to date on the latest changes in accounting rules and regulations, maintaining a smoothly functioning office, satisfying clients, and attracting new clients. But they are not a team because they do not work intensely and regularly with one another toward a specific common goal. Each accountant concentrates on serving the needs of his or her own clients.

group Two or more people who interact with each other to reach certain goals or meet certain needs.

team A group whose members work intensely with each other to achieve a specific common goal or objective.

Throughout this chapter, when we use the term *group* we are referring to both groups *and* teams. As you might imagine, because members of teams work intensely together, teams can sometimes be difficult to form and it may take time for members to learn how to effectively work together. In this section, we look at the organizational contributions made by groups and teams.

Groups and Teams as Performance Enhancers

One of the main advantages of using groups is the opportunity to obtain a type of synergy: People working in teams are able to produce more or higher quality outputs than would have been produced if each person had worked separately and all their individual efforts had been combined. The essence of synergy is captured in the saying "The whole is more than the sum of its parts." Factors that can contribute to synergy in groups include the ability of group members to bounce ideas off one another, to correct one another's mistakes, to solve problems immediately as they arise, to bring a diverse knowledge base to bear on a problem or goal, and to accomplish work that is too vast or all-encompassing for any one individual to achieve on his or her own.

To take advantage of the potential for synergy in groups, managers need to make sure that groups are composed of members who have complementary skills and knowledge relevant to the group's work. The opening case provides an example. At IDEO, synergies are created by bringing together all the different functions needed to create and produce a product in a cross-functional team (a team composed of members from different departments or functions). For instance, artists, writers, biologists, designers, engineers, and marketing experts work together as members of a team to design a new product or solve a social problem.

At IDEO, the skills and expertise of the mechanical engineers complement the contributions of the artists and vice versa. Managers also need to give groups enough autonomy so that the groups, rather than the manager, are solving problems and determining how to achieve goals and objectives, as is true in the cross-functional teams at IDEO. To promote synergy, managers need to empower their subordinates and be coaches, guides, and resources for groups while refraining from playing a more directive or supervisory role. The potential for synergy in groups may be the reason why more and more managers are incorporating empowerment into their personal leadership styles (see Chapter 9).

Groups, Teams, and Responsiveness to Customers

Being responsive to customers is not always easy. In manufacturing organizations, for example, customers' needs and desires for new and improved products have to be balanced against engineering constraints, production costs and feasibilities, government safety regulations, and marketing challenges. Being responsive to customers often requires the wide variety of skills and expertise found in different departments and at different levels in an organization's hierarchy. Sometimes, for example, employees at lower levels in an organization's hierarchy, such as sales representatives for a computer company, are closest to its customers and the most attuned to their needs. However, lower-level employees like salespeople often lack the technical expertise needed to

Two people are often better than one in creating a high-performing organization.
BeanRibbon/Shutterstock

come up with new product ideas; such expertise is found in the research and development department. Bringing salespeople, research and development experts, and members of other departments together in a group or cross-functional team can enhance responsiveness to customers by increasing the skills and expertise available. Consequently, when managers form a team, they need to make sure that the diversity of expertise and knowledge needed to be responsive to customers exists within the team; this is why cross-functional teams are so popular. At IDEO, everyone on staff, from the managers to the "rule-breakers," comes together to solve problems and meet customers' needs.

In a cross-functional team, the expertise and knowledge in different organizational departments are brought together in the skills and knowledge of the team members. Managers of high-performing organizations are careful to determine which types of expertise and knowledge are required for teams to be responsive to customers, and they use this information in forming teams.

Teams and Innovation

Innovation—the implementation of creative ideas for new products, new technologies, new services, or even new organizational structures—is essential for organizational effectiveness. Often an individual working alone does not possess the extensive and diverse set of skills, knowledge, and expertise required for successful innovation. Managers can better encourage innovation by creating teams of diverse individuals who together have the knowledge relevant to a particular type of innovation, rather than by relying on individuals working alone. Using teams to innovate has other advantages as well. First, team members can often uncover one another's errors or false assumptions; an individual acting alone would not be able to do this. Second, team members can critique one another's approaches when need be and build off one another's strengths while compensating for weaknesses (one of the advantages of devil's advocacy, discussed later in this chapter).

To further promote innovation, managers are well advised to empower teams and make their members fully responsible and accountable for the innovation process. The manager's role is to provide guidance, assistance, coaching, and the resources team members need and *not* to closely direct or supervise their activities. At IDEO, rather than follow orders or scripts developed by management, managers provide people with the skills and confidence they need to deal with problems on their own. To speed innovation, managers also need to form teams in which each member brings some unique resource to the team, such as engineering prowess, knowledge of production, marketing expertise, or financial savvy. Successful innovation sometimes requires that managers form teams with members from different countries and cultures. Amazon uses teams to spur innovation, and many of the unique features on its website that enable it to be responsive to customers and meet their needs have been developed by teams. For example, it was a team that developed "Search Inside the Book," which allows customers to search and read content from over 100 000 books.[11]

Groups and Teams as Motivators

Managers often decide to form groups and teams to accomplish organizational goals and then find that using groups and teams brings additional benefits. Members of groups, and especially members of teams (because of the higher intensity of interaction in teams), are likely to be more highly motivated and satisfied than they would have been while working on their own. The experience of working alongside other highly charged and motivated people can be very stimulating. Team members more readily see how their efforts and expertise directly contribute to the achievement of team and organizational goals, and they feel personally responsible for the outcomes or results of their work. This has been the case at IDEO.

The increased motivation and satisfaction that can accompany the use of teams can also lead to other outcomes, such as low absenteeism and turnover. Working in a group or team can also satisfy organizational members' needs for engaging in social interaction and feeling connected to other people. For workers who perform highly stressful jobs, such as hospital emergency and operating room staff, group membership can be an important source of social support and motivation. Family members or friends may not be able to fully understand or appreciate some sources of work stress that these group members experience first-hand. Moreover, group members may cope better with work stressors when they are able to share them with other members of their group. In addition, groups often devise techniques to relieve stress, such as the telling of jokes among hospital operating room staff.

Why do managers in all kinds of organizations rely so heavily on groups and teams? Effectively managed groups and teams can help managers in their quest for high performance, responsiveness to customers, and employee motivation. Before explaining how managers can effectively manage groups, however, we will describe the types of groups that are formed in organizations.

Types of Groups and Teams

LO2 Identify the different types of groups and teams that help managers and organizations achieve their goals.

To achieve their goals of high performance, responsiveness to customers, innovation, and employee motivation, managers can form various types of groups and teams (see Figure 10.3). **Formal groups** are those managers establish to achieve organizational goals. Formal work groups can be **cross-functional teams** composed of members from different departments, and/or **cross-cultural teams** composed of members from different cultures or countries, such as the teams at global automakers.

> **formal groups** Groups that managers establish to achieve organizational goals.
>
> **cross-functional team** A group of individuals from different departments brought together to perform organizational tasks.
>
> **cross-cultural teams** Formal work groups composed of members from different cultures or countries.

Top-management teams are responsible for developing the strategies that produce an organization's competitive advantage; most have between five and seven members. Managers in pharmaceuticals, computers, electronics, electronic imaging, and other high-tech industries often create **research and development teams** to develop new products.

> **top-management team** (1) Groups composed of the CEO, the president, and the heads of the most important departments; (2) Teams that are responsible for developing the strategies that produce an organization's competitive advantage.
>
> **research and development teams** Teams whose members have the expertise and experience needed to develop new products.

Subordinates who report to the same supervisor form a **department**. Examples of departmental groups include the salespeople at Hudson's Bay who report to the same supervisor, the employees of a small swimming pool sales and maintenance company who report to a general manager, the telephone

FIGURE 10.3

Types of Groups and Teams in Organizations

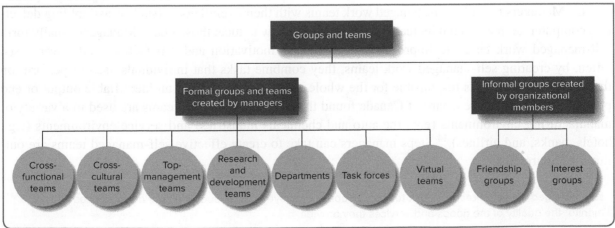

operators at Manulife Financial insurance company who report to the same supervisor, and workers on an automobile assembly line at Ford Canada who report to the same first-line manager.

department A group composed of subordinates who report to the same supervisor; also called a unit.

Managers form **task forces** to accomplish specific goals or solve problems in a certain period; task forces are sometimes called *ad hoc committees.* When Vancouver Island–based Myra Falls copper and zinc mine was purchased by Swedish-controlled Boliden AB, the mine had been facing labour strife for years.[12] Boliden sent over a new mine manager to help get things in order. His first job was to set up five task forces geared to key problem areas. For instance, the ground support task force found that the previous owners had neglected a number of safety problems. The recommendations of the task forces were followed, and $15 million worth of improvements were done. This sent a strong signal to employees that the new management team was concerned about its employees. Task forces can be a valuable tool for busy managers who do not have the time to explore an important issue in depth on their own.

task forces Cross-functional teams charged with solving a specific problem or addressing a specific issue within a fixed timeframe.

Sometimes organizations need to address a long-term or enduring problem or issue, such as how to contribute most usefully to the local community or how to make sure that the organization provides opportunities for potential employees with disabilities. Task forces that are relatively permanent are often referred to as **standing committees**. Membership in standing committees changes over time. Members may have, for example, a two- or three-year term on the committee and then rotate off. Memberships expire at varying times so that there are always some members with experience on the committee. Managers form and maintain standing committees to make sure that important issues continue to be addressed.

standing committees A relatively permanent task force charged with addressing long-term, enduring problems or issues facing an organization.

Self-managed (or self-directed) work teams are teams whose members are empowered and have the responsibility and autonomy to complete identifiable pieces of work. On a day-to-day basis, team members decide what the team will do, how it will do it, and which team members will perform specific tasks.[13] Managers provide self-managed work teams with their overall goals (such as assembling defect-free computer keyboards) but let team members decide how to meet those goals. Managers usually form self-managed work teams to improve quality, increase motivation and satisfaction, and lower costs. Often, by creating self-managed work teams, they combine tasks that individuals used to perform on their own, so the team is responsible for the whole set of tasks that yield an identifiable output or end product. The Conference Board of Canada found that self-directed work teams are used in a variety of manufacturing environments (e.g., the auto and chemicals industries) and service environments (e.g., hotels, banks, and airlines).[14] Steps managers can take to create effective self-managed teams are outlined in Figure 10.4.[15]

self-managed (or self-directed) work teams Groups of employees who supervise their own activities and monitor the quality of the goods and services they provide.

FIGURE 10.4

Creating Effective Self-Managed Teams

- Give teams enough responsibility and autonomy to be truly self-managing. Refrain from telling team members what to do or solving problems for them even if you (as a manager) know what should be done.

- Make sure that a team's work is sufficiently complex so that it entails a number of different steps or procedures that must be performed and results in some kind of finished end product.

- Carefully select members of self-managed work teams. Team members should have the diversity of skills needed to complete the team's work, have the ability to work with others, and want to be part of a team.

- Recognize that self-managed work teams need guidance, coaching, and support, not direct supervision. Managers should be a resource for teams to turn to when needed.

- Analyze what type of training team members need, and provide it. Working in a self-managed work team often requires that employees have more extensive technical and interpersonal skills.

Managers in a wide variety of organizations have found that self-managed work teams help the organization achieve its goals.[16] However, self-managed work teams can run into trouble. Case studies of Canadian plastics companies made it absolutely clear that teamwork is appropriate to certain types of workplaces and not to others.[17] Canadian General Tower Limited had mixed results with using self-directed teams. At the plant's dry laminating facility, such teams were abandoned after no significantly positive results could be observed. The company does, however, operate a small distribution centre in Brantford, Ontario, where the employees work in a self-directed team environment and no grievances or turnover have resulted.

Problems with self-managed teams include members' reluctance to discipline one another by, for example, firing members or withholding bonuses from members who are not performing up to par.[18] They are also reluctant to evaluate each other's performance and determine pay levels. One reason for team members' discomfort may be the close personal relationships and friendship groups they sometimes develop with each other. In addition, sometimes members of self-managed work teams actually take longer to accomplish tasks, such as when team members have difficulties coordinating their efforts.

Virtual teams are teams whose members rarely or never meet face to face and instead interact by using various forms of information technology such as email, computer networks, telephones, faxes, and video conferences and apps such as What's App, Twitter, and Facebook. As organizations become increasingly global and have operations in far-flung regions of the world, and as the need for specialized knowledge increases due to advances in technology, virtual teams allow managers to create teams to solve problems or explore opportunities without being limited by the need for team members to be working in the same geographic location.[19]

virtual teams Teams whose members rarely or never meet face to face and interact by using various forms of information technology such as email, computer networks, telephones, faxes, and video conferences.

Take the case of an organization that has manufacturing facilities in Australia, Canada, the United States, and Mexico, and is encountering a quality problem in a complex manufacturing process. Each of its manufacturing facilities has a quality control team that is headed by a quality control manager.

The vice-president for production does not try to solve the problem by forming and leading a team at one of the four manufacturing facilities; instead, she forms and leads a virtual team composed of the quality control managers of the four plants and the plants' general managers. Team members communicate via email and video conferencing, and a wide array of knowledge and experience is utilized to solve the problem.

The principal advantage of virtual teams is that they enable managers to disregard geographic distances and form teams whose members have the knowledge, expertise, and experience to tackle a particular problem or take advantage of a specific opportunity.[20] Virtual teams can include members who are not employees of the organization itself. For example, a virtual team might include members of an organization that is used for outsourcing. More and more companies are either using or exploring the use of virtual teams.[21]

Increasing globalization is likely to result in more organizations relying on virtual teams to a greater extent.[22] One of the major challenges members of virtual teams face is building a sense of camaraderie and trust among team members who rarely, if ever, meet face to face. To address this challenge, some organizations schedule recreational activities, such as ski trips, so that virtual team members can get together. Other organizations make sure that virtual team members have a chance to meet in person soon after the team is formed and then schedule periodic face-to-face meetings to promote trust, understanding, and cooperation in the teams.[23] The need for such meetings is underscored by research that suggests that while some virtual teams can be as effective as teams that meet face to face, virtual team members might be less satisfied with teamwork efforts and have fewer feelings of camaraderie or cohesion. (Group cohesiveness is discussed in more detail later in the chapter.)[24]

Research also suggests that it is important for managers to keep track of virtual teams and intervene when necessary by, for example, encouraging members of teams who do not communicate often enough to monitor their team's progress and make sure that team members actually have the time and are recognized for their virtual teamwork.[25] Additionally, when virtual teams are experiencing downtime or rough spots, managers might try to schedule face-to-face team time to bring team members together and help them focus on their goals.[26] Some virtual teams periodically meet face to face to promote trust, understanding, and cooperation in the team. Figure 10.5 outlines the steps managers can take to create effective virtual teams.[27]

FIGURE 10.5

Creating Effective Virtual Teams

When forming virtual teams

- Include a few members who already know each other, other members who are very well connected to people outside of the team, and, when possible, members who have volunteered to be a part of the team.

- Create an online site where team members can learn more about each other and the kinds of work they are engaged in, and a shared online workspace that team members can access around the clock.

- Set up regular, frequent communication.

- Ensure that virtual team projects are perceived as meaningful, interesting, and important by their members to promote and sustain their motivation.

The groups described so far are *formal groups* created by managers. Sometimes organizational members, managers or nonmanagers, form groups because they feel that groups will help them achieve their own goals or meet their own needs (for example, the need for social interaction). Groups formed in this way are **informal groups**. Four nurses who work in a hospital and have lunch together twice a week constitute an informal group.

informal groups Groups that managers or nonmanagerial employees form to help achieve their own goals or meet their own needs.

Friendship groups are informal groups composed of employees who enjoy one another's company and socialize with one another. Members of friendship groups may have lunch together, take breaks together, or meet after work for meals, sports, or other activities. Friendship groups help satisfy employees' needs for interpersonal interaction, can provide needed social support in times of stress, and can contribute to people's feeling good at work and being satisfied with their jobs. Managers themselves often form friendship groups. The informal relationships that managers build in friendship groups can often help them solve work-related problems because members of these groups typically discuss work-related matters and offer advice.

friendship groups Informal groups composed of employees who enjoy one another's company and socialize with one another.

Employees form informal **interest groups** when they seek to achieve a common goal related to their membership in an organization. Employees may form interest groups, for example, to encourage managers to consider instituting flexible working hours, providing on-site child care, improving working conditions, or more proactively supporting environmental protection. Interest groups can provide managers with valuable insights into the issues and concerns that are foremost in employees' minds. They also can signal the need for change.

interest groups Informal groups composed of employees seeking to achieve a common goal related to their membership in an organization.

Group Dynamics

LO3 Explain how different elements of group dynamics influence the functioning and effectiveness of groups and teams.

How groups and teams function and how effective they will ultimately be depends on a number of characteristics and processes known collectively as **group dynamics**. In this section, we discuss five key elements of group dynamics: *group size and roles; group leadership; stages of group development; group norms;* and *group cohesiveness.* As we mentioned earlier in the chapter, teams and groups are not the same thing, though some of their processes are similar. Thus, much of what we call group dynamics here also applies to teams.

group dynamics The ways in which group members interact, determining the effectiveness of the group.

Group Size and Roles

Managers need to take group size and group roles into account as they create and maintain high-performing groups and teams.

GROUP SIZE

The number of members in a group can be an important determinant of members' motivation and commitment and of group performance. There are several advantages to keeping a group relatively small—between two and nine members. Compared with members of large groups, members of small groups tend to do the following:

- interact more with each other and find it easier to coordinate their efforts;
- be more motivated, satisfied, and committed;
- find it easier to share information; and
- be better able to see the importance of their personal contributions for group success.

FOCUS ON   *The Social Economy*

Vibrant Communities Canada

In communities across Canada, business leaders, all levels of government, voluntary agencies, and people living in poverty are forming multi-sector round-tables to seek solutions to poverty in a collaboration called Vibrant Communities Canada—Cities Reducing Poverty. This collaboration rests on five core principles: poverty reduction over poverty alleviation; work comprehensively to address root causes of poverty; build on the existing assets in a community; bring people together from all sectors; and learn together to scale up change.

The collaboration is committed to significantly reducing the human, social, and economic costs of poverty. Through a connected learning community of 100 communities, the shared goal is to align poverty-reduction strategies and build collaboration among cities, all provinces, and the federal government, resulting in reduced poverty for one million Canadians.

For example, Vibrant Communities Calgary has members from diverse organizations including Alberta Health Services, Aspen Family and Community Network Society, Brown Bagging for Calgary's Kids, Burns Memorial Fund, Calgary ACSW Social Workers for Social Justice, Calgary Catholic Family Services, Calgary Chamber of Commerce, Calgary Economic Development, Calgary Transit, Calgary Winter Club, Calgary Workers Resource Centre, City of Calgary, Disability Action Hall, Ipsos Reid, Momentum, Multiple Sclerosis Society, The Parkland Institute, REAP: Respect for Earth and All People, The Salvation Army, Sheldon Chumir Foundation for Ethics and Leadership, the United Way of Calgary and Area, and Viable Calgary. These organizations represent business, government, social services, police, health, transit, labour, faith groups, and environmental groups. Vibrant Communities firmly believes that sustainable poverty reduction is best addressed through collaboration across all sectors and includes people with lived experience of poverty to harness diverse perspectives and solutions.

1. What types of groups or teams does Vibrant Communities Canada promote to tackle the complex social problem of poverty reduction?

2. What can community leaders do to promote cohesiveness among such a diverse group of people?

Source: Tamarack Institute.

Recognizing these advantages, Nathan Myhrvold, former chief technology officer at Microsoft Corporation, found that eight is the ideal size for the types of R&D teams he would form to develop new software.[28] A disadvantage of small groups is that members have fewer resources available to accomplish their goals.

Large groups—with 10 or more members—also offer some advantages. They have at their disposal more resources to achieve group goals than do small groups. These resources include the knowledge, experience, skills, and abilities of group members as well as their actual time and effort. Large groups also have advantages stemming from the **division of labour**—splitting the work to be performed into particular tasks and assigning tasks to individuals. Individuals who specialize in particular tasks are likely to become skilled at performing those tasks and contribute significantly to high group performance.

> **division of labour** Splitting the work to be performed into particular tasks and assigning tasks to individual workers.

Large groups suffer a number of problems, including greater communication and coordination difficulties and lower levels of motivation, satisfaction, and commitment. It is more difficult to share information and coordinate activities when you are dealing with 16 people rather than 8. Moreover, members of large groups might not feel that their efforts are really needed and sometimes might not even feel a part of the group.

In deciding on the appropriate size for any group, managers attempt to gain the advantages of small-group size and, at the same time, form groups with sufficient resources to accomplish their goals and have a well-developed division of labour. As a general rule, groups should have no more members than necessary to achieve a division of labour and provide the resources needed to achieve group goals. In R&D teams, for example, group size is too large when

- members spend more time communicating what they know to others rather than applying what they know to solve problems and create new products;
- individual productivity decreases; and
- group performance suffers.[29]

GROUP ROLES

A **group role** is a set of behaviours and tasks that a member of a group is expected to perform because of his or her position in the group. Members of cross-functional teams, for example, are expected to perform roles relevant to their special areas of expertise. In our earlier example of cross-functional teams at IDEO, it is the role of designers on the teams to break down preconceived ideas of what is appropriate, what is possible, and how products should look; the role of engineers to produce prototypes; and the role of an anthropologist to make sure the product will be perceived as attractive and appealing to the clients. The roles of members of top-management teams are shaped primarily by their areas of expertise—production, marketing, finance, research and development—but members of top-management teams also typically draw on their broad-based expertise as planners and strategists.

> **group role** A set of behaviours and tasks that a member of a group is expected to perform because of his or her position in the group.

In forming groups and teams, managers need to communicate clearly the expectations for each group role, what is required of each member, and how the different roles in the group fit together to accomplish group goals. Managers also need to realize that group roles change and evolve as a group's tasks and

Managers communicate the expectations for each group role and what is required of each member.
rawpixelimages/Dreamstime.com/Getstock.com

goals change and as group members gain experience and knowledge. Thus, to get the performance gains that come from experience or "learning by doing," managers should encourage group members to take the initiative to modify their assigned roles by taking on extra responsibilities as they see fit. This process, called **role making**, can enhance individual and group performance.

> **role making** Taking the initiative to modify an assigned role by taking on extra responsibilities.

Beyond the simple roles that each person fulfills in order to complete the task at hand, two major kinds of roles need to be discussed: task-oriented roles and maintenance roles. **Task-oriented roles** are performed by group members to make sure that the group accomplishes its tasks. **Maintenance roles** are carried out to make sure that team members have good relationships. For teams to be effective there needs to be some balance between task orientation and relationship maintenance. Table 10.1 identifies a number of task-oriented and maintenance roles that you might find in a team.

> **task-oriented roles** Roles performed by group members to make sure the task gets done.
> **maintenance roles** Roles performed by group members to make sure there are good relationships among group members.

In self-managed work teams and some other groups, group members themselves are responsible for creating and assigning roles. Many self-managed work teams also pick their own team leaders. When group members create their own roles, managers should be available in an advisory capacity, helping group members effectively settle conflicts and disagreements. At Johnsonville Foods, for example, the position titles of first-line managers were changed to "advisory coach" to reflect the managers' new role vis-à-vis the self-managed work teams they oversee.[30]

Group Leadership

All groups and teams need leadership. Indeed, as we discussed in detail in Chapter 9, effective leadership is a key ingredient for high-performing groups, teams, and organizations. Sometimes managers assume the leadership role, as is the case in many department-type groups and top-management teams.

TABLE 10.1

Roles Required for Effective Group Functioning

	Function	Description	Example
Roles that build task accomplishment	Initiating	Stating the goal or problem, making proposals about how to work on it, and setting time limits.	"Let's set up an agenda for discussing each of the problems we have to consider."
	Seeking information and opinions	Asking group members for specific factual information related to the task or problem, or for their opinions about it.	"What do you think would be the best approach to this, Jack?"
	Providing information and opinions	Sharing information or opinions related to the task or problems.	"I worked on a similar problem last year and found..."
	Clarifying	Helping one another understand ideas and suggestions that come up in the group.	"What you mean, Sue, is that we could...?"
	Elaborating	Building on one another's ideas and suggestions.	"Building on Don's idea, I think we could..."
	Summarizing	Reviewing the points covered by the group and the different ideas stated so that decisions can be based on full information.	"I'll keep track of the important points we discuss on the whiteboard."
	Consensus testing	Periodic testing about whether the group is nearing a decision or needs to continue discussion.	"Is the group ready to decide about this?"
Roles that build and maintain a group	Harmonizing	Mediating conflict among other members, reconciling disagreements, and relieving tensions.	"Don, I don't think you and Sue really see the question that differently."
	Compromising	Admitting error at times of group conflict.	"Well, I'd be willing to change if you provided some help on..."
	Gatekeeping	Making sure all members have a chance to express their ideas and feelings and preventing members from being interrupted.	"Sue, we haven't heard from you on this issue."
	Encouraging	Helping a group member make his or her point and establishing a climate of acceptance in the group.	"I think what you started to say is important, Jack. Please continue."

Source: D. Ancona, T. Kochan, M. Scully, J. Van Maanen, D.E. Westney. "Team Processes," in *Managing for the Future* (Cincinnati, OH: South-Western College Publishing 1996), p. 9. Reprinted by permission of Cengage.

Or a manager may appoint a member of a group who is not a manager to be group leader or chairperson, as is the case in a task force or standing committee. In other cases, group or team members may choose their own leaders, or a leader may emerge naturally as group members work together to achieve group goals. When managers empower members of self-managed work teams, they often let group members choose their own leaders. Some self-managed work teams find it effective to rotate the leadership role among their members. Whether leaders of groups and teams are managers or not and whether they are appointed by managers (often referred to as *formal leaders*) or emerge naturally in a group (often referred to as *informal leaders*), they play an important role in ensuring that groups and teams perform up to their potential.

Stages of Group Development

As many managers overseeing self-managed teams have learned, it sometimes takes a self-managed work team two or three years to perform up to its true capabilities.[31] As their experience suggests, what a group is capable of achieving depends in part on its stage of development. Knowing that it takes considerable time for self-managed work teams to get up and running has helped managers have realistic expectations for new teams and know that they need to provide new team members with considerable training and guidance.

Every group's development over time is somewhat unique. However, researchers have identified five stages of group development that many groups seem to pass through (see Figure 10.6).[32] The model shows how individuals move from being independent to working interdependently with group members. Members develop new skills from working collaboratively and thus group work can transform individuals into team players. Managers play a role at each stage in managing the interpersonal processes.

- *Forming.* Members try to get to know each other and reach a common understanding of what the group is trying to accomplish and how group members should generally behave. During this stage, managers should attempt to reduce anxieties and uncertainty by striving to make each member feel like a valued part of the group.

- *Storming.* Group members experience conflict and disagreements because some members do not wish to submit to the demands of other group members. Power struggles and disputes may arise over who should lead the group. Self-managed work teams can be particularly vulnerable during the storming stage. Managers need to resolve any conflict at this stage to make sure that it does not get out of hand and lead to dysfunction. Types of conflicts and measures to resolve it are discussed later in this chapter. At the end of this stage a relatively clear hierarchy of leadership emerges in the team.

- *Norming.* Interpersonal conflicts are resolved and close ties between group members develop, and the team develops cohesiveness. A strong sense of team identity, feelings of friendship and camaraderie

FIGURE 10.6

Five Stages of Group Development

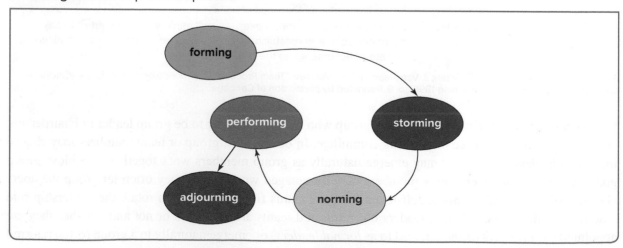

emerge. Group members arrive at a consensus about how group members should behave toward one another. These acceptable standards of behaviour that are shared by members are called *norms*. When agreed to and accepted by the team, norms act as a means of influencing the behaviour of team members with minimal external control from managers. Managers do play a role in ensuring that the norms that are developed by the team are high-performance norms.

- *Performing*. The real work of the group gets accomplished during this stage. Team energy goes from getting to know each other to performing the task at hand. Depending on the type of group in question, managers need to take different steps at this stage to help ensure that groups perform effectively. Managers of departments need to make sure that group members are motivated and that they are effectively supporting group members. Managers overseeing self-managed work teams have to empower team members and make sure that teams are given enough responsibility and autonomy at the performing stage.

- *Adjourning*. This stage applies only to groups that eventually are disbanded, such as task forces. For permanent teams, performing is the last stage in their development. During adjourning, a group is dispersed. Sometimes adjourning takes place when a group completes a finished product, such as when a task force evaluating the pros and cons of providing on-site child care produces a report supporting its recommendation.

Temporary groups, such as task forces, have been found to not follow the five-stage development model. The *punctuated-equilibrium model* describes the pattern of development for temporary groups with deadlines to meet. This model is outlined in Figure 10.7. Essentially, there are two phases of group development in this model, with a moment of transition between them. In phase one, the members of the group clarify and accept the goals of the team and the direction it will take to achieve the objectives. This initial phase is a period of *inertia,* where the members of the group are locked into a fixed course of action. Managers may notice that team members often fail to act on getting things done in this early period, or that members carry out their tasks in an uncoordinated manner. The team's performance level is low. At some point closer to the mid-point from the initial meeting and the deadline for the project, the group moves out of the inertia phase and recognizes that activities need to be done and tasks need to be accomplished. This is the transition point from phase one to phase two. In phase two a new direction and

FIGURE 10.7

Punctuated-Equilibrium Model of Team Development

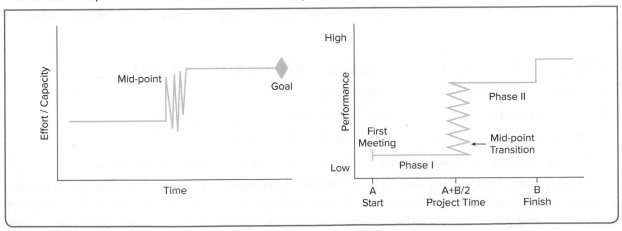

new perspectives on the project are adopted like a burst of energy that gets members moving. The revised direction sets another equilibrium point for the next period of inertia. The plans are carried out that were revised during the transition from phase one to phase two to complete the project.

The example of student teams assigned end-of-term projects illustrates the punctuated-equilibrium model well. At the initial meeting, the assignment is discussed and clarified and tasks and timelines are divided among members. Members get to know each other and try to evaluate each other's strengths and weaknesses. The group might meet regularly to discuss how they are carrying out their tasks. Then around mid-term, they re-assess progress and move to make necessary changes. This is the transition to phase two. Activities are accelerated to complete the project by the deadline. The second phase is a period of higher performance levels in terms of effort and capacity, spurred on by the looming deadline.

Managers need a flexible approach to group development and need to keep attuned to the different needs and requirements of groups at the various stages.[33] Above all else, and regardless of the stage of development, managers need to think of themselves as *resources* for groups and recognize that the stages of development are not linear. Groups can move between the different stages as different events affect its development. Thus, managers should always be trying to find ways to help groups and teams function more effectively.

Group Norms

All groups, whether top-management teams, self-managed work teams, or departments, need to control their members' behaviour to ensure that the group performs well and meets its goals. Roles as well as group norms control behaviour in groups.[34] **Group norms** are shared guidelines or rules for behaviour that most group members follow. Groups develop norms for a wide variety of behaviours, including working hours, the sharing of information among group members, how certain group tasks should be performed, and even how members of a group should dress.

> **group norms** Shared guidelines or rules for behaviour that most group members follow.

Managers should encourage members of a group to develop norms that contribute to group performance and the attainment of group goals. These could include group norms that dictate each member of a cross-functional team should always be available for the rest of the team when his or her input is needed, return phone calls as soon as possible, inform other team members of travel plans, and give team members a phone number at which he or she can be reached when travelling on business. Virtual teams such as those at Ryder System Inc. in Mississauga, Ontario, established such norms as how often to have conference calls and how often they should meet face to face in order to increase their ability to communicate effectively.

CONFORMITY TO AND DEVIANCE FROM GROUP NORMS

Group members conform to norms for three reasons:

1. They want to obtain rewards and avoid punishments.
2. They want to imitate group members whom they like and admire.
3. They have internalized the norm and believe it is the right and proper way to behave.[35]

Consider the case of Robert King, who conformed to his department's norm of attending a fundraiser for a community food bank. King's conformity could be due to (1) his desire to be a member of the group in good standing and to have friendly relationships with other group members (rewards), (2) his copying the behaviour of other members of the department whom he respects and who always attend the fundraiser (imitating other group members), or (3) his belief in the merits of supporting the activities of the food bank (believing that is the right and proper way to behave).

Failure to conform, or deviance, occurs when a member of a group strays away from a group norm. Deviance signals that a group is not controlling one of its members' behaviours. Groups generally respond to members who behave defiantly in one of three ways[36]:

1. The group might try to get the member to change his or her deviant ways and conform to the norm. Group members might try to convince the member of the need to conform, or they might ignore or even punish the deviant. For example, in a Johnsonville Foods plant, Liz Senkbiel, a member of a self-managed work team responsible for weighing sausages, failed to conform to a group norm dictating that group members should periodically clean up an untidy interview room. Because Senkbiel refused to take part in the team's cleanup efforts, team members reduced her monthly bonus by about $225 for a two-month period.[37] Senkbiel clearly learned the costs of deviant behaviour in her team.

2. The group might expel the member.

3. The group might change the norm to be consistent with the member's behaviour.

That last alternative suggests some deviant behaviour can be functional for groups when performance norms are low. Deviance is functional for a group when it causes group members to stop and evaluate norms that may be dysfunctional but that are taken for granted by the group. Often, group members do not think about why they behave in a certain way or why they follow certain norms. This can stifle innovation. Deviance can cause group members to reflect on their norms and change them when appropriate, such as when a new employee comes up with a new procedure because she was not aware of "the right way" to do something, and everyone realizes her suggestion is a better way. This is why IDEO is so successful at creating innovative products—the team members deliberately challenge accepted standards in order to stimulate creative thinking. Innovative teams have "rule-breakers."

Deviance from group norms can increase the performance of an organization.
Purestock/SuperStock

Take the case of a group of receptionists in a beauty salon who followed the norm that all appointments would be handwritten in an appointment book and, at the end of each day, the receptionist on duty would enter the appointments into the salon's computer system, which printed out the hairdressers' daily schedules. One day, a receptionist decided to enter appointments directly into the computer system at the time they were being made, bypassing the appointment book. This deviant behaviour caused the other receptionists to think about why they were using the appointment book in the first place, since all appointments could be entered into the computer directly. After consulting with the owner of the salon, the group changed its norm. Now appointments are entered directly into the computer, which saves time and cuts down on scheduling errors.

ENCOURAGING A BALANCE OF CONFORMITY TO AND DEVIANCE FROM GROUP NORMS

In order for groups and teams to be effective and help an organization gain a competitive advantage, they need to have the right balance of conformity and deviance (see Figure 10.8). A group needs a certain level of *conformity* to ensure that it can control members' behaviour and channel it in the direction of high performance and group goal accomplishment. At IDEO, conformity to a few central norms is emphasized within teams. These norms include understanding what the team is working on (the product, market, or client need), observing real people in their natural environments, visualizing how new products might work and be used, evaluating and refining product prototypes, encouraging wild ideas, and never rejecting an idea simply because it sounds too crazy!

The extent of conformity and reactions to deviance within groups are determined by group members themselves. The three reasons why people in groups conform, discussed earlier—to obtain rewards and avoid punishment, to be like the people they admire, and/or because of the belief that it is the right and

FIGURE 10.8

Balancing Conformity and Deviance in Groups

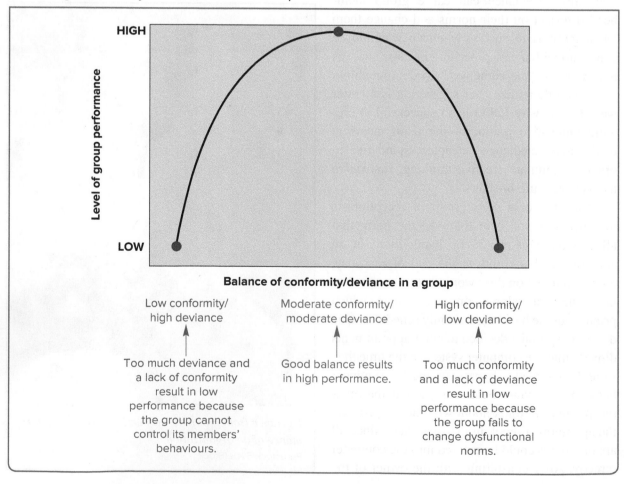

FIGURE 10.9

Changing Established Norms

- First, managers can be role models for the groups and teams they oversee. When managers encourage and accept employees' suggestions for changes in procedures, do not rigidly insist that tasks be accomplished in a certain way, and admit when a norm that they once supported is no longer functional, they signal to group members that conformity should not come at the expense of needed changes and improvements.

- Second, managers should let employees know that there are always ways to improve group processes and performance levels and thus opportunities to replace existing norms with norms that will better enable a group to achieve its goals and perform at a high level.

- Third, managers should encourage members of groups and teams to periodically assess the appropriateness of their existing norms.

proper way to behave—are powerful forces that more often than not result in group members' conforming to norms. Sometimes these forces are so strong that deviance rarely occurs in groups, and when it does, it is stamped out quickly.

Managers can take several steps to ensure that there is enough tolerance of deviance in groups so that group members are willing to deviate from dysfunctional norms and reflect on the appropriateness of the violated norm and change the norm if necessary. See Figure 10.9.

Group Cohesiveness

Another important element of group dynamics that affects group performance and effectiveness is **group cohesiveness**, the degree to which members are attracted or loyal to their group or team.[38] When group cohesiveness is high, individuals strongly value their group membership, find the group very appealing, and have strong desires to remain part of the group. When group cohesiveness is low, group members do not find their group particularly appealing and have little desire to retain their group membership. Research suggests that managers should aim to have a moderate level of cohesiveness in the groups and teams they manage because that is most likely to contribute to an organization's competitive advantage.

group cohesiveness The degree to which members are attracted or loyal to a group.

DETERMINANTS OF GROUP COHESIVENESS

Four factors contribute to the level of group cohesiveness (see Figure 10.10).[39] By influencing these *determinants of group cohesiveness,* managers can raise or lower the level of cohesiveness to promote moderate levels of cohesiveness in groups and teams.

- *Group size*—To promote cohesiveness in groups, when feasible, managers should form groups that are small to medium in size (about 2 to 15 members). If a group is low in cohesiveness and large in size, managers might want to consider the feasibility of dividing the group in two and assigning different tasks and goals to the two newly formed groups.

FIGURE 10.10

Determinants and Consequences of Group Cohesiveness

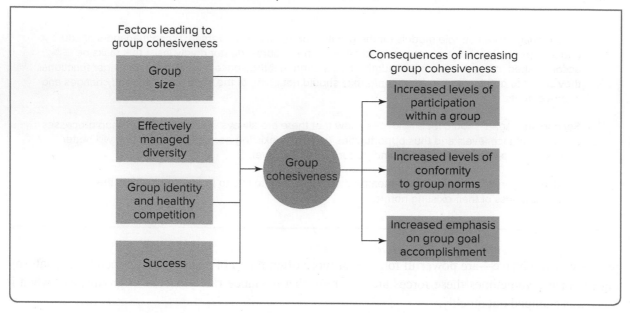

- *Effectively managed diversity*—Diverse groups often come up with more innovative and creative ideas. One reason cross-functional teams are so popular in organizations like IDEO is that the diversity in expertise represented in the teams results in higher levels of team performance. In forming groups and teams, managers need to make sure that the diversity in knowledge, experience, expertise, and other characteristics necessary for group goal accomplishment is represented in the new groups. Managers then have to make sure that this diversity in group membership is effectively managed so that groups will be cohesive.

- *Group identity and healthy competition*—When group cohesiveness is low, managers can often increase it by encouraging groups to develop their own identities or personalities and to engage in healthy competition. This is precisely what managers at Eaton Corporation's manufacturing facility in Lincoln, Illinois, did. Eaton's employees manufacture products such as engine valves, gears, truck axles, and circuit breakers. Managers at Eaton created self-managed work teams to cut costs and improve performance. They realized, however, that the teams would have to be cohesive to ensure that they would strive to achieve their goals. Managers promoted group identity by having the teams give themselves names such as "The Hoods," "The Worms," and "Scrap Attack" (a team striving to reduce costly scrap metal waste by 50 percent). Healthy competition among groups was promoted by displaying measures of each team's performance and the extent to which teams met their goals on a large TV screen in the cafeteria and by rewarding team members for team performance.[40]

  If groups are too cohesive, managers can try to decrease cohesiveness by promoting organizational (rather than group) identity and making the organization as a whole the focus of the group's efforts. Excessive levels of cohesiveness also can be reduced by reducing or eliminating competition among groups and rewarding cooperation.

- *Success*—When it comes to promoting group cohesiveness, there is more than a grain of truth to the saying "Nothing succeeds like success." As groups become more successful, they become increasingly attractive to their members, and their cohesiveness tends to increase. When cohesiveness is low, managers can increase cohesiveness by making sure that a group can achieve some noticeable and visible successes.

Consider a group of salespeople in the housewares department of a medium-size department store. The housewares department was recently moved to a corner of the store's basement. Its remote location resulted in low sales because of infrequent customer traffic in that part of the store. The salespeople, who were generally evaluated favourably by their supervisors and were valued members of the store, tried various initiatives to boost sales, but to no avail. As a result of this lack of success and the poor performance of their department, their cohesiveness started to plummet. To increase and preserve the cohesiveness of the group, the store manager implemented a group-based incentive across the store. In any month, members of the group with the best attendance and punctuality records would have their names and pictures posted on a bulletin board in the cafeteria and would each receive a $50 gift certificate. The housewares group frequently had the best records, and their success on this dimension helped to build and maintain their cohesiveness. Moreover, this initiative boosted attendance and discouraged lateness throughout the store.

CONSEQUENCES OF GROUP COHESIVENESS

There are three major consequences of increasing group cohesiveness: *level of participation within a group, level of conformity to group norms,* and *emphasis on group goal accomplishment* (see Figure 10.10).[41]

As group cohesiveness grows, the extent of group members' participation within the group increases. Increasing levels of group cohesiveness result in increasing levels of conformity to group norms. This is a good thing for the organization when the performance norms are high. But when performance norms are low, groups need a good dose of deviance to shake things up and adopt better working habits. And finally, as group cohesiveness grows, emphasis on group goal accomplishment also increases within a group.

A moderate level of cohesiveness motivates group members to accomplish both group and organizational goals. A moderate level of group cohesiveness helps ensure that group members take an active part in the group and communicate effectively with each other. The reason managers may not want to encourage high levels of cohesiveness is illustrated by the example of two cross-functional teams responsible for developing new toys at a large toy company. Members of the highly cohesive Team Alpha often have lengthy meetings that usually start with non-work-related conversations and jokes, meet more often than most of the other cross-functional teams in the company, and spend a good portion of their time communicating the ins and outs of their department's contribution to toy development to other team members. Members of the moderately cohesive Team Beta generally have efficient meetings in which ideas are communicated and discussed as needed, do not meet more often than necessary, and share the ins and outs of their expertise with one another to the extent needed for the development process. Teams Alpha and Beta have both developed some top-selling toys. However, it generally takes Team Alpha 30 percent longer to do so than Team Beta. This is why too much cohesiveness can be too much of a good thing. Thus a moderate degree of cohesiveness often yields the best outcome.

As group cohesiveness increases, the emphasis placed on group goal accomplishment also increases within a group. A very strong emphasis on group goal accomplishment, however, does not always lead to organizational effectiveness. For an organization to be effective and gain a competitive advantage, the different groups and teams in the organization must cooperate with one another and be motivated to achieve *organizational goals,* even if doing so sometimes comes at the expense of the achievement of group goals. A moderate level of cohesiveness motivates group members to accomplish both group and organizational goals. High levels of cohesiveness can cause group members to be so narrowly focused on group goal accomplishment that they may strive to achieve group goals no matter what—even when doing so jeopardizes organizational performance overall.

Take, again, the teams at the large toy company as an example. At this company the major goal of two cross-functional teams was to develop new toy lines that were truly innovative, utilized the latest in technology, and were in some way fundamentally distinct from other toys on the market. Team Alpha's high level of cohesiveness contributed to its emphasis on the goal of developing an innovative line of toys; thus, the team stuck with its usual design process. Team Beta, in contrast, realized that speed in developing the new line of toys was

Teams must be motivated to collaborate in order to achieve goals
© Fsstock | Dreamstime.com

an important organizational goal. Producing the new line of toys quickly should take precedence over the goal of developing groundbreaking new toys, at least in the short run. Team Beta's moderate level of cohesiveness contributed to team members' doing what was best for the toy company in this case.

A note of caution: In 1972, psychologist Janis Irving named a phenomenon called "groupthink."[42] The group cohesiveness in groupthink becomes dysfunctional. In other words, the group's decision-making processes become faulty because members do not consider all the alternatives and seek unanimity at the expense of quality decisions. To challenge such groupthink, a critical analysis of how the group makes decisions needs to occur. We now turn to this topic.

Group Decision Making

LO4 Explain how group decision making can be improved.

Many, perhaps most, important organizational decisions are made by groups of managers rather than by individuals. Group decision making is superior to individual decision making in several respects. When managers work as a team to make decisions and solve problems, their choices of alternatives are less likely to fall victim to the biases and errors discussed previously. They are able to draw on the combined skills, competencies, and accumulated knowledge of group members, and thereby improve their ability to generate feasible alternatives and make good decisions. Group decision making also allows managers to process more information and to correct each other's errors. In the implementation phase, all managers affected by the decisions agree to cooperate. When a group of managers makes a decision, as opposed to one top manager making a decision and imposing it on subordinate managers, it is more probable that the decision will be implemented successfully.

Nevertheless, some disadvantages are associated with group decision making. Groups often take much longer than individuals to make decisions. Getting two or more managers to agree to the same solution can be difficult because managers' interests and preferences are often different. In addition, just like decision making by individual managers, group decision making can be undermined by biases. A major source of group bias is *groupthink*.

FIGURE 10.11

Symptoms of Groupthink

- *Illusion of invulnerability.* Group members become overconfident, and this causes them to take extraordinary risks.

- *Assumption of morality.* Group members believe that the group's objectives are morally right, and so they do not debate the ethics of their actions.

- *Rationalized resistance.* No matter how strongly the evidence may contradict their basic assumptions, group members rationalize that their assumptions are correct and that the negative evidence is faulty.

- *Peer pressure.* Members who express doubts about any of the group's shared views are pressured to ignore their concerns and to support the group.

- *Minimized doubts.* Members who have doubts or hold differing points of view may keep silent about their misgivings and even minimize to themselves the importance of their doubts.

- *Illusion of unanimity.* If someone does not speak, it is assumed that he or she agrees with the group. In other words, silence becomes viewed as a "yes" vote.

The Perils of Groupthink

Groupthink is a pattern of faulty and biased decision making that occurs in groups whose members strive for agreement among themselves at the expense of accurately assessing information relevant to a decision.[43] When individuals are subject to groupthink, they collectively embark on a course of action without developing appropriate criteria to evaluate alternatives. Typically, a group rallies around a strong individual and the course of action that the individual supports. Group members become blindly committed to that course of action without evaluating its merits. Commitment is often based on an emotional—rather than objective—assessment of the best course of action. We have all seen the symptoms of the groupthink phenomenon, outlined in Figure 10.11.[44]

groupthink A pattern of faulty and biased decision making that occurs in groups whose members strive for agreement among themselves at the expense of accurately assessing information relevant to a decision.

The data on the consequences of groupthink are mixed. While pressures for agreement and harmony within a group may have the unintended effect of discouraging individuals from raising issues that run counter to majority opinion, recent research suggests some positive outcomes from groupthink. In a study of groupthink in five large corporations, the illusion of invulnerability, the belief in inherent group morality, and the illusion of unanimity often led to greater team performance, counter to what the original groupthink proposals suggest.[45]

Improving Group Decision Making

A variety of steps can be taken to improve group decision making.[46] Managers should encourage group leaders to be impartial in their leadership, and actively seek input from all group members. Leaders should avoid expressing their own opinions in the early stages of discussion.

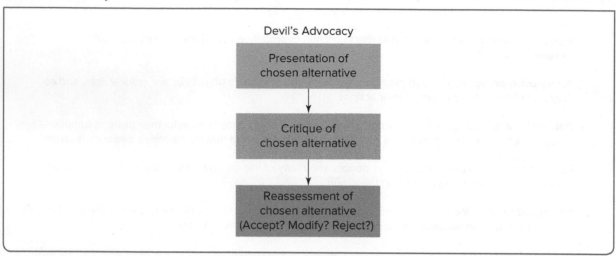

FIGURE 10.12

Devil's Advocacy

One strategy to improve group decision making is to encourage one group member to play the role of the devil's advocate. **Devil's advocacy** is a critical analysis of a preferred alternative to pinpoint its strengths and weaknesses before it is implemented (see Figure 10.12).[47] Typically, one member of the decision-making group plays the role of the devil's advocate. The devil's advocate critiques and challenges the way the group evaluated alternatives and chose one over the others. The purpose of devil's advocacy is to identify all the reasons that might make the preferred alternative unacceptable after all. In this way, decision makers can be made aware of the possible perils of recommended courses of action.

devil's advocacy Critical analysis of a preferred alternative, made by a group member who plays the role of devil's advocate to defend unpopular or opposing alternatives for the sake of argument.

Another way to improve group decision making is to promote diversity in decision-making groups.[48] Bringing together male *and* female managers from various ethnic, national, and functional backgrounds broadens the range of life experiences and opinions that group members can draw from as they generate, assess, and choose among alternatives. Moreover, diverse groups are sometimes less prone to groupthink because group members already differ from each other and thus are less subject to pressures for uniformity. The Swiss firm BrainStore takes advantage of diversity to improve decision making by mixing children and managers together to create innovative products that rely on scalable, replicable processes.[49]

Promoting Group Creativity

To encourage creativity at the group level, organizations can make use of group problem-solving techniques that promote creative ideas and innovative solutions. These techniques can also be used to prevent groupthink and to help managers and employees uncover biases. Here, we look at three group decision-making techniques: *brainstorming,* the *nominal group technique,* and the *Delphi technique.*

BRAINSTORMING

Brainstorming is a group problem-solving technique in which individuals meet face to face to generate and debate a wide variety of alternatives from which to make a decision.[50] Generally, from 5 to 15 individuals meet in a closed-door session and proceed like this:

- One person describes in broad outline the problem the group is to address.
- Group members then share their ideas and generate alternative courses of action.
- As each alternative is described, group members are not allowed to criticize it, and everyone withholds judgment until all alternatives have been heard. One member of the group records the alternatives on a flip chart.
- Group members are encouraged to be as innovative and radical as possible. Anything goes, and the greater the number of ideas put forth, the better. Moreover, group members are encouraged to "piggyback"—that is, to build on each other's suggestions.
- When all alternatives have been generated, group members debate the pros and cons of each and develop a short list of the best alternatives.

brainstorming A group problem-solving technique in which individuals meet face to face to generate and debate a wide variety of alternatives from which to make a decision.

Brainstorming is very useful in some problem-solving situations—for example, when trying to find a new name for a perfume or for a model of car. But sometimes individuals working alone can generate more alternatives. The main reason, it seems, is the **production blocking** that occurs in groups because members cannot always simultaneously make sense of all the alternatives being generated, think up additional alternatives, and remember what they were thinking.[51]

production blocking A loss of productivity in brainstorming sessions due to the unstructured nature of brainstorming.

NOMINAL GROUP TECHNIQUE

To avoid production blocking, the **nominal group technique** is often used. It provides a more structured way of generating alternatives in writing and gives each individual more time and opportunity to generate alternative solutions. The nominal group technique is especially useful when an issue is controversial and when different people might be expected to champion different courses of action. Generally, a small group of people meet in a closed-door session and adopt the following procedures:

- One person outlines the problem to be addressed, and 30 or 40 minutes are allocated for each group member to write down ideas and solutions. Group members are encouraged to be innovative.
- Individuals take turns reading their suggestions to the group. One person writes the alternatives on a flip chart. No criticism or evaluation of alternatives is allowed until all alternatives have been read.
- The alternatives are then discussed, one by one, in the sequence in which they were first proposed. Group members can ask for clarifying information and critique each alternative to identify its pros and cons.
- When all alternatives have been discussed, each group member ranks all the alternatives from most preferred to least preferred, and the alternative that receives the highest ranking is chosen.[52]

nominal group technique A decision-making technique in which group members write down ideas and solutions, read their suggestions to the whole group, and discuss and then rank the alternatives.

DELPHI TECHNIQUE

Both nominal group technique and brainstorming require people to meet together to generate creative ideas and engage in joint problem solving. What happens if people are in different cities or in different parts of the world and cannot meet face to face? Videoconferencing is one way to bring distant people together to brainstorm. Another way is to use the **Delphi technique**, a written approach to creative problem solving.[53] The Delphi technique works like this:

- The group leader writes a statement of the problem and a series of questions to which participating individuals are to respond.

- The questions are sent to the managers and departmental experts who are most knowledgeable about the problem; they are asked to generate solutions and send the questionnaire back to the group leader.

- The group leader records and summarizes the responses. The results are then sent back to the participants, with additional questions to be answered before a decision can be made.

- The process is repeated until a consensus is reached and the most suitable course of action is clear.

Delphi technique A decision-making technique in which group members do not meet face to face but respond in writing to questions posed by the group leader.

Managers must take steps to ensure that teams are performing at high levels. We now turn to how managers can encourage high performance levels by teams.

Managing Groups and Teams for High Performance

LO5 Describe how managers can create high-performing teams.

Now that you have a good understanding of the reasons why groups and teams are so important for organizations; the types of groups that managers create; and group dynamics, group decision making, and the perils of groupthink, we consider additional steps that managers can take to make sure groups and teams perform highly and contribute to organizational effectiveness. Managers who want top-performing groups and teams need to (1) motivate group members to achieve organizational goals, (2) reduce social loafing, and (3) help groups manage conflict effectively.

Motivating Group Members to Achieve Organizational Goals

When work is difficult, tedious, or requires a high level of commitment and energy, managers cannot assume that group members will always be motivated to work toward the achievement of organizational goals. Consider the case of a group of house painters who paint the interiors and exteriors of new homes for a construction company and are paid on an hourly basis. Why should they strive to complete painting jobs quickly and efficiently if doing so will just make them feel more tired at the end of the day and they will not receive any tangible benefits? It makes more sense for the painters to adopt a more relaxed approach, to take frequent breaks, and to work at a leisurely pace. This relaxed approach, however, impairs the construction company's ability to gain a competitive advantage because it raises costs and increases the time needed to complete a new home.

Managers can motivate members of groups and teams to reach organizational goals and create a competitive advantage by making sure that the individual members themselves benefit when the group or team performs highly. Members must benefit from personal growth and be accountable for their part in the production of collective work products or outputs. In addition, in order for a team to be a high-performance team, the collective work products must satisfy or exceed organizational goals.[54] If members of a self-managed work team know that they will receive a percentage of any cost savings that the team discovers and implements, they probably will try to cut costs. For example, Canadian Tire offers team incentives to employees. "Secret" retail shoppers visit the outlets on a regular basis and score them on such factors as cleanliness, the manner in which their transaction was processed, and the types of products offered, using a 100-point scoring system. Scores above a particular threshold provide extra compensation that is shared by the team. Xerox Canada, through its XTRA program, rewards districts for achieving profit and customer satisfaction targets. Everyone in the district shares equally in the bonuses.

Managers often rely on some combination of individual and group-based incentives to motivate members of groups and teams to work toward reaching organizational goals and a competitive advantage. When individual performance within a group can be assessed, pay is often determined by individual performance or by both individual and group performance. When individual performance within a group cannot be assessed accurately, then group performance should be the key determinant of pay levels. Many companies that use self-managed work teams base team members' pay in part on team performance.[55] A major challenge for managers is to develop a fair pay system that will lead to both high individual motivation and high group or team performance. In addition to monetary rewards, benefits that managers can make available to group members when a group performs highly could also include equipment and computer software, awards and other forms of recognition, and choice future work assignments. For example, members of self-managed work teams that develop new software at companies such as Microsoft often value working on interesting and important projects, and so members of teams that perform highly are rewarded with interesting and important new projects.

At IDEO, the innovative design firm profiled in the opening case, managers motivate team members by making them feel important. As Tom Kelley, IDEO's former general manager (now a partner), put it, "When people feel special, they'll perform beyond your wildest dreams."[56] To make IDEO team members feel special, IDEO managers plan unique and fun year-end parties, give teams the opportunity to take time off if they feel they need or want to, encourage teams to take field trips, and see pranks as a way to incorporate fun into the workplace.[57]

> *"When people feel special, they'll perform beyond your wildest dreams."*
>
> Tom Kelley, partner, IDEO

Reducing Social Loafing in Groups

We have been focusing on the steps that managers can take to encourage high levels of performance in groups. Managers, however, need to be aware of an important downside to group and teamwork: the potential for social loafing, which reduces group performance. **Social loafing** is the tendency of individuals to put forth less effort when they work in groups than when they work alone.[58] Have you ever watched one or two group members who never seemed to be pulling their weight? Have you ever worked in a student club or committee in which some members always seemed to be missing meetings and never volunteered for activities? Have you ever had a job in which one or two of your co-workers seemed to be slacking off because they knew that you or other members of your work group would make up for their low levels of effort? If you have, you have witnessed social loafing in action. When individuals within a team are not held accountable for their efforts, they are less likely to put forth to their full potential.

social loafing The tendency of individuals to put forth less effort when they work in groups than when they work alone.

Social loafing can occur in all kinds of groups and teams and in all kinds of organizations. It can result in lower group performance and may even prevent a group from reaching its goals. Fortunately, managers can take steps to reduce social loafing and sometimes completely eliminate it. Here, we look at three such steps (Figure 10.13):

1. *Making sure that individual contributions to a group are identifiable.* Some people may engage in social loafing when they work in groups because they think that they can hide in the crowd—that no one will notice if they put forth less effort than they should. Other people may think that if they put forth high levels of effort and make substantial contributions to the group, their contributions will not be noticed and they will receive no rewards for their work—so why bother?[59]

   One way in which managers can effectively eliminate social loafing is by making individual contributions to a group identifiable so that group members perceive that low and high levels of effort will be noticed and individual contributions evaluated.[60] Managers can accomplish this by assigning specific tasks to group members and holding them accountable for their completion. Take the case of a group of eight employees responsible for reshelving returned books in a large public library in Vancouver. The head librarian was concerned that there was always a backlog of seven or eight carts of books to be reshelved, even though the employees never seemed to be particularly busy and some even found time to sit down and read newspapers and magazines. The librarian decided to try to eliminate the apparent social loafing by assigning each employee sole responsibility for reshelving

FIGURE 10.13

Three Ways to Reduce Social Loafing

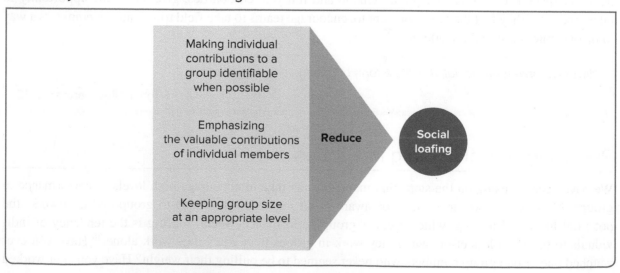

a particular section of the library. Because the library's front-desk employees sorted the books by section on the carts as they were returned, holding the shelvers responsible for particular sections was easily accomplished. Once the shelvers knew that the librarian could identify their effort or lack of effort, there were rarely any backlogs of books to be reshelved.

Sometimes the members of a group can cooperate to eliminate social loafing by making individual contributions identifiable. For example, in a small security company, members of a self-managed work team who assemble control boxes for home alarm systems start each day by deciding who will perform which tasks that day and how much work each member and the group as a whole should strive to accomplish. Each team member knows that, at the end of the day, the other team members will know exactly how much he or she has accomplished. With this system in place, social loafing never occurs in the team. Each team member is committed to their own success and the success of every other member. Remember, however, that in some teams, individual contributions cannot be made identifiable.

2. *Emphasizing the valuable contributions of each individual group member.* Another reason why social loafing may occur is that people sometimes think that their efforts are unnecessary or unimportant when they work in a group. They feel the group will accomplish its goals and perform at an acceptable level whether or not they personally perform at a high level. To counteract this belief, when managers form groups they should assign individuals to a group on the basis of the valuable contributions that *each* person can make to the group as a whole. Individuals who feel their contributions matter will be less likely to engage in social loafing.

3. *Making sure that the group size is not too large.* As size increases, identifying individual contributions becomes increasingly difficult and members are increasingly likely to think that their individual contributions are not very important. To overcome this, managers should form groups with no more members than are needed to accomplish group goals and perform at a high level.[61]

Helping Groups to Manage Conflict Effectively

At some point or other, practically all groups experience conflict either within the group (*intragroup conflict*) or with other groups (*intergroup conflict*). Individuals often have turbulent working relationships that call for managers to take steps to help individuals manage conflict and disagreements. Types of conflict that emerge within groups and what managers can do to handle conflict effectively is discussed below.

Task-related conflict (or *constructive conflict*) occurs when the members of the group perceive a problem or have a disagreement about the nature of the task or project, not in the way the members are relating to one another. This type of conflict is relatively easy to resolve by seeking clarification about the nature of the task or problem to be solved. **Relationship conflict**, on the other hand, occurs when members of the group perceive each other's attitudes as the problem. Differences in opinions are viewed as personal attacks that threaten to derail the project.

Too much conflict can be dysfunctional for a high-performing organization.
© Paulus Rusyanto | Dreamstime.com

> **task-related conflict** Members of the group perceive a problem or have a disagreement about the nature of the task or project.
>
> **relationship conflict** Members of the group perceive each other's attitudes as a problem.

Organizational conflict often arises as the result of communication breakdowns among groups. **Organizational conflict** is the discord that arises when the goals, interests, or values of different individuals or groups are incompatible and those individuals or groups block or thwart each other's attempts to achieve their objectives.[62]

> **organizational conflict** The discord that arises when the goals, interests, or values of different individuals or groups are incompatible and those individuals or groups block or thwart each other's attempts to achieve their objectives.

Conflict is an inevitable part of organizational life because the goals of different stakeholders are often incompatible. For example, while shareholders want to maximize their return on investment (ROI) which may include cost cutting by reducing wages paid to workers, employees seek stable employment and fair wages. Organizational conflict also can exist between departments and divisions that compete for resources or even between managers who may be competing for promotion to the next level in the organizational hierarchy.

Though many people dislike conflict, it is not always dysfunctional. Too little conflict can be as bad as too much conflict, but a medium level of conflict can encourage a variety of perspectives that improve organizational functioning and effectiveness and help decision making. Conflict is a force that needs to be managed rather than eliminated.[63] Managers should never try to eliminate all conflict but rather should try to keep conflict at a moderate and functional level to promote change efforts that benefit the organization. To deal with conflict effectively, managers should understand the sources of conflict in organizations and understand how individuals behave when they are engaged in conflict.

Sources of Organizational Conflict

Organizational conflict can happen between individuals, within a group or department, between groups or departments, or even across organizations. Conflict can arise for a variety of reasons. Within organizations conflict occurs for such reasons as overlapping authority, task interdependencies, incompatible evaluation or reward systems, scarce resources, status inconsistencies, and incompatible goals and time horizons (see Figure 10.14).[64]

OVERLAPPING AUTHORITY

Recall from Chapter 6 the organizational structure called a *matrix* structure. The matrix structure groups people and resources by function and product. Team members from different functional areas come together in a cross-functional team to develop new products. This kind of structure is very flexible and allows for creative innovation in product development. The drawback, as you recall, is that team members report to two bosses: the manager of the functional area, and the leader of the product team. As you can imagine, this dual reporting mechanism may cause conflicting demands on team members who do not know which manager to satisfy first. Also, functional and team managers may come into conflict over precisely who is in charge of which team members and for how long. Overlapping authority, as in the case with the matrix structure, can be a source of conflict.

FIGURE 10.14

Sources of Conflict in Organizations

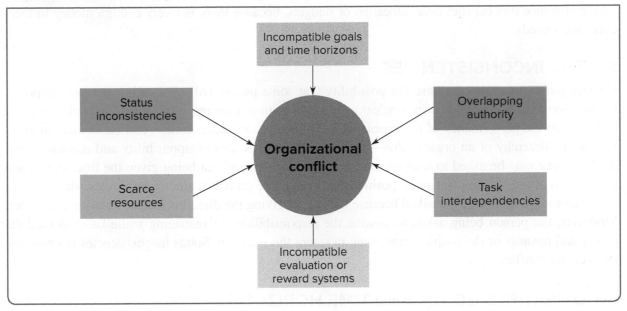

TASK INTERDEPENDENCIES

When people and work units depend on other people and work units for information, materials, or assistance, *task interdependence* exists. Highly interdependent work units require better coordination, communication, and mutual adjustment to maintain work performance. The higher the level of task interdependence, the greater the risk of conflict, because there is a greater chance that each side will disrupt or interfere with the other side's work. Take, for example, the production process of a soft drink manufacturer. The workers that fill, pack, and ship the full bottles depend on the workers who create the glass bottles to send them down the line in an orderly and timely fashion. If there is a problem with the production of the glass bottles, the work at the other end of the line is disrupted.

INCOMPATIBLE EVALUATION OR REWARD SYSTEMS

Often managers develop employee performance and reward systems that create conflict among groups because they contradict and run counter to each group's goals. Continuing with the soft drink manufacturing example, conflict may arise if the bottle producers and the fillers and packers are evaluated for producing different outcomes. Let's say the bottle producers are evaluated on the quantity of bottles produced and forwarded down the line for filling. Those workers are rewarded for meeting or exceeding the goals set by their manager for the number of bottles produced per shift. At the other end of the production line, the fillers and packers are evaluated on product quality and receive bonuses for minimizing customer complaints and returns. The fillers and packers are therefore motivated to reject any bottles that don't meet quality standards. But the fewer bottles rejected by employees at the filling end, the bigger the bonuses of employees at the bottle-making end. The way that managers designed the evaluation and reward system of the two work groups creates conflict between them. Bottle makers complain the fillers are too picky about quality and the fillers don't like the bottle makers questioning their quality control decisions.

SCARCE RESOURCES

When resources are scarce, such as when cutbacks have to be made, people are motivated to compete with others who also need those resources to achieve their objectives. Division heads and plant managers may experience this conflict over allocation of budgets, because there is rarely enough money to meet everyone's needs.

STATUS INCONSISTENCIES

Unclear job expectations increase the possibility that some people will be working at cross purposes. Often referred to as *role ambiguity,* unclear sets of expectations over responsibilities can lead to conflict and weaken the performance of an organization. Titles carry not only status—that is, formal authority within the hierarchy of an organization—but also expectations about responsibility and accountability. An employee may be asked to take on some managerial tasks without being given the title, status, and recognition of the formal managerial position. This can cause problems among employees who feel they don't have to do what they are asked because the person giving the direction has no status as a manager. Moreover, the person being asked to assume the responsibilities of managing while being denied the power and rewards of the position may come to resent the situation. Status inconsistencies in organizations create conflict.

INCOMPATIBLE GOALS AND TIME HORIZONS

One of the main sources of conflict is incompatible goals and time horizons among people or departments. Consider again the relationship between the bottle makers and the bottle fillers on the production line of the soft drink manufacturer. The fillers want to avoid complaints about product quality, whereas the bottle makers want to minimize the number of units rejected by the fillers. The fillers achieve their goal by being meticulous about the quality of bottles packaged and delivered to clients, but this conflicts with the bottle makers' goal of producing as many bottles as possible. These competing objectives cause conflict.

Sometimes different departments have different time constraints for completing their work which creates tension between them. For example, the production department of a magazine sets a limit on when the last advertisement has to be booked for the next issue to ensure there is enough time for production and printing. This conflicts with the interests of the salespeople. The salespeople want to close as many sales as possible to maximize their commission. One more day of sales could make a significant difference to their take-home pay, so they constantly try to push back the closing date.

Similarly, R&D departments are usually operating on a long-term time frame when they develop new products. Product deadlines are set so that marketing and sales departments can create campaigns to promote the new products within a particular budget year. If the research and development of a new product extends beyond the anticipated time frame, the marketing and sales department might lose their allotted budget. The pressure to finalize the product so that the marketing can begin can create conflict.

Conflict Resolution Approaches

Regardless of the source of the conflict, knowing how individuals handle conflict is an important skill for the manager who may have to intervene to resolve it. As 19th-century American philosopher and psychologist William James said, "Whenever you're in conflict with someone, there is one factor that can make the difference between damaging your relationship and deepening it. That factor is attitude."[65] The behaviours for handling conflict fall along two dimensions: *cooperativeness* (the degree to which one

FIGURE 10.15

Dimensions of Conflict-Handling Behaviours

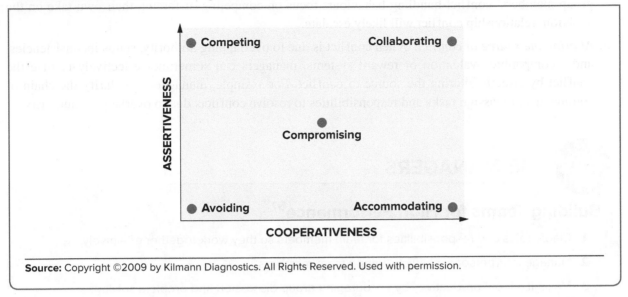

party tries to satisfy the other party's concerns) and *assertiveness* (the degree to which one party tries to satisfy his or her own concerns).[66] This can be seen in Figure 10.15. From these two dimensions emerge five conflict-handling behaviours:

- *Avoiding.* Withdrawing from conflict.
- *Competing.* One person tries to satisfy his or her own interests, without regard to the interests of the other party.
- *Compromising.* Each party is concerned about its own goal accomplishment and the goal accomplishment of the other party and is willing to engage in a give-and-take exchange and to make concessions until a reasonable resolution of the conflict is reached.
- *Accommodating.* One person tries to please the other person by putting the other's interests ahead of his or her own.
- *Collaborating.* The parties to a conflict try to satisfy their goals without making any concessions and instead come up with a way to resolve their differences that leaves them both better off.

When the parties to a conflict are willing to cooperate with each other and devise a solution that each finds acceptable (through compromise or collaboration), an organization is more likely to achieve its goals. Managers should practise the following to diminish and discourage dysfunctional conflict:

1. *Reduce interpersonal hostility by developing high levels of emotional intelligence:* Team members with high levels of emotional intelligence are less likely to fly off the handle when disagreements arise (see Chapter 9).
2. *Promote cohesiveness:* Teams with high levels of loyalty and commitment are more tolerant of emotional outbreaks and tend not to become personally offended when the conversation gets heated.
3. *Promote positive group norms:* Supportive group norms such as encouraging open and honest discussion and practising maintenance roles such as "gatekeeping" that promote participation can diminish relationship conflict.

4. *Collaborating conflict-handling behaviour:* When conflicting members of the group can collaborate by asserting their interests and point of view clearly, without being aggressive, and genuinely desire to have a positive outcome to the disagreement, a win–win situation can result. On the other hand, if group members' conflict-handling behaviours focus on competing or forcing their own take on the situation, relationship conflict will likely escalate.

5. *Altering the source of conflict.* When conflict is due to overlapping authority, status inconsistencies, and incompatible evaluation or reward systems, managers can sometimes effectively resolve the conflict by directly altering the source of conflict. For example, managers can clarify the chain of command and reassign tasks and responsibilities to resolve conflicts due to overlapping authority.

TIPS FOR MANAGERS

Building Teams for High Performance[67]

1. Clarify roles and responsibilities for team members so they work together effectively.

2. Manage interpersonal conflicts among team members.

3. Maximize team productivity by encouraging group discussion and problem solving.

4. Overcome organizational, management, and employee barriers to teamwork through the focus on enhancing the emotional intelligence of team members.

5. Identify and manage team rewards effectively.

Chapter 10

SUMMARY AND REVIEW

connect

LO1   Groups, Teams, and Organizational Effectiveness   A group is two or more people who interact with each other to reach certain goals or meet certain needs. A team is a group whose members work intensely with each other to achieve a specific common goal or objective. Groups and teams can contribute to organizational effectiveness by enhancing performance, increasing responsiveness to customers, increasing innovation, and being a source of motivation for their members.

LO2   Types of Groups and Teams   Formal groups are groups that managers establish to achieve organizational goals; they include cross-functional teams, cross-cultural teams, top-management teams, research and development teams, departments, task forces, self-managed work teams, and virtual teams. Informal groups are groups that employees form because they believe that the groups will help them achieve their own goals or meet their needs; they include friendship groups and interest groups.

LO3   Group Dynamics   Key elements of group dynamics are group size and roles, group leadership, group development, group norms, and group cohesiveness. The advantages and disadvantages of large and small groups suggest that managers should form groups with no more members than are needed to provide the human resources the group needs to reach its goals and use a division of labour. A group role is a set of behaviours and tasks that a member of a group is expected to perform because of his or her position in the group. All groups and teams need leadership. Five stages of development that many groups pass through are *forming, storming, norming, performing,* and *adjourning.* Groups with deadlines to meet often follow the punctuated-equilibrium model of group development. Group norms are shared rules of behaviour that most group members follow. To be effective, groups need a balance of conformity to and deviance from group norms. Conformity allows a group to control its members' behaviours in order to achieve group goals; deviance provides the impetus for needed change, innovation, and creativity. Group cohesiveness is the attractiveness of a group or team to its members. As group cohesiveness increases, so, too, do the level of participation and communication within a group, the level of conformity to group norms, and the emphasis on group goal accomplishment. Managers should strive to achieve a moderate level of group cohesiveness in the groups and teams they manage.

LO4 Group Decision Making Managers must be aware of the perils of groupthink, where members strive to reach a decision without considering all the alternatives sufficiently. Managers can minimize groupthink by playing the devil's advocate and foster creativity and innovation to improve decision making by using three techniques. (1) *Brainstorming* involves generating lots of innovative alternatives, without judgment, in a face-to-face environment. The assessment of the alternatives comes after the brainstorm. (2) The *nominal group technique* allows group members to generate alternatives individually and write them down for later consideration by the whole group. (3) The *Delphi technique* is used to solve problems by allowing experts to generate and debate appropriate solutions and courses of action.

LO5 Managing Groups and Teams for High Performance To make sure that groups and teams perform at a high level, managers need to motivate group members to work toward the achievement of organizational goals and reduce social loafing and conflict. Managers can motivate members of groups and teams to work toward the achievement of organizational goals by making sure that members personally benefit when the group or team performs at a high level.

KEY TERMS

brainstorming	group role
cross-functional teams	groupthink
cross-cultural teams	informal groups
Delphi technique	interest groups
department	maintenance roles
devil's advocacy	nominal group technique
division of labour	organizational conflict
formal groups	production blocking
friendship groups	relationship conflict
group	research and development teams
group cohesiveness	role making
group dynamics	self-managed (or self-directed) work teams
group norms	social loafing

standing committees

task forces

task-oriented roles

task-related conflict

team

top-management teams

virtual teams

WRAP-UP TO OPENING CASE

Teams Benefit from Deviance and Conformity at IDEO

Teams at IDEO have many technically gifted members, such as engineers who work on products requiring specialized knowledge; but on the same team with the engineers might be an anthropologist, a biologist, and a social scientist. After having read and understood the concepts in this chapter you should now be able to answer the following questions:

1. *How do teams at IDEO help the organization achieve a competitive advantage?*

   ANSWER: Groups and teams can help an organization gain a competitive advantage because they can (1) enhance its performance, (2) increase its responsiveness to customers, (3) increase innovation, and (4) increase employees' motivation and satisfaction. The design teams at IDEO are a diverse group of employees including designers, engineers, social scientists, and anthropologists, who come together to create a range of innovative products, from a self-sealing drink bottle for sports to medical equipment to flexible shelving for offices. The cross-functional teams draw on the expertise and knowledge from different departments to determine what is required to be responsive to customers. To promote innovation, the self-managed teams are left alone to solve problems that arise, and balance deviance from and conformity to group norms. Working in teams at IDEO can be motivating for the members by stimulating creative problem solving, engaging in social interaction, feeling connected to others, and sharing techniques for relieving stress and dealing effectively with conflict: all key ingredients of creating a competitive advantage.

2. *What types of teams are encouraged in this case?*

   ANSWER: Many types of teams and groups are found in organizations that help managers achieve organizational goals. A team is a group whose members work intensely with each other to achieve a specific common goal or objective. At IDEO, formal, cross-functional teams are formed by managers, where members from different departments are brought together to work toward a common goal. In this case the common goal is to create innovative design products that meet client needs.

3. *How do IDEO managers encourage deviance and conformity to group norms and why is this important for high performance?*

   ANSWER: Group cohesiveness is the degree to which members are attracted and loyal to their group or team. As group cohesiveness increases, members' participation, conformity to group norms, and motivation to achieve group goals increases. Managers at IDEO encourage group cohesion by planning unique and fun year-end parties, giving teams the opportunity to take time off if they feel they need or want to, encouraging teams to take field trips, and seeing pranks as a way to incorporate fun into the workplace. Too much cohesiveness may lead to dysfunctional outcomes for the organization because highly cohesive teams often focus on group goals at the expense of goals that are effective for the organization as a whole. IDEO makes sure that "rule-breakers" are incorporated into each team to ensure a moderate level of deviation from group norms occurs such that innovative and creative problem solving can result. Too much cohesiveness may also result in groupthink, where faulty and biased decision making occurs in groups whose members strive for agreement among themselves at the expense of accurately assessing information relevant to a decision. Managers at IDEO, and managers in general, strive to create moderately cohesive groups and teams to enhance organizational effectiveness and promote high performance.

MANAGEMENT IN ACTION

TOPICS FOR DISCUSSION AND ACTION

LEVEL 1 Knowledge & Comprehension

1. Describe how teams can increase an organization's competitive advantage.
2. Describe the different types of groups and teams found in organizations.
3. Describe three techniques managers can use to improve group decision making and promote creativity.

LEVEL 2 Application & Analysis

4. Explain why and how managers would use self-managed teams to achieve organizational goals. What are some of the disadvantages to using self-managed teams?
5. What steps should managers take to ensure that virtual teams are effective?
6. Describe the task and maintenance roles for effective group functioning. Which do you think are the most important, and why?

LEVEL 3 Synthesis & Evaluation

7. Teams should have a moderate level of cohesiveness and a balance of conformity to and deviance from group norms. Why are these levels important to the performance of the team?
8. Imagine that you are the manager of a hotel. What steps will you take to reduce social loafing by members of the cleaning staff who are responsible for keeping all common areas and guest rooms spotless?
9. Analyze the pitfalls of groupthink. How can group conflict be resolved?

SELF-REFLECTION EXERCISE
Diagnosing Group Failures

Think about the last dissatisfying or discouraging experience you had as a member of a group or team. Perhaps the group did not accomplish its goals, perhaps group members could agree about nothing, or perhaps there was too much social loafing. Now answer the following questions.

1. What type of group was this?

2. Were group members motivated to achieve group goals? Why, or why not?

3. What were the group's norms? How much conformity and deviance existed in the group?

4. How cohesive was the group? Why do you think the group's cohesiveness was at this level? What consequences did this level of group cohesiveness have for the group and its members?

5. Was social loafing a problem in this group? Why, or why not?

6. What could the group's leader or manager have done differently to increase group effectiveness?

7. What could group members have done differently to increase group effectiveness?

SMALL GROUP BREAKOUT EXERCISE
Creating a Cross-Functional Team

Form groups of three or four, and appoint one member as the spokesperson who will communicate your findings to the whole class when called on by the instructor. Then discuss the following scenario:

You are a group of managers in charge of food services for a large university. Recently, a survey of students, faculty, and staff was conducted to evaluate customer satisfaction with the food services provided by the university's eight cafeterias. The results were disappointing, to put it mildly. Complaints ranged from dissatisfaction with the type and range of meals and snacks provided, operating hours, and food temperature, to unresponsiveness to current concerns about the importance of low-carb/high-protein diets and the preferences of vegetarians. You have decided to form a cross-functional team to further evaluate reactions to the food services and to develop a proposal for changes that can be made to increase customer satisfaction.

1. Indicate who should be on this important cross-functional team and why.

2. Describe the goals the team should be trying to achieve.

3. Describe the different roles team members will need to perform.

4. Describe the steps you will take to help ensure that the team has a good balance between conformity and deviance and a moderate level of cohesiveness.

MANAGING ETHICALLY EXERCISE

Moon Fuel uses self-managed teams to develop and produce new websites. Some of the members of the team are engaged in social loafing, and other members of the team are reluctant to say anything. Team members are supposed to provide performance evaluations of each other at the end of each project, but some rate everyone equally to avoid conflict. This practice has caused low morale on the team because hard work results in the same pay as does loafing. Some team members are complaining that it is unethical to rate everyone the same way when individual performances differ so much. One team member has come to you for advice because you are an expert in team performance and ethics. What would you advise this team member to do? How could the team's performance be improved?

MANAGEMENT CHALLENGE EXERCISE
Building Team Spirit[68]

Jim Clemmer, based in Kitchener, Ontario, is a professional speaker, workshop/retreat leader, and author of *Growing the Distance* and *The Leader's Digest*. He says that "team spirit is the catalyst every organization needs to achieve outstanding performance." Indeed, he goes on to say that the "emotional commitment of the people using the tools and executing the plans is what determines whether companies sink or soar." He further explains how companies can kill or build spirit.

Because of your knowledge and skill in team-based performance, you have been called into discussions with the two founding partners and 10 employees of a new specialty tire company about to open its doors in Winnipeg, Manitoba. Many of these people have been friends to this point, but the owners want to get the company going on the right footing, especially because during the planning stage owners had tolerated the use of wireless devices in meetings. They notice now that some members are beginning to resent this "extra presence" while the team is doing its best to communicate. The owners have discovered that bored staff are simply emailing one another—literally "under the table."

1. What do you think is the problem here?
2. What is your best advice regarding team-building for this group?

MANAGEMENT PORTFOLIO PROJECT

Answer the following questions about the organization you have chosen to follow:

1. What types of groups and teams can you identify in this organization?
2. Does this organization use self-managed teams? How are they organized?
3. Does this organization use virtual teams? If so, in what areas of the operation do they function?
4. Can you identify any conflicts in this organization? What caused them, and how would you resolve them?

MANAGEMENT CASE

TEAMS INNOVATE AT W.L. GORE

How can managers promote high motivation, performance, and team innovation?

W.L. Gore & Associates was founded by Wilbert ("Bill") Gore and his wife Genevieve ("Vieve") in the basement of their house in 1958, and the rest has literally been history.[69] Widely recognized for its diverse and innovative products, Gore has more than $3 billion in annual sales and 9500 employees (who are called associates) worldwide.[70] Headquartered in Newark, Delaware, Gore's most widely recognized product is the waterproof fabric Gore-Tex. Gore makes a wide array of products including fabrics for outerwear, medical products used in surgeries, fibers for astronauts' space suits, and Elexir strings for acoustic guitars. While Gore has thousands of products and more than 2000 worldwide patents, most of Gore's products are based on a very adaptable material, expanded polytetrafluoroethylene (ePTFE), a polymer invented by the Gores' son in 1969.[71] A key ingredient to Gore's enduring success is its use of teams to innovate and motivate rather than relying on a hierarchy of managers.[72]

The Gores were 45 years old and the parents of five children when they took the plunge.[73] Prior to starting his own company, Bill Gore worked at DuPont, which helped him realize how teams can be powerful sources of innovation and high performance. As a member of small R&D teams at DuPont, Gore experienced firsthand how inspiring and motivating it can be to work on a self-managed team with the objective to create and innovate and having high levels of autonomy to do so. He reasoned that innovation and high motivation and performance would likely result when as many people as possible in an organization were members of self-managed teams tasked to be innovative with high levels of autonomy. And that is what he set out to accomplish by founding W. L. Gore. Thus, many teams at Gore have the goal of developing innovative new products.[74] While Gore has a CEO (Jason Field) and four divisions (electronics, fabrics, industrial, and medical), there are few managers, and associates do not have supervisors. Gore is structured around a lattice of self-managed teams in which associates and their teams communicate directly with each other whenever the need or desire arises and are tasked with the mission to innovate, perform highly, and to enjoy their work.[75] Personal initiative and high motivation are greatly valued at Gore, and working in self-managed teams with high levels of autonomy fuels new product innovations.[76] Associates working in manufacturing are also empowered to work in self-managed teams.[77]

At Gore, associates recognize leaders who are especially proficient at building great teams and accomplishing goals and willingly become their followers.[78] New hires at Gore are assigned into broad areas—such as R&D, engineering, sales and marketing, information technology, operations management, and human resources—and assigned a sponsor.[79] Sponsors are experienced associates who help newcomers learn the ropes, meet other associates, and acclimatize to Gore's unique culture and values centered around high trust and motivation. When Jim Grigsby, an electrical engineer, was hired by Gore around 15 years ago, his sponsor told him to spend some time meeting other associates and gave him a list of associates it would be good for him to talk with.[80] Having worked for more traditional and hierarchical companies, Grigsby was surprised by this advice. His thinking: "Am I really getting paid just to meet people?" After gaining an appreciation for Gore's collaborative lattice structure and extensive use of self-managed teams weeks later, Grigsby realized that he had received good advice. As he put it, "It becomes apparent that you need these people to get project work done."[81] Ultimately sponsors help newcomers find a team for which they are a good fit. Teams are truly self-managing, so it is up to the team to decide if they want to have newcomers join them, and the newcomers are responsible to the teams they join. Experienced associates are typically members of multiple self-managed teams.[82]

One of the largest 200 privately held companies in the United States, Gore is owned by the Gore family and associates.[83] Associates are awarded a percentage of their salary in shares of the company and also participate in a profit-sharing program. The shares become vested after a certain time period elapses, and associates who leave the company can sell their shares back for cash payouts.[84]

At Gore, associates are accountable to each other and the teams they are members of. Thus, perhaps it is not surprising that associates are reviewed by their peers. Each year information is gathered from around 20 colleagues of each associate and given to a compensation committee in their work unit that determines relative contributions and compensation levels for members of the unit.[85]

Associates thrive in Gore's collaborative and team-based structure. Thus, it is not surprising that Gore has received recognition for being a top employer. For example, Gore has been on *Fortune* magazine's list of the "100 Best Companies to Work For" for 20 consecutive years;[86] and for the sixth consecutive year it was among only 25 companies to make the World's Best Workplaces list.[87] As past president and CEO, Terri Kelly indicated, "– we take great pride in our continued recognition as a top workplace in the

United States and around the world, and we also continue to focus on cultivating an environment where creativity and innovation thrive."[88]

1. What type of team does W.L. Gore and Associates use in their organization structure?

2. Why is the team structure so success at Gore?

END OF PART IV: CONTINUING CASE

CARROT TOPS: MOTIVATING HIGH PERFORMANCE

Janet's team of courteous and knowledgeable drivers know their way around the city. Sometimes, however, she gets complaints from the drivers that the schedules and routes she assigns them lead them to drop off early or late or unable to deliver at all. Some have suggested she over-manages the drivers, that she should empower them to set their own routes and schedules.

To make matters worse, another grocery store manager in the area announced in a press release that they have started home delivery. This is a relatively new store and, fortunately, Janet thought, although they offer organic food, it is of inferior quality. Nevertheless, one of the five drivers Janet supervises has quit and gone to work for the competition. He voiced his dissatisfaction with Janet's management methods to anyone who would listen and was not interested in working out any differences they had. He soon had all the drivers complaining, but not offering any solutions. Janet admits that the organization of the delivery system is ad hoc, understaffed, and could be improved, but she believes that her employees should nevertheless follow her directions. She is their boss, after all!

Drawing on all segments of this case:

1. What type of team structure would you recommend Janet use with the drivers to encourage high performance?

2. Suggest a total rewards strategy for motivating the drivers.

3. Identify an example of groupthink.

4. How can MBO be applied to this case?

5. Is Janet a transformational or transactional leader? Why?

Part V

Controlling

Chapter 11

Managing Control and Operations

LEARNING OUTCOMES

LO1	Define organizational control and describe the steps in the process of control.
LO2	Describe three systems of control used in operations management.
LO3	Identify how organizations monitor and evaluate performance using output controls.
LO4	Discuss how behavioural controls regulate and motivate employees to achieve organizational goals.
LO5	Explain how effective controls help managers gain a competitive advantage.

OPENING CASE

Will CEO Mary Barra's Customer Safety Strategy Work for General Motors?

It's a place no CEO wants to be: testifying in front of the U.S. Congress, trying to account for a design flaw with an ignition switch that led to at least 124 deaths.[1]

But there was General Motors' chief executive, Mary Barra, who prior to taking the top manager's role in 2014 was responsible for the design, engineering, program management, and quality of GM vehicles around the world.[2]

Why in the world would a company with the stellar reputation of General Motors purchase a part that did not meet its own specifications?

Barra's response: "I want to know that as much as you do. It is not the way we do business today. It is not the way we want to design and engineer vehicles for our customers." Later, Barra added that "whatever mistakes were made in the past, we will not shirk from our responsibilities now and in the future. Today's GM will do the right thing."[3]

And so went Barra's strategy—repeatedly asserting that the culture of GM was changing from one where the primary focus was cutting costs, to one where the primary focus is the customer.

"The customer and their safety are at the center of everything we do," Barra said. "All I can tell you," she said, "is (at) today's General Motors, we are focused on safety." GM announced that it had entered into a consent decree with the government that will see the automotive giant pay a $35-million fine and agree to "unprecedented oversight requirements." The deal covers GM's "failure to report a safety defect . . . in a timely manner" and requires it to give investigators full access to the results of its internal probe into the recalls.[4]

AP Photo/Tony Ding

But to understand why GM failed to address major safety problems, experts say, one has to examine the culture at the automaker long before Barra became CEO, and look at the possible link between cost-cutting and quality. "It was a company that in the modern history of General Motors was always dominated by bean counters," said Maryann Keller, an auto analyst for four decades who has written two books on GM. "And bean counters had only one objective and that is make the numbers, at all cost. And sometimes at the sacrifice of things like quality."

Barra conducted an internal probe that resulted in the firing of 15 employees and the instating of new policies that encourage workers to flag production problems.

A huge new investment in the Michigan Tech design facility focussed on measures to anticipate problems and discover and eradicate errors before tragedies occur again. Unfortunately, the new investment resulted in 1000 production jobs lost in Canada.[5]

After reading and understanding the concepts in this chapter, you should be able to answer the following questions:

1. Describe the control systems failure in this case.
2. What kind of control measures did Barra set in place to make sure no such tragedies occur in the future?

Overview

The purpose of organizational control is to provide managers with a means of motivating subordinates to work toward achieving organizational goals, and to provide managers with specific feedback on how well an organization and its members are performing. If one were to imagine an organization as a living body with interconnecting parts and functions, one would see that the organizational structure, discussed in Chapter 5, provides an organization with a skeleton to which organizational control and culture add the muscles, sinews, nerves, and sensations that allow managers to regulate and govern the organization's activities. The managerial functions of planning, organizing, and controlling are inseparable. Effective managers must learn to make them work together harmoniously to avoid disasters such as those faced by General Motors in the opening case.

Figure 11.1 illustrates an overview of this chapter. First, we look in detail at the nature of organizational control and the steps in the control process that managers take to ensure that organizational standards are being met. Next we examine three systems of control used in operations management: feedforward, concurrent, and feedback measures. We then discuss how managers evaluate the outputs of the organization using financial ratios, goal setting, and operating budgets, and how they motivate their employees to achieve standards and goals; the two main types of control are *output* and *behavioural*. Finally, we discuss how *innovative* and *conservative* cultures shape managerial approaches to planning, organizing, leading, and controlling,[6] and how control mechanisms affect building a competitive advantage. By the end of this chapter, you will appreciate the rich variety of control measures available to managers and understand why developing an appropriate control system is vital to increasing the performance of an organization and its members.

FIGURE 11.1

Overview of Managing Control

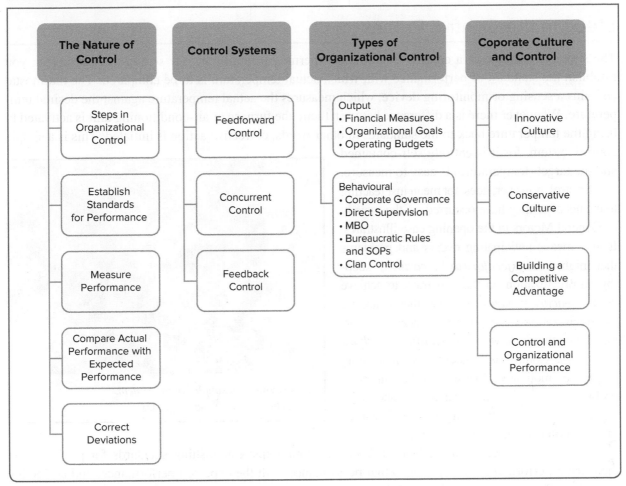

What Is Organizational Control?

LO1 | Define organizational control and describe the steps in the process of control.

As noted in Chapter 1, controlling is the process by which managers regulate, monitor, and evaluate how effectively and efficiently an organization and its members are achieving organizational goals and taking action to maintain or improve performance. As discussed in previous chapters, in *planning* and *organizing,* managers develop the organizational strategy and then create the structure that they hope will allow the organization to use resources most effectively to create value for customers or beneficiaries. In *controlling,* managers monitor and evaluate whether their organization's strategy and structure are working as intended, how they could be improved, and how they might be changed if they are not working.

Moreover, managers are not just concerned with bringing the organization's performance up to some predetermined standard; they want to push that standard forward, to encourage employees at all levels to find new ways to raise performance and gain a competitive advantage.

Steps in the Control Process

The simplest example of a control system is the thermostat in a home. By setting the thermostat, you establish the standard of performance with which actual temperature is to be compared. The thermostat contains a sensing or monitoring device, which measures the actual temperature against the desired temperature. Whenever there is a difference between them, the furnace or air-conditioning unit is activated to bring the temperature back to the standard. In other words, corrective action is initiated. This is a simple control system, for it is entirely self-contained and the target (temperature) is easy to measure.

Control, however, does not mean just reacting to events after they have occurred, as the tragedy of General Motors in the opening case illustrates. It also means anticipating events and problems that might occur (*feedforward measures*), keeping an organization on the best track to achieve goals (*concurrent measures*), and then changing the organization to respond to whatever opportunities or threats have been identified (*feedback measures*). Control is concerned with keeping employees motivated, focused on the important problems confronting the organization, and working together to make the changes that will help an organization perform better over time.

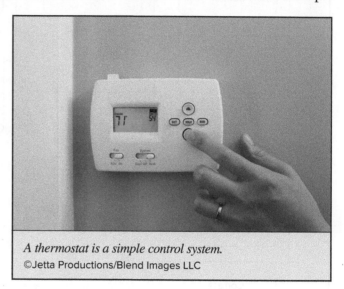

A thermostat is a simple control system.
©Jetta Productions/Blend Images LLC

The control process can be broken down into four steps: establishing standards for performance, measuring performance, comparing actual performance with the expected performance, and correcting deviations if necessary (see Figure 11.2).[7]

STEP 1: ESTABLISH STANDARDS FOR PERFORMANCE

At Step 1 in the control process, managers decide on the standards of performance, goals, or targets that they will use to evaluate the performance of either the entire organization or some part of it, such as a division, a function, or an individual. The standards are the criteria against which results are measured. The standards of performance that managers select measure efficiency, quality, responsiveness to customers, and innovation.[8] Managers can set a variety of *output standards,* including, for example, time, operating costs, inventory levels, market share, return on investment, and other financial ratios that measure profitability. *Output standards* refer to the quantity of the service or product the employee is to produce. For example, *time standards* refer to how long it is supposed to take to complete a task. Some companies, for instance, instruct staff that all emails must be answered within 24 hours. *Operating costs* measure the efficiency of production by monitoring and evaluating the actual costs associated with producing goods and services. Top managers might set a corporate goal of "reducing operating costs by 10 percent for the next three years" to increase efficiency. Also, a company might set *behavioural standards,* which refer to the quality of the actions employees take in achieving organizational goals. Behavioural standards can govern such factors as hours worked, punctuality, dress code, or how one

FIGURE 11.2

Steps in Organizational Control

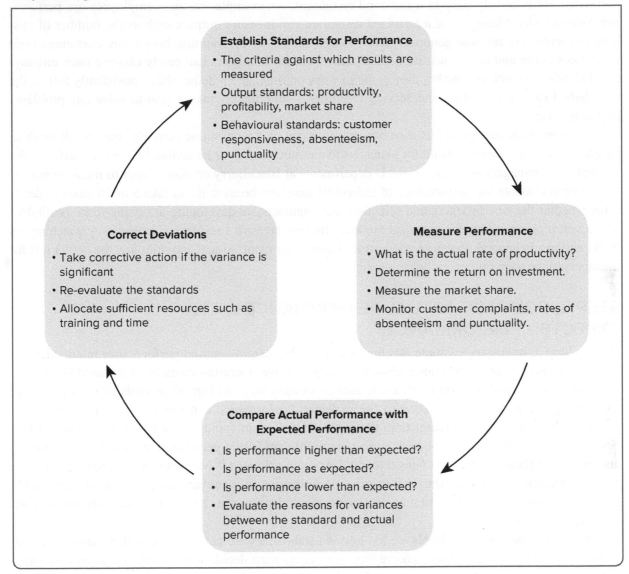

Establish Standards for Performance
- The criteria against which results are measured
- Output standards: productivity, profitability, market share
- Behavioural standards: customer responsiveness, absenteeism, punctuality

Measure Performance
- What is the actual rate of productivity?
- Determine the return on investment.
- Measure the market share.
- Monitor customer complaints, rates of absenteeism and punctuality.

Compare Actual Performance with Expected Performance
- Is performance higher than expected?
- Is performance as expected?
- Is performance lower than expected?
- Evaluate the reasons for variances between the standard and actual performance

Correct Deviations
- Take corrective action if the variance is significant
- Re-evaluate the standards
- Allocate sufficient resources such as training and time

interacts with customers. A manager of a retail clothing store might set a goal for customer service of "greeting the customer within 60 seconds of entering the store."

Managers must be careful to choose standards of performance that are not harmful in unintended ways. If managers focus on just one issue (such as efficiency) and ignore others (such as quality), managers may end up hurting their organization's performance, as the opening case on GM illustrates. Their focus on cost cutting at the expense of quality resulted in defective ignition switches being installed in GM vehicles and several lives were lost.

STEP 2: MEASURE PERFORMANCE

Once managers have decided which standards or targets they will use to evaluate performance, the next step in the control process is to measure actual performance. In practice, managers can measure or evaluate two things: (1) the actual *outputs* that result from the behaviour of their members and (2) the *behaviours* themselves (hence the terms *output control* and *behavioural control*).[9]

Sometimes both outputs and behaviours can be easily measured. Measuring outputs and evaluating behaviour are relatively easy in a fast-food restaurant, for example, because employees are performing routine tasks. Managers of a fast-food restaurant can measure outputs such as the number of customers served and revenue generated from sales quite easily by counting how many customers their employees serve and how much money customers spend. Managers can easily observe each employee's behaviour—such as whether they come to work on time, and whether they consistently follow the established rules for greeting and serving customers—and quickly take action to solve any problems that may arise.

When an organization and its members perform complex, nonroutine activities that are difficult to measure, it is much more difficult for managers to measure outputs or behaviour.[10] It is very difficult, for example, for managers in charge of R&D departments at BlackBerry or Bombardier to measure performance or to evaluate the performance of individual members because it can take 5 or 10 years to determine whether the new products that scientists and engineers are developing are going to be profitable. Moreover, it is impossible for a manager to measure how creative a research scientist is by watching his or her actions. In general, the more nonroutine or complex organizational activities are, the harder it is for managers to measure outputs or behaviours.[11]

STEP 3: COMPARE ACTUAL PERFORMANCE WITH EXPECTED PERFORMANCE

During Step 3, managers evaluate whether—and to what extent—actual performance results deviate from the standards of performance chosen in Step 1. Have operating costs been reduced by 10 percent over three years? Do the retail associates greet customers within 60 seconds of their arriving? Comparing the actual performance to the expected performance can yield three possible results. Either the performance is greater than the standard, less than standard, or has met the standard. If performance is higher than expected, managers might decide that performance standards are too low and may raise them for the next period to challenge subordinates.[12] Managers at Japanese companies are well known for the way they try to raise performance in manufacturing settings by constantly raising performance standards to motivate managers and employees to find new ways to reduce costs or increase quality.

However, if performance levels are too low and standards were not reached, or if standards were set so high that employees could not achieve them, managers must decide whether the deviation is substantial enough to warrant taking corrective action.[13] A variance analysis can be used to determine if corrective action is appropriate; see Figure 11.3. If managers are to take any form of corrective action, Step 4 is necessary.

STEP 4: CORRECT DEVIATIONS

The final step in the control process is to evaluate the results and take corrective action if necessary to meet expected performance levels. Corrective action can focus on the root of the problem when there is a significant gap between actual and expected outputs or behaviours. Whether performance standards have been met or not, managers can learn a great deal during this step: If managers decide that the level of performance is unacceptable, they must try to solve the problem. Sometimes, performance problems occur because the standard was too high—for example, perhaps the cost reduction target of 10 percent over 3 years was too optimistic and impossible to achieve. In this case, adopting

FIGURE 11.3

Variance Analysis

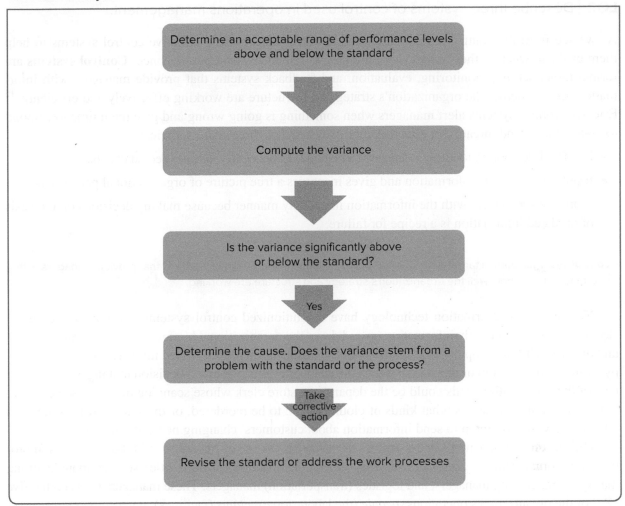

more realistic standards can reduce the gap between actual performance and desired performance levels. However, if managers determine that something in the situation is causing the problem, then to raise performance they will need to change the way in which resources are being used.[14] Perhaps the latest technology is not being used, perhaps workers lack the training they need to ensure customer responsiveness, perhaps the organization needs to buy its inputs or assemble its products abroad to compete against low-cost rivals, or perhaps it needs to restructure itself or re-engineer its work processes to increase efficiency. If managers decide that the level has been achieved or exceeded, they can consider whether the standard set was too low. However, they might also consider rewarding employees for a job well done.

Establishing targets and designing measurement systems can be difficult for managers because of the high level of uncertainty in the organizational environment. Recall from Chapter 2 that the greater the level of uncertainty, the less likely managers are able to predict what might happen. Thus, it is vital for managers to design control systems to alert them to problems so that the issues can be dealt with before they become threatening.

Control Systems and Operations Management

LO2 | Describe three systems of control used in operations management.

As we see from the control process described above, managers need effective control systems to help them evaluate whether they are staying on target with their planned performance. **Control systems** are formal target-setting, monitoring, evaluation, and feedback systems that provide managers with information about whether the organization's strategy and structure are working effectively and efficiently.[15] Effective control systems alert managers when something is going wrong and give them time to respond to opportunities and threats. An effective control system has three characteristics:

- It is flexible enough to allow managers to respond, as necessary, to unexpected events.
- It provides accurate information and gives managers a true picture of organizational performance.
- It provides managers with the information in a timely manner because making decisions on the basis of outdated information is a recipe for failure.

control systems Formal target-setting, monitoring, evaluation, and feedback systems that provide managers with information about how well the organization's strategy and structure are working.

New forms of information technology have revolutionized control systems because they ease the flow of accurate and timely information up and down the organizational hierarchy and between functions and divisions. Today, employees at all levels of the organization routinely feed information into a company's information system or network and start the chain of events that affect decision making at some other part of the organization. This could be the department-store clerk whose scanning of purchased clothing tells merchandise managers what kinds of clothing need to be reordered, or the salesperson in the field who uses a wireless laptop to send information about customers' changing needs or problems.

Operations management is the process of managing the use of materials and other resources in producing an organization's goods and services. Operations managers include titles such as manufacturing managers, purchasing managers, and logistics (transportation) managers. These managers focus on the five "Ps" of the organization's operations: *people* (the labour force), *plants* (facilities), *parts* (inputs), *processes* (technology and work flow), and *planning and control systems* (standards and measures for quality control).

operations management The process of managing the use of materials and other resources in producing an organization's goods and services.

A **production system** is the system that an organization uses to acquire inputs, convert inputs into outputs, and dispose of the outputs (goods or services). **Operations managers** are managers who are responsible for managing an organization's production system. They do whatever it takes to transform inputs into outputs. Their job is to manage the three stages of production—acquisition of inputs, control of conversion processes, and disposal of goods and services—and to determine where operating improvements might be made in order to increase quality, efficiency, and responsiveness to customers and so give an organization a competitive advantage.

production system The system an organization uses to acquire inputs, convert the inputs into outputs, and dispose of the outputs.

operations managers Managers who are responsible for managing an organization's production system.

FIGURE 11.4

Production System

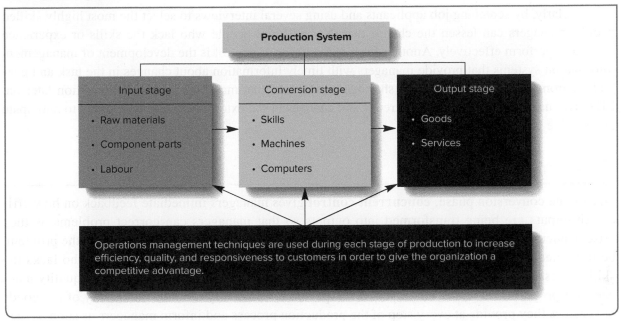

In managing a production system, operations managers focus on the three stages of the process of taking the raw materials and transforming them into a useable finished product or service. Control systems are developed to measure performance at each stage (see Figure 11.4).

Feedforward Control

Before the work begins, managers use **feedforward control** to anticipate possible problems that they can then avoid once the work is underway.[16] For example, by giving stringent product specifications to suppliers in advance (a form of performance target), an organization can control the quality of the inputs it receives from its suppliers and thus avoid potential problems at the conversion stage (see Figure 11.5). As we saw in the opening case, General Motors failed to control the quality of the auto ignition part and did not detect the problem until several deaths resulted.

FIGURE 11.5

Three Systems of Control

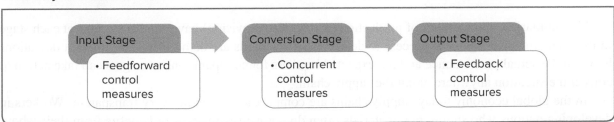

feedforward control Control that allows managers to anticipate and deal with potential problems before they occur.

Similarly, by screening job applicants and using several interviews to select the most highly skilled people, managers can lessen the chance that they will hire people who lack the skills or experience needed to perform effectively. Another form of feedforward control is the development of management information systems that provide managers with timely information about changes in the task and general environments, such as a supply shortage of an input, that may impact their organization later on. Effective managers always monitor trends and changes in the external environment to try to anticipate and resolve problems.

Concurrent Control

During the conversion phase, **concurrent control** gives managers immediate feedback on how efficiently inputs are being transformed into outputs so that managers can correct problems as they arise. Concurrent control alerts managers to the need for quick reaction to the source of the problem, be it a defective batch of inputs, a machine that is out of alignment, or an employee who lacks the skills necessary to perform a task efficiently. Concurrent control is at the heart of total quality management programs, in which employees are expected to constantly monitor the quality of the goods or services they provide at every step of the production process and inform managers as soon as they discover problems. One of the strengths of Toyota's production system, for example, is that individual employees are given the authority to push a button to stop the assembly line whenever they discover a quality problem. When all problems have been corrected, the result is a finished product that is much more reliable.

concurrent control Control that gives managers immediate feedback on how efficiently inputs are being transformed into outputs so that managers can correct problems as they arise.

Feedback Control

Once the work is completed, managers use **feedback control** to provide information about customers' reactions to goods and services so that corrective action can be taken if necessary. For example, a feedback control system that monitors the number of customer returns alerts managers when defective products are being produced, and a system that measures increases or decreases in product sales alerts managers to changes in customer tastes so they can increase or reduce the production of specific products.

feedback control Control that gives managers information about customers' reactions to goods and services so that corrective action can be taken if necessary.

To summarize, all processes of production (and service provision) have control systems at each stage in the operations management process to determine if standards are being met. If significant deviations between the actual performance and the expected level are found, operations managers can take action to correct the situation anywhere along the supply chain.

In the global economy today, supply chains are complex and often not very transparent. Workers in developing nations who supply raw materials often do not get the rewards or benefits from their labour that are expected elsewhere. An ethical movement toward fair trade instead of free trade was the inspiration for the organization featured in our Focus on the Social Economy box, Ten Thousand Villages. Increasingly, consumers are demanding fair trade principles in operations management.

FOCUS ON *The Social Economy*

Ten Thousand Villages: A History of Helping Artisans

Ten Thousand Villages is the oldest and largest fair trade organization in North America, selling artisan-crafted personal accessories, home décor, and gift items from around the globe. They are a nonprofit program of Mennonite Central Committee (MCC), the relief and development agency of Mennonite and Brethren in Christ churches in North America. Ten Thousand Villages has its roots in the work begun by Edna Ruth Byler in 1946.

It was in 1946 that Edna Ruth Byler, an MCC worker, visited volunteers in Puerto Rico who were teaching sewing classes in an effort to help improve the lives of women living in poverty. From this trip, Edna brought home several pieces of embroidery to sell to friends and neighbours. The pieces became quite popular and she soon added cross-stitch needlework from Palestinian refugees and hand-carved Haitian woodenware to her inventory.

In the early 1970s, the flourishing project moved out of Byler's basement and became SELFHELP CRAFTS, an official MCC program. Thousands of loyal customers and volunteers have helped to build this program into the strong alternative trading organization that, in 1996, became known as Ten Thousand Villages.

Commerce with a Conscience

Men and women around the world have a simple dream—to earn an honest living, provide a home, food, and education for their children, and be gainfully employed in a job that brings dignity and joy. Ten Thousand Villages partners with thousands of talented artisans in a healthy business relationship.

Often referred to as "Fair Trade," the philosophy of helping to build a sustainable future is based on the principle that trade should have a conscience. Through Fair Trade, artisans receive respect, dignity, and hope from working hard and earning fair value for their work.

Ten Thousand Villages is a nonprofit Fair Trade Organization (FTO). FTOs are non-governmental organizations designed to benefit artisans, not to maximize profits. They market products from handicraft and agricultural organizations based in low-income countries, providing consumers with products that have been fairly purchased from sustainable sources.

Ten Thousand Villages is a member of the World Fair Trade Organization (WFTO), a global network of Fair Trade Organizations—a coalition of handicraft and agricultural producer organizations and Fair Trade organizations from both the north and the south. WFTO's mission is to improve the livelihood and well-being of disadvantaged producers by linking and promoting Fair Trade organizations and speaking out for greater justice in world trade. Over 270 FTOs in 60 countries form the basis of this network.

1. Visit the World Fair Trade Organization website and research its role in improving the lives of producers in poor countries.

2. How can operations managers practise feedforward control measures that ensure ethical and fair trade principles in managing production systems?

Source: ©Ten Thousand Villages Canada.

Output Control

LO3 | Identify how organizations monitor and evaluate performance using output controls.

Managers need to determine internal control measures that will motivate employees and ensure that they perform effectively. In the following sections, we consider the types of output and behavioural controls that managers use to regulate and motivate employees and coordinate organizational activities, no matter what specific organizational structure is in place.

Mechanisms to Monitor Output

All managers develop a system of output control for their organizations. First, they choose the goals or output performance standards or targets that they think will best measure factors such as efficiency, quality, innovation, and responsiveness to customers. Then they measure to see whether the performance goals and standards are being achieved at the corporate, divisional, functional, and individual levels of the organization. The three main mechanisms that managers use to assess output or performance are financial measures, organizational goals, and operating budgets.

FINANCIAL MEASURES OF PERFORMANCE

Top managers are most concerned with overall organizational performance and use various financial measures to evaluate performance. The most common are *profit ratios, liquidity ratios, leverage ratios,* and *activity ratios.* They are discussed below and summarized in Table 11.1.[17]

- *Profit ratios* measure how efficiently managers are using the organization's resources to generate profits. *Return on investment (ROI),* an organization's net profit after taxes divided by its total assets, is the most commonly used financial performance measure because it allows managers of one organization to compare performance with that of other organizations. ROI allows managers to assess an organization's competitive advantage. *Gross profit margin* is the difference between the amount of revenue generated by a product and the resources used to produce the product. This measure provides managers with information about how efficiently an organization is using its resources and about how attractive customers find the product. It also provides managers with a way to assess how well an organization is building a competitive advantage. *Operating margin* is calculated by dividing a company's operating profit (the amount it has left after all the costs of making the product and running the business have been deducted) by sales revenues. This measure tells managers how efficiently an organization is using its resources; every successful attempt to reduce costs will be reflected in increased operating profit, for example. Also, operating margin is a

Financial measures illustrate the level of efficiency in organizations.
©Stefan Malloch I Dreamstime.com

TABLE 11.1

Four Measures of Financial Performance

Profit Ratios		
Return on investment	$= \dfrac{\text{Net profit after taxes}}{\text{Total assets}}$	Measures how well managers are using the organization's resources to generate profits. A simple ROI can be thought of as gains minus investment costs divided by investment costs.
Operating margin	$= \dfrac{\text{Total operating profit}}{\text{Sales revenue}}$	A measure of how much percentage profit a company is earning on sales; the higher the percentage, the better a company is using its resources to make and sell the product.
Gross profit margin	$= \dfrac{\text{Sales revenue} - \text{Cost of good sold}}{\text{Sales revenue}}$	The difference between the amount of revenue generated from the product and the resources used to produce the product.
Liquidity Ratios		
Current ratio	$= \dfrac{\text{Current assets}}{\text{Current liabilities}}$	Do managers have resources available to meet claims of short-term creditors?
Quick ratio	$= \dfrac{\text{Current assets} - \text{Inventory}}{\text{Current liabilities}}$	Can managers pay off claims of short-term creditors without selling inventory?
Leverage Ratios		
Debt-to-assets ratio	$= \dfrac{\text{Total debt}}{\text{Total assets}}$	To what extent have managers used borrowed funds to finance investments?
Times-covered ratio	$= \dfrac{\text{Profit before interest and taxes}}{\text{Total interest charges}}$	Measures how far profits can decline before managers cannot meet interest charges. If ratio declines to less than 1, the organization is technically insolvent.
Activity Ratios		
Inventory turnover	$= \dfrac{\text{Cost of goods sold}}{\text{Inventory}}$	Measures how efficiently managers are turning inventory over so excess inventory is not carried.
Days sales outstanding	$= \dfrac{\text{Accounts receivable}}{\dfrac{\text{Total sales}}{360}}$	Measures how efficiently managers are collecting revenues from customers to pay expenses.

means of comparing one year's performance to another; for example, if managers discover operating margin has improved by 5 percent from one year to the next, they know their organization is building a competitive advantage.

- *Liquidity ratios* measure how well managers have protected organizational resources so as to be able to meet short-term obligations. The *current ratio* (current assets divided by current liabilities) tells managers whether they have the resources available to meet the claims of short-term creditors. The *quick ratio* tells whether they can pay these claims without selling inventory.

- *Leverage ratios* such as the *debt-to-assets ratio* and the *times-covered ratio* measure the degree to which managers use debt (borrow money) or equity (issue new shares) to finance ongoing operations. An organization is highly leveraged if it uses more debt than equity. Debt can be risky when net income or profit fails to cover the interest on the debt—as some people learn too late when their paycheques do not allow them to pay off their credit cards.

- *Activity ratios* provide measures of how well managers are creating value from organizational assets. *Inventory turnover* measures how efficiently managers are turning inventory over so that excess inventory is not carried. *Days sales outstanding* provides information on how efficiently managers are collecting revenue from customers to pay expenses.

The objectivity of financial measures of performance is the reason why so many managers use them to assess the efficiency and effectiveness of their organizations. When an organization fails to meet performance standards such as ROI, revenue, or stock price targets, managers know that they must take corrective action. Thus, financial controls tell managers when a corporate reorganization might be necessary, when they should sell off divisions and exit from businesses, or when they should rethink their corporate-level strategies.[18]

While financial information is an important output control, on its own it does not provide managers with all the information they need about whether the plans they have made are being met. Financial results inform managers about the results of decisions they have already made; they do not tell managers how to find new opportunities to build competitive advantage in the future. To encourage a future-oriented approach, top managers, in their planning function, establish organizational goals that provide direction to middle and first-line managers. As part of the control function, managers evaluate whether those goals are being met.

ORGANIZATIONAL GOALS

Once top managers, in consultation with lower-level managers, have set the organization's overall goals, they then establish performance standards for the divisions and functions. These standards specify for divisional and functional managers the level at which their units must perform if the organization is to reach its overall goals.[19] For instance, if the goals for the year include improved sales, quality, and innovation, sales managers might be evaluated for their ability to increase sales, materials managers for their ability to increase the quality of inputs or lower their costs, and R&D managers for the number of products they innovate or the number of patents they receive. By evaluating how well performance matches up to the goals set, managers at all levels can determine whether the plans they had made are being met, or whether adjustments need to be made in either the plans or the behaviours of managers and employees. Thus goals can be a form of control by providing the framework for what is evaluated and assessed.

Output control is used at every level of the organization, and it is vital that the goals set at each level harmonize with the goals set at other levels so that managers and other employees throughout the organization work together to attain the corporate goals that top managers have set.[20] It is also important that goals be set appropriately so that managers are motivated to accomplish them. If goals are set at an impossibly high level, managers might work only half-heartedly to achieve them because they are certain they will fail. In contrast, if goals are set so low that they are too easy to achieve, managers will not be motivated to use all their resources as efficiently and effectively as possible. Research suggests that the best goals are *specific, difficult goals*—goals that challenge and stretch managers' ability but are

Operating budgets are an output control measure.
©doockie/Getty Images

not out of reach and do not require an impossibly high expenditure of managerial time and energy. Such goals are often called *stretch goals*.

Deciding what is a specific, difficult goal and what is a goal that is too difficult or too easy is a skill that managers must develop. Based on their own judgment and work experience, managers at all levels must assess how difficult a certain task is, and they must assess the ability of a particular subordinate manager to achieve the goal. If they do so successfully, challenging, interrelated goals—goals that reinforce one another and focus on achieving overall corporate objectives—will energize the organization.

OPERATING BUDGETS

Once managers at each level have been given a goal or target to achieve, the next step in developing an output control system is to establish operating budgets that regulate how managers and employees reach those goals. An **operating budget** is a blueprint that states how managers intend to use organizational resources to achieve organizational goals efficiently. Typically, managers at one level allocate to subordinate managers a specific amount of resources to produce goods and services. Once they have been given a budget, these lower-level managers must decide how to allocate resources for different organizational activities. They are then evaluated for their ability to stay within budget and to make the best use of available resources.

> **operating budget** A budget that states how managers intend to use organizational resources to achieve organizational goals.

Large organizations often treat each division as a singular or stand-alone responsibility centre. Corporate managers then evaluate each division's contribution to corporate performance. Managers of a division may be given a fixed budget for resources and evaluated for the amount of goods or services they can produce using those resources (this is a *cost* or *expense* budget approach). Or managers may be asked to maximize the revenues from the sales of goods and services produced (a *revenue* budget approach). Managers also may be evaluated on the difference between the revenues generated by the sales of goods and services and the budgeted cost of making those goods and services (a *profit* budget approach). Japanese companies' use of operating budgets and challenging goals to increase efficiency is instructive in this context.

In summary, three components—objective financial measures, performance standards derived from goals, and appropriate operating budgets—are the essence of effective output control. Most organizations develop sophisticated output control systems to allow managers at all levels to maintain an accurate picture of the organization so that they can move quickly to take corrective action as needed.[21] Output control is an essential part of management.

Problems with Output Control

A number of issues exist with output controls. When designing an output control system, managers must be careful to avoid some pitfalls, as shown in Figure 11.6. First, they must be sure that their output standards motivate managers at all levels and do not cause managers to behave in inappropriate ways to achieve organizational goals. Scotia McLeod's control system of rewarding brokers for each individual trade they made ended up creating "churning." Brokers advised clients to trade too much, and this led to investigations by regulatory bodies, as well as fines and discipline against the brokerages and individual brokers, as professional ethics were called into question.

FIGURE 11.6

Pitfalls of Output Control

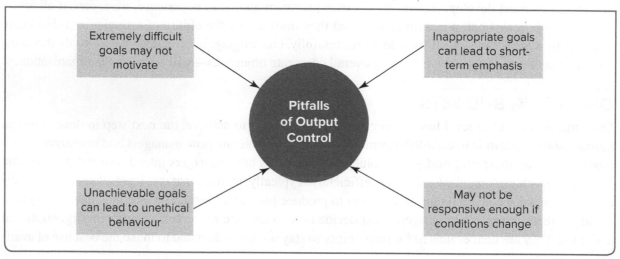

Problems can also occur if the standards that are set turn out to be unrealistic. Suppose that top managers give divisional managers the goal of doubling profits over a three-year period. This goal seems challenging and reachable when it is jointly agreed upon, and in the first two years profits go up by 70 percent. In the third year, however, an economic recession hits and sales plummet. Divisional managers think it is increasingly unlikely that they will meet their profit goal. Failure will mean losing the substantial monetary bonus tied to achieving the goal. How might managers behave to try to preserve their bonuses?

One course of action they might take is to find ways to reduce costs, since profit can be increased either by raising revenues or by reducing costs. Thus, divisional managers might cut back on expensive research and development activities, delay maintenance on machinery, reduce marketing expenditures, and lay off middle managers and employees to reduce costs so that at the end of the year they will make their target of doubling profits and will receive their bonuses. This tactic might help them achieve a short-term goal—doubling profits—but such actions could hurt long-term profitability or ROI (because a cutback in R&D can reduce the rate of product innovation, a cutback in marketing will lead to the loss of customers, and so on).

The long term is what corporate managers should be most concerned about. Thus, top managers must consider carefully how flexible they should be when using output control. If conditions change (as they will because of uncertainty in the task and general environments), it is probably better for top managers to communicate to managers lower in the hierarchy that they are aware of the changes taking place and are willing to revise and lower goals and standards. Indeed, most organizations schedule yearly revisions of their five-year plan and goals.

Second, the inappropriate use of output control measures can lead managers and employees to behave unethically. If goals are too challenging, employees may be motivated to behave unethically toward customers, as sometimes happens in brokerage firms. Scotia McLeod has moved to a fee-based system to change the way in which its brokers are rewarded in order to reduce potential ethical conflicts.

The message is clear: Although output control is a useful tool for keeping managers and employees at all levels motivated and the organization on track, it is only a guide to appropriate action. Output controls need to be flexible enough to accommodate changes in the organization's environment. Therefore, managers must be sensitive to how they use output control and constantly monitor its effects at all levels in the organization.

 # Behavioural Control

LO4	Discuss how behavioural controls regulate and motivate employees to achieve organizational goals.

Organizational structure is often viewed as a way of achieving control by designating who reports to whom and what the responsibilities of each individual are. However, structure by itself does not provide any mechanism that motivates managers and nonmanagerial employees to behave in ways that make the structure work or even improve the way it works—hence the need for control. Output control is one way to motivate people; behaviour control is another. In this section, we begin by examining the ways that managerial behaviour can be held accountable through *corporate governance* principles. We end with a discussion of four mechanisms that managers can use to keep employee behaviour on track and make organizational structures work as they are designed to work: *direct supervision, management by objectives, bureaucratic rules and standard operating procedures,* and *clan control* (see Figure 11.7).

Corporate Governance and Control

After the Enron and WorldCom scandals arose around corporate financial reporting in the early twenty-first century, the ways that top managers account for and report their performance has been called into question. Canadian-born CEO of WorldCom Bernard Ebbers made dubious accounting judgments that misrepresented the actual performance level of the company in an effort to keep the share price high and investors happy. Instead, the fraudulent activity landed him in jail, and the company went bankrupt. In the case of Enron, CFO Andrew Fastow set up accounting practices that allowed him to defraud investors as well as disguise the declining performance to shareholders. These and other more recent financial

FIGURE 11.7

Types of Output and Behavioural Controls

Output Controls	Behavioural Controls
• Financial Measures	• Corporate Governance
• Organizational Goals	• Direct Supervision
• Operating Budgets	• Management by Objectives
	• Bureaucratic Rules and SOPs
	• Clan Control

scandals around the world, such as Satyam in India, Nortel Networks, Goldman Sachs, Hollinger Inc., Bank of America, and Facebook, have resulted in reforms to the way that corporations approach corporate governance and accountability. **Corporate governance practices** are the processes companies use to be accountable to stakeholders, including investors, employees, the environment, and communities. The failure of the self-governing practices of corporations has led shareholders, particularly institutional investors, to become more active in controlling the management of their assets and scrutinizing top managerial behaviour.

> **corporate governance practices** The processes companies use to be accountable to stakeholders, including investors, employees, the environment, and communities.

How do companies make managerial behaviour accountable? Take tech giant BlackBerry, for example. The company's annual income grew by 45 000 percent in its first 10 years of operation when it was called Research In Motion (RIM). With such rapid growth, how did the company maintain control and compliance to regulatory standards in accounting? They didn't. A review found accounting errors in connection with the administration of certain stock options between February 2002 and August 2006. The review resulted in some significant changes to BlackBerry's governance structure. First, the roles of chairman of the board and CEO were separated. The chair became a nonexecutive role after Jim Balsillie voluntarily stepped down but maintained the position of co-CEO with Mike Lazaridis, who also held the position of president of the company. Second, an oversight committee of the board of directors was formed to implement changes to the company's board, audit committee, compensation committee, and nominating committee, and to change various management roles. Although no employees were asked to leave the company as a result of the uncovering of errors in governance, BlackBerry did have to restate several years of financial statements and made significant changes to its organizational structure as a result.

"We are satisfied with the thoroughness of the review and we believe that the resulting enhancements to governance and controls will make RIM even stronger as it continues to grow and lead in the thriving market it pioneered," said James Estill and John Richardson, who sat on the Special Committee investigating the issue, in a joint statement. "It must also be said that we have the utmost confidence in Jim Balsillie and the senior management team. Over the last 10 years, incredible results have been accomplished under their stewardship, including an increase in RIM's annual revenue by more than 45 000 percent and an increase in RIM's share price by more than 10 000 percent. These results speak loudly about the management team and the value of their leadership to RIM and its shareholders."[22] In 2012, after market share declined, RIM's co-CEOs stepped down and passed the reins to Thorsten Heins. Unexpectedly, Balsillie then resigned from the board of directors, while Lazaridis remained.

In light of these developments, the role of the board of directors has undergone substantial reform. Nell Minow, the editor of The Corporate Library, an independent U.S.-based research firm that rates boards of directors of public companies and compiles research on corporate governance issues, put the matter like this: "[B]oards of directors are like subatomic particles—they behave differently when they are observed."[23] To encourage boards and top managers to do their jobs in a more transparent and effective way, government legislation and guidelines set out by stakeholder groups have been developed. In 2002, the *Sarbanes-Oxley Act* was passed in the United States, imposing considerable demands on board members of publicly traded companies with respect to accountability. Similar, but far less tough, rules were adopted in Canada in 2004 by the Canadian Securities Commission. Principles and guidelines go beyond promoting accountability in financial matters.

> *"Boards of directors are like subatomic particles—they behave differently when they are observed."*
>
> Nell Minow, editor of The Corporate Library

Transparent corporate governance systems and adopting a sustainability strategy are increasingly important control measures for creating a competitive advantage, as more vigilant shareholders are also more socially responsible in terms of demanding economic, environmental, and social impact returns (triple-bottom-line returns).

Direct Supervision

The most immediate and potent form of behaviour control is direct supervision by managers who actively monitor and observe the behaviour of their subordinates, educate subordinates about the behaviours that are appropriate or inappropriate, and intervene to take corrective action as needed. When managers personally supervise subordinates, they lead by example and in this way can help subordinates develop and increase their own skill levels (leadership is the subject of Chapter 9). Thus, control through personal supervision can be a very effective way of motivating employees and promoting behaviours that increase effectiveness and efficiency.[24]

Nevertheless, certain problems are associated with direct supervision:.

- It is very expensive. A manager can personally manage only a small number of subordinates effectively. Therefore, direct supervision requires a lot of managers, and this will raise costs.

- It can demotivate subordinates if they feel that they are not free to make their own decisions. Subordinates may avoid responsibility if they feel that their manager is waiting to reprimand anyone who makes the slightest error.

- For many jobs, direct supervision is simply not feasible. The more complex a job is, the more difficult it is for a manager to evaluate how well a subordinate is performing.

For all of these reasons, output control is usually preferred to behaviour control. Indeed, output control tends to be the first type of control that managers at all levels use to evaluate performance.

Direct supervision has both advantages and disadvantages for behaviour control.
Copyright 2007, Mike Watson Images Limited/Glow Images

Management by Objectives

Recall that we introduced you to management by objectives (MBO) in Chapter 8 on managing motivation. To provide a framework within which to evaluate subordinates' behaviour and, in particular, to allow managers to monitor progress toward achieving goals, many organizations implement some version of MBO.

Management by objectives is a system of evaluating subordinates for their ability to achieve specific organizational goals or performance standards.[25] Most organizations make some use of management by objectives because it is pointless to establish goals and then fail to communicate the goals and their measurement to employees.

From a control perspective, the important element of MBO is Step 3: Managers and their subordinates need to periodically review the subordinates' progress toward meeting goals. Managers and employees who achieve their goals receive greater rewards than those who fall short. (The issue of how to design reward systems to motivate managers and other organizational employees is also discussed in Chapter 8.)

In companies that decentralize responsibility for the production of goods and services to empowered teams and cross-functional teams, management would review the accomplishments of the team, and then the rewards would be linked to team performance as well as the performance of any one team member. For either the individual or team situation, MBO creates the conditions for providing standards that are evaluated.

Cypress Semiconductor offers an interesting example of how IT can be used to manage the MBO process quickly and effectively. In the fast-moving semiconductor business a premium is placed on organizational adaptability. At Cypress, CEO T. J. Rodgers was facing a problem. How could he control his growing, 1500-employee organization without developing a bureaucratic management hierarchy? Rodgers believed that a tall hierarchy hinders the ability of an organization to adapt to changing conditions. He was committed to maintaining a flat and decentralized organizational structure with a minimum of management layers. At the same time, he needed to control his employees to ensure that they perform in a manner consistent with the goals of the company.[26] How could he achieve this without resorting to direct supervision and the management hierarchy that it implies?

To solve this problem, Rodgers implemented an online information system through which he can manage what every employee and team is doing in his fast-moving and decentralized organization. Each employee maintains a list of 10 to 15 goals, such as "Meet with marketing for new product launch" or "Make sure to check with customer X." Noted next to each goal are when it was agreed upon, when it is due to be finished, and whether it has been finished. All of this information is stored on a central computer. Rodgers claims that he can review the goals of all employees in about four hours and that he does so each week.[27] How is this possible? He manages by exception and looks only for employees who are falling behind. He then calls them, not to scold but to ask whether there is anything he can do to help them get the job done. It takes only about half an hour each week for employees to review and update their lists. This system allows Rodgers to exercise control over his organization without resorting to the expensive layers of a management hierarchy and direct supervision.

Bureaucratic Rules and SOPs

When direct supervision is too expensive and management by objectives is inappropriate, managers might turn to another mechanism to shape and motivate employee behaviour: bureaucratic control. **Bureaucratic control** is control by means of a comprehensive system of rules and **standard operating procedures (SOPs)** that standardize the behaviour of divisions, functions, and individuals. All organizations use bureaucratic rules and procedures, but some use them more than others.[28]

bureaucratic control Control of behaviour by means of a comprehensive system of rules and standard operating procedures.

standard operating procedures (SOPs) (1) Written instructions describing the exact series of actions that should be followed in a specific situation; (2) Rules and policies that standardize behaviours.

Rules and SOPs guide behaviour and specify what employees are to do when they confront a problem that needs a solution. It is the responsibility of a manager to develop rules that allow employees to perform their activities efficiently and effectively. When employees follow the rules that managers have developed, their behaviour is *standardized*—actions are performed in the same way time and time again—and the outcomes of their work are predictable. In addition, to the degree that managers can make employees' behaviour predictable, there is no need to monitor the outputs of behaviour because standardized behaviour leads to standardized outputs.

Suppose a worker at Toyota comes up with a way to attach exhaust pipes that reduces the number of steps in the assembly process and increases efficiency. Always on the lookout for ways to standardize procedures, managers make this idea the basis of a new rule: "From now on, the procedure for attaching the exhaust pipe to the car is as follows. . . ." If all workers followed the rule to the letter, every car would come off the assembly line with its exhaust pipe attached in the new way, and there would be no need to check exhaust pipes at the end of the line. In practice, mistakes and lapses of attention do happen, so output control is used at the end of the line, and each car's exhaust system is given a routine inspection. However, the number of quality problems with the exhaust system is minimized because the rule (bureaucratic control) is being followed.

Service organizations such as retail stores and fast-food restaurants try to standardize the behaviour of employees by instructing them on the correct way to greet customers or the appropriate way to serve or bag food. Employees are trained to follow the rules that have proven to be most effective in a particular situation. The better trained the employees are, the more standardized is their behaviour and the more trust managers can have that outputs (such as food quality) will be consistent.

Inconsistent behaviour and undesired behaviour on the part of employees, such as not showing up for work, coming late, and performing poorly should be formally addressed through discipline. **Discipline** is administering punishment when undesired behaviours are exhibited, in an attempt to decrease the frequency of those behaviours. It is based on learning theory (discussed in Chapter 8). Management introduces an unpleasant stimulus, such as a reprimand or withholding pay, when, for example, an employee performs poorly executed work. If discipline is given in an objective, fair, and consistent way that makes clear to the employee what the undesired behaviour is, it is a valuable form of managerial control. Management uses varying degrees of penalties

Standardizing component parts and behaviour can lead to effective and efficient operations.
©Ka2shka | Dreamstime.com

when administering discipline according to the nature of the infraction. After a series of written reprimands for continually being late for work, the next step might be docking pay and then temporary suspension. Severe penalties, such as termination of employment, would be used for behaviours such as theft and sabotage. The objective is to achieve compliance with the organization's goals and standards through the least severe reprimand possible. See Figure 11.8.

discipline Managerial control through administering punishment when undesired workplace behaviours, such as absenteeism, lack of punctuality, and low performance, are exhibited, in an attempt to decrease their frequency.

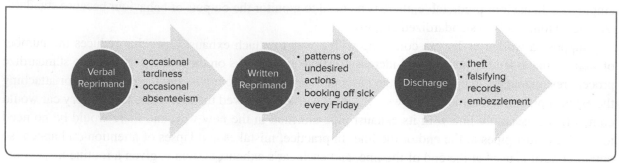

FIGURE 11.8

Progressive Discipline

PROBLEMS WITH BUREAUCRATIC CONTROL

All organizations make extensive use of bureaucratic control because rules and SOPs effectively control routine organizational activities. With a bureaucratic control system in place, managers can manage by exception and intervene and take corrective action only when necessary. However, managers need to be aware of a number of problems associated with bureaucratic control because these problems can reduce organizational effectiveness.[29]

First, establishing rules is always easier than discarding them. Organizations tend to become overly bureaucratic over time if managers do everything according to the rule book. When the amount of red tape becomes too great, decision making slows, and managers react slowly to changing conditions. This slowness can harm an organization's survival if quicker new competitors emerge.

Second, because rules constrain and standardize behaviour and lead people to behave in predictable ways, people may become so used to automatically following rules that they stop thinking for themselves. By definition, new ideas do not come from blindly following standardized procedures. Similarly, the pursuit of innovation implies a commitment by managers to discover new ways of doing things; innovation, however, is incompatible with the use of extensive bureaucratic control.

Managers must therefore be sensitive about the way they use bureaucratic control. It is most useful when organizational activities are routine and well understood and employees are making programmed decisions such as in mass-production settings or in a routine service setting, for example in restaurants and stores such as Tim Hortons, Canadian Tire, and Midas. Bureaucratic control is not nearly as useful in situations where nonprogrammed decisions have to be made and managers have to react quickly to changes in the organizational environment.

Clan Control

Professionals such as scientists, engineers, doctors, and professors often have jobs that are relatively ambiguous in terms of standard operating procedures and which may require individualized response based on the situation.

How can managers try to control and regulate the behaviour of their subordinates when personal supervision is of little use, when rules cannot be developed to tell employees what to do, and when outputs and goals cannot be measured at all or can be measured usefully only over long periods? One source of control increasingly being used by organizations is **clan control**—the shared norms and values of organizational members, which relies on a strong organizational culture. This form of

TIPS FOR MANAGERS

Control

1. Make a list of "must-do" items that need to be accomplished to get the job done (an efficiency task).

2. Make another list of "must-do" items that need to be accomplished, taking into consideration the people who will complete the work (an effectiveness task).

3. Involve employees in training programs that will not only help them do a better job but also meet your control targets (e.g., safety, better financial reporting, etc.).

4. Remember that finding the right balance of control for your organization works better with an open and inclusive corporate culture.

control is also increasingly being used in organizations that value innovation and want to empower their employees.

clan control Control exerted on individuals and groups in an organization by shared values, norms, standards of behaviour, and expectations.

HOW CLAN CONTROL WORKS

As we discussed in Chapter 1, organizational culture is the shared set of beliefs, expectations, values, norms, and work routines that influences how members of an organization relate to one another and work together to achieve organizational goals. William Ouchi used the term *clan control* to describe the control exerted on individuals and groups in an organization by shared values, norms, standards of behaviour, and expectations. The control arising from clan control is not an externally imposed system of constraints, such as direct supervision or rules and procedures, but constraints that come from organizational culture. That is, employees internalize organizational values and norms and then let these values and norms guide their decisions and actions. Just as people in society at large generally behave in accordance with socially acceptable values and norms—such as the norm that people should line up at the checkout counters in supermarkets—so are individuals in an organizational setting mindful of the force of organizational values and norms.

Clan control is an important source of control for two reasons. First, it makes control possible in situations where managers cannot use output or behaviour control. Second, and more importantly, when a strong and cohesive set of organizational values and norms is in place, employees focus on thinking about what is best for the organization in the long run—all their decisions and actions become oriented toward helping the organization perform well. For example, a teacher spends personal time after school coaching and counselling students; an R&D scientist works 80 hours a week, evenings and weekends, to help speed up a late project; a sales clerk at a department store runs after a customer who left a credit card at the cash register. Many researchers and managers believe that employees of some organizations go out of their way to help their organization because the organization has a strong and cohesive organizational culture—a culture that controls employee attitudes and behaviours. Strong bureaucratic control is less likely to foster positive attitudes and behaviours that encourage employees to go above and beyond.

Control Mechanisms and Gaining a Competitive Advantage

LO5 | Explain how effective controls help managers gain a competitive advantage.

Control systems are intended to make organizations more successful. As we see in Figure 11.9,[30] they help managers adapt to change and uncertainty; discover irregularities and errors; reduce costs, increase productivity, or add value; detect opportunities; deal with complexity; and decentralize decision making and facilitate teamwork.

1. *Adapt to change and uncertainty.* We described in Chapter 2 how managers face uncertain task-specific and external environments. New suppliers and customers can appear as well as new technologies and regulations. Control systems help managers anticipate these changes and be prepared for them.

2. *Discover irregularities and errors.* There may be problems with quality control, customer service, or even human resource management. Control systems help managers uncover these problems before they become too serious to overcome.

3. *Reduce costs, increase productivity, or add value.* Control systems can be used to reduce labour or production costs, to improve productivity, or to add value to a product, making it more attractive to a customer.

4. *Detect opportunities.* Control systems can help managers identify new markets, demographic changes, new suppliers, and other opportunities.

5. *Deal with complexity.* When organizations become large, it sometimes becomes impossible to know what the different units are doing. This is particularly the case when two companies merge. There may be redundancies in product lines or employees. Control systems help managers deal with these complexities.

6. *Decentralize decision making and facilitate teamwork.* When control systems are in place, managers can allow employees to make more decisions, and work in teams.

FIGURE 11.9

The Importance of Control

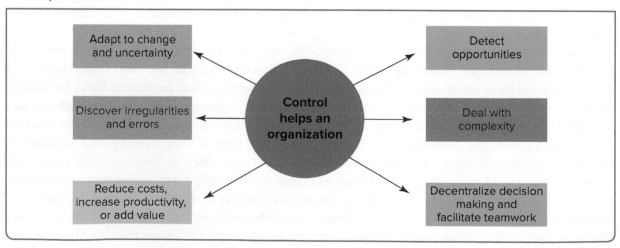

How Culture Controls Managerial Action

Recall from Chapter 1 that the way in which organizational culture shapes and controls behaviour is evident in the way managers perform their four main functions—planning, organizing, leading, and controlling—when they work in different types of organizations (see Table 11.2). As we revisit these functions here, we continue to distinguish between two kinds of top managers: (1) those who create organizational values and norms that encourage creative, *innovative,* and adaptive behaviour and (2) those who encourage a *conservative,* cautious approach in their subordinates. We noted earlier that both kinds of values and norms may be appropriate in different situations.

PLANNING

Top managers in an organization with an *innovative* culture are likely to encourage lower-level managers to take part in the planning process and develop a flexible approach to planning. They are likely to be willing to listen to new ideas and to take risks involving the development of new products.

In contrast, top managers in an organization with *conservative* values are likely to emphasize formal, top-down planning. Suggestions from lower-level managers are likely to be subjected to a formal review, which can significantly slow down decision making. Although this deliberate approach may improve the quality of decision making in a nuclear power plant, it also can have unintended consequences. At conservative IBM, for example, before its more recent turnaround, the planning process became so formalized that managers spent most of their time assembling complex slide shows and overheads to defend their current positions rather than thinking about what they should be doing to keep IBM abreast of the changes taking place in the computer industry.

ORGANIZING

Valuing creativity, managers in an *innovative* culture are likely to try to create an organic structure, one that is flat, with few levels in the hierarchy, and in which authority is decentralized so that employees are encouraged to work together to find solutions to ongoing problems. A product team structure may be very suitable for an organization with an innovative culture.

In contrast, managers in a *conservative* culture are likely to create a well-defined hierarchy of authority and establish clear reporting relationships so that employees know exactly whom to report to and how to react to any problems that arise.

TABLE 11.2

How Culture Controls Managerial Functions

	Type of Organization	
Managerial Function	**Conservative**	**Innovative**
Planning	Formal, top-down planning	All managers encouraged to participate in decision making
Organizing	Well-defined hierarchy of authority and clear reporting relationships	Organic, flexible structure
Leading	Rigid MBO and constant monitoring	Managers lead by example Encourage risk taking
Controlling	Bureaucratic control Closed-door corporate governance	Clan control Transparent corporate governance

LEADING

In an *innovative* culture, managers are likely to lead by example, encouraging employees to take risks and experiment. They are supportive regardless of employees succeeding or failing.

In contrast, managers in a conservative culture are likely to develop a rigid management by objectives system and to constantly monitor subordinates' progress toward goals, overseeing their every move.

CONTROLLING

As this chapter makes clear, there are many control systems that managers can adopt to shape and influence employee behaviour. The control systems managers choose reflect how they want to motivate organizational members and keep them focused on organizational goals. Managers who want to encourage the development of *innovative* values and norms that encourage risk taking choose output and behaviour controls that match this objective. They are likely to choose output controls that measure performance over the long run and develop a flexible MBO system suited to the long and uncertain process of innovation.

In contrast, managers who want to encourage the development of conservative values choose the opposite combination of output and behaviour controls. They rely heavily on direct supervision and bureaucratic rules and regulations that keep subordinates in check, based on fear of punishment and discipline. Sometimes managers who are hired by a company do not fit into the existing culture. Calgary-based WestJet fired CEO Steve Smith, who was far more controlling than the company's culture warranted. WestJet's founders sent a strong message to the employees by firing Smith in a year when the company had done very well financially.

The values and norms of an organization's culture strongly affect the way managers perform their management functions. The extent to which managers buy into the values and norms of their organization shapes their view of the world and their actions and decisions in particular circumstances.[31] In turn, the actions that managers take can have an impact on the performance of the organization. Thus, organizational culture, managerial action, and organizational performance are linked together.

Although organizational culture can give rise to managerial actions that ultimately benefit the organization, this is not always the case. As we will see in Chapter 12, sometimes culture can become so much a part of the organization that it becomes difficult to effect change and improve performance.[32] For example, Wayne Sales, the former CEO of Canadian Tire, tried desperately to revitalize customer service in the company's stores. Canadians had become so used to poor service that employees did not see the need to change. However, with increased competition from Home Depot Canada, RONA, Home Hardware, and Lowe's Canada, lack of customer service is a big issue. Sales set out to "drive away the chain's 'crappy tire' image" by changing the control systems to encourage employees to be more customer-focused.[33]

Organizational Control and Building a Competitive Advantage

To understand the importance of organizational control, consider how it helps managers obtain superior efficiency, quality, responsiveness to customers, and innovation—the four building blocks of competitive advantage.

To determine how efficiently they are using their resources, managers must be able to accurately measure how many units of inputs (raw materials, human resources, and so on) are being used to produce a unit of output. Managers also must be able to measure how many units of outputs (goods and services) are being produced. A control system contains the measures or yardsticks that allow managers to assess how efficiently the organization is producing goods and services. Moreover, if managers experiment with changing the way the organization produces goods and services to find a more efficient way of producing them, these measures tell managers how successful they have been. For example, when managers at GM decided to adopt a product team structure to design, engineer, and manufacture new car models, they used measures such as time taken to design a new car and cost savings per car produced to evaluate how well the new structure worked in comparison with the old structure. They found that the new one performed better. Without a control system in place, managers have no idea how well their organization is performing and how its performance can be improved—information that is becoming increasingly important in today's highly competitive environment.

Today, much of the competition among organizations revolves around increasing the quality of goods and services. In the car industry, for example, cars within each price range compete against one another in features, design, and reliability. Thus, whether a customer will buy a Ford Taurus, GM Grand Prix, Chrysler Sebring, Toyota Camry, or Honda Accord depends significantly on the quality of each product. Organizational control is important in determining the quality of goods and services because it gives managers feedback on product quality. If the managers of carmakers consistently measure the number of customer complaints and the number of new cars returned for repairs, or if school principals measure how many students drop out of school or how achievement scores on nationally based tests vary over time, they have a good indication of how much quality they have built into their product—be it an educated student or a car that does not break down. Effective managers create a control system that consistently monitors the quality of goods and services so that they can make continuous improvements to quality—an approach to change that gives them a competitive advantage.

Managers can also help make their organizations more responsive to customers if they develop a control system that allows them to evaluate how well customer-contact employees are performing their jobs. Monitoring employee behaviour can help managers find ways to increase employees' performance levels, perhaps by revealing areas in which skill training can help employees or by finding new procedures that allow employees to perform their jobs better. When employees know that their behaviours are being monitored, they may also have more incentive to be helpful and consistent in how they act toward customers. To improve customer service, for example, GM regularly surveys customers about their experiences with particular dealers. If a dealership receives too many customer complaints, GM's managers investigate the dealership to uncover the sources of the problems and suggest solutions; if necessary, they might even threaten to reduce the number of cars a dealership receives to force the dealer to improve the quality of its customer service.

Finally, controlling can raise the level of innovation in an organization. Successful innovation takes place when managers create an organizational setting in which employees feel empowered to be creative and in which authority is decentralized to employees so that they feel free to experiment and take risks. Deciding on the appropriate control systems to encourage risk taking is an important management challenge in developing an innovative organizational culture.

Chapter 11

SUMMARY AND REVIEW

☰ connect

LO1 **What Is Organizational Control?** Controlling is the process that managers use to regulate, monitor, and evaluate how efficiently and effectively an organization and its members are performing the activities necessary to reach organizational goals. When goals are not met, managers can take corrective action to get back on track. Controlling is a four-step process: (1) establishing standards for performance, (2) measuring performance, (3) comparing actual performance with expected performance, and (4) correcting deviations after determining the cause.

LO2 **Control Systems and Operations Management** Control systems set targets, monitor and evaluate performance, and help managers make sure the organization is working effectively and efficiently to reach its goals. Three systems of control are used by operations and supply chain managers: *feedforward* control, used to control inputs; *concurrent* control, used during the conversion stage; and *feedback* control, used to provide information to managers in the post-production stage.

LO3 **Output Control** Output controls and behavioural controls are used to regulate, coordinate, and motivate employees. The main mechanisms to monitor output are financial measures of performance, organizational goals, and operating budgets.

LO4 **Behavioural Control** Corporate governance practices control managerial behaviour, while the main mechanisms to shape employee behaviour and induce employees to work toward achieving organizational goals are direct supervision, management by objectives, bureaucratic control based on standard operating procedures, and clan control, which operates on a strong organizational culture where individuals and groups share values, norms, standards of behaviour, and expectations.

LO5 **Control Mechanisms and Gaining a Competitive Advantage** Establishing appropriate control measures helps managers adapt to change and uncertainty; discover irregularities and errors; reduce costs, increase productivity or add value; detect opportunities; deal with complexity; and decentralize decision making and facilitate teamwork. The type of organizational culture affects how managers plan, organize, lead, and control resources and people. Control processes allow managers to assess how efficiently the organization is producing goods and services, how responsive it is to customer needs, how innovative the culture is, and how to increase the quality of goods and services produced to gain a competitive advantage. Organizational control is important because it helps managers increase performance.

KEY TERMS

bureaucratic control

clan control

concurrent control

control systems

corporate governance practices

discipline

feedback control

feedforward control

operating budget
operations management
operations managers

production system
standard operating procedures (SOPs)

WRAP-UP TO OPENING CASE

Will CEO Mary Barra's Customer Safety Strategy Work for General Motors?

Why in the world would a company with the stellar reputation of General Motors purchase a part that did not meet its own specifications? After having read and understood the concepts in this chapter you should now be able to answer the following questions:

1. *Describe the control systems failure in this case.*

    ANSWER: Control systems help managers anticipate, detect, and correct errors and irregularities. Feedforward measures check the quality of inputs into the production of goods and services. Concurrent measures check the goods and services during the process of production, and feedback systems take place after the goods and services have been produced and often after they have been consumed. In this case, the focus on reducing operating costs at the expense of quality assurance resulted in faulty ignition switches being installed in GM vehicles. At least 124 deaths occurred as a consequence of poor feedforward control measures that should have detected problems with the inventory of ignition switches prior to them being installed in the vehicles. Proper specifications to suppliers and rigorous testing before assembly production would have detected the problem and prevented the deaths. The unfortunate feedback from the users of the vehicles—their deaths after driving the vehicles and GM's subsequent recall of the vehicles post-production, was the way the managers got the information they needed to take corrective action to prevent such tragedies in the future.

2. *What kind of control measures did Barra set in place to make sure no such tragedies occur in the future?*

    ANSWER: As the top manager at GM, Mary Barra set out control measures for how every resource is used in the company to achieve organizational goals. Her operations management team set up performance standards for outputs and employee behaviour to rebalance the focus on increasing efficiency through cost cutting with concern for customer safety and quality. Feedforward measures that ensure quality inputs—parts such as the ignition switch—should be monitored to ensure specifications (standards) are being met prior to being used in the assembly production. Concurrent control during the process of production could be achieved by randomly testing a vehicle on the assembly line at fixed intervals of time, to allow managers to detect errors and address them before production is finished. Customer complaints and tragic incidents the involving injury or death of the customer is the worst type of feedback for any manager. Fixing the problems after the product or service reaches the consumer allows managers to set new standards for continuous improvement in the production process but should not be the primary way they gather information on quality concerns. GM under Barra could adopt an innovative culture that would help the control systems and measures be flexible and responsive to changing environments, help reduce uncertainty, and lead to gaining a competitive advantage through higher performance.

MANAGEMENT IN ACTION

TOPICS FOR DISCUSSION AND ACTION

LEVEL 1 Knowledge & Comprehension

1. Define organizational control and how it contributes to competitiveness. Why is it important to overall organizational performance?

2. Describe the four steps in the process of control.

3. Describe three systems of control managers use in operations management.

LEVEL 2 Application & Analysis

4. Identify the main methods of output and behaviour control, and discuss their advantages and disadvantages as means of coordinating and motivating employees.

5. Why is it important to involve subordinates in the control process?

6. What is clan control and how does it affect the way employees behave?

LEVEL 3 Synthesis & Evaluation

7. What types of controls would you expect to find most used in (a) a hospital, (b) the Armed Forces, and (c) a city police force? Why?

8. Watch a YouTube video on the culture at Google. What types of control measures are evident in this video?

9. Explain how *innovative* and *conservative* cultures control managerial action. Which type of corporate culture would you prefer to work in and why?

SELF-REFLECTION EXERCISE

Your parents have indicated that they are expecting a big party for their 25th wedding anniversary and that you are in charge of planning it. Develop a timeline for carrying out the project, and then identify ways to monitor progress in planning for the party. How will you know that your plans have been successful? At what critical points do you need to examine your plans to make sure that everything is on track?

SMALL GROUP BREAKOUT EXERCISE
How Best to Control the Sales Force?

Form groups of three or four, and appoint one member as the spokesperson who will communicate your findings to the whole class when called on by the instructor. Then discuss the following scenario:

You are the regional sales managers of an organization that supplies high-quality windows and doors to building supply centres nationwide. Over the last three years, the rate of sales growth has slackened. There is increasing evidence that to make their jobs easier, salespeople are primarily servicing large customer accounts and ignoring small accounts. In addition, the salespeople are not dealing promptly with customer questions and complaints, and this inattention has resulted in a drop in after-sales service. You have talked about these problems, and you are meeting to design a control system to increase both the amount of sales and the quality of customer service.

1. What type of control do you think will best motivate the salespeople to achieve these goals?
2. What relative importance do you put on (1) output control, (2) behaviour control, and (3) organizational culture in this design?

MANAGING ETHICALLY EXERCISE

You are a manager of a group of 10 employees in their twenties. They are very innovative and are not accustomed to tight rules and regulations. Managers at the company want order and control on every front. Your team is fighting the rules and regulations, which is creating an ethical dilemma for you. They are being very productive and innovative but clearly not in the way top management wants things run. You have been asked to bring more order to your team. You really like your team and think they are effective but feel certain they will leave if they are forced to conform. The company needs their expertise and energy to remain competitive in the high-tech world. What would you do?

MANAGEMENT CHALLENGE EXERCISE
Save the Children Project

Assume your professor has asked you to consult and manage the design of a special "Save the Children" innovative program that 10 teams of five students in your course will be working on. Save the Children Canada will be acting as final judge on the winning program submitted by different colleges and universities. You must manage 10 teams; because of the shortness of time for this request, the innovative program will need aspects designed by each team, as no one team can do it all. Hence, all 10 teams will have contributed to the finished product. Your professor will be grading you on how well you actually manage, motivate, and put into action controls to help each team function at optimal levels.

1. What is your plan to control the operations of the teams in such a way that they function optimally?

MANAGEMENT PORTFOLIO PROJECT

Answer the following questions about the organization you have chosen to follow:

1. What are the main types of control used by management to monitor and evaluate the performance of the organization and employees?

2. Are these methods of control appropriate, given the organization's strategy and culture?

3. What recommendations would you make with respect to the organizational control of this enterprise?

MANAGEMENT CASE

THINKING OF QUITTING? THE BOSS KNOWS[34]

Employers want to know who has one foot out the door.

As turnover becomes a bigger worry—and expense—in a tightening labor market, companies including Wal-Mart Stores Inc., Credit Suisse Group AG and Box Inc. are analyzing a vast array of data points to determine who is likely to leave.

The idea, say people who run analytics teams, is to give managers early warning so they can take action before employees jump ship.

Corporate data crunchers play with dozens of factors, which may include job tenure, geography, performance reviews, employee surveys, communication patterns and even personality tests to identify flight risks, a term human-resources departments sometimes use for people likely to leave.

The data often reveal a complex picture of what motivates workers to stay—and what causes them to look elsewhere.

At Box, for example, a worker's pay or relationship with his boss matters far less than how connected the worker feels to his team, according to an analysis from human-resources analytics firm Culture Amp. At Credit Suisse, managers' performance and team size turn out to be surprisingly powerful influences, with a spike in attrition among employees working on large teams with low-rated managers.

Human-resources software company Ultimate Software Group Inc. has a product that assigns clients' employees, and even its own workers, individual "retention predictor" numbers, similar to a credit score, to indicate the likelihood that a worker will leave.

As the employment picture improves, companies are focusing more on retaining workers, largely because replacing them is costly. The median cost of turnover for most jobs is about 21% of an employee's annual salary, according to the Center for American Progress, a liberal-leaning think tank.

William Wolf, Credit Suisse's global head of talent acquisition and development, says a one-point reduction in unwanted attrition rates saves the bank $75 million to $100 million a year.

No single piece of data predicts whether an employee will stay or go, though many employers wish it were so. Data scientists create models to predict which workers might leave a company in the near future, combining a range of variables and testing the predictions over time.

"One of the things that people want to find is that one nugget, that key thing that correlates with someone leaving, but it is never that simple," says Thomas Daglis, a data scientist at Ultimate Software.

Employers may not mind that some employees are at risk of leaving, though companies stress that they are using the data to find ways to improve retention, and not nudge people out.

Those caveats aside, data scientists who study retention say they have found some meaningful correlations.

VoloMetrix Inc., which examines HR data as well as anonymized employee email and calendar data, found that it could predict flight risk up to a year in advance for employees who were spending less time interacting with certain colleagues or attending events beyond required meetings. And Ultimate Software found a correlation between a client's employees who waived their benefits coverage and those who left the company.

The big challenge for employers is what, exactly, to do with the information. Some aren't sure how to approach employees at risk of leaving.

"Our goal is to never say the only reason we are coming to talk to you is because an algorithm told us to do so," says John Callery, director of people analytics at AOL Inc., which recently started working with workforce analytics firm Visier Inc. on a program to help predict attrition down to the individual employee.

For the past three years, Credit Suisse has studied what happens to employees over time, including raises, promotions, and life transitions, to predict whether they will choose to stay or leave the bank in the subsequent year. Changing jobs makes people "sticky," or likely to stay on, says Mr. Wolf, who oversees the bank's people analytics team. Yet as recently as five years ago, fewer than half of open jobs at the bank were posted, and most went to outsiders.

About a year and a half ago, the bank launched a global effort allowing its workers to raise their hands for internal moves. Credit Suisse recruiters now post 80% of open jobs, and cold-call employees when jobs open up.

After observing that some who volunteered to be considered for internal moves ended up leaving for jobs elsewhere, bank recruiters began using attrition probability estimates in deciding which employees to target when positions opened up.

Some 300 people have been promoted through the internal program; many of those people, Mr. Wolf says, might have left otherwise. "We believe we've saved a number of them from taking jobs at other banks."

To kindle closeness among team members, and help forestall attrition, Box has encouraged managers to throw more social events, recognize team-based work and hold more mentoring meetings between senior leaders and newer employees. Since workers were more likely to leave if they didn't see clear career opportunities at the company, it has sought to improve at pointing out career possibilities for individual workers and encouraging "stretch" assignments.

Semiconductor maker Micron Technology Inc. is using data in its efforts to reduce turnover among first-year employees, who have about a 20% world-wide attrition rate, largely driven by manufacturing personnel.

Among its early findings, Micron discovered that workers were more likely to leave if they felt their job hadn't been accurately described when they were hired, so the company is trying to create clearer job descriptions. Micron also found that people who relocated for a job were more likely to leave, but it isn't sure why.

"It's very delicate how you approach things," says Timothy Long, the company's director of workforce analytics and systems. "The idea is to determine, what can we do to get [people] to stay?"

Companies also are trying to predict when workers might leave their positions, but not necessarily the company. Wal-Mart is trying to determine in advance which employees are likely to get promoted so that it can line up replacements more quickly. The company says it promotes some 160,000 to 170,000 people a year.

"If we can tell three months in advance [that a position is going to be open], we can start hiring and training people. You don't want the jobs vacant for that long a time," says Elpida Ormanidou, Wal-Mart's vice president of global people analytics.

1. What is the business problem and question in this case?

2. From the case, identify one example of a:

   a. Feedforward control measure

   b. Concurrent control measure

   c. Feedback control measure

Chapter 12

Managing Change

LEARNING OUTCOMES

LO1	Understand what organizational change is and how it relates to the internal and external environment.
LO2	Explain some common models of organizational change.
LO3	Understand how organizational change relates to an organization's culture.
LO4	Explain the relationship among entrepreneurship, innovation, and organizational change.
LO5	Describe the challenges managers face in managing organizational change in a unionized workplace.

OPENING CASE

Loblaw Shareholders Reject Living Wage, Independent Board Chair Proposals[1]

Shareholders of Canada's largest grocer rejected a proposal that Loblaw Companies Ltd. determine the feasibility of paying its employees a living wage—one that varies by location and is calculated by its cost of living.

"Socially responsible companies contribute to the economic well-being of communities by providing direct and indirect employment preferably at rates that reflect the true cost of living. We believe the living wage reflects those costs," said a speaker from Vancity Investment Management Ltd., which submitted the shareholder proposal at Loblaw's annual general meeting of shareholders Thursday.

The proposal called for Loblaw to review the feasibility, cost and benefits of implementing a living wage policy for its employees, suppliers and contractors. It asked for the company to report findings to shareholders by the end of the year.

A living wage is an hourly rate set by looking at an area's typical expenses such as food, housing, transportation, child care and other expenses. It is calculated annually.

In Metro Vancouver, workers paid a living wage would receive $20.91 per hour, according to a report from the Canadian Centre for Policy Alternatives. If two adults worked full-time at that wage, they could support a family of four, according to the report.

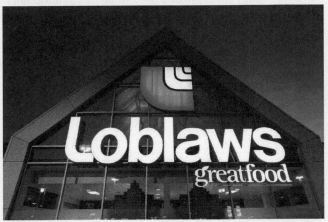

ZUMA Press, Inc./Alamy Stock Photo

In comparison, the province's minimum wage is currently $11.35 per hour, but will increase to $12.65 on June 1.

Loblaw's board of directors recommended shareholders vote against the proposal in its annual proxy circular. It reasoned the proposal over-simplifies compensation practices and won't give the company the flexibility it needs, saying the board must ensure compensation practices "are flexible enough to allow the company to maintain its competitive position and adapt in an ever-changing retail landscape."

Additionally, the "enormous time and resources" it would take to undergo the review is an inefficient use of resources, it said, and the policy would not have any bearing on workers covered by collective bargaining agreements.

The speaker countered some of these arguments when presenting the proposal at the meeting, saying the analysis would provide a factual basis for evaluating how fair the company's compensation policies are and is an efficient use of resources as it would assure shareholders the company is a responsible employer.

CEO Galen G. Weston pointed shareholders to the recommendation made in the proxy circular to vote against the proposal before adding that fair compensation and employment practices are central to Loblaw's success, but the question of fair wages is both important and tremendously complex.

While Loblaw encourages the debate, he said, "we believe that this important public policy issue is best considered by our public institutions as it is far wider in scope than one company, even one as large as Loblaw."

Ninety-seven per cent of proxies received in advance of Thursday's meeting, which represent a majority of eligible votes, voted against the proposal, he said.

At the meeting, the majority of shareholders followed suit. Though no final tally was immediately provided.

One disgruntled shareholder further questioned Weston on the issue during the meeting's question-and-answer period. He said he wasn't clear on how many more resources it would take for Loblaw to conduct the analysis beyond the work it has already done around the impact rising minimum wages in some provinces would have on the company.

"This is a national public policy question," Weston responded, to which the shareholder retorted that it is not.

Shareholders also rejected a second proposal at the meeting, asking the board to institute an independent chair of the board. Currently, Weston also serves as chairman.

An independent chair would be particularly useful at the company, the proposal stated, where it was revealed last year it participated in an alleged industry-wide bread price-fixing scheme.

The board recommended shareholders vote against the proposal, and the majority followed its directive.

After reading and understanding the concepts in this chapter, you should be able to answer the following questions:

1. Summarize the change issues this case.
2. Apply Kotter's model of change to this case.

Overview

Most managers will at one point or another engage in innovation and change when it is necessary to adapt to new internal and external organizational environments. Changes in technology, strategy, organizational structure, and culture may be necessary to take advantage of opportunities and counter any threats facing an organization to ensure sustainability. But, as we all know, change is difficult. It often means giving up privilege and power by some and in many cases also involves empowering others. This is clearly illustrated in the opening case where shareholders would have their return on investment reduced and workers would increase their purchasing power if the proposed change was adopted. Either way, change means the status quo has shifted and uncertainty and resistance to the shift are likely to follow. So how do managers deal with change?

In this chapter, we look at what constitutes organizational change, how organizational change affects the management process, and theories of how to manage change successfully. We also look at the role that entrepreneurship plays in creating organizational change and innovation and how managers can foster an innovative climate that is motivating for employees to take risks and embrace change. We end the chapter with a look at the unique challenges facing managers in unionized workplaces when initiating and implementing change. See Figure 12.1 for an overview of topics. By the end of this chapter, you will understand how an innovative culture helps convey meaning and purpose to employees and the vital role that change plays in building competitive advantage and creating a high-performing organization.

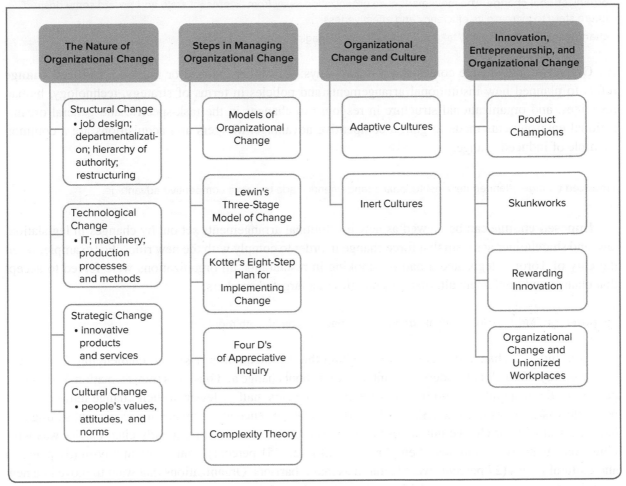

FIGURE 12.1

Overview of Managing Change Topics

Organizational Change

LO1 | Understand what organizational change is and how it relates to the internal and external environment.

Organizational change <u>can affect</u> practically <u>all aspects</u> of organizational functioning, including organizational structure, strategies, control systems, groups and teams, as well as the human resource management system and critical organizational processes such as communication, motivation, and leadership. **Organizational change** is the movement of an organization away from its present state and toward some desired future state to increase its efficiency and effectiveness. Organizational change <u>can bring alterations</u> in the ways managers carry out the critical tasks of planning, organizing, leading, and controlling and the ways they perform their managerial roles. Thus, all changes in the organization need to be carried out within the context of <u>examining</u> the organization's <u>internal</u> environment—HRM, strategy, technology, structure, and culture. <u>Adaptive and innovative</u> cultures facilitate the initiation and development of new ideas; nevertheless, implementing change is often met with <u>resistance</u>. The people who take responsibility for a change initiative are known as **change agents.** Change agents can be employees acting as intrapreneurs, discussed later in this chapter, or managers and outside consultants.

---

organizational change The movement of an organization away from its present state and toward some desired future state to increase its efficiency and effectiveness.

change agents People who take responsibility for managing change initiatives.

Organizational change comes about in two ways: it is either induced or imposed. **Induced change** refers to planned new institutional arrangements and policies in terms of strategy, technology, human resources, and organizational structure in response to changes in the task-specific and general organizational environments made to gain a competitive advantage. Mergers and acquisitions are a common example of induced change.

within business world

---

induced change Planned new institutional arrangements made to gain a competitive advantage.

---

govt

Imposed change can be viewed as new institutional arrangements set out by changes in legislation, law, and shareholder activism that force change in order to comply with the new rules. For example, when the City of Toronto legislated a ban on smoking in restaurants, all organizations were forced to accept that change and implement alternative strategies that targeted smokers.

---

imposed change New institutional arrangements made to comply with regulations.

---

from outside

Even induced change that comes from within the organization is risky and challenging. In a recent online survey,[2] 600 global leaders were interviewed about change and business transformation. Fifty-eight percent of the respondents said that over the past five years, half or fewer of their change initiatives had been successful. For the United States, the participant experience was worse, with 75 percent stating that half or fewer of their change initiatives had been successful. The most frequently cited barrier was winning over the hearts and minds of employees at all levels (51 percent). Management buy-in (31 percent) and cultural issues (27 percent) were featured as major barriers. Organizations that want to move in a new direction, such as mergers, acquisitions, divestitures, or global expansions, must alter structures, policies, behaviours, and beliefs in order to get from "how we've always done it" to how things will be done in the future. Thus, all changes in the organization need to be carried out within the context of examining and changing the organization's leadership (Chapter 9) and culture (Chapter 1). Turnaround leaders, such as John Chen at BlackBerry, are very good at articulating the vision of the future state the organization intends to move toward, but getting people to change the way they have always done things in terms of norms and behaviours—or changes in any organizational activities—often results in resistance. Sometimes the leaders themselves are resistant to change driven by stakeholders, as we saw in the opening case.

While it is difficult to analyze organizational change that is imposed from outside, in the next part of this chapter we look at the dimensions of

Changes in policies often meet with resistance.
Design Pics/Kristy-Anne Glubish

FIGURE 12.2

Types of Organizational Change Affecting Management Processes

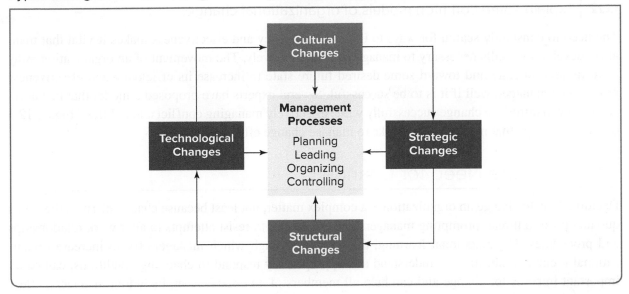

organizational change when organizational change is induced from within. Figure 12.2 outlines the types of change we find in organizations when the changes are <u>induced or planne</u>d. Organizational change can affect practically all aspects of organizational functioning, including organizational structure, critical operational processes involving technology, new product development, and changes in the cultural norms and values of the organization. **Structural changes** in an organization involve any changes in the way the organization is designed, planned, and controlled including how authority is allocated and how departments and activities are integrated and coordinated. Bombardier changed its structure when it created a skunkworks for the "C" series jet (see the discussion of skunkworks later in this chapter). **Technological changes** occur when operational processes and methods are redesigned to be more efficient. For example, point-of-sale technology allows organizations in retail and food services to track sales and order inventory in one transaction. **Strategic changes** occur when new ideas are developed and innovation occurs—that is, creative ideas are implemented resulting in new products or services. The "C" series regional jet is a new product from Bombardier. **Cultural changes** are shifts in the shared set of beliefs, expectations, values, norms, and work routines that influence how members of an organization relate to one another and work together to achieve organizational goals. Paying a living wage to employees at Loblaws would mean embracing a whole new set of principles on how wages are set. <u>Training and development</u> play a critical role in moving people's beliefs and attitudes from the way things have always been done to the new, desired state. Organizational change can bring alterations in the ways managers carry out all the critical tasks in planning, organizing, leading, and controlling and the ways they perform their managerial roles.

structural changes Any change in the design and management of an organization.

technological changes Changes that relate to an organization's operational processes.

strategic changes A change in the products and services offered by the organization.

cultural changes A shift in the shared set of beliefs, expectations, values, norms, and work routines that influence how members of an organization relate to one another and work together to achieve organizational goals.

Steps in Managing Organizational Change

LO2 | Explain some common models of organizational change.

The need to constantly search for ways to improve efficiency and effectiveness makes it vital that managers develop the skills necessary to manage change effectively. The movement of an organization away from its present state and toward some desired future state to increase its efficiency and effectiveness needs to be managed well if it is to be successful. Several experts have proposed a model that managers can follow to introduce change successfully while effectively managing conflict and politics.[3] Figure 12.3 outlines the steps that managers must take to manage change effectively.

Assessing the Need for Change

Deciding how to change an organization is a complex matter, not least because change disrupts the status quo and poses a threat, prompting managers and employees to resist attempts to alter work relationships and procedures. Organizational learning, the process through which managers try to increase organizational members' abilities to understand and appropriately respond to changing conditions, can be an important impetus for change and can help all members of an organization, including managers, effectively make decisions about needed changes.

Assessing the need for change calls for two important activities: *recognizing that there is a problem* and *identifying its source.* Sometimes the need for change is obvious, such as when an organization's market share is suffering. Often, however, managers have trouble determining that something is going wrong because problems develop gradually; organizational performance may slip for a number of years before it becomes obvious. Even if there is no problem with current performance, implementing a new idea or innovation will require changes in structure, strategy, and control processes—and therein lies the problem. Thus, during the first step in the change process, managers need to recognize a problem that requires change and identify its source.

Often, a **performance gap,** the disparity between desired and actual performance, signals that there is a problem. By looking at performance measures—such as falling market share or profits, rising costs, or employees' failure to meet their established goals or stay within budgets—managers can see whether change is needed. These measures are provided by organizational control systems (discussed in Chapter 11). Other things—for example, implementing sustainability measures; new, creative ideas; or

---

FIGURE 12.3

Four Steps in the Organizational Change Process

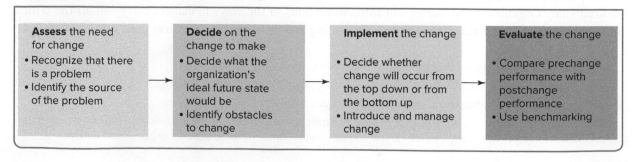

Assess the need for change
- Recognize that there is a problem
- Identify the source of the problem

Decide on the change to make
- Decide what the organization's ideal future state would be
- Identify obstacles to change

Implement the change
- Decide whether change will occur from the top down or from the bottom up
- Introduce and manage change

Evaluate the change
- Compare prechange performance with postchange performance
- Use benchmarking

technologies that increase efficiencies—precipitate the need for a change. In the era of ebusiness, rapid technological changes are forcing traditional land-based, bricks-and-mortar business to radically change operations to compete with low cost competitors. Shareholder activism, as illustrated in the opening case, is increasingly driving change in large publicly traded corporations.

performance gap A disparity between desired and actual performance levels.

Deciding on the Change to Make

Once managers have identified the source of the problem, they must decide what they think the organization's ideal future state would be. In other words, they must decide where they would like their organization to be in the future—what kinds of goods and services it should be offering, what its business-level strategy should be, how the organizational structure should be changed, and so on. During this step, managers also must engage in planning how they are going to attain the organization's ideal future state. Companies transforming to ebusiness create customer value by using networked computing to improve internal communications among employees and external communications with customers, suppliers, and strategic partners. But changing from a "bricks-and-mortar" to a "clicks-and-mortar" organization presents significant challenges to today's managers.

This step in the change process also includes identifying obstacles or sources of resistance to change (discussed in more detail in the next section). Managers must analyze the factors that may prevent the company from reaching the proposed future state. Obstacles to change are found at the corporate, divisional, departmental, and individual levels of the organization.

Corporate-level changes in an organization's strategy or structure—even seemingly trivial changes—may significantly affect how divisional and departmental managers behave. Suppose that to compete with low-cost foreign competitors, top managers decide to increase the resources spent on state-of-the-art machinery and reduce the resources spent on marketing or R&D. The power of manufacturing managers would increase, and the power of marketing and R&D managers would fall. This decision would alter the balance of power among departments and might lead to increased politics and conflict as departments start fighting to retain their status in the organization. Similarly, workers' interests in attaining a living wage conflict with shareholders' interests in maximizing their return on investment. An organization's present culture, strategy, and structure are powerful obstacles to change.

The same obstacles to change exist at the divisional and departmental levels as well. Division managers may differ in their attitudes toward the changes that top managers propose and will resist those changes if their interests and power seem threatened. Managers at all levels usually fight to protect their power and control over resources. Given that departments have different goals and time horizons, they may also react differently to the changes that other managers propose. When top managers are trying to reduce costs, for example, sales managers may resist attempts to cut back on sales expenditures if they believe that problems stem from the manufacturing managers' inefficiencies.

At the individual level, too, people are often resistant to change because change brings uncertainty, and uncertainty brings stress. For example, older individuals may resist the introduction of ebusiness technology because they are uncertain about their abilities to learn it and effectively use it.

These obstacles make organizational change a slow process. Managers must recognize these potential obstacles to change and take them into consideration. Some obstacles can be overcome by improving communication and integrating mechanisms so that all organizational members are aware of both the need for change and the nature of the changes being made. Empowering employees and inviting them to take part in the planning for change also can help overcome resistance and reduce employees' fears. Emphasizing big-picture goals, such as organizational effectiveness and gaining a competitive advantage can make organizational members who resist a change realize that the change is ultimately in everyone's best interests because it will increase organizational performance. The larger and more complex an organization is, the more complex is the change process.

Introducing the Change

Generally, managers can introduce and manage change from the top down or from the bottom up.[4] **Top-down change** is implemented quickly: top managers identify the need for change, decide what to do, and then move speedily to introduce the changes throughout the organization. For example, top managers may decide to restructure and downsize the organization and then give divisional and departmental managers specific goals to achieve. With top-down change, the emphasis is on making the changes quickly and dealing with problems as they arise.

> **top-down change** Change that is introduced quickly throughout an organization by upper-level managers.

Bottom-up change is typically more gradual. Top managers consult with middle and first-line managers about the need for change. Then, over time, these low-level managers work with nonmanagerial employees to develop a detailed plan for change. A major advantage of bottom-up change is that it can reduce uncertainty and resistance to change. The emphasis in bottom-up change is on participation and on keeping people informed about what is going on, thus minimizing resistance from employees.

> **bottom-up change** Change that is introduced gradually and involves managers and employees at all levels of an organization.

Evaluating the Change

The last step in the change process is to evaluate how successful the change effort has been in improving organizational performance.[5] Using measures such as changes in market share, profits, or the ability of managers to meet their goals, managers compare how well an organization is performing after the change with how well it was performing before.

 FOR MANAGERS

Introducing Change

1. Explaining the reasons for the change, the need for the change, the logic behind the change, the benefits of the change, or other seemingly rational approaches may fail.

2. Logical explanations often fail because they are viewed as "uncaring" and people feel their emotional concerns are unheard.

3. Respond to the affected people by confirming their emotional concerns.

Managers also can use **benchmarking,** comparing their performance on specific dimensions with the performance of high-performing organizations to decide how successful the change effort has been. For example, when Xerox was doing poorly in the 1980s, it benchmarked the efficiency of its distribution operations against those of L.L. Bean, the efficiency of its central computer operations against those of John Deere, and its marketing abilities against those of Procter & Gamble. Those companies are renowned for their skills in those different areas, and by studying how they performed, Xerox was able to dramatically increase its own performance.

benchmarking Comparing performance on specific dimensions with the performance of high-performing organizations.

Models of Organizational Change

Interestingly enough, there is a fundamental tension or need to balance two opposing forces that influences the way organizations change. Organizations and their managers need to be able to control their activities and make their operations routine and predictable. At the same time, however, organizations have to be responsive to the need for innovation and change, and managers and employees have to "think on their feet" and realize when they need to depart from routines to be responsive to unpredictable events. See Figure 12.4. Employees need to feel that they have the autonomy to depart from routines as necessary to increase innovation without being punished by rigid rules and regulations. It is for this reason that many researchers believe that the highest-performing organizations are those that are constantly changing—and thus become experienced at doing so—in their search to become more efficient and effective. The need to constantly search for ways to improve efficiency and effectiveness makes it vital that managers develop the skills necessary to manage change effectively.

FIGURE 12.4

Organizational Control and Change

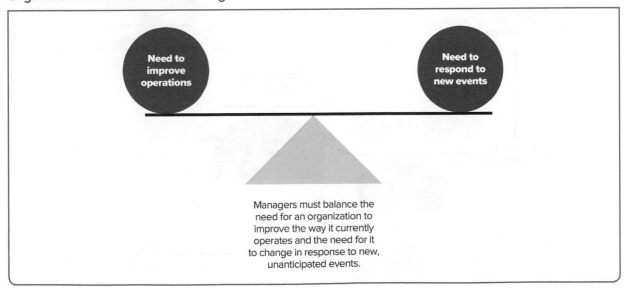

Managers must balance the need for an organization to improve the way it currently operates and the need for it to change in response to new, unanticipated events.

LEWIN'S THREE-STAGE MODEL OF CHANGE

Kurt Lewin identified a three-stage process that organizations could use to manage change successfully: *unfreeze* the status quo, *move* to a new state, and *refreeze* the new change to make it permanent.[6]

Organizations in their ordinary state reflect the status quo. To move toward a new state, unfreezing is necessary. Unfreezing, the process by which an organization overcomes the resistance to change, can occur in one of three ways, as shown in Figure 12.5. **Driving forces,** which direct behaviour away from the status quo, can be increased. **Restraining forces,** which hinder movement from the existing equilibrium, can be decreased. And thirdly, one can also combine the first two approaches.

> **driving forces** Forces that direct behaviour away from the status quo.
>
> **restraining forces** Forces that prevent movement away from the status quo.

Individuals generally resist change for two primary reasons:

1. *Fear.* People fear the unknown. The perception that change can lead to a loss of power and privilege can hold weight, especially when resources and budgets need to be reallocated. There can be winners and losers in the change process.

2. *Doubt.* If people doubt the legitimacy of the change, or perceive it not to be in the best interests of the organization and its shareholders, they are likely to act as a restraining force against the change.

Managers can take action to break down that resistance:

- They can communicate the desired outcome or future state clearly and seek input from others.

- They can increase the driving forces by promising new rewards or benefits if stakeholders work toward the change.

FIGURE 12.5

Lewin's Model of Change

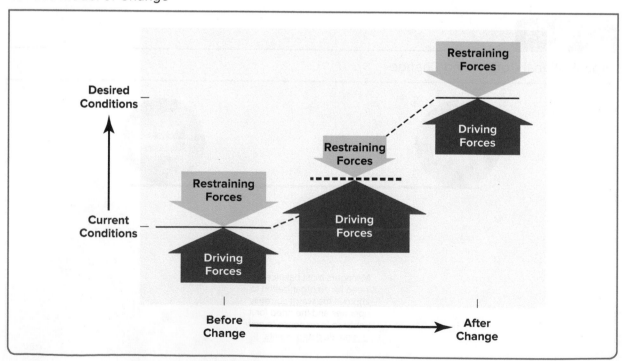

- Managers can also remove some of the restraining forces. For instance, if employees fear change because they do not know how to use the new technology, training could be given to reduce that fear.

- When resistance to change is extremely high, managers may have to work on both the driving forces and the restraining forces for unfreezing to be successful.

- As a last resort, managers may use their formal power to withhold rewards in order to persuade employees to adopt new institutional changes.

Moving involves getting the change process itself underway. Once change has been implemented, the behaviours have to be refrozen so that they can be sustained over time. Otherwise, change is likely to be short-lived, and employees are likely to go back to the previous state. Refreezing balances the driving and restraining forces to prevent the old state from arising again.

To refreeze the change, managers need to put permanent driving forces into place. For instance, the new bonus system could reinforce specific new changes. Over time, the norms of the employee work groups and managers will also help solidify the change if senior managers have sufficiently reinforced the new behaviour.

KOTTER'S EIGHT-STEP PLAN FOR IMPLEMENTING CHANGE

Building on Lewin's three-step model, John Kotter, a professor at Harvard University, created a more detailed eight-step plan for implementing change. See Figure 12.6. The first four steps relate to Lewin's "unfreezing" stage. Steps 5 to 7 represent the "moving" phase, and the final step is necessary for "refreezing" the new behaviours and norms.

FOUR D'S OF APPRECIATIVE INQUIRY

A unique approach to change management comes from appreciative inquiry (AI). Here, managers and employees collaborate on identifying the internal strengths of the organization and envisioning what it

---

FIGURE 12.6

Kotter's Eight-Step Plan for Implementing Change

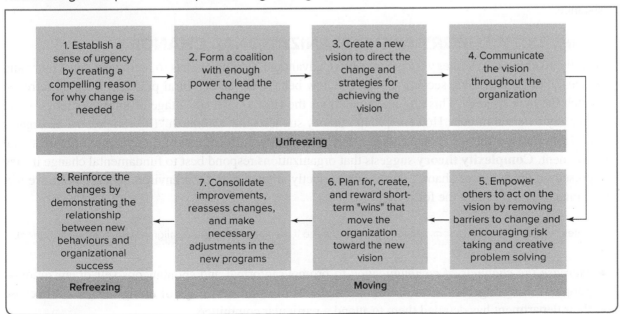

FIGURE 12.7

The "Four D's" of Appreciative Inquiry

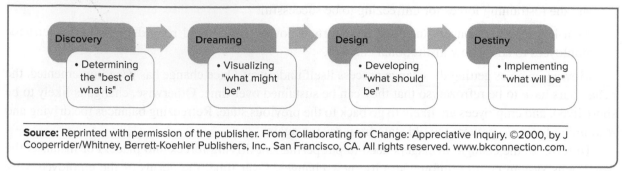

Discovery
- Determining the "best of what is"

Dreaming
- Visualizing "what might be"

Design
- Developing "what should be"

Destiny
- Implementing "what will be"

Source: Reprinted with permission of the publisher. From Collaborating for Change: Appreciative Inquiry. ©2000, by J Cooperrider/Whitney, Berrett-Koehler Publishers, Inc., San Francisco, CA. All rights reserved. www.bkconnection.com.

could look like in the future. It combines brainstorming (see Chapter 3) and SWOT analysis (discussed in Chapter 4). Rather than being problem-focused, AI builds a vision of the future of the organization on its current strengths and core competencies. The process is often facilitated by outside consultants and can take place over several days. The appreciative inquiry process consists of "Four D's," or steps, illustrated in Figure 12.7.

- *Discovery:* People in this step identify what is good about their jobs, what the strengths of the organization are as a whole, and the positive aspects of how their department or work groups operate.
- *Dreaming:* Drawing on the strengths identified in the discovery step, employees envision possible futures for the organization over a period of time, say five years.
- *Design:* Flowing from the dreaming stage, members develop a common vision of what qualities the organization will have and how it will be structured.
- *Destiny:* Typically, in this stage, participants discuss how to implement the dream and design. Action plans are written and implementation strategies developed to facilitate the creation of the new desired state for the organization.

This participative strategy for managing change creates a positive, collaborative culture which reduces resistance.

COMPLEXITY THEORY AND ORGANIZATIONAL CHANGE

Typically, to embrace a strategy for a competitive advantage, a company has to learn new behaviours and practices until they become second nature. The new behaviours and cultural practices must be refrozen to match the new strategy. This alignment positions the firm to take advantage of internal strengths and counter any external threats. However, Ralph Stacey suggests that too much "fit" can prevent an organization from making the necessary changes that would allow it to compete in a dynamic organizational environment. **Complexity theory** suggests that organizations respond best to fundamental change if they are poised on the "edge of chaos"; that is, not perfectly aligned with their environments. To achieve this state, managers have to do the following:

complexity theory Organizations respond best to change if they are not perfectly aligned with their environment.

- *Increase the channels of communication* to promote informal and spontaneous self-organization— people coming together because they are motivated to find new ways of doing things, not because their department has detailed them to attend a particular committee.

- *Not dictate agendas* or set specific objectives but identify problems or pose paradoxes for groups to resolve. For example, how can we be both a successful innovator and a low-cost producer? Set rules and establish the constraints for the debate; do not try to predict outcomes.

- *Rotate people regularly* so that they do not get stale and can both disseminate their own expertise and gain insights from other parts of the business. Bring in outsiders with different backgrounds and cultures. Involve people at the periphery of the organization who have not yet been fully absorbed into the culture.

- *Avoid overreliance on an incumbent management team.* In many firms, the further up the hierarchy you go, the greater is the attachment to the existing dominant logic and the closer the adherence to the status quo. We should therefore identify change agents below the top.

- *Tolerate parallel developments.* In a world where the future is inherently unknowable and everything is to play for, sticking too closely to the knitting can be disastrous. Permit experimentation and learn from failure.

- *Avoid excessive "fit."* To challenge the status quo, there needs to be enough organizational slack for the firm to develop the future "recipe" alongside the existing one.

- *Try to reduce anxiety.* Since change is threatening and likely to induce anxiety and defensive behaviour, fear needs to be reduced by offering realistic terms: for example, continued employment in return for total flexibility.[7]

Complexity theory suggests that fixed notions such as mission statements, developing core competencies, and leadership may be suitable for firms operating in a stable environment but have little relevance to those confronting the necessities for fundamental change to remain competitive today. Complexity theory focuses more on processes and organizational dynamics that question the traditional notion that strategy can be planned and programmed.

Organizational Change and Culture

LO3 | Understand how organizational change relates to an organization's culture.

Adaptive Cultures versus Inert Cultures

Whether a company's culture is adaptive or inert either facilitates or obstructs change. Organizations with entrepreneurial, flexible cultures, such as high-tech companies, are much easier to change than are organizations with more rigid cultures such as those sometimes found in large bureaucratic organizations—for example the RCMP or, as the opening case illustrated, Loblaws.

Many researchers and managers believe that employees of some organizations go out of their way to help the organization because it has a strong and cohesive organizational culture—an *adaptive culture* that encourages positive attitudes and behaviours that foster creativity and innovation. Adaptive cultures, such as that at WestJet and 3M Canada, are cultures whose values and norms help an organization to build momentum and to grow and change as needed to achieve its goals and be effective. By contrast, *inert cultures* are those that lead to values and norms that fail to motivate or inspire employees; they lead to stagnation and often failure over time, and can inspire resistance to change. What leads to an adaptive or inert culture?

Researchers have found that organizations with strong adaptive cultures, like 3M Canada, WestJet, Google, and IBM, invest in their employees. They demonstrate their commitment to their members by, for example, emphasizing the long-term nature of the employment relationship and trying to avoid layoffs. These companies develop long-term career paths for their employees and invest heavily in training and development to increase employees' value to the organization. In these ways, resistance to change is minimized, because everyone is on the same page.

In adaptive cultures employees often receive rewards linked directly to their performance and

Innovation thrives at Google.
dpa picture alliance/Alamy Stock Photo

to the performance of the company as a whole. Sometimes, employee stock ownership plans (ESOPs) are developed in which workers as a group are allowed to buy a significant percentage of their company's stock. Workers who are owners of the company have additional incentive to develop skills that allow them to perform highly and search actively for ways to improve quality, efficiency, and performance. At Shaw Media Inc., for example, employees are able to buy Shaw stock at a steep discount; this allows them to build a sizable stake in the company over time.

Some organizations, however, develop cultures with values that do not include protecting and increasing the worth of their human resources as a major goal. Their employment practices are based on short-term employment according to the needs of the organization and on minimal investment in employees who perform simple, routine tasks and are paid minimum wage rather than a living wage. Moreover, employees are not often rewarded based on their performance and thus have little incentive to improve their skills or otherwise invest in the organization to help it to achieve goals. If a company has an inert culture, poor working relationships frequently develop between the organization and its employees, and instrumental values of noncooperation, loafing, and performance norms of output restriction are common. Resistance to change can be sizable in organizations that have inert cultures.

Moreover, an adaptive culture develops an emphasis on entrepreneurship and respect for the employee and allows technological changes, changes in products or services, and organizational structures, such as the cross-functional team structure, to empower employees to make decisions and motivate them to succeed. By contrast, in an inert culture, employees are content to be told what to do and have little incentive or motivation to perform beyond minimum work requirements. As you might expect, the emphasis is on close supervision and hierarchical authority, which result in a culture that makes it difficult to adapt to a changing environment.

Innovation, Entrepreneurship, and Organizational Change

LO4 | Explain the relationship among entrepreneurship, innovation, and organizational change.

The intensity of competition today, particularly from agile, small companies, has made it increasingly important for large, established organizations to promote and encourage a culture of intrapreneurship to raise the level of **innovation,** the implementation of creative ideas in an organization. As we discussed in Chapter 1, managers are responsible for supervising the use of human and other resources to achieve effective and efficient organizational goals. **Entrepreneurs,** by contrast, are the people who notice opportunities and take responsibility for mobilizing the resources necessary to produce new and improved goods and services in a new organization.

---

innovation The implementation of creative ideas in an organization.

entrepreneurs People who notice opportunities and take responsibility for mobilizing the resources necessary to produce new and improved goods and services.

Essentially, entrepreneurs bring about change to companies and industries because they see new and improved ways to use resources to create products customers will want to buy. At the same time, entrepreneurs who start new business ventures are responsible for all the initial planning, organizing, leading, and controlling necessary to make their idea a reality. Thus, entrepreneurs are an important source of creativity in the organizational world. If their idea is viable and entrepreneurs do attract customers, then their business grows and then they need to hire managers who will take responsibility for organizing and controlling all the specific functional activities—such as marketing, accounting, and manufacturing—necessary for a growing organization to be successful.

Typically, entrepreneurs assume the substantial risk associated with starting new businesses (many new businesses fail), and they receive all the returns or profits associated with the new business venture. These people are the Ted Rogerses (founder of Rogers Communications Inc.) of the world who make vast fortunes when their businesses succeed. Or they are among the millions of people who start new business ventures only to lose their money when their businesses fail. Despite the fact that an estimated 80 percent of small businesses fail in the first three to five years, by some estimates 38 percent of men and 50 percent of women in today's workforce want to start their own companies.[8]

Social entrepreneurs are individuals who pursue initiatives and opportunities to address social problems and unmet needs in order to improve society and well-being, such as reducing poverty, increasing literacy, protecting the natural environment, or reducing substance abuse.[9] Their motivation is not primarily private profit maximization. Rather, social entrepreneurs are motivated by the desire to help others and the environment. Social entrepreneurs seek to mobilize resources to solve social problems through creative solutions.[10] Social entrepreneurs create enterprises with social missions. A pioneer social entrepreneur, Muhammad Yunus, founder of the Grameen Bank that provides micro credit to poor rural people to start businesses, has said, "We can think about a social business as a selfless business whose purpose is to bring an end to a social problem. In this kind of business, the company makes a profit—but no one takes the profit. Because the company is dedicated entirely to the social cause, the whole idea of making personal profit is removed from the business. The owner can take back over a period of time only the amount invested."[11] While social entrepreneurs often face challenges in raising funds to support their initiatives, their options are increasing as more and more investors look for innovative ways to achieve a sustainable social impact. The term **social innovation** refers to finding new ways of solving social problems such as poverty, homelessness, and food security. The Focus on the Social Economy box discusses a good example of social innovation.

---

social entrepreneurs Individuals who pursue initiatives and opportunities and mobilize resources to address social problems and needs in order to improve society and well-being through creative solutions.

social innovation Developing new ways of solving social problems.

Entrepreneurship does not just end once a new business is founded. Entrepreneurship carries on inside an organization over time, and many people throughout an organization take responsibility for developing innovative goods and services. For example, managers, scientists, or researchers employed by existing companies engage in entrepreneurial activity when they develop new or improved products. To distinguish these individuals from entrepreneurs who found their own businesses, employees of existing organizations who notice opportunities for product or service improvements and are responsible for managing the development process are known as **intrapreneurs.** In general, then, **entrepreneurship** is the mobilization of resources to take advantage of an opportunity to provide customers with new or improved goods and services; intrapreneurs engage in entrepreneurship within an existing company.

intrapreneurs Employees of existing organizations who notice opportunities for product or service improvement and are responsible for managing the development process.

entrepreneurship The mobilization of resources to take advantage of an opportunity to provide customers with new or improved goods and services.

An interesting relationship exists between entrepreneurs and intrapreneurs. Many intrapreneurs become dissatisfied when their superiors decide not to support or to fund new product ideas and development efforts that the intrapreneurs think will succeed. Organizations with rigid, inflexible

FOCUS ON   *The Social Economy*

Vibrant Communities Canada: Cities Reducing Poverty

In April 2011, Tamarack—An Institute for Community Engagement invited nine cities and a small number of provincial and national network representatives to a meeting in Kitchener, Ontario to discuss the power and potential of developing a learning network of cities collaborating together to reduce poverty. The cities included five Vibrant Communities partners and four other cities/regions with collaborative roundtables. At the conclusion of the meeting, the nine cities and regional partners returned to their communities, shared the results of the discussions, and formally affirmed their commitment to working collaboratively in the development of the Cities Reducing Poverty effort. Together, these cities/regions determined the following aspiration and path for moving forward.

Vision: To create Vibrant Communities by significantly reducing the human, social, and economic cost of poverty for Canadian cities.

Mission: To create a connected learning community of 100 Canadian cities or regions with multi-sector roundtables addressing poverty reduction. The goal is to create aligned poverty reduction strategies in cities, provinces, and the federal government, resulting in reduced poverty for 1 million Canadians.

They aim to actively recruit and engage multi-sector poverty roundtables in all provinces and territories in a way that respects local priorities and approaches.

A number of cities reported a 10 percent reduction in poverty, impacting the lives of 202 931 low-income Canadians.

1. Apply the four steps in the change process from Figure 12.2 to Vibrant Communities Canada.

Source: Adapted by permission of the Tamarack Institute.

organizational cultures do not support the kind of creative risk taking that is necessary to foster innovation. What do intrapreneurs do who feel that they are getting nowhere? Very often intrapreneurs decide to leave their employers and start their own organizations to take advantage of their new product ideas. In other words, intrapreneurs become entrepreneurs and found companies that may compete with the companies they left.

Many of the world's most successful organizations have been started by frustrated intrapreneurs who became entrepreneurs. William Hewlett and David Packard left Fairchild Semiconductor, an early industry leader, when managers of that company would not support Hewlett and Packard's ideas; their company soon outperformed Fairchild. Compaq Computer was founded by Rod Canion and some of his colleagues, who left Texas Instruments (TI) when managers there would not support Canion's idea that TI should develop its own personal computer. To prevent the departure of talented people, organizations need to take steps to promote a culture that encourages internal entrepreneurship, innovation, and change.

> *"We can think about a social business as a selfless business whose purpose is to bring an end to a social problem."*
>
> Muhammad Yunus, 2006 Nobel Peace Prize Winner and Social Entrepreneur

As we discussed in Chapter 3, a learning organization encourages all employees to identify opportunities and solve problems, thus enabling the organization to continuously experiment, improve, and increase its ability to provide customers with new and improved goods and services. The higher the level of intrapreneurship, the higher will be the level of creativity, learning, and *innovation,* the implementation of creative ideas in an organization creating change. How can organizations promote innovation and intrapreneurship? See Figure 12.8.

Product Champions

One way to promote intrapreneurship is to encourage individuals to assume the role of a **product champion,** a manager who takes ownership of a project and provides the leadership and vision that take a product from the idea stage to the final customer. 3M Canada, a company well known for its attempts to

FIGURE 12.8

The Process of Innovation

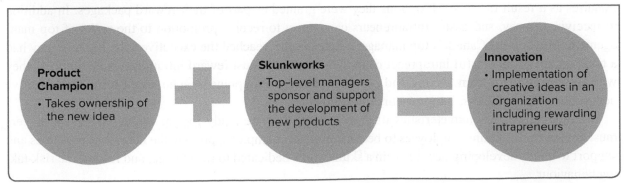

promote intrapreneurship, encourages all its managers to become product champions and identify new product ideas. A product champion becomes responsible for developing a business plan for the product. Armed with this business plan, the champion appears before 3M Canada's product development committee, a team of senior 3M Canada managers who probe the strengths and weaknesses of the plan to decide whether it should be funded. If the plan is accepted, the product champion assumes responsibility for product development.

> **product champion** A manager who takes "ownership" of a project and provides the leadership and vision that take a product from the idea stage to the final customer.

Skunkworks

The idea behind the product champion role is that employees who feel ownership for a project are inclined to act like outside entrepreneurs and go to great lengths to make the project succeed. Using skunkworks and new venture divisions can also strengthen this feeling of ownership. A **skunkworks** is a group of intrapreneurs who are deliberately separated from the normal operation of an organization—for example, from the normal chain of command—to encourage them to devote all their attention to developing new products. The idea is that if these people are isolated, they will become so intensely involved in a project that development time will be relatively brief and the quality of the final product will be enhanced. The term *skunkworks* was coined at the Lockheed Corporation, which formed a team of design engineers to develop special aircraft such as the U2 spy plane. The secrecy with which this unit functioned and speculation about its goals led others to refer to it as "the skunkworks." Bombardier's small-bodied regional jet, called the "C" series, was similarly developed.

> **skunkworks** A group of intrapreneurs who are deliberately separated from the normal operation of an organization to encourage them to devote all their attention to developing new products.

Rewarding Innovation

To encourage managers to bear the uncertainty and risk associated with the hard work of entrepreneurship, it is necessary to link performance to rewards. Increasingly, companies are rewarding intrapreneurs on the basis of the outcome of the product development process. Intrapreneurs are granted large bonuses if their projects succeed, or they are granted stock options that can make them millionaires if the product sells well. Both Microsoft and Google, for example, have made hundreds of their employees multimillionaires as a result of the stock options they were granted as part of their reward packages. In addition to receiving money, successful intrapreneurs can expect to receive promotion to the ranks of top management. Most of 3M Canada's top managers, for example, reached the executive suite because they had a track record of successful intrapreneurship. Organizations must reward intrapreneurs equitably if they wish to prevent them from leaving and becoming outside entrepreneurs who might form a competitive new venture. Nevertheless, intrapreneurs frequently do so.

To summarize the characteristics of organizations that are ready for embracing change, managers must empower risk-taking employees to become product champions, provide the necessary resources and support to teams developing new ideas in a skunkworks dedicated to the change, and reward the risk-taking behaviour.

Managing Change in a Unionized Environment

LO5 Describe the challenges managers face in managing organizational change in a unionized workplace.

When managers work in a unionized environment, they may have some other considerations to deal with when facing the challenge of managing change. Two consultants who have worked with a number of Canadian organizations in recent years note four essential elements for managing change in a unionized environment.[12]

Don't think outside the box, Think like there is NO BOX!

How can organizations remain competitive in a dynamic environment?
©Ayse Ezgi Icmeli | Dreamstime.com

- *An effective system for resolving day-to-day issues.* Employees should have alternatives to the formal grievance process so that they feel they can be heard easily. If the workplace is open to hearing workers' issues, this will underscore a commitment to participation and empowerment.

- *A jointly administered business education process.* Because union leaders and their members become uneasy about the effects of change on jobs, education can help employees understand the need for change. Making them more aware of company performance helps them better understand the decisions the company makes.

- *A jointly developed strategic vision for the organization.* Giving union members the opportunity to be involved in setting the vision lets them focus on how change can be made, rather than whether it should be made. The vision "should describe performance expectations, work design, organizational structure, the supply chain, governance, pay and rewards, technology, education and training, operating processes, employee involvement, employment security, and union–management roles and relations."[13]

- *A nontraditional, problem-solving method of negotiating collective agreements.* Managers need to create an atmosphere of tolerance and willingness to listen. Expanding the traditional scope of bargaining to include complex issues such as strategic plans is also helpful. Management resists bargaining over these issues, but when managers do bargain, it communicates a commitment to working jointly with unionized employees.

In summary, managers face several challenges in balancing innovation, creating a high-performance culture, and implementing organizational change successfully. Innovation—implementing new creative ideas to gain a competitive advantage—happens in companies whose organizational culture is based on norms and values which support individual creativity and organizational learning and risk taking. Managers must appropriately reward individual intrapreneurs for new ideas, even if in the end they do not come to market. Employees and managers who feel empowered to work on new solutions, without risk of repercussion, create an adaptive organizational culture that can better cope with organizational change. Changes in any aspect of an organization's operations, strategy, or structure may result in resistance from employees and managers who would rather maintain the status quo than give up any power or privilege. Managers must adopt techniques to overcome resistance. The challenge is for managers to balance the need for smooth, predictable operations with the need to respond quickly to changes in the environment to maintain or gain a competitive advantage. Companies who are ever-ready for change as it arises are more likely to have innovative, adaptive organizational cultures and be high-performing organizations.

✱ Managing organizational change is key to an organization's performance. In responding to the threats and opportunities in the environment, managers must be alert to the need to align new strategies and structures. Innovation and change is more successful in organizations with entrepreneurial and adaptive cultures. High-performing organizations are those whose managers are attuned to the need to continually modify the way they operate, and who adopt techniques to foster innovative, adaptive organizational cultures and organizational learning—such as empowered work groups and teams, and benchmarking—to overcome resistance to change and remain competitive in a global world.

Chapter 12

SUMMARY AND REVIEW

connect

LO1 **Organizational Change** Organizational change is the movement of an organization away from its present state and toward some desired future state to increase its efficiency and effectiveness. When organizational change is either induced from inside the organization or imposed from outside, changes in the technology, structure, strategy, and organizational culture affect the management processes of planning, organizing, leading, and controlling.

LO2 **Steps in Managing Organizational Change** Managing organizational change is one of managers' most important and difficult tasks. Four steps in the organizational change process are assessing the need for change, deciding on the change to make, introducing the change, and evaluating how successful the change effort has been. A central challenge for managers is to balance the need for predictable, stable work patterns with the need to respond to changes in the environment by innovating and changing strategy and structure. Kurt Lewin suggests a three-stage process to manage change: (1) the status quo is unfrozen, (2) the organization moves to the desired state, and (3) the changes are refrozen to make them permanent. John Kotter developed an eight-stage process of change. Complexity theory suggests that to effectively deal with change, managers must create flexible systems that teeter on the "edge of chaos" rather than rigid, permanent structures.

LO3 **Organizational Change and Culture** *Adaptive* organizational cultures are better able to embrace change than are *inert* cultures, because the positive attitudes and behaviours help the organization build momentum toward the new environment and reduce resistance.

LO4 **Innovation, Entrepreneurship, and Organizational Change** Innovation is the implementation of creative ideas within an organization. Employees are more motivated to initiate change and innovate when the organizational culture is supportive and flexible. Managers can promote innovation by creating product champions, creating skunkworks, and rewarding employees for taking risks.

LO5 **Managing Change in a Unionized Environment** To manage change in a unionized environment it is important to resolve day-to-day issues, provide education about the change, work together on developing a vision for the organization, and establish new, cooperative problem-solving arrangements. A high-performance culture based on norms and values that support innovation and risk taking is better adapted to organizational change.

KEY TERMS

benchmarking

bottom-up change

change agents

complexity theory

cultural changes

driving forces

entrepreneurs

entrepreneurship

imposed change

induced change

innovation

intrapreneurs

organizational change

performance gap

product champion

restraining forces

skunkworks

social entrepreneurs

social innovation

strategic changes

structural changes

technological changes

top-down change

WRAP-UP TO OPENING CASE

Loblaw Shareholders Reject Living Wage, Independent Board Chair Proposals

Shareholders of Canada's largest grocer rejected a proposal that Loblaw Companies Ltd. determine the feasibility of paying its employees a living wage—one that varies by location and is calculated by its cost of living.

After having read and understood the concepts in this chapter, you should now be able to answer the following questions:

1. *Describe the change issues in this case.*

   ANSWER: Change involves moving from a current state to a future desired state. The current state of compensation policy at Loblaws is based on minimum wage. A group of activist shareholders tabled a proposal at the Annual General Meeting to increase compensation for employees to a "living wage" which is substantially higher than the minimum wage. The desired future state for this group is a world where workers can meet the basic needs of their families. This vision is not shared by all stakeholders. In the end, the shareholders (investors) voted against the proposal to change the wage structure at Loblaws. Also proposed was a separation of the positions of Board Chair and CEO. Currently, the two positions are held by the same person. Activist shareholders propose the separation to ensure that management behaviour has sufficient governance and oversight. This change proposal was also voted down at the AGM, suggesting that the forces of resistance to the changes were stronger than the driving forces for the changes.

2. *Apply Kotter's model of change to this case.*

   ANSWER: Kotter's theory of organizational change involves eight steps; The first four steps encourage 'unfreezing' the status quo; Steps 5 to 7 represent the 'moving' toward the desired change state, and Step 8 is necessary for normalizing the change initiative. In this case, the shareholder activists proposed two major institutional changes to the way Loblaw operates at the Annual General Meeting (AGM) of shareholders. The first change initiative was to institute a "living wage" compensation commitment instead of paying employees minimum wages. The second was to separate the functions of governance and oversight from the daily operations of the company by not allowing the CEO to hold the Board Chair position. The proposal made a compelling case for why the changes are necessary, citing the cost of living for a family of four in Vancouver and avoiding the appearance of conflict of interest respectively (Step 1). The shareholders who brought the proposals to the AGM began the process of building a coalition around this new socially responsible vision (Step 2) and used the AGM to communicate the vision to the decision-making body (Steps 3 & 4), the common stockholder investors who have the right to table and vote on proposals brought to the meeting (Step 5). Their arguments were not compelling enough to convince the shareholders to vote for the proposals which would have meant going against the management directive to vote against them. However, the fact that the proposals were heard, discussed, and voted on could be considered a short-term 'win' that may move the organization further toward the proposed changes in the future (Step 6). Had the proposals been voted for, they would have had to make the necessary changes and adjustments to institute the new programs (Step 7) and, over time, conducted the research necessary to demonstrate that the changes to the status quo resulted in favourable outcomes for the organization. This might translate into better labour relations and transparency in governance, resulting in an enhanced reputation for social responsibility and increased market share.

MANAGEMENT IN ACTION

TOPICS FOR DISCUSSION AND ACTION

LEVEL 1 Knowledge & Comprehension

1. What is organizational change? How does it affect the management processes of planning, organizing, leading and controlling?

2. Describe the four steps in managing organizational change.

3. Explain Lewin's three-stage model of change.

LEVEL 2 Application & Analysis

4. What are the advantages of using appreciative inquiry (AI) when managing organizational change?

5. What can managers do to reduce individual resistance to change?

6. Interview a manager about a change effort that he or she was involved in. What issues were involved? What problems were encountered? What was the outcome of the change process?

LEVEL 3 Synthesis & Evaluation

7. Analyze the difficulties managers face when trying to introduce organizational change. How might they overcome some of these difficulties?

8. How would you apply Kotter's eight-step plan for implementing change in an organization moving from a functional organizational structure to a divisional structure?

9. Discuss and evaluate the importance of complexity theory in change management.

SELF-REFLECTION EXERCISE

Think of something that you would like to change in your personal life. It could be your study habits, your fitness and nutrition, the way you interact with others, or anything else that is of interest to you. What values and assumptions have encouraged the behaviour that currently exists (i.e., the one you want to change)?

What driving and restraining forces can you address in order to make the desired change?

SMALL GROUP BREAKOUT EXERCISE
Reducing Resistance to Advances in Information Technology

Form groups of three or four, and appoint one member as the spokesperson who will communicate your findings to the whole class when called on by the instructor. Then discuss the following scenario:

You are a member of a team of managers in charge of information and communications in a large consumer products corporation. Your company has already introduced many advances in information technology. Managers and employees have access to voice mail, email, the Internet, your company's own intranet, and groupware.

Many employees use the new technology, but the resistance of some is causing communication problems. For example, all managers have email addresses and computers in their offices, but some refuse to turn their computers on, let alone send and receive email. These managers feel that they should be able to communicate as they have always done—in person, over the phone, or in writing. Thus, when managers who are unaware of their preferences send them email messages, those messages are never retrieved.

Moreover, the resistant managers never read company news sent by email. Another example of the resistance that your company is encountering concerns the use of groupware. Members of some work groups do not want to share information with others electronically.

Although you do not want to force people to use the technology, you want them at least to try it and give it a chance. You are meeting today to develop strategies for reducing resistance to the new technologies.

1. One resistant group of employees is made up of top managers. Some of them seem computer-phobic. They have never used, and do not want to start using, personal computers for any purpose, including communication. What steps will you take to get these managers to give their PCs a chance?

2. A second group of resistant employees consists of middle managers. Some middle managers resist using your company's intranet. Although these middle managers do not resist the technology per se and use their PCs for multiple purposes, including communication, they seem to distrust the intranet as a viable way to communicate and get things done. What steps will you take to get these middle managers to take advantage of the intranet?

3. A third group of resistant employees is made up of members of groups and teams that do not want to use the groupware that has been provided to them. You think that the groupware could improve their communication and performance, but they seem to think otherwise. What steps will you take to get these members of groups and teams to start using groupware?

MANAGING ETHICALLY EXERCISE

Some organizations, such as Arthur Andersen and Enron, seem to have developed norms and values that caused their members to behave in unethical ways. When and why might a strong norm that encourages high performance become one that can cause people to act unethically? How can organizations prevent their values and norms becoming "too strong"?

MANAGEMENT CHALLENGE EXERCISE

Assume you are the CEO of a medium-size company that makes window coverings similar to Hunter Douglas blinds and duettes. Your company has a real cost advantage in terms of being able to make custom window coverings at costs that are relatively low in the industry. However, the performance of your company has been lackluster. To make needed changes and improve performance, you met with the other top managers in your company and charged them with identifying problems and missed opportunities in each of their areas and coming up with an action plan to address the problems and take advantage of opportunities.

The operations manager argued that to compete with low-cost foreign competitors, the company should decide to increase the resources spent on state-of-the-art machinery and reduce the resources spent on marketing or R&D. The sales and marketing managers differed in their attitudes toward the changes that the operations manager proposed. While the operations manager is trying to reduce costs, the sales and marketing managers believe that the organizational problems stem from the manufacturing managers' inefficiencies.

You approve the operations manager's action plan, even though you recognized there may be resistance and organizational conflict as a result of the changes. You ask the managers to implement the plan in a timely fashion and monitor the effects of the initiatives monthly for the next 8 to 12 months.

A year later, most of the managers are reporting no signs of improvement. You are confused and starting to question your leadership capabilities and approach to change.

1. Identify the need for a change.
2. Identify the driving and restraining forces found in the firm. List these forces.
3. What are you going to do to improve the performance and effectiveness of your company?

MANAGEMENT PORTFOLIO PROJECT

Answer the following questions about the organization you have chosen to follow:

1. Describe the organizational culture of the firm you are following.
2. Has the organization undergone a significant change in the last decade? Describe the driving and restraining forces that operated in this change.
3. If the organization was to experience a significant change in the future, what steps could be taken to ensure that the change takes hold?

MANAGEMENT CASE

THE UBER BUSINESS MODEL: DRIVING DISRUPTION

The Uber business model is transforming business as usual. Will it destroy traditional models?

The Uber model, based on connecting people who need a ride—like a taxi service—with independent drivers who provide the service through an app for smartphones, is revolutionizing the taxi industry. It offers more flexible payment options than taxis, is cheaper for customers, and offers flexible working hours for drivers. Customers love it and traditional taxi drivers hate it, deeming the new model illegal and calling on politicians to stop it.

Toronto City Council voted to bring in regulations that would make the service more compliant with industry standards, including reducing the starting cost of a cab fare from $4.25 to $3.25 and making it illegal for Uber to connect customers to unlicensed drivers. Uber said it has no intentions of complying and will continue to operate in Toronto.[14] Vancouver City Council and provincial regulators have outright rejected Uber, but it appears that it's here to stay: Uber is already in over 200 cities in 45 countries.[15] The model is part of the new sharing economy infiltrating several industries. There is Airbnb, the home-sharing platform, a dog-walking service app called Wag!, a home cleaning company called Handy, and same-day grocery services—Instacart and Urbery, to name just two. All of them use the same model: customers connect with people offering the services in their local communities through an app, bypassing traditional service-industry delivery methods.[16]

Whenever innovation emerges within an industry, the change has adopters and detractors. When Roger Hardy found a better way to serve eyewear customers using the Web and a state-of-the-art manufacturing plant that rendered old-school optometrist and optician models costly and slow, he was labelled disruptive.[17] Amazon, the online portal that started selling books and severely challenged traditional bricks-and-mortar bookstores, now sells just about everything online, including furniture, thereby transforming the whole retail industry. But detractors argue that the bigger issues of fair labour relations and safety measures that go along with traditional models should be upheld—in the case of Uber, to protect both the independent driver and the customer. Standardized insurance and safety measures such as training, vehicle inspections, and criminal background checks for drivers, they argue, should be mandatory for Uber-based businesses.

1. What are the driving forces and the restraining forces in this case?

END OF PART V: CONTINUING CASE

CARROT TOPS: CONTROLLING OPERATIONS

When Mel Harvey decided to start selling his own Carrot Tops brand-name products, he decided to outsource the production. Finding a reliable source of fresh produce from local organic farmers and producers has been a stumbling block to his success, even though he hired Janet Khan to head up produce procurement and logistics. When suppliers deliver organic produce to the store, Janet has to check every box for quality and quantity. If it meets her approval, it then gets stored in the walk-in refrigerators until it is ready to be put out for consumers. When the produce has been out for a while, one of Janet's employees goes around and cuts back the dead and dying leaves to present the produce in the best, most appealing manner. The employees must log their activity on the floor. Janet makes sure the produce is up to par by observing her employees while they work and by reviewing their logs. If employees fail to meet the standards Janet sets, their hours could be cut. Janet doesn't tolerate laziness. Occasionally, a customer will return some produce, claiming it was not fresh enough. Janet tries to avoid these complaints before they happen. Hiring the right people in the first place and training them well is where she begins.

Recently, Mel met with Janet to discuss a new point-of-sale technology system he is considering for the store. The mobile app would be carried around by the employees who stock the shelves with groceries. It would eliminate the traditional checkout-counter process and mean that several cashiers would be laid off. Janet is anxious about letting staff go and thinks that customer service would be compromised. Mel counters with the cost savings to the company and the efficiency the new technology would bring to operations. The question is, how will they get the staff to embrace the new change?

Drawing on all segments of this case:

1. How are feedforward, concurrent, and feedback controls illustrated by Janet?
2. How could Janet use MIS to better manage relations with suppliers?
3. How could Mel use MBO to control Janet's performance?
4. Characterize Janet as either an innovative or conservative manager.
5. Suggest how Janet should manage change in this case.
6. What can Janet do to motivate the drivers and create an entrepreneurial culture?

Glossary

360-degree appraisals Performance appraisals by peers, subordinates, superiors, and sometimes clients who are in a position to evaluate a manager's performance.

A

ability tests Assess the skills necessary to perform the job well.

accommodative approach Moderate commitment to social responsibility; willingness to do more than the law requires, if asked.

administrative model An approach to decision making that explains why decision making is an inherently uncertain and risky process and why managers usually make satisfactory rather than optimum decisions.

ambiguous information Information that can be interpreted in multiple and often conflicting ways.

applications software Software designed for a specific task or use.

artificial intelligence (AI) Behaviour performed by a machine that, if performed by a human being, would be called "intelligent."

attitude A collection of feelings and beliefs.

attraction–selection–attrition (ASA) framework A model that explains how personality may influence organizational culture.

authority The power to hold people accountable for their actions and to allocate organizational resources.

B

B2B marketplaces Internet-based trading platforms set up to connect buyers and sellers in an industry.

barriers to entry Factors that make it difficult and costly for a company to enter an industry.

behavioural interview questions Questions that ask candidates how they dealt with a situation they encountered on the job in the past.

benchmarking Comparing performance on specific dimensions with the performance of high-performing organizations.

bias The systematic tendency to use information about others in ways that result in inaccurate perceptions.

blended value Organizations in the social economy that create both social impact and economic value.

bottom-up change Change that is introduced gradually and involves managers and employees at all levels of an organization.

boundaryless career A career that is not attached to or bound to a single organization and consists of a variety of work experiences in multiple organizations.

boundaryless organization An organization whose members are linked by computers, faxes, computer-aided design systems, and video teleconferencing, and who rarely, if ever, see one another face to face.

bounded awareness The tendency for people to overlook important information that bears on the decision-making process.

bounded rationality Cognitive limitations that constrain one's ability to interpret, process, and act on information.

brainstorming A group problem-solving technique in which individuals meet face to face to generate and debate a wide variety of alternatives from which to make a decision.

brand loyalty Customers' preference for the products of organizations.

bureaucracy A formal system of organization and administration designed to ensure efficiency and effectiveness.

bureaucratic control Control of behaviour by means of a comprehensive system of rules and standard operating procedures.

business-level plan Includes (1) the long-term divisional goals that will allow the division to meet corporate goals, and (2) the division's business-level strategy and structure necessary to achieve divisional goals.

business-level strategy Outlines the specific methods a division, business unit, or organization will use to compete effectively against its rivals in an industry.

business-to-business (B2B) commerce Trade that takes place between companies using technology and the Internet to link and coordinate the value chains of different companies.

business-to-business (B2B) networks A group of organizations that join together and use software to link themselves to global suppliers and distributors to increase efficiency and effectiveness.

business-to-customer (B2C) commerce Trade that takes place between a company and individual customers using technology and the Internet.

C

cafeteria-style benefit plans   Plans from which employees can choose the benefits that they want.

career plateau   A position from which the chances of being promoted or obtaining a more responsible job are slight.

certainty   The state of environmental forces that is stable enough to predict possible outcomes of decisions.

chain of command   The linkage of reporting relationships from the top management to the lowest levels in the organization.

change agents   People who take responsibility for managing change initiatives.

charismatic leaders   Enthusiastic, self-confident leaders who are able to communicate clearly their vision of how good things could be.

clan control   Control exerted on individuals and groups in an organization by shared values, norms, standards of behaviour, and expectations.

classical model   A prescriptive approach to decision making based on the idea that the decision maker can identify and evaluate all possible alternatives and their consequences and rationally choose the most suitable course of action.

codes of ethics   Formal standards and rules, based on beliefs about right or wrong, that managers can use to make appropriate decisions in the best interests of their stakeholders.

coercive power   The ability to persuade someone to do something that he or she otherwise would not.

collective agreement   A mutually agreed upon set of provisions that govern working conditions between a union and an employer for a set period of time.

collective bargaining   Negotiations between labour unions and managers to resolve conflicts and disputes about issues such as working hours, wages, working conditions, and job security.

collective impact   Public, private, and nonprofit organizations working together to solve social problems.

communication   The sharing of information between two or more individuals or groups to reach a common understanding.

competitive advantage   The ability of one organization to outperform other organizations because it produces desired goods or services more efficiently and effectively than competitors do.

competitors   Organizations that produce goods and services that are similar to a particular organization's goods and services.

complexity theory   Organizations respond best to change if they are not perfectly aligned with their environment.

conceptual skills   The ability to analyze and diagnose a situation and to distinguish between cause and effect.

concurrent control   Control that gives managers immediate feedback on how efficiently inputs are being transformed into outputs so that managers can correct problems as they arise.

consideration   Behaviour indicating that a manager trusts, respects, and cares about subordinates.

contingency models of leadership   Models of leadership that take into account the variables in the situation or context in which leadership occurs.

control systems   Formal target-setting, monitoring, evaluation, and feedback systems that provide managers with information about how well the organization's strategy and structure are working.

controlling   Evaluating how well an organization is achieving its goals and taking action to maintain or improve performance; one of the four principal functions of management.

co-opetition   Arrangements in which firms compete vigorously with one another, while also cooperating in specific areas to achieve economies of scale.

core competency   The specific set of departmental skills, knowledge, and experience that allows one organization to outperform another.

corporate governance practices   The processes companies use to be accountable to stakeholders, including investors, employees, the environment, and communities.

corporate-level plan   Top management's decisions concerning the organization's mission and goals, overall (corporate-level) strategy, and structure.

corporate-level strategy   Specifies in which industries and national markets an organization intends to compete and why.

cost-leadership strategy   Driving the organization's costs down below the costs of its rivals.

Creating Shared Value (CSV)   Policies and operating practices that enhance the competitiveness of a company while simultaneously advancing the economic and social conditions in the communities in which it operates.

creativity   A decision maker's ability to discover original and novel ideas that lead to feasible alternative courses of action.

crisis management plans   Plans formulated to deal with possible future crises.

cross-cultural teams Formal work groups composed of members from different cultures or countries.

cross-functional team A group of individuals from different departments brought together to perform organizational tasks.

cultural changes A shift in the shared set of beliefs, expectations, values, norms, and work routines that influence how members of an organization relate to one another and work together to achieve organizational goals.

customer relationship management (CRM) A technique that uses IT to develop an ongoing relationship with customers to maximize the value an organization can deliver to them over time.

customers Individuals and groups that buy the goods and services that an organization produces.

D

decentralizing decision-making authority Giving lower-level managers and nonmanagerial employees the right to make important decisions about how to use organizational resources.

decision making The process of analyzing options and making determinations about specific organizational goals and courses of action.

decision support system An interactive, computer-based management information system that managers can use to make nonroutine decisions.

decoding Interpreting and trying to make sense of a message.

defensive approach Minimal commitment to social responsibility; willingness to do what the law requires and no more.

Delphi technique A decision-making technique in which group members do not meet face to face but respond in writing to questions posed by the group leader.

demographic forces Outcomes of changes in the characteristics of a population, such as age, gender, ethnic origin, race, sexual orientation, and social class.

department A group composed of subordinates who report to the same supervisor; also called a unit.

departmentalization Grouping jobs together into units to best match the needs of the organization's environment, strategy, technology, and human resources.

deregulation Opening industries previously operated and controlled by the state to free market competition.

development Building the knowledge and skills of organizational members so that they will be prepared to take on new responsibilities and challenges.

developmental consideration Behaviour a leader engages in to support and encourage followers and help them develop and grow in the job.

devil's advocacy Critical analysis of a preferred alternative, made by a group member who plays the role of devil's advocate to defend unpopular or opposing alternatives for the sake of argument.

differentiation strategy Distinguishing an organization's products from the products of competitors in dimensions such as product design, quality, or after-sales service.

discipline Managerial control through administering punishment when undesired workplace behaviours, such as absenteeism, lack of punctuality, and low performance, are exhibited, in an attempt to decrease their frequency.

distributors Organizations that help other organizations sell their goods or services to customers.

diversity Differences among people in age, gender, race, ethnicity, ability, and sexual orientation.

division of labour Splitting the work to be performed into particular tasks and assigning tasks to individual workers.

divisional structure An organizational structure composed of separate business units within which are the functions that work together to produce a specific product for a specific customer.

driving forces Forces that direct behaviour away from the status quo.

E

e-commerce Trade that takes place between companies, and between companies and individual customers, using technology and the Internet.

economic forces Interest rates, inflation, unemployment, economic growth, and other factors that affect the general health and well-being of a nation or the regional economy of an organization.

economies of scale Cost advantages associated with large operations.

effective career management Ensuring that at all levels in the organization there are well-qualified workers who can assume more responsible positions as needed.

effectiveness A measure of the appropriateness of the goals an organization is pursuing and of the degree to which the organization achieves those goals.

efficiency A measure of how well or productively resources are used to achieve a goal.

emotional intelligence The ability to understand and manage one's own moods and emotions and the moods and emotions of other people.

emotions Intense, relatively short-lived feelings.

employee engagement Activities that managers engage in to ensure that fair and consistent treatment of all employees is maintained.

employee recognition programs Management expressions of interest, approval, and appreciation for a job well done by individuals or groups of employees.

employee stock options Financial instruments that entitle the bearer to buy shares of an organization's stock at a certain price during a certain period of time or under certain conditions.

employee-centred leaders Leaders who place a strong emphasis on the well-being of employees and interpersonal relations.

encoding Translating a message into understandable symbols or language.

enterprise resource planning (ERP) systems Multi-module application software packages that coordinate the functional activities necessary to move products from the design stage to the final customer stage.

entrepreneurs People who notice opportunities and take responsibility for mobilizing the resources necessary to produce new and improved goods and services.

entrepreneurship The mobilization of resources to take advantage of an opportunity to provide customers with new or improved goods and services.

environmental change The degree to which forces in the task and general environments change and evolve over time.

equity theory A theory of motivation that focuses on people's perceptions of the fairness of their work outcomes relative to their work inputs.

equity The justice, impartiality, and fairness to which all organizational members are entitled.

ethical dilemma The quandary people find themselves in when they have to decide if they should act in a way that might help another person or group even though doing so might go against their own self-interest.

ethics ombudsperson An ethics officer who monitors an organization's practices and procedures to ensure that they are ethical.

ethics Moral principles or beliefs about what is right or wrong.

expectancy theory The theory that motivation will be high when employees believe that high levels of effort will lead to high performance, that high performance will lead to the attainment of rewards, and rewards will be desired by the employee.

expectancy In expectancy theory, a perception about the extent to which effort will result in a certain level of performance.

expert power Power that is based in the special knowledge, skills, and expertise that a leader possesses.

expert system A management information system that utilizes human knowledge embedded in computer software to solve problems that ordinarily require human expertise.

external environment The forces operating beyond the boundaries of an organization that affect how the organization functions.

extinction Stopping the performance of dysfunctional behaviours by eliminating whatever is reinforcing them.

extrinsically motivated behaviour Behaviour that is performed to acquire material or social rewards or to avoid punishment.

F

facilities layout The operations management technique whose goal is to design the machine–worker interface to increase production system efficiency.

feedback control Control that gives managers information about customers' reactions to goods and services so that corrective action can be taken if necessary.

feedforward control Control that allows managers to anticipate and deal with potential problems before they occur.

filtering Withholding part of a message out of the mistaken belief that the receiver does not need or will not want the information.

first-line managers Managers who are responsible for the daily supervision and coordination of nonmanagerial employees.

flexible manufacturing Operations management techniques that attempt to reduce the setup costs associated with a production system.

focused differentiation strategy Serving only one segment of the overall market and trying to be the most differentiated organization serving that segment.

focused low-cost strategy Serving only one segment of the overall market and being the lowest-cost organization serving that segment.

formal appraisals Appraisals conducted at a set time during the year and based on performance dimensions and measures that were specified in advance.

formal groups Groups that managers establish to achieve organizational goals.

franchising A corporate-level strategy that licenses the rights to use the brand name and trademarks of the franchiser to an independent owner (the franchisee) in exchange for a lump-sum payment and a percentage of sales.

free-trade doctrine The idea that if each country specializes in the production of the goods and services that it can produce most efficiently, this will make the best use of global resources.

friendship groups Informal groups composed of employees who enjoy one another's company and socialize with one another.

functional managers Managers who supervise the various functions—such as manufacturing, accounting, and sales—within a division.

functional structure An organizational structure composed of all the departments that an organization requires to produce its goods or services.

functional-level plan States the goals that the managers of each function will pursue to help their division attain its business-level goals.

functional-level strategy A plan of action that managers of individual functions can follow to improve the ability of each function to perform its task-specific activities in ways that add value to an organization's goods and services and thereby increase the value customers receive.

functions Units or departments in which people have the same skills or use the same resources to perform their jobs.

G

Gantt chart A graphic bar chart managers use to schedule tasks in a project showing what tasks need to be done, who will do them, and by what timeframe.

general environment The political, economic, socio-cultural, technological, and international/global forces (PESTI) that affect an organization and its task environment.

Generation Y Also known as *millennials;* people born between 1981 and 1992.

geographic division An organizational structure in which each region of a country or area of the world is served by a self-contained division.

glass ceiling An invisible barrier that prevents women from advancing as far as they should in some organizations.

global forces Outcomes of changes in international relationships primarily due to declining trade barriers; changes in nations' economic, political, and legal systems; and changes in technology that allow reliable and instantaneous communication.

global organizations Organizations that operate and compete in more than one country.

globalization The set of forces that lead to integrated social systems so that nations become increasingly interdependent and similar.

goal A desired future outcome that an organization strives to achieve within a specified timeframe.

goal-setting theory A theory that focuses on identifying the types of goals that are most effective in producing high levels of motivation and performance and explaining why goals have these effects.

grapevine An informal communication network among people in organizations.

group cohesiveness The degree to which members are attracted or loyal to a group.

group dynamics The ways in which group members interact, determining the effectiveness of the group.

group norms Shared guidelines or rules for behaviour that most group members follow.

group role A set of behaviours and tasks that a member of a group is expected to perform because of his or her position in the group.

group Two or more people who interact with each other to reach certain goals or meet certain needs.

groupthink A pattern of faulty and biased decision making that occurs in groups whose members strive for agreement among themselves at the expense of accurately assessing information relevant to a decision.

H

Hawthorne effect Workers' productivity is affected more by observation or attention received than by physical work setting.

Herzberg's motivator-hygiene theory A need theory that distinguishes between motivator needs (related to the nature of the work itself) and hygiene needs (related to the physical and psychological context in which the work is performed). Herzberg proposed that motivator needs must be met in order for motivation and job satisfaction to be high. This theory is also known as the *two-factor theory.*

heuristics Rules of thumb that simplify decision making.

hierarchy of authority An organization's chain of command, specifying the relative authority of each manager.

hierarchy of needs An arrangement of five basic needs that, according to Maslow, motivate behaviour. Maslow proposed that the lowest level of unmet needs is the prime motivator and that only one level of needs is motivational at a time.

hostile work environment sexual harassment Telling lewd jokes, displaying pornography, making sexually oriented remarks about someone's personal appearance, and other sex-related actions that make the work environment unpleasant.

human relations movement Advocates behaviour and leadership training of supervisors to elicit worker cooperation and improve productivity.

human resource management (HRM) Activities that managers engage in to attract and retain employees and to ensure that they perform at a high level and contribute to the accomplishment of organizational goals.

human resource planning Activities that managers use to forecast their current and future needs for human resources.

hybrid structure The structure of a large organization that has many divisions and simultaneously uses many different organizational structures.

I

impact investing Investments that seek to solve social or environmental problems and generate financial returns to the investor.

imposed change New institutional arrangements made to comply with regulations.

individual ethics Personal standards that govern how individuals interact with other people.

induced change Planned new institutional arrangements made to gain a competitive advantage.

industry-specific or task environment The set of forces and conditions that affect an organization's ability to obtain inputs and dispose of its outputs because they influence managers on a daily basis.

inequity Lack of fairness.

informal appraisals Unscheduled appraisals of ongoing progress and areas for improvement.

informal groups Groups that managers or nonmanagerial employees form to help achieve their own goals or meet their own needs.

informal organization The system of behavioural rules and norms that emerge in work groups.

information distortion Changes in the meaning of a message as the message passes through a series of senders and receivers.

information overload A superabundance of information that increases the likelihood that important information is ignored or overlooked and tangential information receives attention.

information richness The amount of information that a communication medium can carry and the extent to which the medium enables sender and receiver to reach a common understanding.

initiating structure Behaviours that managers engage in to define and structure their role and the roles of their subordinates in order to achieve organizational goals.

innovation (1) The implementation of creative ideas in an organization. (2) The process of creating new goods and services or developing better ways to produce or provide goods and services.

input Anything a person contributes to his or her job or organization.

instrumental value A mode of conduct that an individual seeks to follow.

instrumentality In expectancy theory, a perception about the extent to which performance will result in the attainment of rewards.

integrating mechanisms Ways to increase effective and efficient communication and coordination among departments and divisions.

integrating role The responsibility to increase coordination and integration across departments or divisions to achieve performance gains.

intellectual stimulation Behaviour a leader engages in to make followers aware of problems and view these problems in new ways, consistent with the leader's vision.

intentional discrimination The illegal practice of deliberately using prohibited grounds, such as race, religion, and sex, when making employment decisions.

interest groups Informal groups composed of employees seeking to achieve a common goal related to their membership in an organization.

internal environment The forces operating within an organization and stemming from the organization's strategy, structure, and culture.

interpersonal skills The ability to understand, alter, lead, and control the behaviour of other individuals and groups.

intrapreneurs Employees of existing organizations who notice opportunities for product or service improvement and are responsible for managing the development process.

intrinsically motivated behaviour Behaviour that is performed for its own sake.

intuition Ability to make sound decisions based on past experience and immediate feelings about the information at hand.

inventory The stock of raw materials, inputs, and component parts that an organization has on hand at a particular time.

J

jargon Specialized language that members of an occupation, group, or organization develop to facilitate communication among themselves.

job analysis Identifying the tasks, duties, and responsibilities that make up a job and the knowledge, skills, and abilities needed to perform the job.

job design The process by which managers decide how to divide the work to be done into specific jobs.

job enlargement Increasing the number of different tasks in a given job by changing the division of labour.

job enrichment Increasing the degree of responsibility a worker has over his or her job.

job satisfaction The collection of feelings and beliefs that managers have about their current jobs.

job simplification Reducing the number of tasks that each worker performs.

judgment Ability to develop a sound opinion based on one's evaluation of the importance of the information at hand.

just-in-time inventory system A system in which parts or supplies arrive at an organization when they are needed, not before.

K

knowledge management system A company-specific virtual information system that allows workers to share their knowledge and expertise and find others to help solve ongoing problems.

L

labour relations The activities that managers engage in to ensure that they have effective working relationships with the labour unions that represent their employees' interests.

lateral moves Job changes that entail no major changes in responsibility or authority levels.

leader substitute Characteristics of subordinates or characteristics of a situation or context that act in place of the influence of a leader and make leadership unnecessary.

leader An individual who is able to exert influence over other people to help achieve group or organizational goals.

leader–member relations The extent to which followers like, trust, and are loyal to their leader; can be good or poor.

leadership The process by which an individual exerts influence over other people and inspires, motivates, and directs their activities to help achieve group or organizational goals.

leading Articulating a clear vision and energizing and empowering organizational members so that everyone understands his or her individual role in achieving organizational goals; one of the four principal functions of management.

learning organization An organization in which managers try to maximize the ability of individuals and groups to think and behave creatively and thus maximize the potential for organizational learning to take place.

learning theories Theories that focus on increasing employee motivation and performance by linking the outcomes that employees receive to the performance of desired behaviours and the attainment of goals.

learning A relatively permanent change in knowledge or behaviour that results from practice or experience.

legitimate power The authority that a manager has by virtue of his or her position in an organization's hierarchy.

liaison roles The responsibility for coordinating with the other functional departments or divisions.

line manager Someone in the direct line or chain of command who has formal authority over people and resources at lower levels.

linear career A career consisting of a sequence of jobs in which each new job entails additional responsibility, a greater impact on an organization, new skills, and upward movement in an organization's hierarchy.

M

maintenance roles Roles performed by group members to make sure there are good relationships among group members.

management by objectives (MBO) A formal system of evaluating subordinates on their ability to achieve specific organizational goals or performance standards.

management by wandering around (MBWA) A face-to-face communication technique in which a manager walks around a work area and talks informally with employees about issues and concerns.

management information systems (MIS)   Electronic systems of interconnected components designed to collect, process, store, and disseminate information to facilitate management decision making, planning, and control.

management   The planning, organizing, leading, and controlling of resources to achieve organizational goals effectively and efficiently.

manager   A person who is responsible for supervising the use of an organization's resources to achieve its goals.

market segment division   An organizational structure in which each kind of customer is served by a self-contained division; also called customer divisional structure.

matrix team   An organizational structure that simultaneously groups people and resources by function and by product.

mechanistic structure   An organizational structure in which authority is centralized at the top of the hierarchy, tasks and roles are clearly specified, and employees are closely supervised.

medium   The pathway through which an encoded message is transmitted to a receiver.

merit pay plan   A compensation plan that bases pay on performance.

message   The information that a sender wants to share.

middle managers   Managers who supervise first-line managers and are responsible for finding the best way to use resources to achieve organizational goals.

minimum chain of command   The idea that top managers should always construct a hierarchy with the fewest levels of authority necessary to efficiently and effectively use organizational resources.

mission statement   A broad declaration of an organization's purpose that identifies the organization's products and customers and distinguishes the organization from its competitors.

mood   A feeling or state of mind.

motivation   Psychological forces that determine the direction of a person's behaviour in an organization, a person's commitment or effort, and a person's persistence.

N

national culture   The set of values that a society considers important and the norms of behaviour that are approved or sanctioned in that society.

need for achievement   The extent to which an individual has a strong desire to perform challenging tasks well and to meet personal standards for excellence.

need for affiliation   The extent to which an individual is concerned about establishing and maintaining good interpersonal relations, being liked, and having the people around him or her get along with each other.

need for power   The extent to which an individual desires to control or influence others.

need theories   Theories of motivation that focus on what needs people are trying to satisfy at work and what outcomes will satisfy those needs.

need   A requirement or necessity for survival and well-being.

needs assessment   An assessment to determine which employees need training or development and what type of skills or knowledge they need to acquire.

negative reinforcement   Eliminating or removing undesired outcomes once people have performed organizationally functional behaviours.

network structure   A series of global strategic alliances that an organization creates with suppliers, manufacturers, and/or distributors to produce and market a product.

networking   The exchange of information through a group or network of interlinked computers.

noise   Anything that hampers any stage of the communication process.

nominal group technique   A decision-making technique in which group members write down ideas and solutions, read their suggestions to the whole group, and discuss and then rank the alternatives.

nonprogrammed decision making   Nonroutine decision making that occurs in response to unusual, unpredictable opportunities and threats.

nonverbal communication   The encoding of messages by means of facial expressions, body language, and styles of dressing.

norms   Unwritten, informal codes of conduct that prescribe how people should act in particular situations and that are considered important by most members of a group or organization.

O

obstructionist approach   Disregard for social responsibility; willingness to engage in and cover up unethical and illegal behaviour.

operant conditioning theory   The theory that people learn to perform behaviours that lead to desired consequences and learn not to perform behaviours that lead to undesired consequences.

operating budget   A budget that states how managers intend to use organizational resources to achieve organizational goals.

operating system software   Software that tells computer hardware how to run.

operations information system   A management information system that gathers, organizes, and summarizes comprehensive data in a form that managers can use in their nonroutine coordinating, controlling, and decision-making tasks.

operations management   The process of managing the use of materials and other resources in producing an organization's goods and services.

operations managers   Managers who are responsible for managing an organization's production system.

optimum decision   The most appropriate decision in light of what managers believe to be the most desirable future consequences for their organization.

organic structure   An organizational structure in which authority is decentralized to middle and first-line managers and tasks and roles are left ambiguous to encourage employees to cooperate and respond quickly to the unexpected.

organizational behaviour   The study of factors that impact how workers respond to and act in an organization.

organizational change   The movement of an organization away from its present state and toward some desired future state to increase its efficiency and effectiveness.

organizational citizenship behaviours (OCBs)   Behaviours that are not required of organizational members but that contribute to and are necessary for organizational efficiency, effectiveness, and competitive advantage.

organizational commitment   The collection of feelings and beliefs that managers have about their organization as a whole.

organizational conflict   The discord that arises when the goals, interests, or values of different individuals or groups are incompatible and those individuals or groups block or thwart each other's attempts to achieve their objectives.

organizational culture   The shared set of beliefs, expectations, values, norms, and work routines that influence how individuals, groups, and teams interact with one another and cooperate to achieve organizational goals.

organizational design   The process by which managers make specific organizing choices that result in a particular kind of organizational structure.

organizational environment   The set of forces and conditions that can affect the way an organization operates.

organizational learning   The process through which managers seek to improve employees' desire and ability to understand and manage the organization and its task environment.

organizational performance   A measure of how efficiently and effectively a manager uses resources to satisfy customers and achieve organizational goals.

organizational socialization   The process by which newcomers learn an organization's values and norms and acquire the work behaviours necessary to perform jobs effectively.

organizational structure   A formal system of both task and reporting relationships that coordinates and motivates organizational members so that they work together to reach organizational goals.

organizations   Collections of people who work together and coordinate their actions to achieve goals and desired future outcomes.

organizing   Structuring workplace relationships so organizational members work together to achieve organizational goals; one of the four principal functions of management.

orientation   The introduction to the culture, norms, policies, values, and vision and mission of the organization.

outcome   Anything a person gets from a job or organization.

outsource   To use outside suppliers and manufacturers to produce goods and services.

overpayment inequity   Inequity that exists when a person perceives that his or her own outcome – input ratio is greater than the ratio of a referent.

P

path-goal theory   A contingency model of leadership proposing that leaders can motivate subordinates by helping them find the right path to achieve personal and organizational goals.

pay level   The relative position of an organization's pay incentives in comparison with those of other organizations in the same industry employing similar kinds of workers.

pay structure   The arrangement of jobs into categories that reflect their relative importance to the organization and its goals, levels of skill required, and other characteristics.

perception   The process through which people select, organize, and interpret sensory input to give meaning and order to the world around them.

performance appraisal   The evaluation of employees' job performance and contributions to their organization.

performance feedback   The process through which managers share performance appraisal information with subordinates, give subordinates an opportunity to reflect on their own performance, and develop, with subordinates, plans for the future.

performance gap   A disparity between desired and actual performance levels.

performance level   How efficient and effective an organization is in achieving its goals.

performance-simulation tests   Measure the candidate's ability to perform actual job tasks.

personal leadership style   The ways a manager chooses to influence others and how they approach planning, organizing, and controlling.

personality tests   Measure personality traits and characteristics relevant to job performance.

personnel replacement charts   Graphic illustrations of current positions, who holds them, and whether they have the skills and qualifications necessary for succession planning.

physical ability tests   Measure physical strength and stamina.

planning   Identifying and selecting appropriate goals and courses of action; one of the four principal functions of management.

policy   A general guide to action.

political forces   Outcomes of changes in laws and regulations, such as the deregulation of industries, the privatization of organizations, and increased emphasis on environmental protection.

Porter's Five Forces model   A technique managers use to analyze the potential profitability of entering and competing in a particular industry.

position power   The amount of legitimate, reward, and coercive power that a leader has by virtue of his or her position in an organization; can be strong or weak.

positive reinforcement   Giving people outcomes they desire when they perform organizationally functional behaviours.

potential competitors   Organizations that are not currently in a task environment but have the resources to enter if they so choose.

privatization   Selling organizations once owned and operated by the state to individuals or corporations.

proactive approach   Strong commitment to social responsibility; eagerness to do more than the law requires and to use organizational resources to promote the interests of all organizational stakeholders.

process reengineering   The fundamental rethinking and radical redesign of business processes to achieve dramatic improvements in critical measures of performance such as cost, quality, service, and speed.

process theories   Theories that explain the processes by which employee behaviour can be aroused and then directed.

product champion   A manager who takes "ownership" of a project and provides the leadership and vision that take a product from the idea stage to the final customer.

product division   An organizational structure in which each product line or business is handled by a self-contained division.

product/project team   An organizational structure in which employees are permanently assigned to a cross-functional team and report only to the project team manager or to one of his or her direct subordinates.

production blocking   A loss of productivity in brainstorming sessions due to the unstructured nature of brainstorming.

production system   The system an organization uses to acquire inputs, convert the inputs into outputs, and dispose of the outputs.

production-oriented leaders   Leaders who place a strong emphasis on task-related and goal-achievement behaviours.

professional ethics   Standards that govern how members of a profession make decisions when the way they should behave is not clear-cut.

programmed decision making   Routine, virtually automatic decision making that follows established rules or guidelines.

prosocially motivated behaviour   Behaviour that is performed to benefit or help others.

punishment   Administering an undesired or negative consequence when dysfunctional behaviour occurs.

Q

quid pro quo sexual harassment   Asking or forcing an employee to perform sexual favours in exchange for some reward or to avoid negative consequences.

R

realistic job preview (RJP)   Communicating the good and bad aspects of a job to a candidate to prevent mismatched expectations and high turnover.

receiver   The person or group for which a message is intended.

recruitment   Activities that managers use to develop a pool of qualified candidates for open positions.

referent power   Power that comes from subordinates' and co-workers' respect, admiration, and loyalty.

reinforcer   Any stimulus that causes a given behaviour to be repeated.

relationship conflict   Members of the group perceive each other's attitudes as a problem.

reliable selection technique   A test or tool that yields consistent results when repeated.

reputation   The esteem or high repute that individuals or organizations gain when they behave ethically.

research and development teams   Teams whose members have the expertise and experience needed to develop new products.

resources   Resources include assets such as people and their skills, know-how, and experience; machinery; raw materials; computers and information technology; and patents, financial capital, and loyal customers and employees.

restraining forces   Forces that prevent movement away from the status quo.

reward power   The ability of a manager to give or withhold tangible and intangible rewards.

role making   Taking the initiative to modify an assigned role by taking on extra responsibilities.

role   The specific tasks that a person is expected to perform because of the position he or she holds in an organization.

rule   A formal, written guide to action.

rumours   Unofficial pieces of information of interest to organizational members but with no identifiable source.

S

satisficing   Searching for and choosing acceptable, or satisfactory, ways to respond to problems and opportunities, rather than trying to make the best decision.

scenario planning   The generation of multiple forecasts of future conditions followed by an analysis of how to respond effectively to each of those conditions; also called *contingency planning*.

scientific management   The systematic study of relationships between people and tasks to increase efficiency.

selection   The process that managers use to determine the relative qualifications of job applicants and the individuals' potential for performing well in a particular job.

self-efficacy   A person's belief about his or her ability to perform a behaviour successfully.

self-managed (or self-directed) work teams   Groups of employees who supervise their own activities and monitor the quality of the goods and services they provide.

self-reinforcers   Any desired or attractive outcome or reward that a person gives to himself or herself for good performance.

sender   The person or group wishing to share information.

sexual harassment   Unwelcome behaviour of a sexual nature in the workplace that negatively affects the work environment or leads to adverse job-related consequences for the employee.

simple structure   An organizational structure where the owner is the general manager responsible for the activities in all the functions.

situational interview questions   Questions that ask candidates how they would respond to a particular work situation in the future.

situational leadership theory (SL)   A contingency model of leadership that focuses on the followers' readiness.

skunkworks   A group of intrapreneurs who are deliberately separated from the normal operation of an organization to encourage them to devote all their attention to developing new products.

social audit   A tool that allows managers to analyze the profitability and social returns of socially responsible actions.

social economy   A bridging concept for organizations that have social objectives central to their mission and their practice, and either have explicit economic objectives or generate some economic value through the services they provide and purchases that they undertake.

social entrepreneurs   Individuals who pursue initiatives and opportunities and mobilize resources to address social problems and needs in order to improve society and well-being through creative solutions.

social innovation   Developing new ways of solving social problems.

social learning theory   A theory that takes into account how learning and motivation are influenced by people's thoughts and beliefs and their observations of other people's behaviour.

social loafing   The tendency of individuals to put forth less effort when they work in groups than when they work alone.

social responsibility   A manager's duty or obligation to make decisions that promote the well-being of stakeholders and society as a whole.

social structure   The arrangement of relationships between individuals and groups in a society.

societal ethics Standards that govern how members of a society deal with each other on issues such as fairness, justice, poverty, and the rights of the individual.

socio-cultural forces Pressures emanating from the social structure of a country or society or from the national culture.

span of control The number of subordinates who report directly to a manager.

spiral career A career consisting of a series of jobs that build on each other but tend to be fundamentally different.

staff manager Someone responsible for managing a support function, such as finance or human resources.

stakeholders Persons, groups, and institutions directly affected by the activities and decisions of an organization.

standard operating procedures (SOPs) (1) Written instructions describing the exact series of actions that should be followed in a specific situation; (2) Rules and policies that standardize behaviours.

standing committees A relatively permanent task force charged with addressing long-term, enduring problems or issues facing an organization.

steady-state career A career consisting of the same kind of job during a large part of an individual's work life.

stereotype Simplistic and often inaccurate belief about the typical characteristics of particular groups of people.

strategic alliance A formal agreement that commits two or more companies to exchange or share their resources in order to produce and market a product.

strategic changes A change in the products and services offered by the organization.

strategic human resource management The process by which managers design the components of a human resource management system to be consistent with each other, with other elements of organizational architecture, and with the organization's strategy and goals.

strategic leadership The ability of the CEO and top managers to convey a compelling vision of what they want the organization to achieve to their subordinates.

strategy formulation Analysis of an organization's current situation followed by the development of strategies to accomplish the organization's mission and achieve its goals.

strategy A cluster of decisions about what goals to pursue, what actions to take, and how to use resources to achieve goals.

structural changes Any change in the design and management of an organization.

structured interview Formal, standardized questions are asked in a set sequence.

suppliers Individuals and organizations that provide an organization with the inputs and resources that it needs to produce and sell goods and services.

sustainability Decisions that protect the environment, promote social responsibility, respect cultural differences, and provide an economic benefit.

SWOT analysis A planning exercise in which managers identify organizational strengths (S) and weaknesses (W), and environmental opportunities (O) and threats (T) relative to the competition.

systematic errors Errors that people make over and over again and that result in poor decision making.

T

tariff A tax that a government imposes on goods imported into one country from another.

task forces Cross-functional teams charged with solving a specific problem or addressing a specific issue within a fixed timeframe.

task structure The extent to which the work to be performed is clear-cut so that a leader's subordinates know what needs to be accomplished and how to go about doing it; can be high or low.

task-oriented roles Roles performed by group members to make sure the task gets done.

task-related conflict Members of the group perceive a problem or have a disagreement about the nature of the task or project.

team A group whose members work intensely with each other to achieve a specific common goal or objective.

technical skills Job-specific knowledge and techniques that are required to perform an organizational role.

technological changes Changes that relate to an organization's operational processes.

technological forces Outcomes of changes in the technology that managers use to design, produce, or distribute goods and services.

technology The combination of skills and equipment that managers use in the design, production, and distribution of goods and services.

terminal value A lifelong goal or objective that an individual seeks to achieve.

Theory X The assumption that workers will try to do as little as possible and avoid further responsibility unless rewarded or punished for doing otherwise.

Theory Y   The assumption that workers will do what is best for an organization if given the proper work setting, opportunity, and encouragement.

time horizon   The intended duration of a plan.

top managers   Managers who establish organizational goals, decide how departments should interact, and monitor the performance of middle managers.

top-down change   Change that is introduced quickly throughout an organization by upper level managers.

top-management team   (1) Groups composed of the CEO, the president, and the heads of the most important departments; (2) Teams that are responsible for developing the strategies that produce an organization's competitive advantage.

total reward strategy   A total reward strategy encompasses both intrinsically and extrinsically motivating factors.

training   Teaching organizational members how to perform their current jobs and helping them acquire the knowledge and skills they need to be effective performers.

transactional leadership   Leaders who guide their subordinates toward expected goals by rewarding them for high performance and reprimanding them for low performance, with no expectation of exceeding expected behaviour.

transaction-processing system   A management information system designed to handle large volumes of routine, recurring transactions.

transformational leadership   Leadership that makes subordinates aware of the importance of their jobs and performance to the organization and aware of their own needs for personal growth, and that motivates subordinates to work for the good of the organization.

transitory career   A career in which a person changes jobs frequently and in which each job is different from the one that precedes it.

U

uncertainty   The state of environmental forces that is so dynamic that managers cannot predict the probable outcomes of a course of action.

underpayment inequity   Inequity that exists when a person perceives that his or her own outcome – input ratio is less than the ratio of a referent.

unintentional discrimination   Unfair practices and policies that have an adverse impact on specific groups for reasons unrelated to the job.

unstructured interview   Unplanned questions asked as points of interest arise in the conversation.

V

valence   In expectancy theory, how desirable each of the rewards available from a job or organization is to a person.

valid selection technique   A test or tool that measures the candidates' likely success or failure in performing the job.

value system   The terminal and instrumental values that are guiding principles in an individual's life.

verbal communication   The encoding of messages into words, either written or spoken.

vicarious learning   Learning that occurs when the learner becomes motivated to perform a behaviour by watching another person perform it and be reinforced for doing so; also called *observational learning*.

virtual teams   Teams whose members rarely or never meet face to face and interact by using various forms of information technology such as email, computer networks, telephones, faxes, and video conferences.

vision statement   A broad declaration of the big picture of the organization and/or a statement of its dreams for the future.

W

work specialization   The degree to which the job is focused on particular tasks or multiple tasks.

worker-requirements questions   Questions that ask candidates about their willingness to work under specific job conditions.

workplace harassment   Any behaviour directed toward an employee that is known to be or ought to be known to be offensive and unwelcome.

Endnotes

Appendix A

1. F.W. Taylor, *Shop Management* (New York: Harper, 1903); F.W. Taylor, *The Principles of Scientific Management* (New York: Harper, 1911).
2. L.W. Fry, "The Maligned F. W. Taylor: A Reply to His Many Critics," *Academy of Management Review* 1 (1976), 124–29.
3. J.A. Litterer, *The Emergence of Systematic Management as Shown by the Literature from 1870–1900* (New York: Garland, 1986).
4. D. Wren, *The Evolution of Management Thought* (New York: Wiley, 1994), 134.
5. C. Perrow, *Complex Organizations,* 2nd ed. (Glenview, IL: Scott, Foresman, 1979).
6. M. Weber, *From Max Weber: Essays in Sociology,* ed. H.H. Gerth and C.W. Mills (New York: Oxford University Press, 1946), 331.
7. See Perrow, *Complex Organizations,* Ch. 1, for a detailed discussion of these issues.
8. L.D. Parker, "Control in Organizational Life: The Contribution of Mary Parker Follett," *Academy of Management Review* 9 (1984), 736–45.
9. P. Graham, *M.P. Follett—Prophet of Management: A Celebration of Writings from the 1920s* (Boston: Harvard Business School Press, 1995).
10. M.P. Follett, *Creative Experience* (London: Longmans, 1924).
11. E. Mayo, *The Human Problems of Industrial Civilization* (New York: Macmillan, 1933); F.J. Roethlisberger and W.J. Dickson, *Management and the Worker* (Cambridge, MA: Harvard University Press, 1947).
12. D.W. Organ, "Review of *Management and the Worker,* by F.J. Roethlisberger and W.J. Dickson," *Academy of Management Review* 13 (1986), 460–64.
13. Ibid.
14. D. Roy, "Banana Time: Job Satisfaction and Informal Interaction," *Human Organization* 18 (1960), 158–61.
15. For an analysis of the problems in distinguishing cause from effect in the Hawthorne studies and in social settings in general, see A. Carey, "The Hawthorne Studies: A Radical Criticism," *American Sociological Review* 33 (1967), 403–16.
16. D. McGregor, *The Human Side of Enterprise* (New York: McGraw-Hill, 1960).
17. Ibid., 48.

Appendix B

1. Written by J.W. Haddad, Professor, School of Business Management, Seneca College of Applied Arts and Technology, Toronto, Canada.
2. I suggest using *PlanWrite Business Plan Writer Deluxe 2006,* McGraw-Hill Irwin, ISBN-13: 978-0-07-328146-9, ISBN-10: 0-07-328146-8.
3. This is not a full resumé. The full resumés of the management team can be included in the Appendices. For this section of the business plan, simply state what experience and/or credentials make the manager suitable for the role they are taking on within the venture.
4. Website: www.statcan.gc.ca/subjects-sujets/standard -norme/naics-scian/2002/naics-scian02l-eng.htm.
5. Website: www.restaurantscanada.org. Accessed January 18, 2018.
6. Website: www.statcan.gc.ca. CANISM Table 355-0008. Accessed January 18, 2018.
7. Website: www.bizpal.ca/index_e.shtml.
8. Website: www.thebodyshop.com.au/infopage.cfm? pageID=53.
9. Website: www.dnb.ca/default.htm.
10. www.statcan.gc.ca.

Appendix C

1. J.H. Greenhaus, *Career Management* (New York: Dryden Press, 1987).
2. L. Lovelle, "A Payday for Performance" *Business Week,* April 18, 2005, pp. 78–80.
3. M.J. Driver, "Careers: A Review of Personal and Organizational Research," in C.L. Cooper and I. Robertson (eds.), *International Review of Industrial and Organizational Psychology* (New York: Wiley, 1988).
4. Ibid.
5. M.J. Driver, "Careers: A Review of Personnel and Organizational Research," in C.L. Cooper and I. Robertson, eds., *International Review of Industrial and Organizational Psychology* (New York: Wiley, 1988).
6. Career Path (recruitment material provided by Dillard's, Inc., 1994).
7. J.H. Greenhaus, *Career Management* (New York: Dryden Press, 1987).
8. M.B. Arthur, "The Boundaryless Career: A New Perspective for Organizational Inquiry," *Journal of Organizational Behavior* 15 (1994), 295–306; M.B. Arthur and D.M. Rousseau, *The Boundaryless Career: A New Employment Principle for a New Organizational Era* (New York: Oxford University Press, 1996), 237–55; "Introduction: The Boundaryless Career as a New Employment Principle," in M.B. Arthur and D.M. Rousseau (eds.) *The Boundaryless Career: A New Employment Principle for a New Organizational Era* (New York: Oxford University Press, 1996), 3–20; L.T. Eby et al., "Predictors of Success in the Era of the Boundaryless Career," *Journal of Organizational Behavior* 24 (2003), 689–708; S.C. de Janasz, E. Sullivan and V. Whiting, "Mentor Networks and Career Success: Lessons for Turbulent Times," *Academy of Management Executive* 17, no. 4 (2003), 78–91.
9. N. Griffin, "Personalize Your Management Development," *Harvard Business Review,* March 2003, 113–19.
10. Driver, "Careers: A Review of Personal and Organizational Research."
11. Greenhaus, *Career Management.*
12. J.L. Holland, *Making Vocational Choices: A Theory of Careers* (Englewood Cliffs, NJ: Prentice Hall, 1973).
13. Greenhaus, *Career Management.*
14. Ibid.
15. G. Dreher and R. Ash, "A Comparative Study of Mentoring Among Men and Women in Managerial, Professional, and Technical Positions," *Journal of Applied Psychology* 75 (1990), 525–35; T.A. Scandura, "Mentorship and Career Mobility: An Empirical Investigation," *Journal of Organizational Behavior* 13 (1992), 169–74; D.B. Turban and T.W. Dougherty, "The Role of Protégé Personality in Receipt of Mentoring and Career Success," *Academy of Management Journal* 37 (1994), 688–702; W. Whitely, W. Dougherty, and G.F. Dreher, "Relationship of Career Mentoring and Socioeconomic Origin to Managers' and Professionals' Early Career Success," *Academy of Management Journal* 34 (1991), 331–51.
16. T.P. Ference, J.A.F. Stoner, and E.K. Warren, "Managing the Career Plateau," *Academy of Management Review* 2 (1977), 602–12.

Appendix D

1. The view of quality as including reliability goes back to the work of W. Edwards Deming and Joseph Juran. See A. Gabor, *The Man Who Discovered Quality* (New York: Times Books, 1990).
2. D. F. Abell, *Defining the Business: The Starting Point of Strategic Planning* (Englewood Cliffs, NJ: Prentice Hall, 1980).
3. M. E. Porter, *Competitive Advantage* (New York: Free Press, 1985).
4. B. O'Brian, "Flying on the Cheap," *The Wall Street Journal,* October 26, 1992, A1; B. O'Reilly, "Where Service Flies Right," *Fortune,* August 24, 1992, 116–17; A. Salpukas, "Hurt in Expansion, Airlines Cut Back and May Sell Hubs," *The Wall Street Journal,* April 1, 1993, A1, C8.
5. www.crm.com, 2012.
6. www.crm.com, 2006.
7. The view of quality as reliability goes back to the work of Deming and Juran; see Gabor, *The Man Who Discovered Quality.*
8. See also D. Garvin, "What Does Product Quality Really Mean?" *Sloan Management Review* 26 (Fall 1984), 5–44; P. B. Crosby, *Quality Is Free* (New York: Mentor Books, 1980); Gabor, *The Man Who Discovered Quality.*
9. www.jdpa.com, 2015.
10. J. Griffiths, "Europe's Manufacturing Quality and Productivity Still Lag Far behind Japan's," *Financial Times,* November 4, 1994, 11.
11. S. McCartney, "Compaq Borrows Wal-Mart's Idea to Boost Production," *The Wall Street Journal,* June 17, 1994, B4.
12. P. Nemetz and L. Fry, "Flexible Manufacturing Organizations: Implications for Strategy Formulation," *Academy of Management Review* 13 (1988), 627–38; N. Greenwood, *Implementing Flexible Manufacturing Systems* (New York: Halstead Press, 1986).
13. M. Williams, "Back to the Past," *The Wall Street Journal,* October 24, 1994, A1.
14. G. Stalk and T. M. Hout, *Competing Against Time* (New York: Free Press, 1990).
15. For an interesting discussion of some other drawbacks of JIT and other "Japanese" manufacturing techniques, see S. M. Young, "A Framework for Successful Adoption and Performance of Japanese Manufacturing Practices in the United States," *Academy of Management Review* 17 (1992), 677–701.
16. T. Stundza, "Massachusetts Switch Maker Switches to Kanban," *Purchasing,* November 16, 2000, 103.
17. B. Dumaine, "The Trouble with Teams," *Fortune,* September 5, 1994, 86–92.
18. See C. W. L. Hill, "Transaction Cost Economizing, National Institutional Structures, and Competitive Advantage: The Case of Japan," *Organization Science* (1995), 119–31; M. Aoki, *Information, Incentives, and Bargaining in the Japanese Economy* (Cambridge: Cambridge University Press, 1989).
19. J. Hoerr, "The Payoff from Teamwork," *BusinessWeek,* July 10, 1989, 56–62.
20. M. Hammer and J. Champy, *Reengineering the Corporation* (New York: Harper Business, 1993), 35.
21. Ibid., 46.
22. Ibid.
23. For example, see V. Houlder, "Two Steps Forward, One Step Back," *Financial Times,* October 31, 1994, 8; Amal Kumar Naj, "Shifting Gears," *The Wall Street Journal,* May 7, 1993, A1; D. Greising, "Quality: How to Make It Pay," *BusinessWeek,* August 8, 1994, 54–59.

Chapter 1

1. http://www.brickbeer.com/sites/brick_corporate/files/2016_annual_report.pdf. Accessed November 5, 2017.
2. http://www.brickbeer.com/investors/history/. Accessed Jan. 26, 2015.
3. http://www.brickbeer.com/sites/brick_corporate/files/2014_annual_report.pdf. Accessed Jan. 26, 2015.
4. https://www.linkedin.com/in/seantbyrne. Accessed Jan. 26, 2015.
5. G.R. Jones, *Organizational Theory* (Reading, MA: Addison-Wesley, 1995).
6. Jack Quarter, Laurie Mook, and Ann Armstrong, *Understanding the Social Economy: A Canadian Perspective* (Toronto: University of Toronto Press, 2009).
7. Ibid, p. 4.
8. Imagine Canada and Canadian Policy Research Networks, 2006. "Building Blocks for Strong Communities—Key Findings and Recommendations." Accessed May 20, 2012.
9. Brick Brewing Company, http://www.newswire.ca/en/releases/archive/March2011/17/c3677.html. Accessed March 18, 2011.
10. P. Drucker, *Management: Tasks, Responsibilities, Practices* (New York: Harper and Row, 1974).
11. J.P. Campbell, "On the Nature of Organizational Effectiveness," in P.S. Goodman, J.M. Pennings, and Associates, *New Perspectives on Organizational Effectiveness* (San Francisco: Jossey-Bass, 1977).
12. M.J. Provitera, "What Management Is: How It Works and Why It's Everyone's Business," *Academy of Management Executive* 17 (August 2003), 152–54.
13. "CEO Salaries," *Toronto Star,* http://www.thestar.com/staticcontent/917086. Accessed Sept. 21, 2011.
14. J.G. Combs and M.S. Skill, "Managerialist and Human Capital Explanations for Key Executive Pay Premium: A Contingency Perspective," *Academy of Management Journal* 46 (February 2003), 63–74.
15. G.R. Jones, *Organizational Theory* (Reading, MA: Addison-Wesley, 1995).
16. P.F. Drucker, *Management Tasks, Responsibilities, and Practices* (New York: Harper and Row, 1974).
17. G. Dixon, "Clock Ticking for New CEOs," *The Globe and Mail,* May 8, 2001.
18. http://www.newswire.ca/en/releases/archive/May2011/12/c3818.html. Accessed Sept. 21, 2011.
19. http://www2.brickbeer.com/. Accessed Sept. 21, 2011.
20. J. Kotter, *The General Managers* (New York: Free Press, 1992).
21. C.P. Hales, "What Do Managers Do? A Critical Review of the Evidence," *Journal of Management Studies* (January 1986), 88–115; A.I. Kraul, P.R. Pedigo, D.D. McKenna, and M.D. Dunnette, "The Role of the Manager: What's Really Important in Different Management Jobs," *Academy of Management Executive* (November 1989), 286–293.
22. A.K. Gupta, "Contingency Perspectives on Strategic Leadership," in D.C. Hambrick (ed.), *The Executive Effect: Concepts and Methods for Studying Top Managers* (Greenwich, CT: JAI Press, 1988), pp. 147–178.
23. D.G. Ancona, "Top Management Teams: Preparing for the Revolution," in J.S. Carroll (ed.), *Applied Social Psychology and Organizational Settings* (Hillsdale, NJ: Erlbaum, 1990); D.C. Hambrick and P.A. Mason, "Upper Echelons: The Organization as a Reflection of Its Top Managers," *Academy of Management Journal,* 9, 1984, pp. 193–206.
24. T.A. Mahony, T.H. Jerdee, and S.J. Carroll, "The Jobs of Management," *Industrial Relations* 4 (1965), 97–110; L. Gomez-Mejia, J. McCann, and R.C. Page, "The Structure of Managerial Behaviours and Rewards," *Industrial Relations* 24 (1985), 147–154.
25. R.L. Katz, "Skills of an Effective Administrator," *Harvard Business Review,* September–October 1974, pp. 90–102.
26. Ibid.
27. P. Tharenou, "Going Up? Do Traits and Informal Social Processes Predict Advancing in Management?" *Academy of Management Journal* 44 (October 2001), 1005–18.

28. C.J. Collins and K.D. Clark, "Strategic Human Resource Practices, Top Management Team Social Networks, and Firm Performance: The Role of Human Resource Practices in Creating Organizational Competitive Advantage," *Academy of Management Journal* 46 (December 2003), 740–52.

29. H. Mintzberg, "The Manager's Job: Folklore and Fact," *Harvard Business Review,* July–August 1975, pp. 56–62.

30. H. Mintzberg, *The Nature of Managerial Work* (New York: Harper and Row, 1973).

31. Ibid.

32. M. Rokeach, *The Nature of Human Values* (New York: Free Press, 1973).

33. Ibid.

34. A.P. Brief, *Attitudes In and Around Organizations* (Thousand Oaks, CA: Sage, 1998).

35. D.W. Organ, *Organizational Citizenship Behavior: The Good Soldier Syndrome* (Lexington, MA: Lexington Books, 1988).

36. J.M. George and A.P. Brief, "Feeling Good—Doing Good: A Conceptual Analysis of the Mood at Work—Organizational Spontaneity Relationship," *Psychological Bulletin* 112 (1992), 310–29.

37. W.H. Mobley, "Intermediate Linkages in the Relationship between Job Satisfaction and Employee Turnover," *Journal of Applied Psychology* 62 (1977), 237–40.

38. C. Hymowitz, "Though Now Routine, Bosses Still Stumble during Layoff Process," *The Wall Street Journal,* June 25, 2007, B1; J. Brockner, "The Effects of Work Layoffs on Survivors: Research, Theory and Practice," in B.M. Staw and L.L. Cummings, eds., *Research in Organizational Behavior,* vol. 10 (Greenwich, CT: JAI Press, 1988), 213–55.

39. Hymowitz, "Though Now Routine."

40. Ibid.

41. Ibid.

42. Goodman, "U.S. Job Losses in December Dim Hopes for Quick Upswing."

43. M. Luo, "For Small Employers, Rounds of Shedding Workers and Tears," *The New York Times,* May 7, 2009, A1, A3.

44. N. Solinger, W. van Olffen, and R.A. Roe, "Beyond the Three-Component Model of Organizational Commitment," *Journal of Applied Psychology* 93 (2008), 70–83.

45. J. E. Mathieu and D. M. Zajac, "A Review and Meta-Analysis of the Antecedents, Correlates, and Consequences of Organizational Commitment," *Psychological Bulletin* 108 (1990), 171–94.

46. D. Watson and A. Tellegen, "Toward a Consensual Structure of Mood," *Psychological Bulletin* 98 (1985), 219–35.

47. Watson and Tellegen, "Toward a Consensual Structure of Mood."

48. J. M. George, "The Role of Personality in Organizational Life: Issues and Evidence," *Journal of Management* 18 (1992), 185–213.

49. H.A. Elfenbein, "Emotion in Organizations: A Review and Theoretical Integration," in J.P. Walsh and A.P. Brief, eds., *The Academy of Management Annals,* vol. 1 (New York: Lawrence Erlbaum Associates, 2008), 315–86.

50. J.P. Forgas, "Affect in Social Judgments and Decisions: A Multi-Process Model," in M. Zanna, ed., *Advances in Experimental and Social Psychology,* vol. 25 (San Diego, CA: Academic Press, 1992), 227–75; J.P. Forgas and J.M. George, "Affective Influences on Judgments and Behavior in Organizations: An Information Processing Perspective," *Organizational Behavior and Human Decision Processes* 86 (2001), 3–34; J.M. George, "Emotions and Leadership: The Role of Emotional Intelligence," *Human Relations* 53 (2000), 1027–55; W.N. Morris, *Mood: The Frame of Mind* (New York: Springer-Verlag, 1989).

51. George, "Emotions and Leadership."

52. J.M. George and K. Bettenhausen, "Understanding Prosocial Behavior, Sales Performance, and Turnover: A Group Level Analysis in a Service Context," *Journal of Applied Psychology* 75 (1990), 698–709.

53. George and Brief, "Feeling Good—Doing Good"; J.M. George and J. Zhou, "Understanding When Bad Moods Foster Creativity and Good Ones Don't: The Role of Context and Clarity of Feelings," *Journal of Applied Psychology* 87(2002), 687–697; A.M. Isen and R.A. Baron, "Positive Affect as a Factor in Organizational Behavior," in B.M. Staw and L.L. Cummings, eds., *Research in Organizational Behavior,* vol. 13 (Greenwich, CT: JAI Press, 1991), 1–53.

54. J. M. George and J. Zhou, "Dual Tuning in a Supportive Context: Joint Contributions of Positive Mood, Negative Mood, and Supervisory Behaviors to Employee Creativity," *Academy of Management Journal* 50 (2007), 605–22; J.M. George, "Creativity in Organizations," in J.P. Walsh and A.P. Brief, eds., *The Academy of Management Annals,* vol. 1 (New York: Lawrence Erlbaum Associates, 2008), 439–77.

55. J.D. Greene, R.B. Sommerville, L.E. Nystrom, J.M. Darley, and J.D. Cohen, "An FMRI Investigation of Emotional Engagement in Moral Judgment," *Science,* September 14, 2001, 2105–08; L. Neergaard, "Brain Scans Show Emotions Key to Resolving Ethical Dilemmas," *Houston Chronicle,* September 14, 2001, 13A.

56. George and Zhou, "Dual Tuning in a Supportive Context."

57. George and Zhou, "Dual Tuning in a Supportive Context"; J.M. George, "Dual Tuning: A Minimum Condition for Understanding Affect in Organizations?" *Organizational Psychology Review,* no. 2 (2011), 147–64.

58. R.C. Sinclair, "Mood, Categorization Breadth, and Performance Appraisal: The Effects of Order of Information Acquisition and Affective State on Halo, Accuracy, Informational Retrieval, and Evaluations," *Organizational Behavior and Human Decision Processes* 42 (1988), 22–46.

59. D. Goleman, *Emotional Intelligence* (New York: Bantam Books, 1994); J.D. Mayer and P. Salovey, "The Intelligence of Emotional Intelligence," *Intelligence* 17 (1993), 433–42; J.D. Mayer and P. Salovey, "What Is Emotional Intelligence?" in P. Salovey and D. Sluyter, eds., *Emotional Development and Emotional Intelligence: Implications for Education* (New York: Basic Books, 1997); P. Salovey and J.D. Mayer, "Emotional Intelligence," *Imagination Cognition, and Personality* 9 (1989–1990), 185–211.

60. S. Epstein, *Constructive Thinking* (Westport, CT: Praeger, 1998).

61. "Leading by Feel," *Inside the Mind of the Leader,* January 2004, 27–37.

62. P.C. Early and R.S. Peterson, "The Elusive Cultural Chameleon: Cultural Intelligence as a New Approach to Intercultural Training for the Global Manager," *Academy of Management Learning and Education* 3, no. 1 (2004), 100–15.

63. George, "Emotions and Leadership"; S. Begley, "The Boss Feels Your Pain," *Newsweek,* October 12, 1998, 74; D. Goleman, *Working with Emotional Intelligence* (New York: Bantam Books, 1998).

64. "Leading by Feel," *Inside the Mind of the Leader,* January 2004, 27–37.

65. George, "Emotions and Leadership."

66. J. Zhou and J.M. George, "Awakening Employee Creativity: The Role of Leader Emotional Intelligence," *Leadership Quarterly* 14 (2003), 545–68.

67. H.M. Trice and J.M. Beyer, *The Cultures of Work Organizations* (Englewood Cliffs, NJ: Prentice-Hall, 1993).

68. J.B. Sörensen, "The Strength of Corporate Culture and the Reliability of Firm Performance," *Administrative Science Quarterly* 47 (2002), 70–91.

69. "Personality and Organizational Culture," in B. Schneider and D.B. Smith, eds., *Personality and Organizations* (Mahwah, NJ: Lawrence Erlbaum, 2004), 347–69; J.E. Slaughter, M.J. Zickar, S. Highhouse, and D.C. Mohr, "Personality Trait Inferences about Organizations: Development of a Measure and Assessment of Construct Validity," *Journal of Applied Psychology* 89, no. 1 (2004), 85–103.

70. T. Kelley, *The Art of Innovation: Lessons in Creativity from IDEO, America's Leading Design Firm* (New York: Random House, 2001).

71. "Personality and Organizational Culture."

72. B. Schneider, "The People Make the Place," *Personnel Psychology* 40 (1987), 437–53.

73. "Personality and Organizational Culture."

74. Ibid.

75. B. Schneider, H.B. Goldstein, and D.B. Smith, "The ASA Framework: An Update," *Personnel Psychology* 48 (1995), 747–73; J. Schaubroeck, D.C. Ganster, and J.R. Jones, "Organizational and Occupational Influences in the Attraction–Selection–Attrition Process," *Journal of Applied Psychology* 83 (1998), 869–91.

76. Kelley, *The Art of Innovation.*

77. www.ideo.com, February 5, 2008.

78. Kelley, *The Art of Innovation.*

79. "Personality and Organizational Culture."

80. Kelley, *The Art of Innovation.*

81. Ibid.

82. D.C. Feldman, "The Development and Enforcement of Group Norms," *Academy of Management Review* 9 (1984), 47–53.

83. G.R. Jones, *Organizational Theory, Design, and Change* (Upper Saddle River, NJ: Prentice-Hall, 2003).

84. H. Schein, "The Role of the Founder in Creating Organizational Culture," *Organizational Dynamics* 12 (1983), 13–28.

85. Anthony Grnak, John Hughes, and Douglas Hunter, *Building the Best, Lessons from Inside Canada's Best Managed Companies* (Toronto: Viking Canada, 2006).

86. J.M. George, "Personality, Affect, and Behavior in Groups," *Journal of Applied Psychology* 75 (1990), 107–116.

87. J. Van Maanen, "Police Socialization: A Longitudinal Examination of Job Attitudes in an Urban Police Department," *Administrative Science Quarterly* 20 (1975), 207–28.

88. www.intercotwest.com/Disney; M.N. Martinez, "Disney Training Works Magic," *HRMagazine,* May 1992, 53–57.

89. P.L. Berger and T. Luckman, *The Social Construction of Reality* (Garden City, NY: Anchor Books, 1967).

90. H.M. Trice and J.M. Beyer, "Studying Organizational Culture through Rites and Ceremonials," *Academy of Management Review* 9 (1984), 653–69.

91. "Bonding and Brutality: Hazing Survives as a Way of Forging Loyalty to Groups," *Maclean's,* January 30, 1995, p. 18.

92. Aaron Karp, "WestJet's Value Proposition," *Air Transport World,* January 1, 2011. http://atwonline.com/airline-finance-data/article/WestJet-s-value-proposition-1231. Accessed Oct. 25, 2011.

93. B. Ortega, "Wal-Mart's Meeting Is a Reason to Party," *The Wall Street Journal,* June 3, 1994, p. A1.

94. Website: www.senecac.on.ca/.

95. D. Akin, "Big Blue Chills Out: A Canadian Executive Leads the Campaign to Turn IBM into Cool Blue," *Financial Post (National Post),* October 11, 1999, pp. C1, C6.

96. A. Rafaeli and M.G. Pratt, "Tailored Meanings: On the Meaning and Impact of Organizational Dress," *Academy of Management Review,* January 1993, pp. 32–55.

97. R.L. Katz, "Skills of an Effective Administrator," *Harvard Business Review,* September–October 1974, pp. 90–102.

98. P. Tharenou, "Going Up? Do Traits and Informal Social Processes Predict Advancing in Management?" *Academy of Management Journal* 44 (October 2001), 1005–18.

99. C.J. Collins and K.D. Clark, "Strategic Human Resource Practices, Top Management Team Social Networks, and Firm Performance: The Role of Human Resource Practices in Creating Organizational Competitive Advantage," *Academy of Management Journal* 46 (December 2003), 740–52.

100. William Boston, "Volkswagen CEO Resigns as Car Maker Races to Stem Emissions Scandal," The Wall Street Journal, www.wsj.com, September 23, 2015.

Chapter 2

1. Based on Kerri Capell et al.,"IKEA: How the Swedish Retailer Became a Global Cult Brand," *BusinessWeek,* November 14, 2005. https://www.bloomberg.com/news/articles/2005-11-13/ikea. Accessed June 11, 2018.

2. L.J. Bourgeois, "Strategy and Environment: A Conceptual Integration," *Academy of Management Review* 5 (1985), 25–39.

3. Peterson, Hayley. 'Inside Sears' Death Spiral, *Business Insider,* Jan 8, 2017. http://www.businessinsider.com/sears-failing-stores-closing-edward-lampert-bankruptcy-chances-2017-1. Web. October 22, 2017.

4. "Business: Link in the Global Chain," *The Economist,* June 2, 2001, 62–63.

5. Kerri Capell et al., "IKEA: How the Swedish Retailer Became a Global Cult Brand," *BusinessWeek,* November 14, 2005. https://www.bloomberg.com/news/articles/2005-11-13/ikea. Accessed June 11, 2018.

6. M.E. Porter, *Competitive Advantage* (New York: Free Press, 1985).

7. Kerri Capell et al., "IKEA: How the Swedish Retailer Became a Global Cult Brand," *BusinessWeek,* November 14, 2005. https://www.bloomberg.com/news/articles/2005-11-13/ikea. Accessed June 11, 2018.

8. "Researching Your Competition," StatsLink Canada, © John White, GDSourcing—Research & Retrieval 2006. Website: www.stats-link-canada.com/Industry-Competitors.html. Accessed May 15, 2008.

9. Gaurav Kheterpal, "Shaw Losing the War for Western Canada," April 17, 2012, http://www.thetelecomblog.com/2012/04/17/shaw-losing-the-war-for-western-canada/. Accessed Jan. 3, 2015.

10. D.I. Jung and B.J. Avolio, "Opening the Black Box: An Experimental Investigation of the Mediating Effects of Trust and Value Congruence on Transformational and Transactional Leadership," *Journal of Organizational Behavior,* December 2000, 949–64; B.M. Bass and B.J. Avolio, "Transformational and Transactional Leadership: 1992 and Beyond," *Journal of European Industrial Training,* January 1990, 20–34.

11. J. Porras and J. Collins, *Built to Last: Successful Habits of Visionary Companies* (New York: HarperCollins, 1994).

12. For a detailed discussion of the importance of the structure of law as a factor explaining economic change and growth, see D.C. North, *Institutions, Institutional Change and Economic Performance* (Cambridge: Cambridge University Press, 1990).

13. Barbara Shecter, "Cineplex Snaps Up Rival," *Financial Post,* Tuesday, June 14, 2005, pp. FP1, 6. See also Richard Blackwell, "Movie Marriage Promises Blockbuster Savings," *The Globe and Mail,* Wednesday, June 22, 2005, p. B3; and Gayle MacDonald, "Movie Boss Has Best Seat in the House," *The Globe and Mail,* Wednesday, June 15, 2005, pp. B1, 4.

14. "When Fortune Frowned: A Special Report on the World Economy," *The Economist,* October 11, 2008, p. 3.

15. World Economic Forum.

16. www.canada.com/topics/news/story.html?id=c3a67e3b-1aef-4daf-a768-a54eedb80185. Accessed Oct. 11, 2008.

17. N. Goodman, *An Introduction to Sociology* (New York: HarperCollins, 1991); C. Nakane, *Japanese Society* (Berkeley: University of California Press, 1970).

18. "A Female CEO may be the Answer to more women on Boards, surveys show," *Financial Post*, June 6, 2016. Web. Accessed Oct 23, 2017.

19. Ibid.

20. "Canada's Seniors Population to Jump, Workforce Decline by 2063, in 50 Years, One-Quarter of Canadians Will be Over 65," CBC News. Accessed Jan. 3, 2015.

21. "Long-Term Global Demographic Trends: Reshaping the Geopolitical Landscape," Central Intelligence Agency, July 2001, p. 5. https://www.cia.gov/library/reports /general-reports-1/Demo_Trends_For_Web.pdf. Accessed Sept. 28, 2011.

22. "Demographic Time Bomb: Mitigating the Effects of Demographic Change in Canada," Report of the Standing Senate Committee on Banking, Trade and Commerce, June 2006. Website: www.parl.gc.ca/39/1/parlbus /commbus/senate/Com-e/bank-e/rep-e/rep03jun06-e .htm. Accessed May 15, 2008.

23. J. Schumpeter, *Capitalism, Socialism and Democracy* (London: Macmillan, 1950), p. 68. Also see R.R. Winter and S.G. Winter, *An Evolutionary Theory of Economic Change* (Cambridge, MA: Harvard University Press, 1982).

24. R.B. Reich, *The Work of Nations* (New York: Knopf, 1991).

25. Curry, Bill, 'The ABCS of the TPP,' *The Globe and Mail*, Oct 5, 2015. Web. Accessed Oct 23, 2017.

26. "Newfoundland Announces It Could Reject CETA," *Council of Canadians*, http://www.e-activist.com /eacampaign/action.handleViewInBrowser.do?ea .campaigner.email=yfYDXqBvMoaLSt%2F4mplZ %2FKPt4es%2BR5xiFqvSrIQaOsI=&broadcastId =66703&templateId=47713. Accessed Jan. 27, 2015.

27. NAFTA Rules of Origin: Regional Content Rules. http:// medey.com/pdf/NAFTA%20Rules%20of%20Origin;%20 Regional%20Value%20Content.pdf. Accessed Sept. 30, 2011.

28. "In Praise of the Stateless Multinational," *The Economist*, September 20, 2008, p. 20.

29. Bhagwati, *Protectionism*.

30. For a summary of these theories, see P. Krugman and M. Obstfeld, *International Economics: Theory and Policy* (New York: HarperCollins, 1991). Also see C.W.L. Hill, *International Business* (New York: McGraw-Hill, 1997), chap. 4.

31. A. M. Rugman, "The Quest for Global Dominance," *Academy of Management Executive* 16 (August 2002), 157–60.

32. www.wto.org.com, 2004.

33. www.wto.org.com, 2012.

34. C.A. Bartlett and S. Ghoshal, *Managing across Borders* (Boston: Harvard Business School Press, 1989).

35. C. Arnst and G. Edmondson, "The Global Free-for-All," *BusinessWeek*, September 26, 1994, 118–26.

36. W. Konrads, "Why Leslie Wexner Shops Overseas," *BusinessWeek*, February 3, 1992, 30.

37. "Roll-Up-Rim Contest Wasteful, Critics Say," *The London Free Press*, March 2, 2005. www.canoe.ca/NewsStand /LondonFreePress/News/2005/03/02/946850-sun.html.

38. Bill Mah, "Tim Hortons Contest a Litterbug, Critics Say: Roll Up the Rim Begins," *National Post*, March 1, 2005.

39. R.B. Duncan, "Characteristics of Organization Environment and Perceived Environment," *Administrative Science Quarterly* 17 (1972), 313–327.

40. See "McDonald's USA Food Allergens and Sensitivities Listing." www.mcdonalds.com/app_controller.nutrition .categories.allergens.index.html.

41. Not everyone agrees with this assessment. Some argue that organizations and individual managers have little impact on the environment. See M.T. Hannan and J. Freeman, "Structural Inertia and Organizational Change," *American Sociological Review* 49 (1984), 149–164.

42. "Foreign Investment in Canada, Lie Back and Forget the Maple Leaf," *The Economist*, April 5, 2008, p. 42.

43. A. Shama, "Management Under Fire: The Transformation of Management in the Soviet Union and Eastern Europe," *Academy of Management Executive*, 1993, pp. 22–35.

44. Michael E. Porter and Mark R. Kramer "Creating Shared Value," *Harvard Business Review*, January 2011 ISSUE. https://hbr.org/2011/01/the-big-idea-creating-shared -value. Accessed Jan. 4, 2015.

45. Ibid.

46. Michael E. Porter and Mark R. Kramer. *Op. cit.* Jan. 25, 2015.

47. Anthony Grnak, John Hughes, and Douglas Hunter, *Building the Best, Lessons from Inside Canada's Best Managed Companies* (Toronto: Viking Canada, 2006), p. 86.

48. Ibid, p. 37.

49. Michael Rachlis, "Medicare Made Easy," *The Globe and Mail*, Monday, April 26, 2004, p. A13.

50. Kerri Capell et al., "IKEA: How the Swedish Retailer Became a Global Cult Brand," *BusinessWeek*, November 14, 2005. https://www.bloomberg.com/news/articles /2005-11-13/ikea. Accessed June 11, 2018.

51. Michael E. Porter and Mark R. Kramer. *Op. cit.* Jan. 25, 2015.

52. K. Seiders and L.L. Berry, "Service Fairness: What It Is and Why It Matters," *Academy of Management Executive* 12 (1998), 8–20.

53. Anthony Grnak, John Hughes, and Douglas Hunter, *Building the Best, Lessons from Inside Canada's Best Managed Companies* (Toronto: Viking Canada, 2006).

54. C. Anderson, "Values-Based Management," *Academy of Management Executive* 11 (1997), 25–46.

55. W.H. Shaw and V. Barry, *Moral Issues in Business*, 6th ed. (Belmont, CA: Wadsworth, 1995); and T. Donaldson, *Corporations and Morality* (Englewood Cliffs, NJ: Prentice-Hall, 1982).

56. D.R. Tobin, *The Knowledge Enabled Organization* (New York: AMACOM, 1998).

57. Human Resource Management Video DVD Volume 2, number 3, 2010.

58. *The Economist*, February 4, 2012, p. 8.

59. "Sony Cyber-Attack: North Korea Faces New US Sanctions," January 2, 2015. http://www.bbc.com/news/world-us -canada-30661973. Accessed Jan. 4, 2015.

60. Michael Lewis, "Sony Closing All 14 Stores in Canada," *Toronto Star*, Jan. 15, 2015. http://www.thestar.com /business/2015/01/15/sony-closing-all-14-stores-in-canada .html. Accessed Jan. 25, 2015.

Chapter 3

1. D. Sacks, "The Catalyst," *Fast Company*, October 2006, 59–61.

2. About PUMA, http://about.puma.com/EN/1/, Feb. 13, 2008.

3. Sacks, "The Catalyst."

4. Ibid.

5. "PUMA Progress Update on Greenpeace Detox Campaign," http://about.puma.com/?page_id=10. Accessed Oct. 11, 2011.

6. "Puma Expects 2008 Sales, Profits to Rise—PPR CFO," Jan. 24, 2008, www.reuters.com/articlePrint?articleId =USL2491288920080124, Feb. 13, 2008.

7. Sacks, "The Catalyst."
8. Ibid.
9. http://ca.puma.com/en_CA/home?mktId
   =PS:JDigital:Bing:CA|Brand|X|PUMA|Exact&utm
   _source=bing&utm_medium=cpc&utm_campaign
   =CA|Brand|X|PUMA|Exact&mktId=PS:JDigital
   :Bing:CA|Brand|X|PUMA|Exact&msclkid
   =8220784357251a8e09fc221f9a383539&utm_source
   =bing&utm_campaign=CA%7CBrand
   %7CX%7CPUMA%7CExact&utm_term=Puma&utm
   _content=Neutral%7CX%7CX%7CGeneral%7CCollection.
   Accessed Jan. 15, 2017.
10. http://about.puma.com/en/this-is-puma/strategy.
    Accessed Jan 15, 2018.
11. http://about.puma.com/en/this-is-puma/strategy.
    Accessed Jan 15, 2018.
12. Ibid.
13. http://about.puma.com/en/newsroom/corporate-
    news/2018. Accessed Jan 15, 2018.
14. Ibid.
15. G.P. Huber, *Managerial Decision Making* (Glenview, IL:
    Scott, Foresman, 1993).
16. Sacks, "The Catalyst."
17. "What Steve Jobs Taught Me by Kicking My Butt,"
    Canadian Business, October 10, 2011, p. 17.
18. H.A. Simon, *The New Science of Management*
    (Englewood Cliffs, NJ: Prentice-Hall, 1977).
19. D. Kahneman, "Maps of Bounded Rationality: A Perspective
    on Intuitive Judgment and Choice," Prize Lecture, December
    8, 2002; E. Jaffe, "What Was I Thinking? Kahneman Explains
    How Intuition Leads Us Astray," *American Psychological
    Society* 17, no. 5 (May 2004), 23–26.
20. Alan Kearns, "The Big Career Decisions," *National Post,*
    Wednesday, May 4, 2005, p. FP9. See also the website:
    www.econlib.org/library/Enc/bios/Simon.html.
21. H.A. Simon, *Administrative Behavior* (New York:
    Macmillan, 1947), p. 79.
22. H.A. Simon, *Models of Man* (New York: Wiley, 1957).
23. K.J. Arrow, *Aspects of the Theory of Risk Bearing*
    (Helsinki: Yrjo Johnssonis Saatio, 1965).
24. R.L. Daft and R.H. Lengel, "Organizational Information
    Requirements, Media Richness and Structural Design,"
    Management Science 32 (1986), 554–571.
25. R. Cyert and J. March, *Behavioral Theory of the Firm*
    (Englewood Cliffs, NJ: Prentice-Hall, 1963).
26. J.G. March and H.A. Simon, *Organizations* (New York:
    Wiley, 1958).
27. H.A. Simon, "Making Management Decisions: The Role
    of Intuition and Emotion," *Academy of Management
    Executive* 1 (1987), 57–64.
28. M. H. Bazerman, *Judgment in Managerial Decision
    Making* (New York: Wiley, 1986). Also see Simon,
    Administrative Behavior.
29. M.H. Bazerman, *Judgment in Managerial Decision
    Making* (New York: Wiley, 1986); G.P. Huber, *Managerial
    Decision Making*(Glenview, IL: Scott, Foresman, 1993);
    and J.E. Russo and P.J. Schoemaker, *Decision Traps*
    (New York: Simon and Schuster, 1989).
30. M.D. Cohen, J.G. March, and J.P. Olsen, "A Garbage Can
    Model of Organizational Choice," *Administrative Science
    Quarterly* 17 (1972), 1–25.
31. Ibid.
32. M.H. Bazerman, *Judgment in Managerial Decision
    Making* (New York: Wiley, 1986).
33. P.C. Nutt, *Why Decisions Fail: Avoiding the Blunders
    and Traps That Lead to Debacles* (San Francisco:
    Berrett-Koehler Publishers, 2002); and M.H. Bazerman,
    Judgment in Managerial Decision Making (New York:
    Wiley, 1986).
34. J.E. Russo and P.J. Schoemaker, *Decision Traps* (New
    York: Simon and Schuster, 1989).
35. Ibid.
36. B. Berger, "NASA: One Year after *Columbia*—Bush's New
    Vision Changes Agency's Course Midstream," *Space
    News Business Report,* January 26, 2004, www.space
    .com/spacenews/businessmonday_040126.html.
37. J. Glanz and J. Schwartz, "Dogged Engineer's Effort
    to Assess Shuttle Damage," *The New York Times,*
    September 26, 2003, A1.
38. M.L. Wald and J. Schwartz, "NASA Chief Promises a Shift
    in Attitude," *The New York Times,* August 28, 2003, A23.
39. D. Kahneman and A. Tversky, "Judgment Under Scrutiny:
    Heuristics and Biases," *Science* 185 (1974), pp. 1124–1131.
40. C.R. Schwenk, "Cognitive Simplification Processes in
    Strategic Decision Making," *Strategic Management
    Journal* 5 (1984), 111–128.
41. J.E. Russo and P.J. Schoemaker, *Decision Traps* (New
    York: Simon and Schuster, 1989).
42. Ibid.
43. T.L. Beauchamp and N.E. Bowie (eds.), *Ethical Theory
    and Business* (Englewood Cliffs, NJ: Prentice-Hall, 1979);
    and A. Macintyre, *After Virtue* (South Bend, IN: University
    of Notre Dame Press, 1981).
44. R.E. Goodin, "How to Determine Who Should Get What,"
    Ethics, July 1975, pp. 310–321.
45. "Medical Marijuana Licence Applications Up, But
    Approvals Slow," *The Canadian Press,*http://www.cbc.ca
    /news/politics/medical-marijuana-licence-applications-up
    -but-approvals-slow-1.2752955. Accessed Jan. 27, 2015.
46. C.I. Barnard, *The Functions of the Executive* (Cambridge,
    MA: Harvard University Press, 1948).
47. A.S. Waterman, "On the Uses of Psychological Theory
    and Research in the Process of Ethical Inquiry,"
    Psychological Bulletin 103, no. 3 (1988), 283–298.
48. M.S. Frankel, "Professional Codes: Why, How, and with
    What Impact?" *Ethics* 8 (1989), 109–15.
49. J. Van Maanen and S.R. Barley, "Occupational
    Communities: Culture and Control in Organizations," in B.
    Staw and L. Cummings, eds., *Research in Organizational
    Behavior,* vol. 6 (Greenwich, CT: JAI Press, 1984),
    287–365.
50. Jones, "Ethical Decision Making by Individuals in
    Organizations."
51. G.R. Jones, *Organizational Theory: Text and Cases*
    (Reading, MA: Addison-Wesley, 1997).
52. P.E. Murphy, "Creating Ethical Corporate Structure,"
    Sloan Management Review (Winter 1989), 81–87.
53. "When It Comes to Ethics, Canadian Companies Are All
    Talk and Little Action, A Survey Shows," *Canadian Press
    Newswire,*February 17, 2000.
54. "India IT Boss Quits Over Scandal." http://news.bbc
    .co.uk/2/hi/business/7815031.stm. Accessed Jan. 7, 2009.
55. E. Gatewood and A.B. Carroll, "The Anatomy of
    Corporate Social Response," *Business Horizons,*
    September–October 1981, pp. 9–16.
56. M. Friedman, "A Friedman Doctrine: The Social
    Responsibility of Business Is to Increase Its Profits," *New
    York Times Magazine,*September 13, 1970, p. 33.
57. Quoted in "CSR—Milton Friedman was Right," http://
    www.bathconsultancygroup.com/documents/CSR%20
    -%20Milton%20Friedman%20was%20right.pdf. Accessed
    Oct. 7, 2011.
58. "Mining Could Be More Resourceful," *The Economist,*
    August 16, 2008, p. 64.
59. "Wal-Mart Canada Says Imports from Myanmar Ended in
    Spring," *Canadian Press Newswire,* July 18, 2000.
60. Danielle Sacks, "Working with the Enemy," *Fast Company,*
    September 2007, 74–81. Website: www.fastcompany.com
    /magazine/118/working-with-the-enemy.html.
61. "Environmental Sustainability Report: Wal-Mart Canada,"
    http://admin.csrwire.com/system/report_pdfs/805/
    original/1239375228_Canada.pdf. Accessed Oct. 7, 2011.

62. Ibid.

63. W.G. Ouchi, *Theory Z: How American Business Can Meet the Japanese Challenge* (Reading, MA: Addison-Wesley, 1981).

64. J.B. McGuire, A. Sundgren, and T. Schneewis, "Corporate Social Responsibility and Firm Financial Performance," *Academy of Management Review* 31 (1988), 854–872.

65. "Ecosystems and Human Well-Being: A Report of the Millennium Ecosystem Assessment (MA)," Business and Industry Synthesis Team, 2005. http://www.maweb.org /documents/document.353.aspx.pdf. Accessed Oct. 10, 2011, p. 4.

66. J. Jedras, "Social Workers," *Silicon Valley NORTH,* July 30, 2001, p. 1.

67. M. Friedman, "A Friedman Doctrine: The Social Responsibility of Business Is to Increase Its Profits," *New York Times Magazine,* September 13, 1970, pp. 32, 33, 122, 124, 126.

68. https://iris.thegiin.org/. Accessed Jan 15, 2018.

69. E.D. Bowman, "Corporate Social Responsibility and the Investor," *Journal of Contemporary Business,* Winter 1973, pp. 49–58.

70. Website: www.crestaurant.com.

71. Website: www.vanaqua.org/oceanwise/JackMacDonald, CEO Compass Food Canada, Press Release May 9, 2008. Compass Group Canada takes leading role in sustainable seafood purchasing.

72. Website: www.compass-canada.com/home/media /sustainability_purchasing.pdf.

73. Website: www.imc2.com/Documents/StateOf SustainabilityCommunications.pdf. Accessed Nov. 5, 2008.

74. Website: www.justmeans.com/index. php?action=viewcompanyprofile&id=122&sublinkid=33. Accessed Nov. 5, 2008.

75. See P. Senge, *The Fifth Discipline: The Art and Practice of the Learning Organization* (New York: Doubleday, 1990).

76. T.A. Stewart, "3M Fights Back," *Fortune,* February 5, 1996, pp. 94–99; and T.D. Schellhardt, "David in Goliath," *The Wall Street Journal,* May 23, 1996, p. R14.

77. C. Salter, "FAST 50: The World's Most Innovative Companies," *Fast Company,* March 2008, 73–117.

78. M. Ullmann, "Creativity Cubed: Burntsand Has Found a Novel Program to Motivate Its Most Creative Employees. Can It Work for You?" *SVN Canada,* February 2001, pp. B22–B23.

79. Jennifer Newman and Darryl Grigg, "Managers Struggle with Ethical Questions," *Vancouver Sun,* June 21, 2008. http://www.vancouversun.com/opinion/managers+struggle +with+ethical+decisions/828886/story.html

80. Website: www.cbc.ca.thehour. Accessed Nov. 12, 2008.

Chapter 4

1. Dina Bass, "Microsoft CEO Satya Nadella Looks to Future Beyond Windows," *Bloomberg Business,* February 19, 2015, www.bloomberg.com.

2. A. Chandler, *Strategy and Structure: Chapters in the History of the American Enterprise* (Cambridge, MA: MIT Press, 1962).

3. Ibid.

4. H. Fayol, *General and Industrial Management* (New York: IEEE Press, 1984). Fayol's work was first published in 1916.

5. Ibid.

6. F.J. Aguilar, "General Electric: Reg Jones and Jack Welch," in *General Managers in Action* (Oxford: Oxford University Press, 1992).

7. Aguilar, "General Electric."

8. D.F. Abell, *Defining the Business: The Starting Point of Strategic Planning* (Englewood Cliffs, NJ: Prentice-Hall, 1980).

9. C.W. Hofer and D. Schendel, *Strategy Formulation: Analytical Concepts* (St. Paul, MN: West, 1978).

10. R. Phelps, C. Chan, S.C. Kapsalis, "Does Scenario Planning Affect Firm Performance?" *Journal of Business Research,* March 2001, pp. 223–232.

11. Paul J.H. Schoemaker, "Are You Ready for Global Turmoil?" *BusinessWeek,* April 25, 2008. Website: www .businessweek.com/print/managing/content/apr2008 /ca20080429_312634.htm.

12. Hill and McShane, *Principles of Management* (New York: McGraw-Hill/Irwin, 2008), p. 111.

13. J.A. Pearce, "The Company Mission as a Strategic Tool," *Sloan Management Review,* Spring 1992, 15–24.

14. A. Chandler, *Strategy and Structure: Chapters in the History of the American Enterprise* (Cambridge, MA: MIT Press, 1962).

15. P.C. Nutt and R.W. Backoff, "Crafting Vision," *Journal of Management Inquiry,* December 1997, p. 309.

16. D.F. Abell, *Defining the Business: The Starting Point of Strategic Planning* (Englewood Cliffs, NJ: Prentice-Hall, 1980).

17. Amazon.com, FAQs. Accessed March 18, 2015.

18. J.A. Pearce, "The Company Mission as a Strategic Tool," *Sloan Management Review,* Spring 1992, 15–24.

19. http://www.campbellsoupcompany.com/about-campbell/. Accessed March 18, 2015.

20. G. Hamel and C.K. Prahalad, "Strategic Intent," *Harvard Business Review,* May–June 1989, 63–73.

21. D.I. Jung and B.J. Avolio, "Opening the Black Box: An Experimental Investigation of the Mediating Effects of Trust and Value Congruence on Transformational and Transactional Leadership," *Journal of Organizational Behavior,* December 2000, 949–64; B.M. Bass and B.J. Avolio, "Transformational and Transactional Leadership: 1992 and Beyond," *Journal of European Industrial Training,* January 1990, 20–34.

22. J. Porras and J. Collins, *Built to Last: Successful Habits of Visionary Companies* (New York: HarperCollins, 1994).

23. George T. Doran. "There's a S.M.A.R.T. Way to Write Management's Goals and Objectives," *Management Review (AMA Forum),* November 1981, pp. 35–36.

24. E.A. Locke, G.P. Latham, and M. Erez, "The Determinants of Goal Commitment," *Academy of Management Review* 13 (1988), 23–39.

25. K.R. Andrews, *The Concept of Corporate Strategy* (Homewood, IL: Irwin, 1971).

26. Peter Drucker, "The Next Society," *The Economist,* 2001.

27. Cited in *The Economist,* "Dealing with the Downturn: Make Love—and War," August 9, 2008, p. 57; Adam M. Brandenburger and Barry J. Nalebuff, *Co-opetition: A Revolution Mindset* (New York: Bantam Double Day, 1997).

28. *The Economist,* "Dealing with the Downturn: Make Love—and War," August 9, 2008, p. 57.

29. "Samsung, the Next Big Bet," *The Economist,* October 1, 2011. From the print edition. http://www.economist.com /node/21530976. Accessed Oct. 19, 2011.

30. M.E. Porter, *Competitive Strategy* (New York: Free Press, 1980).

31. Gordon Pitts, "Ganong Boss Aims for Sweet Spot," *The Globe and Mail,* March 3, 2003, p. B4.

32. C.W.L. Hill, "Differentiation versus Low Cost or Differentiation and Low Cost: A Contingency Framework," *Academy of Management Review,* 13, 1988, pp. 401–412.

33. For details see J.P. Womack, D.T. Jones, and D. Roos, *The Machine That Changed the World* (New York: Rawson Associates, 1990).

34. M.E. Porter, *Competitive Strategy* (New York: Free Press, 1980).

35. www.cott.com, 2008.

36. Nickels et al., *Understanding Canadian Business* (Toronto: McGraw-Hill Ryerson, 2005).
37. Tara Perkins, "Legacy at a Crossroads," *The Globe and Mail,* August 15, 2009, B1.
38. Carly Weeks, "Campbell's Adding Salt Back to Its Soups," *The Globe and Mail,* Last updated Friday, Jul. 15, 2011. http://www.theglobeandmail.com/life/health/new-health/health-news/Campbell's-adding-salt-back-to-its-soups/article2097659/. Accessed Oct. 19, 2011.
39. Website: www.thegreendoor.ca/.
40. Website: http://web.ustpaul.uottawa.ca/en.
41. Website: www.ottawaplus.ca/portal/profile.do?profileID=45274.
42. J. Lee, "The Apparel Industry's Answer to Global Water Shortages," *Triple Pundit,* March 12, 2015, www.triplepundit.com.
43. K. Drennan, "Reduce Your Wardrobe's Water Footprint," *Green Living,* accessed March 12, 2015, www.greenlivingonline.com.
44. "Water Pollution," *Eco360,* accessed March 12, 2015, www.sustainablecommunication.org.
45. D. Ferris, "Nike, Adidas Want to Dye Your Shirt with No Water," *Forbes,* accessed March 12, 2015, www.forbes.com.
46. "Water Pollution."
47. L. Kaye, "Clothing to Dye For: The Textile Sector Must Confront Water Risks," *The Guardian,* accessed March 12, 2015, www.theguardian.com.
48. R. Hosseini, "Recycling Water to Make Your Jeans," (blog) www.levistrauss.com, accessed March 12, 2015.
49. "Nike Moves to Water-Free, Chemical-Free Dyeing," *GreenBiz,* accessed March 12, 2015, www.greenbiz.com.
50. A. Brettman, "6 Questions about Nike's Water-Less Fabric Dyeing Technology," *The Oregonian,* accessed March 12, 2015, www.oregonlive.com.
51. P. Meister, "One Million Yards of Water-Saving DryDye Fabric—and Counting!" *Adidas Group* blog, accessed March 12, 2015, http://blog.adidas-group.com.
52. Company website, "Nike, Inc., Unveils ColorDry Technology and High-Tech Facility to Eliminate Water and Chemicals in Dyeing," http://news.nike.com, accessed March 12, 2015.

Chapter 5

1. "Samsung Electronics Appoints New Executive Leadership in Major Organizational Realignment," January 12, 2010. http://www.samsung.com/us/news/newsRead.do?news_seq=16596&page=1. Accessed Oct. 22, 2011.
2. "Samsung Electronics Names New CEO," Reuters, Monday December 19, 2009, http://www.reuters.com/article/2009/12/15/us-samsungelec-ceo-idUSTRE5BE05T20091215. Accessed Oct. 23, 2011.
3. Sea-Jin Chang, *Sony versus Samsung* (John Wiley and Sons, 2008), p. 128.
4. "Samsung and Its Attractions," *The Economist,* October 1, 2011. From the Print Edition. http://www.economist.com/node/21530984. Accessed Oct. 22, 2011.
5. "Samsung, the Next Big Bet," *The Economist,* October 1, 2011. From the Print Edition. http://www.economist.com/node/21530976. Accessed Oct. 22, 2011.
6. https://news.samsung.com/global/fast-facts. Accessed January 19, 2018.
7. https://news.samsung.com/global/samsung-electronics-rises-to-no-6-in-interbrands-best-global-brands-2017. Accessed Jan 19, 2018.
8. P.R. Lawrence and J.W. Lorsch, *Organization and Environment* (Boston: Graduate School of Business Administration, Harvard University, 1967).
9. G.R. Jones, *Organizational Theory: Text and Cases* (Reading, MA: Addison-Wesley, 1995).
10. J. Child, *Organization: A Guide for Managers and Administrators* (New York: Harper and Row, 1977).
11. F.W. Taylor, *The Principles of Scientific Management* (New York: Harper, 1911).
12. R.W. Griffin, *Task Design: An Integrative Approach* (Glenview, IL: Scott, Foresman, 1982).
13. Ibid.
14. J.R. Hackman and G.R. Oldham, *Work Redesign* (Reading, MA: Addison-Wesley, 1980).
15. J.R. Galbraith and R.K. Kazanjian, *Strategy Implementation: Structure, System, and Process,* 2nd ed. (St. Paul, MN: West, 1986).
16. P.R. Lawrence and J.W. Lorsch, *Organization and Environment* (Boston: Graduate School of Business Administration, Harvard University, 1967).
17. G.R. Jones, *Organizational Theory: Text and Cases* (Reading, MA: Addison-Wesley, 1995).
18. P.R. Lawrence and J.W. Lorsch, *Organization and Environment* (Boston: Graduate School of Business Administration, Harvard University, 1967).
19. R.H. Hall, *Organizations: Structure and Process* (Englewood Cliffs, NJ: Prentice-Hall, 1972); and R. Miles, *Macro Organizational Behaviour* (Santa Monica, CA: Goodyear, 1980).
20. A.D. Chandler, *Strategy and Structure* (Cambridge, MA: MIT Press, 1962).
21. G.R. Jones and C.W.L. Hill, "Transaction Cost Analysis of Strategy–Structure Choice," *Strategic Management Journal* 9 (1988), 159–172.
22. Kaya Morgan, "FRED SMITH—Federal Express Renegade." Website: www.islandconnections.com/edit/smith.htm. Accessed July 15, 2008.
23. http://www.arcticco-op.com/
24. Ibid. Accessed March 24, 2015.
25. S.M. Davis and P.R. Lawrence, *Matrix* (Reading, MA: Addison-Wesley, 1977); and J.R. Galbraith, "Matrix Organization Designs: How to Combine Functional and Project Forms," *Business Horizons* 14 (1971), 29–40.
26. L.R. Burns, "Matrix Management in Hospitals: Testing Theories of Matrix Structure and Development," *Administrative Science Quarterly* 34 (1989), 349–368.
27. C.W.L. Hill, *International Business* (Homewood, IL: Irwin, 1997).
28. G.R. Jones, *Organizational Theory: Text and Cases* (Reading, MA: Addison-Wesley, 1995).
29. G.S. Capowski, "Designing a Corporate Identity," *Management Review,* June 1993, 37–38.
30. J. Marcia, "Just Doing It," *Distribution,* January 1995, 36–40.
31. Anthony Grnak, John Hughes, and Douglas Hunter, *Building the Best, Lessons from Inside Canada's Best Managed Companies* (Toronto: Viking Canada, 2006), p. 154.
32. P. Blau, "A Formal Theory of Differentiation in Organizations," *American Sociological Review,* 35, 1970, pp. 684–695.
33. http://corporate.mcdonalds.com/mcd/our_company/leadership.html. Accessed January 19, 2018.
34. J. Child, *Organization: A Guide for Managers and Administrators* (New York: Harper and Row, 1977).
35. Information about Ducks Unlimited from "Salute! Celebrating the Progressive Employer," advertising supplement, Benefits Canada, March 1999, p. Insert 1–23; and www.ducksunlimited.ca.
36. Ibid.
37. P.M. Blau and R.A. Schoenherr, *The Structure of Organizations* (New York: Basic Books, 1971).
38. G.R. Jones, *Organizational Theory: Text and Cases* (Reading, MA: Addison-Wesley, 1995).
39. Marina Strauss, "Leadership Secrets of the Invisible Man," *The Globe and Mail Report on Business,* May 2011, pp. 56–62.

40. Lawrence and Lorsch, *Organization and Environment,* 50–55; www.dell.com, 2012.
41. J.R. Galbraith, *Designing Complex Organizations* (Reading, MA: Addison-Wesley, 1977), chap. 1; Galbraith and Kazanjian, *Strategy Implementation,* chap. 7.
42. Lawrence and Lorsch, *Organization and Environment,* 55.
43. T. Burns and G.M. Stalker, *The Management of Innovation* (London: Tavistock, 1961).
44. L.A. Perlow, G.A. Okhuysen, and N.P. Repenning, "The Speed Trap: Exploring the Relationship between Decision Making and Temporal Context," *Academy of Management Journal* 45 (2002), 931–955.
45. P.R. Lawrence and J.W. Lorsch, *Organization and Environment* (Boston: Graduate School of Business Administration, Harvard University, 1967).
46. R. Duncan, "What Is the Right Organizational Design?" *Organizational Dynamics,* Winter 1979, pp. 59–80.
47. T. Burns and G.R. Stalker, *The Management of Innovation* (London: Tavistock, 1966).
48. Scott Peterson, "Good Leaders Empower People," *National Post,* Wednesday, May 18, 2005, p. FP9.
49. D. Miller, "Strategy Making and Structure: Analysis and Implications for Performance," *Academy of Management Journal,* 30, 1987, pp. 7–32.
50. A.D. Chandler, *Strategy and Structure* (Cambridge, MA: MIT Press, 1962).
51. J. Stopford and L. Wells, *Managing the Multinational Enterprise* (London: Longman, 1972).
52. J. Woodward, *Management and Technology* (London: Her Majesty's Stationery Office, 1958).
53. C. Perrow, *Organizational Analysis: A Sociological View* (Belmont, CA: Wadsworth, 1970).
54. Gareth Jones, *Essentials of Contemporary Management* 2ce, McGraw-Hill Ryerson, 2007.
55. Globe and Mail. http://www.theglobeandmail.com/report -on-business/loblaw-closes-deal-to-buy-shoppers-drug -mart/article17723887/. Accessed March 25, 2015.

Chapter 6

1. http://www.cbc.ca/news/technology/amazon-go-grocery -store-1.4497862?cmp=rss. Accessed January 23, 2018.
2. https://www.bnn.ca/amazon-opens-first-automated-grocery -store-in-seattle-1.974750. Accessed January 23, 2018.
3. http://www.cbc.ca/news/business/walmart-scan-and-go -app-self-checkout-1.4364434. Accessed Jan 23, 2018.
4. Ibid.
5. C.A. O'Reilly and L.R. Pondy, "Organizational Communication," in S. Kerr (ed.), *Organizational Behavior* (Columbus, OH: Grid, 1979).
6. E.M. Rogers and R. Agarwala-Rogers, *Communication in Organizations* (New York: Free Press, 1976).
7. Deena Waisberg, "Dress Code Still in Force Though It's Stinking Hot," *National Post,* Saturday, August 6, 2005, FW3.
8. Kamal Fatehi, *International Management* (Upper Saddle River, NJ: Prentice Hall, 1996).
9. D.A. Adams, P.A. Todd, and R.R. Nelson, "A Comparative Evaluation of the Impact of Electronic and Voice Mail on Organizational Communication," *Information & Management,* 24, 1993, pp. 9–21.
10. "On the Road," *Newsweek,* June 6, 1994, p. 8.
11. Based on S.P. Robbins and P.L. Hunsaker, *Training in Interpersonal Skills: TIPS for Managing People at Work,* 2nd ed. (Upper Saddle River, NJ: Prentice-Hall, 1996), ch. 3.
12. R.L. Daft, R.H. Lengel, and L.K. Trevino, "Message Equivocality, Media Selection, and Manager Performance: Implications for Information Systems," *MIS Quarterly* 11 (1987), 355–366; R.L. Daft and R.H. Lengel, "Information Richness: A New Approach to Managerial Behavior and Organization Design," in B.M. Staw and

L.L. Cummings (eds.), *Research in Organizational Behavior*(Greenwich, CT: JAI Press, 1984).
13. R.L. Daft, *Organization Theory and Design* (St. Paul, MN: West, 1992).
14. Ibid.
15. T.J. Peters and R.H. Waterman Jr., *In Search of Excellence* (New York: Harper and Row, 1982); T. Peters and N. Austin, *A Passion for Excellence: The Leadership Difference* (New York: Random House, 1985).
16. "Lights, Camera, Meeting: Teleconferencing Becomes a Time-Saving Tool," *The Wall Street Journal,* February 21, 1995, p. A1.
17. "E-Mail Abuse: Workers Discover High-Tech Ways to Cause Trouble in the Office," *The Wall Street Journal,* November 22, 1994, p. A1; and "E-Mail Alert: Companies Lag in Devising Policies on How It Should Be Used," *The Wall Street Journal,* December 29, 1994, p. A1.
18. J. Kay, "Someone Will Watch Over Me: Think Your Office E-Mails Are Private? Think Again," *National Post Business,* January 2001, pp. 59–64.
19. www.ibm.com, 2001.
20. Turban, *Decision Support and Expert Systems.*
21. B. Power, "Artificial Intelligence Is Almost Ready for Business," *Harvard Business Review,* accessed April 27, 2015, https://hbr.org.
22. https://magazine.marsdd.com/. *The Future of Artificial Intelligence.* Accessed February 28, 2018.
23. https://magazine.marsdd.com/26-, things-you-need-to -know-about-ai-766337a47371. Accessed February 28, 2018.
24. https://magazine.marsdd.com/26-things-you-need-to -know-about-ai-766337a47371. Accessed February 28, 2018.
25. F. Burnson, "Compare Enterprise Resource Planning (ERP) Software," *Software Advice,* accessed April 28, 2015, www.softwareadvice.com.
26. https://magazine.marsdd.com/26-things-you-need-to-know -about-ai-766337a47371. Accessed February 28, 2018.
27. Frost & Sullivan, Future of Artificial Intelligence, April 2016, cited in https://magazine.marsdd.com/26-things -you-need-to-know-about-ai-766337a47371. Accessed February 28, 2018.
28. G.R. Jones and J.M. George, *Essentials of Contemporary Management,* 4th ed. (New York: McGraw-Hill Irwin, 2011).
29. https://hootsuite.com/about?icn=footernav&ici=About+Us. Accessed April 13, 2015.
30. http://signup.hootsuite.com/pro-ent-na-english-r10 /?utm_source=bing&utm_medium=cpc&utm_campaign =selfserve-bau-na-en--ca-pua-bing_search_branded _alpha-&utm_term=hootsuite?msclkid =ed4717688bb117a565774ded514c7025. Accessed February 15, 2018.
31. http://marketingland.com/report-sprout-social-hootsuite -tweetdeck-are-top-ranked-social-management-tools -121698. Accessed April 13, 2015.

Chapter 7

1. http://fortune.com/best-companies/four-seasons-hotels -91/. Accessed February 15, 2018.
2. "Four Seasons Employees Name Company to *Fortune* '100 Best Companies to Work For' List," www .fourseasons.com/about_us/press_release_280.html, February 22, 2008.
3. Ibid.
4. Ibid.
5. Ibid; "Creating the Four Seasons Difference," www.businessweek.com/print/innovate/content /jan2008/id20080122_671354.htm, February 22, 2008.
6. J.M. O'Brien, "100 Best Companies to Work For—A Perfect Season," *Fortune,* February 4, 2008, 64–66; "Creating the Four Seasons Difference."

7. Ibid.; "Four Seasons Employees Name Company to *Fortune* '100 Best Companies to Work For' List."
8. O'Brien, "100 Best Companies to Work For—A Perfect Season."
9. "Creating the Four Seasons Difference."
10. O'Brien, "100 Best Companies to Work For—A Perfect Season."
11. Ibid.
12. Ibid.
13. Ibid.
14. http://fortune.com/best-companies/four-seasons-hotels -resorts/. Accessed February 15, 2018.
15. Ibid.; "Creating the Four Seasons Difference"; "Four Seasons Employees Name Company to *Fortune* '100 Best Companies to Work For' List."
16. C.D. Fisher, L.F. Schoenfeldt, and J.B. Shaw, *Human Resource Management* (Boston: Houghton Mifflin, 1990).
17. P.M. Wright and G.C. McMahan, "Theoretical Perspectives for Strategic Human Resource Management," *Journal of Management* 18 (1992), 295–320.
18. L. Baird and I. Meshoulam, "Managing Two Fits for Strategic Human Resource Management," *Academy of Management Review* 14 (1989), 116–128; J. Milliman, M. Von Glinow, and M. Nathan, "Organizational Life Cycles and Strategic International Human Resource Management in Multinational Companies: Implications for Congruence Theory," *Academy of Management Review* 16 (1991), 318–339; R.S. Schuler and S.E. Jackson, "Linking Competitive Strategies with Human Resource Management Practices," *Academy of Management Executive* 1 (1987), 207–219; P.M. Wright and S.A. Snell, "Toward an Integrative View of Strategic Human Resource Management," *Human Resource Management Review* 1 (1991), 203–225.
19. Website: www.fedpubs.com/subject/legis/clc.htm. Accessed Aug. 31, 2009.
20. Website: www.hc-sc.gc.ca/ewh-semt/occup-travail /whmis-simdut/index-eng.php. Accessed Aug. 31, 2009.
21. See the various provincial and territorial documents.
22. Website: www.ccohs.ca/. Accessed Aug. 31, 2009.
23. For example, Website: www.gov.pe.ca/law/statutes /pdf/o-01_01.pdf. Accessed Aug. 31, 2009.
24. http://fortune.com/best-companies/four-seasons-hotels -resorts/. Accessed February 15, 2018.
25. http://www.statcan.gc.ca/daily-quotidien/100309 /dq100309a-eng.htm. Accessed Jan. 29, 2015.
26. Colin Perkel, "Highly Educated Immigrants Still Lag in Earnings," *Toronto Star,* May 1, 2008. www.thestar.com /Canada/Census/article/420336. Accessed May 18, 2008.
27. Calgary Economic Development, "The Changing Profile of Calgary's Workforce Labour Force Profile," *CalgaryWorks,* June 2006, p. 32. Website: www. calgaryeconomicdevelopment.com/files/CED%20 reports/LabourForce_SP04.pdf. Accessed May 18, 2008; see also Derek Sankey, "The Many Faces of Diversity," *National Post,* FP WORKING, Wednesday, April 9, 2009, WK3.
28. J.E. Butler, G.R. Ferris, and N.K. Napier, *Strategy and Human Resource Management* (Cincinnati, OH: South Western, 1991); P.M. Wright and G.C. McMahan, "Theoretical Perspectives for Strategic Human Resource Management," *Journal of Management* 18 (1992), 295–320.
29. E. Porter, "Send Jobs to India? U.S. Companies Say It's Not Always Best," *The New York Times,* April 28, 2004, A1, A7.
30. D. Wessel, "The Future of Jobs: New Ones Arise; Wage Gap Widens," *The Wall Street Journal,* April 2, 2004, A1, A5; "Relocating the Back Office," *The Economist,* December 13, 2003, 67–69.
31. Porter, "Send Jobs to India?"
32. Ibid.
33. "Learning to Live with Offshoring," *BusinessWeek,* January 30, 2006, 122.
34. M. Lewis, "BCE Appoints Alcan Recruit 'Chief Talent Officer,'" *Financial Post (National Post),* May 24, 2001, p. C11.
35. E.L. Levine, *Everything You Always Wanted to Know About Job Analysis: A Job Analysis Primer* (Tampa, FL: Mariner, 1983).
36. R.L. Mathis and J.H. Jackson, *Human Resource Management,* 7th ed. (St. Paul, MN: West, 1994).
37. S.L. Rynes, "Recruitment, Job Choice, and Post-Hire Consequences: A Call for New Research Directions," in M.D. Dunnette and L.M. Hough (eds.), *Handbook of Industrial and Organizational Psychology,* vol. 2 (Palo Alto, CA: Consulting Psychologists Press, 1991), pp. 399–444.
38. R. Sharpe, "The Life of the Party? Can Jeff Taylor Keep the Good Times Rolling at Monster.com?" *BusinessWeek,* June 4, 2001 (*BusinessWeek* Archives); D.H. Freedman, "The Monster Dilemma," *Inc.* Magazine, May 2007, 77–78; P. Korkki, "So Easy to Apply, So Hard to Be Noticed," *The New York Times,* July 1, 2007, BU16.
39. www.monster.com, June 2001.
40. www.jobline.org, Jobline press releases, May 8, 2001. Accessed June 20, 2001.
41. Stephanie Rosenbloom, "Savvy Job Hunters Work the Web," *National Post,* FP WORKING, Wednesday, May 7, 2008, WK2.
42. R.M. Guion, "Personnel Assessment, Selection, and Placement," in M.D. Dunnette and L.M. Hough (eds.), *Handbook of Industrial and Organizational Psychology,* vol. 2 (Palo Alto, CA: Consulting Psychologists Press, 1991), pp. 327–397.
43. T. Joyner, "Job Background Checks Surge," *Houston Chronicle,* May 2, 2005, D6.
44. Ibid.; "ADP News Releases: Employer Services: ADP Hiring Index Reveals Background Checks Performed More Than Tripled Since 1997," Automatic Data Processing, Inc., June 3, 2006, www.investquest.com /iq/a/aud/ne/news/adp042505background.htm.
45. http://corporate.mcdonalds.com/mcd/our_company /leadership.html. Accessed January 19, 2018.
46. R.A. Noe, J.R. Hollenbeck, B. Gerhart, and P.M. Wright, *Human Resource Management: Gaining a Competitive Advantage* (Burr Ridge, IL: Irwin, 1994).
47. J. Flint, "Can You Tell Applesauce from Pickles?" *Forbes,* October 9, 1995, 106–8.
48. Tavia Grant, "Colour Them Controversial," *The Globe and Mail,* Wednesday, May 21, 2008, C1, 4. See also Caitlin Crawshaw, "Questionnaires Test Job Seeker's Patience," *National Post,* Wednesday, May 14, 2008, FP15.
49. J. Flint, "Can You Tell Applesauce from Pickles?"
50. "Wanted: Middle Managers, Audition Required," *The Wall Street Journal,* December 28, 1995, p. A1.
51. Murad Hemmadi, "The End of Bad Hiring Decisions," *Canadian Business,* January 2015, p. 12.
52. I.L. Goldstein, "Training in Work Organizations," in M.D. Dunnette and L.M. Hough (eds.), *Handbook of Industrial and Organizational Psychology,* vol. 2 (Palo Alto, CA: Consulting Psychologists Press, 1991), pp. 507–619.
53. T.D. Allen, L.T. Eby, M.L. Poteet, E. Lentz, and L. Lima, "Career Benefits Associated with Mentoring for Protégés: A Meta-Analysis," *Journal of Applied Psychology* 89, no. 1 (2004), 127–36.
54. P. Garfinkel, "Putting a Formal Stamp on Mentoring," *The New York Times,* January 18, 2004, BU10.
55. Ibid.
56. Allen et al., "Career Benefits Associated with Mentoring"; L. Levin, "Lesson Learned: Know Your Limits; Get Outside Help Sooner Rather Than Later," *BusinessWeek Online,* July 5, 2004, www.businessweek.com; "Family, Inc.,"

BusinessWeek Online, November 10, 2003, www
.businessweek.com; J. Salamon, "A Year with a Mentor;
Now Comes the Test," *The New York Times,* September
30, 2003, B1, B5; E. White, "Making Mentorships Work,"
The Wall Street Journal, October 23, 2007, B11.

57. Garfinkel, "Putting a Formal Stamp on Mentoring."

58. A.P. Carnevale and S.C. Stone, "Diversity: Beyond the
Golden Rule," *Training & Development,* October 1994,
pp. 22–39.

59. "Selling Equity," *Financial Post Magazine,* September
1994, pp. 20–25.

60. C.D. Fisher, L.F. Schoenfeldt, and J.B. Shaw, *Human
Resource Management* (Boston: Houghton Mifflin, 1990).

61. Fisher et al., *Human Resource Management;* G.P.
Latham and K.N. Wexley, *Increasing Productivity through
Performance Appraisal* (Reading, MA: Addison-Wesley,
1982).

62. M.A. Peiperl, "Getting 360 Degree Feedback Right,"
Harvard Business Review, January 2001, 142–47.

63. A. Harrington, "Workers of the World, Rate Your
Boss!" *Fortune,* September 18, 2000, 340, 342; www
.ImproveNow.com, June 2001.

64. J. Flynn and F. Nayeri, "Continental Divide over Executive
Pay," *BusinessWeek,* July 3, 1995, 40–41

65. J.A. Byrne, "How High Can CEO Pay Go?" *BusinessWeek,*
April 22, 1996, 100–106.

66. A. Borrus, "A Battle Royal against Regal Paychecks,"
BusinessWeek, February 24, 2003, 127; "Too Many
Turkeys," *The Economist,* November 26, 2005, 75–76; G.
Morgenson, "How to Slow Runaway Executive Pay," *The
New York Times,* October 23, 2005, 1, 4; S. Greenhouse,
The Big Squeeze: Tough Times for the American Worker
(New York: Alfred A. Knopf, 2008); "Trends in CEO Pay,"
AFL-CIO, http://www.aflcio.org/Corporate-Watch/CEO-
Pay-and-the-99/ Trends-in-CEO-Pay, April 26, 2012.

67. https://www.policyalternatives.ca/newsroom/news-
releases/record-breaking-ceo-pay-now-209-times-more-
average-worker. Accessed February 15, 2018.

68. https://www.policyalternatives.ca/publications/monitor
/monitor-januaryfebruary-2018. Accessed February 15,
2018.

69. "Executive Pay," *BusinessWeek,* April 19, 2004, 106–110.

70. "Home Depot Chief's Pay in 2007 Could Reach $8.9m,"
The New York Times, Bloomberg News, January 25,
2007, C7; E. Carr, "The Stockpot," *The Economist, A
Special Report on Executive Pay,* January 20, 2007,
6–10; E. Porter, "More Than Ever, It Pays to Be the Top
Executive," *The New York Times,* May 25, 2007, A1, C7.

71. https://www.canada.ca/en/employment-social-
development/services/collective-bargaining-data/
work-stoppages/work-stoppages-year-sector.html#H2_1.
Accessed February 15, 2018.

72. https://www.canada.ca/en/employment-social-
development/services/collective-bargaining-data/
reports/union-coverage.html. Accessed February 15,
2018.

73. Ishak Saporta, "Managers' and Workers' Attitudes toward
Unions in the U.S. and Canada." *Relations Industrielles/
Industrial Relations.* Website:http://findarticles.com/p
/articles/mi_hb4388/is_n3_v50/ai_n28662583/.
Accessed Aug. 2, 2009.

74. www.servicecanada.gc.ca/eng/cs/fas/as/contracting
/harass_policy.shtml. Accessed July 13, 2009.

75. Ibid.

76. https://canadasafetycouncil.org/working-bully/. Accessed
Sept 21, 2018.

77. "Vic Toews Promises New RCMP Discipline Legislation:
Government Promises to Help RCMP Deal with Problem
Officers," CBC News. http://www.cbc.ca/news/canada
/british-columbia/story/2012/05/29/bc-rcmp-discipline
-law.html. Accessed May 30, 2012.

78. B. Carton, "Muscled Out? At Jenny Craig, Men Are Ones
Who Claim Sex Discrimination," *The Wall Street Journal,*
November 29, 1994, pp. A1, A7.

79. R.L. Paetzold and A.M. O'Leary-Kelly, "Organizational
Communication and the Legal Dimensions of Hostile
Work Environment Sexual Harassment," in G.L. Kreps
(ed.), *Sexual Harassment: Communication Implications*
(Cresskill, NJ: Hampton Press, 1993).

80. M. Galen, J. Weber, and A.Z. Cuneo, "Sexual Harassment:
Out of the Shadows," *Fortune,* October 28, 1991, pp.
30–31.

81. http://www.stopstreetharassment.org/2018/02
/newstudy2018/. Accessed February 18, 2018.

82. A.M. O'Leary-Kelly, R.L. Paetzold, and R.W. Griffin, "Sexual
Harassment as Aggressive Action: A Framework for
Understanding Sexual Harassment," paper presented
at the annual meeting of the Academy of Management,
Vancouver, August 1995.

83. "Employers Underestimate Extent of Sexual Harassment,
Report Says," *The Vancouver Sun,* March 8, 2001, p. D6.

84. Information in this paragraph based on Ian Jack, "Magna
Suit Spotlights Auto Industry Practices," *The Financial
Post Daily,* September 10, 1997, p. 1.

85. S.J. Bresler and R. Thacker, "Four-Point Plan Helps Solve
Harassment Problems," *HR Magazine,* May 1993,
pp. 117–124.

86. http://fortune.com/best-companies/four-seasons-
hotels-91/. Accessed Jan. 29, 2015.

87. Lee-Anne Goodman, "Unpaid Interns in Canada May
Number as Many as 300,000: Report," The
Canadian Press, posted May 20, 2014; http://www
.huffingtonpost.ca/2014/05/20/unpaid-interns-canada
-female_n_5360177.html. Accessed Sept. 17, 2015.

88. Lee-Anne Goodman, "Unpaid Internships Backlash
Growing in Canada," The Canadian Press, March 2,
2014; http://www.huffingtonpost.ca/2014/03/02/unpaid
-internships-canada_n_4885626.html. Accessed Sept.
17, 2015.

89. Daniel Tencer, "Bank of Canada's Stephen Poloz:
Long-Term Jobless Youth Should Work for Free,"
Huffington Post Canada, November 4, 2014; http://www
.huffingtonpost.ca/2014/11/04/stephen-poloz-youth-work
-for-free_n_6101144.html. Accessed Sept. 17, 2015.

90. Marjo Johne, "The Ins and Outs of Internships," *The
Globe and Mail,* Tuesday, Dec. 14, 2010; http://www
.theglobeandmail.com/report-on-business/careers
/career-advice/the-ins-and-outs-of-internships
/article1319780/. Accessed Sept. 17, 2015.

Chapter 8

1. R. Kanfer, "Motivation Theory and Industrial and
Organizational Psychology," in M.D. Dunnette and L.M.
Hough (eds.), *Handbook of Industrial and Organizational
Psychology,* 2nd ed., vol. 1 (Palo Alto, CA: Consulting
Psychologists Press, 1990), pp. 75–170.

2. N. Nicholson, "How to Motivate Your Problem People,"
Harvard Business Review, January 2003, 57–65.

3. A.M. Grant, "Does Intrinsic Motivation Fuel the Prosocial
Fire? Motivational Synergy in Predicting Persistence,
Performance, and Productivity," *Journal of Applied
Psychology* 93, no. 1 (2008), 48–58.

4. Ibid.; C.D. Batson, "Prosocial Motivation: Is It Ever Truly
Altruistic?" in L. Berkowitz, ed., *Advances in Experimental
Social Psychology,* vol. 20 (New York: Academic Press,
1987), 65–122.

5. Antony Bugg-Levine and Jed Emerson, *Impacting
Investing, Transforming How We Make Money While
Making a Difference* (San Francisco: Jossey-Bass, 2011),
p. xii.

6. Grant, "Does Intrinsic Motivation Fuel the Prosocial Fire?"

7. A.H. Maslow, *Motivation and Personality* (New York: Harper and Row, 1954); and J.P. Campbell and R.D. Pritchard, "Motivation Theory in Industrial and Organizational Psychology," in M.D. Dunnette (ed.), *Handbook of Industrial and Organizational Psychology*(Chicago: Rand McNally, 1976), pp. 63–130.

8. R. Kanfer, "Motivation Theory and Industrial and Organizational Psychology," in M.D. Dunnette and L.M. Hough (eds.), *Handbook of Industrial and Organizational Psychology,* 2nd ed., vol. 1 (Palo Alto, CA: Consulting Psychologists Press, 1990), pp. 75–170.

9. S. Ronen, "An Underlying Structure of Motivational Need Taxonomies: A Cross-Cultural Confirmation," in H.C. Triandis, M.D. Dunnette, and L.M. Hough (eds.), *Handbook of Industrial and Organizational Psychology,* vol. 4 (Palo Alto, CA: Consulting Psychologists Press, 1994), pp. 241–269.

10. N.J. Adler, *International Dimensions of Organizational Behavior,* 2nd ed. (Boston: P.W.S.-Kent, 1991); G. Hofstede, "Motivation, Leadership and Organization: Do American Theories Apply Abroad?" *Organizational Dynamics,* Summer 1980, pp. 42–63.

11. F. Herzberg, *Work and the Nature of Man* (Cleveland: World, 1966).

12. N. King, "Clarification and Evaluation of the Two-Factor Theory of Job Satisfaction," *Psychological Bulletin,* 74, 1970, pp. 18–31; and E.A. Locke, "The Nature and Causes of Job Satisfaction," in M.D. Dunnette (ed.), *Handbook of Industrial and Organizational Psychology* (Chicago: Rand McNally, 1976), pp. 1297–1349.

13. D.C. McClelland, *Human Motivation* (Glenview, IL: Scott, Foresman, 1985); D.C. McClelland, "How Motives, Skills, and Values Determine What People Do," *American Psychologist* 40 (1985), 812–25; D.C. McClelland, "Managing Motivation to Expand Human Freedom," *American Psychologist* 33 (1978), 201–10.

14. D.G. Winter, *The Power Motive* (New York: Free Press, 1973).

15. M.J. Stahl, "Achievement, Power, and Managerial Motivation: Selecting Managerial Talent with the Job Choice Exercise," *Personnel Psychology* 36 (1983), 775–89; D.C. McClelland and D.H. Burnham, "Power Is the Great Motivator," *Harvard Business Review* 54 (1976), 100–10.

16. R.J. House, W.D. Spangler, and J. Woycke, "Personality and Charisma in the U.S. Presidency: A Psychological Theory of Leader Effectiveness," *Administrative Science Quarterly* 36 (1991), 364–96.

17. G.H. Hines, "Achievement, Motivation, Occupations, and Labor Turnover in New Zealand," *Journal of Applied Psychology* 58 (1973), 313–17; P.S. Hundal, "A Study of Entrepreneurial Motivation: Comparison of Fast- and Slow-Progressing Small Scale Industrial Entrepreneurs in Punjab, India," *Journal of Applied Psychology* 55 (1971), 317–23.

18. R.A. Clay, "Green Is Good for You," *Monitor on Psychology,* April 2001, pp. 40–42.

19. T.R. Mitchell, "Expectancy-Value Models in Organizational Psychology," in N.T. Feather (ed.), *Expectations and Actions: Expectancy-Value Models in Psychology* (Hillsdale, NJ: Erlbaum, 1982), pp. 293–312; V.H. Vroom, *Work and Motivation* (New York: Wiley, 1964).

20. N. Shope Griffin, "Personalize Your Management Development," *Harvard Business Review* 8, no. 10 (2003), 113–119.

21. Kevin Cox, "Irving Oil Fuels Its Leaders," *The Globe and Mail,* Wednesday, April 21, 2004, C1, 3.

22. T.J. Maurer, E.M. Weiss, and F.G. Barbeite, "A Model of Involvement in Work-Related Learning and Development Activity: The Effects of Individual, Situational, Motivational, and Age Variables," *Journal of Applied Psychology* 88, no. 4 (2003), 707–24.

23. J.S. Adams, "Toward an Understanding of Inequity," *Journal of Abnormal and Social Psychology* 67 (1963), 422–36.

24. J.S. Adams, "Toward an Understanding of Inequity," *Journal of Abnormal and Social Psychology* 67 (1963), 422–436; J. Greenberg, "Approaching Equity and Avoiding Inequity in Groups and Organizations," in J. Greenberg and R.L. Cohen (eds.), *Equity and Justice in Social Behavior* (New York: Academic Press, 1982), pp. 389–435; J. Greenberg, "Equity and Workplace Status: A Field Experiment," *Journal of Applied Psychology* 73 (1988), 606–613; and R.T. Mowday, "Equity Theory Predictions of Behavior in Organizations," in R.M. Steers and L.W. Porter, (eds.), *Motivation and Work Behavior* (New York: McGraw-Hill, 1987), pp. 89–110.

25. E.A. Locke and G.P. Latham, *A Theory of Goal Setting and Task Performance* (Englewood Cliffs, NJ: Prentice-Hall, 1990).

26. Locke and Latham, *A Theory of Goal Setting and Task Performance;* J.J. Donovan and D.J. Radosevich, "The Moderating Role of Goal Commitment on the Goal Difficulty–Performance Relationship: A Meta-Analytic Review and Critical Analysis," *Journal of Applied Psychology* 83 (1998), 308–315; and M.E. Tubbs, "Goal Setting: A Meta-Analytic Examination of the Empirical Evidence," *Journal of Applied Psychology* 71 (1986), 474–483.

27. P.F. Drucker, *The Practice of Management* (New York: Harper & Row, 1954).

28. S.J. Carroll and H.L. Tosi, *Management by Objectives: Applications and Research* (New York: Macmillan, 1973).

29. R. Rodgers and J. E. Hunter, "Impact of Management by Objectives on Organizational Productivity," *Journal of Applied Psychology*76 (1991), 322–26.

30. M.B. Gavin, S.G. Green, and G.I. Fairhurst, "Managerial Control Strategies for Poor Performance over Time and the Impact on Subordinate Reactions," *Organizational Behavior and Human Decision Processes* 63 (1995), 207–21.

31. W.C. Hamner, "Reinforcement Theory and Contingency Management in Organizational Settings," in H. Tosi and W.C. Hamner, eds., *Organizational Behavior and Management: A Contingency Approach* (Chicago: St. Clair Press, 1974).

32. B.F. Skinner, *Contingencies of Reinforcement* (New York: Appleton-Century-Crofts, 1969).

33. H.W. Weiss, "Learning Theory and Industrial and Organizational Psychology," in Dunnette and Hough, *Handbook of Industrial and Organizational Psychology,* 171–221.

34. Hamner, "Reinforcement Theory and Contingency Management."

35. A. Bandura, *Principles of Behavior Modification* (New York: Holt, Rinehart and Winston, 1969); A. Bandura, *Social Learning Theory* (Englewood Cliffs, NJ: Prentice Hall, 1977); T.R.V. Davis and F. Luthans, "A Social Learning Approach to Organizational Behavior," *Academy of Management Review* 5 (1980), 281–90.

36. A.P. Goldstein and M. Sorcher, *Changing Supervisor Behaviors* (New York: Pergamon Press, 1974); F. Luthans and R. Kreitner, *Organizational Behavior Modification and Beyond* (Glenview, IL: Scott, Foresman, 1985).

37. Bandura, *Social Learning Theory;* Davis and Luthans, "A Social Learning Approach to Organizational Behavior"; Luthans and Kreitner, *Organizational Behavior Modification and Beyond.*

38. A. Bandura, "Self-Reinforcement: Theoretical and Methodological Considerations," *Behaviorism* 4 (1976), 135–55.

39. Hammonds, "Growth Search."

40. B. Elgin, "Managing Google's Idea Factory," *BusinessWeek,* October 3, 2005, 88–90.

41. A. Bandura, *Self-Efficacy: The Exercise of Control* (New York: W.H. Freeman, 1997); J.B. Vancouver, K.M. More, and R.J. Yoder, "Self-Efficacy and Resource Allocation: Support for a Nonmonotonic, Discontinuous Model," *Journal of Applied Psychology* 93, no. 1 (2008), 35–47.

42. A. Bandura, "Self-Efficacy Mechanism in Human Agency," *American Psychologist* 37 (1982), 122–27; M.E. Gist and T.R. Mitchell, "Self-Efficacy: A Theoretical Analysis of Its Determinants and Malleability," *Academy of Management Review* 17 (1992), 183–211.

43. Ibid.

44. "Development Opportunities Top Factor in Reward Fairness: Study," *HR Reporter,* July 25, 2011. http://www.hrreporter.com/articleview?&articleid=10847&headline=development-opportunities-top-factor-in-reward-fairness-study. Accessed Oct. 26, 2011.

45. E.E. Lawler III, *Pay and Organization Development* (Reading, MA: Addison-Wesley, 1981).

46. Based on S.E. Gross and J.P. Bacher, "The New Variable Pay Programs: How Some Succeed, Why Some Don't," *Compensation & Benefits Review,* January–February 1993, p. 51; and J.R. Schuster and P.K. Zingheim, "The New Variable Pay: Key Design Issues," *Compensation & Benefits Review,* March–April 1993, p. 28.

47. Peter Brieger, "Variable Pay Packages Gain Favour: Signing Bonuses, Profit Sharing Taking Place of Salary Hikes," *Financial Post (National Post),* September 13, 2002, p. FP5.

48. E. Beauchesne, "Pay Bonuses Improve Productivity, Study Shows," *The Vancouver Sun,* September 13, 2002, p. D5.

49. "Hope for Higher Pay: The Squeeze on Incomes Is Gradually Easing Up," *Maclean's,* November 25, 1996, pp. 100–101.

50. Source: http://www.greatest-inspirational-quotes.com/inspirational-business-quotes.html

51. Lawler, *Pay and Organization Development.*

52. Ibid.

53. Ibid.

54. "Stock Option," *Encarta World English Dictionary,* June 28, 2001, www.dictionary.msn.com; personal interview with Professor Bala Dharan, Jones Graduate School of Business, Rice University, June 28, 2001.

55. Personal interview with Professor Bala Dharan.

56. Ibid.

57. A.J. Michels, "Dallas Semiconductor," *Fortune,* May 16, 1994, 81.

58. M. Betts, "Big Things Come in Small Buttons," *Computerworld,* August 3, 1992, 30.

59. M. Boslet, "Metal Buttons Toted by Crop Pickers Act as Mini Databases," *The Wall Street Journal,* June 1, 1994, B3.

60. C.D. Fisher, L.F. Schoenfeldt, and J.B. Shaw, *Human Resource Management* (Boston: Houghton Mifflin, 1990); B.E. Graham-Moore and T.L. Ross, *Productivity Gainsharing* (Englewood Cliffs, NJ: Prentice Hall, 1983); A.J. Geare, "Productivity from Scanlon Type Plans," *Academy of Management Review* 1 (1976), 99–108.

61. J. Labate, "Deal Those Workers In," *Fortune,* April 19, 1993, 26.

62. K. Belson, "Japan's Net Generation," *BusinessWeek,* March 19, 2001 (*BusinessWeek* Archives, June 27, 2001).

63. K. Belson, "Taking a Hint from the Upstarts," *BusinessWeek,* March 19, 2001 (*BusinessWeek* Archives, June 27, 2001); "Going for the Gold," *BusinessWeek,* March 19, 2001 (*BusinessWeek* Archives, June 27, 2001); "What the Government Can Do to Promote a Flexible Workforce," *BusinessWeek,* March 19, 2001 (*BusinessWeek* Archives, June 27, 2001).

64. Courtney Shea, "Real Motivation Comes from Within: You Either Want to Succeed or You Don't," *Canadian Business,* Jan. 2015, pp. 19–20. Reprinted by permission of Courtney Shea.

Chapter 9

1. "Red Hat stock up 47% after $34B US takeover by IBM", Thomson Reuters. Posted: Oct 29, 2018. https://www.cbc.ca/news/business/ibm-red-hat-tech-stock-1.4882327?cmp=rss. Accessed Oct 29, 2018.

2. "Great Leaders Are Comfortable with Who They Are," Opensource.com, http://opensource.com/14/3/leadership-tips-red-hat-earn-respect, May 5, 2014.

3. I. Faletski, "Yes, You Can Make Money with Open Source,"*Harvard Business Review,* http://blogs.hbr.org/2013/01/yes-you-can-make-money-with-op/, May 5, 2014.

4. Faletski, "Yes, You Can Make Money with Open Source"; "Red Hat—About Red Hat," www.redhat.com/about/, May 5, 2014; "Red Hat Inc—Form 10-K," EDGAR Online, http://files.shareholders.com/downloads/RHAT/3149726759x0x51193125-14157171/1087423/final.pdf, May 6, 2014.

5. "James Whitehurst: Executive Profile & Biography," *Businessweek,* http://investing.businessweek.com/research/stocks/people/person.asp?personId=1474206&ticker=RHT, May 5, 2014; "Red Hat—Jim Whitehurst," www.redhat.com/about/company/management/bios/management-team-jim-whitehurst-bio, May 5, 2014.

6. "James Whitehurst: Executive Profile & Biography."

7. J. Haden, "What's Your Mission?" *Inc.,* April 12, 2013; "Great Leaders Are Comfortable with Who They Are"; J. Bort, "Red Hat CEO: My Employees and I Cuss at Each Other," *Business Insider,* www.businessinsider.com/red-hat-ceo-cussing-at-employees-2013-9, May 5, 2014.

8. Haden, "What's Your Mission?", "Great Leaders Are Comfortable with Who They Are"; Bort, "Red Hat CEO: My Employees and I Cuss at Each Other"; L.K. Ohnesorge, "Red Hat CEO Jim Whitehurst Doubles as a Cloud Computing Evangelist and Entrepreneur Advisor," http://upstart.bizjournals.com/entrepreneurs/hot-shots/2014/05/04/passion-drives-red-hat-jim-whitehurst.html?page=all, May 5, 2014.

9. Haden, "What's Your Mission?"; "Great Leaders Are Comfortable with Who They Are"; Bort, "Red Hat CEO: My Employees and I Cuss at Each Other."

10. Haden, "What's Your Mission?";" Great Leaders Are Comfortable with Who They Are"; Bort, "Red Hat CEO: My Employees and I Cuss at Each Other"; P. High, "Red Hat CEO Jim Whitehurst Opens Up," *Forbes,* www.forbes.com/sites/peterhigh/2012/12/11/red-hat-ceo-jim-whitehurst-opens-up/, May 5, 2014.

11. "Red Hat CEO Jim Whitehurst to Deliver Keynote Address at the Cloud Factory," www.redhat.com/about/news/press-archive/2014/4/red-hat-ceo-jim-whitehurst-to-deliver-keynote-address-at-the-cloud-factory, May 5, 2014.

12. "Planet Earth's Premiere Enterprise Technology Conference," The Cloud Factory, http://thecloudfactory.io/story/, May 6, 2014.

13. https://theprovince.com/technology/ibm-pursues-amazon-into-cloud-with-33-billion-red-hat-takeover/wcm/dfa54d1c-b9a2-468e-a180-a07e8bd1cf01. Accessed October 29, 2018.

14. G. Yukl, *Leadership in Organizations,* 2nd ed. (New York: Academic Press, 1989); and R.M. Stogdill, *Handbook of Leadership: A Survey of the Literature* (New York: Free Press, 1974).

15. J.P. Kotter, "What Leaders Really Do," *Harvard Business Review,* May–June 1990, pp. 103–111.

16. R.N. Kanungo, "Leadership in Organizations: Looking Ahead to the 21st Century," *Canadian Psychology* 39, no. 1–2 (1998), 77. For more evidence of this consensus, see N. Adler, *International Dimensions of Organizational Behavior,* 3rd ed. (Cincinnati, OH: South Western College Publishing), 1997; R.J. House, "Leadership in the Twenty-First Century," in A. Howard (ed.), *The Changing Nature of Work* (San Francisco: Jossey-Bass), 1995, pp. 411–450;

R.N. Kanungo and M. Mendonca, *Ethical Dimensions of Leadership*(Thousand Oaks, CA: Sage Publications, 1996); and A. Zaleznik, "The Leadership Gap," *Academy of Management Executive* 4, no. 1 (1990), 7–22.

17. H. Mintzberg, *Power In and Around Organizations* (Englewood Cliffs, NJ: Prentice-Hall, 1983); and J. Pfeffer, *Power in Organizations* (Marshfield, MA: Pitman, 1981).

18. R.P. French Jr. and B. Raven, "The Bases of Social Power," in D. Cartwright and A.F. Zander (eds.), *Group Dynamics* (Evanston, IL: Row, Peterson, 1960), pp. 607–623.

19. M. Loeb, "Jack Welch Lets Fly on Budgets, Bonuses, and Buddy Boards," *Fortune,* May 29, 1995, 146.

20. Max Weber, "The Types of Authority and Imperative Coordination," *The Theory of Social and Economic Organization* (NY: Oxford University Press), translated by A.M. Henderson and Talcott Parsons, 1949.

21. B.M. Bass, Bass and Stogdill's *Handbook of Leadership: Theory, Research, and Managerial Applications,* 3rd ed. (New York: Free Press, 1990); R.J. House and M.L. Baetz, "Leadership: Some Empirical Generalizations and New Research Directions," in B.M. Staw and L.L. Cummings (eds.), *Research in Organizational Behavior,* vol. 1 (Greenwich, CT: JAI Press, 1979), pp. 341–423; S.A. Kirpatrick and E.A. Locke, "Leadership: Do Traits Matter?" *Academy of Management Executive* 5, no. 2 (1991), 48–60; G. Yukl, *Leadership in Organizations,* 2nd ed. (New York: Academic Press, 1989); and G. Yukl and D.D. Van Fleet, "Theory and Research on Leadership in Organizations," in M.D. Dunnette and L.M. Hough (eds.), *Handbook of Industrial and Organizational Psychology,* 2nd ed., vol. 3 (Palo Alto, CA: Consulting Psychologists Press, 1992), pp. 147–197.

22. E.A. Fleishman, "Performance Assessment Based on an Empirically Derived Task Taxonomy," *Human Factors* 9 (1967), 349–366; E.A. Fleishman, "The Description of Supervisory Behavior," *Personnel Psychology* 37 (1953), 1–6; A.W. Halpin and B.J. Winer, "A Factorial Study of the Leader Behavior Descriptions," in R.M. Stogdill and A.I. Coons (eds.), *Leader Behavior: Its Description and Measurement* (Columbus Bureau of Business Research, Ohio State University, 1957); and D. Tscheulin, "Leader Behavior Measurement in German Industry," *Journal of Applied Psychology* 56 (1971), 28–31.

23. R. Likert, *New Patterns of Management* (New York: McGraw-Hill, 1961); and N.C. Morse and E. Reimer, "The Experimental Change of a Major Organizational Variable," *Journal of Abnormal and Social Psychology* 52 (1956), 120–129.

24. David Sirota, Louis A. Mischkind, and Michael Irwin Meltzer, "Nothing Beats an Enthusiastic Employee," *The Globe and Mail,*Friday, July 29, 2005, C1.

25. E.A. Fleishman and E.F. Harris, "Patterns of Leadership Behavior Related to Employee Grievances and Turnover," *Personnel Psychology* 15 (1962), 43–56.

26. F.E. Fiedler, *A Theory of Leadership Effectiveness* (New York: McGraw-Hill, 1967); and F.E. Fiedler, "The Contingency Model and the Dynamics of the Leadership Process," in L. Berkowitz (ed.), *Advances in Experimental Social Psychology* (New York: Academic Press, 1978).

27. R.J. House and M.L. Baetz, "Leadership: Some Empirical Generalizations and New Research Directions," in B.M. Staw and L.L. Cummings (eds.), *Research in Organizational Behavior,* vol. 1 (Greenwich, CT: JAI Press, 1979), pp. 341–423; L.H. Peters, D.D. Hartke, and J.T. Pohlmann, "Fiedler's Contingency Theory of Leadership: An Application of the Meta-Analysis Procedures of Schmidt and Hunter," *Psychological Bulletin* 97 (1985), 274–285; and C.A. Schriesheim, B.J. Tepper, and L.A. Tetrault, "Least Preferred Co-Worker Score, Situational Control, and Leadership Effectiveness: A Meta-Analysis

of Contingency Model Performance Predictions," *Journal of Applied Psychology* 79 (1994), 561–573.

28. P. Hersey and K.H. Blanchard, "So You Want to Know Your Leadership Style?" *Training and Development Journal,* February 1974, pp. 1–15; and P. Hersey and K.H. Blanchard, *Management of Organizational Behavior: Utilizing Human Resources,* 6th ed. (Englewood Cliffs, NJ: Prentice-Hall, 1993).

29. Cited in C.F. Fernandez and R.P. Vecchio, "Situational Leadership Theory Revisited: A Test of an Across-Jobs Perspective," *Leadership Quarterly* 8, no.1 (1997), 67.

30. M.G. Evans, "The Effects of Supervisory Behavior on the Path–Goal Relationship," *Organizational Behavior and Human Performance* 5 (1970), 277–298; M.G. Evans, "Leadership and Motivation: A Core Concept," *Academy of Management Journal* 13 (1970), 91–102; R.J. House, "A Path–Goal Theory of Leader Effectiveness," *Administrative Science Quarterly,* September 1971, pp. 321–338; R.J. House and T.R. Mitchell, "Path–Goal Theory of Leadership," *Journal of Contemporary Business,* Autumn 1974, p. 86; M.G. Evans, "Leadership," in S. Kerr (ed.), *Organizational Behavior* (Columbus, OH: Grid Publishing, 1979); R.J. House, "Retrospective Comment," in L.E. Boone and D.D. Bowen (eds.), *The Great Writings in Management and Organizational Behavior,*2nd ed. (New York: Random House, 1987), pp. 354–364; M.G. Evans, "Fuhrungstheorien, Wegzieltheorie" (trans. G. Reber), in A. Kieser, G. Reber, and R. Wunderer (eds). *Handworterbuch Der Fuhrung,* 2nd ed. (Stuttgart, Germany: Schaffer Poeschal Verlag, 1995), pp. 1075–1091; and J.C. Wofford and L.Z. Liska, "Path–Goal Theories of Leadership: A Meta-Analysis," *Journal of Management* 19 (1993), 857–876.

31. R. McQueen, "The Long Shadow of Tom Stephens: He Branded MacBlo's Crew as Losers, Then Made Them into Winners," *Financial Post (National Post),* June 22, 1999, pp. C1, C5.

32. S. Kerr and J.M. Jermier, "Substitutes for Leadership: Their Meaning and Measurement," *Organizational Behavior and Human Performance* 22 (1978), 375–403; P.M. Podsakoff, B.P. Niehoff, S.B. MacKenzie, and M.L. Williams, "Do Substitutes for Leadership Really Substitute for Leadership? An Empirical Examination of Kerr and Jermier's Situational Leadership Model," *Organizational Behavior and Human Decision Processes* 54 (1993), 1–44.

33. S. Kerr and J.M. Jermier, "Substitutes for Leadership: Their Meaning and Measurement," *Organizational Behavior and Human Performance* 22 (1978), 375–403; and P.M. Podsakoff, B.P. Niehoff, S.B. MacKenzie, and M.L. Williams, "Do Substitutes for Leadership Really Substitute for Leadership? An Empirical Examination of Kerr and Jermier's Situational Leadership Model," *Organizational Behavior and Human Decision Processes* 54 (1993), 1–44.

34. https://waterstonehc.com/cma/awards/winners/. Accessed March 7, 2018.

35. A. Bryman, "Leadership in Organizations," in S.R. Clegg, C. Hardy, and W.R. Nord (eds.), *Handbook of Organization Studies*(London: Sage Publications, 1996), pp. 276–292.

36. J.M. Howell and B.J. Avolio, "The Leverage of Leadership," in *Leadership: Achieving Exceptional Performance,* supplement prepared by the Richard Ivey School of Business, *The Globe and Mail,* May 15, 1998, pp. C1, C2.

37. Ibid.

38. B.M. Bass, *Leadership and Performance Beyond Expectations* (New York: Free Press, 1985); B.M. Bass, Bass and Stogdill's *Handbook of Leadership: Theory, Research, and Managerial Applications,* 3rd ed. (New York:

Free Press, 1990); and G. Yukl and D.D. Van Fleet, "Theory and Research on Leadership in Organizations," in M.D. Dunnette and L.M. Hough (eds.), *Handbook of Industrial and Organizational Psychology,* 2nd ed., vol. 3 (Palo Alto, CA: Consulting Psychologists Press, 1992), pp. 147–97.

39. B.M. Bass, *Leadership and Performance Beyond Expectations* (New York: Free Press, 1985); B.M. Bass, Bass and Stogdill's *Handbook of Leadership: Theory, Research, and Managerial Applications,* 3rd ed. (New York: Free Press, 1990); and G. Yukl and D.D. Van Fleet, "Theory and Research on Leadership in Organizations," in M.D. Dunnette and L.M. Hough (eds.), *Handbook of Industrial and Organizational Psychology,* 2nd ed., vol. 3 (Palo Alto, CA: Consulting Psychologists Press, 1992), pp. 147–197.

40. Anthony Grnak, John Hughes, and Douglas Hunter, *op.cit.,* p. 195.

41. *Op cit.,* note 75.

42. Cited in B.M. Bass and B.J. Avolio, "Developing Transformational Leadership: 1992 and Beyond," *Journal of European Industrial Training,* January 1990, p. 23.

43. J.M. Howell and B.J. Avolio, "The Leverage of Leadership," in *Leadership: Achieving Exceptional Performance,* supplement prepared by the Richard Ivey School of Business, *The Globe and Mail,* May 15, 1998, p. C2.

44. B.M. Bass, Bass and Stogdill's *Handbook of Leadership;* B.M. Bass and B.J. Avolio, "Transformational Leadership: A Response to Critiques," in M.M. Chemers and R. Ayman (eds.), *Leadership Theory and Research: Perspectives and Directions* (San Diego: Academic Press, 1993), pp. 49–80; B.M. Bass, B.J. Avolio, and L. Goodheim, "Biography and the Assessment of Transformational Leadership at the World Class Level," *Journal of Management* 13 (1987), 7–20; J.J. Hater and B.M. Bass, "Supervisors' Evaluations and Subordinates' Perceptions of Transformational and Transactional Leadership," *Journal of Applied Psychology* 73 (1988), 695–702; R. Pillai, "Crisis and Emergence of Charismatic Leadership in Groups: An Experimental Investigation," *Journal of Applied Psychology* 26 (1996), 543–562; J. Seltzer and B.M. Bass, "Transformational Leadership: Beyond Initiation and Consideration," *Journal of Management* 16 (1990), 693–703; and D.A. Waldman, B.M. Bass, and W.O. Einstein, "Effort, Performance, Transformational Leadership in Industrial and Military Service," *Journal of Occupation Psychology* 60 (1987), 1–10.

45. R. Pillai, C.A. Schriesheim, and E.S. Williams, "Fairness Perceptions and Trust as Mediators of Transformational and Transactional Leadership: A Two-Sample Study," *Journal of Management* 25 (1999), 897–933.

46. J.A. Conger and R.N. Kanungo, "Behavioral Dimensions of Charismatic Leadership," in J.A. Conger, R.N. Kanungo, and Associates, *Charismatic Leadership* (San Francisco: Jossey-Bass, 1988).

47. J.A. Conger and R.N. Kanungo, *Charismatic Leadership in Organizations* (Thousand Oaks, CA: Sage, 1998).

48. "Building a Better Boss," *Maclean's,* September 30, 1996, p. 41.

49. T. Dvir, D. Eden, B.J. Avolio, and B. Shamir, "Impact of Transformational Leadership on Follower Development and Performance: A Field Experiment," *Academy of Management Journal* 45, no. 4 (2002), 735–744; R.J. House, J. Woycke, and E.M. Fodor, "Charismatic and Noncharismatic Leaders: Differences in Behavior and Effectiveness," in J.A. Conger and R.N. Kanungo, *Charismatic Leadership in Organizations* (Thousand Oaks, CA: Sage, 1998), pp. 103–104; D.A. Waldman, B.M. Bass, and F.J. Yammarino, "Adding to Contingent-Reward Behavior: The Augmenting Effect of Charismatic Leadership," *Group & Organization Studies,* December 1990, pp. 381–394; S.A. Kirkpatrick and E.A. Locke, "Direct and Indirect Effects of Three Core Charismatic Leadership Components on Performance and Attitudes," *Journal of Applied Psychology,* February 1996, pp. 36–51; and J.A. Conger, R.N. Kanungo, and S.T. Menon, "Charismatic Leadership and Follower Outcome Effects," paper presented at the 58th Annual Academy of Management Meetings, San Diego, CA, August 1998.

50. J.M. Howell and P.J. Frost, "A Laboratory Study of Charismatic Leadership," *Organizational Behavior & Human Decision Processes* 43, no. 2, April 1989, pp. 243–269.

51. "Building a Better Boss," *Maclean's,* September 30, 1996, p. 41.

52. A. Elsner, "The Era of CEO as Superhero Ends Amid Corporate Scandals," globeandmail.com, July 10, 2002.

53. http://www.canadianbusiness.com/leadership/blackberry-ceo-john-chen-turnaround-interview/. Accessed April 24, 2015.

54. Ibid.

55. http://www.michaelleestallard.com/3-practices-ceos-can-learn-girl-scouts. Accessed April 24, 2015.

56. Ibid.

57. http://whatsyourtech.ca/2015/04/20/almost-a-tenth-of-the-highest-paid-executive-positions-in-canada-are-held-by-women/. Accessed April 25, 2015.

58. http://www.catalyst.org/knowledge/statistical-overview-women-, workforce. Accessed March 7, 2018.

59. Ibid.

60. Ibid.

61. A.H. Eagly and B.T. Johnson, "Gender and Leadership Style: A Meta-Analysis," *Psychological Bulletin* 108 (1990), 233–256.

62. Ibid.

63. *The Economist,* "Workers Resent Scoldings from Female Bosses," *Houston Chronicle,* August 19, 2000, 1C.

64. Eagly and Johnson, "Gender and Leadership Style: A Meta-Analysis."

65. Ibid.

66. Ibid.

67. A.H. Eagly, S.J. Karau, and M.G. Makhijani, "Gender and the Effectiveness of Leaders: A Meta-Analysis," *Psychological Bulletin* 117 (1995), pp. 125–145.

68. Ibid.

69. R. Calori and B. Dufour, "Management European Style," *Academy of Management Executive* 9, no. 3 (1995), 61–70.

70. Ibid.

71. J.M. George and K. Bettenhausen, "Understanding Prosocial Behavior, Sales Performance, and Turnover: A Group-Level Analysis in a Service Context," *Journal of Applied Psychology* 75 (1990), 698–709.

72. T. Sy, S. Cote, and R. Saavedra, "The Contagious Leader: Impact of the Leader's Mood on the Mood of Group Members, Group Affective Tone, and Group Processes," *Journal of Applied Psychology* 90, no. 2 (2005), 295–305.

73. N.M. Ashkanasy and C.S. Daus, "Emotion in the Workplace: The New Challenge for Managers," *Academy of Management Executive* 16, no. 1 (2002), 76–86; and J.M. George, "Emotions and Leadership: The Role of Emotional Intelligence," *Human Relations* 53 (2002), 1027–1055.

74. J.M. George, "Emotions and Leadership: The Role of Emotional Intelligence," *Human Relations* 53 (2000), 1027–1055.

75. J. Zhou and J.M. George, "Awakening Employee Creativity: The Role of Leader Emotional Intelligence," *The Leadership Quarterly* 14, no. 45 (August–October 2003), 545–68.

76. Ibid.
77. Ibid.
78. http://www.canadianbusiness.com/innovation/emotional -intelligence-for-higher-income/. Accessed April 25, 2015.
79. Adapted from Harvey Schachter, "Monday Morning Manager," *The Globe and Mail,* Monday, July 3, 2006. Reprinted by permission of Harvey Schachter.
80. Jerry Manas. *Napoleon on Project Management: Timeless Lessons in Planning, Execution, and Leadership.* Toronto: Nelson Business, 2006, 288 pages.

Chapter 10

1. T. Kelley and J. Littman, *The Art of Innovation* (New York: Doubleday, 2001); "ideo.com: Our Work," www.ideo.com /portfolio. June 19, 2006. http://www.ideo.com, 4/29/2011.
2. B. Nussbaum, "The Power of Design," *BusinessWeek,* May 17, 2004, pp. 86–94; "ideo.com: About Us: Teams," www.ideo.com/about/index.asp?x=1&y=1, June 19, 2006.
3. "ideo.com: About Us: Teams," www.ideo.com/about/ index.asp?x=1&y=1, June 19, 2006; "ideo.com: About Us: Teams," www.ideo.com/about/index.asp?x=1&y=1, April 18, 2008; "Teams—IDEO," http://www.ideo.com/culture /teams/ March 15, 2010.
4. Nussbaum, "The Power of Design."
5. Kelley and Littman, *The Art of Innovation.*
6. Kelley and Littman, *The Art of Innovation;* www.ideo.com; "1999 Idea Winners," *BusinessWeek,* June 7, 1999, *BusinessWeek*Archives.
7. Nussbaum, "The Power of Design; "ideo.com: About Us: Teams."
8. P. Booth, *Challenge and Change: Embracing the Team Concept, Report 123–94,* Conference Board of Canada, 1994.
9. Cited in C. Joinson, "Teams at Work," *HRMagazine,* May 1999, p. 30; and P. Strozniak, "Teams at Work," *Industry Week,* September 18, 2000, p. 47.
10. T.M. Mills, *The Sociology of Small Groups* (Englewood Cliffs, NJ: Prentice-Hall, 1967); M.E. Shaw, *Group Dynamics* (New York: McGraw-Hill, 1981).
11. A. Deutschman, "Inside the Mind of Jeff Bezos," *Fast Company,* August 2004, 50–58; and "Amazon.com Digital Media Technology," http://media-server.amazon .com/jobs/jobs.html, June 19, 2006.
12. P. Willcocks, "Yours and Mine? Can the New Owner of the Once-Troubled Myra Falls Copper and Zinc Mine Near Campbell River Forge a New Relationship With Workers and Their Union to Create a True Partnership?" *BCBusiness Magazine,* September 2000, pp. 114–120.
13. J.A. Pearce II and E.C. Ravlin, "The Design and Activation of Self-Regulating Work Groups," *Human Relations* 11 (1987), 751–782.
14. P. Booth, *Challenge and Change: Embracing the Team Concept, Report 123–94,* Conference Board of Canada, 1994.
15. B. Dumaine, "Who Needs a Boss?" *Fortune,* May 7, 1990, pp. 52–60; and J.A. Pearce II and E.C. Ravlin, "The Design and Activation of Self-Regulating Work Groups," *Human Relations* 11 (1987), 751–782.
16. B. Dumaine, "Who Needs a Boss?" *Fortune,* May 7, 1990, pp. 52–60; and A.R. Montebello and V.R. Buzzotta, "Work Teams That Work," *Training & Development* (March 1993), 59–64.
17. http://www.cpsc-ccsp.ca/Employee%20Retention /Canadian%20General%20Tower%20Limited.htm. Canadian General Tower Limited. Accessed June 9, 2012.
18. T.D. Wall, N.J. Kemp, P.R. Jackson, and C.W. Clegg, "Outcomes of Autonomous Work Groups: A Long-Term Field Experiment," *Academy of Management Journal* 29 (1986), 280–304.
19. W.R. Pape, "Group Insurance," *Inc.* (Inc. Technology Supplement), June 17, 1997, pp. 29–31; A.M. Townsend, S.M. DeMarie, and A.R. Hendrickson, "Are You Ready for Virtual Teams?" *HRMagazine,* September 1996, pp. 122–126; and A.M. Townsend, S.M. DeMarie, and A.M. Hendrickson, "Virtual Teams: Technology and the Workplace of the Future," *Academy of Management Executive*12, no. 3 (1998), 17–29.
20. A.M. Townsend, S.M. DeMarie, and A.R. Hendrickson, "Are You Ready for Virtual Teams?" *HRMagazine,* September 1996, pp. 122–126.
21. W.R. Pape, "Group Insurance," *Inc.* (Inc. Technology Supplement), June 17, 1997, pp. 29–31; and A.M. Townsend, S.M. DeMarie, and A.R. Hendrickson, "Are You Ready for Virtual Teams?" *HRMagazine,* September 1996, pp. 122–126.
22. B. Geber, "Virtual Teams," *Training* 32, no. 4 (August 1995), 36–40; T. Finholt and L.S. Sproull, "Electronic Groups at Work," *Organization Science* 1 (1990), 41–64.
23. Geber, "Virtual Teams."
24. E.J. Hill, B.C. Miller, S.P. Weiner, and J. Colihan, "Influences of the Virtual Office on Aspects of Work and Work/Life Balance," *Personnel Psychology* 31 (1998), 667–83; S.G. Strauss, "Technology, Group Process, and Group Outcomes: Testing the Connections in Computer-Mediated and Face-to-Face Groups," *Human Computer Interaction* 12 (1997), 227–66; M.E. Warkentin, L. Sayeed, and R. Hightower, "Virtual Teams versus Face -to-Face Teams: An Exploratory Study of a Web-Based Conference System," *Decision Sciences*28, no. 4 (Fall 1997), 975–96.
25. S.A. Furst, M. Reeves, B. Rosen, and R.S. Blackburn, "Managing the Life Cycle of Virtual Teams," *Academy of Management Executive* 18, no. 2 (May 2004), 6–20.
26. Ibid.
27. Gratton, "Working Together . . . When Apart."
28. A. Deutschman, "The Managing Wisdom of High-Tech Superstars," *Fortune,* October 17, 1994, pp. 197–206.
29. Ibid.
30. J.S. Lublin, "My Colleague, My Boss," *The Wall Street Journal,* April 12, 1995, pp. R4, R12.
31. R.G. LeFauve and A.C. Hax, "Managerial and Technological Innovations at Saturn Corporation," *MIT Management,* Spring 1992, 8–19.
32. B.W. Tuckman, "Developmental Sequences in Small Groups," *Psychological Bulletin* 63 (1965), 384–399; and B.W. Tuckman and M.C. Jensen, "Stages of Small Group Development," *Group and Organizational Studies* 2 (1977), 419–427.
33. C.J.G. Gersick, "Time and Transition in Work Teams: Toward a New Model of Group Development," *Academy of Management Journal* 31 (March 1988), 9–41; C.J.G. Gersick, "Marking Time: Predictable Transitions in Task Groups," *Academy of Management Journal* 32 (June 1989), 274–309.
34. J.R. Hackman, "Group Influences on Individuals in Organizations," in M.D. Dunnette and L.M. Hough (eds.), *Handbook of Industrial and Organizational Psychology,* 2nd ed., vol. 3 (Palo Alto, CA: Consulting Psychologists Press, 1992), pp. 199–267.
35. Ibid.
36. Ibid.
37. J.S. Lublin, "My Colleague, My Boss."
38. L. Festinger, "Informal Social Communication," *Psychological Review* 57 (1950), 271–282; and M.E. Shaw, *Group Dynamics* (New York: McGraw-Hill, 1981).
39. D. Cartwright, "The Nature of Group Cohesiveness," in D. Cartwright and A. Zander, eds., *Group Dynamics*, 3rd ed. (New York: Harper & Row, 1968); L. Festinger, S. Schacter, and K. Black, *Social Pressures in Informal Groups* (New York: Harper & Row, 1950); Shaw, *Group Dynamics.*

40. T.F. O'Boyle, "A Manufacturer Grows Efficient by Soliciting Ideas from Employees," *The Wall Street Journal,* June 5, 1992, A1, A5.

41. J.R. Hackman, "Group Influences on Individuals in Organizations," in M.D. Dunnette and L.M. Hough (eds.), *Handbook of Industrial and Organizational Psychology,* 2nd ed., vol. 3 (Palo Alto, CA: Consulting Psychologists Press, 1992), pp. 199–267; and M.E. Shaw, *Group Dynamics* (New York: McGraw-Hill, 1981).

42. Janis Irving, *Victims of Groupthink* (Boston: Houghton Mifflin, 1972). See also Janis Irving, *Groupthink: Psychological Studies of Policy Decisions and Fiascos,* 2nd ed. (Boston: Houghton Mifflin, 1982).

43. I.L. Janis, *Groupthink: Psychological Studies of Policy Decisions and Fiascoes,* 2nd ed. (Boston: Houghton Mifflin, 1982).

44. Ibid.

45. J.N. Choi and M.U. Kim, "The Organizational Application of Groupthink and Its Limitations in Organizations," *Journal of Applied Psychology* 84 (1999), 297–306.

46. See N.R.F. Maier, *Principles of Human Relations* (New York: Wiley, 1952); I.L. Janis, *Groupthink: Psychological Studies of Policy Decisions and Fiascoes,* 2nd ed. (Boston: Houghton Mifflin, 1982); and C.R. Leana, "A Partial Test of Janis' Groupthink Model: Effects of Group Cohesiveness and Leader Behavior on Defective Decision Making," *Journal of Management,* Spring 1985, pp. 5–17.

47. See R.O. Mason, "A Dialectic Approach to Strategic Planning," *Management Science* 13 (1969), 403–414; R.A. Cosier and J.C. Aplin, "A Critical View of Dialectic Inquiry in Strategic Planning," *Strategic Management Journal* 1 (1980), 343–356; I.I. Mitroff and R.O. Mason, "Structuring III—Structured Policy Issues: Further Explorations in a Methodology for Messy Problems," *Strategic Management Journal* 1 (1980), 331–342.

48. Mary C. Gentile, *Differences That Work: Organizational Excellence Through Diversity* (Boston: Harvard Business School Press, 1994).

49. http://www.brainstore.com/en/tools. Accessed April 21, 2015.

50. T.J. Bouchard Jr., J. Barsaloux, and G. Drauden, "Brainstorming Procedure, Group Size, and Sex as Determinants of Problem Solving Effectiveness of Individuals and Groups," *Journal of Applied Psychology* 59 (1974), 135–138.

51. L. Thompson and L.F. Brajkovich, "Improving the Creativity of Organizational Work Groups," *Academy of Management Executive* 17, no. 1 (2003), 96–111, B. Mullen, C. Johnson, and E. Salas, "Productivity Loss in Brainstorming Groups: A Meta-Analytic Integration," *Basic and Applied Social Psychology* 12, no. 1 (1991), 3–23; and M. Diehl and W. Stroebe, "Productivity Loss in Brainstorming Groups: Towards the Solution of a Riddle," *Journal of Personality and Social Psychology* 53 (1987), 497–509.

52. D.H. Gustafson, R.K. Shulka, A. Delbecq, and W.G. Walster, "A Comparative Study of Differences in Subjective Likelihood Estimates Made by Individuals, Interacting Groups, Delphi Groups, and Nominal Groups," *Organizational Behavior and Human Performance* 9 (1973), 280–291.

53. N. Dalkey, *The Delphi Method: An Experimental Study of Group Decision Making* (Santa Monica, CA: Rand Corp., 1989).

54. Jon R. Katzenbach, Douglas K. Smith, *The Wisdom of Teams, Creating High-performance Teams,* McKinsey and Company, 1993.

55. Lublin, "My Colleague, My Boss."

56. T. Kelley and J. Littman, *The Art of Innovation* (New York: Doubleday, 2001).

57. Ibid.

58. P.C. Earley, "Social Loafing and Collectivism: A Comparison of the United States and the People's Republic of China," *Administrative Science Quarterly* 34 (1989), 565–581; J.M. George, "Extrinsic and Intrinsic Origins of Perceived Social Loafing in Organizations," *Academy of Management Journal* 35 (1992), 191–202; S.G. Harkins, B. Latane, and K. Williams, "Social Loafing: Allocating Effort or Taking it Easy," *Journal of Experimental Social Psychology* 16 (1980), 457–465; B. Latane, K.D. Williams, and S. Harkins, "Many Hands Make Light the Work: The Causes and Consequences of Social Loafing," *Journal of Personality and Social Psychology* 37 (1979), 822–832; and J.A. Shepperd, "Productivity Loss in Performance Groups: A Motivation Analysis," *Psychological Bulletin* 113 (1993), 67–81.

59. George, "Extrinsic and Intrinsic Origins"; G.R. Jones, "Task Visibility, Free Riding, and Shirking: Explaining the Effect of Structure and Technology on Employee Behavior," *Academy of Management Review* 9 (1984), 684–95; K. Williams, S. Harkins, and B. Latane, "Identifiability as a Deterrent to Social Loafing: Two Cheering Experiments," *Journal of Personality and Social Psychology* 40 (1981), 303–11.

60. S. Harkins and J. Jackson, "The Role of Evaluation in Eliminating Social Loafing," *Personality and Social Psychology Bulletin* 11 (1985), 457–65; N.L. Kerr and S.E. Bruun, "Ringelman Revisited: Alternative Explanations for the Social Loafing Effect," *Personality and Social Psychology Bulletin* 7 (1981), 224–231; Williams et al., "Identifiability as a Deterrent to Social Loafing."

61. B. Latane, "Responsibility and Effort in Organizations," in P.S. Goodman, ed., *Designing Effective Work Groups* (San Francisco: Jossey-Bass, 1986); Latane et al., "Many Hands Make Light the Work"; I.D. Steiner, *Group Process and Productivity* (New York: Academic Press, 1972).

62. J.A. Litterer, "Conflict in Organizations: A Reexamination," *Academy of Management Journal* 9 (1966), 178–186; S.M. Schmidt and T.A. Kochan, "Conflict: Towards Conceptual Clarity," *Administrative Science Quarterly* 13 (1972), 359–370; and R.H. Miles, *Macro Organizational Behavior* (Santa Monica, CA: Goodyear, 1980).

63. S.P. Robbins, *Managing Organizational Conflict: A Nontraditional Approach* (Englewood Cliffs, NJ: Prentice-Hall, 1974); and L. Coser, *The Functions of Social Conflict* (New York: Free Press, 1956).

64. L.R. Pondy, "Organizational Conflict: Concepts and Models," *Administrative Science Quarterly* 2 (1967), 296–320; and R.E. Walton and J.M. Dutton, "The Management of Interdepartmental Conflict: A Model and Review," *Administrative Science Quarterly* 14 (1969), 62–73.

65. http://thinkexist.com/quotations/conflict/. Accessed Feb. 25, 2012.

66. K.W. Thomas, "Conflict and Negotiation Processes in Organizations," in M.D. Dunnette and L.M. Hough (eds.), *Handbook of Industrial and Organizational Psychology,* 2nd ed., vol. 3 (Palo Alto, CA: Consulting Psychologists Press, 1992), pp. 651–717.

67. Adapted from the American Management Association, "How to Build High-Performance Teams," Self-Study Course. Website: www.amanet.org/selfstudy/b13759.htm.

68. Adapted from Jim Clemmer, "Team Spirit Built From the Top," *The Globe and Mail,* Friday, November 26, 2004, C1.

69. G. Hamel, *The Future of Management* (Boston, MA: Harvard Business School Press, 2007); "Our History," https://www.gore.com/about/the-gore-story#our-history. Accessed Oct 30, 2018.

70. "About Gore," https://www.gore.com/about. Accessed Oct 30, 2018.

71. Hamel, *The Future of Management;* "Our History," https://www.gore.com/about/the-gore-story#our-history. Accessed Oct 30, 2018.
72. Ibid.
73. Ibid.
74. Ibid.
75. "Gore Culture," www.gore.com/en_xx/aboutus/culture /index.html. Accessed Oct 30, 2018.
76. G. Hamel, *The Future of Management,* (Boston, MA: Harvard Business School Press, 2007); "Our History," https://www.gore.com/about/the-gore-story#our-history. Accessed Oct 30, 2018.
77. R.E. Silverman, "Who's the Boss? There Isn't One," *The Wall Street Journal,* sec. Careers, June 20, 2012, B1, B8.
78. G. Hamel, *The Future of Management,* (Boston, MA: Harvard Business School Press, 2007); "Our History," https://www.gore.com/about/the-gore-story#our-history. Accessed Oct 30, 2018.
79. Ibid.; "Opportunities for Professionals at Gore," www .gore.com/en_xx/careers/professionals/index.html, May 20, 2014.
80. Silverman, "Who's the Boss? There Isn't One."
81. Ibid.
82. Hamel, *The Future of Management;* "Our History."
83. "Our History," https://www.gore.com/about/the-gore -story#our-history. Accessed Oct 30, 2018.
84. Hamel, *The Future of Management;* "Our History."
85. Hamel, *The Future of Management.*
86. https://www.gore.com/about/the-gore -story#section30051. Accessed Oct 30, 2018.
87. https://www.gore.com/news-events/press-release /gore-recognized-as-one-of-worlds-best-multinational -workplaces-2017. Accessed Oct 30, 2018.
88. "W.L. Gore & Associates Named a Top U.S. Workplace in 2014," www.gore.com/en_xx/news/FORTUNE-2014 .html_May 19, 2014.

Chapter 11

1. Leah Fessler, GM CEO May Barra says too many women quit their jobs for the wrong reason, QUARTZ at WORK, http://www.work.qz.com. February 6, 2018. Accessed May 7, 2018.
2. http://www.gm.com/company/corporate-officers/mary -barra. Accessed May 15, 2015.
3. Phil Lebeau and Jeff Pohlman, http://www.nbcnews.com /storyline/gm-recall/can-ceo-mary-barra-change-general -motors-corporate-culture-n107521. Accessed March 25, 2015.
4. Phil Lebeau and Jeff Pohlman, op.cit.
5. http://www.wsj.com/articles/gm-plans-5-4-billion-in-u-s -plant-investments-1430404230. Accessed May 15, 2015.
6. W.G. Ouchi, "Markets, Bureaucracies, and Clans," *Administrative Science Quarterly* 25 (1980), 129–141.
7. E.E. Lawler III and J.G. Rhode, *Information and Control in Organizations* (Pacific Palisades, CA: Goodyear, 1976).
8. C.W.L. Hill and G.R. Jones, *Strategic Management: An Integrated Approach,* 4th ed. (Boston: Houghton Mifflin, 1997).
9. W.G. Ouchi, "The Transmission of Control Through Organizational Hierarchy," *Academy of Management Journal* 21 (1978), 173–192.
10. W.G. Ouchi, "The Relationship between Organizational Structure and Organizational Control," *Administrative Science Quarterly* 22 (1977), 95–113.
11. W.G. Ouchi, "Markets, Bureaucracies, and Clans," *Administrative Science Quarterly* 25 (1980), 129–141.
12. W.H. Newman, *Constructive Control* (Englewood Cliffs, NJ: Prentice-Hall, 1975).
13. J.D. Thompson, *Organizations in Action* (New York: McGraw-Hill, 1967).
14. R.N. Anthony, *The Management Control Function* (Boston: Harvard Business School Press, 1988).
15. P. Lorange, M. Morton, and S. Ghoshal, *Strategic Control* (St. Paul, MN: West, 1986).
16. H. Koontz and R.W. Bradspies, "Managing Through Feedforward Control," *Business Horizons,* June 1972, pp. 25–36.
17. W.G. Ouchi, "Markets, Bureaucracies, and Clans," *Administrative Science Quarterly* 25 (1980), 129–141.
18. C.W.L. Hill and G.R. Jones, *Strategic Management: An Integrated Approach,* 4th ed. (Boston: Houghton Mifflin, 1997).
19. R. Simons, "Strategic Orientation and Top Management Attention to Control Systems," *Strategic Management Journal* 12 (1991), 49–62.
20. B. Woolridge and S.W. Floyd, "The Strategy Process, Middle Management Involvement, and Organizational Performance," *Strategic Management Journal* 11 (1990), 231–41.
21. J.A. Alexander, "Adaptive Changes in Corporate Control Practices," *Academy of Management Journal* 34 (1991), 162–193.
22. "RIM Provides Status Update and Reports on Results of Internal Review of Stock Option Grants by Special Committee." Website: http://press.rim.com/financial /release.jsp?id=1193. Accessed July 29, 2009.
23. Quoted in www.corpgov.net/. Accessed Aug. 1, 2009.
24. G.H.B. Ross, "Revolution in Management Control," *Management Accounting* 72 (1992), 23–27.
25. P. F. Drucker, *The Practice of Management* (New York: Harper & Row, 1954).
26. www.cypress.com, 2001.
27. B. Dumaine, "The Bureaucracy Busters," *Fortune,* June 17, 1991, 46.
28. D.S. Pugh, D.J. Hickson, C.R. Hinings, and C. Turner, "Dimensions of Organizational Structure," *Administrative Science Quarterly* 13 (1968), 65–91.
29. P.M. Blau, *The Dynamics of Bureaucracy* (Chicago: University of Chicago Press, 1955).
30. A. Kinicki and B.K. Williams, "Management: A Practical Introduction" (Boston: McGraw-Hill Irwin, 2003).
31. S. Mcgee, "Garish Jackets Add to Clamor of Chicago Pits," *The Wall Street Journal,* July 31, 1995, p. C1.
32. K.E. Weick, *The Social Psychology of Organization* (Reading, MA: Addison-Wesley, 1979).
33. J. McCann, "Cutting the Crap," *National Post Business,* March 2001, pp. 47–57.
34. Rachel Emma Silverman and Nikki Walker, "Thinking of Quitting? The Boss Knows," *The Wall Street Journal,* March 14, 2015, pp. A1—A2.

Chapter 12

1. Aleksandra Sagan, "Loblaw shareholders reject living wage, independent board chair proposals," *Canadian Business Magazine,* May 3, 2018. http://www .canadianbusiness.com/business-news/loblaw -shareholders-reject-living-wage-independent-board -chair-proposals/. Accessed May 8, 2018. Reprinted by permission of The Canadian Press.
2. Website: www.EIU.com. Accessed July 22, 2009.
3. L. Brown, "Research Action: Organizational Feedback, Understanding and Change," *Journal of Applied Behavioral Research* 8 (1972), 697–711; P.A. Clark, *Action Research and Organizational Change* (New York: Harper and Row, 1972); and N. Margulies and A.P. Raia (eds.), *Conceptual Foundations of Organizational Development* (New York: McGraw-Hill, 1978).
4. Economist Intelligence Unit, E-Business Transformation. Website: http://store.eiu.com/product/313436031.html. Accessed Aug. 18, 2009.

5. W.L. French, "A Checklist for Organizing and Implementing an OD Effort," in W.L. French, C.H. Bell, and R.A. Zawacki (eds.), *Organizational Development and Transformation* (Homewood, IL: Irwin, 1994), pp. 484–495.

6. K. Lewin, *Field Theory in Social Science* (New York: Harper and Row, 1951).

7. Ian Turner, "Strategy, Complexity and Uncertainty." Website: www.poolonline.com/archive/iss1fea5.html. Accessed Aug. 2, 2009. Based on Ralph Stacey.

8. T. Lonier, "Some Insights and Statistics on Working Solo," www.workingsolo.com.

9. I.N. Katsikis and L.P. Kyrgidou, "The Concept of Sustainable Entrepreneurship: A Conceptual Framework and Empirical Analysis," *Academy of Management Proceedings,* 2007, 1–6, 6p, web.ebscohost.com/ehost /delivery?vid=7&hid=102&sid=434afdf5-5ed9 -45d4-993b-, January 24, 2008; "What Is a Social Entrepreneur?" http://ashoka.org/social_entrepreneur, February 20, 2008; C. Hsu, "Entrepreneur for Social Change," October 31, 2005, U.S.News.com, www .usnews.com/usnews/news/articles/051031/31drayton .htm; D.M. Sullivan, "Stimulating Social Entrepreneurship: Can Support From Cities Make a Difference? *Academy of Management Perspectives,* February 2007, 78.

10. Ibid.

11. Muhammad Yunus, *Building Social Business: The New Kind of Capitalism That Serves Humanity's Most Pressing Needs* (New York: Public Affairs, 2010), p. xvii. http://tamarackcommunity.ca/cities_reducing_poverty. html?gclid=COqHlve9zsUCFQuMaQodTEUADg. Accessed May 19, 2015.

12. J.R. Stepp and T.J. Schneider, "Fostering Change in a Unionized Environment," *Canadian Business Review,* Summer 1995, pp. 13–16.

13. Ibid. Source: http://www.canadianbusiness.com /companies-and-industries/can-sobeys-change-leaders -and-conquer-western-canada-at-the-same-time/. Mar 14, 2014 Quentin Casey. Accessed May 19, 2015.

14. Jennifer Pagliaro and Betsy Powell, "Toronto Council Votes to Regulate Uber," *Toronto Star,* Wednesday, September 30, 2015. Accessed Oct. 1, 2015.

15. Marcus Wohlsen, "Uber's Biggest Danger Is Its Business Model, Not Bad PR," *Wired,* Aug. 29, 2014, http://www .wired.com/2014/08/the-peril-to-uber-is-its-business -model-not-bad-pr/. Accessed Oct. 1, 2015.

16. Molly Reynolds, "Why Every Business Model May Soon Look Like Uber's," *Inc.,* http://www.inc.com /molly-reynolds/is-our-future-heading-toward-the-uber -business-model.html. Accessed Oct. 1, 2015.

17. Roger Hardy, "Why Disruption Shouldn't Be a Dirty Word," http://www.profitguide.com/manage-grow /innovation/why-disruption-shouldnt-be-a-dirty -word-78426. Accessed May 19, 2015.

Index

A

Abbott, Ida, 270
ability tests, 266
absenteeism, 185, 321, 353, 376
abuse of authority, 282
Access to Information Act, 232
accommodating, 405
accommodative approach, 115
accountability, 27
accounting scandals, 358
accuracy, 133
achievement, 295, 309
achievement-oriented behaviours, 351
*Act Respecting the Protection of Personal
     Information in the Private Sector,* 232
active listeners, 227
activity ratios, 429, 430
ad hoc committees, 378
Adams, J. Stacey, 314
adaptive culture, 463–464
Adidas, 159
adjourning, 387
administrative model, 94–97
   incomplete information, 96
   nature of rationality, 95
   satisficing, 96–97
AdvancedCare.com, 178
affiliation, need for, 309
affirmative nods, 227
Afghanistan, 55
aging population, 55
Agricultural Data Systems, 329
All-Channel network, 228
alternative scenarios, 173
Amazon.com, 49, 140, 216, 243–244, 475
ambiguous information, 96
analytic style, 107
analytical communicator, 221, 222
analytics, 241
answering machines, 231
Aon Consulting, 221
appeals procedure, 279
Apple Computer, 30, 47, 105, 121, 138,
     139, 145, 218
applications software, 235
appreciative inquiry, 461–462
Arthur Andersen, 113
artificial intelligence (AI), 237–238
ASA processes, 25–26
assertiveness, 405
assumption of morality, 395
attention, 226–227
attitude change, 54
attitudes, 20, 21–23
attraction-selection-attrition (ASA)
     framework, 25–26
Auditor General of Canada, 55
Australia, 53
authority, 82, 197
   allocation of authority, 197–200
   decentralizing decision-making authority,
      200–201
   hierarchy of authority, 197, 198

minimum chain of command, 200
overlapping authority, 402
tall and flat organizations, 199–200
autonomy, 185, 308
avoiding, 405

B

background information, 263–264
Ballmer, Steve, 129
Balsillie, Jim, 434
banking systems, 53
Barra, Mary, 417–418, 445–446
barriers to entry, 49–51, 145
Barron, Millard, 352
B2B marketplaces, 239
B2B network structures, 180, 194–196
BCE, 258
the Beatles, 121
behaviour appraisals, 272–273
behavioural control, 422, 433–439
   bureaucratic rules, 436–438
   clan control, 438–439
   corporate governance, 433–435
   direct supervision, 435
   management by objectives (MBO),
      435–436
   standard operating procedures (SOPs),
      436–437
   types of, 433
behavioural decision-making style, 107
behavioural interview questions,
     265, 266
behavioural model, 344–346
behavioural standards, 420
Bell, 48, 290
Bell, Alexander Graham, 121
benchmarking, 16, 459
benefits, 250–251, 278
Benimadhu, Prem, 327
Bertone, Antonio, 89
Best Buy Co. Inc., 149
best sales practices, AD–4
Bezos, Jeff, 140
bias, 270, 271
   cognitive biases, 97, 104–106
   confirmation bias, 105
   in decision making, 104–106
   overconfidence bias, 105
   perceptual biases, 220
   prior hypothesis bias, 105
   representativeness bias, 105
"big, hairy, audacious goals (BHAGs), 141
Birkinshaw, Julian, 127
Black, Conrad, 114–115
BlackBerry, 67, 70–71, 121, 218, 358–359,
     434, 454
Blanchard, Ken, 349
blended value, 5
blogs, 232–233
board of directors, 434
body language, 223
Bombardier Inc., 67

bonus, 328–329
bots, 238
bottom-up change, 458
boundaryless career, 294
boundaryless organization, 196
boundaryless structure, 181
bounded awareness, 95
bounded rationality, 95
brainstorming, 397
brand loyalty, 50
Branson, Richard, 92, 105, 106
break-even analysis, 173
Brick Brewing Co. Limited, 3–4, 6,
     9, 11, 14
Brickman, Jim, 3
British Columbia, 233
Bromley, Stan, 270
Bryan, J.P., 352
budgeting systems, 138
Bugg-Levine, Antony, 303, 304
Built to Last, 141
bullying, 282
bureaucracy, 82
bureaucratic control, 436
bureaucratic red tape, 83
bureaucratic rules, 436–438
bureaucratic theory, 82–83
business-level plan, 136
business-level strategy, 136, 148–151
business plan, 161
   appendices, 173
   components of, 162
   executive summary, 162–163
   financial plan, 172–173
   marketing plan, 166–169
   nondisclosure statement, 162
   operating and control systems plan,
      171–172
   organizational plan, 169–171
   profile of industry or sector, 165
   profile of product or service, 165
   profile of the organization, 163–165
business-to-business (B2B) commerce, 239
business-to-business (B2B) networks,
     16, 196
business-to-customer (B2C) commerce, 239
business units, 133
Byler, Edna Ruth, 427
Byrne, Sean, 3, 14, 17, 34–35

C

cafeteria-style benefit plans, 278–279
Calgary Economic Development Report,
     254
Campbell's Soup Company, 141, 154
Canada
   banking system, 53
   changing attitudes, 54
   health and safety net legislation, 252
   nonprofit and voluntary sector, 6
   social structure, 53
Canada Labour Code, 252, 279